Lecture Notes in Artificial Intelligence   8810

Subseries of Lecture Notes in Computer Science

T0212605

Lecture Notes in Artificial Intelligence 8810

Subseries of Lecture Notes in Computer Science

LNAI Series Editors

Randy Goebel
University of Alberta, Edmonton, Canada
Yuzuru Tanaka
Hokkaido University, Sapporo, Japan
Wolfgang Wahlster
DFKI and Saarland University, Saarbrücken, Germany

LNAI Founding Series Editor

Joerg Siekmann
DFKI and Saarland University, Saarbrücken, Germany

ne Editors

le Brugali
ersità degli Studi di Bergamo, Department of Engineering
Marconi 5, 24044 Dalmine, Italy
il: brugali@unibg.it

, Broenink
ersity of Twente, Faculty EE-Math-CS
Institute, Robotics and Mechatronics Group
3ox 217, 7500 AE Enschede, The Netherlands
il: j.f.broenink@utwente.nl

en Kroeger
ord University, Artificial Intelligence Laboratory
ord, CA 94305-9010, USA
il: t@kroe.org

e A. MacDonald
ersity of Auckland, Faculty of Engineering
rical and Computer Engineering, Science Centre - Mathphysic
incess Street, Auckland 1010, New Zealand
il: b.macdonald@auckland.ac.nz

0302-9743   e-ISSN 1611-3349
978-3-319-11899-4   e-ISBN 978-3-319-11900-7
10.1007/978-3-319-11900-7
ger Cham Heidelberg New York Dordrecht London

ry of Congress Control Number: 2014950057

5 Sublibrary: SL 7 – Artificial Intelligence

ger International Publishing Switzerland 2014

ting: Camera-ready by author, data conversion by Scientific Publishing Services, Chennai, India

on acid-free paper

r is part of Springer Science+Business Media (www.springer.com)

Davide Brugali   Jan F. Broenink
Torsten Kroeger   Bruce A. MacDona

Simulation, Mod and Programmin for Autonomous I

4th International Conference, SIMPA
Bergamo, Italy, October 20-23, 2014
Proceedings

 Springer

Preface

Robots are versatile machines that are increasingly being used not only to perform dirty, dangerous, and dull tasks in manufacturing industries, but also to achieve societal objectives, such as enhancing safety in transportation, reducing the use of pesticide in agriculture, helping people with health conditions, providing companionship, and improving efficacy in the fight against crime and civilian protection.

Compared to the manufacturing workcell, a public road, a cornfield, a hospital, a home, or a crime scene are open-ended environments, which require autonomous robots to be equipped with advanced cognitive capabilities, such as perception, planning, monitoring, coordination, and control in order to cope with unexpected situations reliably and safely.

In this scenario, the cost of creating new robotics products is significantly related to the complexity of developing software control systems that are robust, dependable, and whose correct behavior can be certified. This complexity can be managed by exploiting system engineering methodologies and tools that build on the power of software models and domain-specific programming languages to analyze, design, simulate, implement, test, and deploy complex robotic control systems.

The series of the International Conference on Simulation, Modeling, and Programming for Autonomous Robots (SIMPAR) is organized to foster research in the above topics. Gathering the most recent works in this field enhances the reusability of software for robotics and pushes research forward swiftly.

The 2014 event of SIMPAR was held at the "Giovanni XXIII" Conference Center in Bergamo, Italy during October 20–23. It followed the previous works of the first SIMPAR 2008 in Venice, Italy, the second SIMPAR 2010 in Darmstadt, Germany, and the third SIMPAR 2012 in Tsukuba, Japan and provided a forum for concentrated discussions on the topics of interest.

The number of submitted papers has increased steadily up to 62 for the SIMPAR 2014 event. Also the paper quality has increased significantly, which is demonstrated by the 49 contributed papers collected in this book. 41 papers were presented during regular sessions, while the remaining eight papers were presented as posters. Each submitted paper received at least two reviews by the members of a carefully selected international Program Committee.

We also had two impressive plenary talks presented by Raffaello D'Andrea (ETH Zurich, Swizerland) and Nate Koenig (Open Source Robotics Foundation, USA). A third plenary talk was planned to be given by Mike Stilman (Georgia Tech, USA), who passed away following an apparent accident in Atlanta on May 6th 2014, leaving all robotics community bereft of an emerging leader in humanoid robotics research.

We want to gratefully thank all Program Committee members and all other reviewers, supporters, organizers, and volunteers who contributed to this year's event of SIMPAR. Without their efforts, it would not be possible to hold this important conference.

October 2014

Davide Brugali
Jan Broenink
Torsten Kroeger
Bruce MacDonald

Organization

Program Committee

Martin Adams	Universidad de Chile, Chile
Hoseok Ahn	University of Auckland, New Zealand
Rachid Alami	LAAS, France
Monica Anderson	University of Alabama, USA
Noriaki Ando	AIST, Japan
Marcelo Ang	National University of Singapore, Singapore
Soumela Atmatzidou	Aristotle University of Thessaloniki, Greece
Ravi Balasubramanian	Oregon State University, USA
Kostas Bekris	Rutgers University, USA
Spring Berman	Arizona State University, USA
Geoffrey Biggs	AIST, Japan
Stan Birchfield	Clemson University, USA
Jan Broenink	University of Twente, The Netherlands
Davide Brugali	Università degli Studi di Bergamo, Italy
Zack Butler	Rochester Institute of Technology, USA
Mario Campos	Universidade Federal de Minas Gerais, Brazil
Stefano Carpin	University of California at Merced, USA
Filippo Cavallo	Scuola Superiore Sant'Anna, Italy
Heping Chen	Texas State University, USA
Ian Chen	Open Source Robotics Foundation, USA
Toby Collett	Auckland, New Zealand
Nikolaus Correll	University of Colorado at Boulder, USA
Anthony Cowley	University of Pennsylvania, USA
Mehmet Dogar	Massachusetts Institute of Technology, USA
Evan Drumwright	George Washington University, USA
Lars-Peter Ellekilde	University of Southern Denmark, Denmark
Vlad Estivill-Castro	Griffith University, Australia
Alessandro Farinelli	Verona University, Italy
David Feil-Seifer	University of Southern California, USA
Nicholas Gans	University of Texas at Dallas, USA
Luiz M. Garcia Gonçalves	Univ. Federal do Rio Grande do Norte, Brazil
Giuseppina Gini	Politecnico di Milano, Italy
Antoni Grau	Technical University of Catalonia, Spain
Takayuki Kanda	ATR, Japan
Hyun Kim	ETRI, South Korea
Jaehong Kim	ETRI, South Korea
Tomasz Kornuta	Warsaw University of Technology, Poland

Massimiliano Zecca   Loughborough University, UK
Hong Zhang   University of Alberta, Canada
Cezary Zielinski   Warsaw University of Technology, Poland
Uwe Zimmerman   KUKA Laboratories, Germany

Additional Reviewers

Baumann, Oliver   Muxfeldt, Arne
Hochgeschwender, Nico   Raibulet, Claudia
Kim, Doik   Roop, Partha
Kluth, Jan-Henrik   Taylor, James
Lu, Yan   Was, Jaroslaw
Mobilio, Marco

Table of Contents

Simulation

Modeling

Programming

Architectures

Methods and Tools

Systems and Applications

Making Time Make Sense in Robotic Simulation

James R. Taylor, Evan M. Drumwright, and Gabriel Parmer

Department of Computer Science, George Washington University, USA
{jrt,drum,gparmer}@gwu.edu

Abstract. Typical dynamic robotic simulators model the rigid body dynamics of robots using ordinary differential equations (ODEs). Such software libraries have traditionally focused on simulating the rigid body dynamics robustly, quickly, and accurately toward obtaining consistent dynamics performance between simulation and *in situ*. However, simulation practitioners have generally yet to investigate maintaining *temporal* consistency within the simulation: given that simulations run at variable rates, how does the roboticist ensure the robot's control software (controller, planners, and other user-level processes) runs at the same rate that it would run in the physical world? This paper describes an intersection of research between Robotics and Real-Time Operating Systems that investigates mechanisms for addressing this problem.

Introduction

Dynamic robotic simulators are one of the most widely used software tools in the field of Robotics today. Some of the recent focus on these simulations has been making them faster (*e.g.*, as with `Gazebo` in the DARPA Robotics Challenge), but one ongoing goal for rigid body simulations in general has been greater physical accuracy. The desire is that the simulations should evince physical behavior as close as possible to the real world, whether that closeness is measured quantitatively (as shown in recent experiments by Vose *et al.* [8]) or qualitatively (as can be seen in the unusual behavior observed in rigid "toys" like the Rattleback [4]). Clearly, Robotics will benefit as the physical accuracy of these systems becomes more faithful to reality: planning, optimization, and validation are just a few areas that can reap substantial improvements with better physical fidelity.

Our recent work [7] has broached an issue that has been safely ignorable for simulating dynamics for computer gaming and computer animation applications (the original focus of some popular simulation libraries like `Gazebo` and `ODE`): the *temporal consistency* between the simulation library and the "user level" software (controllers, planners, perception loops) for directing the robot. This issue arises because the simulation software does not simulate at the rate of "wall clock" time; as a result, the user level software—which may be expected to feed commands to and pull state from the simulation at roughly the same rate it would perform those operations on a physically situated robot—can not be expected to exhibit similar performance in simulation as *in situ*.

This paper continues investigating the issue of temporally consistent simulation. In addition to the general scheduling mechanisms and accurate timing of

D. Brugali et al. (Eds.): SIMPAR 2014, LNAI 8810, pp. 1–12, 2014.

a controller interfaced with dynamics that we explored in our previous work, we have further developed our infrastucture to ensure time consistent sharing of system resources among multiple controllers and planning processes. Additionally, we use a simple experiment to demonstrate the effect that neglect of this issue can have on robotic systems.

1   Background

1.1   Conventional Robotic Simulation Paradigm: The *Callback Model*

Current simulation architectures leverage a simple model whereby the dynamics executes for steps of time, and after each step the simulator invokes a call-back function which defines the planning and control for the system. This function can access dynamics state and it can actuate the system by adding virtual forces and torques. Importantly, the callback function can execute for an unbounded amount of time, without the time in the simulator progressing at all. The implication of this is that a significantly intelligent planner with correspondingly large computation times will execute on the *exact* environment it used as input, thus ignoring planner computation time. If this system were transplanted into a real environment the physical state of the system would diverge from the plan, possibly irreparably, by the time such a planner returned a sequence of controls for the system.

1.2   Simulation Components

Simulators integrate user defined client components together with dynamics libraries into a single framework such that a particular scenario may be evaluated. We define *client processes* to be the set of controllers and planners evaluated in such a system. Multiple robots might be simulated, each with sets of client processes. Collections of robots and environmental obstacles form a scenario. Each of the robots has a set of sensors and actuators that are controlled by the client processes in the system.

1.3   Temporal Requirements

Temporally consistent simulation attempts to ensure temporal consistency between different software components, and a simulation environment (*cf.* the notion of consistency for real-time aware, distributed shared memory accesses in Singla *et al.* [6]). The goal of temporally consistent simulation is not adhering execution to real-time, but rather ensuring consistency between the virtual progress of the dynamics, and the computational progress of the robotics software.

Real-time operating systems (RTOS) could be used to provide the same functionality as our temporally consistent simulation design on Linux, but would surprisingly not provide many additional assurances. The focus of RTOSes is often to control and bound latency for I/O. As temporally consistent simulation replaces traditional I/O with interfaces for coordinator and dynamics interactions, such RTOS facilities are superfluous.

A difficulty in providing a temporally consistent simulation infrastructure is that the timing requirements for the client processes vary significantly, and that they require accurate timing from the system. A system's sensors and actuators often have a natural frequency at which they provide environmental data or take actuation commands. Correspondingly, controllers are often executed at a rate closely tied to those sensor and actuator frequencies (i.e. their rates of input/output), and thus execute in a *periodic* manner. Specifically, they are activated by the OS every N milliseconds, at which points they do their computation, and block waiting for the next periodic activation. Note that if a controller *overruns* its computation, it might finish execution only after an activation. This is often called *missing a deadline*, and can result in instability. In contrast, planners often execute irregularly, do as much computation as is required, and provide their output as fast as they can, but not on a tight schedule as with controllers. These computations are often called *best-effort*. Planners often also provide higher-level sets of commands to the controllers via Inter-Process Communication (IPC) channels.

In a temporally consistent simulation, the activations of periodic controllers must be as time-accurate as possible, and the computation for the planners must not interfere adversely with the controller's ability to meet deadlines. The most difficult timing requirements, however, derive from the interactions between client processes and the external world, and between client processes. If the simulated time within the dynamics gets too far ahead of the amount of time that the client processes have executed, then sensor data will reference data "in the future". Alternatively, if the simulated time in the dynamics lags behind computation, then actuator commands will be sent to stale dynamics state. Comparably, the planner and controllers must be temporally kept in sync for the same reason. This is at the core of temporal consistency: all aspects of the simulation environment must proceed at rates that are realistic, and in sync.

1.4 System Scheduling toward Temporally Consistent Simulation

In attempting to address temporally consistent simulation, this research requires an infrastructure that can control not only the rate of progress of a dynamics engine (which is often provided naturally by it's API), but also of the *execution progress* of multiple client process computations. Put another way, the temporally consistent system infrastructure requires control over the scheduling of the system. Unfortunately, there is a *semantic gap* between what scheduling facilities the kernel of the system provides (often a black-box), and what is required by the simulation architecture. Many previous research projects in the area of operating systems have attempted to solve this problem. For example, [5] and [3] provide system infrastructures that are extensible, enabling normal user-level processes to define their own scheduling policies. However, they both require drastic system changes to provide these infrastructures. Alternatively,

[2] and [1] attempt to create an environment in existing systems in which some of the timing characteristics can be controlled by user-level code. Our research continues with this trend by creating a multi-process simulation environment in which the *coordinator* plays the role that the kernel traditionally takes: it controls system scheduling (i.e. the interleaving of different client processes, and the dynamics), and communication. However, it is designed to execute at user-level using only the facilities and APIs provided by a POSIX-compliant OS such as Linux. Thus, users need not modify their underlying systems at all.

The coordinator must address three main challenges: (1) how can Linux's POSIX-like API be leveraged to control scheduling and communication; (2) how can abstractions be provided to client processes so that they read sensor data, send actuator commands, and communicate via IPC normally; and (3) how can client computation be scheduled alongside the dynamics engine's virtual time?

2   OS Facilities for Temporally Consistent Simulation

2.1   Timing Facilities

The goal of the temporally consistent system is to ensure that for a number of client processes, and the dynamics, time progresses consistently for all. A key concept for temporally consistent systems is the maximum deviation in this progress, which we define in the following. We denote each of the client processes and dynamics as $\{p_0, \ldots, p_n\} \in P$. $p_i \in P$ has executed (or had simulated time progress) an amount of time e_i^t by time t within a given simulation infrastructure. Each periodic process blocks waiting for its next activation, thus essentially moving its own computational progress forward by the amount of time it waits, w_i^t. This wait time is common for controllers that activate periodically, but don't use all execution time until their next activation. Thus we define the temporal drift of the system, Δ, as such:

$$\Delta = \max_{\forall t}\{ \max_{\forall p_i \in P} (e_i^t + w_i^t) - \min_{\forall p_i \in P} (e_i^t + w_i^t)\}$$

Intuitively, Δ is the maximum deviation in temporal progress between any two parts of a simulation. A perfectly temporally consistent system is one in that $\Delta = 0$, while a traditional callback-driven simulator with a planner that always executes for more time than a step in the dynamics has $\Delta = \infty$ as $t \to \infty$.

Commodity hardware features timing facilities that are based on somewhat granular units of time. For example, timer ticks provide preemptive execution to prevent system starvation from a single process, which occur at a minimum fixed interval (for example, 100 or 1000 times a second). POSIX-based operating systems provide APIs for accessing timers and execution accounting facilities. Thus, the granularity for executing processes on modern systems is somewhat large. If this is bounded by 10ms (the timer inter-arrival on our system), then $\Delta \geq 10$ms. Thus our temporally consistent system attempts to minimize Δ within the confines of the hardware and OS provisions. However, we have found that the choice of the OS facility used for this timing has a large impact on the accuracy of timing in the system.

Accounting for Execution Time. To track the execution progress of a client process, traditional OS facilities (such as those used in the `time` and `top` programs) have a very large granularity, and an unbounded error. Instead of relying on these very coarse grained mechanisms, we use the cycle-accurate *time stamp counter* register that is available on most processors. It is a 64 bit value that counts the number of cycles elapsed in the processor, and is accessible on x86 and x86-64 processors through the `rdtsc` instruction. To maintain accurate time using `rdtsc`, the system must (1) know the processor speed; (2) maintain a consistent processor speed (or, alternatively use "invariant time stamps" in modern processors); and (3) all client processes and the coordinator must remain active on only one, shared processor core. For (1), we read the processor speed from the `/proc` file-system, for (2), we disable all power saving and throttling features, and for (3), we confine the measured process to run on a single processor core using the `sched_setaffinity(.)` system-call family. Thus our system can cycle-accurately account for the execution time (e_i^t) of each client process.

Accounting for Wait Time. To track the wait-time (w_i^t) for a process, our system provides an API similar to `setitimer` which enables recurring, periodic activations. Controllers use our API to schedule periodic activations, and after their computation for a specific activation is complete, they become inactive waiting for the next activation. The system tracks this elapsed wait time until the process is again executed. Notably, this wait time does signal some temporal progress for those controllers, even though it does not include computation time, thus why we consider it in the calculation of Δ.

Granularity of Preemption. For any scheduling system to control the execution of unknown computation (that might, for example, contain an infinite loop), preemption is required. A significant flaw of the callback model is that it executes the planner non-preemptively – the simulator cannot stop the planner when it has executed for too long. The hardware provides timer interrupts as its basic mechanism for preemption. POSIX provides a number of facilities for notification of timer interrupts. Our coordinator uses signals associated with the timer to receive these notifications. When the hardware causes a timer tick, the OS vectors it into a user-level signal that switches away from the previously executing client process (*e.g.*, planner), and to the coordinator, where scheduling decisions can be made. This, combined with the accurate execution time explained above, provides the temporally consistent system with the main facilities it requires to manage timing.

2.2 System Scheduling

The default scheduling policy in Linux is SCHED_OTHER that makes no guarantees on when any thread in the system will make progress. In contrast, it also includes two real-time policies for first-in-first-out, non-premptive, fixed priority scheduling, and preemptive (round-robin), fixed priority scheduling—SCHED_FIFO and

SCHED_RR, respectively. These policies are *predictable* in that if two processes both want to run on the CPU, the higher priority one will always be chosen to execute. A process can be set to be scheduled using any of these policies via the sched_setparam system call.

Context Switching. We take advantage of the predictable behavior afforded by these kernel scheduling policies to implement our own scheduling policy in the coordinator. The coordinator itself always executes at the highest priority. The client process it wants to switch to will be given the next highest priority. To finish the switch to that process, the coordinator will block waiting for timer interrupts, actuator commands, blocking notifications, and IPC (blocking on multiple sources in POSIX can be done with select). If any of these are detected, it will wake, and immediately activate (as it is highest priority). Whenever the coordinator executes, it makes a scheduling decision about which client process/dynamics should run next to optimize for a minimal Δ.

Process Blocking. In attempting to override the scheduling policies of the kernel, the coordinator must consider the case when a client process blocks. For simplicity, in this work, we assume that the client processes only block waiting for timeouts (periodic controllers), or waiting for sensor data. Without accounting for blocking, the coordinator might lose control of the system: if the process that is supposed to be executing instead blocks, then the kernel will take over and choose the next highest thread to execute, which might not be in the time consistent system, thus invalidating the coordinator's execution accounting.

2.3 Interprocess Communication

Communication between client processes (*e.g.*, the planner sending commands to the controller), sensor data requests, and actuator commands require the coordinator to mediate the communication. Each client process is given access to two pipes that are used to (1) block the process waiting for an event (*e.g.,*. IPC, sensor data), or (2) send a notification to the coordinator that the process is sending data (*e.g.*, IPC, actuator commands). The coordinator is awakened by such notifications and can decide where to copy the data (it is in shared memory) or how to manipulate the dynamics.

3   Time Consistent Simulator Design

The time consistent simulator must manage multiple conflicting goals. On the one hand, the timing requirements of controllers require the meeting of deadlines (*i.e.*, an accurate activation time), and on the other, temporal consistency is required to have a clear mapping between actual system execution, and simulated execution. As the simulated environment must support multiple robots and varied software infrastructures with rich communication structures, it must be highly flexible. This section covers the implementation of the infrastructure, and details how it integrates with the OS facilities from Section 2.

3.1   Hierarchical Scheduling and Threads

To handle the required generality, we use a hierarchical scheduling framework [5]. Such systems define a tree of schedulers. The leaves of the tree are client processes, and the dynamics. When activated, the *root* scheduler determines from its children which to execute (*i.e.* it makes a scheduling decision), and does so using a polymorphic method invocation to `dispatch` the child. If the child is a leaf, then the dispatch function will either (1) use the context switch mechanism described in Section 2.2, or (2) make an invocation into the dynamics to step the simulated time forward. However, as the system is hierarchical, the dispatched child could be a scheduler itself. The key insight here is that each of the schedulers in the hierarchy can define different scheduling policies.

Scheduling Policies. There are two policies we use in the system, one to maintain minimal temporal consistency, and the another to do strict priority-based scheduling. As a general rule, the schedulers close to the root are concerned with temporal consistency, while those that represent an actual scheduler on a robot are concerned with maintaining accurate timing for the system controllers, thus placing them at a higher priority than the planners. Though more scheduling policies could be added, we found that these are sufficient.

Example Use of Hierarchical Scheduling. The system set-up we use in Section 4 includes a dynamics engine and two robots, one with both a planner and a controller, and the other with a simple controller. All of the three threads for the robots, and the dynamics must be scheduled. Thus, we organize the system with a single root scheduling for consistent timing between each robot, and the dynamics. The robot with both the planner and the controller has each under a scheduler with the fixed-priority policy, with priority going to the controller. The hierarchical arrangement of schedulers and the dynamics and client processes is essential to properly schedule given the different goals of different parts of the system, and to enable the simulation of complex, possibly multi-robot systems.

Maintaining Proper Accounting in the Hierarchy. Just as scheduling decisions follow a chain from the root to a leaf, the accounting for execution time and progress must go from leaves down toward the root, so that scheduling decisions can be made at each scheduler based on an accurate rendition of how much temporal progress all of its children have made. For this, we aggregate the execution times of all children, unless they are all blocked waiting for sensor data, in which case we determine that child's progress to be the minimum of those block times.

3.2   Coordinator Design

The coordinator is the heart of the system and orchestrates all execution. The hierarchical scheduling policy is executed in the coordinator, and when a dispatch is made to a client process, the coordinator goes through the following steps: (1) swap the priorities of the previously active client process, and the one we want to switch to (Section 2.2), (2) take a time-stamp reading (Section 2.1), and (3) block the coordinator (on `select`) waiting for an event (timer tick or request for sensor data). As the coordinator (which is highest priority) blocks, the system naturally switches to the new process, thus completing a context switch. Unblocking the coordinator (and subsequent blocking of the active client) is accomplished by writing notifications to the pipes that will wake the main coordinator thread of execution. Client processes explicitly notify the coordinator of servicing needs and scheduling demands by sending `read`, `write`, and `idle` notifications including timestamp to the coordinator which result in yielding by the client process and rescheduling per their scheduling policy. The coordinator also implements a real-time monotonic timer via `timer_create` that periodically sends a `timer` notification including timestamp. The timer notification ensures the coordinator interrupts a long running (typically *best-effort*) client process such that all client processes (especially *periodic*) are given fair access to the processor on a regular basis and no client process can starve all others.

Table 1. Process Priority Assignment

Priority	Level	Process	Description
p_c	ℓ_0	coordinator	highest real-time priority for the OS
$p_c - 1$	ℓ_1	active client	the currently dispatched client
$p_c - 2$	ℓ_2	block detection	reserved for a block detection process
$p_c - 3$	ℓ_3	waiting clients	all other waiting (or blocked) clients

Coordinator Initialization. System boot-up is a delicate process that we detail here. Upon initialization, the coordinator is bound to the CPU, set as a real-time process with highest priority ℓ_0 (Table 1), opens pipes for IPC, opens the shared memory, intializes the dynamics system, creates all client processes, and initializes the timer. Creation of a client process involves wrapping the process with a client thread, forking a new process, scheduling with the system as a real-time process and with real-time priority ℓ_3, binding to the same CPU as the coordinator, disabling console interaction, and launching the executable file via `execl`. Console interaction is disabled after the fork by forwarding `stdin`, `stout`, and `stderr` to `/dev/null` to minimize blocking system calls within these processes, which might disturb the coordinator's control over timing. When a client process is dispatched, the coordinator raises the client system priority from ℓ_3 to ℓ_1, and yields to the dispatched child by blocking via `select`. When the client process publishes any notification to the coordinator, the coordinator unblocks, preempts the client process, and lowers the client system priority from ℓ_1 to ℓ_3.

3.3   Client Process

A client process is an external main function program that must provide facilities for opening the shared buffer, for sending read, write, and idle notifications on prescribed channels, and for executing its own computation code. A client process must be preregistered with the simulation such that it is linked to the corresponding dynamic body, is described as a controller or planner, is classi-fied as either periodic or best-effort, and has IPC facilites prepared. Forking the coordinator and executing the external program, inserts the external pro-gram into the process space of the coordinator as a child process and inherits the established IPC channels. Notifications of process reads indicate requests for simulation state (e.g., reading sensor data). The coordinator services these reads using shared memory to pass data. Client process writes correspond to either a controller sending commands to actuators, which are correspondingly interpreted to manipulate dynamics state, or they correspond to a planner send-ing the plan to the controller via the coordinator. Finally, client processes send idle notifications to the coordinator to yield until the next activation (e.g., for periodic controllers).

4   Experimental Validation

Our experiments aim to illustrate the performance discrepancy between systems using callback functions and our time consistent system. The experiments have been designed to reflect our experience with building software for both simu-lated and physically situated robots; this decision results in a few discrepancies between the time consistent and callback-based systems that will be noted below.

Our experimental scenario uses a predator-prey scenario with two identical "space ships" (i.e., rigid bodies moving freely in SE(3) via application of forces). The ships are constrained to move within a cubic region of space; when a ship attempts to move out of this region, a spring-like penalty force pushes it back toward the free region.

4.1   Predator and Prey Behavior

The prey is driven by a simple control policy, which enacts either a random walk (we save the seed so that we can reproduce the walk across trials) or a fleeing behavior, depending on the distance of the predator. The prey flees by moving directly away from the predator using limited force.

The predator uses kinodynamic planning to chase the prey by exploiting the latter's deterministic behavior when the predator gets sufficiently close. Indeed, given ample planning time, the predator should be able to plan to intercept the prey by using the prey's deterministic movement model and an inverse dynamics model (that determines the requisite forces to achieve a target acceleration).

Planning and Control. We instituted our own kinodynamic planning mecha-nism which applies controls, integrates its models of the predator and prey for-ward in time, and finds a plan that brings the predator closer to the prey. Our initial efforts used OMPL, but the inherent multi-threaded nature of the library and its use of wall-clock time for determining when the planner should termi-nate confounded our system's efforts to schedule the planning process. Using wall-clock for process timing assumes that the process will not be scheduled-out, so the planning time parameter in running OMPL in the context of a real-time system can only be considered an idealized upper bound. The planner is allowed to execute for a maximum time (1.0s) and the resulting plan is not executed beyond a maximum duration (0.1s); beyond this point the open loop execution of the plan by the predator tends to lead to it becoming dynamically unstable.

The planner is called differently on the time consistent and callback-based systems. On the callback-based system, the planner is called only when all of the commands from a previous plan have been executed (or the plan has become stale by going over the maximum allowable duration). The time consistent system calls a planner in a manner analogous to operation on a real robot: (1) before a plan arrives, the predator executes "no-op" commands (*i.e.*, it applies no force and no torque); (2) the planner attempts to find a plan (the predator continues to execute "no-op"s at this time); (3) when a plan is found, the predator begins executing the plan and immediately calls the planner to begin planning again; (4) the planner keeps executing that plan until the sequence of commands is complete or the planner notifies the controller that a new plan is available.

The predator controller uses a composite feedforward (*i.e.*, the planned commands) and negative-feedback controller to account for error between its current state and the desired outcome. The prey uses a simple control policy only.

4.2   Time Consistent System and Callback-Based-Systems

The time consistent system was built on top of an otherwise unmodified version of Moby. For comparison we used two callback-based systems, "vanilla" Moby and Gazebo/ODE. Each simulation was run with a 0.01s dynamics time step, a maximum planning time of 1.0s, a planning step size of 0.01s, and both controllers running at a frequency of 100Hz. Our experiments were run on Linux kernel 3.2.0 ("vanilla" Ubuntu 12.04) using a 2.80GHz Intel Xeon quad-core processor.

4.3   Experimental Specifications

All scenarios start in the same configuration with the predator and prey halted and separated by ten meters and a flee triggering distance of five meters. Scenarios were simulated for twenty seconds of simulation time, and each experimental trial consisted of running the scenario with identical random seed for the prey using the three systems: Gazebo, "vanilla" Moby, and modified Moby (the time consistent system).

4.4   Experimental Results

The results of our experiments, depicted in Figure 1, show that the simulations based on the callback model yield virtually identical statistical behavior while the time consistent simulation exhibits dissimilar behavior. Because the simulation state is frozen during planning in the callback model simulations, the predator is consistently able to plan from its current state to the current state of the prey, which allows it to maintain close proximity at nearly all times. The statistical distributions for the callback-based systems are centered within the flee triggering distance with a maximum distance equal to the initial distance. In the time consistent simulations, the predator is able to approach the prey for only short durations and the statistical distribution is centered more closely to the starting distance and exhibits high variance. Animated renderings of the simulations show that the predator tracks the prey very closely in the `Gazebo` and "vanilla" `Moby` simulations while the predator generally undershoots or over-shoots the prey's position in the time accurate system.

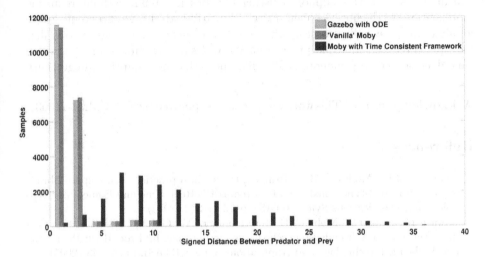

Fig. 1. Histogram showing the instantaneous distances between predator and prey over ten trials (2,000 samples per trial). Systems based on the callback model are effectively able to plan while the predator and prey are frozen in time, while the time consistent system must plan and act in real time. Consequently, the predator is able to stay much closer to the prey in the systems based on the callback model.

The predator in the callback-based systems is able to maintain much smaller distances to the prey solely because the predator's planner is able to execute proportionally for much longer without the danger of plans becoming stale. At the end of 20 simulated seconds, the planner in the traditional callback-based systems consumed on average 188 seconds, thus yielding $\Delta = 168.01$ seconds. The ratio of planner execution time (1.0s) to planner frequency (0.1s) indicates that the planner runs for 10 times longer per second than the simulated time progresses and approximates $\Delta = 10t$. In contrast, $\Delta = 0.003$ seconds for the time consistent system; though Δ is non-zero (due to intrinsic hardware limitations), its value is independent of the time that the simulation runs.

In a follow-up experiment, we measured the overhead of our components for enforcing temporal consistency. For a single trial, the overall system ran twenty seconds of simulation time in a real-time of 21.22 seconds during which the system spent 0.42 seconds coordinating, 20.21 seconds running planners and controllers, and 0.59 seconds stepping dynamics. From this result, we estimate our framework adds 2% of overhead, which we argue is acceptable.

5   Future Work

For future work, we will investigate augmenting our system to increase time accounting accuracy by detecting unconstrained blocking system events (which most non-real-time software triggers) and client process unblocking events, which will allow us to better support existing libraries like OMPL without requiring modifications to the libraries themselves. To take full advantage of current system architectures, we will also scale the coordinator scheduling system to utilize multiple cores and multiple processors. We will support simulations for which time does not proceed monotonically (like those that use adaptive integration).

Acknowledgements. This work was partially supported by NSF CMMI-110532.

References

1. Anderson, J.H., Mollison, M.S.: Bringing theory into practice: A userspace library for multicore real-time scheduling. In: Proc. IEEE Real-Time and Embedded Technology and Applications Symp (RTAS), pp. 283–292 (2013)
2. Aswathanarayana, T., Niehaus, D., Subramonian, V., Gill, C.: Design and performance of configurable endsystem scheduling mechanisms. In: Proc. IEEE Real-Time and Embedded Technology and Applications Symp. (RTAS), pp. 32–43 (2005)
3. Ford, B., Susarla, S.: Cpu inheritance scheduling. In: Proc. USENIX Symp. on Operating Systems Design and Implementation (OSDI), pp. 91–105 (1996)
4. Mirtich, B.: Impulse-based Dynamic Simulation of Rigid Body Systems. PhD thesis, University of California, Berkeley (1996)
5. Parmer, G., West, R.: HiRes: A system for predictable hierarchical resource management. In: Proc. IEEE Real-Time and Embedded Technology and Applications Symp. (RTAS) (2011)
6. Singla, A., Ramachandran, U., Hodgins, J.: Temporal notions of synchronization and consistency in beehive. In: Proc. ACM Symp. on Parallel Algorithms and Architectures, SPAA 1997, pp. 211–220. ACM, New York (1997)
7. Taylor, J.R., Drumwright, E.M., Parmer, G.: Temporally consistent simulation of robots and their controllers. In: Proc. ASME Intl. Design Engr. Tech. Conf. and Comput. and Inform. in Engr. Conf., Buffalo, NY (2014)
8. Vose, T., Umbanhowar, P., Lynch, K.M.: Friction-induced velocity fields for point parts sliding on a rigid oscillated plate. Intl. J. of Robotics Res. (June 2009)

Simulation and HRI Recent Perspectives with the MORSE Simulator

Séverin Lemaignan[1], Marc Hanheide[2], Michael Karg[3], Harmish Khambhaita[4], Lars Kunze[5], Florian Lier[6], Ingo Lütkebohle[7], and Grégoire Milliez[4]

[1] CHILI Lab., EPFL, Lausanne, Switzerland
[2] Centre for Autonomous Systems, University of Lincoln, UK
[3] IAS, Technische Universität München, Germany
[4] LAAS/CNRS, Université de Toulouse, France
[5] Intelligent Robotics Lab., University of Birmingham, UK
[6] CITEC, Bielefeld University, Germany
[7] Machine Learning and Robotics Lab., Universität Stuttgart, Germany

Abstract. Simulation in robotics is often a love-hate relationship: while simulators do save us a lot of time and effort compared to regular deployment of complex software architectures on complex hardware, simulators are also known to evade many of the real issues that robots need to manage when they enter the real world. Because humans are the paragon of dynamic, unpredictable, complex, real world entities, simulation of human-robot interactions may look condemn to fail, or, in the best case, to be mostly useless. This collective article reports on five independent applications of the MORSE simulator in the field of human-robot interaction: It appears that simulation is already useful, if not essential, to successfully carry out research in the field of HRI, and sometimes in scenarios we do not anticipate.

1 Introduction

The use of simulators for human-robot interaction (HRI) encompasses a variety of use-cases, from prototyping through evaluation to anticipatory simulation at runtime. It however suffers from a specific integration problem: Simulation in HRI requires to model robots in all their complexity *plus* a mean of representing and interacting with human agents. We therefore believe that an important stepping stone for a wider use of simulation in HRI is the availability of an integrated, easy-to-use framework that can encompass all currently important use-cases, and that provides an integration interface for developers *and* end-users of HRI simulation. In particular, we feel that it must be both easy to install and use, and offer adequate domain abstractions to facilitate development and integration. This paper presents how recent work using the *Modular OpenRobots Simulation Engine* [2] (MORSE, figure 1) attempts to address this challenge.

We will first review the range of current use-cases for simulation in HRI, then introduce MORSE with a focus on its HRI specific features, and finally demonstrate and discuss MORSE's versatility through several case studies. The

D. Brugali et al. (Eds.): SIMPAR 2014, LNAI 8810, pp. 13–24, 2014.

Fig. 1. Simulation and HRI: A PR2 and a human avatar in MORSE

case studies also illustrate the collective nature of this article: We report on contributions and experiences in human-robot interaction simulation from five unrelated projects, conducted by different people in different organizations, only sharing the MORSE simulator as common simulation platform.

HRI and Simulation

Applications of Simulation in HRI. In the HRI literature, several distinct goals for the use of simulation can be discerned. Without claim to completeness, we categorize them into *1*) prototyping, *2*) human modeling, *3*) interactive simulation, and *4*) anticipatory simulation.

The most well-known use-case is probably *prototyping*: The use of a simulator to reconstruct and run experiments in a simulated target situation prior to real-world evaluation. Apart from convenience, reasons to do so include simulation of unsafe situations (*e.g.* navigation in narrow spaces [18,9] or crowds [6]), and exploration of edge cases (*e.g.* humans not paying attention [10,5]).

Human modeling is one way of realizing human agents in simulation. [3] present for example a pedestrian model which has been evaluated against a large-scale database of recorded human movements. When detailed motion or other actions (such as speaking) is required, cognitive models have often been used [19], and recently also in HRI [22]. It is probably safe to say that such models are still far from general, but already quite useful for specific situations.

A problem with these approaches is the significant up-front effort required for modeling. Therefore, some research has explored the use of game engines in what we call *interactive simulation*: a real human controls a simulated human avatar interactively. While not fully automated, it allows reliable capture of interaction data for later analysis. This has been used for a long time in tele-operation settings [24] and also more recently for so-called "crowd-sourcing" work [1].

A very different use of simulation is *anticipatory simulation*. Here, a simulator is used *at runtime*, to be able to quickly explore the likely consequences of robotic actions. This uses simulation engines mainly to support spatial computations, *e.g.* to compute social metrics such as walking comfort [9] or proxemics [7]. The general goal is to enable the system to choose an action based on these metrics.

We believe it is clear that these use-cases benefit from each other. Particularly prototyping requires models, which could be manually specified, learned from real-world data, or learned interactively through the simulator.

Simulators for HRI. Softwares used for HRI simulation are currently fairly diverse, and can be distinguished by their use-cases. Prototyping work often uses "standard" robot simulators such as USARSim [14] (commonly used for rescue robotics applications but also beyond), or Gazebo [11] (though Gazebo's human agent support is currently limited) and MORSE [2].

In contrast, work in models or more advanced use-cases such as interactive or anticipatory simulation currently uses custom software – this is true for all of the papers cited in the previous sections at least. The pedestrian modeling community seems to share some tools, *e.g.* the work by Treuille et al [23] is known to have been re-used, but it has no connection to robot simulators.

Both standard robot simulators and pedestrian simulators use fairly coarse human models. In contrast, work in the Embodied Virtual Agent (EVA) community usually provides higher-level functionality, such as simulated emotion dynamics, behavior generation based on action primitives, conversational dialogue systems, and up to cognitive simulations. However, integrating these into a coherent system with an acceptable interface remains challenging [4].

As stated before, we think that the integration of these diverse functionalities into standard robot simulators would be an ideal next step, making specialized tools available to a much wider audience, and thus likely also identifying new avenues for improvements.

HRI and the MORSE Simulator

All five projects that are presented in this article rely on the domain-independent MORSE simulator as simulation platform. MORSE is an open-source tool developed for academic robotic research with contributions from over 15 institutions worldwide. It extends the Blender *Game Engine*, a 3D engine which features shader-based 3D rendering and physics simulation (BULLET physics engine). This allows for semi-realistic simulation of complex environments. The MORSE components (sensors and actuators) exchange data with the robotics software via middleware bindings (*Software In The Loop* architecture). Four middlewares designed for robotics are currently supported, including ROS and YARP, as well as a generic socket-based protocol. This design aims at providing a seamless experience when switching back and forth between the simulator and the physical robot. Standard robotic platforms, actuators and sensors (more than 50 components) are provided and enable fast creation of simulation scenarios, while custom components and behaviors can be added via simple Python scripts.

MORSE also introduces a concept of *abstraction levels*: sensors and actuators may expose several levels of abstraction, corresponding to different level of realism. For instance, users may choose if the odometry sensor returns only a curvilinear distance, a dX, dY, dZ differential vector, or the absolute position of the robot (integrated odometry). This allows users that are testing low-level components to do so, while users working at higher abstraction levels (typically in HRI) do not have to run full robotic software stacks (and thus, benefit from a lighter environment) and can work in a more deterministic environment. This feature can be finely controlled, on a per-component basis.

For HRI applications, MORSE provides a human avatar that can be fully controlled (displacement, gaze, grasping of objects, interactions with the environment like turning lights on, opening drawers, doors...) from a first-person-shooter perspective. This enables the researcher to quickly setup and test human-robot interactions with a tele-operated human model, hence with realistic human behaviors. As presented in [13], the human avatar can be controlled using a Kinect-like device. The same avatar can also be programmatically controlled by external scripts, like any robot in MORSE. With standard MORSE actuators like the *waypoint* actuator, the researcher can for instance pre-define paths that the human avatar will follow in a simulated environment.

2   HRI Simulation: Five Scenarios

To illustrate how simulation can support research in HRI, we present in the next sections five case-studies. The first three scenarios, *Situation Assessment for HRI and Simulated Feedback*, *An Expectations Framework for Domestic Robot Assistants* and *Preliminary Testing of Human-Aware Navigation Planner* illustrate the typically use-case for simulation: rather complex virtual environments are created where human presence plays a central role, and HRI algorithms are tested in a convenient and repeatable way. Note that, while we introduce here *simulation-only* scenarios, they all are test-cases of experiments that have been conducted on real robots: simulation is used here to support real-world deployments.

The fourth scenario, *Data Acquisition through Automatic Scene Generation* shows how simulation is used as an alternative source of input to train robots to behave in human environments, and the last scenario, *Automated Execution of Prototype HRI Experiments*, presents how the simulator can be used to provide automatic testing of human-aware behaviors, fully integrated to the software development workflow. Each of the presentations follow the same structure: we first introduce the scenario, we then highlight how simulation has been leveraged and its benefits, and we finally mention some of the shortcomings of the tool.

2.1   Situation Assessment for HRI and Simulated Feedback

When studying human-robot interaction, understanding the environment in which agents will interact is a key issue. In this first application, MORSE provides

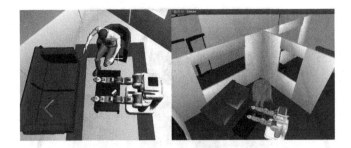

Fig. 2. On the left side, the MORSE environment; on the right side, the same environment, as perceived by the robot in the SPARK situation assessment module

a virtual environment that we use to harness situation assessment algorithms (performed by a software called SPARK [17], for SPAtial Reasoning and Knowledge) that also include human-centered *perspective taking*. The robot updates its knowledge in SPARK using its own position, human position and objects seen through abstracted, symbolic cameras provided by MORSE (so-called *semantic* cameras). In this particular scenario (figure 2), the human is sitting in a couch and ask the robot to bring specific objects that may be in another room (Pick-Place-Carry task).

Benefits of the Simulation. The direct benefits of relying on MORSE for the development of the situation assessment algorithms is the low-cost of deployment (manual testing on physical systems is labour-intensive), as well as the repeatability of the experimental conditions, important to assess the algorithmic improvements. Also, relying on MORSE effectively supports collaboration between the partners involved in this project (MaRDi project[1]): our partners are also using MORSE simulation to test their software and collect data with the same environment in their laboratory, where they focus on dialog processing. They can train their dialog system using MORSE feedback to test the robot behaviors [16].

2.2 An Expectations Framework for Domestic Robot Assistants

In this scenario, an apartment is simulated in which a domestic service robot is living together with a person (figure 3). A PR2 robot is controlled via ROS and the CRAM reactive plan language, which is used on several other real robots. The robots' duty is to observe the person performing different activities and detect unexpected situations based on the validation of different types of expectations [8]. The detection of such unexpected behavior can help future domestic service robots to better assess situations and adapt their actions to human behavior.

Benefits of the Simulation. The use of the MORSE simulator enabled us to set up a large testbed by reusing the real robot control layer via the ROS middleware

---

[1] http://mardi.metz.supelec.fr

Fig. 3. A simulated apartment with a domestic service robot and a person

and easy-to-generate unpredictable human behaviors using the human component of MORSE. Setting up of such an apartment in a real-world setting, together with a suitable sensor setup and a reliable robot control, would not only introduce huge costs but would also be a time-consuming task which can distract researchers from their actual research focus. The use of the simulated scenario enables us to gain many insights into the problem domain in a scenario that would not been possible within our project, while the algorithms were eventually validated on the real robot, inside a smaller real-world environment.

The human component of MORSE enabled us to test and validate our approach dynamically in a variety of situations. Since it can be controlled in real-time like in a 3D computer game while at the same time, a robot can be simulated by state-of-the-art components, it is possible to generate a multitude of situations on which the robot has to react. This greatly supported our project to gain insights about our approach, detect weak points and make improvements.

2.3   Preliminary Testing of Human-Aware Navigation Planner

To evaluate the improvements in the human-aware navigation planner developed at LAAS we carried out a user study. An experiment was set up, where a robot encounters a human crossing its path (at 90° angle to each other) while the robot is moving forward to its navigation goal. For preliminary testing of the planning algorithm, our lab area was simulated in MORSE. This simulated environment was extensively used to review the algorithm before it was deployed on the PR2 robot to carry out real-world experiments (whose results have been published in [21]).

Benefits of the Simulation. Development of human-robot interaction algorithms often require iterative process of prototyping, testing and reviewing. Setting up and experiment and testing of robot navigation algorithms especially for large environments involving humans is time consuming and is subject to availability of lab resources while working in a shared lab between different groups of researchers. Full support of the PR2 robot model among others, availability of a human model, and a convenient way of setting up experiment environment using Blender software were the most prominent features for choosing MORSE as the simulation environment for these experiments. Since MORSE already provides ROS bindings for the PR2 robot and human pose it requires minimal effort to switch between real-world and simulated environments.

As a consortium member in the EU project SPENCER[2], we plan to develop novel algorithms for robot navigation in large populated environments, e.g. airports. In the future we plan to use MORSE to simulate such large environment with multiple human models. This will certainly push the limits of simulation for HRI and hopefully provide new benchmarks.

2.4   Data Acquisition through Automatic Scene Generation

This fourth study proposes a different perspective on the role of simulation in HRI: simulating credible human environments to train systems to appropriately react to them: autonomous mobile robots that are to help and assist people in care homes, households, and at other workplaces have to understand how human activities affect the dynamics of objects in the environment. That is, robots need to know, when, where and how people manipulate objects and how they arrange and structure them in space. In the context of the STRANDS project[3] we aim for robots that understand the long-term, spatio-temporal relationships of objects and activities of people. In the scenario described here, we looked in particular at learning qualitative spatial relations of objects on office desks. As an accurate classification and pose estimation of objects on real-world office desks is still a challenging and difficult task for current robot perception systems we acquired a data set of object arrangements using the MORSE simulator. For this, we first bootstrapped an object statistics from manually labeled images of real office desks, and secondly, automatically generated a set of physically possible desktop scenes (figure 4). Based on the generated data we learned relational models of object arrangements on desks. The learnt models enabled a robot to predict the position of an object given a landmark. We employed these models to effectively guide a simulated and a real robot in object search tasks and evaluated its performance [12].

Benefits of the Simulation. First, the automatic scene generation (made easy by the use of Python to "program" the simulation scenes) and annotation of object arrangements in simulation is useful for the acquisition of large amounts of data over short periods of time. The generated data enabled us to design, implement and to evaluate our methods for predicting object locations before having a real-world data set in place. Secondly, the generation of object arrangements can increase the variability of scenes in human-robot experiments in general. Given the dynamics of objects in the real world it is important not to oversimplify human-robot experiments in simulated environments but make them as realistic as possible (in a controlled way). Finally, in future work, we plan to use the

---

[2] http://www.spencer.eu

[3] http://www.strands-project.eu

Fig. 4. Automatically generated scenes of office desks

generated desktop scenes in web-applications to crowdsource Natural Language descriptions of object arrangements and commands for robots from Internet users.

2.5   Automated Execution of Prototype HRI Experiments

In human-robot interaction studies, robots often indicate behavioral variability that may influence the experiment's final outcome. However, manual testing on physical systems is usually the only way to prevent this, but remains labour-intensive. To tackle this issue, we introduced *early automated prototype testing* [15] that consists of: a simulation environment, a software framework for automated bootstrapping of prototype systems, execution verification of system components, automated result assessment of experiments and a Continuous Integration (CI) server to centralize experiment execution. In our setup we bootstrap and execute a simulated prototype system on a CI server and assess the results in each run. In this particular scenario, a robot must report the location of a virtual human in a domestic environment. Both the robot and the human are moving in the scene and meet in front of a table.

The goal of this simulation setup is to incrementally decrease the level of abstraction until a satisfactory/sufficient degree of "realism" to make an assumption about real world behavior, is reached — in an integrated and continuous approach. In order to achieve this goal, we make use of two essential MORSE features: *a)* the human avatar that can be steered (set waypoints) interactively via middleware and *b)* a *semantic* camera that extracts the location of a specific entity in the simulation environment. The semantic camera is attached to the robot. If the human enters the robot's field of view, the location is reported and sent via middleware. After each CI run, the recorded movement trajectory of the human avatar is assessed (plotted) and archived. We have explicitly chosen to simplify the extraction of the location of the human to acquire a ground truth in the first iterations of the simulation. As an example, a system component (running outside of the simulation) that is intended to classify whether there is a human in front of a robot, by fusing multiple sensory inputs, can be evaluated based on this ground truth. Subsequently, we are able to exchange/add diverse virtual sensors, *i.e.* add a simulated laser scanner to build a person hypothesis for instance, thus gradually develop, assess and implement more complex scenarios.

Benefits of the Simulation. First of all, the interactive (remotely controllable) human avatar is useful to include a dynamic, yet not too realistic, human component in this setup. Secondly, the level of abstraction of different sensors, *i.e.* semantic camera versus virtual laser scanner enables us to gradually raise the level of complexity/realism and test different algorithms based on abstract and almost realistic sensor inputs. Lastly, the chance to deploy MORSE in a Continuous Integration environment, *i.e.* automatically run simulation scripts, generates an additional benefit.

3   Discussion: Towards Unification

While the five scenarios that we present here implement different use-cases, they actually cover similar approaches, while relying on the same simulator: study 2.1 shows how MORSE can be thought as a computation engine, 2.2 exploits the human agent in a computer game style, 2.3 uses MORSE for assessing and tuning the performance of algorithms, and scenario 2.4, while somewhat unique, still share similarities with Garrell et al., in that a model for object positions is trained on real-world data. Finally, the use-case presented in 2.5 proposes a different approach, with a focus on continuous testing, and can arguably be seen as the natural progression of using simulators for evaluation, extended here to cover HRI scenarios.

From this perspective, one may consider that the experiments recently conducted in the MORSE community around the simulation of HRI applications constitute the first steps towards building an unifying platform for HRI simulation, with two additional features: its *programmability* (simulation scenarios are Python scripts) and its concept of *abstraction levels* that provides an effective way to focus simulation on a particular problem by hiding irrelevant simulation artifacts.

These diverse use-cases support the idea that simulation is not only actually useful as a support tool for development of human-robot applications, but also *enables* new research techniques in HRI. *Continuous Integration* illustrates this point: while HRI experiments are considered as notoriously difficult to deploy, test and repeat, we show here how a simulator may enable automated testing of more and more complex scenarios, including long-term interaction.

Several issues are also raised and must be clearly stated. In its current state, the MORSE simulator provides only an incomplete model of the environment. Sounds/speech models are incomplete, and human models do not yet provide good enough accuracy, both at the level of the user interface (some actions can not be done with the interactive avatar), and at the simulation level (poor/missing walking cycles for instance). Finally, the overall convenience of MORSE for HRI could be improved, for instance by providing more assets (furnitures, objects) related to human environments. These issues, that are mostly technical and could be addressed at the software level, show that simulators dedicated to HRI application still need to mature. In that regard, the next section presents some of the directions that are currently researched.

The Next Steps

Several noteworthy developments related to HRI are currently shaping up in the MORSE community. We outline below some of them, that suggest new applications that we believe are relevant to HRI research.

A first line of investigation relates to the procedural generation of a variety of realistic human models. MAKEHUMAN is such an open-source tool that generates anatomically, kinetically and visually realistic human models. This software has a tight integration with Blender, and MORSE is soon to provide as well seamless integration with MAKEHUMAN models. This will bring a wide range of characters to feed the simulations, and extend testing environments with gender/size/age/skin color variances.

Besides being able to control a human avatar in simulation programmatically and deterministically, the possibility to automatically generate believable and realistic crowd behaviors is being explored. In this context, the objective is to adopt in MORSE technologies previously developed for computer games to generate trajectories that control the MORSE avatars. Based on the idea of *social forces*, the work of [20] is to be adapted to provide believable and realistic movement of several humans within MORSE. This implementation would provide a more realistic and dynamic environment to study human-robot spatial interaction and to provide a testbed for human-aware motion planning, to give two exemplary use-cases.

Another line of investigation looks at *embedding* the researcher into the robotic simulation. The purpose of such efforts is to provide a life-like immersive simulation environment that would allow at the same time ecologically valid human behaviors and repeatable, lightweight interaction settings. In [13], we presented how a human agent could interact with a virtual robot through a deictic interface based on a Kinect. Two distinct projects are currently looking into extending this approach, one (at Bielefeld University) aiming at integrating emerging Virtual Reality devices (like Occulus Rift) with MORSE, the other one (MarDI project) developing a virtual reality cave, that include 360° projections and spatialized sound.

Also often suggested, the *on-line* deployment of HRI simulations could efficiently support large scale HRI studies. The simulator and specific interaction scenarios would be embedded in a dedicated webpage and users would control a human avatar from their webbrowsers. This would potentially enable collection of large behavioral datasets. While MORSE development in that direction has yet to start, Breazeal et al. presented an initial attempt in that direction in [1] and the Gazebo simulator features a limited WebGL client that act as a proof-of-concept of on-line robotic simulation.

4   Conclusion

These examples and ideas hopefully give a picture of the lively landscape of the "Simulation for HRI" community, that has built itself around the MORSE simulator. In the introduction, we mentioned how simulation in HRI had to address in parallel constraints stemming from *robotic simulation* and *virtual agent simulation*, while remaining a lightweight, easy-to-use tool. We are certainly not yet there, much remains to be imagined, refined and achieved. Yet MORSE is already deployed in several institutions as a platform that efficiently supports research in human-robot interaction. As an open-source project, we strive for new use-cases and ideas, and warmly welcome researchers that would like to join the effort.

Acknowledgment. This research has received funding from the European Union (FP7/2007-2013) under grant agreements FP7-600623 (STRANDS) and FP7-600877 (SPENCER).

References

1. Breazeal, C., DePalma, N., Orkin, J., Chernova, S., Jung, M.: Crowdsourcing human-robot interaction: New methods and system evaluation in a public environment. Journal of Human-Robot Interaction 2(1), 82–111 (2013)
2. Echeverria, G., Lemaignan, S., Degroote, A., Lacroix, S., Karg, M., Koch, P., Lesire, C., Stinckwich, S.: Simulating complex robotic scenarios with MORSE. In: Noda, I., Ando, N., Brugali, D., Kuffner, J.J. (eds.) SIMPAR 2012. LNCS, vol. 7628, pp. 197–208. Springer, Heidelberg (2012)
3. Garrell, A., Sanfeliu, A.: Model validation: Robot behavior in people guidance mission using DTM model and estimation of human motion behavior. IEEE Transactions on Intelligent Robots and Systems (IROS), 5836–5841 (2010)
4. Gratch, J., Rickel, J., André, E., Cassell, J., Petajan, E., Badler, N.: Creating interactive virtual humans: Some assembly required. IEEE Intelligent Systems 17(4), 54–63 (2002)
5. Guzzi, J., Giusti, A., Gambardella, L.M., Theraulaz, G., Di Caro, G.A.: Human-friendly robot navigation in dynamic environments. In: IEEE International Conference on Robotics and Automation (ICRA), pp. 423–430. IEEE (2013)
6. Henry, P., Vollmer, C., Ferris, B., Fox, D.: Learning to navigate through crowded environments. In: IEEE International Conference on Robotics and Automation (ICRA), pp. 981–986. IEEE (2010)
7. Hoffman, G., Breazeal, C.: Effects of anticipatory perceptual simulation on practiced human-robot tasks. Autonomous Robots 28(4), 403–423 (2010)
8. Karg, M., Kirsch, A.: An expectations framework for domestic robot assistants. In: Conference on Advances in Cognitive Systems, pp. 77–92 (2013)
9. Kidokoro, H., Kanda, T., Brscic, D., Shiomi, M.: Will I bother here? – A robot anticipating its influence on pedestrian walking comfort. In: 8th ACM/IEEE International Conference on Human-Robot Interaction (HRI), pp. 259–266. IEEE (2013)

10. Knepper, R.A., Rus, D.: Pedestrian-inspired sampling-based multi-robot collision avoidance. In: 21st IEEE International Symposium on Robot and Human Interactive Communication (RO-MAN), pp. 94–100. IEEE (2012)
11. Koenig, N., Howard, A.: Design and use paradigms for Gazebo, an open-source multi-robot simulator. In: IEEE/RSJ International Conference on Intelligent Robots and Systems (IROS), vol. 3, pp. 2149–2154. IEEE
12. Kunze, L., Kumar, K., Hawes, N.: Indirect object search based on qualitative spatial relations. In: IEEE International Conference on Robotics and Automation (ICRA), May 31-June 7 (2014)
13. Lemaignan, S., Karg, M., Mainprice, M., Kirsch, A., Alami, R.: Human-robot interaction in the MORSE simulator. In: 7th ACM/IEEE International Conference on Human-Robot Interaction (HRI). Late Breaking Reports (2012)
14. Lewis, M., Wang, J., Hughes, S.: USARSim: Simulation for the study of human-robot interaction. Journal of Cognitive Engineering and Decision Making 1(1), 98–120 (2007)
15. Lier, F., Lütkebohle, I., Wachsmuth, S.: Towards automated execution and evaluation of simulated prototype HRI experiments. In: 9th ACM/IEEE Conference on Human-Robot Interaction (HRI). Late Breaking Reports (2014)
16. Milliez, G., Ferreira, E., Fiore, M., Alami, R., Lefèvre, F.: Simulating human-robot interactions for dialogue strategy learning. In: Brugali, D., Broenink, J., Kroeger, T., MacDonald, B. (eds.) SIMPAR 2014. LNCS (LNAI), vol. 8810, pp. 62–73. Springer, Heidelberg (2014)
17. Milliez, G., Warnier, M., Clodic, A., Alami, R.: A framework for endowing interactive robot with reasoning capabilities about perspective-taking and belief management. In: Proceedings of the 23rd IEEE International Symposium on Robot and Human Interactive Communication (2014)
18. Sisbot, E.A., Marin-Urias, L.F., Alami, R., Simeon, T.: A human aware mobile robot motion planner. Transactions on Robotics 23(5), 874–883 (2007)
19. Sun, R.: Cognition and multi-agent interaction: From cognitive modeling to social simulation. Cambridge University Press (2006)
20. Szymanezyk, O., Duckett, T., Dickinson, P.: Agent-based crowd simulation in airports using games technology. In: Nguyen, N.-T. (ed.) Transactions on CCI VIII. LNCS, vol. 7430, pp. 192–213. Springer, Heidelberg (2012)
21. Kruse, T., Khambhaita, H., Kirsch, A., Alami, R.: Evaluating directional cost models in navigation. In: 9th ACM/IEEE Conference on Human-Robot Interaction (HRI), Bielefeld, Germany (2014)
22. Trafton, G., Hiatt, L., Harrison, A., Tamborello, F., Khemlani, S., Schultz, A.: Act-R/E: An embodied cognitive architecture for human-robot interaction. Journal of Human-Robot Interaction 2(1), 30–55 (2013)
23. Treuille, A., Cooper, S., Popović, Z.: Continuum crowds. ACM Transactions on Graphics (TOG) 25, 1160–1168 (2006)
24. Wang, J., Lewis, M., Hughes, S., Koes, M., Carpin, S.: Validating USARsim for use in HRI research. Human Factors and Ergonomics Society Annual Meeting 49(3), 457–461 (2005)

A Dynamic Simulator
for Underwater Vehicle-Manipulators

Olivier Kermorgant

ICube Laboratory, Université de Strasbourg, France
kermorgant@unistra.fr

Abstract. In this paper we present a dynamic simulator for intervention autonomous underwater vehicles. Prototyping and testing of such robots is often tedious and costly, and realistic simulation can greatly help validating several aspects of the project. In order to benefit from existing software, the presented system is integrated with ROS, through the Gazebo dynamic simulator, and the underwater image rendering UWSim. The whole approach allows realistic rendering of dynamic multi-robot simulation, with contact physics, buoyancy, hydrodynamic damping and low-level PID control. This paper details the modeling choices that are done and exposes how to build its own AUV model. Integration with other ROS programs is exposed, and a simulation shows an example of behavior during a black box recovery mission.

1 Introduction

A strong trend in underwater robotics is the use of autonomous underwater vehicles instead of the classical Remotely Operated Vehicles and maned submersibles. Risk and cost are highly reduced, as it is never easy to deploy a team on a surface vessel or operators in a submersible. However, experimentation with AUV's is very difficult, because of the environment and the nature of the vehicle. Small experiments can be carried in water tanks, for example low-level control and basic prototyping, but this already requires space and resources. Higher-level experiments like navigation, waypoint following, seabed mapping or sensor-based control are designed to be carried in open environments, which involves high costs, human resources and are highly time consuming. Furthermore, in most autonomous underwater experiment the researchers do not have full knowledge of what is happening underwater, which is another difficulty during early development stages.

For these reasons, simulators have been developed in order to help prototyping AUV control and design. They allow having a full real-time access to all data during an experiment, and thus make it possible to greatly improve the AUV before going into the real experiments. A survey of AUV simulator has been carried in 2008 [6]. Since then, the robotic community got used to the ROS framework [2] which acquired its own AUV simulator, called UWSim [8]. This simulator has been used extensively in the Trident project, and renders realistic images

D. Brugali et al. (Eds.): SIMPAR 2014, LNAI 8810, pp. 25–36, 2014.
© Springer International Publishing Switzerland 2014

(a) Gazebo view.   (b) UWSim view.

Fig. 1. Rendering comparison between Gazebo (a) and UWSim (b). osgOcean allows UWSim to render automatically water color, visibility, floating particles and other underwater characteristics.

through OpenSceneGraph[1] (OSG) and osgOcean[2]. OSG is an open source 3D graphics application, while osgOcean was developped to render realistic underwater images in OSG. Fig. 1 gives an example of comparison between classical and underwater-oriented rendering. Embedded cameras, basic sonar and other AUV sensors are supported, and multiple underwater or surface vehicles can be present in the same simulation, which allows carrying experiments that would be very difficult in the real environment.

A drawback still present in the current state of the art is the absence of dynamic AUV simulation. Indeed, UWSim is only a kinematic simulator, with an external dynamic module that has to be coded in Matlab and only handles single-body vehicles. It is thus limited to kinematic control in the case of intervention AUV's (I-AUV), that carry a robotic arm. Several works have been using UWSim to show advanced whole-body control schemes [1,4], but the simulations lack realism. On the other hand, the ROS community is used to the Gazebo simulator [5], that was designed mostly for ground robots. This simulator handles dynamics, contact physics and is very versatile through its plugin-based design. A good example of Gazebo extension is the recent Hector Quadrotor package [7] that proposes quadrotor UAV simulation. However, as seen in Fig. 1a the rendering is of course far less satisfactory for underwater environments.

The purpose of this paper is to present an integration between Gazebo and UWSim, in order to achieve both dynamic and visually realistic I-AUV simulation. In this work we focus on the low-level dynamics, as higher-level control schemes or navigation tasks can already be implemented through the numerous ROS packages. The proposed simulator, called free-floating Gazebo[3], aims to

---

[1] http://www.openscenegraph.org

[2] http://code.google.com/p/osgocean

[3] https://github.com/freefloating-gazebo

be flexible, letting each user specifying the characteristics of his own (I-)AUV. A typical scenario would be to use CFD software or water tank experiments to estimate the hydrodynamics coefficients of the vehicle. This parameters can then be used in the proposed simulator in order to allow real-time simulation of navigation or sensor-based missions, which leads to a good compromise between computation cost and realism compared to pure kinematics simulators.

The paper is organized as follows. In Section 2 the simulated dynamics are described together with their implementation in the robot model. Section 3 presents the low-level PID control that is included in the simulator, allowing to control the I-AUV in position, velocity or effort depending on the controller design. The integration with other programs such as high-level control is then exposed in Section 4. Finally, an experiment is detailed in Section 5, showing the recovery of a black box.

2   Description and Simulation of a Submerged Object

The simulation is carried through two separate Gazebo plugins:

- A world plugin that simulates the overall buoyancy direction and water surface, together with the water current. The current may be varying but is assumed to be the same in the whole environment.
- A model plugin that handles low-level control through thruster effort (vehicle body) or joint torque (embedded arm).

We first describe the overall simulated dynamics before going into implementation details.

2.1   Dynamic Model

Gazebo performs dynamic simulation and takes as inputs the forces and torques that acts on a body. Through plugins, it is possible to add any kind of effort and thus to consider an hydrodynamic model. In this section we describe the dynamic model of a robot link and the approximations that are carried in the implementation.

We denote $\mathbf{p}$ the pose of a robot link expressed in the world frame, and $\mathbf{v}$ the velocity screw expressed in the local frame. In this case, the general form of the state-space dynamic model of the link yields [3]:

$$\mathbf{M}\dot{\mathbf{v}} = \mathbf{G}(\mathbf{v})\mathbf{v} + \mathbf{d}(\mathbf{v}) + \boldsymbol{\tau}_g + \boldsymbol{\tau}_u + \boldsymbol{\tau}_e \qquad (1)$$

$$\dot{\mathbf{p}} = \mathbf{J}\mathbf{v} \qquad (2)$$

where the parameters are defined as:

- $\mathbf{M}$ is the inertia matrix. It is the sum of the rigid body inertia matrix $\mathbf{M}_d$ and the added inertia matrix $\mathbf{M}_a$ due to the fluid. Besides of the mass that can be measured directly, the values of $\mathbf{M}_d$ and $\mathbf{M}_a$ are usually determined empirically. The error on $\mathbf{M}_a$ can be quite large and we will not consider this matrix in the model.

- **G(v)** represents the Coriolis and centrifugal forces. It is also the combination of the corresponding dynamic $\mathbf{G}_d$ and hydrodynamic $\mathbf{G}_a$ matrices, that are computed from the inertia matrices. For the same reason as $\mathbf{M}_a$, the matrix $\mathbf{G}_a$ is considered null.
- **d(v)** is the hydrodynamic damping force, or parasitic drag. Its values are also usually poorly known, but this effect cannot be ignored in the underwater case.
- $\boldsymbol{\tau}_g$ is the combination of the gravity and the buoyancy forces and induced torques. In most vehicles, the center of gravity and the center of buoyancy are vertically aligned in order to produce a keel effect that stabilizes the roll of the vehicle.
- $\boldsymbol{\tau}_u$ represents the forces and torques that are added by the user. In our case, we consider additional forces through several thrusters that can be placed on the AUV body. No other kind of motors (for example fins) are considered. For the links related to the robotic arm, the applied torque and forces correspond to the joint efforts.
- $\boldsymbol{\tau}_e$ regroups the other forces and torques applied to the robot link. This corresponds to the interactions with other robot links or through contact points with other objects, which are modeled by the Gazebo simulator.
- **J** is the transformation matrix between the world frame and the link frame.

Because of the usual modeling uncertainties and the low velocity of the vehicle, the added inertia and Coriolis forces are not taken into account. All additional efforts related to the hydrodynamic effects are considered into the damping force $\mathbf{d(v)}$, which is a quadratic function of the velocity between the robot link and the water velocity:

$$\mathbf{d(v)} = -\mathbf{k}^\top |\mathbf{v} - \mathbf{J}^{-1}\mathbf{v}_c| (\mathbf{v} - \mathbf{J}^{-1}\mathbf{v}_c) \tag{3}$$

where **k** expresses the damping coefficients and $\mathbf{v}_c = (\boldsymbol{v}_c, 0)$ is the water velocity expressed in the world frame and has null angular values.

The same modeling is used for non-actuated objects that may be present in the simulation. A free-floating buoy or an object lying on the seabed are also subject to buoyancy and hydrodynamic drag, and a robot that interacts with such objects will have to cope with the corresponding force. We now detail the implementation of the given model.

2.2   Implementation

World Plugin for Hydrodynamics. The water velocity $\mathbf{v}_c$ and the buoyancy direction are taken into account in a world plugin, The Gazebo simulator subscribes to a ROS topic that gives the intensity and direction of the water current. It is thus possible to have the current vary if needed. The buoyancy direction is of course opposed to the gravity, and becomes null as the vehicle goes above the surface. A Gazebo world file is given and handles this plugin.

We use additional tags in the URDF[4] to handle buoyancy and damping related to a given link or object. This allows giving the position of the center of buoyancy with regards to the link frame, together with the compensation coefficient that indicates the percentage of gravity that is compensated. In most I-AUV this coefficient is slightly greater than 1, meaning that without external effort the vehicle tends to come to the surface. Here is an example of these additional tags:

```
<buoyancy>
     <compensation>1.01</compensation>
     <origin xyz= ".5 0 .2"/>
     <limit radius=".5"/>
     <damping xyz="40 80 80"/>
</buoyancy>
```

The `<limit>` tag indicates where the buoyancy force begins to decrease when approaching the water surface. In I-AUV simulation we are mostly interested in controlling the vehicle when it is entirely underwater, therefore no complex computation are carried to handle the surface approach: the buoyancy force applied to a given link simply decreases to zero when the link is near the surface.

Model Plugin for Thruster Control. Thrusters are also defined in the URDF. For each thruster the maximum effort is given, together with the mapping between the thrust direction and the body frame:

```
<link>base_link</link>
<bodyCommandTopic>body_command</bodyCommandTopic>
<jointCommandTopic>joint_command</jointCommandTopic>
<!-- for each thruster, map to XYZ+RPY and maximum effort -->
<thruster>
     <map>-1 0 0 0 0 ${-body_width/2}</map>
     <effort>30</effort>
</thruster>
```

It is thus possible to simulate thruster saturation and to handle it in the control law. For now all thrusters are assumed to be fixed on the same link, which is defined as base_link in the given example. This tag is read by the model plugin to allow low-level control. In the given example, we see that the Gazebo simulator will listen to thruster forces on the body_command topic, and to joint efforts on the joint_command topic. These efforts can be generated from a high-level force controller, or more usually from the low-level controller that is included in the simulator. We now detail the implementation of this controller.

3   Low-Level PID Control

In this section we describe the PID controller of the AUV simulator. Because of the numerous uncertainties on the dynamic model, it is very tedious to design

---

[4] Universal Robot Description File.

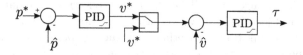

Fig. 2. Cascaded PID, here in position control. The position PID outputs a velocity setpoint that is then followed with the velocity PID.

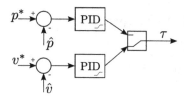

Fig. 3. Parallel PID, here in velocity control. Both the position and the velocity PID's output the desired effort.

a AUV advanced force controller. The usual approach is to have a high-level controller that generates position or velocity setpoints for the body and the arm, and a low-level PID controller that ensures the given setpoints are followed.

General Design. A independent ROS node handles the global PID controller, which is implemented as a set of parallel or cascaded controllers depending on the user choice. The two configurations are detailed in Fig. 2 (cascaded) and Fig. 3 (parallel). p^* and v^* correspond to the desired position and velocity of a joint value or a body linear or angular direction. $\hat{p}$ and $\hat{v}$ represents the estimation of the position and of the velocity, coming from the sensors or from an estimation algorithm. The velocity PID is the same in both configuration, but the position PID outputs the velocity setpoint in cascaded mode, and the effort in parallel mode. Dynamic Reconfigure[5] allows real-time gain tuning, and a configuration file is used to store the tuned gains. A ROS service is used to switch between position and velocity control, which are defined independently for the body and the arm.

Anti-windup and Body Thrusters Mapping. The maximum velocities and efforts that are given in the URDF are used for anti-windup inner loops in each PID. In particular, the maximum thruster efforts are mapped to the body directions in order to get the actual controllable directions and their associated maximum effort. No PID are instanciated for non-controllable directions (typically roll, but sometimes also pitch and sway). The position setpoint of the AUV is given in the world frame, while the velocity setpoint are given in the vehicle frame. The several PID outputs represent the desired wrench τ_u^* to apply to the AUV body. This desired wrench is then mapped to the thruster efforts τ_t^* in order to apply the saturation, and mapped back to the actual wrench τ_u to be applied in Gazebo:

---

[5] http://wiki.ros.org/dynamic_reconfigure

$$\boldsymbol{\tau}_u = \mathbf{T}.\boldsymbol{\tau}_t = \mathbf{T}.\mathrm{sat}(\boldsymbol{\tau}_t^*) = \mathbf{T}.\mathrm{sat}(\mathbf{T}^+\boldsymbol{\tau}_u^*) \tag{4}$$

where $\mathbf{T}$ is the mapping matrix between the body directions and the thrusters and $\mathbf{T}^+$ is its Moore-Penrose pseudo-inverse. Another possible strategy in case of thruster saturation is to scale all thruster efforts instead of only applying the saturation:

$$\boldsymbol{\tau}_u = \mathbf{T}.\min_{i=1}^{n_t} \frac{\tau_i^{\max}}{\tau_i^*} \boldsymbol{\tau}_t^* \tag{5}$$

where n_t is the number of thrusters and $\tau_i^{\max}$ is the maximum effort of thruster i. The real-time load of the thrusters is available for logging or high-level control, as we will see in Section 5. We now detail the integration of the simulator with Gazebo, UWSim and higher-level control nodes.

4   Integration

In this section we detail the interactions between the I-AUV simulation in Gazebo, the PID controller, the UWSim visualization and other potential higher-level controllers. First the file integration is mentioned as it is necessary to synchronize the Gazebo and UWSim description files. We then expose and detail an example of graph of nodes.

4.1   File Synchronization

Gazebo and UWSim both have their own approach to describe the robot model, additional moving objects and the world terrain. As UWSim is only a kinematic simulator, the URDF used to describe the robots are usually simpler that the Gazebo ones, that contains all the inertial and collision-related data. On the opposite, the scene file, used to describe the whole world setup in UWSim, contains all information about the considered simulation while the same data is separated in several files when using Gazebo. In this section we briefly expose the synchronization script that helps building lesser-information files from higher ones.

The starting point is the UWSim launchfile that contains the UWSim scene file, that describes the whole setup. This allows retrieving the list of robots URDF files and moving objects, their starting position and the terrain 3D mesh that is used. The URDF files may already exist or need to be generated from existing xacro files, that are used in Gazebo. All starting positions are found in the UWSim scene file, which allows generating a Gazebo model spawner: this ensures that the same objects will be present at the same position in Gazebo and UWSim. Finally, for now UWSim and Gazebo do not use the same convention for file pathes. The pathes are thus adapted on the fly when generating or updating missing files. With such synchronization, an experiment can first be carried only in UWSim with kinematic control for simplicity and debugging, then with the dynamic simulator and low-level PID loops to have a realistic behavior. We now detail the interactions between the several ROS nodes in a typical simulation.

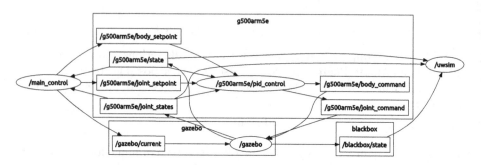

Fig. 4. Auto-generated graph of nodes (round-shaped) and topics (rectangular)

4.2   Node Interactions

This section details the interactions between the simulation node, integrated through plugins in Gazebo, and the other nodes of a typical I-AUV simulation. The graph of nodes is represented in Fig. 4. We can see all moving objects have their own namespace. Here `/g500arm5e` is the robot namespace and re-groups all nodes and topics related to its low-level control, while `/blackbox` is related to a moving black box. Moving objects are considered as non-actuated robots, thus have their own namespaces. The `gazebo` node subscribes to the `/gazebo/current` topic, which allows defining and modifying the water current.

The main controller is called `/main_control`. It reads body and joint positions from the corresponding topics. In this simulation these values are the true ones and come directly from Gazebo. Water current, as well as body and joint position setpoints are generated. These setpoints are handled by the `pid_control` node, which generates the joint effort `joint_command` and the body wrench `body_command`. These topics are read by Gazebo in order to apply the corresponding forces and torques to the vehicle and its arm.

As we can see on the graph, UWSim only receives data in order to visualize the current pose of the I-AUV and of the black box. Still, an embedded camera is simulated in UWSim and the generated images could be used in the main controller to perform visual servoing as shown in [4].

We now expose the simulation results.

5   Experiments

In this section we show an example of behavior of a black box recovering mission.

Experimental Setup. The considered I-AUV is the Girona 500 [9], equipped with a 3-degrees of freedom robot arm mounted with a hook on the end-effector. The AUV body has 5 thrusters, allowing to control all degrees of freedom except for the roll. A keel effect is induced by the relative position of the center of gravity and the center of buoyancy such that the roll is stable. The AUV is slightly lighter than water, thus the two vertical thrusters are always used to stabilize the depth.

(a) End of approach. The hook is lying on the seabed and the arm cannot follow its setpoint.

(b) Lifting. One of the vertical thruster saturates.

(c) Recovery complete.

Fig. 5. UWSim view of the simulation

Simulation Scenario. As the goal is to show the dynamic behavior, position control is in open loop and the PID gains are not well tuned. The scenario includes several steps that illustrate difficulties of underwater interventions:

1. At first only joint control is performed to set the arm in an idle position.
2. At iteration 70, body position control is used to approach the black box. At the end of the approach, around iteration 350, the hook will touch the seabed and thus the arm will not be able anymore to follow its setpoint.
3. At iteration 520, the joint setpoint is changed to prepare the recovery
4. At iteration 820, the body position setpoint is changed to go up and recover the box, which is entirely carried by the AUV after iteration 840. Because of the weight of the box, some joints and some thrusters will be saturated at this time.

Fig. 5 depicts the I-AUV in various steps. At the end of the approach (Fig. 5a), the hook slightly hits the seabed, which will appear on the joint measurements. Fig. 5b shows the beginning of the recovery, which corresponds to some oscillations and to the saturation of a vertical thruster. In Fig. 5c the I-AUV has recovered the black box and is going up. Because of the weight of the black box, some joints are saturated.

Body Position Control. The overall behavior of the body control is shown in Fig. 6. The vertical dotted lines correspond to the key-iterations that are mentioned above. The measurement rate is 30 Hz. The low-level PID controllers ensure the body position and orientation setpoints are followed after iteration 70 (beginning of body position control). Interaction with the black box is clearly visible from iteration 840. As soon as the box is entirely recovered, small oscillations appear on the orientation error (Fig. 6b). This is due to the fact that the box behaves like a pendulum when carried by the recovering hook, and induces some perturbations on the vehicle position control.

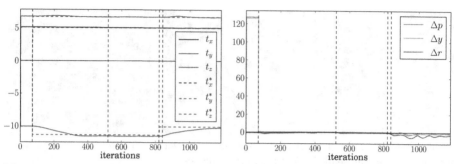

(a) Body position (plain) and setpoint (dotted). Surge (blue), sway (green) and heave (red).

(b) Body orientation error in degree. Roll (magenta), pitch (cyan) and yaw (yellow).

Fig. 6. 3D behavior of the I-AUV body. The heave (red) follows its setpoint after iteration 70, while the orientation error (b) is null even if small oscillations appear when lifting the black box after iteration 840.

Thruster Load. The described body behaviors also appear in Fig. 7, that represents the thruster load in percent. When gived a new position setpoint at iteration 70, we see one of the vertical thruster (cyan) is saturated. This explains the slow reaching of the heave setpoint (red) in Fig. 6a. From iteration 350 the hook is lying on the seabed. The load is thus reduced on the vertical thruster. It is saturated again after iteration 820, when the new position setpoint makes the I-AUV go up.

The oscillations of the orientation error in Fig. 6b are also visible in Fig. 7 after iteration 820. The thruster load oscillations are more important than the orientation error, which means the PID controllers of the thrusters manage to greatly reduce the perturbation induced by the carrying of the black box.

Joint Behavior. The behavior of the 3-degrees of freedom arm is represented in Fig. 8. First the setpoints are followed but when the hook comes in contact with the seabed at iteration 350, the arm is stuck between the ground and the I-AUV body and it becomes impossible to follow the position setpoint. The setpoint changes at iteration 520, making it possible to be followed again. Once the arm begins to lift the black box at iteration 820, the joint effort limits clearly appear as the shoulder and elbow cannot cope with the weight of the black box.

Discussion. The whole experiment demonstrates the dynamic simulation, together with contact physics between the hook and both the seabed and the black box. Dynamic coupling is clearly visible when lifting the box, as its pendulum-like oscillation are passed on the whole I-AUV. The PID controllers of the thrusters manage stabilizing the body position, but the arm still oscillates and cannot follow its position setpoint due to the limits on joint efforts. The overall simulation

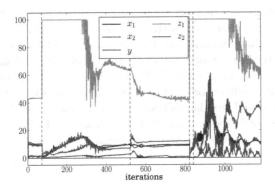

Fig. 7. Thruster load in percent. Surge/yaw (blue and green), sway (red) and heave/pitch (cyan and magenta).

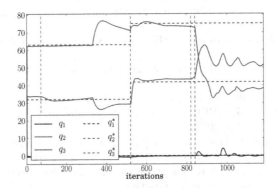

Fig. 8. Joint positions and setpoints. Slew (blue), shoulder (green) and elbow (red). The hook touching the seabed is clearly visible at iteration 350, as the arm cannot ensure its position setpoint. Oscillations appear after iteration 820 because of effort limits.

shows that dynamic simulation of a I-AUV raises realistic difficulties that are possible to try and solve in the simulated environment, before having to perform real experiments.

6 Conclusion

We have presented a dynamic simulator for intervention autonomous underwater vehicles. Through the ROS framework, it was possible to use both the dynamic simulation capabilities of Gazebo and the realistic underwater rendering of UWSim. The considered modeling is focused on the main effects due to hydrodynamic forces, that are drag and buoyancy. A possible improvement is to take into account the added inertia and Coriolis, but these effects are difficult to quantify precisely. That is why all uncertainties are here considered in the damping coefficients $d(v)$. Additional URDF tags allows defining the buoyancy and damping parameters of each robot link or other moving object, such as the black box that is considered in the example. The presented experiment was designed to show that dynamic simulation can be used to reproduce realistic difficulties such as thruster or joint effort limit, collision and uncertainties on the setpoint following. As in real I-AUV, this can be due to non-optimal tuning of the low-level controllers, or on the uncertainties on the hydrodynamic parameters. The proposed simulation framework can thus be used to validate new algorithms for sensor-based control or state estimation. In future works we will focus on underwater sensors in order to perform realistic sensor-based missions.

References

1. Casalino, G., Zereik, E., Simetti, E., Torelli, S., Sperinde, A., Turetta, A.: Agility for underwater floating manipulation: Task & subsystem priority based control strategy. In: IEEE/RSJ Int. Conf. on Intelligent Robots and Systems, Vilamoura, Portugal, pp. 1772–1779 (September 2012)
2. Cousins, S.: Welcome to ros topics. IEEE Robotics & Automation Magazine 17(1), 13–14 (2010)
3. Fossen, T.I.: Guidance and control of ocean vehicles, vol. 199. Wiley, New York (1994)
4. Kermorgant, O., Pétillot, Y., Dunnigan, M.: A global control scheme for free-floating vehicle-manipulators. In: IEEE/RSJ Int. Conf. on Intelligent Robots and Systems, Tokyo, Japan (November 2013)
5. Koenig, N., Howard, A.: Design and use paradigms for gazebo, an open-source multi-robot simulator. In: IROS, vol. 3, pp. 2149–2154. IEEE (2004)
6. Matsebe, O., Kumile, C.: A review of virtual simulators for autonomous underwater vehicles (auvs). In: Navigation, Guidance and Control of Underwater Vehicles, Killaloe, Ireland, vol. 2, pp. 31–37 (2008)
7. Meyer, J., Sendobry, A., Kohlbrecher, S., Klingauf, U., von Stryk, O.: Comprehensive simulation of quadrotor uAVs using ROS and gazebo. In: Noda, I., Ando, N., Brugali, D., Kuffner, J.J. (eds.) SIMPAR 2012. LNCS, vol. 7628, pp. 400–411. Springer, Heidelberg (2012)
8. Prats, M., Pérez, J., Fernández, J.J., Sanz, P.J.: An open source tool for simulation and supervision of underwater intervention missions. In: IEEE/RSJ Int. Conf. on Intelligent Robots and Systems, Vilamoura, Portugal, pp. 2577–2582 (October 2012)
9. Ribas, D., Ridao, P., Magí, L., Palomeras, N., Carreras, M.: The girona 500, a multipurpose autonomous underwater vehicle. In: IEEE OCEANS, Santander, Spain, pp. 1–5 (June 2011)

Extending Open Dynamics Engine
for the DARPA Virtual Robotics Challenge

John M. Hsu and Steven C. Peters

Open Source Robotics Foundation, 419 N. Shoreline Blvd, Mountain View, CA 94041, USA
{hsu,scpeters}@osrfoundation.org
http://osrfoundation.org

Abstract. The DARPA Virtual Robotics Challenge (VRC)[1] was a cloud-based robotic simulation competition. Teams competed by writing control software for a humanoid robot to perform disaster response tasks in real-time simulation. Simulating the physics and sensors of a humanoid robot in real-time presented challenges related to the trade-off between simulation accuracy and computational time. The Projected Gauss-Seidel (PGS) iterative solver was chosen for its performance and robustness, but it lacks the accuracy and the fidelity required for reliable simulation of task-level behaviors. This paper presents the modeling decisions and algorithmic improvements made to the Open Dynamics Engine (ODE) physics solver that improved PGS accuracy and fidelity without sacrificing its real-time simulation performance in the VRC. These improvements allowed for stable simulation regardless of user input during the VRC, and supported reliable contact dynamics during VRC tasks without violating the near real-time requirement.

1 Introduction

The DARPA Robotics Challenge (DRC) is a competition with the goal of improving robotic systems for use in disaster response. With sufficient mobility and dexterity, robots may assist technicians and emergency responders in dangerous environments. The DRC will test the ability of robots to complete tasks relevant to disaster response, such as walking on uneven terrain, driving a utility vehicle, opening doors, climbing industrial ladders, and threading a fire hose into a standpipe.

In addition to physical testing in the DRC Trials and DRC Finals, the DRC also included the Virtual Robotics Challenge (VRC), in which teams wrote control software for a simulated humanoid robot. The Open Source Robotics Foundation (OSRF) provided an open-source cloud-based simulator for the disaster response tasks using a model of the Atlas robot from Boston Dynamics [2] and the dexterous Sandia hand [3].

When selecting the simulation tasks for the VRC, it was necessary to consider the difficulty of accurately simulating tasks using Newton-Euler equations of motion with a Coulomb friction approximation. The following high-level tasks were chosen: walk across various terrains, drive a utility vehicle, and thread a fire hose into a standpipe. These tasks require simulation of dynamic balancing, walking on uneven terrain, ingress/egress of a utility vehicle, manipulation of vehicle controls (pedals, gear shift, steering), vehicle dynamics, and object manipulation with a dexterous hand.

D. Brugali et al. (Eds.): SIMPAR 2014, LNAI 8810, pp. 37–48, 2014.

2   Literature Review

There are numerous approaches to modeling rigid body dynamics with frictional contacts. Explicit penalty methods apply restorative forces to "penalize" collisions between rigid bodies as contacts arise. For example, the Hertz model [4], is an idealized model of material deformation and contact forces for spherical surfaces that is often applied as an explicit penalty force. Constraint-based methods formulated as a Linear Complementarity Problem (LCP) attempt to resolve all contact (and constraint) forces simultaneously when collisions are detected. Examples of constraint-based methods using velocity-impulse formulated as an LCP include [5,6,7,8]. These methods can have performance advantages when compared with pure penalty based methods due to reduced numerical stiffness. This is mostly due to the fact that penalty methods can require very small time steps for stability while simulating dynamic walking and grasping.

The strategies for solving the constraint based LCP problem mainly fall into two categories: iterative and direct (pivoting) methods. This paper presents improvements to the iterative Projected Gauss-Seidel solver that exists within the Open Dynamics Engine (ODE). Note that ODE also includes a direct method that is based on Lemke's algorithm [9], which is an extension of Dantzig's algorithm [10].

An important aspect to consider when formulating the equations for articulated rigid body dynamics is the internal state representation. In maximal coordinate formulations, such as ODE, each rigid body has six degrees of freedom. Articulation is encoded as equality constraints on the dynamic states. This approach yields convenient sparse matrix structures, such as a block diagonal mass matrix and a sparse constraint Jacobian. Additionally, the approach treats contact and articulation constraints in a uniform manner. In contrast, formulations based on internal (or generalized) coordinates (often using Featherstone's algorithm [11,12]) consider articulation implicitly by adding the system degrees of freedom with each articulation joint. This yields more accurate kinematics and a smaller mass matrix, though the mass matrix structure is no longer sparse. There was some discussion prior to the VRC regarding the relative merit of maximal and generalized coordinates [13], though a robust comparison is not presented here.

3   Modeling and Fidelity Considerations

This section presents the modeling decisions that were made to improve real-time performance while maintaining sufficient physical accuracy.

The Atlas robot is a humanoid robot manufactured by Boston Dynamics Inc. (BDI), with 28 hydraulically actuated degrees of freedom [2]. The kinematics, rigid body inertias, 3D mesh collision shapes, maximum joint angles, velocities, and torques were provided by BDI. In the absence of details about the hydraulic systems, each joint was modeled as a pin joint with torque control subject to position, velocity, and torque limits. The torque and speed limits were not coupled with a torque-speed curve. Static joint friction was not modeled, though viscous damping (proportional to joint velocity) was applied at the joints in a heuristic manner to improve solver stability. Contact friction was modeled as Coulomb friction using a friction pyramid (see Section 4.6).

Although a full set of 3D concave meshes was provided for the Atlas robot, each collision shape was approximated by a union of convex sphere, box, and cylinder collision primitives. It was found that the collision primitives exhibited faster collision detection and more robust contact resolution than the 3D meshes [14].

Some physical interactions were approximated due to insufficient fidelity at the required level of real-time performance. Threading a fire hose, for example, involves contact between millimeter-scale features. Instead of modeling the fine contact geometry, a screw joint was dynamically created when the fire hose coupling was sufficiently aligned with the standpipe. The coupling could be rotated in one direction to connect or in the opposite direction to release the coupling. Sitting in the seat of a utility vehicle was another challenge, as the seat was modeled as a rigid body. This caused difficulty in finding a stable seating position. To remedy this, a viscous damping field was created on the surface of the seat. This partially mitigated the problem, though stable sitting in the vehicle proved a continual challenge in the VRC [15].

4 Open Dynamics Engine

This section presents the algorithms used by Open Dynamics Engine (ODE) [16]. ODE represents rigid body states with maximal coordinates, in which each rigid body has six degrees of freedom, and articulation and contact constraints are enforced by adding constraint equations. Please see ODE's User Manual [17] for general documentation.

4.1 Unconstrained Rigid Body Dynamics

The notation for maximal coordinates is borrowed from [18], and it is assumed that all vectors are expressed in the world frame unless otherwise specified. Each rigid body has an associated coordinate frame with center of gravity (c.g.) position $\bar{x}$ and orientation quaternion $\bar{q}$. The coordinate frames evolve in time according to

$$\bar{x}_t = \dot{\bar{x}}, \bar{q}_t = (1/2)\bar{\omega}\bar{q} \tag{1}$$

with $\dot{\bar{x}}$ and $\bar{\omega}$ representing linear and angular velocity. The velocities evolve according to the Newton-Euler equations of motion, which are expressed as

$$m\ddot{\bar{x}}_t = \bar{f}, \bar{L}_t = \bar{\tau}$$

where m is the mass; $\bar{f}$ and $\bar{\tau}$ are the net force and torque; $\bar{L} = \bar{\bar{I}}\bar{\omega}$ is the angular momentum with inertia tensor $\bar{\bar{I}} = \bar{\bar{R}}\bar{\bar{D}}\bar{\bar{R}}^T$, rotation matrix $\bar{\bar{R}}(\bar{q})$, and body-frame inertia tensor $\bar{\bar{D}}$. For a single unconstrained rigid body, this can be re-written as:

$$\begin{bmatrix} m\bar{\bar{\delta}} & \bar{\bar{0}} \\ \bar{\bar{0}} & \bar{\bar{I}} \end{bmatrix} \begin{bmatrix} \ddot{\bar{x}} \\ \dot{\bar{\omega}} \end{bmatrix} = \begin{bmatrix} \bar{f} \\ \bar{\tau} - \bar{\omega} \times \bar{\bar{I}}\bar{\omega} \end{bmatrix} \tag{2}$$

where $\bar{\bar{\delta}}$ is the identity matrix.

For a system with multiple rigid bodies, augmented variables are defined for each body b: velocity vector $\bar{v}_b = [\dot{\bar{x}}_b^T, \bar{\omega}_b^T]^T$; block diagonal mass matrix $\bar{\bar{m}}_b = diag(m_b\bar{\bar{\delta}}, \bar{\bar{I}}_b)$;

and effort vector $\bar{e}_b = [\bar{f}_b^T, (\bar{\tau}_b - \bar{\omega}_b \times \bar{\bar{I}}_b \bar{\omega})^T]^T$. The dynamics in equation 2 can then be expressed as:

$$\bar{\bar{m}}_b \dot{\bar{v}}_b = \bar{e}_b \tag{3}$$

For a system of N rigid bodies, system variables are defined as the velocity states $\bar{v} = [\bar{v}_1^T, \bar{v}_2^T, ...\bar{v}_N^T]^T$; the block diagonal system mass matrix $\bar{\bar{M}} = diag(\bar{\bar{m}}_1, \bar{\bar{m}}_2, ..., \bar{\bar{m}}_N)$; and the system effort vector $\bar{E} = [\bar{e}_1^T, \bar{e}_2^T, ...\bar{e}_N^T]^T$. The unconstrained system dynamics from 3 are then given as:

$$\bar{\bar{M}} \dot{\bar{v}} = \bar{E} \tag{4}$$

4.2   Articulation and Contact Constraints

Articulation and contact are encoded through a set of nonlinear constraints on rigid body position and orientation, with articulation using equality constraints $h_e(\bar{x}, \bar{q}) = 0$, and contact using inequality constraints $h_i(\bar{x}, \bar{q}) \geq 0$.

To avoid nonlinearities, the position constraints are differentiated to yield linear velocity constraints of the form

$$\bar{\bar{J}} \bar{v} = \bar{c} \tag{5}$$

where $\bar{\bar{J}}$ is the constraint Jacobian matrix and $c_e = 0, c_i >= 0$, for articulation equality constraints and contact inequality constraints, respectively. The velocity constraints are adjoined to the equations of motion using a vector of Lagrange multipliers $\bar{\lambda}$ as:

$$\bar{\bar{M}} \dot{\bar{v}} = \bar{E} + \bar{\bar{J}}^T \bar{\lambda} \tag{6}$$

4.3   Discretization

The dynamics in equation 6 are discretized over a time interval Δt using a first-order Euler method as $\dot{\bar{v}} \Delta t = \bar{v}^{n+1} - \bar{v}^n$, and rearranged to yield the difference equation for constrained rigid body dynamics in matrix form as

$$\begin{bmatrix} (1/\Delta t)\bar{\bar{M}} & -\bar{\bar{J}}^T \\ \bar{\bar{J}} & 0 \end{bmatrix} \begin{bmatrix} \bar{v}^{n+1} \\ \bar{\lambda} \end{bmatrix} = \begin{bmatrix} (1/\Delta t)\bar{\bar{M}}\bar{v}^n + \bar{E} \\ \bar{c} \end{bmatrix} \tag{7}$$

Assuming that the constraints are satisfied implicitly at the next time step $(t + \Delta t)$, $\bar{\bar{J}}\bar{v}^{n+1} = \bar{c}$, the Lagrange multipliers $\bar{\lambda}$ are computed by left multiplying 7 by $\bar{\bar{J}}\bar{\bar{M}}^{-1}$ as

$$[\bar{\bar{J}}\bar{\bar{M}}^{-1}\bar{\bar{J}}^T]\bar{\lambda} = \frac{\bar{c}}{\Delta t} - \bar{\bar{J}}[\frac{\bar{v}^n}{\Delta t} + \bar{\bar{M}}^{-1}\bar{E}] \tag{8}$$

Solving 8 yields the necessary constraint forces $\bar{\lambda}$ for forward dynamics. This equation is solved using an iterative Projected Gauss Seidel algorithm, omitted here for brevity.

Given $\bar{\lambda}$, the rigid body velocities $\bar{v}^{n+1}$ are computed from equation 7. The positions x^{n+1} and orientations q^{n+1} are computed by integrating equation 1 using the velocity value v^{n+1} to give semi-implicit stability.

Note that the Lagrange multipliers for inequality constraints are initially computed by solving 8 but are afterwards projected into their proper domains.

4.4 Constraint Error Correction

Rigid body dynamics solvers with fixed time stepping schemes will encounter instances where two rigid bodies intersect. Constraint violation can also be caused by position drift from numerical errors during integration and unconverged iterative solvers.

One approach is to backup simulation and take smaller time steps until a non-penetrating contact has been made. Physics engines such as Simbody [19] uses this variable time stepping approach.

On the other hand, ODE adds a position constraint correction term. The position constraint error is evaluated for each constraint and expressed at timestep n as $\bar{h}^n$. It is added to the velocity constraint equation with coefficient β (also known as error reduction parameter **ERP** inside ODE).

$$\bar{J}\bar{v} + \frac{\beta}{\Delta t}\bar{h}^n = \bar{c} \qquad (9)$$

This term can be considered a form of Baumgarte stabilization [20]. It is used to restore constraint error to zero when $\beta = 1$ with a first-order Euler integrator, though values less than 1 are used in practice.

The constraint error correction term can be added into 8 as

$$[\bar{\bar{J}}\bar{\bar{M}}^{-1}\bar{J}^T]\bar{\lambda} = \frac{\bar{c}}{\Delta t} - \frac{\beta}{\Delta t^2}\bar{h}^n - \bar{\bar{J}}[\frac{\bar{v}^n}{\Delta t} + \bar{\bar{M}}^{-1}\bar{E}] \qquad (10)$$

4.5 Constraint Force Mixing and Spring-Damper

An interesting concept called Constraint Force Mixing (**CFM**) was applied by Smith in ODE to stabilize the pivoting Lemke's solver. It was also implemented in the standard PGS algorithm in ODE. The approach adds a term $(1/\Delta t)\bar{\bar{C}}\bar{\lambda}$ to equation 10, where $\bar{C}$ is a diagonal positive semidefinite matrix composed of CFM parameters. With the right-hand side of 10 abbreviated as rhs, the equation is rewritten as follows:

$$\left[\bar{\bar{J}}\bar{\bar{M}}^{-1}\bar{J}^T + \tfrac{1}{\Delta t}\bar{\bar{C}}\right]\bar{\lambda} = rhs \qquad (11)$$

An extremely useful application of the **CFM** and **ERP** parameters is that they map a constraint directly to an equivalent spring and damper system with stiffness k_p and viscous dissipation k_d properties:

$$ERP = \frac{k_p\Delta t}{k_p\Delta t + k_d} \qquad CFM = \frac{1}{kp\Delta t + k_d} \qquad (12)$$

See Catto [21] for a derivation of equivalence between these parameters.

Effectively, any spring damper system can be implemented using **CFM** and **ERP**. Most importantly, the spring damper system solution is obtained implicitly as part of the overall LCP system, without the numerical stiffness problems experienced by explicit spring dampers.

4.6   Coulomb's Friction Approximation Constraints

Given a frictional constraint with contact normal $\bar{f}_{cn}$ and corresponding frictional force $\bar{f}_\mu$ along the direction satisfying the maximum dissipation principle [22], the governing equations can be posed as velocity constraints:

$$\bar{J}_{fric}\bar{v} = \bar{c}_{fric} \tag{13}$$

The corresponding $\bar{\lambda}_\mu$ is projected into a corresponding solution space based on Coulomb's law: $\|\bar{f}_\mu\| \leq \mu \bar{f}_{cn}$. Solving equation 13 yields a solution for frictional contact based on Coulomb's friction cone if the direction of maximum dissipation $\bar{j}_\mu$ is determined.

To avoid computing the direction of maximum dissipation, the frictional constraints can be split into two or more spanning vectors on the contact surface manifold [22]. This approximates the friction cone as a pyramid. The corresponding constraint equations become:

$$\bar{J}_{fric}\bar{v} = \begin{bmatrix} \cdots & \bar{j}_{cn} & \cdots & \bar{j}_{\mu_1} & \cdots \\ \cdots & \bar{j}_{cn} & \cdots & \cdots & \bar{j}_{\mu_2} \end{bmatrix} \begin{bmatrix} \cdots & \bar{v}_{cn}^T & \cdots & \bar{v}_{\mu_1}^T & \bar{v}_{\mu_2}^T \end{bmatrix}^T = \bar{c}_{fric} \tag{14}$$

with corresponding unknowns $\bar{\lambda}_{\mu_1}$ and $\bar{\lambda}_{\mu_2}$, to be projected into their corresponding solution spaces at each iteration based on

$$\|\bar{f}_{\mu_1}\| \leq \mu_1 \bar{f}_{cn}, \ \|\bar{f}_{\mu_2}\| \leq \mu_2 \bar{f}_{cn}. \tag{15}$$

This approach yields anisotropic friction, but is much faster than the friction cone.

5   Modifications to Projected Gauss-Seidel Solver within Open Dynamics Engine

ODE is a robust solver that provides an excellent starting point for a fast dynamics simulator with tunable accuracy. There were some inadequacies, however, that needed to be addressed before using it in the VRC. This section will discuss some of the work done to improve the dynamics solver in ODE.

5.1   Contact Constraint Correction with Position Projection (Split Impulse)

The problem with the existing correction method in ODE (described in section 4.4) is that the **ERP** term adds non-physical energy to the system every time an interpenetration occurs. Alternatively, if **ERP** is zero, the solution will not correct for interpenetration and the rigid bodies in contact may *drift* into deeper constraint violations. A method similar to the Split Impulse method was introduced in ODE to cope with position errors caused by fixed time step interpenetration, unconverged iterative PGS residual and numerical integration errors.

For this method, the LCP equations 7 are solved twice, with β to yield $\bar{v}_\beta^{n+1}$ and without β to yield $\bar{v}^{n+1}$. Note the two equations can be solved in parallel. The velocity vector without β ($\bar{v}^{n+1}$) is used as the next velocity vector, while the velocity vector with β ($\bar{v}_\beta^{n+1}$) is integrated in 1 to yield the next position $\bar{x}^{n+1}$ and orientation $\bar{q}^{n+1}$.

The proposed position projection correction approach effectively *teleports* the overlapping objects away from each other without introducing excess energy into the system. At the velocity level, contact constraints are seen as non-penetrating inelastic impacts if PGS converges fully.

For example, a box on the ground plane with initial collision interpenetration of 1 centimeter will correct its position until resting contact is achieved without gaining energy if position projection is turned on. Figure 1a shows box position trajectory and velocity with and without position projection correction.

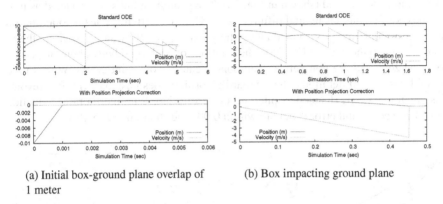

(a) Initial box-ground plane overlap of 1 meter

(b) Box impacting ground plane

Fig. 1. Trajectory of box model interactions with ground plane with and without position correction (**ERP = 1**)

In addition to more stable interpenetration correction, position projection correction is ideal for modeling completely inelastic impacts as demonstrated in figure 1b.

5.2   Convergence Acceleration by Static and Dynamics Invariant Inertia Ratio Reduction

The large-mass-ratio problem [23] is a well known issue for iterative LCP solvers. As the solution is updated via row-sweep, the impulse flux propagating across constraints is effectively throttled by the smallest Eigenvalue of the global constraint matrix $\bar{\bar{J}}\bar{\bar{M}}^{-1}\bar{\bar{J}}^{T}$.

The Atlas and Sandia hand models contain large inertia ratios across some of the constraints. The Atlas model has an inertia ratio of ~ 9017 across the ankle joint causing PGS to converge slowly. With a limited number of PGS inner iterations, this causes joint constraint violations, noise in the dynamics solution and an inability to dynamically control articulated bodies.

During the VRC, issues with PGS convergence were raised (see discussion [24]), and various constraint stabilization methods (e.g. [25]) were suggested. While constraint stabilization is a promising future research direction, an intermediate solution was found which stabilizes the solution for the Atlas model by inertia ratio reduction.

The method for modifying the Atlas model inertias to stabilize simulation is summarized below, with detailed documentation available in Bitbucket pull request [26].

Given two bodies with bilateral constraint Jacobian $\bar{J}_b$, the bodies' moments of inertia in constrained directions can be re-distributed to reduce the inertia ratio. The moment of inertia of a body along an arbitrary unit line vector $\bar{S}$ can be computed by $\bar{I}^L = \bar{S}^T \bar{\bar{I}} \bar{S} \cdot \bar{S} \bar{S}^T$. Redistributing the moments of inertia components about the line vector for the two connected bodies is done by modifying the original moment of inertias for both bodies $\bar{I}_i^{new} = \bar{I}_i + \alpha(\bar{I}_j^L - \bar{I}_i^L)$, where $\alpha \in [0, 1]$ controls the distribution ratio. This inertia redistribution is recomputed on every simulation update step.

To illustrate the effect of inertia ratio reduction, a double pendulum with an large inertia ratio is considered (shown in Fig. 2a). The pendulum links are modeled as uniform boxes of equal density and different size. This size difference leads to an inertia ratio over 6000. Gravity is applied along the y-axis $g_y = -9.81$ and also along the z-axis $g_z = 1$ (into the page in Fig. 2a). The rotations of each rigid body about the x-axis should be zero, but the non-zero g_z component causes constraint errors. With a time step of 1 ms and 50 iterations, the standard algorithm goes unstable with full revolutions about the x-axis (labeled as pitch in top of Fig. 2b). With inertia ratio reduction enabled, the constraint error is held to within 0.001 rad (bottom of Fig. 2b).

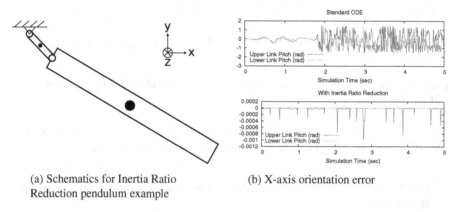

(a) Schematics for Inertia Ratio
Reduction pendulum example

(b) X-axis orientation error

Fig. 2. Constraint error in rotations about the x-axis for a double pendulum with high inertia ratio, before and after inertia ratio reduction

Since reducing the inertia ratio modifies the inertia of rigid bodies, it may change the behavior of bodies with large angular velocity due to gyroscopic effects. It was not observed to be a problem during the VRC.

5.3   Implicit Joint Spring Dampers

In lieu of simulating friction, viscous joint damping is extremely useful in stabilizing overall dynamics of the simulation. For the VRC, implicit joint damping was applied by adding a constraint to the joint degree of freedom, and adjusting the **ERP** and **CFM** values to set its spring stiffness k_p to zero and its viscous damping coefficient k_d to an estimated value[1]. Equations 12 and 12 were used to construct a joint damping constraint, and enforce joint damping implicitly through the constraint.

---

[1] A back of the envelope estimate of realistic joint viscous damping coefficients.

Another requirement for making VRC manipulation tasks solvable was indefinite grasp-hold of an object by the Sandia hand in simulation. Contact chatter and vibration have been a major obstacle in stable and robust contact dynamics in simulated grasping. Many high fidelity approaches exist [27,28], but the VRC required an approach compatible with real-time speeds. In one example demonstrated in figure 4a, the Atlas robot with the Sandia hand is seen holding an object of significantly larger uniform density mass (5.39 kg) than the individual finger links (~ 0.01 kg and principle moments of inertia on the order of $\sim 1e - 6$ kg $\cdot$ m^2) in contact with the object. The robot eventually loses grasp of the object because: the object drifts due to high frequency chatter of the finger links and insufficient contact force is transmitted from the arm in motion to the grasped object through the finger links due to lack of PGS convergence. With sufficient joint viscous damping, however, high frequency chatter is reduced while additional contact forces are transmitted from the finger joints to the finger-object contact constraints to make the grasp stable. In the limit where viscous damping coefficient approaches infinity, the finger joint becomes effectively a fixed joint.

This approach helps overall simulation stability, but errors due to PGS nonconvergence are still visible in finger contact simulation due to the fact that PGS has not fully converged.

5.4 PGS Row Ordering and Residual Smoothing

Contact friction drift was a major challenge for the Atlas robot while standing with a dynamically controlled balancing behavior. Approaches to achieving drift-free dynamic standing and grasping using ODE with $\lesssim 50$ inner iterations are being investigated. This would allow real-time simulation of Atlas with Sandia hands on a typical Intel i7 CPU architecture. One possible solution for improving ODE accuracy was to increase the number of inner iterations to above ~ 250, which severely degraded simulation performance to $\lesssim 0.4\times$ real-time. An alternative is to optimize the order of the constraints in the Jacobian matrix as described in equation 10. The constraint rows were arranged in the following order: bilateral, contact normal, and contact friction. At the very end, the friction contraints received an additional 10 iterations. This appeared to speed up convergence and reduce contact chatter.

In addition to solving the frictional directions last in PGS, high frequency oscillations in the frictional contact solutions are reduced by smoothing the contact normal and frictional (non-bilateral) constraints via an exponential smoothing filter $\lambda_{k+1}^{n+1} = (1 - \varepsilon)\lambda_k^{n+1} + \varepsilon\lambda^n$, where k denotes the PGS inner iteration number within a time step and ε was hard coded to 0.01 for the VRC.

Figure 3a is an example of Atlas grasping a cylinder indefinitely after row reordering and residual smoothing. In this example, all contact normals are perpendicular to gravity, so friction forces are keeping the cylindrical object from falling out of the grasp. Figure 3b shows the frictional drift of the Atlas feet with and without row reordering and residual smoothing.

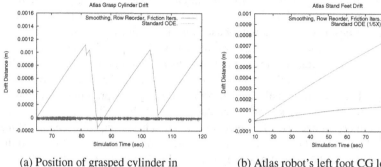

(a) Position of grasped cylinder in Sandia hand

(b) Atlas robot's left foot CG location while standing

Fig. 3. Absolute position drift with and without row reorder and residual smoothing

5.5 Warm Starting PGS

Warm starting Gauss-Seidel iterations can help accelerate PGS convergence by starting inner iterations for each time step with the solution from the previous time step (i.e. use $\bar{\lambda}^n$ as the initial guess for $\bar{\lambda}^{n+1}$ in equation 10). Even for a very simple system without contact constraints, however, warm starting PGS must be applied with care as shown in the following example.

Potential pitfalls of warm starting PGS can be demonstrated with a pendulum attached to the inertial frame via a revolute joint constraint. Figure 4a) depicts Atlas robot holding an uniform density 5.39 kilogram cylindrical shaped object. As demonstrated in figure 4b, $\sim 50\%$ warm starting, i.e. $\bar{\lambda}^{n+1} = \beta \bar{\lambda}^n$ where $\beta = 0.5$, does show some reduction in solution chatter over both 0% and 100% warm starts. Note that from our experience, 100% warm start with the solution from the previous time step can result in non-convergence.

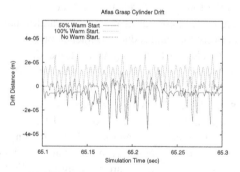

(a) Atlas with Sandia hand holding a 5.39 kg cylindrical object

(b) Effect of warm start values on cylinder vertical position drift

Fig. 4. Effect of warm start values on contact chatter and slip during grasping

6   Conclusions

This paper presented the solver algorithm used by the Open Dynamics Engine as well as numerous modifications made during the VRC to stabilize the constrained rigid body dynamics solution and accelerate convergence of the iterative solver.

Without sacrificing real-time dynamics performance, we were able to improve PGS solution for stable contact during dynamic standing and grasping behaviors, maintain overall system stability and prevent divergence in physics solutions. These achievements made the VRC possible from a physics perspective.

A benchmark of the Atlas dynamic walking behavior is shown in figure 5, the resulting simulator performance and constraint violation errors are compared against the number of PGS inner iterations performed at every time step. Figure 5 indicates that at 50 PGS iterations, we were near an optimal trade-off point between constraint error and simulation speed.

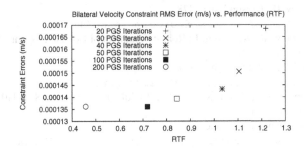

Fig. 5. Plot of Gazebo real-time factor (RTF) vs. bilateral constraint error with varying iterations for Atlas robot with hands performing dynamic walk

Acknowledgment. This work is not possible without the collaborative contributions from the DARPA support team, Boston Dynamics team and the Open Source Robotics Foundation (OSRF) team. This work was supported in part by DARPA contract HR0011-12-C-0111.

References

1. Defense Advanced Research Project Agency (DARPA), DARPA Robotics Challenge (DRC) and Virtual Robotics Challenge (VRC),
   http://theroboticschallenge.org/about
2. Boston Dynamics, Boston Dynamics Atlas Robot,
   http://www.bostondynamics.com/robot_Atlas.html
3. Open Source Robotics Foundation, Sandia Hand Project Webpage,
   https://bitbucket.org/osrf/sandia-hand
4. Stronge, W.: Rigid body collisions with friction. Proceedings of the Royal Society of 431(1881), 169–181 (1990)

5. Brogliato, B., ten Dam, A., Paoli, L., Genot, F., Abadie, M.: Numerical simulation of finite dimensional multibody nonsmooth mechanical systems. Applied Mechanics Reviews 55(2), 107 (2002)
6. Anitescu, M., Potra, F.: Formulating dynamic multi-rigid-body contact problems with friction as solvable linear complementarity problems. Nonlinear Dynamics 14, 231–247 (1997)
7. Trinkle, D., Stewart, D.E., Trinkle, J.C.: An implicit time-stepping scheme for rigid body dynamics with inelastic collisions and coulomb friction. International Journal for Numerical Methods in Engineering 39(15), 2673–2691 (1996)
8. Pang, J., Trinkle, J.: Complementarity formulations and existence of solutions of dynamic multi-rigid-body contact problems with coulomb friction. Mathematical Programming 73(2), 199–226 (1995)
9. Cottle, R., Pang, J.-S., Stone, R.E.: The Linear Complementarity Problem (2009)
10. Cottle, R., Dantzig, G.: Complementary pivot theory of mathematical programming. Linear Algebra and its Applications, 103–125 (1968)
11. Featherstone, R.: A short course on Spatial Vector Algebra the easy way to do rigid body dynamics (2005)
12. Featherstone, R.: Rigid Body Dynamics Algorithms. Springer US, Boston (2008)
13. Smith, J., Gerkey, B.: Drcsim issue #378,
    https://bitbucket.org/osrf/drcsim/issue/378
14. Bridson, R., Fedkiw, R., Anderson, J.: Robust Treatment of Collisions, Contact and Friction for Cloth Animation (1994)
15. Koolen, T., Hsu, J., et al.: Drcsim issue #320,
    https://bitbucket.org/osrf/drcsim/issue/320
16. Smith, R.: Open Dynamics Engine ODE. Multibody Dynamics Simulation Software,
    http://www.ode.org
17. Smith, R.: Open Dynamics Engine ODE. User's Manual,
    http://opende.sourceforge.net/wiki/index.php/Manual
18. Weinstein, R., Teran, J., Fedkiw, R.: Dynamic simulation of articulated rigid bodies with contact and collision. IEEE Trans. Visualization and Computer Graphics 12(3), 365–374 (2006)
19. Sherman, M.A., Seth, A., Delp, S.L.: Simbody: multibody dynamics for biomedical research. In: Procedia IUTAM, vol. 2, pp. 241–261 (January 2011)
20. Baumgarte, J.: Stabilization of constraints and integrals of motion in dynamical systems. Computer Methods in Applied Mechanics and Engineering 1(1), 1–16 (1972)
21. Catto, E.: Soft Constraints reinventing the spring. In: Game Developer Conference (2011)
22. Stewart, D.E.: Rigid-Body Dynamics with Friction and Impact. SIAM Review 42(1), 3 (2000)
23. Silcowitz, M., Niebe, S., Erleben, K.: Nonsmooth Newton Method for Fischer Function Reformulation of Contact Force Problems for Interactive Rigid Body Simulation (2009)
24. Atkeson et al.: Simulating hands is killing performance,
    http://answers.gazebosim.org/question/1427
25. Atkeson et al.: Constraint stabilization methods discussion,
    http://www.cs.cmu.edu/~cga/drc/constraint-stabilization.html
26. Inertia tweaks, https://bitbucket.org/osrf/drcsim/pull-request/157
27. Zhang, L., Betz, J., Trinkle, J.: Comparison of simulated and experimental grasping actions in the plane. In: First International Multibody Dynamics... (2010)
28. Drumwright, E., Shell, D.: A robust and tractable contact model for dynamic robotic simulation. In: Proc. ACM symposium on Applied Computing, pp. 1176–1180. ACM (2009)

Control and Scheduling Co-design
for a Simulated Quadcopter Robot:
A Model-Driven Approach

Matteo Morelli and Marco Di Natale

Institute of Communication, Information and Perception (TeCiP)
Scuola Superiore Sant'Anna, 56124 Pisa, Italy
{matteo.morelli,marco.dinatale}@sssup.it

Abstract. The Model-based development of robotics applications relies on the definition of models of the controls that abstract the computation and communication platform under the synchronous assumption. Computation, scheduling and communication delays can affect the performance of the controls in way that are possibly significant, and an early evaluation allows to select the best control compensation or the best HW/SW implementation platform. In this paper we show a case study of the application of the open T-Res framework, an environment for the co-simulation of controls and real-time scheduling, on a quadcopter model example, highlighting the possible tradeoffs in the selection of the scheduling strategy and priority assignment.

1 Introduction

Model-based development of robotics controls is an industrial reality. The MAT-LAB/Simulink tool from Mathworks is a very popular framework used to define the controls functionality and the model of the controlled plant, and provides for the simulation and verification of hybrid systems. In Simulink, however, the model execution is simulated according to the synchronous reactive (SR) paradigm, in which all the computations and communications are assumed to complete within the interval between two events in logical time (formally referred to as *synchronous assumption*). When the (controller) model is implemented in software and its implementation executes on a real architecture of CPUs and communication links, computation, scheduling and communication delays may exceed what is prescribed by the synchronous assumption and the jitters and latencies may affect the performance of the controls. The impact of these delays is often evaluated late, at testing time, with significant costs, additional development cycles and possible changes to the hardware architecture.

An early evaluation of the impact of the hardware and software implementation is desirable and requires the co-simulation of the controller functionality, the plant model, and the computation, scheduling and communication hardware and software platform. The simulation requires a model of the software tasks and the messages exchanged over the networks. To support such a co-simulation

D. Brugali et al. (Eds.): SIMPAR 2014, LNAI 8810, pp. 49–61, 2014.

in the popular Simulink environment we developed the T-Res open project [3] and a framework supporting its use.

Our framework merges methods and tools of the MDE (Model Driven Engineering [15]) approach in a development flow in which Simulink models are used to define the functionality of the controls and SysML models define the hardware execution platform and the task model of the controls implementation. After the functionality is mapped for execution on the platform model, defining the structure of the tasks and messages, the execution and transmission times are estimated (or measured) and the Simulink model can be annotated with blocks that allow the simulation of the scheduling, computation and communication latencies, allowing to fine tune the control logic or the task and message model (possibly with their priorities), or evaluate different scheduling policies.

The evaluation of the impact of the scheduling on the controls performance allows to overcome the often myopic assumption that all control loops/tasks are of type hard real-time. In reality, several systems may miss deadlines without losing stability, and indeed, several systems (including fuel injection [8]) actually operate in spite of deadline misses, at the boundary of overload conditions.

MDE approaches have become popular in robotics and several MDE Integrated Development Environments (IDEs) and Domain-Specific Languages (DSLs) are available. BRIDE[1] is an IDE based on Eclipse developed in the BRICS project [1]. It targets the automatic generation of platform-specific code for component-based frameworks from a graphical (abstract) model of the system architecture and its SW components (the BRICS Component Model [6]). BRIDE uses model-to-model (M2M) transformations to generate framework-specific code for the communication, configuration, composition and coordination of ROS [16] and Orocos-RTT [7] components. The declarative description of robotics architectures and SW deployment using a DSL is described in [13] with a hierarchy of architectural concepts for HW and SW, inspired by AADL [4]. However, the properties of HW and SW that define the timing behavior of components are not included. The SmartSoftMDSD toolchain [17] supports non-functional properties for design-time real-time schedulability analysis. The framework allows the graphical modeling of applications in Papyrus[2], and provides M2M transformations to construct a platform-specific model for schedulability analysis using Cheddar [18]. However, it should be considered that in reality the scheduling choices affect the performance of the robot controller in a way that is different from the simple binary (safe/not safe) outcome provided by schedulability analysis.

Some IDE provide DSLs for the algorithmic description of behaviors. V^3CMM [5] is a modeling language that provides a simplified version of UML activity diagrams, to model the sequential flow of execution within components. RobotML [11] is a DSL aiming at the design of robotic applications in Papyrus and their deployment to multiple target execution platforms (and simulators).

---

[1] http://www.best-of-robotics.org/bride/

[2] http://www.eclipse.org/papyrus/

It uses a specialization of UML state machines for the modeling of the behavior of generated component implementations. RobotML enables (simplistic) modeling of platform-specific non-functional properties of SW components, that are used to create models for third-party real-time schedulability analyzers. Hence, it suffers the same drawbacks of the SmartSoftMDSD toolchain.

Virtual Path [14] is a HW-SW co-Design method that includes Simulink in the development flow, to create executable models representing the controls. In [19], Wätzoldt *et al.* adapt the automotive toolchain to the development of robotic systems. The design methodology uses Simulink for the simulation of robot functionalities, and Embedded Coder for the generation of the implementation. AUTOSAR models and tools (e.g., SystemDesk [12]) are used to combine hard and soft real-time tasks in a system view and analyze the scheduling feasibility.

Finally, TrueTime [9] is a freeware Matlab/Simulink-based simulation tool that allows to model multi-task real-time kernels and networks in simulation models for networked embedded control systems and study the (simulated) impact of lateness and deadline misses on controls. Because of the monolithic architecture and the number of code artifacts that are needed for system configuration, the current TrueTime implementation is hardly compatible with an automatic model generation flow.

2   From the Simulink Model of the Controls to the Platform and Implementation Design

In the development flow considered in our work (summarized in Figure 1), a *Simulink functional model* of the controls executing in the abstract logical time (zero delays) is the starting point. The *functional model* is created by importing in EMF a Simulink model that includes the controller part and the model of the plant. The Simulink model must comply with the restriction that there is a decomposition level in which the controller part consists of a collection of subsystems and each subsystem only contains periodic blocks with the same period (each subsystem is single-rate).

A Matlab script uses the Simulink modeling API to parse the model structure and export an XML view of the controller subsystems. The XML conforms to a schema created in accordance with an Eclipse Ecore meta-model, defined for representing the execution constraints that apply to the Simulink subsystems and preserving the structural properties of the Simulink model, such as the types and interfaces of the blocks and the connections among the blocks, and also the information related to the timed execution events, including rate and partial order of execution constraints.

After the functional model is imported in the Eclipse EMF framework, a QVTo model-to-model transformation is executed to import the model in SysML, leveraging a profile definition for SR systems. Generic `Block` entities are mapped to standard SysML blocks; `Subsystem` entities are mapped to `SRSubsystem`

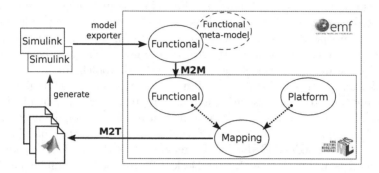

Fig. 1. The development flow for the proposed Model-Driven approach

instances. The input/output ports and the corresponding connections are suitably translated from the source model (Ecore) to the destination model (SysML).

Here, it is extended with the platform and mapping models. For the modeling of the hardware (HW) part of the *execution platform* we rely on the concepts provided in MARTE. It introduces the `HwProcessor` stereotype, which matches the concept of CPU and provides the attribute `nbCores` to specify the number of cores, thus enabling the modeling of multi-core architectures.

For the modeling of basic software (BSW) components and for the deployment of BSW modules onto the HW we define our own taxonomy of stereotypes, since those in MARTE are mostly cumbersome, come with a large number of properties and are in turn quite difficult to be mastered by the system designer. The `BswRTOS` package provides a set of stereotypes to model RTOS concepts (Figure 2). The stereotype `BswRTOS` denotes an RTOS and inherits from the general block concept of SysML. The RTOS (kernel) contains a scheduler, denoted as `BswScheduler`, which is responsible for executing tasks according a given scheduling policy.

The *mapping model* represents the execution of functional elements by tasks and the allocation of tasks on cores. Concurrent execution contexts are classified in terms of `Process` and `Thread` instances. A `Thread` is contained in a `Process`, is characterized by a `priority` value and runs on one of the system cores under the control of an RTOS. Specializations of `Thread` are `AperiodicThread` and `PeriodicThread` (with its `period`).

The mapping model also specifies a set of dependencies that define mappings/deployments as extensions of the standard SysML Allocation concept. The `FunctionToThreadMap` denotes the mapping of a functional subsystem into a `Thread`. When multiple subsystems are mapped into the same `Thread`, the attribute `mapOrder` defines how their execution will be serialized in the generated thread code. The SysML profile for mapping is shown in Figure 3.

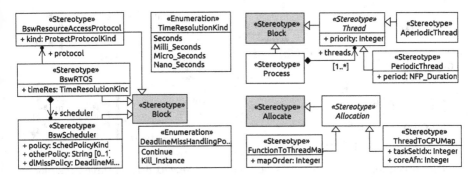

Fig. 2. Structure of the `BswRTOS` meta-model

Fig. 3. Structure of the `Mapping` meta-model

3   Time and Resource Aware Simulation in Simulink

The simulation of the control functions considering task implementations with finite execution times and RTOS scheduling delays is enabled by integrating Simulink and a RT scheduling simulator in the T-Res [3] co-simulation framework. T-Res is designed according to object-oriented design patterns to provide an easy integration with any RT simulator.

The Simulink master simulation engine computes the model updates at *major steps*: time instants in which the inputs and outputs of the blocks are updated. Major steps include all the periodic activation times of tasks, as well as the aperiodic events that lead to the activation of other tasks.

T-Res is implemented as a set of custom blocks that execute at all major steps, interact with the Simulink engine and capture all the relevant events from the simulated environment. Every time a major step occurs, the block implementing the RTOS kernel is invoked and processes (if there is any) the task arrival events. These events are forwarded to the underlying RT scheduling simulator and cause an update of its internal structure. Then, the kernel block queries the scheduling simulator to determine future events (execution completions and context switches) and uses the Simulink API to define major steps in the simulation at all the points in time in which a task scheduling event occurs.

In a RT simulator, tasks execute according to a model of (time-consuming) computations. T-Res assumes that the execution of a task is split in units that are atomic from the standpoint of execution time granularity, but can be preempted, called *segments*, informally corresponding to the execution of a function called by the task main code. Each segment is identified by an execution time and all segments in a task are executed according to a pre-defined sequence. Segments represent the execution of Simulink subsystems and their execution order in a task must match the order of execution of subsystems. The time duration of each segment corresponds to the execution time of the code implementing the subsystem. The start and completion times of the segments correspond to the times in which the corresponding subsystems read or sample their inputs and produce their outputs. The activation of the Simulink subsystems is changed from

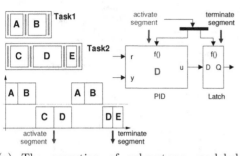 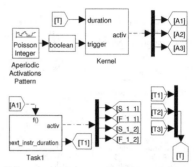

(a) The execution of subsystems modeled through segments.

(b) **Kernel** driving three **Task** blocks (top), and **Task** with two segments (bottom).

Fig. 4. Execution model of segments and interfaces of T-Res blocks

periodic to function activated and a latch barrier is added on all their outputs. Figure 4a shows the activation mechanism: when a segment starts executing, the subsystem is activated; the output signals are latched and enabled when the segment terminates. The signals activating a subsystem (and its input sampling) and its output latch are generated by the task blocks upon the beginning of the execution and the completion of the task segment.

The actual implementation of T-Res relies on two custom blocks, namely **Kernel** and **Task**, implemented as C++ S-Functions. Blocks' input/output interfaces are shown in Figure 4b. The block **Task** models one instance of a task that consists of the serialized execution of the segments/subsystems. **Task** is a triggered subsystem, executed on the occurrence of a function call event received on its port **f()**. Its output port **activ** issues activation and termination events to the task segments; port **next_instr_duration** outputs a scalar signal representing the duration of next segment executed by the task. The duration of segments is set by a variable in the Matlab workspace. The computation time of a segment can be fixed or random (e.g., uniform and exponential distributions).

The block **Kernel** models an event-based RT kernel and the scheduler inside it on a single- or multi-core computer node. It is responsible for keeping the scheduling simulation aligned with the system simulation. At each activation, it checks for any aperiodic requests. If there is any, it activates the corresponding aperiodic tasks. Next, it advances the RT scheduler simulator. Two types of events are relevant for the simulation: the *segment completion* and *task completion*. In the first case, **Kernel** reads the input signal on the port **duration** and dynamically creates a new instruction for the corresponding task. In the second case, **Kernel** resets the internal state of the corresponding task. A number of parameters configure the (simulated) kernel such as the scheduling policy and the number of cores of the computer node. Parameters are set through the **Kernel** mask dialog. T-Res is open-source and is released under the terms of the 3-Clause BSD License. Currently, it features a concrete implementation of the adapter layer based on RTSim [2], which is available under the GNU GPLv2+.

4   Case Study: Quadcopter Attitude Control

The application of the methodology and an example of analysis results are shown using a model of a quadcopter.

4.1   Functional, Platform and Mapping Models

The quadcopter is required to lift off and fly in a circle at constant altitude, while spinning slowly around its Z-axis. The adopted control scheme (shown in Figure 5a) is taken from [10] with minor changes introduced to comply with our design restrictions. The original model in [10] contains multiple functional loops at the top level of the model hierarchy dedicated to set-point generation and flight control. Each loop has been included in a Simulink subsystem. The constantly increasing signal for the desired yaw angle, originally generated by a Ramp block in [10], is now obtained from the set of blocks of Figure 5b that use the output of an external Clock block as time source. In Figure 5b, start represents the time at which the block begins generating the signal, X0 is the initial value of the output and the the rate of change of the generated signal is influenced by the parameters of the block Step. This is because subsystems mapped into segments cannot contain continuous time blocks (such as Ramp).

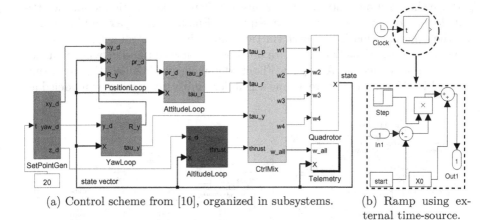

(a) Control scheme from [10], organized in subsystems.   (b) Ramp using external time-source.

Fig. 5. Models used for the quadcopter flight-control scheme

The set-points of the desired circular path and the desired yaw and altitude are generated by the subsystem SetPointGen. Quadrotor implements the motion of vehicle. The inputs are the speeds of the four rotors; the output is the 12-element state vector with the position, velocity, orientation and orientation rate of the quadcopter. The actual vehicle velocity is assumed to be estimated by an inertial navigation system or GPS receiver (i.e., there is no velocity estimator in the Simulink model).

The control strategy involves multiple nested loops that compute the required thrust and torques so that the quadcopter moves to set-points. Position control has a two-level hierarchical structure: the subsystem `AttitudeLoop` implements the inner loop, which uses the current and desired roll and pitch angles and angular rates to control the vehicle's attitude and to provide damping (to slow down the dynamics). The subsystem `PositionLoop` realizes the outer loop, which controls the XY-position of the flyer by generating changes in roll and pitch angles so as to provide a component of thrust in the direction of the desired motion. Finally, yaw angle and altitude are controlled by proportional-derivative (PD) controllers, respectively implemented by the subsystems `YawLoop` and `AltitudeLoop`.

In practice, control loops are implemented as real time tasks, with finite execution times, running at different rates under the control of a scheduler. Typical execution rates range from 10Hz for reading (generating) set-points to 50Hz (or more) for controlling the vehicle attitude. To investigate how the performances of control code are actually affected by computation and scheduling delays, a structural view of the Simulink model of controls is first exported to Ecore and then *automatically* translated into a SysML model in Papyrus, where it is extended with the models of platform and mapping (deployment).

Figure 6a shows a (partial) view of an implementation model of controls consisting of four periodic tasks. `Task_spr` runs every 100ms and reads the set-points. `Task_pos` uses the set-points and the current state of the vehicle to perform the position control. Every 20ms, it executes the position loop, the attitude loop and the control mixer, in sequence. Finally, `Task_yaw` and `Task_alt` use the same information to perform yaw and altitude control with a period of 50ms and 25ms, respectively. Figure 6b shows a view of the deployment model of tasks to a single-core Autopilot/Flight Management Unit (FMU) board running a Fixed Priority (FP) real-time scheduler. Subsystems are now modeled as

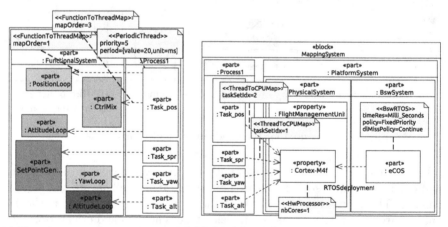

(a) Function-to-task mapping model. (b) Models of Autopilot board (with BSW) and of task-to-platform mapping.

Fig. 6. Functional, platform and mapping models

executing with execution times randomly generated according to uniform distributions (Figure 8b). Once the task priorities are specified, the mapping model includes all the information needed to automatically generate and connect the kernel and task blocks to the original Simulink model.

4.2   Back-Annotated Functional Model

The Acceleo M2T transformation processes the mapping model and generates a collection of Matlab scripts that contain the back-annotation commands. The execution of the Matlab scripts produces the Simulink model of Figure 7.

One instance of kernel block (**Kernel1**) and four instances of task blocks (the names are the same of the corresponding SysML modeling artifacts) are added to the functional model.

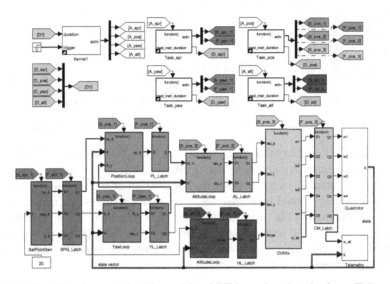

Fig. 7. Attitude control with models of RT kernel and tasks from T-Res

Kernel1 outputs task-activation signals in the order specified by the **taskSetIdx** attributes of the «**ThreadToCPUMap**» allocations in the mapping model. Activation signals are forwarded to task blocks through the **Goto-From** connections labeled A_spr, A_pos, A_yaw, and A_alt. Similarly, tasks communicate the duration of the next segment to **Kernel1** through the **Goto-From** connections labeled D_spr, D_pos, D_yaw, and D_alt.

Each control subsystem is transformed to a triggered subsystem and a latch barrier is added on its outputs. Task blocks manage the activation and termination signals of the (control) subsystems executing in the segments.

Figure 8a shows a snapshot of the generated Matlab code that adds the **Kernel1** block, and configures its parameters. All parameters are available from the platform model and their values are set through the Matlab function **set_param()**. The timing properties and the type of tasks in the task-set are

```
% - Add and configure the Kernel block
kern1 = 'quadcopter_bn/Kernel1';
add_block('t_res/Kernel', kern1);
set_param(kern1, 'taskset_descr_name','task_set_descr');
set_param(kern1, 'scheduling_policy', 'FIXED_PRIORITY');
```

(a) Matlab commands for the generation of block `Kernel1`.

```
% Description of timing properties of task set
task_set_descr = {...
  % type          %iat        %rdl        %ph   % prio
  'PeriodicTask', 100*0.001, 100*0.001, 0.0, 0; ... % spr
  'PeriodicTask', 20*0.001,  20*0.001,  0.0, 5; ... % pos
  'PeriodicTask', 50*0.001,  50*0.001,  0.0, 15; ... % yaw
  'PeriodicTask', 25*0.001,  25*0.001,  0.0, 10; ... }; %alt

% Sequences of pseudo instructions (task codes)
spr_instrs = {'delay(unif(0.001,0.002))'};
pos_instrs = {...
  'delay(unif(0.005,0.008))'; ... % PositionLoop
  'delay(unif(0.003,0.007))'; ... % AttitudeLoop
  'delay(unif(0.002,0.004))'; ... };% CtrlMix
yaw_instrs = {'delay(unif(0.004,0.006))'};
alt_instrs = {'delay(unif(0.008,0.009))'};
```

(b) Definition of type and timing properties of tasks.

Fig. 8. Matlab commands for the configuration of kernel and task blocks

described by the variable `task_set_descr` in Figure 8b (cell array). Tasks types and periods (or interarrival times) are available from the mapping model. Relative deadlines coincide with periods and activation offsets are set to zero. All task periods are expressed in *milliseconds*, therefore a time-scale constant equal to 0.001 is generated. The duration of segments executed by each task is described by a Matlab cell array of strings (Figure 8b). Each string that describes the computation time of a segment is available from the `execTime` attributes of the «SRSubsystem» block instances.

4.3   Scheduling Selection and Priority Assignments

All design refinements, be them minor (e.g., changing the scheduling policy) or more prominent (e.g., mapping functional subsystems to a different task-set), are realized at SysML level to keep platform and mapping models in synch with the generated Matlab code for back-annotations.

Initially, `Task_spr` is given the highest priority; the other tasks' priorities are assigned according to their period, so that the shorter the period the higher the priority (Rate Monotonic rule). In this case, computation times and scheduling delays induce deadline misses of tasks `Task_yaw` and `Task_alt`, that do not affect much the altitude control, as shown in Figure 9a, but degrade the performances of circular path-following significantly (Figure 9b). This fact is easily explained if one considers that the low-priority task `Task_yaw`, which drives the high-priority task `Task_pos` (that controls the XY-position of the flyer), is repeatedly subject

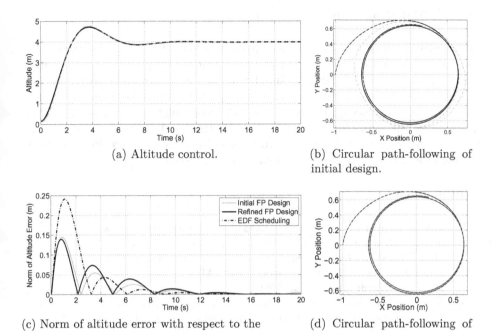

(a) Altitude control.

(b) Circular path-following of initial design.

(c) Norm of altitude error with respect to the pure functional control.

(d) Circular path-following of refined design.

Fig. 9. Simulation results. Comparison of trajectories and errors for different scheduling and priority assignments.

to preemption from the mid-priority task `Task_alt`, and that this prevents the preservation of SR communication flows between `Task_yaw` and `Task_pos`, with respect to the pure functional control model of Figure 5a.

The analysis indicates that the response time of task `Task_yaw` has a significant impact on the effectiveness of the control action, and suggests to raise its priority to a value greater than the one of `Task_alt`. Figure 9d shows the simulation results of circular path-following in the refined design. `Task_yaw` has now a priority level greater than `Task_alt` and meets all its deadlines; consequently, the control behavior is closer to the pure functional one. On the other hand, `Task_alt` misses more deadlines than in the initial design and the altitude control performs slightly worse, as shown in Figure 9c (dark line vs light line). However, it is still controlled with a reasonable error, which makes the refined design preferable. As an additional option, we tried an application of the Earliest Deadline First (EDF) dynamic scheduling policy, which results in a slightly worse performance of the altitude control (dashed line of Figure 9c) and path following performance similar to that of the refined priority model (not shown in the graphs but practically overlapping with the dark line).

5 Conclusions and Future Work

The paper presents a case study application of a MDE framework for the definition of the execution platform and the impact of the computation and communication delays and the T-Res co-simulation framework to a quadcopter model. The example shows how the selection of task priorities and scheduler models can affect the performance of the controls and the co-simulation environment allows to quantify the errors for different options. Future work includes the extension of the modeling and co-simulation framework to networked architectures and messages and the evaluation on a distributed case-study.

References

[1] BRICS - Best practice in robotics, http://www.best-of-robotics.org/
[2] RT-Sim – Real-Time system SIMulator, http://rtsim.sssup.it/
[3] T-Res – Time and Resource Simulator, http://retis.sssup.it/tres/
[4] Architecture Analysis & Design Language (AADL),
    http://standards.sae.org/as5506b/
[5] Alonso, D., Vicente-Chicote, C., Ortiz, F., Pastor, J., Alvarez, B.: V3cmm: a 3-view
    component meta-model for model-driven robotic software development. Journal
    of Software Engineering for Robotics 1(1), 3–17 (2010)
[6] Bruyninckx, H., Klotzbücher, M., Hochgeschwender, N., Kraetzschmar, G., Gherardi, L., Brugali, D.: The BRICS Component Model: A Model-based Development
    Paradigm for Complex Robotics Software Systems. In: Proc. of the 28th Annual
    ACM Symposium on Applied Computing, pp. 1758–1764 (2013)
[7] Bruyninckx, H., Soetens, P., Koninckx, B.: The Real-Time Motion Control Core
    of the Orocos Project. In: IEEE International Conference on Robotics and Automation, pp. 2766–2771 (2003)
[8] Buttle, D.: Real-time in the prime-time. Keynote presentation. In: Euromicro
    ECRTS Conference (July 2012)
[9] Cervin, A., Henriksson, D., Lincoln, B., Eker, J., Årzén, K.E.: How does control
    timing affect performance? Analysis and Simulation of Timing using Jitterbug and
    TrueTime 23(3), 16–30 (2003)
[10] Corke, P.I.: Robotics, Vision & Control: Fundamental Algorithms in Matlab.
    Springer (2011)
[11] Dhouib, S., Kchir, S., Stinckwich, S., Ziadi, T., Ziane, M.: RobotML, a domain-
    specific language to design, simulate and deploy robotic applications. In: Noda,
    I., Ando, N., Brugali, D., Kuffner, J.J. (eds.) SIMPAR 2012. LNCS, vol. 7628,
    pp. 149–160. Springer, Heidelberg (2012)
[12] dSPACE GmbH: SystemDesk, http://www.dspace.com/en/pub/home/products/
    sw/system_architecture_software/systemdesk.cfm
[13] Hochgeschwender, N., Gherardi, L., Shakhirmardanov, A., Kraetzschmar, G., Brugali, D., Bruyninckx, H.: A Model-Based Approach to Software Deployment in
    Robotics. In: 2013 IEEE/RSJ International Conference on Intelligent Robots and
    Systems (IROS), pp. 3907–3914 (November 2013)
[14] Nickl, M., Jörg, S., Hirzinger, G.: The virtual path: The domain model for the design of the MIRO surgical robotic system. In: 9th International IFAC Symposium
    on Robot Control, IFAC, Gifu, Japan, pp. 97–103 (2009)

[15] Object Management Group: Model Driven Architecture (MDA), http://www.omg.org/mda/specs.htm

[16] Quigley, M., Conley, K., Gerkey, B., Faust, J., Foote, T.B., Leibs, J., Wheeler, R., Ng, A.Y.: ROS: an open-source Robot Operating System. In: ICRA Workshop on Open Source Software (2009)

[17] Schlegel, C., Steck, A., Brugali, D., Knoll, A.: Design Abstraction and Processes in Robotics: From Code-Driven to Model-Driven Engineering. In: Ando, N., Balakirsky, S., Hemker, T., Reggiani, M., von Stryk, O. (eds.) SIMPAR 2010. LNCS, vol. 6472, pp. 324–335. Springer, Heidelberg (2010)

[18] Singhoff, F., Legrand, J., Nana, L., Marcé, L.: Cheddar: a flexible real time scheduling framework. In: Proceedings of the ACM International Conference on Ada (SIGAda), pp. 1–8 (2004)

[19] Wätzoldt, S., Neumann, S., Benke, F., Giese, H.: Integrated software development for embedded robotic systems. In: Noda, I., Ando, N., Brugali, D., Kuffner, J.J. (eds.) SIMPAR 2012. LNCS, vol. 7628, pp. 335–348. Springer, Heidelberg (2012)

Simulating Human-Robot Interactions for Dialogue Strategy Learning

Grégoire Milliez[1], Emmanuel Ferreira[2], Michelangelo Fiore[1], Rachid Alami[1], and Fabrice Lefèvre[2]

[1] CNRS, LAAS, 7 avenue du colonel Roche, 31077 Toulouse, France,
Université de Toulouse, UPS, INSA, INP, ISAE, LAAS, 31077 Toulouse, France
{gregoire.milliez,michelangelo.fiore,rachid.alami}@laas.fr
[2] LIA, Université d'Avignon BP1228 - 84911 Avignon Cedex 9, France
{emmanuel.ferreira,fabrice.lefevre}@univ-avignon.fr

Abstract. Many robotic projects use simulation as a faster and easier way to develop, evaluate and validate software components compared with on-board real world settings. In the human-robot interaction field, some recent works have attempted to integrate humans in the simulation loop. In this paper we investigate how such kind of robotic simulation software can be used to provide a dynamic and interactive environment to both collect a multimodal situated dialogue corpus and to perform an efficient reinforcement learning-based dialogue management optimisation procedure. Our proposition is illustrated by a preliminary experiment involving real users in a Pick-Place-Carry task for which encouraging results are obtained.

1 Introduction

Simulation softwares are highly needed in robotic projects. By using simulators, roboticists can evaluate and validate their works on the chosen level of abstraction in a sandbox that limits the risk-taking. In this way, projects relying on high level computation (e.g. interaction, dialogue, supervision), can use a simulator to abstract lower levels (e.g. navigation, image processing, localisation) and avoid their related issues to interfere during the system evaluation. Furthermore, the simulation setup can also be useful to assess parts of the development before any attempt of costly integration on the on-board robotic platform.

In the present study, we specifically focus on Human-Robot Interaction (HRI). In the simulation context, two distinct solutions can be adopted to integrate humans in the loop: 1. modelling and implementing their behaviours and actions, and 2. dealing with tele-operation to control human avatars.

The first solution has the advantage of automatization and does not require manual manipulation. So, this solution is less time consuming and easier to run. However, depending on the human features required, it may be really difficult to have a realistic human model. Humans are complex entities with reactions and behaviours nearly impossible to consistently synthesize. This solution is usually

D. Brugali et al. (Eds.): SIMPAR 2014, LNAI 8810, pp. 62–73, 2014.
© Springer International Publishing Switzerland 2014

used for studies that do not involve the most complex sides of human behaviours, such as navigation or manipulation.

The second solution consits in having the simulated human controlled by a real human operator. By doing so, the complexity of the experimentation rises as an actual human is required to operate the human avatar. However, the avatar in the simulator will have a far more realistic behaviour. To do so, the simulator must have a realistic environment rendering and the human control must be natural and close enough to the real world.

HRI projects that focus on situated dialogue usually investigate tasks that seem to be within the scope or already implemented in HRI simulator, such as a Pick-Place-Carry scenario [1], robot bartender [2] or navigation tasks in a virtual environment [3]. Nevertheless, few works consider the simulation setup as the way to carry out situated dialogue corpus acquisition as well as a test-bed for an efficient online dialogue policy learning. Indeed, most of the previous works in situated dialogue for HRI resorted to a preliminary Wizard-of-Oz (WoZ) experiment, where a human remotely operates the robot [4,2,5]. However, the WoZ technique is both time consuming and an expensive method.

In this article we present how a robotic simulation software, in which the human is integrated, can help to train a dialogue system for realistic HRI from scratch. In Section 2 we explain how we simulated HRI scenarios with the open-source robotic simulator MORSE. In Section 3 we show how we used the simulator along with a robotic architecture, and finally in Section 4 we expose the integration with the dialogue system and give some testing results. In last Section 5, we discuss the outcome of this preliminary study and future work.

2   MORSE as HRI Simulator

2.1   Why MORSE for HRI?

In the robotic field, many simulators are available. We can name the Player/Stage/Gazebo suite [6], the integrated simulation platform OpenHRP [7], the cross-platform software architecture OpenRAVE [8] or even the commercial simulator V-REP [9]. However, only a few of them are very well suited to HRI. They generally limit human agent behaviours to relatively simple motions and interaction capacities which is one of the reasons why HRI simulations so far have been carried out in *tele-operation* settings, where only the robot and the environment, but not the human agent, are actually simulated. Robotic simulators USARSim [10] and MORSE [11,12] are both used in dozens of HRI studies due to their explicit support for controlling a human agent. However, the latter has several specific advantages that motivated our choice.

MORSE is an open-source simulator, with a very active community, that was developed specifically for robotic simulation. It supports a wide range of middleware (e.g. ROS, YARP, pocolibs) as well as reliable implementations of realistic sensors and actuators which ease the integration on real robotic platforms afterwards. Moreover, MORSE offers an adaptable simulation setup by allowing virtual robots to interact with the virtual environment through both realistic sensors/actuators and higher level ones. Thereby, roboticists can control the related computation cost of low level data processing by exploiting high level outputs from unrealistic components. For example, MORSE provides both a vision camera and a semantic camera sensor. While the first camera provides a rough image (i.e. raw pixels) as output, the second one gives directly the names of the perceived objects and their positions in the scene. The latter sensor avoids practitioners to perform object recognition and localization processes when focusing on higher level issues.

Furthermore, MORSE relies on the Blender Game Engine, a real-time 3D runtime integrated to the open-source Blender modelling toolkit, for both advanced 3D (OpenGL shader) and physics simulation (based on the BULLET physics engine). This setup allows realistic rendering of complex environment and provides an immersive graphical user interface, which is a required feature for HRI modelling.

In MORSE, the human avatar can be controlled by a human operator or directly through external scripts as any other robot.

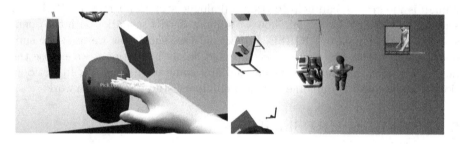

Fig. 1. Human avatar grabbing an object controlled by an operator (left image) and human in 3rd person perspective (right image)

In the first case, the operator controls the virtual human in an immersive way (see Figure 1) in terms of displacement, gaze, and interactions on the environment, such as object manipulation (e.g. grasp/released an object). To go even further in realistic human incorporation in the simulator, a motion capture actuator allows to control the human avatar directly by using an external device. So, a Kinect sensor collects human gestures and sends the posture data to move the human avatar accordingly. Furthermore, a Nintendo wiimote can jointly be used to manage its action (e.g. grasp/released an object).

In the second case, the avatar is programmatically controlled by using standard MORSE actuators. As an example, it is possible to use a waypoint actuator on the human to define a path he has to follow.

2.2   Scenario Implementation

In our scenario, a disabled human is in her apartment and has a robot to assist her to perform everyday life chores. The goal is to make the robot understand, by reasoning on human speech, gestures and the environment, human's requests concerning objects. Objects are limited here to graspable items such as books, DVDs and mugs, that have diverse colors and a unique identifier.

The PR2 robot is used in the simulator as it is our real platform at LAAS-CNRS. PR2 is already present in MORSE models, making it directly usable. We add a symbolic camera (MORSE semantic camera) sensor to the standard model so that it can perform object recognition and also a teleport actuator to move it to a designated position (while saving the time of the true displacement). We also add a human avatar with first person representation to have realistic inputs of speech and behaviour of human users. We use a virtual model of the physical environment in which the real robot will be tested (see Figure 2).

Fig. 2. Scenario environment in MORSE

At the start of the simulation, a script randomly positions objects in prede-fined areas (such as over kitchen table, living-room table, bedroom shelf etc.), called *manipulation areas*. This allows us to use different environment configurations without changing the initialization files (MORSE builder script).

2.3   Actions Library

To get a more interactive and realistic simulation and also for the user to evaluate the fulfilment of her request (e.g. does the robot bring the appropriate object), we have developed a library of high-level and abstract actions that the robot will be able to perform.

The list of abstract actions is as followed:

- To explore the environment and bring an object to the human, the robot needs to be able to move to manipulation areas. To do so, we use the teleport actuator of MORSE. This actuator moves instantaneously the robot to a given place. We define a script function to move the robot to each manipulation area that has been defined. In this way the robot can go to each position to pick objects or explore an area to get some contextual information.
- The robot is able to scan a manipulation area. To make this action possible a symbolic camera is added to the robot on its head. We then move the head sequentially to scan the environment.
- The robot has to grab an object. To perform this action the grasp service of the PR2 is used. We specify the name of the object it has to grab and if the object is close to robot's hand it will be attached to it. In a similar way, we added a function to drop an object that takes as parameter the manipulation area where it should be dropped to. The robot will drop the object on top of the corresponding furniture.
- The last action is giving the object to the human. It consists in moving the robot to the human position and deploying the arm of the robot toward the human to give her the object. We simply use the robot armature actuator to control the robot's arm.

3   Integration with Robotic System

3.1   SPARK for Spatial Reasoning

To achieve geometric reasoning and to get the environment through robot perception SPARK [13] (SPAtial Reasoning and Knowledge) was used on our robot. To do the same in our simulated environment we need to get data from MORSE. We briefly explain here how we linked SPARK with MORSE and then what is obtained from this integration.

SPARK gets three kinds of input: object identifier and position, human position and posture and robot position and posture.

To obtain the object position in SPARK, we use the semantic camera on the robot head. This sensor can export the position and name of objects in view field. This data is sent using a middleware and is then read by SPARK to position the object in its representation. Concerning human and robot, we attach a pose sensor to them and we export their armature configuration. In this way SPARK can read the position and posture of the robot and human through the middleware, requesting only a mapping to match the MORSE joint representation with the SPARK one.

SPARK uses robot perception data to build the environment as seen by the robot. It also computes geometrical facts such as topological description of object's position (Book isOn table), agents affordances (Book is visibleBy Human) and knowledge of agents (Human hasKnownLocation Book). These high level data will be used to enrich the dialogue context.

3.2   Robotic System

By using SPARK as a link in the system, we are able to use a full robotic architecture with MORSE. This architecture, shown in Figure 3, is composed of several modules:

- Supervision System: the component in charge of commanding the other components of the system in order to complete a task.
- HATP: the Human-Aware Task Planner [14], based on a Hierarchical Task Network (HTN) refinement [15]. HATP is able to produce plans for the robot actions as well as for the other participants (humans or robots).
- Collaboration Planners: this set of planners are used in joint actions such as handover to estimate the user intentions and selects an action to perform.
- SPARK: the Spatial Reasoning and Knowledge component, as explained in 3.1.
- Knowledge Base: the facts produced by the geometric and temporal reasoning component are stored in a central symbolic knowledge base. This base maintains a different model for each agent, allowing to represent divergent beliefs.
- Human Planners: a set of human aware motion, placement and manipulation planners [16].

Our system is able, using SPARK, to create different representations of the world for itself and for the other agents, which are then stored in the Knowledge Base. In this way the robot can take into account what each agent can see, reach and know when creating plans. Using HATP the robot can create a plan constituted by different execution streams for every present agent.

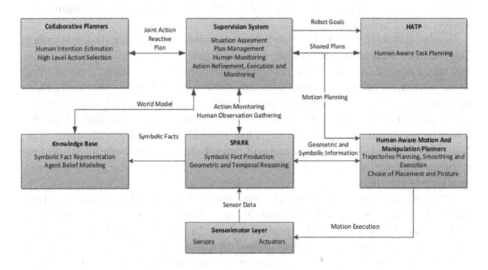

Fig. 3. Robotic system architecture

The interaction process is designed to be flexible. Users are able to issue commands to the robot but the robot is also able to plan on its own to execute complex goals and to adapt its plan to user actions. Human actions are monitored using SPARK by creating Monitor Spheres associated to items deemed interesting in a given context. A Monitor Sphere is a spheric area surrounding a point that can be associated to different events, like the hand of a human entering into it. The system is explained in more details in [17].

4   Learning Dialogue Strategies

4.1   Dialogue Management

In this study the robot is dedicated to help a human achieving a specific object manipulation task. Thereby, multimodal dialogues are employed to solve ambiguities and to request missing information until task completion (i.e. full command execution) or failure (i.e. explicit user disengagement or wrong command execution). In this setup, the robot, more precisely the Dialogue Manager (DM), is responsible for taking appropriate multimodal dialogue decisions to fulfil the user's goal based on uncertain dialogue contexts.

To do so, the dialogue management problem is cast as a Partially Observable Markov Decision Process (POMDP). In this setup, the agent maintains a distribution over possible dialogue states, called the belief state in the literature, and interacting with its perceived environment using a dialogue policy learned by means of a Reinforcement Learning (RL) algorithm [18]. This mathematical framework has been successfully employed in the Spoken Dialogue System (SDS) field (e.g. [19,20,21]) as well as to manage dialogue in HRI context (e.g. [22,1]). Indeed, this framework explicitly handles parts of the inherent uncertainty of the information which the DM has to deal with (erroneous speech recognitions, misrecognized gestures, etc.).

Recent attempts in SDS have shown the possibility to learn a dialogue policy from scratch with a limited number (several hundreds) of interactions [23,24,25] and the potential benefit of this technique compared to the classical use of WoZ or to develop a well-calibrated user simulator [23]. Following the same idea, we employ a sample-efficient learning algorithm, namely the Kalman Temporal Differences (KTD) framework [26,25], which enables us to learn and adapt the robot behaviour in an online setup. That is while interacting with users. The main shortcoming of the chosen method consists in the very poor initial performances. However, solutions as those proposed in [27,28] can be easily adopted to alleviate this limitation.

Although objectively artificial, the presented robotic simulation platform provides a very interesting test-bed module for online dialogue learning. Indeed, a better control over the global experimental conditions can be achieved (e.g. environment instantiation, sensors equipped by the robot). Thereby, comparisons between different approaches and configurations are facilitated. Furthermore, this solution reduces the subjects' recruitment costs without strongly hampering their natural expressiveness (due to the capacities offered by the simulator).

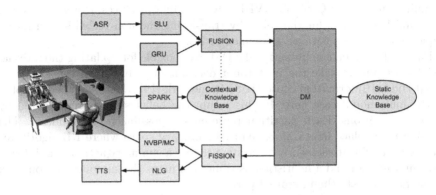

Fig. 4. Architecture of the multimodal and situated dialogue system

4.2 Architecture

The multimodal dialogue architecture considered in our experiments is presented in Figure 4. Twelve components are responsible of the overall functioning of this dialogue system.

The four orange ones are those which are implicated in the user's input management, speech and gesture modalities in our case. Thus, the combination of the Google Web Speech API[1] for Automatic Speech Recognition (ASR) and a custom-defined grammar parser for Spoken Language Understanding (SLU) are used to perform speech recognition and understanding. The Gesture Recognition and Understanding (GRU) module simply catches the gesture-events generated by our spatial reasoner during the course of the interaction. Then, the Fusion module temporally aligns the monomodal inputs then merge them with custom-defined rules. Finally, the result of the fusion (i.e. N-best list of interpretation hypotheses and their related confidence scores) becomes the input of the multimodal DM.

The three blue components are responsible of the context modelling. SPARK, previously presented in 3, for both detecting the user gestures and generating the per-agent spatial facts (perspective taking) which are used to dynamically feed the contextual knowledge base. These two modules are responsible of per-agent knowledge modelling which allows the robot to reason over different perspectives on the world. Furthermore, we also make use of a static knowledge base containing the list of all available objects (even those not perceived) and their related static properties (e.g. color).

The four yellow components are dedicated to the output restitution. So, the Fission module splits the abstract system action into verbal and non-verbal ones. The spoken output is produced by chaining a template-based Natural Language Generation (NLG) module with a Text-To-Speech Synthesis (TTS) component based on the commercial Acapela TTS system[2]. The Non-verbal Behaviour

---

[1] https://www.google.com/intl/en/chrome/demos/speech.html
[2] http://www.acapela-group.com/index.html

Planning and Motor Control (NVBP/MC) module produces arm gestures and head and body poses for the robot by translating the non-verbal action into a sequence of abstract actions, as defined in 2.3.

Finally, the green component is the DM, responsible for updating the internal belief state and to take the next robot decision. It is based on the POMDP-based Hidden Information State (HIS) framework [19] which has been adapted to the multimodal case here. In this setup, the belief state is represented by a set of partitions. Each partition represents a possible user command. The decision takes place into a more reduced summary space where RL algorithms are tractable. So, at each turn the system choose a summary action (e.g. inform, confirm, execute) and a heuristic-based method maps the summary action back to the master state (hand-crafted part).

Concerning the DM policy, the sample-efficient KTD-SARSA RL algorithm [25] was used in combination with the Bonus Greedy exploration scheme to enable the online learning of a dialogue policy from scratch. A reward function is defined to penalise the DM by -1 for each dialogue turn and reward it by $+20$ if the right command is performed at the end of the interaction, 0 otherwise. More details about this setup are available in [27,28].

4.3   Experimental Setup and Results

In this "proof of concept" study we chose to deal with a limited expert panel, composed of 6 subjects (2 females and 4 males of around 25 years old), in order to focus on the capacity of the system to learn from scratch using a limited set of interactions. The advantage is that the collected data sufficiently explore the state and action spaces during the online learning to be exploited in offline learning (using batch samples).

At the beginning of each dialogue, a specific goal (here a command) is randomly generated taking into account the simulated environment settings and the current interaction history in order to select a possible command. For example, "You want the robot to give you the white book on the kitchen table". No experimenter has any idea of the chosen configuration of the system with which he is interacting. So, we basically compare a hand-crafted expert dialogue policy (noted HDC) to a learned one (noted LEARNED). The latter was trained using a small set of expert users which first performed 60 dialogues in an online learning setting.

In the complete multimodal architecture, each interaction takes from 7 to 10 minutes to complete (objects detection, robot movements, etc.). So, without loss of generality, a practical workaround to speed-up the testing process consisted in using a fixed representation of the scene (a screenshot from the human point of view) and a web-based multimodal GUI instead of the full simulation setup. Overall, 84 dialogues for both the two proposed systems were recorded with 6 distinct subjects. At the end of each interaction users evaluated the system in terms of task completion. The learned policy were configured to act greedily according to the value function. Results are those gathered in test condition where exploration is not allowed. All the dialogues were recorded both in terms of audio and various kinds of meta-information (e.g. ASR N-Best list, dialogue manager detected gestures and related timestamps, etc.) but also high level annotations (e.g. environment settings, pursued goal, task success). As an illustration, a short interaction, translated from French, is given in Table 1.

Table 1. Example of a multimodal dialogue

	DA	hello()
R1	NLG/TTS	Can I help you ?
	ASR	Can you put the book in my bedroom?
U1	SLU	inform(action=move,desc=in,room=bedroom)
	DA	confreq(type=book,position)
R2	NLG/TTS	Sorry but where is the book you are talking about?
	ASR	I am talking about this one
U3	SLU	inform(idobj=?)
	GRU	pointsAt BLUE_BOOK 1395848705.31
R3	DA	execute(action=move,destination=bedroom_bedsidetable, idobj=BLUE_BOOK,position=livingroom_table,type=book, color=blue)
	NVBP/MC	move(BLUE_BOOK,livingroom_table,bedroom_bedsidetable)
	NLG/TTS	Ok, I will put the blue book on your bedside table

The results obtained are 14.3 for the HDC method and 17.6 for the LEARNED one. These results are given in terms of mean discounted cumulative rewards [18]. According to the reward function definition, this metric expresses in a single real value the two variables of improvement, namely the success rate (accuracy) and the number of turns until dialogue end (time efficiency). So, here the HDC policy manages the dialogue with 86% of success rate in an average of 4.8 turns against respectively 93% and 2.9 turns for the LEARNED one. The difference observed between the two methods can be mainly explained by a more accurate and less frequent usage of request of confirmation as well as an expected more fined-grained uncertainty management for the LEARNED method. Thus, these results clearly both demonstrates the ability of the overall architecture (simulation software + multimodal dialogue system) to learn an efficient dialogue policy using few dialogue examples and shows the interest of considering RL methods rather than a hand-crafted fixed and suboptimal policy. Indeed, only 60 training dialogues are enough to outperform the HDC by more than 3 points.

5 Summary and Future Work

In this paper we show how the MORSE simulator is used to build a scenario for HRI and how we used a robotic system along with this simulator to provide situated data to train the dialogue system. Using the MORSE simulator along with a robotic system was very helpful for us as it allows several partners to work with the same environment even being at different physical places and allows to train the system without using the actual robot, making it much easier for trainers. We believe this configuration is close enough to reality to efficiently train the dialogue system. Anyhow as we have not yet deployed the dialogue system on the robotic platform this affirmation still needs to be proved. These metrics will be carried out in a future work.

Acknowledgments. This work has been supported by l'Agence Nationale pour la Recherche under project reference ANR-12-CORD-0021 (MaRDi).

References

1. Lucignano, L., Cutugno, F., Rossi, S., Finzi, A.: A dialogue system for multimodal human-robot interaction. In: Proceedings of the 15th ACM on International Conference on Multimodal Interaction, pp. 197–204. ACM (2013)
2. Stiefelhagen, R., Ekenel, H.K., Fugen, C., Gieselmann, P., Holzapfel, H., Kraft, F., Nickel, K., Voit, M., Waibel, A.: Enabling multimodal human–robot interaction for the karlsruhe humanoid robot. IEEE Transactions on Robotics 23(5), 840–851 (2007)
3. Byron, D.K., Fosler-Lussier, E.: The osu quake 2004 corpus of two-party situated problem-solving dialogs. In: Proceedings of the 15th Language Resources and Evaluation Conference (LREC 2006) (2006)
4. Prommer, T., Holzapfel, H., Waibel, A.: Rapid simulation-driven reinforcement learning of multimodal dialog strategies in human-robot interaction. In: INTER-SPEECH (2006)
5. Rieser, V., Lemon, O.: Learning effective multimodal dialogue strategies from wizard-of-oz data: Bootstrapping and evaluation. In: ACL, pp. 638–646 (2008)
6. Rusu, R.B., Maldonado, A., Beetz, M., Gerkey, B.P.: Extending Player/Stage/Gazebo towards cognitive robots acting in ubiquitous sensor-equipped environments. In: Proceedings of the IEEE International Conference on Robotics and Automation (ICRA) Workshop for Network Robot Systems (2007)
7. Nakaoka, S., Hattori, S., Kanehiro, F., Kajita, S., Hirukawa, H.: Constraint-based dynamics simulator for humanoid robots with shock absorbing mechanisms. In: IEEE/RSJ International Conference on Intelligent Robots and Systems (IROS 2007) (2007)
8. Diankov, R.: Automated Construction of Robotic Manipulation Programs. PhD thesis, Carnegie Mellon University, Robotics Institute (August 2010)
9. Freese, M., Singh, S., Ozaki, F., Matsuhira, N.: Virtual robot experimentation platform V-REP: A versatile 3D robot simulator. In: Ando, N., Balakirsky, S., Hemker, T., Reggiani, M., von Stryk, O. (eds.) SIMPAR 2010. LNCS, vol. 6472, pp. 51–62. Springer, Heidelberg (2010)
10. Lewis, M., Wang, J., Hughes, S.: Usarsim: Simulation for the study of human-robot interaction. Journal of Cognitive Engineering and Decision Making 2007, 98–120 (2007)
11. Echeverria, G., Lemaignan, S., Degroote, A., Lacroix, S., Karg, M., Koch, P., Lesire, C., Stinckwich, S.: Simulating complex robotic scenarios with MORSE. In: Noda, I., Ando, N., Brugali, D., Kuffner, J.J. (eds.) SIMPAR 2012. LNCS, vol. 7628, pp. 197–208. Springer, Heidelberg (2012)

12. Lemaignan, S., Hanheide, M., Karg, M., Khambhaita, H., Kunze, L., Lier, F., Lütkebohle, I., Milliez, G.: Simulation and HRI recent perspectives with the MORSE simulator. In: Brugali, D., Broenink, J., Kroeger, T., MacDonald, B. (eds.) SIMPAR 2014. LNCS (LNAI), vol. 8810, pp. 13–24. Springer, Heidelberg (2014)
13. Milliez, G., Warnier, M., Clodic, A., Alami, R.: A framework for endowing interactive robot with reasoning capabilities about perspective-taking and belief management. In: Proceedings of the 23rd IEEE International Symposium on Robot and Human Interactive Communication (2014)
14. Alili, S., Montreuil, V., Alami, R.: HATP Task Planner for social behavior control in Autonomous Robotic Systems for HRI. In: The 9th International Symposium on Distributed Autonomous Robotic Systems (2008)
15. Nau, D., Au, T.C., Ilghami, O., Kuter, U., Murdock, J.W., Wu, D., Yaman, F.: SHOP2: An HTN Planning System. Journal of Artificial Intelligence Research, 379–404 (2003)
16. Sisbot, E.A., Clodic, A., Alami, R., Ransan, M.: Supervision and Motion Planning for a Mobile Manipulator Interacting with Humans (2008)
17. Fiore, M., Clodic, A., Alami, R.: On planning and task achievement modalities for human-robot collaboration. In: International Symposium on Experimental Robotics, Marrakech/Essaouira, June 15-18 (2014)
18. Sutton, R., Barto, A.: Reinforcement learning: An introduction. IEEE Transactions on Neural Networks 9(5), 1054–1054 (1998)
19. Young, S., Gašić, M., Keizer, S., Mairesse, F., Schatzmann, J., Thomson, B., Yu, K.: The hidden information state model: A practical framework for pomdp-based spoken dialogue management. Computer Speech and Language 24(2), 150–174 (2010)
20. Thomson, B., Young, S.: Bayesian update of dialogue state: A pomdp framework for spoken dialogue systems. Computer Speech and Language 24(4), 562–588 (2010)
21. Pinault, F., Lefèvre, F.: Unsupervised clustering of probability distributions of semantic graphs for pomdp based spoken dialogue systems with summary space. In: IJCAI 7th KRPDS Workshop (2011)
22. Roy, N., Pineau, J., Thrun, S.: Spoken dialogue management using probabilistic reasoning. In: ACL (2000)
23. Gašić, M., Jurčíček, F., Keizer, S., Mairesse, F., Thomson, B., Yu, K., Young, S.: Gaussian processes for fast policy optimisation of pomdp-based dialogue managers. In: SIGDIAL (2010)
24. Sungjin, L., Eskenazi, M.: Incremental sparse bayesian method for online dialog strategy learning. Journal on Selected Topics in Signal Processing 6, 903–916 (2012)
25. Daubigney, L., Geist, M., Chandramohan, S., Pietquin, O.: A comprehensive reinforcement learning framework for dialogue management optimization. Journal on Selected Topics in Signal Processing 6(8), 891–902 (2012)
26. Geist, M., Pietquin, O.: Kalman temporal differences. Journal of Artificial Intelligence Research (JAIR) 39, 483–532 (2010)
27. Ferreira, E., Lefèvre, F.: Social signal and user adaptation in reinforcement learning-based dialogue management. In: Proceedings of the 2nd Workshop on Machine Learning for Interactive Systems: Bridging the Gap Between Perception, Action and Communication, pp. 61–69. ACM (2013)
28. Ferreira, E., Lefèvre, F.: Expert-based reward shaping and exploration scheme for boosting policy learning of dialogue management. In: 2013 IEEE Workshop on Automatic Speech Recognition and Understanding (ASRU), pp. 108–113. IEEE (2013)

A Simulation Based Architecture
for the Development of an Autonomous All
Terrain Vehicle

Gianluca Bardaro, Davide Antonio Cucci, Luca Bascetta,
and Matteo Matteucci

Dipartimento di Elettronica, Informazione e Bioingegneria, Politecnico di Milano,
Piazza Leonardo da Vinci 32, 20133 Milano, Italy

Abstract. In this work we describe a simulation environment for an autonomous all-terrain mobile robot. To allow for extensive test and verification of the high-level perception, planning, and trajectory control modules, the low-level control systems, the sensors, and the vehicle dynamics have been modeled and simulated by means of the V-Rep 3D simulator. We discuss the overall, i.e., high and low-level, software architecture and we present some validation experiments in which the behavior of the real system is compared with the corresponding simulations.

1 Introduction

In this work we present an Autonomous All-Terrain Robot developed starting from a commercial, fuel-powered, All-Terrain Vehicle (ATV), i.e., a YAMAHA GRIZZLY 700. This robot is characterized by an Ackermann steering kinematic and the original vehicle commands have been replaced by servomechanisms controlling the handlebar position, the throttle, and the brake. Multiple sensors have been fitted on the robot to perform perception activities: two laser range-finders, a stereo camera rig, a GPS, an Inertial Measurement Unit (IMU), as well as, wheel and handlebar encoders.

Given the physical dimensions of the robot, the typical operating environment, and the complexity of the system architecture, it has been quite challenging to develop and test all the software components, especially in early stages of development. The main difficulties come from the intrinsic complexity in operating the robot, the little repeatability of experiments, the time consuming activity of fault detection and isolation. Moreover, meteorological and space issues further affected field evaluation, either because a suitable test area was not always available for experiments, and because of safety issues for the vehicle itself, which have a high roll-over risk, and for the people working with it.

To address these challenges we developed a simulation environment in which the vehicle and its sensors are substituted by a simulator in a way that is transparent with respect to the high-level perception and control software architecture. In contrast with respect to classical hardware-in-the-loop techniques, in which key elements of the real system, which might be difficult to model, replace their simulated counterpart, here the real system and the environment are replaced with models without changes in the robot control software.

D. Brugali et al. (Eds.): SIMPAR 2014, LNAI 8810, pp. 74–85, 2014.

In our work we employed the Virtual Robot Experimentation Platform (V-REP) [7], a physical simulator which relies on a distributed and modular approach and allows to model complex scenarios in which multiple sensors and actuators operate asynchronously at various rates. Other simulator were available, such as Gazebo [10], which is mainly focused on robotic applications, and Dymola [4], which instead focuses on highly accurate multi-domain, multi-body, physical, simulations. We decided to use V-REP instead of Dymola because of its capability in simulating the vehicle sensors and we preferred V-REP to Gazebo for its ease of use. The high-level perception and control architecture of the robot is implemented relying on the Robot Operating System [13], an open source framework which has recently become popular in the literature for its turn-on-and-go functionalities, easiness of deployment, large community, and support.

The use of simulators is common in robotics and several works related to the use of a simulator in the development of an autonomous all terrain robot, and autonomous robots in general, have been presented in the literature: in [9] a high fidelity model, including sensors, is developed to study the behavior of an autonomous ATV, focusing on the simulation itself, rather than the integration with the robot architecture. A simulator is also used in [8] in the actual robot architecture for real-time path planning, where the aim is to foresee potential collisions and change the plan accordingly. In [12], the SimRobot simulator is introduced and example applications in the RoboCup competition are discussed.

This work is organized as follows: in Section 2 the overall robot architecture is briefly discussed. Next we move to the high-level perception and control modules implemented employing the ROS framework. In Section 3 we present the simulation environment and we discuss sensor and vehicle models. Finally, in Section 4 we validate our approach comparing the behavior of the simulated system with the real one during autonomous trajectory following experiments.

2   The Quadrivio ATV

In this section we briefly review the vehicle specifications and the developed hardware and software architectures. The original vehicle used is a YAMAHA GRIZZLY 700 (see Figure 1a), a commercial fuel-powered utility ATV, specifically designed for agriculture work. For the purposes of the project, the vehicle cover has been removed and substituted with an aluminum one; this new cover allows to easily accommodate for control hardware and sensors. Furthermore, the vehicle has been equipped with three low-level servomechanisms, each one with its own control loop, to automatically regulate the steer position, the throttle aperture and the braking force [2][3]. Figure 1b shows the vehicle after customization. The main characteristics of the vehicle are listed in Table 1.

2.1   The Hardware Architecture

In order to allow for teleoperation and autonomous navigation, an on-board hardware/software control architecture has been developed.

(a) Original YAMAHA GRIZZLY 700   (b) Quadrivio ATV

Fig. 1. On the left the original all-terrain vehicle, on the right the vehicle after the changes to make it autonomous

The architecture is divided in two different layers: the higher level is developed using ROS and is responsible for acquiring data from external sensors, such as GPS, magnetometer, Inertial Measurement Unit (IMU), cameras and laser range-finders. Moreover, it hosts the modules for localization, path planning, high-level trajectory control and autonomous driving. The lower level acts as an interface between the vehicle servomechanisms and the ROS architecture: it receives desired setpoints from the higher level, reads the handlebar angle, throttle ratio, vehicle speed measurements and runs the low-level control loops.

To implement such an architecture that includes high-level and low-level tasks, a multi-layered and multiprocessor hardware/software architecture is required, which consists of: an industrial PLC, which allows a good compromise between the hard real-time requirements and high-level programming, and a standard i5 PC, on which runs the high-level ROS architecture (perception, localization,

Table 1. Vehicle characteristics

Main characteristics of the vehicle

Engine type	686cc, 4-stroke, liquid-cooled, 4 valves
Drive train	2WD, 4WD, locked 4WD
Transmission	V-belt with all-wheel engine braking
Brakes	dual hydraulic disc (both f/r)
Suspensions	independent double wishbone (both f/r)
Steering System	Ackermann
Dimensions (LxWxH)	2.065 x 1.180 x 1.240 m
Weight	296 Kg (empty tank)

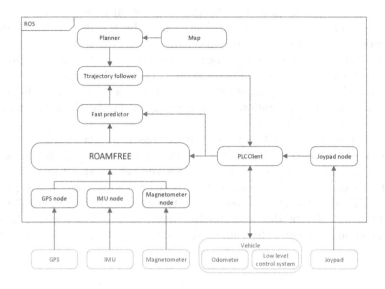

Fig. 2. The real system architecture

obstacle avoidance, medium-long range navigation, planning, etc.). Communication between the two layers is obtained through an Ethernet link.

2.2 The Software Architecture

Figure 2 shows the main modules of the high-level software architecture and their relations with the external sensors and the vehicle servomechanisms. These modules live as independent applications running on the standard PC and the communication between them is guaranteed by the ROS middleware.

The core part of the perception architecture consists in the localization node, which is based on ROAMFREE [5]. This open source framework provides out-of-the-box 6-DOF pose tracking fusing the information coming from an arbitrary number of information sources such as wheel encoders, inertial measurement units, and so on[1]. In ROAMFREE, high-level measurement models are used to handle raw sensor readings and provide calibration parameters to account for distortions, biases, misalignments between sensors and the main robot reference frame. The information fusion problem is formulated as a fixed-lag smoother and it runs in real time thanks to efficient implementations of the inference algorithms (for further details see [6], and [11]). At the present stage of development the localization module estimates the robot poses exploiting vehicle kinematic data (i.e., the handlebar position and the rear wheel speed), GPS, magnetometer, and the gyroscopes in the inertial measurement unit.

---

[1] http://roamfree.dei.polimi.it

The pose estimate is generated by the localization node at a frequency of 20 Hz. However, due to the latencies introduced by the ROS network, delays in the trajectory control loop which affect the system stability can occasionally arise. In order to prevent the detrimental effects of these delays, we introduced a predictor node. This node computes a prediction of the future robot pose at a frequency of 50 Hz; this prediction is based on the latest available global pose estimate and on the integration of the Ackermann kinematic model with the kinematic readings from the vehicle.

Given a map and a goal, a planner node, based on the SBPL library [1], produces a global path, which is then fed to a lower level trajectory following module. This module computes setpoints for the vehicle speed and handlebar angle, based on the current pose and velocity estimates, and on the planned trajectory. These setpoints are sent to the low-level regulators by a ROS node communicating with the PLC, which additionally acts as a multiplexer between the autonomous drive and the manual setpoints, depending on the current operating mode.

3   The Simulation Environment

The software architecture in Figure 2 has been designed introducing a decoupling layer between the real robot and the high-level perception and control software. This layer is composed by ROS nodes that respectively handle the GPS and the IMU sensors, and the communication module between the standard PC and the PLC. In this section we describe how we have replaced the real vehicle with a physical simulator and how we set up vehicle and sensor models so that they accurately mimic the real robot.

3.1   The Simulator

The vehicle simulator was developed using V-Rep [14], a software for robot modelling offering an accurate physics simulation. This software has been chosen for some of its features that fit particularly well with the requirements of our application. First of all, it is simple to set up and use with its integrated development environment, it has a library with various examples of robots already modeled, and one of them is particularly similar to our vehicle in terms of kinematics and suspension geometry. Another important feature is the possibility to control every object in the simulation with a remote API, that allows the integration with ROS, making it suitable for interacting with our software architecture.

One important issue which has to be addressed in coupling a simulator with a control architecture is to make sure that they share a global time reference. In our case, this was obtained enabling the use_sim_time parameter in ROS and having V-Rep publishing the current simulation time on the clock ROS topic. This is particularly useful when challenging simulations are run which involve complex terrain or environments and cannot be carried out in real-time.

(a) The customized model   (b) Suspensions and Ackermann steering

Fig. 3. The vehicle model used in simulation

3.2 The Vehicle Model

V-Rep offers multiple built-in vehicle models. We chose one that shares the Ackermann steering and the suspension geometry with our vehicle and we customized it to match the Quadrivio ATV specifications. The vehicle characteristics required to set up the model are listed in Table 2, while Figure 3a shows the customized model in which it is possible to see the image from the camera and the trace of the laser range-finder on the terrain. Figure 3b shows details of the Ackermann steering and suspensions.

The next step in vehicle simulation was to ensure the real vehicle and the simulation model share the same dynamic and kinematic behavior. In particular, we required that the step response for the handlebar and the speed loops on the real vehicle and in simulation were similar. As we are not interested in reproducing the engine behavior or in studying the dynamics of the steering motion control system, but only in simulating the overall vehicle dynamics, the simulator does not include an accurate model of the steering column and of the engine. Instead, the steer and speed loops, both based on a PID controller, were

Table 2. Model parameters

Vehicle model specifications.

Track	1920 mm
Wheelbase	1250 mm
Front wheel (WxH)	201 x 635 mm
Rear wheel (WxH)	247 x 635 mm
Weight (estimated)	390 kg

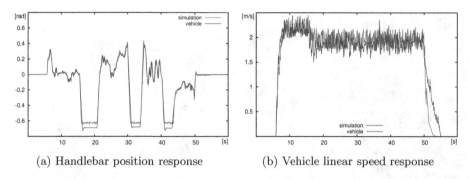

(a) Handlebar position response   (b) Vehicle linear speed response

Fig. 4. Plot of the vehicle actuators step responses on the real vehicle and on the the simulated one

directly modelled in such a way that the simulated responses of these controlled systems were as close as possible to the experimental ones.

We recorded data for the handlebar step response of the real vehicle and then we tuned the PID regulators that control the handlebar column in the V-Rep simulator so that the simulated vehicle handlebar position step response matches the one of the real vehicle. In particular, setpoints for the handlebar position and vehicle speed were recorded while being sent to the real vehicle, then we feed the simulated vehicle with the same setpoints, allowing to tune the simulator response. Figure 4a shows a comparison between the handlebar response for the real vehicle (blue line) and the simulated one (red line). It is possible to see that the two behaviors substantially match, but the simulated steer cannot reach a value as high as the real one, because of geometric limitations in the original model. However, we obtained a reasonable behavior in common operation ranges.

For the speed step response we implemented a custom PID controller, which controls the torque applied to the motor joint minimizing the error over the target speed. It was not possible to use the one integrated in the simulator because the model uses a motorized joint, which models an electric motor, while the vehicle has a fuel-powered engine with a significantly different characteristic. After the tuning with field data of the motor PID, we obtained a good matching behavior in the acceleration phases, while there is still a slight difference in deceleration due to the difficulties in modeling the engine braking when the throttle setpoint is suddenly decreased (see Figure 4b).

3.3   The Sensor Models

After modeling the vehicle we added the sensors: GPS, IMU, magnetometer and odometer. Most of them were already available in V-Rep, but they lacked the ROS integration and they did not account for noise and fault situations.

The sensors are realized with a "two layers" approach; the first layer is implemented directly inside the simulator, it consists in the sensors itself and a script that prepares and publishes ROS messages. The second layer is outside the simulator and it consists in a ROS node that reads the messages published by the simulator and converts them into a format which matches the one produced by sensors on the real vehicle. This double conversion has the aim of obtaining the decoupling between the simulator and the high-level perception and control architecture; indeed, from the point of view of the high-level architecture, there is no difference between the real sensors and the simulated ones.

The following are the sensor we have simulated with a brief description:

- GPS: V-Rep provides already a simulated GPS providing x/y/z-coordinates which are compatible with the East-North-Up (ENU) reference frame used in our architecture, so no further conversion was needed. The node coupled with this sensor builds the correct ROS message introducing some Gaussian noise (derived from real data) and allows to model random downtimes, to simulate for real world GPS unavailability;
- IMU: models for accelerometers and gyroscopes are provided by the simulator out of the box. The raw readings are published as ROS messages and converted in the desired format;
- Magnetometer: to implement this sensor we extract the current vehicle model orientation with respect to the global fixed reference frame; from it we can compute a simulated value for the Earth magnetic field reading in the sensor reference frame. However, on the real vehicle, hard and soft iron distortion affect the magnetometer readings. These are considered by employing the sensor model presented in [15], whose parameters have been calibrated by means of the sensor self-calibration capabilities of the ROAMFREE sensor fusion framework;
- Odometer: the vehicle rear wheel speed and the current handlebar position are extracted from the current status of the relevant joints in V-Rep, and a TCP socket is employed to communicate with the PLCClient ROS node, in a way that mimics the behavior of the X20 industrial PLC.

Moreover, there are two sensors that are simulated but not currently used for localization:

- Laser: the simulator provides a laser scanner out of the box. The associated script required some adjustment to publish the correct ROS message;
- Camera: V-Rep offers a highly customizable vision sensor that we used to realize a camera that matched our needs.

Figure 5 shows how the overall architecture changes when the simulator substitutes the vehicle and the real sensors. Every sensor now is substituted by its simulated counterpart, yet nothing changes from the point of view of the perception and control modules, since the communication is done on the same ROS topics. The PLCClient, in charge of communicating with the low-level control of the vehicle, interacts with a simulated low-level control system through a local socket connection. Inside the simulator a script converts setpoints from the PLCClient into setpoints of the model joints, another one collects odometry and sends it back to the ROS node. Migration from the simulated environment and the real vehicle is simple and requires only the change of few parameters.

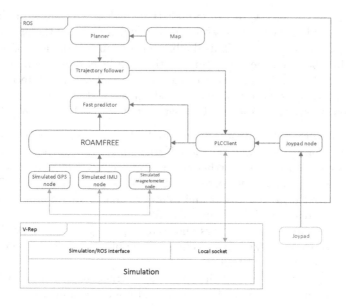

Fig. 5. Overall architecture in the simulation setup

4   Experimental Evaluation

In this section we discuss some autonomous trajectory following experiments done on the real vehicle and in the simulation environment. We employ an eight-shaped trajectory originating 1 meter ahead with respect to the current pose of the robot. The two circles have a diameter of respectively 18 and 12.5 meters.

Figure 6 shows the results of six experiments done with the real vehicle, in it we have plotted the reference path, the robot position, estimated by ROAMFREE, and the raw GPS readings. Especially in the first experiment (Figure 6a), but also in the other ones, it is possible to see how the trajectory is followed with reasonable accuracy, and with ROAMFREE being able to account for substantial multi-path effect compromising GPS readings.

Figure 7, instead, shows the results of the same experiments done with the simulator. In this case the GPS, like all the other sensors, is simulated and it is possible to appreciate its simulated faulty behavior. The robot position is estimated using measurements given by the simulated sensors as they were real, no special configuration is necessary to use them.

In Figure 7a, and 7b, it is possible to see that multipath effect compromises the real GPS sensor readings. This happens when the receiver tracks a replica of the GPS signal which is reflected by environmental features such as buildings and trees. This effect is hard to model and it has not been simulated in V-Rep, even though, if we restrict to its effect on localization, a noise model which accounts for a random transformation to be applied occasionally on the GPS readings could be considered.

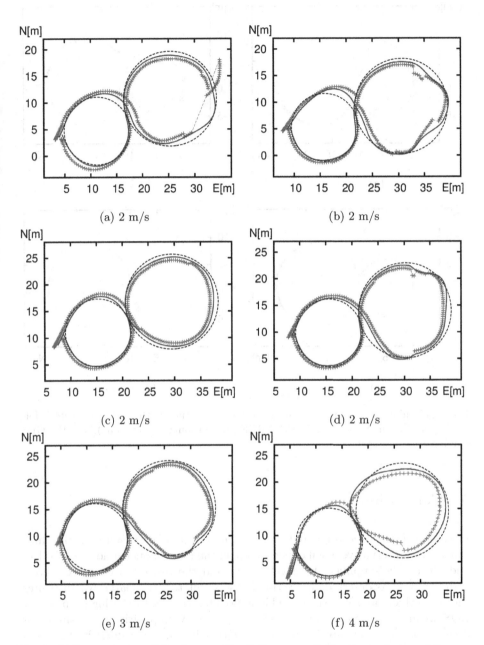

(a) 2 m/s

(b) 2 m/s

(c) 2 m/s

(d) 2 m/s

(e) 3 m/s

(f) 4 m/s

Fig. 6. Online trajectory following results. Reference path for the trajectory follower (black dashed line), the ROAMFREE position output (blue line), and the GPS readings (red crosses).

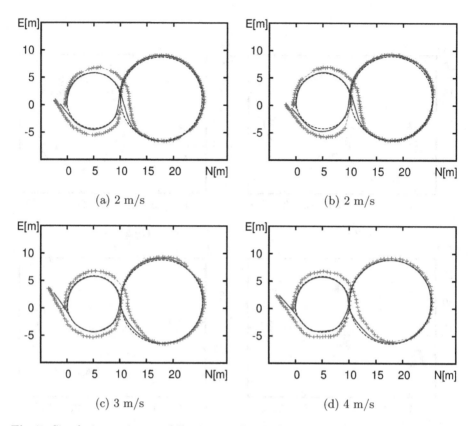

(a) 2 m/s   (b) 2 m/s

(c) 3 m/s   (d) 4 m/s

Fig. 7. Simulation trajectory following results. Reference path for the trajectory follower (black dashed line), the ROAMFREE position output (blue line), and the GPS readings (red crosses).

5   Conclusions

In this work we have presented and validated a simulated environment which provides an alternative when experiments on the real robots cannot be afforded, and ultimately simplifies the development and the testing of complex robotic architectures. As described in Section 3, the simulator transparently substitutes the real vehicle and its sensors. This is possible thanks to the highly modular ROS architecture and to the native integration of V-Rep with it. The simulator does not account for latency of sensors, either internal or caused by the communication, and this makes a simulation more ideal than we would like it to be, therefore a possible improvement to the current work could be addition of latency to sensors. The next step is to exploit the features of V-Rep to test the robot on rough terrains, since the simulator permits to add complex terrains that can be difficult to find in the real world, or that are too risky for the vehicle.

References

1. http://wiki.ros.org/sbpl
2. Bascetta, L., Magnani, G.A., Rocco, P., Zanchettin, A.M.: Design and implementation of the low-level control system of an all-terrain mobile robot. In: 2009 International Conference on Advanced Robotics (ICAR), pp. 1–6. IEEE (2009)
3. Bascetta, L., Cucci, D., Magnani, G., Matteucci, M., Osmankovic, D., Tahirovic, A.: Towards the implementation of a mpc-based planner on an autonomous all-terrain vehicle. In: Proceedings of Workshop on Robot Motion Planning: Online, Reactive, and in Real-time (IEEE/RJS IROS 2012), pp. 1–7 (2012), http://cs.stanford.edu/people/tkr/iros2012/schedule.php
4. Brück, D., Elmqvist, H., Mattsson, S.E., Olsson, H.: Dymola for multi-engineering modeling and simulation. In: Proceedings of Modelica, Citeseer (2002)
5. Cucci, D.A., Matteucci, M.: Position tracking and sensors self-calibration in autonomous mobile robots by gauss-newton optimization. In: 2014 IEEE International Conference on Robotics and Automation (ICRA). IEEE (to appear, 2014)
6. Cucci, D.A., Matteucci, M.: On the development of a generic multi-sensor fusion framework for robust odometry estimation. Journal of Software Engineering for Robotics 5(1), 48–62 (2014)
7. Freese, M., Singh, S., Ozaki, F., Matsuhira, N.: Virtual robot experimentation platform V-REP: A versatile 3D robot simulator. In: Ando, N., Balakirsky, S., Hemker, T., Reggiani, M., von Stryk, O. (eds.) SIMPAR 2010. LNCS, vol. 6472, pp. 51–62. Springer, Heidelberg (2010)
8. Hellstrom, T., Ringdahl, O.: Real-time path planning using a simulator-in-the-loop. International Journal of Vehicle Autonomous Systems 7(1), 56–72 (2009)
9. Jayakumar, P., Smith, W., Ross, B.A., Jategaonkar, R., Konarzewski, K.: Development of high fidelity mobility simulation of an autonomous vehicle in an off-road scenario using integrated sensor, controller, and multi-body dynamics. Tech. rep., DTIC Document (2011)
10. Koenig, N., Howard, A.: Design and use paradigms for gazebo, an open-source multi-robot simulator. In: Proceedings of 2004 IEEE/RSJ International Conference on Intelligent Robots and Systems (IROS 2004), vol. 3, pp. 2149–2154. IEEE (2004)
11. Kümmerle, R., Grisetti, G., Strasdat, H., Konolige, K., Burgard, W.: g^2o: A general framework for graph optimization. In: 2011 IEEE International Conference on Robotics and Automation (ICRA), pp. 3607–3613. IEEE (2011)
12. Laue, T., Spiess, K., Röfer, T.: SimRobot – A general physical robot simulator and its application in roboCup. In: Bredenfeld, A., Jacoff, A., Noda, I., Takahashi, Y. (eds.) RoboCup 2005. LNCS (LNAI), vol. 4020, pp. 173–183. Springer, Heidelberg (2006)
13. Quigley, M., Gerkey, B., Conley, K., Faust, J., Foote, T., Leibs, J., Berger, E., Wheeler, R., Ng, A.: ROS: an open-source robot operating system. In: ICRA Workshop on Open Source Software, vol. 3 (2009)
14. Rohmer, E., Singh, S., Freese, M.: V-REP: A versatile and scalable robot simulation framework. In: IEEE/RSJ International Conference on Intelligent Robots and Systems, pp. 1321–1326 (2013)
15. Vasconcelos, J., Elkaim, G., Silvestre, C., Oliveira, P., Cardeira, B.: Geometric approach to strapdown magnetometer calibration in sensor frame. IEEE Transactions on Aerospace and Electronic Systems 47(2), 1293–1306 (2011)

Applying Simulation and a Domain-Specific Language for an Adaptive Action Library

Jacob Pørksen Buch, Johan Sund Laursen, Lars Carøe Sørensen,
Lars-Peter Ellekilde, Dirk Kraft, Ulrik Pagh Schultz,
and Henrik Gordon Petersen

The Mærsk Mc-Kinney Møller Institute,
University of Southern Denmark, Odense, Denmark
{jpb,josl,lcs,lpe,kraft,ups,hgp}@mmmi.sdu.dk

Abstract. In this paper, we present the status of ongoing research aimed at tackling the issues of programming robots for small-size productions where fast set-up times, quick changeovers and easy adjustments are essential. We use a probabilistic approach where uncertainties are taken into account, making the deterministic requirements of an assembly process less strict. Concretely, actions from an action library are modelled through parameters, simulation is used to facilitate learning of uncertainty-tolerant actions, and a Domain-Specific Language (DSL) is used to convert the abstractly specified actions into corresponding executable actions. The approach is tested on an application example from industry.

1 Introduction

Extending robotic automation to the wide range of industrial applications with low volumes, high variance, high flexibility, capability to handle inaccuracies, etc. is a driving force for research in a range of topics such as computer vision, haptic and tactile sensing, advanced online robot programming, programming by demonstration, human-robot interaction and co-operation and modularization (plug-and-produce). Somewhat in between all these topics is the problem of how to develop structures that enable algorithms and software components to be reused for other applications - in literature often referred to as "action libraries" or "skills". However, the stored components in these structures have the drawbacks that there are no easy to use tools for generating the components and it is rather cumbersome to adjust the components to new scenarios.

We have therefore designed a concept to quickly derive complete solutions for new automation tasks by the following steps: In the *hardware definition step (S0)*, the user manually configures the system and in the *hardware modeling step (S1)*, a computer model of the platform is developed using the software library RobWork [5]. In the *sequencing step (S2)*, the assembly task is divided into a sequence of reusable actions. This is performed manually, but planning tools as [6] may be applied at a later stage. In the *action evaluation step (S3)*, we perform experimental studies of the new actions using both simulated and real

D. Brugali et al. (Eds.): SIMPAR 2014, LNAI 8810, pp. 86–97, 2014.

experiments and in the *parameter selection step (S4)*, we use these results to select optimal parameters for the action. In the *sequence testing step (S5)*, we combine results from the actions to perform simulated and real execution tests of the complete action sequences and in the *deployment step (S6)*, the final solution is chosen based on the results in S5 and then tested and possibly further refined. Noticed that there are feedback options in these steps so that if an outcome of a given step is not satisfactory, choices made in previous steps may be modified.

In this paper, we address three main components that are necessary to develop the system: In step S3, the amount of experiments is often quite large due to the size of the possible solution space even though human intuition is applied. We therefore need to perform experiments in simulation, which require **mathematical models and simulation techniques of the involved processes**. The simulation techniques are also combined and used in step S5. The actions must be formalized in a new way in order to handle inaccuracies while they can still be combined. This requires a new **probabilistic action library**. We will present this action library and discuss how the probabilistic part can also be sequenced. Combining a user interface with an action library of the complexity that we envisage (important for steps S2, S5, S6) will be a cumbersome task. We therefore present our ideas of a **new Domain-Specific Language (DSL)** supporting an interface for programming the new task in this way. We present our goals with these three components and the current status in developing them. Using a small real-world example, we demonstrate that our system is capable of solving a task that is sensitive to pose uncertainties and tight fits, which normally would have been difficult to solve using tradition methods. In the example we create a parameterised action and use simulation to find parameters, making the action more tolerant to the uncertainties. The adaptive action is instantiated and interfaced using our DSL.

The paper is structured with Section 2 discussing related work, Section 3 describing the system description and detailing the three main components, and Section 4 containing the demonstration. The paper is concluded in Section 5.

2   State of the Art

Methods for facilitating robotics in small batch productions are an important issue [7]. Systems such as softRobot [1] are focused on achieving improvements in large-scale industrial robot applications, but the ideas about object-oriented robot programming, separation of real and non-real time, integration of sensors and expandability are also viable for small batch productions. Other systems (e.g. RoboEarth [18] and KnowRob [16]) are focused on frameworks for robot knowledge sharing independent of specific hardware, done through web based databases and generic components and general skills applied to specific robots.

The system that we suggest is targeted at small batch production and in contrast to most previous work, it uses a probabilistic approach for its sub-symbolic representations. The probabilistic properties are exploited through simulation enabling us to find the action parameters best able to handle the uncertainties in the system, which is inspired from work with grasp affordance densities [4].

An important part of this work is the existence of a software library for reuse and sharing of functionality. Such are often referred to as skill or action libraries [2,10,9], and contains a set of actions which has pre- and postconditions together with prediction and evaluation functionalities. In these papers, skills or actions are assumed to be deterministic and of a fairly static nature. Here our work differentiates itself by explicitly modelling uncertainties and considering actions as something which need to be learned for a given application.

To actually learn actions, we need to rely on process simulation, which is a wide field having received much attention. In recent years much focus has been on dynamic simulation for e.g. grasping [3,19], whereas simulation of processes such as welding [11] and painting [8] have been used for decades. In this work we will utilize the simulator in RobWork [5] aimed at grasping and assembly.

Domain-Specific Languages can be used to create minimalistic interfaces for complex systems [1], and are thus relevant for having an easy-to-use system. Projects such as [15] aim at converting and re-engineering the current vendor specific DSLs into extensible robotics APIs to be used in the context of general purpose languages. Other projects, e.g. [17], create DSLs for the new and more abstract action and skill based robotics systems. Articles such as [13], [14], [12] tackle the subject of portability and separation of configuration and coordination in DSLs for programming robots, which is similar to the approach taken here. Unlike these existing systems, our DSL is however focused on interfacing and instantiating the adaptive actions while easily allowing the user to complement the DSL programs with more traditional robot programming.

3   Simulation and DSL for an Adaptive Action Library

Based on the vision described in Section 1, a layered system architecture was developed. The architecture consists of the following 4 layers:

Workcell Simulation/Actual Hardware: The bottom layer consists of the actual hardware and a simulation of the system. The actual hardware is chosen in the hardware definition step (S0) according to the needs of the task and from which the models for the simulation is made in hardware modeling step (S1). These components enable a complete test of the system in both simulation and real world as required for sequence testing step (S5) and deployment step (S6).

Modular Hardware Interface: To be usable interchangeably and also in a modular fashion to solve different automation problems both the actual hardware set-ups as well as the simulated workcell need to implement the same software interfaces. For that purpose, a set of common interfaces has been developed and is used to connect the bottom layer with higher layers in the architecture. An example is the general robot interface where robot commands like *joint-control* are provided. Actions in the system will only depend on these interfaces, making them independent of the actual hardware. The modularity of the hardware interface extends beyond the robot and includes digital and analogue I/O, grippers, sensors etc. This component provides a basis for usage of hardware near actions in the sequencing step (S2).

Action Library (Simulation Tool): Besides the basic and hardware-near actions provided through the modular interface, we are interested in structuring more complex actions, which is provided by the third layer. Reuse of previous experiences and the use of simulation and learning serves to concretise and instantiate the concept of an action to an actual execution. A simulation component is used as part of this layer to predict action outcomes for given parameters, thereby allowing the selection of suitable actions. More details on the action library and simulation can be found in Sections 3.1 and 3.2. These components are used in the action evaluation step (S3) and parameter selection step (S4).

Domain-Specific Language: Hardware and simulation is interfaced from actions within the action library, but also from the highest layer which is the overall system interface, provided in the form of a Domain Specific Language (DSL). The DSL enables the user to closely integrate hardware-near calls with the more abstract and high-level actions in an easy and intuitive way. For more details please see Section 3.3. In our work we use the DSL in the sequencing step (S2).

3.1   Action Library

In order to reduce the set-up time of assembly tasks, knowledge from previous executions should be exploited. We wish to achieve this not by asking an expert to realize the system, but by a library of assembly actions. The action library can be seen as a collection of all the actions (such as grasping, peg-in-hole and screwing) necessary for accomplishing a given assembly task. An action from this library should be able to improve its performance through learning and reuse of prior performance data to influence further execution. The action library is used in the sequencing step (S2) by providing a set of action choices and in the action evaluation step (S3) by the possibility to reuse previous results.

Any action has a definition A, a set of parameters π_A, a precondition $\Omega_i(A)$ and a postcondition $\Omega_f(A)$.[1] Unlike other action libraries, we have a strong emphasis on encoding and active handling of uncertainties as this is crucial for achieving the necessary robustness without fixating all objects accurately prior to task execution. In an action sequence each action A has a probabilistic precondition $x_i \in \Omega_i(A)$ where x_i denotes the specific state of the relevant parts of the overall scene and $\Omega_i(A)$ denotes the admissible states prior to executing the action. The action produces a postcondition $x_f \in \Omega_f(A)$ where x_f denotes the specific state of the relevant parts of the overall scene invoked by the action and $\Omega_f(A)$ denotes the set of possible states of x_f. To illustrate how we encode uncertainties, assume that x_i is not known precisely but rather taken from a probability density $\rho_i(x)$ on the set $\Omega_i(A)$. The action will then produce an outcome formally defined by a probability density $P_A(\rho_i, \pi_A)$ on $\Omega_f(A)$ where π_A denotes the action parameters. It is then easy to see that actions

---

[1] In our work pre- and postconditions can include two different types and combinations thereof, one being regions in continuous spaces (e.g., the Euclidean space), the other being classic discrete planning predicates (e.g., object_in_hand).

$A = \{A^{(1)}, \ldots, A^{(K)}\}$ where $\Omega_f(A^{(k)}) \subseteq \Omega_i(A^{(k+1)})$ can be sequenced with a resulting map $P_A(\rho_i, \pi_A) = \left\{ P_A^{(K)} \circ P_A^{(K-1)} \circ \ldots P_A^{(1)} \right\}(\rho_i)$ where π_A contains the parameters of all the actions and where ρ_i is the probability density on $\Omega_i(A^{(1)})$ prior to the first action and $P_A(\rho_i)$ is the probability density on $\Omega_i(A^{(K)})$ after the last action. Thus, if we know the probability distribution ρ_i prior to execution of the action sequence, we can use this framework to optimize the complete action with respect to a target distribution $P_A(\rho_i, \pi_A)$ on the postcondition.

In the longer run we expect to be able to improve the system by (a) being able to use already learned actions as sub-components of new actions and by (b) using experiences the system made with one action to help improve other actions. For this a similarity metric of actions (and potentially objects) will be required. The inclusion of additional information required for action chaining, task verification, planning and re-planning will also be explored at a later stage.

Action Learning by Simulation and Real World Experiments. The action can gain its knowledge about how to execute in a good way from both simulation and real world experiments. In both cases learning in higher dimensions become a problem since the space composed of the precondition $\Omega_i(A)$ and the action parameters π_A can be huge. It is therefore necessary to apply efficient learning techniques to avoid exhaustive search in this space. As mentioned (see Section 1, the action evaluation step (S3) and the parameter selection step (S4)) the idea is that by learning in simulation a good indication on how the action could be performed in real world (in terms of parameters π_A) can be obtained.

The learning is currently terminated after the simulation of the action has been performed and suitable knowledge obtained, but in the future it could also continue with real world executions adapting these to the unmodelled particularities of the real situation.

3.2   Simulation

An important component in the system is the availability of a realistic dynamical simulator that can simulate complete action. The simulator takes the action A, the action parameters π_A and the initial state of the relevant parts x_i. The aim of the simulator is then to calculate the state of the system consisting of only the relevant parts as accurate as possible while executing an action A. By sampling initial states from an assumed probability density ρ_i and by sampling action parameters π_A, it is possible to estimate the function $P_A(\rho_i, \pi_A)$. This sampling in simulation, instead of performing the corresponding real experiments, significantly reduces costs and time. In order for the actions to take full advantage of the simulator and to make implementation of new actions easier, a generic interface decoupling the actions and the simulation tool is used. This allows several actions to use the same tool, without having a separate implementation of the simulation tool for each action. Through this interface, the actions specify their intended motions of objects through a sequence of commands. The actions also specify success criteria such as the final intended position of objects and force limits. This use of simulation is in the third layer of our system Action Library (Simulation Tool). It is mostly used in the action evaluation step (S3) and to help with selecting good action parameters (parameter selection step (S4)).

Tests of complete assembly tasks (in the sequence testing step (S5)) can also be carried out in simulation as represented by the box "Workcell simulation". Here, all parts in the scene are simulated and these simulations are thus typically much more expensive than those above. However, when these simulations are applied, the action parameters have been chosen and thus it is only necessary to sample the initial density ρ_i. By simulating the full assembly task on the complete scene, we may be able to predict unexpected pitfalls in the assembly execution before the solution is implemented on the real set-up. The workcell simulation is interfaced to the rest of the system in the same way as the hardware module to make switching with the real set-up as easy as possible.

3.3 Domain-Specific Language

In order to specify and solve industrial assembly problems, individual actions need to be orchestrated and order in the right way (a part of the sequencing step (S2), see Section 1). To reduce the complexity of programming with these actions and to keep programming simple, a Domain-Specific programming language is used. This DSL is developed as an internal DSL in C++ to remain tightly integrated with the development of the underlying framework of actions and hardware set-up. The aim of the DSL is to allow users to quickly reconfigure and program the robot with new tasks even though these tasks might consist of complicated assembly operations and actions.

The DSL allows the user to integrate low level and hardware-near actions with the action library and function calls of a high abstraction level. We use a model-based approach where an internal metamodel is instantiated and subsequently interpreted. This approach is intended to enable future extensions of the DSL, such as exception-style error handling, concurrency, and arbitrary specification of assembly sequences. In a system where the goal is to reduce changeover times and allow for easy reconfiguration, there is a need for being able to easily add and reuse hardware, change execution sequences and make adjustment to the program. We believe that this can be achieved by creating a clear separation between imperative and declarative code.

The BNF of the *abstract syntax* of our DSL is shown in Fig. 1 (omitting syntactic noise due to the use of an internal DSL). The declarative parts consist of metainformation associated with the assembly items *(Item)*, IO-operations *(IO)*, and joint configurations *(JointConf)*. IO-operations can be combined and specified with wait commands to allow for greater control of external equipment. These declarations are then used to specify an imperative sequence of operations *(Sequence)*. These sequences consist of move commands, actions from the action library, I/O-operations, control commands and previously defined sequences. In our DSL it is therefore possible to declare hardware-related actions, allowing them to be used imperatively along with the high level and abstract actions,

$$
\begin{array}{ll}
P & := (\ \textit{Item} \mid \textit{IO} \mid \textit{JointConf} \mid \textit{Sequence}\ )\ * \\
\textit{Item} & := \underline{\text{item}}\ N_{\text{item}}\ (\ \underline{\text{keyframe}}\ N\ \textit{coordinate}*) \\
\textit{IO} & := \underline{\text{IOoperation}}\ N_{\text{io}}\ \textit{Primitive}* \\
\textit{JointConf} & := \underline{\text{JointConfiguration}}\ N_{\text{joint}}\ \textit{vector} \\
\textit{Sequence} & := \underline{\text{sequence}}\ N\ \textit{Action}* \\
\textit{Primitive} & := \underline{\text{setLow}} \mid \underline{\text{bit}}\ n \mid \underline{\text{sleep}}\ n \mid \ldots \\
\textit{Action} & := \underline{\text{move}}\ N_{\text{joint}} \mid \underline{\text{call}}\ N_{\text{action}}(N_{\text{item}}*) \mid \underline{\text{io}}\ N_{\text{io}} \mid \underline{\text{wait}}\ n \mid \ldots \\
\end{array}
$$

$N \in$ names, $n \in \mathbb{R}$, *coordinate* specifies coordinates, *vector* $\in \mathbb{R}^n$

Fig. 1. BNF of the abstract syntax for the internal DSL

effectively creating a building block structure where actions can be combined, modelled and reused.

Current implementations of action libraries often requires a large number of parameters before being able to instantiate an action [13,1]. These parameters specify detailed information on how the actions are performed. It is is our goal that the parameters specified in the DSL are based on action descriptions, such that they reflect the sequence of operations instead of how to perform the action. In a peg-in-hole action for instance, rather than having the parameters specifying the orientation of the peg, the parameters specify which end of the peg is used. This approach leads to missing parameters for the individual actions but our goal is to learn these parameters from previous action executions and simulation. Continuing the example, the action might have previous experience with one peg, some of which can be applied to another peg. An important factor is then how can we define similarity between actions or objects in a discretised fashion.

We solve the problem of filling in missing parameters by using "key-frames". Key-frames are meta-data associated with the assembly objects that along with an identifier represent important object positions.

4   Demonstrating the System Concept

This section aims to illustrate how we can apply our concepts and methods to a small real application where a tube is inserted into a nut. The DSL is used to program the task sequence (sequencing step (S2)). Since the action library does initially not contain any action suitable for this task, a new action is defined and learning is applied. This illustrates how we use simulation to estimate $P_A(\rho_i, \pi_A)$ (action evaluation step (S3)). The automatic selection of the action parameters π_A (parameter selection step (S4)) is not addressed in this paper and is therefore done manually. Finally execution of the task sequence on the real set-up (deployment step (S6)) is performed.

In the experiment the robot is moved to an initial configuration, where a peg-in-hole action is performed and learning through simulation is applied. In this action the robot inserts a tube into a tight-fitting union nut placed in a fixture. The robot then moves the tube with the nut away from the fixture.

Listing 1.1. The code written in the DSL to run the demonstration

```
1   //Platform specific information     17   JointConfiguration
2   IOoperations().                     18     initialPosition     = {3.425, -1.0...},
3     manipulation("gripper_open").     19     liftedPosition      = {3.379, -1.2...},
4       setLow().bit(0).sleep(0.5).     20     changeTubePosition = {3.817, -1.1...};
5     manipulation("gripper_close").    21
6       setHigh().bit(0).sleep(0.5);    22
7                                       23   //Sequence specification
8   //Scenario declarative information  24   sequence("reliability_test").
9   item("Tube").                       25     move() << initialPosition;
10    addKeyFrame("Peg_TCP").           26     pegInHole("Tube","Nut").
11      x(0).y(0).z(-0.046).            27     move() << liftedPosition
12      rx(0).ry(0).rz(0);              28               << changeTubePosition;
13                                      29     io("gripper_open").
14  item("Nut").                        30     wait(3.0).
15    addKeyFrame("Hole_TCP").          31     io("gripper_close").
16      z(0.0075);                      32     end();
```

Sequencing the Assembly Task through DSL. The DSL allows the user to execute the actions from the action library along with hardware near functionalities. The program in Listing 1.1 is the program used to conduct the real world experiments. In the DSL, a model of the sequence and actions are first constructed. The model is then interpreted and executed on the platform.

The program moves the robot to an initial position, calls the peg-in-hole action, moves the tube and nut out of the fixture and to a final position. Before the user can specify this sequence, the declarative part of the program has to be created (I/Os: line 1-6 , key-frames: line 8 to 16, joint configurations: line 17 to 20) in Listing 1.1. After that the sequence, which calls the action, is specified (line 22 - 31). Notice that the call to the insertion action is marked with *italics*.

Creating an Action Suitable for Learning and Execution. When the action is called from the DSL, it needs to learn good parameters, since no prior data for the action is available. The peg-in-hole action, A, is denoted by the four parameters $\pi_A = \{x, \theta, \phi, y\}$. These parameters are visualized in Fig. 2: x is the perpendicular distance from the plane of the hole to the middle of the peg defined by their respective key-frames. θ is the angle of the peg in the first linear motion. ϕ is the approach direction of the peg in the first linear motion. y is the distance from the calculated contact point between peg and hole to the rotation point of a circular motion. Based on the key-frames and the parameters the action is concretised as illustrated in Fig. 2.

The evaluation of the action in simulation is done using two criteria. For A to succeed the peg has to be inside the nut after the first linear movement and placed inside the nut after the last, as shown in Fig. 2. By trying different sets of parameters, data about the success/failure region $P_A(\rho_i, \pi_A)$ is obtained.

To simplify the complexity of the learning and for illustration purposes, two of the the four parameters in π_A is kept constant in this work. As a result

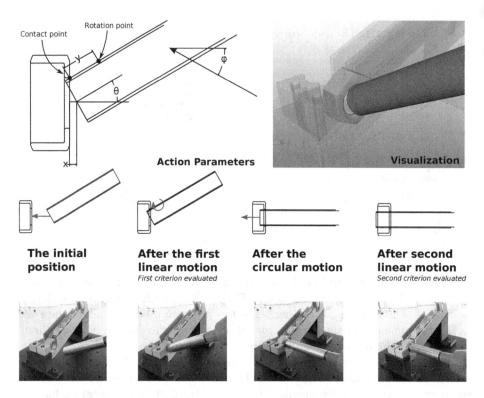

Fig. 2. Top left: the action parameters. **Top right:** visualization of a simulation. **Bottom:** Action movement visualised with corresponding execution.

the search for solutions was done within the parameter space of $\phi = 0°$, $y = 10\,mm$. $x \in [-3; 7]\,mm$ and $\theta \in [15; 45]°$ with step sizes of $1\,mm$ and $3°$ respectively.

Pose uncertainties $\rho_i(x)$ are approximated in simulation as the relative uncertainty between peg and hole. The positional change is handled by drawing two values from a normal distribution both with zero mean and a standard deviation of $1\,mm$, and adding them to the x- and y-position of the peg. Additionally a rotational disturbance is added by rotating the peg around a random direction vector in the xy-plane[2]. The magnitude of the rotation is again drawn from a normal distribution with zero mean and a standard deviation of $0.01\,rad$. Extreme values is removed by drawing a new value if it diverges by more than two standard deviations. These levels of uncertainties are based on empirical tests.

Obtaining an Action Probability Density Map from Simulation. In our simple experiment, we choose the set of postconditions to be $\Omega_f(A) =$

---

[2] The reason for not adding positional changes in the z-direction is that the peg has the same length and is grasped in the same way each time. By not adding rotational changes in the z-direction the peg is seen as perfectly circular in simulation.

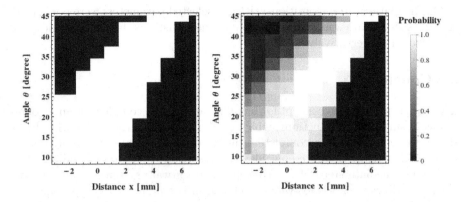

Fig. 3. The simulation result of the peg-in-hole action with varying x and θ. Left: without perturbations. Right: success-probability with 30 perturbations.

$\{nut\_on\_cyl, \neg nut\_on\_cyl\}$. We estimate $P_A(\rho_i, \pi_A)$ by performing a simple uniform sampling of their intervals. In Fig. 3, we show our results. The left image shows the resulting "Probability" $\equiv \{P_A(\rho_i, \pi_A)\}(nut\_on\_cyl)$ without perturbations. Not surprisingly, only pure black and white colour appear, indicating that each set of action parameters leads to a deterministic result of either success or failure. When taking the pose uncertainties ρ_i into account each sample point needs to be experimentally evaluated multiple times where the perturbation in each experiment is randomly selected from the distribution ρ_i. The right image shows our results. As can be seen, there is a clear structure indicating that it was sampled sufficiently to suppress noise to a reasonable level. Moreover, we obtain a pure white region indicating a promising set of action parameters.

Simulation shows that the direct approach with a low angle is more likely to fail. It also shows that big x-values are likely to fail, as big x-values mean that the turning of the tube will happen before the tube is even partly inside the nut. This violates the first evaluation criteria.

Choosing an Appropriate Set of Parameters to Execute the Action.
It will in general be a difficult optimization and learning task to derive a (close to) optimal set of action parameters taking into account the whole sequence and a potentially large set of parameters. The results from the simulation document this. Running all the simulation took around 18 hours[3].

In this paper, we emphasize illustrating the overall functionality, so this task is carried out manually by inspecting Fig. 3. The chosen values for these parameters for the action execution are: $\pi_A = \{x = 1\,mm, \theta = 30°, \phi = 0°, y = 10\,mm\}$.

Executing the Assembly Sequence in the Real World. To execute the sequence on the platform, the parameters π_A and key-frames is used to calculate a Cartesian path between peg and hole. Using inverse kinematics this was transformed into configurations and executed on the real platform.

---

[3] Using *one* core of a Intel Core i7-4600U at 2.1GHz processor with 8GiB of memory.

On the platform 100 repetitions with the selected parameters were performed. A 100% success rate was achieved, which seems realistic as the uncertainties used were chosen conservatively.

5   Conclusion

This article presented a concept for handling automated complex assembly operations in small size productions, which encompasses the process from hardware set-up to deployment of a complete solution for an automated assembly tasks.

In particular, we presented our ideas for a software system for handling some of the intermediate steps of the concept. The software system is based on developing a library of actions where each action is handled using a probabilistic approach and we showed how the system can derive solutions that are able to robustly handle spatial uncertainties and thereby limit the need for a very deterministic behaviour. We also presented an internal Domain-Specific Language for programming the system.

An application example was chosen to showcase architecture and principles of the system. We illustrated that our system can handle a peg-in-hole type operation with tight fits, which would often fail with a traditional approach due to spatial uncertainties. The chosen example could only be used for presenting a small subset of the overall functionality that we have in mind. In the coming period, we will extend our development to more advanced examples with substantial action sequencing and by this show the full potential of our system.

Acknowledgements. This work was supported by The Danish Council for Strategic Research through the CARMEN project. The authors would like to thank the people at Danish Technological Institute for their support with the platform used for the experiments.

References

1. Angerer, A., Hoffmann, A., Schierl, A., Vistein, M., Reif, W.: Robotics API: Object-Oriented Software Development for Industrial Robots. Journal of Software Engineering of Robotics 4, 1–22 (2013)
2. Bøgh, S., Nielsen, O.S., Pedersen, M.R., Krüger, V., Madsen, O.: Does your robot have skills? In: Proceedings of the 43rd International Symposium on Robotics (ISR 2012) (2012)
3. Ciocarlie, M., Lackner, C., Allen, P.: Soft finger model with adaptive contact geometry for grasping and manipulation tasks. In: World Haptics 2007: Second Joint EuroHaptics Conference and Symposium on Haptic Interfaces for Virtual Environment and Teleoperator Systems, pp. 219–224 (2007)
4. Detry, R., Kraft, D., Kroemer, O., Bodenhagen, L., Peters, J., Krger, N., Piater, J.: Learning grasp affordance densities. Paladyn. Journal of Behavioral Robotics 2(1), 1–17 (2011)
5. Ellekilde, L.P., Jorgensen, J.A.: Robwork: A flexible toolbox for robotics research and education. In: Robotics (ISR), 2010 41st International Symposium on and 2010 6th German Conference on Robotics (ROBOTIK), pp. 1–7 (June 2010)

6. Fikes, R.E., Nilsson, N.J.: STRIPS: A new approach to the application of theorem proving to problem solving. Artificial Intelligence 2(3-4), 189–208 (1971)
7. Haegele, M., Skordas, T., Sagert, S., Bischoff, R., Brogårdh, T., Dresselhaus, M.: White paper — industrial robot automation (2005),
   http://www.euron.org/miscdocs/docs/euron2/year2/dr-14-1-industry.pdf
8. Hertling, P., Hog, L., Larsen, R., Perram, J.W., Petersen, H.G.: Task Curve Planning for Painting Robots -Part I: Process Modeling and Calibration. IEEE Transactions on Robotics and Automation 12(2), 324–330 (1996)
9. Huckaby, J., Vassos, S., Christensen, H.I.: Planning with a task modeling framework in manufacturing robotics. In: 2013 IEEE/RSJ International Conference on Intelligent Robots and Systems (IROS), pp. 5787–5794. IEEE/RSJ (2013)
10. Huckaby, J., Christensen, H.: A taxonomic framework for task modeling and knowledge transfer in manufacturing robotics. In: Proc. 26th AAAI Cognitive Robotics Workshop, pp. 94–101 (2012)
11. Jeberg, P., Holm, H., Madsen, O.: Automatic weld planning by finite element simulation and iterative learning. Welding Journal 87(9), 219S–228S (2008)
12. Klotzbücher, M., Biggs, G., Bruyninckx, H.: Pure coordination using the coordinator–configurator pattern. In: 3rd International Workshop on Domain-Specific Languages and models for ROBotic Systems (DSLRob 2012) (2013)
13. Klotzbücher, M., Bruyninckx, H.: Coordinating Robotic Tasks and Systems with rFSM Statecharts. Journal of Software Engineering for Robotics 3(1), 28–56 (2012)
14. Klotzbücher, M., Smits, R., Bruyninckx, H., De Schutter, J.: Reusable hybrid force-velocity controlled motion specifications with executable Domain Specific Languages. In: 2011 IEEE/RSJ International Conference on Intelligent Robots and Systems, pp. 4684–4689 (September 2011)
15. Mühe, H., Angerer, A., Hoffmann, A., Reif, W.: On reverse-engineering the kuka robot language. In: 1st International Workshop on Domain-Specific Languages and Models for ROBotic Systems (DSLRob 2010) (2010)
16. Tenorth, M., Beetz, M.: Knowrob knowledge processing for autonomous personal robots. In: IEEE/RSJ International Conference on Intelligent Robots and Systems, IROS 2009, pp. 4261–4266. IEEE (2009)
17. Thomas, U., Hirzinger, G., Rumpe, B., Schulze, C., Wortmann, A.: A new skill based robot programming language using uml/p statecharts. In: 2013 IEEE International Conference on Robotics and Automation (ICRA), pp. 461–466 (May 2013)
18. Waibel, M., Beetz, M., D'Andrea, R., Janssen, R., Tenorth, M., Civera, J., Elfring, J., Gálvez-López, D., Häussermann, K., Montiel, J., Perzylo, A., Schießle, B., Zweigle, O., van de Molengraft, R.: Roboearth - a world wide web for robots. Robotics & Automation Magazine 18(2), 69–82 (2011)
19. Zhang, L., Betz, J., Trinkle, J.C.: Comparison of simulated and experimental grasping actions in the plane. In: First International Multibody Dynamics Symposium (2010)

Simulation Environment for Multi-robot Cooperative 3D Target Perception

André Dias[1], Jose Almeida[1], Nuno Dias[1], Pedro Lima[2], and Eduardo Silva[1]

[1] INESC TEC, INESC Technology and Science,
ISEP/IPP, School of Engineering,
Porto, Portugal
{adias,jma,ndias,eaps}@lsa.isep.ipp.pt
[2] Institute for Systems and Robotics,
Instituto Superior Técnico, Universidade de Lisboa,
Lisbon, Portugal
pal@isr.ist.utl.pt

Abstract. Field experiments with a team of heterogeneous robots require human and hardware resources which cannot be implemented in a straightforward manner. Therefore, simulation environments are viewed by the robotic community as a powerful tool that can be used as an intermediate step to evaluate and validate the developments prior to their integration in real robots. This paper evaluates a novel multi-robot heterogeneous cooperative perception framework based on monocular measurements under the MORSE robotic simulation environment. The simulations are performed in an outdoor environment using a team of Micro Aerial Vehicles (MAV) and an Unmanned Ground Vehicle (UGV) performing distributed cooperative perception based on monocular measurements. The goal is to estimate the 3D target position.

1 Introduction

Robotics emerged as a research field and has seen important advances over the last years. There has been an increasing research effort on novel multi-robot cooperative tasks for heterogeneous mobile robotics applications. These continuous developments achieved by the robotic community are driven by an significant number of potential end-user applications where it is necessary to reduce human intervention, including cooperative search and rescue missions[1][2], surveillance[3][4], or recognition and border tasks[5][4]. Therefore, to accomplish this level of end-user applications with teams of robots, there are concepts, such as navigation, perception and control, which must be thoroughly developed, evaluated and validated under different scenarios.

Another point, which cannot be disregarded and is associated with this level of application scenarios, is the human resources required. For instance, if a team of aerial robots is being evaluated while performing a surveillance task, for safety reasons it is necessary to have at least one human operator for each robot, which is not feasible for some research groups. Adding to this, some resources are not

D. Brugali et al. (Eds.): SIMPAR 2014, LNAI 8810, pp. 98–109, 2014.

available, such as the robots and sensors required. Taking these constraints into consideration, simulation environments has been an important support tool by robotics research groups[6][7][8][9][10][11][12], not just to conduct the field experiments successfully, but to ensure that the developments are evaluated and validated prior to being integrated in real robots. For instance, the work from Johannes[10] with a simulation environment developed in Gazebo and integrated with ROS to evaluate the MAV behavior such as flight dynamic, the work from Nathan[12] with Gazebo in distributed formation control of a swarm team of ground robots with the ability to adapt the shape of the formation based on the environment constraints, and the work from Dewan[11] to evaluation the proposed optimization method to perform cooperative exploration between heterogeneous vehicles.

Focusing on the problem of multi-robot cooperative perception and on the outlined constraints associated with the field experiments using a team of robots, this paper evaluates a novel multi-robot heterogeneous cooperative perception framework based on monocular measurements under the open-source MORSE robotic simulation environment[8][9]. The framework, defined as Uncertainty-based Multi-Robot Cooperative Triangulation (UCoT), is capable of estimating the 3D target position based on monocular measurements. Therefore, we propose to validate is behavior under different conditions, for instance, assessing the impact of introducing more robots to the environment and also the robustness of the UCoT to different levels of Gaussian noise associated with the attitude and position sensors.

The MORSE was chosen as the simulation environment, instead of other powerful simulators such as the Gazebo[10][13], because in the context of our requirements MORSE proved to be more versatile, modular, flexible and reusable[8], due to the ability to provide a straightforward implementation of the outdoor scenario composed with heterogeneous types of robots and sensors, like GPS, Laser and Cameras. Moreover, the MORSE is built on the top of the Blender software, which provides the tools required to model new robots and scenarios. Another important key issue from MORSE, is the fact of supporting different middleware used in robotics, such as YARP[14], ROS[15] and MOOS[16].

This paper is outlined as follows: Section 2 presents the framework to be evaluated under the MORSE simulation environment, as well as the mathematical formulation for the Uncertainty-based Multi-Robot Cooperative Triangulation (UCoT). Section 3 presents the architecture associated to the integration of the simulation environment with the UCoT framework and also the developed in Blender of a 3D model of a Unmanned Ground Vehicle (UGV) TIGRE[17]. The UCoT framework is validated in Section 4 with MORSE for an outdoor simulation environment, using a team of Micro Aerial Vehicles (MAV) and an Unmanned Ground Vehicle (UGV) performing cooperative perception based on monocular measurements. The goal is to estimate the 3D target position of a human moving randomly over an outdoor scenario with the effect of the terrain morphology. Section 5 provides the concluding remarks and outlines future work topics.

2   Multi-robot Cooperative Perception Framework

This section introduces the framework to be evaluated by the open-source simulation environment MORSE, which is a multi-robot cooperative perception method, defined as Uncertainty-based Multi-Robot Cooperative Triangulation (UCoT). The main contribution of this method is the ability to estimate 3D information based on monocular measurements, using the relative position and attitude provided by each robot, and based on the geometric constraints derived from the triangulation[18].

The method estimates the 3D target position by establishing a flexible and dynamic geometric baseline between monocular measurements. The uncertainty of the observation model of each robot, position, attitude and image plane pixel target position are modeled using the first order uncertainty propagation, with the assumption that all sources of uncertainty can be modeled as uncorrelated Gaussian noise. The multi-robot cooperative triangulation method has been introduced in [19] and extended based on the uncertainty of the observation model provided by each robot in [20].

In order to support the readout, the notation $^{to}_{from}\xi_n$ is used to denote the transformation matrix *from* one coordinate frame *to* the other. The robot body frame is called $\{B\}$ and the global frame is called $\{W\}$. The upper case notation in bold represents the matrix variables, while the lower case in bold represents the vectors, and finally the lower case represents the scalar variables.

The UCoT architecture framework is outlined in figure 1 and contains the following components:

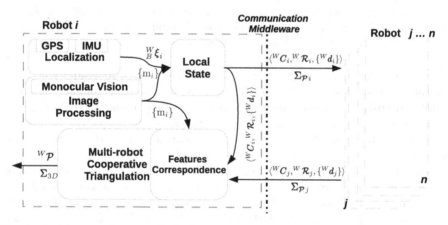

Fig. 1. Architecture Framework for Uncertainty-based Multi-Robot Cooperative Triangulation (UCoT)

– **Localization** is responsible for providing the robots pose to the local state component, described by the following matrix $^W_B\xi$ relatively to the global frame. This information is provided not only by an IMU as $\boldsymbol{u} \overset{\text{def.}}{=} [\phi\ \theta\ \psi]^T$, where (ϕ, θ, ψ) are respectively the roll, pitch and yaw angles, but also by a GPS as $\varsigma \stackrel{\text{def.}}{=} [\lambda \; \varphi \; h]^T$, where (λ, φ, h) are respectively the latitude, longitude and altitude;

- **Local State** provides an output 3 tuple $\langle {}^W C, {}^W \mathcal{R}, \{{}^W d\}\rangle$ relatively to the global frame, composed of the camera position ${}^W C$, attitude ${}^W \mathcal{R}$ and ray vectors $\{{}^W d\}$. These represent the direction vector from the points detected by the monocular vision system $\{m\}$;

- **Feature Correspondence** is responsible for evaluating the tuples shared by other robots relatively to the local state component. This evaluation is performed based on the Euclidean distance between two points projected in the global frame from the intersection rays $\lambda_i^W d_i$ and $\lambda_j^W d_j$, with the perpendicular to both vectors ${}^W d_\perp = \lambda_i^W d_i \perp \lambda_j^W d_j$;

- **Multi-Robot Cooperative Triangulation** is responsible for the 3D target estimation and covariance Σ_{Target} related to all sources of uncertainty, as described in equation (8) for the UCoT method.

2.1   UCoT – Uncertainty Based Multi-robot Cooperative Triangulation

The UCoT method selects the line that is perpendicular to the shortest segment of both rays. Based on the uncertainty associated with the position, attitude and image plane pixel error of each ray, the method will estimate the intersection of both rays by weighing, in a probabilistic manner, their contribution to the 3D target position.

Considering the formulation by Trucco[18] relatively to the mid-point triangulation using a stereo rigid baseline and an extended dynamic baseline, described in [19], it is possible to obtain the following equation:

$$
{}^W P = \Omega_i^W P_i + \Omega_j^W P_j \tag{1}
$$
$$
{}^W P = \Omega_i({}^W C_i + \lambda_i^W d_i) + \Omega_j({}^W C_j + \lambda_j^W d_j)
$$

This equation can represent a dynamic baseline approach relatively to the global frame using a pair of bearing-only systems defined as i, j, where each camera not only knows its own position ${}^W C$ and attitude ${}^W \mathcal{R}$, but also shares the direction vectors ${}^W d$ from the points detected by the monocular vision system $\{m\}$, with the Ω_i and Ω_j being the weight assigned to each bearing-only systems, derived in equation (7).

To ensure that all sources of uncertainty are taken into consideration when estimating the 3D target position, the Σ_{Target} will be estimated based on the assumption that there is uncertainty in the input pixel localization σ_m, as well as in the cameras position σ_ς and attitude σ_u relatively to the global frame. All of them are modeled as uncorrelated zero-mean Gaussian random variables.

$$
\sigma_\varsigma = \begin{bmatrix} \sigma_\lambda & 0 & 0 \\ 0 & \sigma_\varphi & 0 \\ 0 & 0 & \sigma_h \end{bmatrix} \quad \sigma_u = \begin{bmatrix} \sigma_\phi & 0 & 0 \\ 0 & \sigma_\theta & 0 \\ 0 & 0 & \sigma_\psi \end{bmatrix} \quad \sigma_m = \begin{bmatrix} \sigma_{m_x} & 0 \\ 0 & \sigma_{m_y} \end{bmatrix} \tag{2}
$$

Using the first-order uncertainty propagation, it is possible to approximate the distribution of the variables, defined in section 2 as the input state vector $\boldsymbol{\nu}_{(i,j)} = [\boldsymbol{\varsigma}_i, \boldsymbol{u}_i, \boldsymbol{m}_i, \boldsymbol{\varsigma}_j, \boldsymbol{u}_j, \boldsymbol{m}_j]$, from equation (2), as multivariate Gaussians. The $\boldsymbol{\Sigma}_{Target}$ covariance matrix approximately models the uncertainty in the 3D target estimation, which is computed using the noisy measurements of the Multi-Robot Cooperative Triangulation, as follows:

$$\boldsymbol{\Sigma}_{Target} = \boldsymbol{J_P} \boldsymbol{\Lambda}_{i,j} \boldsymbol{J_P}^T \tag{3}$$

where $\boldsymbol{J_P}$ stands for the Jacobian matrix of $^W\boldsymbol{P}$ in equation (2) by

$$\boldsymbol{J_P}_{[3\times16]} = \boldsymbol{\nabla}_{(\boldsymbol{\nu}_{(i,j)})} {}^W\boldsymbol{P}(\boldsymbol{\nu}(i,j)) \tag{4}$$

with $\boldsymbol{\Lambda}_{i,j}$ being the input covariance matrix represented by a diagonal line relatively to all sources of uncertainty present in equation (2) for each monocular vision system

$$\boldsymbol{\Lambda}_{i,j[16\times16]} = \begin{bmatrix} \sigma_{\boldsymbol{\varsigma}_i[3\times3]} & \cdots & & & & \\ \cdots & \sigma_{\boldsymbol{u}_i[3\times3]} & \cdots & & & \\ & \cdots & \sigma_{\boldsymbol{m}_i[2\times2]} & \cdots & & \\ & & \cdots & \sigma_{\boldsymbol{\varsigma}_j[3\times3]} & \cdots & \\ & & & \cdots & \sigma_{\boldsymbol{u}_j[3\times3]} & \cdots \\ & & & & \cdots & \sigma_{\boldsymbol{m}_j[2\times2]} \end{bmatrix} \tag{5}$$

To ensure that all sources of uncertainty provided by each intersection ray are addressed in a probabilistic manner, to obtain the weight associated with each ray, once again it is necessary to estimate the covariance, using the first-order uncertainty propagation, $\boldsymbol{\Sigma_{P_i}}$ and $\boldsymbol{\Sigma_{P_j}}$ related to $^W\boldsymbol{P}_i$ and $^W\boldsymbol{P}_j$, as follows:

$$\begin{aligned} \boldsymbol{\Sigma_{P_i}} = \boldsymbol{J_{P_i}} \boldsymbol{\Lambda}_{i,j} \boldsymbol{J_{P_i}}^T & \quad \boldsymbol{J_{P_i}}_{[3\times16]} = \boldsymbol{\nabla}_{(\boldsymbol{\nu}_{(i,j)})} {}^W\boldsymbol{P}_i \\ \boldsymbol{\Sigma_{P_j}} = \boldsymbol{J_{P_j}} \boldsymbol{\Lambda}_{i,j} \boldsymbol{J_{P_j}}^T & \quad \boldsymbol{J_{P_j}}_{[3\times16]} = \boldsymbol{\nabla}_{(\boldsymbol{\nu}_{(i,j)})} {}^W\boldsymbol{P}_j \end{aligned} \tag{6}$$

where $\boldsymbol{J_{P_i}}$ and $\boldsymbol{J_{P_j}}$ are respectively the Jacobian matrix from $^W\boldsymbol{P}_i$ and $^W\boldsymbol{P}_j$, and $\boldsymbol{\Lambda}_{i,j}$ is the input covariance matrix from equation (5). Therefore, with the uncertainty of each intersection ray $\boldsymbol{\Sigma_{P_i}}$ and $\boldsymbol{\Sigma_{P_j}}$, and the perpendicular vector $^W\boldsymbol{d}_\perp$, the probabilistic weight of each ray is expressed as:

$$\Omega_i = \frac{({}^W\boldsymbol{d}_\perp \boldsymbol{\Sigma_{P_j}} {}^W\boldsymbol{d}_\perp{}^T)^2}{({}^W\boldsymbol{d}_\perp \boldsymbol{\Sigma_{P_i}} {}^W\boldsymbol{d}_\perp{}^T)^2 + ({}^W\boldsymbol{d}_\perp \boldsymbol{\Sigma_{P_j}} {}^W\boldsymbol{d}_\perp{}^T)^2} \quad \Omega_j = \frac{({}^W\boldsymbol{d}_\perp \boldsymbol{\Sigma_{P_i}} {}^W\boldsymbol{d}_\perp{}^T)^2}{({}^W\boldsymbol{d}_\perp \boldsymbol{\Sigma_{P_i}} {}^W\boldsymbol{d}_\perp{}^T)^2 + ({}^W\boldsymbol{d}_\perp \boldsymbol{\Sigma_{P_j}} {}^W\boldsymbol{d}_\perp{}^T)^2} \tag{7}$$

Therefore, combining the weights Ω_i, Ω_j from equation (7) and the dynamic baseline cooperative triangulation equation (2), it is possible to obtain the UCoT Uncertainty-based Multi-Robot Cooperative Triangulation method, as follows:

$$\begin{aligned} {}^W\boldsymbol{P} = & \frac{({}^W\boldsymbol{d}_\perp \boldsymbol{\Sigma_{P_j}} {}^W\boldsymbol{d}_\perp{}^T)^2}{({}^W\boldsymbol{d}_\perp \boldsymbol{\Sigma_{P_i}} {}^W\boldsymbol{d}_\perp{}^T)^2 + ({}^W\boldsymbol{d}_\perp \boldsymbol{\Sigma_{P_j}} {}^W\boldsymbol{d}_\perp{}^T)^2} ({}^W\boldsymbol{C}_i + \lambda_i^W \boldsymbol{d}_i) \\ & + \frac{({}^W\boldsymbol{d}_\perp \boldsymbol{\Sigma_{P_i}} {}^W\boldsymbol{d}_\perp{}^T)^2}{({}^W\boldsymbol{d}_\perp \boldsymbol{\Sigma_{P_i}} {}^W\boldsymbol{d}_\perp{}^T)^2 + ({}^W\boldsymbol{d}_\perp \boldsymbol{\Sigma_{P_j}} {}^W\boldsymbol{d}_\perp{}^T)^2} ({}^W\boldsymbol{C}_j + \lambda_j^W \boldsymbol{d}_j) \end{aligned} \tag{8}$$

3   Simulation Environment

One of the key points in this paper is the ability to evaluate the multi-robot cooperative perception method under a simulation environment, and approximate it as much as possible to a real experimental scenario[19], as depicted in Figure 2.

Fig. 2. Top-Left: Experimental scenario[19]. **Right**: MORSE outdoor simulation environment. **Middle - Left**: UGV TIGRE[17] and MAV Asctec Pelican. **Right**: Simulated robots: MAV and the UGV TIGRE developed based on the TIGRE 3D model. **Bottom - Left**: TIGRE and MAV camera view. **Right**: Simulated TIGRE and MAV camera view.

Therefore, to accomplish this level of similarity, the following items were developed under the MORSE simulation environment:

- Integrate the UCoT framework, as depicted in figure 3, to receive the Camera and Pose sensor, over the middleware ROS, from the MORSE output data stream, and perform image processing equal to the one that has already been developed in [19].
- Over the middleware ROS, share the required 3 tuple $\langle {}^{W}C, {}^{W}\mathcal{R}, \{{}^{W}d\}\rangle$ between robots so that it is possible to estimate the target 3D position based on the UCoT framework.
- Develop the UGV TIGRE[17] with the modifications required by the Blender Game Engine. The rear and the front wheels are attached to the platform so that the vehicle moves based on the Ackerman geometry, with the Blender

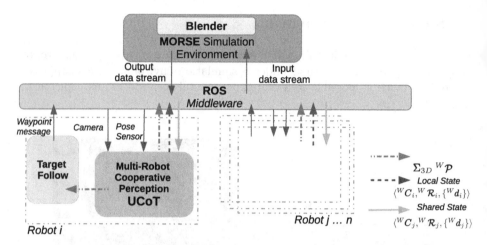

Fig. 3. Architecture between the MORSE simulation environment and the multi-robot cooperative perception framework

simulator being responsible for computing the tyre friction, as well as suspension stiffness, compression and damping.

- Integrate a new component in MORSE, using the Ackerman controller because the TIGRE robot is based on an electric 4-wheel motor bike with Ackerman geometry. The inputs of the Ackerman controller are the steering, force and brake applied to the wheels.

4   Results

This section presents the results from the validation of the UCoT framework in an outdoor simulation environment with MORSE. The framework is evaluated using a team of heterogeneous robots composed of MAVs and an UGV with different values of Gaussian noise applied to position and attitude sensors.

Table 1. Simulated Gaussian noise applied to the position and attitude on each experimental case

Experimental case	Sensor	UGV TIGRE Reference/Model	Gaussian Noise	MAV Quadrotor Reference/Model	Gaussian Noise
I	GPS	RTK Septentrio PolaRx + Base Station	$\sigma_\zeta = \begin{bmatrix} 0.01 & 0 & 0 \\ 0 & 0.01 & 0 \\ 0 & 0 & 0.02 \end{bmatrix}$	NVS08 + Base Station	$\sigma_\zeta = \begin{bmatrix} 0.1 & 0 & 0 \\ 0 & 0.1 & 0 \\ 0 & 0 & 0.2 \end{bmatrix}$
I	IMU	iMAR iNAV-FMS	$\sigma_u = \begin{bmatrix} 0.00035 & 0 & 0 \\ 0 & 0.00035 & 0 \\ 0 & 0 & 0.00087 \end{bmatrix}$	PixHawk PX4	$\sigma_u = \begin{bmatrix} 0.0087 & 0 & 0 \\ 0 & 0.0087 & 0 \\ 0 & 0 & 0.0174 \end{bmatrix}$
II	GPS	RTK Septentrio PolaRx	$\sigma_\zeta = \begin{bmatrix} 0.02 & 0 & 0 \\ 0 & 0.02 & 0 \\ 0 & 0 & 0.04 \end{bmatrix}$	UBlox LEA-5T	$\sigma_u = \begin{bmatrix} 0.5 & 0 & 0 \\ 0 & 0.5 & 0 \\ 0 & 0 & 0.75 \end{bmatrix}$
II	IMU	MicroStrain 3DM-GX1	$\sigma_u = \begin{bmatrix} 0.0087 & 0 & 0 \\ 0 & 0.0087 & 0 \\ 0 & 0 & 0.0174 \end{bmatrix}$	PixHawk PX4	$\sigma_u = \begin{bmatrix} 0.0087 & 0 & 0 \\ 0 & 0.0087 & 0 \\ 0 & 0 & 0.0174 \end{bmatrix}$

The component able to return the position and attitude of each robot is denote in MORSE by *Pose sensor* and include a classe *Modifier* in order to introduce in the simulated data Gaussian noise. Based on this feature provided by MORSE, we applied on each experimental case the values present in table 1. The values are enact on the information provided by the manufacturers but also based on experimental work[19].

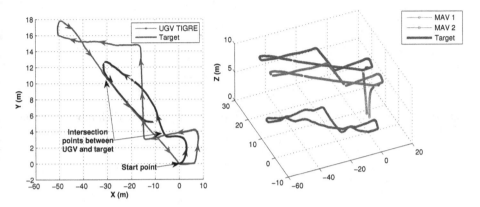

Fig. 4. Trajectory performed by the UGV TIGRE and the MAVs, relative to the target

In both experimental cases, we used a team of heterogeneous robots, composed by two MAVs and a UGV estimating the 3D position of the target based on the UCoT method.

The 3D information from the target was used in the task planner of each robot. Therefore, the UGV had the task of follow and intersect, if possible, the target, while the MAVs follow the target with a fixed geometry between each other and the target, as depicted in figure 4.

The results from the 3D target estimation $^{W}\mathcal{P}$ and the correspondence median and standard deviation error with UCoT framework in both experimental cases are detail in figures 5 - 7, while the covariance Σ_{Target} is expressed in figures 6 - 8.

The median and standard deviation error in both experimental cases, details in figures 5 - 7, present good performance and robustness even went we introduce in experimental case II, more Gaussian noise. The UCoT framework, in order to perform cooperative triangulation, estimate the dynamic baseline between robots based on the position and attitude $\langle^{W}\mathcal{C},^{W}\mathcal{R},\{^{W}\boldsymbol{d}\}\rangle$, therefore it was expected to reveal a huge sensibility to the introduction of Gaussian noise. Although, due the probabilistic approach, the contribution of each monocular measurement is weight Ω to the 3D target estimation position and the result is an accurate multi-robot cooperative perception method.

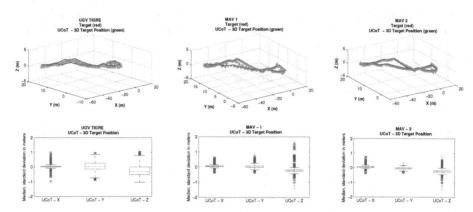

Fig. 5. Experimental case I - Estimated 3D target position $^W\mathcal{P}$ of each robot with the UCoT method

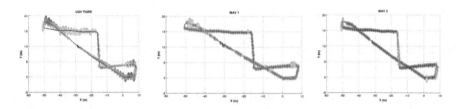

Fig. 6. Top view from the 3D Covariance matrix of the target Σ_{Target} provided by each robot during the experimental case I with the red line representing the target trajectory

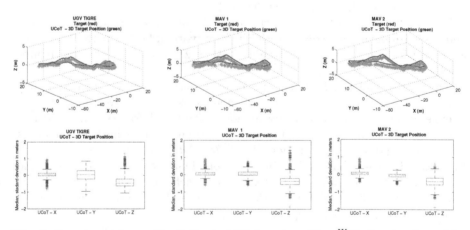

Fig. 7. Experimental case II - Estimated 3D target position $^W\mathcal{P}$ of each robot with the UCoT method

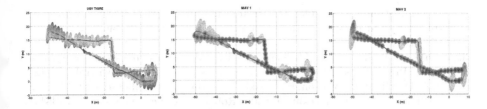

Fig. 8. Top view from the 3D Covariance matrix of the target Σ_{Target} provided by each robot during the experimental case II with the red line representing the target trajectory

5   Conclusions and Future Work

This paper evaluates the Uncertainty-based Multi-Robot Cooperative Triangulation (UCoT) framework under the open-source MORSE simulation environment. The architecture associated with the integration of the simulation environment is presented with the UCoT, as well as the architecture developed in Blender for the UGV TIGRE and the corresponding Ackerman controller component.

The UCoT framework has evaluated using a team of heterogeneous robots composed of MAVs and a UGV with different values of Gaussian noise applied to sensors, as well as with a fixed geometry relatively to the target position.

One limitation found in this work has to do with the integration of more robots in the simulation environment, which is difficult due to the MORSE requirements in terms of computational and graphics resources. Therefore, based on the Multi-node provided by the MORSE, a future research topic could be running the same simulation scenario in separated computers in order to be able to extend the number of robots. This approach can also be used to evaluate the impact that introducing communication constraints will have on the UCoT framework when each robot is sharing the required 3-tuple $\langle {}^{W}\boldsymbol{C}, {}^{W}\boldsymbol{\mathcal{R}}, \{{}^{W}\boldsymbol{d}\} \rangle$ to estimate the 3D information.

Acknowledgments. This work is co-financed by Project "NORTE-07-0124-FEDER-000060" by the North Portugal Regional Operational Programme (ON.2 O Novo Norte), under the National Strategic Reference Framework (NSRF) through the European Regional Development Fund (ERDF) and also by National Funds through the FCT within project PEst-OE/EEI/LA0009/2013.

References

1. Michael, N., Shen, S., Mohta, K., Mulgaonkar, Y., Kumar, V., Nagatani, K., Okada, Y., Kiribayashi, S., Otake, K., Yoshida, K., Ohno, K., Takeuchi, E., Tadokoro, S.: Collaborative mapping of an earthquake-damaged building via ground and aerial robots. Journal of Field Robotics 29(5), 832–841 (2012)

2. Olson, E., Strom, J., Goeddel, R., Morton, R., Ranganathan, P., Richardson, A.: Exploration and mapping with autonomous robot teams. Commun. ACM 56(3), 62–70 (2013)

3. Kushleyev, A., Kumar, V., Mellinger, D.: Towards a swarm of agile micro quadrotors. In: Proceedings of Robotics: Science and Systems, Sydney, Australia (2012)

4. Xu, Z., Douillard, B., Morton, P., Vlaskine, V.: Towards Collaborative Multi-MAV-UGV Teams for Target Tracking. In: 2012 Robotics: Science and Systems Workshop on Integration of Perception with Control and Navigation for Resource-limited, Highly Dynamic, Autonomous Systems (2012)

5. Marino, A., Caccavale, F., Parker, L.E., Antonelli, G.: Fuzzy behavioral control for multi-robot border patrol. In: 17th Mediterranean Conference on Control and Automation, MED 2009, pp. 246–251 (2009)

6. Lächele, J., Franchi, A., Bülthoff, H.H., Robuffo Giordano, P.: SwarmSimX: Realtime simulation environment for multi-robot systems. In: Noda, I., Ando, N., Brugali, D., Kuffner, J.J. (eds.) SIMPAR 2012. LNCS, vol. 7628, pp. 375–387. Springer, Heidelberg (2012)

7. Folgado, E., Rincón, M., Álvarez, J.R., Mira, J.: A multi-robot surveillance system simulated in gazebo. In: Mira, J., Álvarez, J.R. (eds.) IWINAC 2007. LNCS, vol. 4528, pp. 202–211. Springer, Heidelberg (2007)

8. Echeverria, G., Lassabe, N., Degroote, A., Lemaignan, S.: Modular open robots simulation engine: Morse. In: 2011 IEEE International Conference on Robotics and Automation (ICRA), pp. 46–51 (May 2011)

9. Echeverria, G., Lemaignan, S., Degroote, A., Lacroix, S., Karg, M., Koch, P., Lesire, C., Stinckwich, S.: Simulating complex robotic scenarios with MORSE. In: Noda, I., Ando, N., Brugali, D., Kuffner, J.J. (eds.) SIMPAR 2012. LNCS, vol. 7628, pp. 197–208. Springer, Heidelberg (2012)

10. Meyer, J., Sendobry, A., Kohlbrecher, S., Klingauf, U., von Stryk, O.: Comprehensive simulation of quadrotor uAVs using ROS and gazebo. In: Noda, I., Ando, N., Brugali, D., Kuffner, J.J. (eds.) SIMPAR 2012. LNCS, vol. 7628, pp. 400–411. Springer, Heidelberg (2012)

11. Dewan, A., Mahendran, A., Soni, N., Krishna, K.: Heterogeneous ugv-mav exploration using integer programming. In: 2013 IEEE/RSJ International Conference on Intelligent Robots and Systems (IROS), pp. 5742–5749 (November 2013)

12. Michael, N., Kumar, V.: Controlling shapes of ensembles of robots of finite size with nonholonomic constraints. In: Robotics: Science and Systems (2008)

13. Koenig, N., Howard, A.: Design and use paradigms for gazebo, an open-source multi-robot simulator. In: Proceedings of 2004 IEEE/RSJ International Conference on Intelligent Robots and Systems (IROS 2004), vol. 3, pp. 2149–2154 (September 2004)

14. Metta, G., Fitzpatrick, P., Natale, L.: Yarp: Yet another robot platform. International Journal on Advanced Robotics Systems (2006)

15. Quigley, M., Conley, K., Gerkey, B.P., Faust, J., Foote, T., Leibs, J., Wheeler, R., Ng, A.Y.: ROS: an open-source Robot Operating System. In: ICRA Workshop on Open Source Software (2009)

16. Benjamin, M., Schmidt, H., Newman, P., Leonard, J.: Nested autonomy for unmanned marine vehicles with moos-ivp. J. Field Robotics, 834–875 (2010)

17. Martins, A., Amaral, G., Dias, A., Almeida, C., Almeida, J., Silva, E.: Tigre - an autonomous ground robot for outdoor exploration. In: 13th International Conference on Autonomous Robot Systems and Competitions (2013)

18. Trucco, E., Verri, A.: Introductory Techniques for 3-D Computer Vision. Prentice Hall PTR, Upper Saddle River (1998)
19. Dias, A., Almeida, J., Silva, E., Lima, P.: Multi-robot cooperative stereo for outdoor scenarios. In: 2013 13th International Conference on Autonomous Robot Systems (Robotica), pp. 1–6 (April 2013)
20. Dias, A., Almeida, J., Lima, P., Silva, E.: Uncertainty based Multi-Robot Cooperative Triangulation. In: RoboCup Symposium Proceedings, Brasil. LNCS (LNAI). Springer (2014)

Combining Complex Simulations with Realistic Virtual Testing Environments – The eRobotics-Approach for Semantics-Based Multi-domain VR Simulation Systems

Nico Hempe, Ralf Waspe, and Juergen Rossmann

RWTH Aachen University, Aachen, Germany
{hempe,waspe,rossmann}@mmi.rwth-aachen.de

Abstract. Today Virtual Reality (VR) simulation technology is a well-known field of virtual training and engineering and widely applied in research and in the industry. Multi-domain VR simulation systems cover multiple technical and visual aspects not limited to a single task or domain. While current systems mostly neglect the rendering component and provide purely functional graphics and simple virtual environments, we present the concepts of eRobotics and matching system structures to combine complex simulations and realistic virtual environments in a holistic VR simulation system. These environments not only provide attractive visual presentations, they also help to realize close-to-reality testing of virtual prototypes and positively affect the accuracy and performance of simulated components like optical sensors.

Keywords: eRobotics, multi-domain VR simulation systems, real-time computer graphics, semantic world modeling.

1   Introduction

Virtual Prototyping (VP) is an important application in engineering, which allows to experienced a digital model of a product in development prior to construction. By also including the collaboration of the simulated technical components, virtual prototypes can be regarded as Virtual Testbeds (VT), which also allow for the close-to-reality testing and development of the desired systems [15]. For complex technical or mechatronical systems, such as mobile and autonomous robots shown in Figure 1, a large number of different subsystems need to be simulated in order to simulate all desired tasks required for adequate virtual testing.

Multi-domain VR simulation systems cover multiple technical and visual aspects not limited to a single task or domain and can be seen as the top-of-the-range systems regarding VR simulation technology. They provide a framework to bring together various simulation and rendering modules. However in common system structures, the amount of included functionalities is limited due to complexity, compatibility and performance reasons.

D. Brugali et al. (Eds.): SIMPAR 2014, LNAI 8810, pp. 110–121, 2014.

Fig. 1. Simulation of the Seekur Jr mobile robot platform. This Virtual Testbed includes the real-time simulation of the robot itself, as well as several sensors (left: LiDAR sensor; middle: digital camera; right: Time-of-Flight camera) for testing and development of novel navigation approaches.

Especially simulation and rendering tasks rely on different data types and structures in order to perform best, which is the reason why both areas are usually separated into independent frameworks. While rendering-related applications traditionally rely on a scene graph structure, a simulation database may be optimized for other purposes using a completely different data structure, which hardly fit into each other without negatively influencing flexibility, applicability or performance. In particular, simulation-centric applications do not provide the flexibility required to integrate state of the art rendering approaches. Additionally, available virtual environments for engineering systems applied in non-commercial contexts are often purely functional and limited to a single scenario due to the resultant costs and the specific expertise requirements in modeling and real-time rendering. As a consequence, realistic models suitable for the adequate simulation of many different testing scenarios are usually hardly available. While visually attractive imagery drastically increases acceptance of simulation technologies, realistic virtual environments are also beneficial for close-to-reality testing of newly developed systems and approaches in Virtual Testbeds. The presented eRobotics-approach aims to address this issue by combining complex simulations with state of the art computer graphics and realistic virtual testing environments. In Section 2, related work regarding current mobile robot simulators as well as the usage of semantic data for graphics applications will be presented. In Section 3, the eRobotics approach is detailed. Section 4 presents the concepts and structure of the developed system and the semantic database capable to meet eRobotic needs. Section 5 presents current applications in multiple robotic domains that benefit from the eRobotics approach. Finally, Section 6 concludes this work and gives an outlook to future developments.

2   Related Work

2.1   Current Mobile Robotic VR Simulation Systems

In the field of mobile robot simulators which are applied in a broad range of research and development projects, well known VR simulation systems are

USARSim [4], Player/Stage/Gazebo [11], ROAMS [10] and WeBots [13]. Beside physics simulations and rigid body dynamics, these systems also feature the simulation of various sensors, which are important for this domain [19]. As illustrated in Figure 2, these environments often consist of a small, single scenario like an indoor environment with several rooms, an alleyway with several houses or a small outdoor environment, which do not allow for the testing of the system as a whole under various conditions. Even if a few published works try to enhance these virtual environments [2][14], these systems do not provide the technical possibilities to integrate state of the art rendering techniques.

Fig. 2. Screenshots of current mobile robot simulators, which demonstrate typical testing environments. Left: USARSim, middle: Gazebo, right: Webots. Images taken from the developers' websites.

2.2   Semantic World Models and Semantic Data Rendering

Semantic world models consist of elementary facts and rules stored in schemaless graph databases, which allow a set of nodes with dynamic attributes to be arbitrary linked to other nodes through edges [1]. In contrast to predefined data structures like scene graphs, semantic world models are not limited to spatial relations or geometry and can describe the environment more detailed. They can contain almost any kind of data and give complex information about the surrounding; hence, they are perfectly suitable to combine different data structures in a single system database. In order to make graph databases practical for software systems, they can be realized following the object-orientated paradigm. These databases are known as Graph-Oriented Object Databases (GOOD) [7]; however, graphics applications benefit for scene-graph-like structures in order to efficiently apply optimization techniques like culling and batching to grant real-time performance. In order to address this issue, Mendez et al. [12] suggested to separate semantics from rendering in the scene graph by using semantic tags as attributes. Recently, Tobler [20] picked up this idea and suggested a more complete solution by fully separating semantics from rendering in a split scene graph architecture. This structure contains a separate semantic and rendering scene graph following the Model-View-Controller (MVC) design pattern [6]. As the name implies, the MVC pattern allows for the usage of a single model under different environments by separating the model from the system view using a controller that coordinates the translation. The semantic scene graph represents the model as created by the user, the rendering scene graph represents the view necessary for the system environment and the rule objects represent the controller that dynamically translate the model into the system view during graph traversal.

3   The eRobotics Approach

The research field of eRobotics has been established recently in order to help to cope with the inherent complexity of advanced robotics and mechatronics development [18]. It focuses on the use of VR technology to optimize and ease the development process and to significantly cut down the cost. As illustrated on the left part of Figure 3, the aim of eRobotics is to provide a holistic, but comprehensive software tool that covers all common VR domains ranging from education and 3D simulations up to multi-domain simulations. Even in small projects visually pleasing demonstrations of project ideas and results in attractive, immersive virtual worlds as a sales argument for possible follow-up projects must not be neglected.

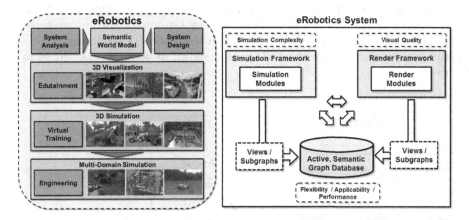

Fig. 3. Left: eRobotic applications cover all aspects of VR. Model descriptions are based on semantic world modeling. Right: The semantic database deals as connecting element between all modules involved.

As illustrated on the right part of the Figure 3, semantic world models stored in a central GOOD database are suitable to match the flexibility requirements and are therefore a key feature of eRobotic systems. The rendering components can benefit from the interpretation of this data, in order to enhance the visual appearance or to generate close-to-reality virtual environments. However, handling strategies need to be applied in order to transfer the data into optimized data structures for efficient usage by the simulation and rendering plugins.

4   A Novel Multi-domain VR Simulation System Architecture

The semantic database also acts as connecting element between the simulation and render framework and provides the inter-communication between both frameworks. Rendering modules can be applied to actively support the simulation process in specific tasks (e.g. optical sensor simulation), to improve the accuracy and performance as shown in a previous publication [16]. However, it is still a challenge to develop a holistic and comprehensive yet sustainable multi-domain VR simulation system, which is easily manageable, extensible and understandable.

4.1   Database Structure

The simulation system is built around the "Versatile Simulation Database" (VSD), a schema-less database kernel. In order to retain semantic information the VSD is an object oriented graph database, which have proven their adaptability to a wide filed of applications, as shown in the overview by [3]. Plugins to the core system can provide data schema needed for specific simulation tasks (such as discrete event or 3D simulation) or they can implement further capabilities, such as a graphical user interface, user interaction or rendering. A very simplified class hierarchy of the VSD core is shown in white on the left of in Figure 4.

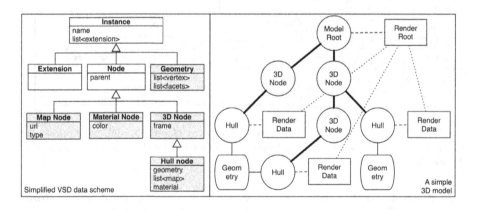

Fig. 4. Left: The VSD core components (white) and a data schema extension for 3D simulation (gray). Right: A multi-graph of a simple 3D model.

All data describing the state of the simulation is held within the database as properties. As shown on the right of Figure 4 the spanning tree [5] of the database is compromised of nodes, with the edges of the graph defined by parent-child relations (depicted as solid black lines) between nodes. Nodes can be augmented by extensions (depicted as boxes).

A multi-graph can be created by attaching any Instance to a reference property, thus defining additional arbitrary sets of edges within the database. This can be useful for modeling different arrangements of instances for special views of the database, such as a rendering graph, as proposed by Tobler [20]. This is shown in Figure 4, where the "Render Root" extension attached to the model root holds links to the render data extensions, which are associated with a hull node. Geometries are held as special references of hull nodes and are not nodes themselves, in order to enforce their position within the model database.

4.2   Optimizing Semantic Data for Rendering Purposes

As illustrated in Figure 5 simulation and rendering plugins can both integrate their desired data elements into the central system database without affecting each other. Plugins can also work with data elements of other plugins if they are known, regardless if they are simulation or rendering related. Finally, the presented active database concept build the ideal basis to realize the MVC pattern. Plugins can integrate transformation rules in order to transform the semantic data graph into system-specific data structures optimized for rendering reasons. For example, the 3D geometry plugin defines a set of semantic nodes (VSD3D), which contain basic nodes like geometric elements, texture nodes, material nodes, etc., that can be used to model the scene in a "natural" fashion. The plugin defines a set of rules which monitor these elements and automatically transforms them into a rendering-optimized data structure. In contrast to the split scene graph approach suggested by Tober [20], our approach keeps track of all related

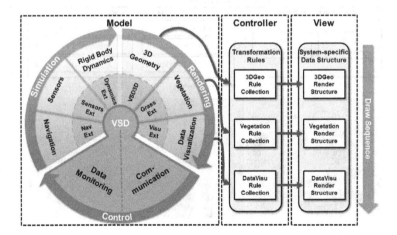

Fig. 5. Illustration of the micro-kernel-based system and plugins, which add new functionalities, semantic elements and transformation rules for the transformation of semantic data structures into rendering-specific ones

semantic nodes and organize them globally, which allows for more efficient implementations of buffer usage, as well as state-sorting and batching approaches. A transform rule collection can contain multiple rule sets to consider different hardware performance characteristics in order to optimize the generated render data structure by applying techniques like LOD or adaptive mesh refinement. As illustrated by the vegetation and data visualization plugins in Figure 5 additional effects can be integrated, which may demand other render or buffer structures.

4.3   Generating Realistic Virtual Environments with Semantic Data Interpretation

Instead of creating virtual environments manually with high effort, the presented system can import semantic data from various data sources like geographic information services (GIS), which are widely available to the public. While common systems only rely the terrain geometry or satellite imagery that can be rendered directly and result in a poor visual representation, the presented system allows to import and interpret provided semantic information in order to generate life-like virtual mappings of the real environment as illustrated in Figure 6. Further details about the newly developed rendering and interpretation techniques have been presented in [9] and [8]. Beside realistic ground vegetation, additional semantic render plugins have been implemented, which feature HDR rendering with changing lighting conditions and shadowing as well as dynamic weather effects in order to properly test the robustness of newly developed image processing approaches of mobile robots under different conditions.

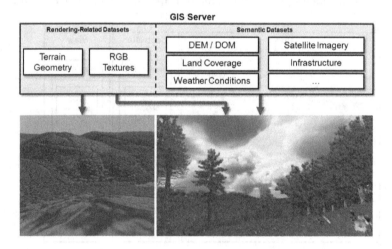

Fig. 6. Semantic data can be imported and interpreted by specific plugins in order to generate realistic mappings of real-world environments

4.4 Rendering-Based Simulation Support

Due to the fact that simulations get more complicated and the accuracy requirements rise with advanced technology development, the calculation power of modern graphics hardware should not be neglected. The simulation of optical sensors is an essential field in most robotic applications. Beside the shown examples to improve the visual quality, the introduced system structure also allows for rendering-supported simulations. A realistic looking virtual environment enhances the realism when using the rendered images as input for digital camera simulations. Advanced rendering techniques can also be applied in order to simulate other optical sensors like time-of-flight cameras or laser range scanners shown in Figure 1 with higher accuracy. Building on that, a GPU-based sensor simulation component was developed, that allows for accurate real-time simulations of optical sensors including various error models using state-of-the-art rendering techniques [16]. Further examples of rendering-based simulation support are data visualization tasks like particle tracing to visualize CFD datasets in realistic environments as shown in the right column of Figure 10.

5 Applications

The virtual environments achievable with the presented multi-domain VR simulation system build the ideal testing ground for mobile robots in advanced Virtual Testbeds. A goal of a recent project was the development of a landmark-based localization framework for use in outdoor environments, able to estimate the current position of mobile systems [17]. Figure 7 compares the results of a semi global matching (SGM) stereo disparity estimation achieved with a real-world testbed (left), a simple virtual testbed (middle) and the advanced Virtual Testbed generated out of semantic data (right).

Fig. 7. Different testing environments for computer vision algorithms and achieved color-coded depth visualizations of the stereo matching results

It becomes clear, that simple virtual models lead to unsatisfactory results which strongly differ from data acquired in real-world tests. The environments generated with the presented system feature life-like, dynamic ground vegetation, which lead to results comparable to those acquired in real-world setups. For an evaluation, we use the ground truth data generated by the simulation system and calculate a disparity map corresponding to the baseline and intrinsic parameters of the stereo camera system which allows to easily assess the stereo matching algorithm directly in units of disparity pixels. The achieved results with a simple and a realistic virtual environment are shown in Figure 8.

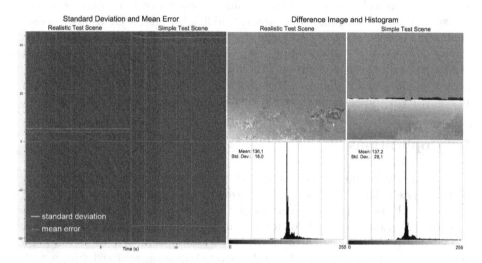

Fig. 8. Comparison of stereo matching results achieved with simple and realistic virtual environments. Left: Mean error and standard deviation between SGM and ground truth disparity data. Right: Difference image and histogram.

While the matching algorithm has problems finding corresponding pixels on plain-colored ground in the simple environment, the matching results with highly detailed ground vegetation are much more reliable. In our test scene, we achieved mean errors of 15 pixels in the simple environment compared to 5 pixels difference in the more realistic one. The difference images in the figure show the signed pixel difference between the ground truth disparity and the stereo estimated disparity shifted towards the middle of the 8 bit gray scale image. The histograms have their peak around the value of 127 with standard deviations of up to 28 using the simple scene and values up to 18 with the more realistic one.

Figure 9 shows another virtual testbed, which demonstrates the aspects of knowledge transfer as well as the possibilities of early, visually pleasing presentation of project ideas. The basic idea of this project was to mount 2D laser scanners on a wood harvester in order to apply the computer vision and localization approaches developed for the Seekur Jr navigation framework. This

navigation system should support the machine operator by guiding him to selected trees in the stand marked for felling in order to to improve the wood
harvesting effectiveness. Due to the usage of the available virtual forest models,
the simulated laser range scanners and the computer vision algorithms developed
for the Seekur Jr project, a fully functional simulation of such a harvester, able
to demonstrate the possibilities and advantages of the project ideas was created
within a short period of time. During the project, the simulation models and
approaches were refined for efficient testing of the newly developed algorithms
before they were applied to the real harvester, which drastically decreases project
costs and development time.

Fig. 9. Real and simulated harvester equipped with 2D laser scanners for forest navigation and harvesting support as an example for knowledge transfer from one project
to another

Fig. 10. Currently, more than 30 eRobotic applications have been realized

Currently, more many eRobotic applications in different domains have been
realized with the presented multi-domain VR simulation system, which benefit
from knowledge transfer from one domain to another, as well as the combination

of complex simulations, semantic world modeling and realistic computer graphics. Further examples are shown in Figure 10, which range from edutainment in the Virtual ISS or in digital city models, over virtual training in the Virtual Forest, up to engineering domains in space robotics.

6   Conclusion and Future Prospects

In this paper, we presented system and database structures to realize the novel eRobotics approach, which aim is to provide a comprehensive software environment to address robotics related issues. Semantic world modeling in combination with the presented active, graph-oriented object database greatly helps to bring together simulation and rendering tasks in a holistic system, without affecting each other in a negative way. While the render component was mostly neglected in scientific contexts in the past, we showed that a powerful render framework is not only helpful to increase the understanding of robotics-related issues, but is also important to realize virtual close-to-reality testing environments. The developed multi-domain VR simulation system builds the optimal basis to deal with the ever increasing complexity of rendering techniques and current computer-aided robotic solutions and keep them manageable. Due to its schema-aware database core that can conveniently be extended in a modular fashion the simulation system is also capable to extend into other domains not related to mobile robotics, such as automation, decision support and discrete event simulation.

Acknowledgments. The work presented in this paper was done as part of the Virtual Forest project. The Virtual Forest project is co-financed by the European Union and the federal state of North Rhine-Westphalia, European Regional Development Fund (ERDF). Europe - Investing in our future.

References

1. Abrial, J.R.: Data semantics. In: Data Base Management: Proc. of the IFIP Workshop Conference on Data Base Management, pp. 1–60 (1974)
2. Alemany, J., Cervera, E.: Design of high quality, efficient simulation environments for usarsim. In: Technical Report ICC 2011-10-1, University Jaume I, Spain (2011)
3. Angles, R., Gutierrez, C.: Survey of graph database models. ACM Computing Surveys 40(1), 1–39 (2008)
4. Balaguer, B., Balakirsky, S., Carpin, S., Lewis, M., Scrapper, C.: Usarsim: a validated simulator for research in robotics and automation. In: Workshop on Robot Simulators: Available Software, Scientific Applications, and Future Trends at IEEE/RSJ (2008)
5. Diestel, R.: Graph Theory, 4th edn. Graduate texts in mathematics, vol. 173. Springer (2012)
6. Gamma, E., Helm, R., Johnson, R.E., Vlissides, J.: Design Patterns: Elements of Reusable Object-Oriented Software. Addison-Wesley (1995)

7. Gyssens, M., Paredaens, J., Van Den Bussche, J., Van Gucht, D.: A graph-oriented object database model. IEEE Transactions on Knowledge and Data Engineering 6(4), 572–586 (1994)

8. Hempe, N., Rossmann, J.: Efficient real-time generation and rendering of interactive grass and shrubs for large sceneries. In: Proc. of the 13th IASTED International Conference on Computer Graphics and Imaging (CGIM), pp. 240–247 (2012)

9. Hempe, N., Waspe, R., Rossmann, J.: Geometric interpretation and optimization of large semantic data sets in real-time vr applications. In: Proc. of the ASME 2012 International Design Engineering Technical Conferences & Computers and Information in Engineering Conference (IDETC/CIE), pp. 1–10 (2012)

10. Jain, A., Huineau, J., Lim, C., Lincoln, W., Pomarantz, M., G., Sohl, S.R.: Roams: Planetary surface rover simulation environment. In: Proc. of iSAIRAS 2003, pp. 19–23 (2003)

11. Keonig, N., Howard, A.: Design and use paradigms for gazebo, an open-source multi-robot simulator. In: Proc. of IEEERSJ International Conference on Intelligent Robots and Systems IROS, vol. 3, pp. 2149–2154 (2004)

12. Mendez, E., Schall, G., Havemann, S., Fellner, D., Schmalstieg, D., Junghanns, S.: Generating semantic 3d models of underground infrastructure. IEEE Computer Graphics and Applications 28(3), 48–57 (2008)

13. Michel, O.: Cyberbotics ltd. webots tm: Professional mobile robot simulation. Int. Journal of Advanced Robotic Systems, 39–42 (2004)

14. Rathnam, R., Pfingsthorn, M., Birk, A.: Incorporating large scale ssrr scenarios into the high fidelity simulator usarsim. In: IEEE International Workshop on Safety, Security and Rescue Robotics, SSRR 2009, pp. 1–6 (2009)

15. Rossmann, J.: The virtual testbed: Latest virtual reality technologies for space robotic applications. In: Proc. of the iSAIRAS 2008, pp. 1–8 (2008)

16. Rossmann, J., Hempe, N., Emde, M., Steil, T.: A real-time optical sensor simulation framework for development and testing of industrial and mobile robot applications. In: Proc. of the 7th German Conference on Robotics (ROBOTIK 2012), pp. 337–342 (2012)

17. Roßmann, J., Wantia, N., Springer, M., Stern, O., Müller, H., Ellsiepen, M.: Rapid generation of 3d navigation maps for extraterrestrial landing and exploration missions: The virtual testbed approach. In: Proc. of the 11th Symposium on Advanced Space Technologies in Robotics and Automation (ASTRA) (2011)

18. Rossmann, J., Schluse, M., Schlette, C., Waspe, R.: A new approach to 3d simulation technology as enabling technology for erobotics. In: Van Impe, J.F.M., Logist, F. (eds.) 1st International Simulation Tools Conference and EXPO 2013 (2013)

19. Staranowicz, A., Mariottini, G.: A survey and comparison of commercial and open-source robotic simulator software. In: Proc. of the 4th International Conference on Pervasive Technologies Related to Assistive Environments, PETRA 2011, vol. 1, pp. 39–42 (2011)

20. Tobler, R.: Separating semantics from rendering: a scene graph based architecture for graphics applications. Visual Computer 27(6-8), 687–695 (2011)

Analysis of Knee-Ankle Orthosis Modelling: An Inverse Dynamics Approach Using Adaptive Coupled Oscillator

Michael Oluwatosin Ajayi[1,2], Karim Djouani[1,2], and Yskandar Hamam[1,3]

[1] Department of Electrical Engineering, Tshwane University of Technology,
Staatsartillerie Road, Pretoria West, Pretoria, South-Africa
[2] University of Paris Est Creteil (UPEC), LISSI, 94400 Vitry Sur Seine, France
[3] LISV, Btiment Boucher, Pole scientifique et technologique de Velizy,
10-12 avenue de l'Europe, 78140 Velizy
{ajayimo,djouanik,hamama}@tut.ac.za

Abstract. In this paper, an inverse dynamics approach by means of adaptive coupled oscillators is used in the modelling and control of a lower limb orthosis applied at the knee and ankle joint level. This design is aimed at providing assistance and rehabilitative measures to humans with lower limb disorders and as such presents a platform for which their mobility performance can be improved. Adaptive oscillators are known to have the capability of learning high level parameters of sinusoidal, quasi-sinusoidal or non-sinusoidal signals (amplitude, frequency and offset). However, the later signal (non-sinusoidal) considered in this paper requires a number of oscillators in parallel to replicate the moving joint regarding filtering via adaptive oscillator. The dynamic model for the knee and ankle are considered to take the form of a damped pendulum model connected by two revolute joints. This maps the input torque of both joints (knee and ankle) to their output trajectories, hence integrating the different forces at the joint level of the different joints. The coupling effect is achieved by the use of coupled Adaptive Frequency Oscillator (AFO) for the estimation of the joint trajectories. Tracking performance for the knee-ankle orthosis is studied for non-sinusoidal reference trajectories, having a global coupling between the joints. The results obtained using SCILAB show a good performance of the controller trajectory tracking capabilities even in the presence of external disturbances.

Keywords: Adaptive Coupled Oscillators, Knee-Ankle Orthosis, Rehabilitation Robotics, Robot-assisted platform.

1 Introduction

The objective of rehabilitation is to perform specific movements that exercise and hence improve motor unit plasticity of the patient thereby influencing motor recovery and minimising functional deficits [1]. Rehabilitation therefore could

D. Brugali et al. (Eds.): SIMPAR 2014, LNAI 8810, pp. 122–133, 2014.

be implemented manually or robotically (i.e. by the use of a robotic tool). Rehabilitation robotics is a branch of robotics which provides a platform for the design of robots in the form of orthosis for the purpose of providing physiotherapy to persons with physical disability. Conventional manual rehabilitation is associated with excessive time, energy and resources (physiotherapist) hence disadvantageous compared to robotic-based rehabilitation [2]. Research on the efficiency of robotic therapy has shown that rehabilitation technologies provide new alternatives for repetitive training sessions that can increase efforts to improve the therapy performance. This is also intended to reduce the burden on physiotherapists and assess quantitatively the level of motor recovery by measuring force and movement patterns [1],[3].

Robotic therapy may be performed on *traditional robotic platforms or robot-assisted platforms* [4]. The former is basically used to drive the patients limb along a pre-specified trajectory using stiff position control as in [5], thereby making the patient passive during the whole training sessions. Although this proved to be a drawback, [2] addressed the possibility for traditional robotic platforms to work in passive and active mode, depending on the recovery stage of the patients.

The "assistance-as-needed" approach as known as the robot-assisted platform helps provide assistance for movement to subjects when they are incapable of completing the movement task [6]. This allows patients to be active during the entire physiotherapy session and assisted only when required, thereby improving the patients muscle activity [7]. In [4], a novel assistance method was proposed for rhythmic movement of the forearm about the elbow using a single adaptive oscillator. The features associated with this method commensurate with that of EMG-based assistive device [8], since its level of assistance is same at steady-state for the subject and virtually no pre-specified trajectory is needed. The objective of this paper is to investigate a rehabilitation protocol method using CPGs (Central pattern generators) to perform rhythmic movements of the lower limb about the knee and ankle. Mechanical coupling about these joints are assumed to be governed by the principle behind the double pendulum dynamic behaviour. This is based on an inverse dynamic approach hence, an estimate of the torques applied to both joints is calculated and the assistance provided to the joints is a feedback of a fraction of the said calculated torques.

CPGs are biological neural networks that produce coordinated multidimensional rhythmic signals, under the control of simple input signals. The building block for the construction of the CPG in this paper is the Adaptive Frequency Oscillator (AFO) developed in [9]. In [10], a variety of different application of the AFO was highlighted. The global problem associated with estimating derivatives of noisy position signal in robotics was addressed in [11]. It thus, proposed a new approach to estimating velocity and acceleration of cyclical/periodic signals using AFOs. Application to biped locomotion control was presented in [12] hereby demonstrating how online learning and modulation of pre-recorded walking trajectories using CPGs limit cycle properties can be achieved. [13] addressed the future of humanoid robots in areas relating to performing periodic tasks. Coupled nonlinear oscillators were used to design CPGs similar to human gait pattern applied in the locomotion of bipedal robot was exploited in [14]. An oscillator-based model-free approach designed for the assistance and rehabilitation protocols as regard walking was also demonstrated in [15].

The main contribution of this paper is to demonstrate the possibility of assisting and rehabilitating patients with both knee and ankle anomalies so as to recuperate their motor functions concurrently using CPGs. Thus, a 2 (two) DOF (degree of freedom) is considered for the knee-ankle orthotic device.

The rest of the paper is organised as follows: Section 2 presents the knee-ankle orthosis system. Section 3 gives the methodology for design of the CPG. The mathematical model of the knee-ankle orthosis is given in Section 4. Section 5 provides the simulation and results of the movement assistance of the knee-ankle joints based on certain physiological parameters. Finally, in Section 6, further work and conclusion is made.

2   Knee-Ankle Orthosis System

In this study, the authors consider a Shank-Foot CAD model as shown in Fig.1 which depicts the knee-ankle orthosis. The CAD model is assumed to incorporate the parameters of the orthosis and the users lower limb (knee and ankle to be precise). The model thus takes into account the flexion/extension of the knee about the revolute joint a and the plantar-flexion/dorsal-flexion of the ankle about b, assuming the motions are performed in a sagittal plane with the subject in a sitting position, hence the mass of the subject's shank and foot link of a single leg are those accounted for in this model. The movements of the knee-ankle orthosis are in the range $0rad \leq \theta \leq 2.35rad$ for the knee and $0rad \leq \theta \leq 0.87rad$ for the ankle. Where 0rad relates to the full knee extension, 2.35rad is the maximum flexion of the knee and $1.57rad$ corresponds to the rest position of the knee. Furthermore, 0rad as regard the ankle movements corresponds to the rest position of the ankle, $0.35rad$ is the maximal ankle dorsal-flexion, while $0.87rad$ denotes the maximal ankle plantar-flexion. The assisted joint positions are required to be measured, so as to determine the human torques required. It should be noted that the system is considered to reflect a controlled movement about its axis and hence seen perform a periodic motion of each link about its pivot. Having known that the system is mechanical coupled via the joints, the movement are said to be coupled and thus achieved by CPG (Adaptive Oscillators) as disscused in section 4.2. This is done to guarantee a global movement since the dynamic model of the shank-foot is treated as a decoupled system. Based on this, the periodic motions is said to assume the dynamics of a damped simple pendulum for each link.

3   CPG Design

This section describes the model of the CPG that is used to provide assistance to the knee-ankle orthosis. The design of the CPG using adaptive oscillators and

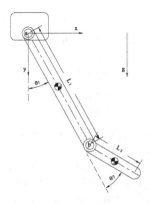

Fig. 1. Shank-Foot model

hence the tuning of the adaptive oscillator for filtering of a two (2) degree of freedom (DOF) along a non-sinusoidal trajectory are explained.

3.1   Adaptive Frequency Oscillator (AFO)

The adaptive frequency Hopf oscillator was first developed in [9] and [10]. For the purpose of simplicity, the augmented phase oscillator explained in [15] and [16] is adopted for the design of the CPGs used for the rhythmic movements needed to be achieved in this paper. The augmented phase oscillator is written as:

$$\dot{\phi} = \omega + \nu F cos\phi$$
$$\dot{\omega} = \nu F cos\phi \tag{1}$$

where ϕ is the phase of the oscillator and ν represents the learning parameter that determines the speed of the phase synchronization to F and must be greater than 0; $\nu \gg 0$. F is the is the periodic input signal to which the oscillator will adapt its frequency while ω controls the frequency of the oscillations, and this is the frequency adapted to the periodic input signal F.

3.2   Coupled AFO

The idea relating to coupled oscillator was used to define a precise way of learning any periodic input signal. This was in particular used to learn non-sinusoidal periodic signals due to the fact that most human movements are not usually sinusoidal. This coupling scheme which is more than just a dynamic Fourier series decomposition of non-sinusoidal periodic signal, was first proposed in [12] and later modified using augmented phase oscillator in [15], as shown below:

$$\dot{\phi}_i = i\omega + \nu F cos\phi_i$$
$$\dot{\omega} = \nu F cos\phi_1$$
$$\dot{\alpha}_i = \eta F sin\phi_i$$
$$F = \theta - \hat{\theta} \tag{2}$$
$$\hat{\theta} = \sum_{i=0}^{N} \alpha_i sin\phi_i$$

where i represents the no. of oscillators in parallel as regard the non-sinusoidal periodic signal and N the total number of oscillators. α_i is the amplitude associated to the main frequency ω, F is the is the periodic input signal to which the oscillator will adapt its frequency while θ signifies the non-sinusoidal periodic signal. $\hat{\theta}$ is the sum of filtered outputs of each oscillator and η is the amplitude integrator gain. Note that only the main frequency ω will learned to F.

Furthermore, the CPG corresponds to one degree of freedom (DOF), therefore, for 2 DOF based on the knee-ankle orthosis 2 CPGs are required. 3 oscillators relate to one CPG. This is in conjunction with the assumed non-sinusoidal trajectories of the knee and ankle respectively. Consequently, in this model, $i = 3$.

4   Mathematical Model

In this section, the building blocks for the entire system are described. The blocks include: the dynamic model, coupled AFO (which includes the signal estimator and the torque estimator) and the human torque. Fig. 2 shows the block diagram of the combined system (human knee and ankle + orthosis).

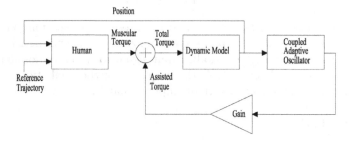

Fig. 2. Block diagram of the human knee and ankle + orthosis

4.1   Dynamic Model

The knee and ankle rhythmic movement of the human lower limb generates two trajectories and therefore the system is modelled as two (2) degree of freedom (DOF). These rhythmic movements are characterised as movements similar to that of a damped pendulum dynamics. The purpose of this has been explained in section 2. Hence the dynamic model for the knee and the ankle can be mathematically written as:

$$\ddot{\theta}_j = I_j^{-1}\left(-m_j g l_j sin\theta_j - b_j \dot{\theta}_j + \tau_j\right) \tag{3}$$

with j is the number of joints which corresponds to two (2) for this particular model with $j = 1$ relating to the knee and $j = 2$ relating to the ankle and I_j symbolises the inertia of the shank/foot. m_j is the mass of the shank/foot, l_j is the equivalent length of the shank/foot, which corresponds to the movement about the knee and ankle joint while b_j represents the damping constants of the shank/foot movement about knee/ankle joints. g signifies the gravitational force, $\ddot{\theta}_j$, $\dot{\theta}_j$, θ_j denotes the knee/ankle angular acceleration, velocity and position respectively and τ_j is the total torques applied to the knee and ankle respectively. The dynamic model block simply retrieves the actual angular position by integrating (3) in relation to each joint level. The generalised coordinate which represent the actual angular position for the knee and ankle can therefore be represented as:

$$\theta = \begin{bmatrix} \theta_1 & \theta_2 \end{bmatrix}^T \tag{4}$$

4.2   Coupled AFO (Joints Coupling)

The coupling of adaptive frequency oscillators to reproduce non-sinusoidal periodic signal for a single joint was explained in Section 3.2. However, the simultaneous rhythmic movement of the knee and ankle joints requires coupling between each CPG which represent each joint. The choice of coupling used could differ, as demonstrated in [12] and [15] respectively.

This paper adapts the global coupling procedures which require a common variable belonging to each CPG controlled by each CPG. Fig. 3 presents a pictorial diagram of the coupling of the CPG with the frequency being the common variable needed to be controlled. The equation of the CPG which incorporates the global coupling between each joint can be written as:

$$\begin{aligned}
\dot{\phi}_i &= i\omega + \nu F_j cos\phi_i \\
\dot{\omega} &= \left(\nu \sum_{j=1}^{G} F_j cos\phi_{1,j}\right)/G \\
\dot{\alpha}_i &= \eta F sin\phi_i
\end{aligned} \tag{5}$$

with j represents the active joint in question; for which in this particular model $j = 1$ relates to the knee, while $j = 2$ relates to the ankle. F_j is the non-sinusoidal periodic signal for each CPG and can be written as $F = \begin{bmatrix} F_1 & F_2 \end{bmatrix}^T$ and ω signifies the frequency and thus initiates the coupling between each CPG. G is the total number of joints while other terms are same as defined in (2).

Fig. 3. Structure of CPG coupling

4.3   Signal Estimator

The non-sinusoidal input signal F_j of the adaptive oscillator is the difference between the knee-ankle angular positions θ_j and the estimated (learned) signal $\hat{\theta}_j$. This can be expressed as below:

$$F = \theta_j - \hat{\theta}_j$$
$$\hat{\theta}_j = \sum_{i=0}^{K} \alpha_{i,j} \, sin\phi_{i,j} \tag{6}$$

The adaptive oscillator estimate of the velocity and acceleration can be written respectively as in [16]:

$$\hat{\dot{\theta}}_j = \sum_{i=0}^{K} \alpha_{i,j} \, \omega cos\phi_{i,j}$$
$$\hat{\ddot{\theta}}_j = -\left(\sum_{i=0}^{K} \alpha_{i,j} \, \omega^2 sin\phi_{i,j} \right) \tag{7}$$

4.4   Torque Estimator

The estimated torques is derived from the dynamic model in (3). The value of which is obtained by introducing the estimates from the adaptive oscillators described in (6) & (7). This forms the basis of the AFO control system. The equation may be described as:

$$\hat{\tau}_j = m_j g l_j sin\hat{\theta}_j - b_j \hat{\dot{\theta}}_j + I_j \hat{\ddot{\theta}}_j \tag{8}$$

with each symbol defined as in section 4.1 but represents its estimated version.

4.5   Human Torque

The human (muscular) torque applied to the device is determined by the PID controller in conjunction with the reference trajectory for the purpose of simulation and it is thus defined as:

$$\tau_{h,j} = K_{p,j} \, e_j + K_{i,j} \int e_j dt + K_{d,j} \, \dot{e}_j \tag{9}$$

where e_j is the error signal which is the difference between the reference trajectories and actual angular positions of the knee/ankle and $K_{p,j}$, $K_{i,j}$, $K_{d,j}$ are the proportional, integral and derivative gains of the controller (human torque) about the knee/ankle.

The total torque τ_j is the sum of the human (muscular) torque $\tau_{h,j}$ and the assistive torque $\tau_{e,j}$:

$$\tau_j = \tau_{h,j} + \tau_{e,j} \tag{10}$$

with $\tau_{e,j} = \kappa_j \hat{\tau}_j$ where κ_j determines the level of assistance applied at the knee/ankle joint. $\kappa_j = 1$ implies full assistance, $\kappa_j = 0.5$ represents 50% assistance and $\kappa_j = 0$ signifies no assistance.

5   Numerical Simulation

In this section, the physiological parameters, the non-sinusoidal periodic reference trajectories chosen for the purpose of this simulation and the eventual results of the simulation are highlighted.

5.1   Reference Trajectories and Physiological Parameters

The reference trajectories are assumed to be the measured angular position of the knee and ankle and chosen to be within the range of motion specified in section 2; they are given as below respectively:

$$\begin{aligned}
\theta_{ref\,1} &= \tfrac{\pi}{12}(sin(2\pi ft) + 0.5cos(\pi ft) + 2.25sin(\tfrac{\pi}{2} ft)) \\
\theta_{ref\,2} &= \tfrac{\pi}{90}(sin(\pi ft) + 0.8cos(\tfrac{\pi}{2} ft) + 0.6sin(\tfrac{\pi}{4} ft))
\end{aligned} \tag{11}$$

with $f = 0.16 Hz$

Furthermore, the physiological parameters of the knee/ankle with respect to the Shank-Foot Model in Fig. 1. were chosen as in Table: 1. below:

Table 1. Physiological Parameters

Parameters	Units	Values
Shank length (L_1)	m	0.2
Foot length (L_2)	m	0.08
Shank mass (m_1)	kg	2.80
Foot mass (m_2)	kg	1.17
Shank inertia (I_1)	$kg.m^2$	0.075
Foot inertia (I_2)	$kg.m^2$	0.012
gravity (g)	m/s^2	9.8
Shank damping Coeffiecient b_1	Nm/s^2	0.4
Foot damping Coeffiecient b_2	Nm/s^2	0.6

Note that the value of the inertia is calculated assuming cylindrical links and thus calculated as $I_i = \tfrac{2}{3}m_i L_i{}^2$.

The PID controller parameters and Adaptive Oscillator parameters are given as; $K_p = 110, K_i = 5.5, K_d = 2$ are same for both knee and ankle PID controllers and the adaptive oscillator parameters values $\eta = 5, \nu = 25$ are the same for each CPG representing the knee or ankle.

5.2   Results

With regards to Section 5.1, the simulation results are given in the figures below.

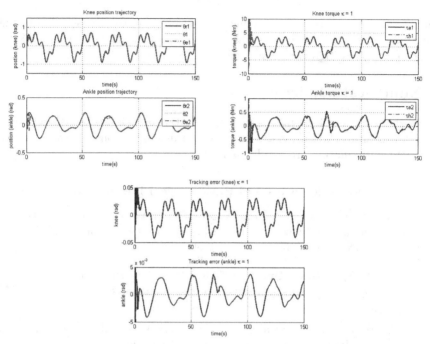

Fig. 4. Top (left): Position trajectory of knee and ankle with adaptive oscillator synchronisation. $\theta_{r1}, \theta_1 \& \theta_{e1}$ represents the reference, actual and estimated angular position trajectories of the knee respectively, while $\theta_{r2}, \theta_1 \& \theta_{e2}$ signifies the reference, actual and estimated angular position trajectories of the ankle in the same other. This same for the top figure in Fig. 6. **Top (right)**: Human (muscular) torque and assistive torque simulation of knee and ankle $\kappa = 1$. $\tau_{e1} \& \tau_{h1}$ defines the assistive torque and human torque for the knee respectively while $\tau_{e2} \& \tau_{h2}$ is same as regard the ankle. This same for Fig. 5 (torque figures only), but with different assistive torques. **Bottom**: Tracking error result of knee and ankle with adaptive oscillator synchronisation. This is a measure of how close the assistive torque follows the human torque of which it is benchmarked, based on the difference between the actual trajectory and the reference trajectory.

5.3   Discussion

As shown in Fig. 4 (top (right)) the adaptive oscillator was able to achieve phase synchronization of all three trajectories which includes the reference, actual and estimated angular positions (knee and ankle). A considerable replication of the reference trajectories was achieved with little finite time convergence of for both positions. This is true for all the conditions which vary from $\kappa = 1$ (full assistance), $\kappa = 0.5$ (50 % assistance) and $\kappa = 0$ (no assistance). By observing Fig. 4

(bottom), the tracking errors for the angular positions (knee and ankle) are relatively small with RMS errors value of $0.01012rad$ for the knee position and $0.00308rad$ for the ankle position.

In Fig.4 (top (right)) and Fig.5 (top (left) & top (right)), the level of assistance offered to the subject and the human torque of the subject is plotted with time. This is to verify the effect of the assistance to the subject during a particular training session. It can be perceived from these figures that as the level of assistance decreases from $\kappa = 1$ to $\kappa = 0$, the human torque required to achieve the proposed task increases. The orthotic device can therefore fully or partially assist the patient bringing into to play the term "assist as needed".

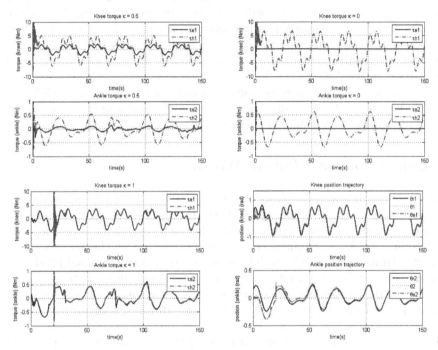

Fig. 5. Top (left): Human (muscular) torque and assistive torque simulation of knee and ankle $\kappa = 0.5$. **Top (right)**: Human (muscular) torque and assistive torque simulation of knee and ankle $\kappa = 0$. **Bottom (left)**: Human and assistive torque simulation of knee and ankle $\kappa = 1$ with disturbance. It shows the interval of applied disturbance in human torque which is between $0 - 20s$. **Bottom (right)**: Position trajectory of knee and ankle with adaptive oscillator synchronisation in the presence of disturbance.

To further authenticate the assistive measures rendered, a disturbance which exemplifies the state of inactivity of the human muscles about the knee and ankle was introduced to the knee-ankle orthotic device (system). Its introduction is at early phase of the training session with full assistive measure to compensate for this muscle inactiveness (i.e. at $0 - 20s$). In real-life circumstances, it could be viewed as an abstraction to the movement of the shank-foot during the training session.

A significant ripple effect on the trajectories of the positions was observed in Fig. 5 (bottom (right)) at the early stage but all the trajectories achieved phase synchronisation at the end of stipulated training session time. This was due to the full assistance given to the subject by the device. Fig. 5 (bottom (left)) virtually demonstrates this effect; having observed that the human torque was abnormal or ineffective between $0 - 20s$, and the effect could be perceived in Fig. 5 (bottom (right)), due to the tracking dificulties encountered as a result of the disturbance.

Initial spikes of the PID controller which generates the human torques can be seen in figures which describes the said torque pattern. This can be eliminated by tuning the PID parameters more efficiently. However, this is for simulation purpose only as the practical use will be to measure the angular position of the periodic motions of the shank and foot about the knee and ankle respectively. This parameter is then used to calculated the human torques in conjuction with the eventual assistive torques via the estimation of the position, velocity and acceleration by the AFO.

The main contribution is to establish a rehabilitation protocol which incorporates the knee and ankle using the *robotic-assisted platform* by means of the AFO and that has been achieved based on the above simulations.

6   Conclusions and Future Works

In this paper, an assistive method for the knee and ankle rehabilitation was proposed. This was achieved by exploiting the rhythmic traits of CPGs (adaptive frequency oscillators) for the purpose of developing a new rehabilitation protocol that requires the knee and ankle concurrent movement with the aid of a global coupling. An inverse dynamic model assumed to be a simple damped pendulum dynamics for each link was used to realise a conceived movement pattern. Using a chosen numerical data, the assistive orthotic device was confirmed to be effective. This was established by mimicking the muscular (human) torque with the aid of a PID controller.

In future works, the authors intend to verify this assistive effect in a lab and also carry out parametric identification by the use of least square method and regression equations of Zatsiorsky [17] which will be achieved by sampling the inverse dynamic model along stipulated trajectories of both the knee and ankle [18]. Furthermore, the final goal will be to implement this control method to specific human gait systems using its inverse dynamic model.

References

1. Iaki, D., Jorge, J.G., Emilio, S.: Lower-Limb Robotic Rehabilitation: Literature Review and Challenges. Journal of Robotics (2011)
2. Kordasz, M., Kuczkowski, K., Sauer, P.: Study on possible control algorithms for lower limb rehabilitation system. In: IEEE International Conference on Rehabilitation Robotics (ICORR), pp. 1–6 (2011)

3. Dollar, A.M., Herr, H.: Lower Extremity Exoskeletons and Active Orthoses: Challenges and State-of-the-Art. IEEE Transactions on Robotics 24, 144–158 (2008)
4. Ronsse, R., Vitiello, N., Lenzi, T., van den Kieboom, J., Carrozza, M.C., Ijspeert, A.J.: Adaptive oscillators with human-in-the-loop: Proof of concept for assistance and rehabilitation. In: 3rd IEEE RAS and EMBS International Conference on Biomedical Robotics and Biomechatronics (BioRob), pp. 668–674 (2010)
5. Colombo, G., Wirz, M., Dietz, V.: Driven gait orthosis for improvement of locomotor training in paraplegic patients. Spinal Cord 39 (2001)
6. Wolbrecht, E.T., Chan, V., Reinkensmeyer, D.J., Bobrow, J.E.: Optimizing Compliant. Model-Based Robotic Assistance to Promote Neurorehabilitation. IEEE Transactions on Neural Systems and Rehabilitation Engineering 16, 286–297 (2008)
7. Israel, J.F., Campbell, D.D., Kahn, J.H., Hornby, T.G.: Metabolic Costs and Muscle Activity Patterns During Robotic- and Therapist-Assisted Treadmill Walking in Individuals With Incomplete Spinal Cord Injury. Physical Therapy 86, 1466–1478 (2006)
8. Sankai, Y.: Leading edge of cybernics: Robot suit hal. In: International Joint Conference SICE-ICASE, pp. P-1–P-2 (2006)
9. Righetti, L., Buchli, J., Ijspeert, A.J.: From dynamic hebbian learning for oscillators to adaptive central pattern generators. In: Proceedings of 3rd International Symposium on Adaptive Motion in Animals and Machines, AMAM, p. 45 (2005)
10. Righetti, L., Buchli, J., Ijspeert, A.J.: Adaptive frequency oscillators and applications. Open Cybernetics and Systemics Journal 3, 64–69 (2009)
11. Ronsse, R., De Rossi, S., Vitiello, N., Lenzi, T., Carrozza, M.C., Ijspeert, A.J.: Real-Time Estimate of Velocity and Acceleration of Quasi-Periodic Signals Using Adaptive Oscillators. IEEE Transactions on Robotics 29, 783–791 (2013)
12. Righetti, L., Ijspeert, A.J.: Programmable central pattern generators: an application to biped locomotion control. In: IEEE International Conference on Robotics and Automation, ICRA, pp. 1585–1590 (2006)
13. Gams, A., Petric, T., Ude, A., Lajpah, L., Zaier, R.: Performing Periodic Tasks: On-Line Learning, Adaptation and Synchronization with External Signals. In: The Future of Humanoid Robots Research and Applications, pp. 3–28 (2012)
14. de Pina Filho, A.C., Dutra, M.S., Santos, L., Raptopoulos, C.: Modelling of Bipedal Robots Using Coupled Nonlinear Oscillators (2006)
15. Ronsse, R., Koopman, B., Vitiello, N., Lenzi, T., De Rossi, S.M.M., van den Kieboom, J., et al.: Oscillator-based walking assistance: A model-free approach. In: IEEE International Conference on Rehabilitation Robotics (ICORR), pp. 1–6 (2011)
16. Rinderknecht, M.D., Delaloye, F.A., Crespi, A., Ronsse, R., Ijspeert, A.J.: Assistance using adaptive oscillators: Robustness to errors in the identification of the limb parameters. In: IEEE International Conference on Rehabilitation Robotics (ICORR), pp. 1–6 (2011)
17. Swevers, J., Ganseman, C., Tukel, D.B., De Schutter, J., Van Brussel, H.: Optimal robot excitation and identification. IEEE Transactions on Robotics and Automation 13, 730–740 (1997)
18. Khalil, W., Dombre, E.: Modelisation, identification et commande des robots: Hermes science publ. (1999)

Optimizing Robotic Team Performance
with Probabilistic Model Checking*

Sagar Chaki, Joseph Giampapa, David Kyle, and John Lehoczky

Carnegie Mellon University, Pittsburgh, PA, USA

Abstract. We present an approach to analytically construct a robotic team, i.e., team members and deployment order, that achieves a specific task with quantified probability of success. We assume that each robot is Markovian, and that robots interact with each other via communication only. Our approach is based on probabilistic model checking (PMC). We first construct a set of Discrete Time Markov Chains (DTMCs) that each capture a specific "projection" of the behavior of an individual robot. Next, given a specific team, we construct the DTMC for its behavior by combining the projection DTMCs appropriately. Finally, we use PMC to evaluate the performance of the team. This procedure is repeated for multiple teams, the best one is selected. In practice, the projection DTMCs are constructed by observing the behavior of individual robots a finite number of times, which introduces an error in our results. We present an approach – based on sampling using the Dirichlet distribution – to quantify this error. We prove the correctness of our approach formally, and also validate it empirically on a mine detection task by a team of communicating Kilobots.

1 Introduction

Autonomous robots are increasingly being used in teams to communicate and achieve tasks in a collaborative manner. Given a collection of robots and a specific mission, a designer solves the coalition formation problem and selects the coordination strategy so as to maximize the chances of mission success. Currently this is done in an ad-hoc manner since navigating the solution space and selecting the best one manually is impossible. This is true even if the designer is able to observe each robot individually to construct a model of its behavior. First, it is not clear which modeling formalism to use. Second, since these models are complex (if they are to be precise) it is impossible to compose them manually to make predictions about the overall behavior of a robotic team.

In this paper, we present an analytic approach to solve a simplified but common version of this problem. Specifically, we assume robots are Markovian, and

* This material is based upon work funded and supported by the Department of Defense under Contract No. FA8721-05-C-0003 with Carnegie Mellon University for the operation of the Software Engineering Institute, a federally funded research and development center. This material has been approved for public release and unlimited distribution. DM-0001326.

D. Brugali et al. (Eds.): SIMPAR 2014, LNAI 8810, pp. 134–145, 2014.

only influence each other via communication (i.e., no physical interaction such as collisions). We call this a communicating multi-robot mission (CMRM). Given a CMRM S and a deadline D, our approach computes the following class of properties: (i) probability of an event e happening when S is executed up to time D; and (ii) expected value of an attribute a of S when it is executed up to time D. We make the following contributions.

First, we formalize a CMRM as a *modal* Discrete Time Markov Chain (DTMC). A modal DTMC consists of a finite set of component DTMCs. Each component DTMC corresponds to a robot, and engages alternately in two kinds of moves: (i) deterministic – the DTMC's state changes instantly according to a "mode-change" function that depends on the current states of the other DTMCs; and (ii) probabilistic – according to its own transition relation; this happens synchronously with the other DTMCs and takes unit time. We show (see Theorem 1) that a modal DTMC is semantically equivalent to a specific combination of the "projections" of its component DTMCs. This result enables us to compute properties of modal DTMCs, and therefore a CMRMs, using existing probabilistic model checkers, such as PRISM [9], that verify DTMCs.

Second, we present an approach to quantify the error in our predictions. In practice, each projection DTMC is constructed by observing and measuring a finite set of runs of the corresponding robot. This means that the DTMC differs from the true DTMC for the robot's behavior. Therefore, predictions based on them lie within an error margin of the correct values. We present an approach that quantifies this error and estimates the correct property value. Specifically, we sample a set of DTMCs "around" the constructed projection, and make prediction using each sample. From these predictions, we use statistical theory to estimate the real property value and the error margin. A key aspect of our sampling procedure is its use of the Dirichlet distribution [7]. To our knowledge, this is a new approach for error estimation in the DTMC context.

Finally, we implement our approach and evaluate it using a team of Kilobots [11]. To construct the projection DTMC for a Kilobot, we: (i) run it and record its actual behavior; (ii) reproduce this behavior in the V-REP [1] simulator using manually tuned parameters; and (iii) construct the projection DTMC from measurements of multiple simulation runs. Using a simulator enables us to perform many runs and lower our error margins. At the same time, tuning the simulation parameters to replicate observed robot behavior grounds our results in reality. We show that our approach yields accurate predictions that match observed results with Kilobot teams. Further details are presented in Section 4.

Related Work. Konur et al. [8] model coordinated robotic behavior in the context of swarms. Like us, they compose individual models of robots into a model of team behavior. However, they assume that all robots have the same behavioral characteristics. This allows them to produce a team model which operates on counts of robots in each state, instead of tracking each robot individually. We do not assume homogeneous robots. Their attempt to track robots individually met untenable state explosion past a team size of 3. Our individual models are significantly more complex, but still due to the use of projections, we were able to verify teams of up to 6 robots.

Ghorbal et al. [4] present an approach for predicting intervals of result probabilities based on intervals of transition probabilities. This addresses the issue of error propagation, but assumes that a true range of probabilities for each transition is known with certainty. Effectively, this is a 100% confidence interval, which is unrealistic . Their approach is fully analytic, while we rely on sampling. They develop a new verification algorithm which is validated on a 21 state model, while we use existing tools and handle systems with thousands of states.

This paper builds on a wide body of work in modeling and verifying probabilistic systems [12]. In particular, probabilistic model checking has been used to verify systems ranging from pacemakers [2], root contention protocols [10] and biological pathways [6]. We extend the application of probabilistic model checking to yet another domain – communicating autonomous multi-robot missions.

The rest of this paper is organized as follows. In Section 2 we present our approach to predict properties of modal DTMCs by combining projections. In Section 3, we present our approach for quantifying error. In Section 4, we present our experimental results, and in Section 5, we conclude.

2   Modal DTMC and Verification

In this section we define modal DTMCs and present an algorithm to compute their properties. We begin with preliminary notation and concepts. Given a set X, a probability density function (PDF) over X is a mapping $\pi : X \mapsto [0, 1]$ such that: $\sum_{x \in X} \pi(x) = 1$. The set of all PDFs over X is denoted by $\Pi(X)$. Given two sets X_1 and X_2, and PDFs $\pi_1 \in \Pi(X_1)$ and $\pi_2 \in \Pi(X_2)$, the joint PDF $\pi_1 \otimes \pi_2 \in \Pi(X_1 \times X_2)$ is defined as follows:

$$\forall (x_1, x_2) \in X_1 \times X_2 \,.\, (\pi_1 \otimes \pi_2)(x_1, x_2) = \pi_1(x_1) \times \pi_2(x_2)$$

A DTMC is a triple (S, I, R) where: (i) S is a finite set of states; (ii) $I \in S$ is the initial state; and (iii) $R : S \mapsto \Pi(S)$ is the transition probability matrix.

We use Probabilistic Computation Tree Logic (PCTL) [5] to express properties. For a PCTL formula φ, and a DTMC S, $S \models \varphi$ is the probability that S satisfies φ. For example, if $\varphi = F(p \vee q)$, then $S \models \varphi$ is the probability that the DTMC eventually reaches a state where either p or q holds, where p and q are propositions that are either TRUE or FALSE in each state. For DTMCs S_1, S_2 we write $S_1 \equiv S_2$ to mean that for every PCTL formula φ, $(S_1 \models \varphi) = (S_2 \models \varphi)$, i.e., S_1 and S_2 satisfy all PCTL formulas with equal probability.

2.1   Modal DTMC

A n-component modal DTMC is a $2n$-tuple $(M_1, \ldots, M_n, \delta_1, \ldots, \delta_n)$ where $M_i = (S_i, I_i, R_i)$ are DTMCs, and:

$$\delta_i : S_i \mapsto 2^{S_1 \times \cdots \times S_{i-1} \times S_{i+1} \times \cdots \times S_n} \times S_i$$

are "mode transition" functions. Informally $\delta_i(s_i) = (E, \bar{s}_i)$ means that if DTMC M_i is in state s_i, and the other DTMCs are in state $e = (s_1, \ldots, s_{i-1}, s_{i+1}, \ldots s_n)$, then either (i) $e \in E$ and M_i makes a mode change by moving to state $\bar{s}_i$; or (ii) $e \notin E$ and M_i remains in state s_i.

Formally, the semantics of the modal DTMC $P = (M_1, \ldots, M_n, \delta_1, \ldots, \delta_n)$, denoted $[\![P]\!]$, is the DTMC $(\tilde{S}, \tilde{I}, \tilde{R})$ where: (i) $\tilde{S} = S_1 \times \cdots \times S_n$; (ii) $\tilde{I} = (I_1, \ldots, I_n)$; and (iii) $\tilde{R} : \tilde{S} \mapsto \Pi(\tilde{S})$ is defined as:

$$\tilde{R}(s_1, \ldots, s_n) = R_1(s_1') \otimes \cdots \otimes R_n(s_n')$$

where for all $i \in [1, n]$, if $\delta_i(s_i) = (E, \bar{s}_i)$ then:

$$(s_1, \ldots, s_{i-1}, s_{i+1}, \ldots s_n) \in E \wedge (s_i' = \bar{s}_i) \bigvee$$
$$(s_1, \ldots, s_{i-1}, s_{i+1}, \ldots s_n) \notin E \wedge (s_i' = s_i)$$

Note that, in the definition of $\tilde{R}(s_1, \ldots, s_n)$ above, state $(s_1', \ldots, s_n')$ denotes the result of (instantaneous) mode change due to exchange of information between the component DTMCs. This is followed by simultaneous probabilistic transition made by each component DTMC (which requires one unit of time), as denoted by the application of $R_1, \ldots, R_n$ to states $s_1', \ldots, s_n'$, respectively, and composing the resulting PDFs via the $\otimes$ operator.

In the rest of the paper, for simplicity of explanation, we consider only a 2-component modal DTMC P, i.e., $P = (M_1, M_2, \delta_1, \delta_2)$. The generalization to an arbitrary (but finite) number of components is done in a natural manner. Our overall goal is to verify a PCTL formula φ over P, the topic of Section 2.2.

2.2   Modal DTMC Verification

For any set X, and $x \in X$, $\Delta(x) \in \Pi(X)$ is the PDF that maps x to 1 and all other elements of X to 0. Recall that our target modal DTMC is $P = (M_1, M_2, \delta_1, \delta_2)$. We verify P by constructing a model based on observing M_1 and M_2 individually. Our approach relies on several key ideas:

1. A state of a component DTMC (i.e., M_1 and M_2) records at least the current time and the time at which the last mode change happened. Thus, each state is of the form (t, m, d) where t is the current time, m is the time of mode change ($m = \infty$ means that mode change has not happened yet), and d is the remaining state information. Thus, the initial state is of the form $(0, \infty, d)$. Also, we know that $m \neq t$ since up to the point of mode change $m = \infty \neq t$, and after the mode change $m < t$.

2. On any execution of the DTMC, a mode change happens at most once, and is instantaneous. Thus,

$$\delta_i(t, m, d) = (E, (\bar{t}, \bar{m}, \bar{d})) \Rightarrow (m = \infty) \wedge (\bar{t} = \bar{m} = t)$$

3. The system is time-bounded, i.e., there is some time $T \geq 0$ at which the system stutters. In terms of the transition relation R, this means that if $s = (T, m, d)$ for some m and d, then $R(s) = \Delta(s)$. For our experiments, the time bound equals the deadline specified in the property.

4. During our individual observations, we can change the mode of M_i at arbitrary time points. This is because a mode change is controlled via software, which we are able to reprogram.

Approach. Our overall approach is as follows:

- Let DTMC $\langle M_i, t \rangle$ be the projection of M_i under the restriction that mode change always happens at time t. Construct all projections $\{\langle M_1, t \rangle \mid 0 \leq t \leq T\}$ and $\{\langle M_2, t \rangle \mid 0 \leq t \leq T\}$ for M_1 and M_2, respectively.
- Construct a DTMC $\widehat{M}$ by "re-combining" the projection DTMCs using the definitions of the mode change functions $\delta_1, \ldots, \delta_n$. Prove that $\widehat{M} = [\![P]\!]$.
- Compute $\widehat{M} \models \varphi$ using a probabilistic model checker, e.g., PRISM [9].

2.3 DTMC Projection

We now define the projection of a DTMC based on mode change time. First define function $\widehat{\delta}_i : S_i \mapsto S_i$ as follows:

$$\forall s_i \in S_i \centerdot \widehat{\delta}_i(s_i) = \bar{s}_i \centerdot \exists E \centerdot \delta_i(s_i) = (E, \bar{s}_i)$$

Thus, $\widehat{\delta}_i$ is the projection of δ_i on the second component of its range, and is well-defined. Let $M_i = (S_i, I_i, R_i)$. Then the projection of M_i under the restriction that mode change always happens at time $\mathbf{t}$ (where $0 \leq \mathbf{t} < T$) is the DTMC $\langle M_i, \mathbf{t} \rangle = (S_i, I_i, \langle R_i, \mathbf{t} \rangle)$ such that $\forall s = (t, m, d) \in S_i$:

$$\langle R_i, \mathbf{t} \rangle(s) = \begin{cases} R_i(\widehat{\delta}_i(s)) & \text{if } t = \mathbf{t} \\ R_i(s) & \text{otherwise} \end{cases}$$

2.4 Combining Projections

Consider the projections $\{\langle M_1, t \rangle \mid t \in [0, T]\}$ and $\{\langle M_2, t \rangle \mid t \in [0, T]\}$ of M_1 and M_2. Define the DTMC $\widehat{M} = (\widehat{S}, \widehat{I}, \widehat{R})$ as follows:

$$\widehat{S} = S_1 \times S_2 \qquad \widehat{I} = (I_1, I_2) \qquad \text{and}$$

$$\forall s_1 \in S_1 \centerdot \forall s_2 \in S_2 \centerdot s_1 = (t_1, m_1, d_1) \land s_2 = (t_2, m_2, d_2) \land$$

$$\delta_1(s_1) = (E_1, \bar{s}_1) \land \delta_2(s_2) = (E_2, \bar{s}_2) \Rightarrow \widehat{R}(s_1, s_2) = A_1 \otimes A_2 \quad \text{where}$$

$$A_1 = \begin{cases} \langle R_1, t_1 \rangle(s_1) & \text{if } s_2 \in E_1 \\ \langle R_1, m_1 \rangle(s_1) & \text{otherwise} \end{cases} \qquad A_2 = \begin{cases} \langle R_2, t_2 \rangle(s_2) & \text{if } s_1 \in E_2 \\ \langle R_2, m_2 \rangle(s_2) & \text{otherwise} \end{cases}$$

We now present our main result, Theorem 1, which states that the combination of projection DTMCs described above is equivalent to the modal DTMC.

Theorem 1. $\widehat{M} = [\![P]\!]$.

Proof. Recall that $\widehat{M} = (\widehat{S}, \widehat{I}, \widehat{R})$ and $[\![P]\!] = (\tilde{S}, \tilde{I}, \tilde{R})$. By definition, we already know that: (i) $\widehat{S} = \tilde{S} = S_1 \times S_2$ and $\widehat{I} = \tilde{I} = (I_1, I_2)$. Hence it suffices to show that $\widehat{R} = \tilde{R}$.

Let $s_1 = (t_1, m_1, d_1)$ and $s_2 = (t_2, m_2, d_2)$. Then $\tilde{R}(s_1, s_2) = R_1(s_1') \otimes R_2(s_2')$. First we show that $R_1(s_1') = A_1$. Let $\delta_1(s_1) = (E_1, \bar{s}_1)$.

Case 1: $s_2 \in E_1$. In this case, $s_1' = \bar{s}_1 = \widehat{\delta}_1(s_1)$. Then $R_1(s_1') = R_1(\widehat{\delta}_1(s_1)) = \langle R_1, t_1 \rangle(s_1) = A_1$.

Case 2: $s_2 \notin E_2$. In this case, $s_1' = s_1$. Recall that $m_1 \neq t_1$. Hence, $\langle R_1, m_1 \rangle(s_1) = R_1(s_1)$. Hence, $R_1(s_1') = R_1(s_1) = \langle R_1, m_1 \rangle(s_1) = A_1$.

In a symmetric manner, we can show that $R_2(s_2') = A_2$. Thus, $\tilde{R}(s_1, s_2) = R_1(s_1') \otimes R_2(s_2') = A_1 \otimes A_2 = \widehat{R}(s_1, s_2)$.

Theorem 1 enables us to compute a property of the modal DTMC P by combining projections of its components to construct DTMC $\widehat{M}$, and then applying probabilistic model checking. In practice, a projection $\langle M_i, t \rangle$ is constructed from observations of multiple runs of the corresponding robot. This inevitably introduces an error in our results. The next section presents our approach to quantify and bound this error.

3 Error Quantification

Suppose we model a real-world system G, e.g., a robot, using a DTMC $\widehat{M}$. For a given PCTL formula φ, let $\widehat{p} = (\widehat{M} \models \varphi)$, i.e., the probability that $\widehat{M}$ satisfies φ, and let $p = (G \models \varphi)$. If the model is perfect, i.e., $\widehat{M} = G$, then $\widehat{p} = p$. However, such perfect modeling is impracticable for several reasons. First, G might not be Markovian. Second, suppose G is Markovian, i.e., $G \equiv M_\diamond$ for some DTMC $M_\diamond$. Note that, in this case, $(M_\diamond \models \varphi) = (G \models \varphi) = p$. However, $\widehat{M}$ might not capture enough *state* to accurately model G; i.e., there could be hidden variables in G resulting in behaviors that are absent in $\widehat{M}$. Finally, $\widehat{M}$ might have the same states as $M_\diamond$, but different *transition probabilities*, and hence diverges from G.

In practice, we should expect transition probabilities to be imprecise. Ultimately, the only approaches to obtain these probabilities for a real-world system are based on intuitive guesses or finite observations of the system. Thus, we should also expect any predictions made by a model to deviate from reality by some margin, where that margin is related to the uncertainty of those transition probabilities. This is the error we seek to quantify.

3.1 Constructing an Approximation

Recall that there exists a DTMC $M_\diamond = (S, I, R)$ such that $M_\diamond \equiv G$. Suppose that each state of $M_\diamond$ corresponds to a known combination of observable characteristics in G. Thus, if we execute a trial of G, and observe it at each discrete time point, then from each observation we can compute the corresponding state of $M_\diamond$. Suppose we execute several trials of G, and record our observations as a list of evidence E, where each evidence $e \in E$ is a sequence of states $\langle s_0, s_1, \ldots, s_k \rangle$ of $M_\diamond$ corresponding to observations of a trial of G at discrete time points.

Using E, we construct a transition probability matrix $\widehat{R} : S \mapsto \Pi(S)$ as follows. Given a sequence of states e, and states $s, \bar{s}$, let $e(s)$ and $e(s, \bar{s})$ denote, respectively, the number of times $\langle s \rangle$ and $\langle s, \bar{s} \rangle$ appear as a subsequence of e. We generalize this to E as follows: $E(s) = \sum_{e \in E} e(s)$ and $E(s, \bar{s}) = \sum_{e \in E} e(s, \bar{s})$. Thus $E(s)$ is the number of times we observe G to reach state s, and $E(s, \bar{s})$ is the number of times we observe G to move from s to $\bar{s}$ in one time step.

Then, we have two cases: (i) if $E(s) = 0$, then $\widehat{R}(s) = \Delta(s)$; (ii) otherwise $\forall \bar{s} \in S . \widehat{R}(s)(\bar{s}) = \frac{E(s,\bar{s})}{E(s)}$. Thus, for states not observed in our trials (case-i) we assume self-transitions. For other states (case-ii) we use the "frequentist" approach. Note that $\widehat{R}$ is a well-defined PDF, and provides the best possible approximation of R given the available evidence E. Then, our approximate DTMC is $\widehat{M} = (S, I, \widehat{R})$. Note that $\widehat{M}$ deviates from $M_\diamond$ only in its transition probabilities.

3.2   Distribution Definitions

The construction of $\widehat{M}$ described in the previous section does not provide any insight into how $\widehat{M} \models \varphi$ relates to $M_\diamond \models \varphi$ (and thus $G \models \varphi$) in terms of error. Note that each possible transition $(s, \bar{s})$ can be viewed as a Bernoulli trial. Thus, statistical methods allow us to estimate the error of each individual transition probability of $\widehat{M}$. However, understanding how these errors – i.e., the difference between R and $\widehat{R}$ – affect error in $\widehat{M} \models \varphi$ is not straightforward.

Let $\mathbb{M}$ be the set of all DTMCs of the form $(S, I, \tilde{R})$, i.e., $\mathbb{M}$ is the set of all DTMCs that have the same states and initial state as $M_\diamond$. Given a real number $r \in [0, 1]$, let $M_r = \{M \in \mathbb{M} \mid (M \models \varphi) \leq r\}$ be the set of DTCMs that satisfy φ with probability at most r. Let $\mathscr{M} = \{M_r \mid r \in [0, 1] \wedge \forall r' \in [0, 1] . r < r' \implies M_r \subset M_{r'}\}$. Note that the elements of $\mathscr{M}$ are strictly ordered by size.

Given evidence E from trials of G, we define the PDF $\widehat{\mathcal{M}_E} \in \Pi(\mathscr{M})$ by the following cumulative density function (CDF):

$$CDF(\widehat{\mathcal{M}_E})(M) = \mathsf{P}(M_\diamond \in M|E) \tag{1}$$

That is, the CDF of $\widehat{\mathcal{M}_E}$ maps each set of DTMCs $M \in \mathscr{M}$ to the probability that some DTMC in M is "correct", and thus equivalent to $M_\diamond$ and G, given the evidence E. Let $\mathrm{dom}(\mathscr{M}) = \{r \in [0, 1] \mid M_r \in \mathscr{M}\}$. Next, given $\widehat{\mathcal{M}_E}$, define a PDF $\widehat{\mathcal{P}_E} \in \Pi(\mathrm{dom}(\mathscr{M}))$ by the following CDF:

$$CDF(\widehat{\mathcal{P}_E})(r) = \mathsf{P}((M_\diamond \models \varphi) \leq r \mid E) \tag{2}$$

Thus, the CDF of $\widehat{\mathcal{P}_E}$ maps r to the probability that G satisfies φ with probability at most r given evidence E. Note that, from (1) and (2), we have:

$$CDF(\widehat{\mathcal{P}_E})(r) = \mathsf{P}(M_\diamond \in M_r \mid E) = CDF(\widehat{\mathcal{M}_E})(M_r) \tag{3}$$

We now show how to construct $\widehat{\mathcal{M}_E}$ and $\widehat{\mathcal{P}_E}$.

3.3   Constructing Distributions

To construct $\widehat{\mathcal{M}_E}$, we define a mapping $T : S \mapsto \Pi(\Pi(S))$ from states to a *PDF over PDFs* of other states to transition to. We use the Dirichlet distribution since it produces sets of variates that sum to one (i.e., a PDF), and it is a conjugate prior for the Multinomial distribution [7]. We define T in several steps. First, we define a prior T^0 to T as:

$$\forall s \in S . \forall \pi \in \Pi(S) : T^0(s)(\pi) = \mathsf{P}(\pi|\boldsymbol{\alpha_s}) = \mathrm{Dirichlet}(\pi|\boldsymbol{\alpha_s})$$

where $\boldsymbol{\alpha_s}$ is a vector of pseudo-counts of prior belief in transition likelihood of transitioning from s to each state in S. Thus, for each $s \in S$, $T^0(s)$ is a Dirichlet distribution with parameters $\boldsymbol{\alpha_s}$. In our implementation, we used the union of the individual robots' DTMCs created during unit testing as the prior.

Next, recall that $E(s, \bar{s})$ is the number of times we observe G to move from state s to $\bar{s}$ in one time step during our trials. Also, $R(s)(\bar{s})$ is the probability of transitioning from s to $\bar{s}$ in $\boldsymbol{M_\diamond}$. Let $\boldsymbol{c_s} = (\forall \bar{s} \in S : E(s, \bar{s}))$ be the vector of counts of transitions from s to each $\bar{s}$. Since $\boldsymbol{M_\diamond}$ perfectly models G, we have:

$$\forall s \in S : \boldsymbol{c_s} \sim \mathrm{Multinomial}(\forall \bar{s} \in S : R(s)(\bar{s}))$$

That is, $\boldsymbol{c_s}$ is drawn from a Multinomial distribution, which the true distribution for state s in G. Finally, given the well known relationship between Multinomial distributions and Dirichlet priors [7], we construct T as the posterior Dirichlet distribution of transition probabilities. In other words:

$$\forall s \in S . \forall \pi \in \Pi(S) . T(s)(\pi) = \mathsf{P}(\pi|\boldsymbol{\alpha_s}, \boldsymbol{c_s}) \propto \mathsf{P}(\boldsymbol{c_s}|\pi) p(\pi|\boldsymbol{\alpha_s})$$
$$= \mathrm{Multinomial}(\boldsymbol{c_s}|\pi) T^0(s)(\pi) = \mathrm{Multinomial}(\boldsymbol{c_s}|\pi) \, \mathrm{Dirichlet}(\pi|\boldsymbol{\alpha_s})$$
$$= \mathrm{Dirichlet}(\pi|\boldsymbol{\alpha_s} + \boldsymbol{c_s})$$

That is, for any state $s \in S$, $T(s)$ is a Dirichlet distribution with parameters $\boldsymbol{\alpha_s} + \boldsymbol{c_s}$. Next, recall that $\widehat{\mathcal{M}_E} \in \Pi(\mathbb{M})$. We define $\widehat{\mathcal{M}_E}$ using T as follows:

$$\forall M = (S, I, \widetilde{R}) \in \mathbb{M} . \widehat{\mathcal{M}_E}(M) = \prod_{s \in S} T(s)(\widetilde{R}(s))$$

That is, for any M which has a set of states and an initial state which are the same as $\boldsymbol{M_\diamond}$, the probability of drawing it from $\widehat{\mathcal{M}_E}$ is the probability of drawing each of its states transition probabilities from the corresponding Dirichlet distributions in T.

Given $\widehat{\mathcal{M}_E}$, we still do not know how to construct $\widehat{\mathcal{P}_E}$, or calculate its statistic measures. Since $\mathbb{M}$ is infinite, an exhaustive construction of $\widehat{\mathcal{P}_E}$ is impossible. Instead, we sample $\widehat{\mathcal{P}_E}$ to generate a vector $\widetilde{\boldsymbol{M_E}}$ of n DTMCs, such that $\forall \widetilde{M} \in \widetilde{\boldsymbol{M_E}} : \widetilde{M} \sim \widehat{\mathcal{M}_E}$. More specifically, we have $\widetilde{\boldsymbol{M_E}} = (\widetilde{M}_1, \ldots, \widetilde{M}_n)$ such that for $1 \leq i \leq n$, $\widetilde{M}_i \sim \widehat{\mathcal{M}_E} = (S, I, \widetilde{R}_i)$ where $\forall s \in S . \widetilde{R}_i(s) = \pi_{is} \sim T(s) \sim \mathrm{Dirichlet}(\boldsymbol{\alpha_s} + \boldsymbol{c_s})$. That is, we construct each DTMC $\widetilde{M}_i$ by drawing the transition probabilities for each of its states from the corresponding Dirichlet distribution in T. The algorithm for drawing variates from Dirichlet distributions is well known [3]. Finally, given $\widetilde{M_E}$, we construct the vector of probabilities $\widetilde{P_E} = \langle r_1, \ldots, r_n \rangle$, such for $1 \leq i \leq n$, $r_i = \widetilde{M_i} \models \varphi$. We compute each r_i using a probabilistic model checker. Our main result is that $\widetilde{P_E}$ is drawn from $\widehat{\mathcal{P}_E}$, as expressed in Theorem 2.

Theorem 2. *If $\widetilde{P_E}$ and $\widehat{\mathcal{P}_E}$ are defined as above, then $\widetilde{P_E} \sim \widehat{\mathcal{P}_E}$.*

Proof. We wish to show that each $\forall r_i \in \widetilde{P_E}$, $r_i \sim \widehat{\mathcal{P}_E}$, or equivalently, $\forall r \in \mathrm{dom}(\mathcal{M}) \cdot \mathsf{P}(r_i \leq r) = CDF(\widehat{\mathcal{P}_E})(r)$. This holds because:

$$\mathsf{P}(r_i \leq r) = \mathsf{P}((M \models \varphi) \leq r \mid M \sim \widehat{M_E})$$
$$= CDF(\widehat{M_E})(\{M \mid (M \models \varphi) \leq r\}) = CDF(\widehat{M_E})(\boldsymbol{M}_r) = CDF(\widehat{\mathcal{P}_E})(r)$$

The last equality follows from (3). This completes the proof.

□

To quantify the error between $\widehat{M} \models \varphi$ and $G \models \varphi$, we analyze $\widetilde{P_E}$ with the usual statistical measurements, and determine whether $\widehat{M}$ is a suitable approximation of G. Specifically, for our experiments, we determine the 5th and 95th percentiles of $\widetilde{P_E}$ to find a 90% credible interval. If this interval is too wide, we narrow it by performing more trials of G to increase the size of E.

Even for a fixed E, our analysis approximately characterizes the true distribution $\widehat{\mathcal{P}_E}$. However, with a sufficiently large number of samples of $\widehat{\mathcal{P}_E}$, i.e., $|\widetilde{P_E}|$, we expect these approximations to approach true values. Since each sample is obtained by running an automated tool (e.g., PRISM), as opposed to running a trial of a physical robot team, it is feasible to construct a sufficiently large $\widetilde{P_E}$.

4   Experimental Results

We validate our approach on an example representing a demining operation by a team of communicating Kilobots. Our tools and examples, and instructions to reproduce our experiments are available at https://db.tt/Wc9tBsNd. All our experiments were done on a 4 core 3.1GHz i5 machine with 4GB of RAM. Kilobots are very simple robots. They can communicate with each other within a very limited range (a few inches) by bouncing infrared signals off the table they are moving on, and they move by vibrating two motors at different speeds. They possess no reliable localization.

The Scenario. A mine has been placed in a culvert beneath a road. The culvert is too small to admit advanced robots, so Kilobots must be used instead. One, two, or three Kilobots are used as a team of sweepers. Each Kilobot enters the culvert, traverses it in search of the mine, and returns to the mouth of the culvert for recovery, and to communicate whether it found the mine. We represent the mine and the base station at the mouth of the culvert by two (static) Kilobots. We place sweeper Kilobots immediately adjacent to the base station on deployment. The mine continually broadcasts a "Mine Here" message, while the base station initially broadcasts a "Base Here" message.

Each sweeper behaves as follows: (i) upon hearing the "Base Here" message for the first time, it begins moving forward; (ii) if it hears no other messages, it turns around at a predefined timeout (2 minutes); (iii) at any time, if it hears a "Mine Here" message or "Mine Found" message it begins transmitting a "Mine Found" message itself; also, if it hasn't turned around yet, it does so; (iv) if the base station hears a "Mine Found" message, it begins transmitting a "Mission Success" message instead; (v) if a sweeper moving backward hears a "Base Here" or "Mission Success" message, it assumes it is in the recovery zone, and stops.

Note that while each robot in our scenario has the same intent, it has a distinct behavior due to its motion characteristic and its release time. In other words, different robots released at the same time would behave differently, and the same robot released at a different time would also behave differently. Moreover, our approach also allows for different robots to have different intents, and perform multiple tasks in sequence or in parallel. This would lead to more complex DTMCs and increased verification time. However, in our experience, PRISM is able to handle systems with millions of reachable states.

Metrics. We use the following three measures of success: (i) f: the probability that at least one Kilobot finds the mine (i.e., transmits "Mine Found"); (ii) s: the probability that the base station knows about the mine (i.e., transmits "Mission Success"); and (iii) r: the expected number of Kilobots that return to the recovery zone, irrespective of whether it found the mine or not. Note that each of these measures provides valuable information about the mission success that is not supplied by the other two.

Modeling Kilobots. We first reproduced our scenario physically in the laboratory using actual Kilobots. We ran the scenario 190 times and noted 7 distinct Kilobot behaviors. Next, reproduced these behaviors in the VREP simulator by tuning the Kilobot model parameters appropriately. Subsequently, all our experiments were done via simulation. This physical-simulation hybrid approach enabled us to perform as many experiments as needed while grounding our results on observed behavior of physical Kilobots.

The Kilobot model in VREP has four parameters, each corresponding to the speed of a motor. To reproduce the observed behavior of a real Kilobot we first manually tuned them to appropriate values. Each VREP simulation is completely deterministic. Next, in order to introduce randomness across different experiments, we modified these parameters at each simulation step to a value selected from a normal distribution with mean equal to its tuned value and standard deviation 25. VREP has a sophisticated physics engine, and our approach produced simulated behaviors that are observably analogous to actual Kilobots.

Constructing Projection DTMCs. We discretized time at 20s units, and space into a 3×8 2-dimensional grid. Since each Kilobot G_i has a maximum turn around time of 120s (when it times out), it has 7 projections corresponding to 0s, 20s, 40s, 60s, 80s, 100s, 120s. We constructed each projection $\langle M_i, t_j \rangle$ by simulating Kilobot G_i 30 times with a pre-programmed turn around time of t_j. Using the results of these simulations as our evidence E, $\langle M_i, t_j \rangle$ is constructed as described in Sec. 3.1.

Table 1. Experiment results (3x8)

Team	f^*	$\widehat{f}$	$\widetilde{f_\mu}$	$\widetilde{f_5}$	$\widetilde{f_{95}}$	s^*	$\widehat{s}$	$\widetilde{s_\mu}$	$\widetilde{s_5}$	$\widetilde{s_{95}}$	r^*	$\widehat{r}$	$\widetilde{r_\mu}$	$\widetilde{r_5}$	$\widetilde{r_{95}}$
3-2-1	1.00	1.00	1.00	1.00	1.00	1.00	0.96	0.96	0.91	0.99	2.20	2.17	2.17	1.97	2.38
4-6-1	1.00	1.00	1.00	1.00	1.00	0.97	0.96	0.96	0.91	0.99	1.67	1.23	1.23	1.14	1.33
4-6-2	1.00	1.00	1.00	1.00	1.00	0.47	0.43	0.43	0.29	0.58	0.83	0.70	0.70	0.55	0.89
5-6-2	1.00	1.00	1.00	1.00	1.00	0.50	0.43	0.43	0.28	0.61	0.83	0.72	0.73	0.53	0.91
5-6-7	1.00	1.00	1.00	1.00	1.00	0.00	0.00	0.00	0.00	0.00	0.43	0.29	0.29	0.19	0.38
6-1-7	1.00	1.00	1.00	1.00	1.00	0.93	0.96	0.96	0.91	0.99	1.57	1.23	1.24	1.14	1.35
6-5-7	1.00	1.00	1.00	1.00	1.00	0.00	0.00	0.00	0.00	0.00	0.20	0.29	0.30	0.19	0.41
7-3-5	1.00	1.00	1.00	1.00	1.00	0.70	0.83	0.83	0.72	0.92	0.70	0.85	0.85	0.73	0.94
7-3-6	1.00	1.00	1.00	1.00	1.00	0.83	0.83	0.84	0.74	0.92	1.17	1.11	1.12	0.95	1.25
7-6-1	1.00	1.00	1.00	1.00	1.00	0.90	0.96	0.96	0.92	0.99	1.63	1.23	1.24	1.13	1.34

Team Selection. To validate our approach we used teams of 3 Kilobots. Since each team is specified by a set of Kilobots and their deployment order, there are 210 such possible teams. For practicality, we validated our approach on ten randomly selected teams as a representative sample. For each team in the sample, we conducted two experiments, which we describe now in more detail.

Experiment One: Predictions Using Projections. First, we computed the predicted values of f, s and r by combining the constructed projections $\langle M_i, t_j \rangle$ as described in Sec. 2.4 and verifying the resulting DTMC using PRISM [9]. These predictions are denoted $\widehat{f}$, $\widehat{s}$, and $\widehat{r}$, respectively and shown in the corresponding column of Table 1. To evaluate the accuracy of these predictions, we also computed the corresponding "observed values" f^*, s^* and r^*. Specifically, each observed value (e.g., f^*) is the average of the corresponding success measure (e.g., f) over 30 simulations of the corresponding team using VREP. During each team simulation (e.g., team 5-6-2), Kilobots are introduced to the scene at 20s intervals in the order specified by the team (e.g., $G_5 \to G_6 \to G_2$). The observed values are shown in the corresponding columns of Table 1. Note that, in each case, the predicted and observed results are close, indicating that our approach is sound, and that our assumptions do not distort results significantly.

Experiment Two: Error Quantification. Next, we computed $(\widetilde{f_\mu}, \widetilde{f_5}, \widetilde{f_{95}})$, $(\widetilde{s_\mu}, \widetilde{s_5}, \widetilde{s_{95}})$, and $(\widetilde{r_\mu}, \widetilde{r_5}, \widetilde{r_{95}})$, which correspond, for each measure, to the mean 5th-percentile, and the mean 95th-percentile of the Dirichlet sampling error estimation method described in section 3. Each mean was computed using 200 Dirichlet samples. The results are also shown in the corresponding columns of Table 1. Note that in most cases, the observed results, e.g., f^*, fall within the 90% confidence interval, e.g., between $\widetilde{f_5}$ and $\widetilde{f_{95}}$.

We also experimented with teams of varying size. The average model checking times were 1.98s, 2.19s, 4.94s, 10.71s, and 42.20s, for team sizes 2 through 6, respectively. For teams of size 7, PRISM ran out of memory on our 4G machine.

5   Conclusion

We presented an approach to analytically construct a team of communicating Markovian robots that achieves a specific task with quantified probability of success. We first construct a set of Discrete Time Markov Chains (DTMCs) that each capture a specific "projection" of the behavior of an individual robot. Next, given a specific team, we construct the DTMC for its behavior by combining the projection DTMCs appropriately. Finally, we compute the performance of the team using Probabilistic Model Checking. The best team is selected by repeating this process for multiple candidates. We also show how to quantify the error in our results due to finite sampling when constructing the projection DTMCs. We prove the correctness of our approach formally, and also validate it empirically on a mine detection task by a team of communicating Kilobots. An important direction for future work is to extend our approach to non-Markovian systems, and also to quantify the error due to discretization of time and space.

References

1. V-REP: Virtual robot experimentation platform (2014)
2. Chen, T., Diciolla, M., Kwiatkowska, M.Z., Mereacre, A.: Quantitative Verification of Implantable Cardiac Pacemakers. In: Proceedings of the 33rd Real-Time Systems Symposium (RTSS 2012), San Juan, PR, USA, pp. 263–272. IEEE Computer Society (December 2012)
3. Devroye, L.: Non-Uniform Random Variate Generation. Springer, New York (1986)
4. Ghorbal, K., Duggirala, P.S., Kahlon, V., Ivančić, F., Gupta, A.: Efficient probabilistic model checking of systems with ranged probabilities. In: Finkel, A., Leroux, J., Potapov, I. (eds.) RP 2012. LNCS, vol. 7550, pp. 107–120. Springer, Heidelberg (2012)
5. Hansson, H., Jonsson, B.: A Logic for Reasoning about Time and Reliability. Formal Aspects of Computing (FACJ) 6(5), 512–535 (1994)
6. Heath, J., Kwiatkowska, M.Z., Norman, G., Parker, D., Tymchyshyn, O.: Probabilistic model checking of complex biological pathways. Theoretical Computer Science (TCS) 391(3), 239–257 (2008)
7. Huang, J.: Maximum likelihood estimation of dirichlet distribution parameters. Technical report, Robotics Institute, Carnegie Mellon University (2005)
8. Konur, S., Dixon, C., Fisher, M.: Analysing robot swarm behaviour via probabilistic model checking. In: Robotics and Autonomous Systems (2011)
9. Kwiatkowska, M., Norman, G., Parker, D.: PRISM 4.0: Verification of Probabilistic Real-Time Systems. In: Gopalakrishnan, G., Qadeer, S. (eds.) CAV 2011. LNCS, vol. 6806, pp. 585–591. Springer, Heidelberg (2011)
10. Kwiatkowska, M.Z., Norman, G., Sproston, J.: Probabilistic Model Checking of Deadline Properties in the IEEE 1394 FireWire Root Contention Protocol. Formal Aspects of Computing (FACJ) 14(3), 295–318 (2003)
11. Rubenstein, M., Ahler, C., Nagpal, R.: Kilobot: A low cost scalable robot system for collective behaviors. In: IEEE Intl. Conf on Robotics and Automation (ICRA), p. 6 (2012)
12. Segala, R.: Modeling and Verification of Randomized Distributed Real-Time Systems. PhD thesis, Massachusetts Institute of Technology, Cambridge, MA, USA, Available as Technical Report MIT/LCS/TR-676 (1995)

Modelling and Analysis of a Redundant Mobile Robot Architecture Using AADL

Geoffrey Biggs[1], Kiyoshi Fujiwara[1], and Keiju Anada[2]

[1] Intelligent Systems Research Institute
National Institute of Advanced Industrial Science and Technology (AIST)
AIST Tsukuba Central 2, Tsukuba, Ibaraki 305-8568, Japan
[2] aRbot, Inc., Japan

Abstract. As the complexity of robots deployed in the real world increases, the use of formal specifications in the development of safety-critical robot systems is becoming increasingly important. A formal specification gives confidence in the correctness, completeness, and accuracy of a system design. In this paper, we present a formal specification of a redundant control architecture for a mobile robot in the form of a model. The model is created using the Architecture Analysis and Design Language (AADL). This formal language allows the model to be analysed to prove system properties of interest. In this case, we are interested in proving the response time of the robot to external obstacles and to internal errors. We present the model and the results of these analyses with the goal of proving that the architecture is sufficiently safe for use in a safe robot wheelchair.

1 Introduction

As with any cyber-physical or embedded system, an important part of designing a robot is specifying the architecture of the control system that turns sensor readings and planned actions into controlled motions of the robot. Sensors, micro-processors, control software, actuators, and the communication buses that connect them must all be designed to provide sufficient capacity, in each respective way, to perform their role in the overall control system.

For system correctness, it is not enough to simply design the control system. It is also necessary to ensure that the design will satisfy the system's requirements. When the system being developed is safety-critical, there is a further need to provide proof that a design is correct and satisfies the system's functional and non-functional requirements.

An approach to both ensuring and proving that a design is suitable is the application of formal methods, including formal specifications of design. The use of formal methods during the design of cyber-physical and embedded systems is becoming increasingly common. There have been several noteworthy projects to produce complete tool chains using formal methods for system design, such as the TOPCASED project [9]. Their continued growth is an indication of the

D. Brugali et al. (Eds.): SIMPAR 2014, LNAI 8810, pp. 146–157, 2014.

success they have had in introducing formally-based methodology to fields such as aerospace and railway development.

Formal methods allow a design to be proven to be correct, in that it contains no mistakes in specification. For example, designed wiring between components can be shown to be correct in such terms as the information carried, or that all necessary connections exist in the design. Formal specifications of behaviour, for example finite automata, can ensure that the system's behaviour is defined for all known inputs. The use of formal methods can reduce the time to develop a system through reduction of other parts of the development process; for example, the IEC 61508 standard for Functional Safety of Programmable Electrical/Electronic Devices specifically states that the use of formal methods in design of software reduces the necessary testing that must be performed [2,3].[1] Analyses performed using a formal method can even aid in debugging problems found during implementation, such as solving a bottleneck in system response by identifying parts of the system that may experience high latencies.

This article describes the application of a formal method during the design of the control system architecture for a safety-monitoring motorised wheelchair. The wheelchair applies robot control technology to avoid collisions when possible and reduce impact forces when not. It also ensures that the wheelchair is robust to failures and is guaranteed to come to a safe stop in the case of one. A formal specification language was used to specify the control architecture of the wheelchair. Formal analyses were performed on this specification to determine such factors as the latency in responding to the appearance of an obstacle, the response time to a failure, and the suitability of the chosen micro-controller hardware. Based on the analyses, we claim that the control system architecture is correct and sufficient to provide reasonable safety to a user of a motorised wheelchair under the analysed scenarios.

The next section discusses the formal specification language used in this work. Following that, the formal model of the control system architecture is given in Section 3. Analysis results are given in Section 4.

2   AADL

The Architecture Analysis and Design Language (AADL) is a modelling language for the formal modelling of embedded system architectures [4]. Its goal is modelling and formally proving the correctness of cyber-physical and embedded system architectures, allowing the architecture of even extremely complex systems to be designed accurately It is a declarative language, focusing on structure rather than behaviour. It supports modelling a system's software structure, the structure of the execution hardware, the mapping of software to execution hardware, and the sensors, actuators and similar devices that provide interfaces to the external world.

---

[1] The standard *requires* the use of formal methods at higher safety integrity levels – see Table A.2 of Part 3 of the standard.

AADL has a formal semantics and fixed syntax. This means that it is possible to check a model for correctness. The capacity to specify properties of all components in the model, including software, processors, and communication buses, allows a developer to perform model analysis to examine properties of the system such as execution time or communication bandwidth utilisation. We describe some analyses in Section 4.

AADL was chosen for this work due to its formality. We have previously used SysML to model the entire wheelchair system, including its control architecture, during the design stages [5]. SysML added structure to the design information that was particularly a benefit in establishing traceability between system requirements and system design; we were able to establish that each functional requirement relating to necessary features of the system was satisfied. However, we found that the semi-formal nature of the SysML model limited its usefulness both for proving design correctness and for analysing properties of the control architecture. By contrast, AADL's formality makes such analyses simple. At the same time, AADL is tightly focused on the embedded control system's structural design, whereas SysML can model a wider range of information such as requirements, testing and behaviour.[2]

There are several tools available for specifying and analysing AADL models. In this work, we use the Open Source AADL Tool Environment (OSATE) tool version 2.0.5 [7]. It provides a compiler for AADL models, syntax and semantic error checkers, a model correctness checker, and several analysis tools including connection analysis, thread execution schedule analysis, and flow latency analysis.

The next section describes our application of AADL to the design of the safety-monitoring wheelchair's control architecture. Our use of the OSATE tool to perform analyses on this model is described in Section 4.

3   Safe Mobile Robot Architecture Model

A model of the control architecture for a safety-monitoring wheelchair, described in [8], has been developed using AADL. This architecture is designed to conform to SIL2 of the IEC 61508 standard for electrical/electronic/programmable electronic safety-related systems [1]. This section briefly summarises the key points of the architecture and describes the model.

3.1   Architecture Description

The control architecture modelled in this work is used to control the wheel speed of a motorised wheelchair. Wheel speed must be controlled in response to velocity command inputs from an external system, such as a human operating a joystick.

The controller provides two safety aspects. The first aspect is safety against collisions. Range sensors cover the wheelchair's entire surroundings, watching for

---

[2] Planned and recently-produced extensions to the AADL standard (known as "annexes") add support for error modelling and requirements modelling.

obstacles. The wheelchair's velocity is limited appropriately when obstacles are near. Additionally, a contact sensor detects impacts on the wheelchair, bringing it to an immediate halt when one is detected.

The second aspect is safety against failures. Redundancy is used in the form of dual CPUs. They each control a single motor/wheel and run identical software (with an exception for configuring one to rotate its motor in the opposite direction). The two CPUs also continuously monitor each other. If a failure is detected, such as non-responsiveness or an incorrect response to a command or sensor input, the partner CPU will halt its own motor.[3]

The redundant controller architecture has been implemented on real hardware. The execution hardware used is two Renesas SH72AW CPUs, one for each redundant motor control unit. These run at 160 MHz and have 96 kB of RAM. Two AC motors are used, one for each wheel/drive unit. Each motor controller/motor combination drives a single wheel. Four Hokuyo UAM-01LP-T301 laser range finders, which are certified to SIL2 of IEC 61508, are used for ranged sensing, and a fault-tolerant strip switch provides contact sensing.

3.2   AADL Model

This section presents an AADL model of the control architecture described in Section 3.1. The model describes only the structural architecture of the wheelchair control system.

The model is organised into several systems and black box devices that are composed to produce the whole control system. This top-level structure is shown in Figures 1 (information connections) and 2 (hardware buses). The laser range finders, touch sensors, and the motors and their related control hardware are all treated as black boxes with known external interfaces and known activity periods.[4] Note also the presence in the model of several buses, such as the wire connections to the sensors and the CAN bus connections to the motors. The presence of execution hardware such as this in the model allows for analysis of sense-compute-actuate latencies and bus bandwidth utilisation. In this model, each individual bus has been specified to allow the analysis of bus bandwidth use.

The two redundant CPUs and the software they execute (named a "control unit" in the discussion below) are each represented by instances of the same sub-system design. This sub-system is shown in Figure 3. Each control unit contains both the software to be executed (the ctrl_proc process) and the computing hardware to execute it. The software itself is divided into five separate tasks, shown in Figure 4. These each have a role in turning sensor and control inputs into motor commands while monitoring safety. Each thread's required real-time execution deadline and processor budget is specified in the model. Modelling the software allows for analysis of processor load and deadline achievement.

---

[3] Halting the motor of the failed CPU is achieved through a watchdog timer on the motor control input of the motor controller and brakes that engage when power is removed.

[4] The activity periods of sensors and actuators are necessary during latency analyses.

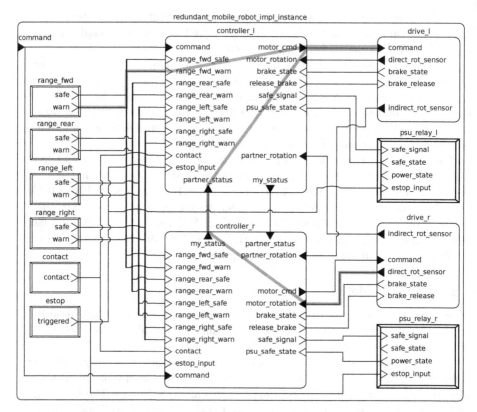

Fig. 1. The information connections at the top level of the control architecture model

The drive units are similarly represented by two instances of the same sub-system design, shown in Figure 5. Each drive unit includes an AC motor (which includes a rotation sensor), a brake, a separate rotation sensor using a different technology to that used in the in-built sensor of the motor, and the motor control unit that turns motor torque commands into AC voltages to drive the motor.

The model contains 796 SLOC of AADL.

4   Formal Analysis

The formal semantics of AADL allow a variety of analyses to be performed on an instantiated model. The limit to what can be analysed is determined by the available tools and the properties provided in the model. This section describes some of the analyses performed on the safety architecture model.

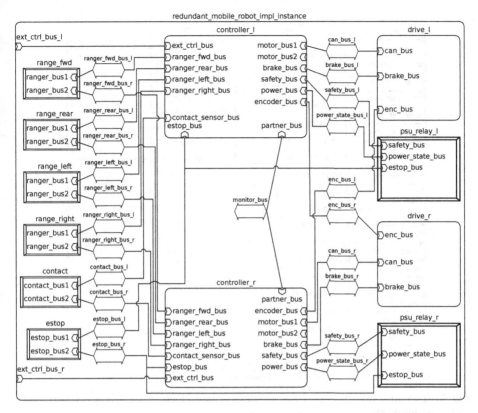

Fig. 2. The buses at the top level of the control architecture model

4.1   Obstacle Response Latency

The response time of an embedded system depends on the latency between receiving an input and producing an output. In AADL, such latencies can be modelled and calculated using *flows* [6]. A flow is a path through a system specified by the model developer. Typically it is from an input (the *source*), through the communication and processing of that input (the *path*), and to an output (the *sink*). Flows may be hierarchically specified, with one flow making use of sub-flows along its path.

We have used flows to analyse two latencies in the control system that are important to safety. The first, described below, is the latency of responding to the detection of an obstacle. The second, described in the next section, is the latency of one drive unit responding to an error in the opposite side's drive unit.

The flow of signals through the control system from a range sensor to the motor controlling a wheel is illustrated in Figures 1 to 5, highlighted in blue.

The results of the latency calculations performed by OSATE for this flow are given in Table 1. The latency is calculated for the worst case. It includes the

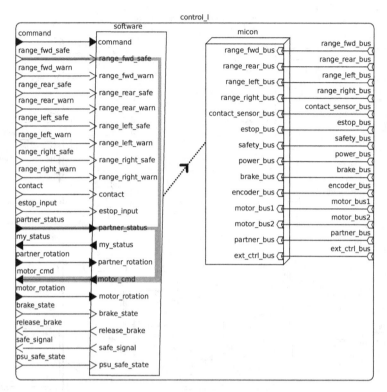

Fig. 3. The structure of one of the redundant control units, including software and execution hardware

maximum possible delay from the range sensor (30 ms, corresponding to its cycle time), delays due to sampling and scheduling of software in the processor, the communication delay across the CAN bus to the motor controller (at a transfer speed of 1 $Mbps$), and the response time of the motor controller and motor itself, excluding physically-limited response time.

The calculated total worst-case latency is 160.064 ms. At the maximum velocity of the robot of 8 km/h, it corresponds to a distance of 0.356 m. At the more common velocity of 4 km/h, it is 0.178 m.

4.2   Partner Monitoring Latency

The worst-case latency of responding to an error has been calculated. The error used is the left drive unit responding to a failure in the right drive unit, manifesting as a mis-match between the right encoder reading and what the right control unit reports for motor rotation. The flow of signals through the control system from the right rotation sensor to the motor controlling the left wheel is illustrated in Figures 1 to 5, highlighted in red.

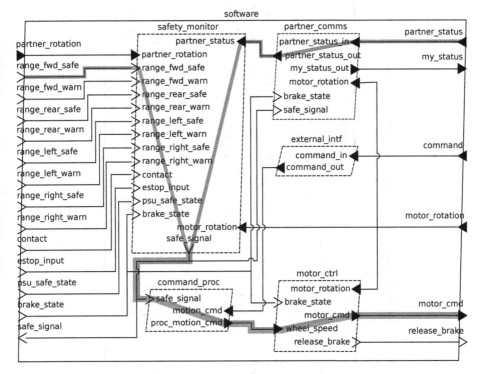

Fig. 4. The structure of the software that executes within each microprocessor

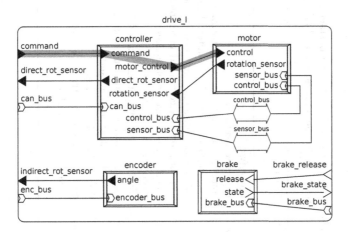

Fig. 5. The structure of each drive unit

Table 1. The latency of responding to an obstacle, as calculated by OSATE. Time columns are the real-time deadline, time due to communication, and additional time.

Model element	Name	Deadline or Connection	Sampling	Flow spec	Additional	Total
device	range_fwd	0.0 μs	0.0 μs	30.0 ms	30.0 ms	30.0 ms
connection	range_fwd.warn → control_l.software.safety_monitor.range_fwd_warn	0.0 μs	0.0 μs	0.0 μs	30.0 ms	30.0 ms
thread	control_l.software.safety_monitor:obs_flow	10.0 ms	10.0 ms	0.0 μs	20.0 ms	40.0 ms
connection	safety_monitor.safe_signal → command_proc.safe_signal	0.0 μs	0.0 μs	0.0 μs	20.0 ms	60.0 ms
thread	control_l.software.command_proc:unsafe_flow	10.0 ms	10.0 ms	0.0 μs	20.0 ms	70.0 ms
connection	command_proc.proc_motion_cmd → motor_ctrl.wheel_speed	0.0 μs	0.0 μs	0.0 μs	20.0 ms	90.0 ms
thread	control_l.software.motor_ctrl:cmd_flow	10.0 ms	10.0 ms	0.0 μs	10.0 ms	100.0 ms
connection	control_l.software.motor_ctrl.motor_cmd → drive_l.controller:command	64.0 μs	0.0 μs	0.0 μs	10.064 ms	100.0 ms
device	drive_l.controller:cmd_flow	50.0 ms	0.0 μs	50.0 ms	60.064 ms	100.0 ms
connection	controller.motor_control → motor.control	0.0 μs	0.0 μs	0.0 μs	60.064 ms	160.064 ms
device	drive_l.motor:cmd_flow_sink	0.0 μs	0.0 μs	0.0 μs	60.064 ms	100.0 ms
Total						160.064 ms

Unfortunately, a bug in the version of OSATE used prevented us from calculating the latency of the complete path. An exception is triggered when calculating the latency of the serial link between the two controllers, preventing the latency calculation from completing. To work around this, we split the flow into two, one for each side of the partner monitoring link.

The latency of the flow from its source to the my_status port of controller_r is given in Table 2. This is the time for the right control unit to produce a status message. The latency of the flow from the partner_status port of controller_l to its sink is given in Table 3. This is the time for the left control unit to detect and respond to the error. As in the previous analysis, it includes the various delays and latencies involved in controlling the motor.

The latency of the serial monitoring link between the two controllers has been calculated as 2.08 *ms*. This is based on a transmission speed of 38400 *bps* and a message size (from the model) of 10 bytes.

Based on the two latency values and the manual calculation of the latency of the serial monitoring link, the total worst-case latency is 142.186 *ms*. At the maximum velocity of the robot of 8 *km/h*, it corresponds to a distance of 0.316 *m*. At the more common velocity of 4 *km.h*, it is 0.158 *m*.

5   Discussion

The latency analyses of the previous section indicate that the control architecture provides safety in the two analysed scenarios. However, we say "indicate" here rather than "prove" due to the problem with the tool mentioned in Section 4.2. The failure in calculating one of the latencies led us to doubt the calculation results, and a manual estimate had to be calculated to confirm they are in the expected range, but even then we do not consider them to be absolute proof.

A formal specification gives confidence in the correctness of the specification. It does so through correctness checks on the specification for internal consistency and consistency with the formal model in use. In our case, these checks are performed when the AADL model is compiled; they confirm that the specification is error-free, but not that the design is error-free.

Analyses on the specification give confidence in the design, and are used to confirm that the design is error-free with regard to the requirements. In the analyses presented in this paper, this is the need for the control architecture to have a sufficiently fast response time.

In both cases, however, we are relying on a tool. Our experience illustrates the importance of having reliable tools; without a tool that can be trusted to be correct, a formal specification drops in value. Manually checking for errors and performing analyses is far less reliable than automated checks and analyses, and automation is essential for large systems.

Fortunately, AADL is a standardised language. There are several for-cost tools in existence that may be more reliable than the free OSATE tool. Our experience shows the need to choose tools carefully, but it does not negate the benefits of AADL.

Table 2. The latency of responding to an error (right controller side), as calculated by OSATE

Model element	Name	Deadline or Connection	Sampling	Flow spec	Additional	Total
device	drive.r.motor	0.0 μs	0.0 μs	0.001 μs	0.001 μs	0.001 μs
Connection	motor.rotation_sensor → controller.rotation_sensor	0.0 μs	0.0 μs	0.001 μs	0.001 μs	0.001 μs
device	drive.r.controller:mot.rot.flow	0.1 μs	0.1 μs	0.101 μs	0.101 μs	0.101 μs
Connection	drive.r.controller:direct_rot_sensor → control.r.software.partner.partner_comms:motor_rotation	32 μs	0.0 μs	32.101 μs	32.101 μs	32.101 μs
thread	control.r.software.partner.partner_comms:motrot.out.flow	10.0 ms	0.0 μs	10.0 ms	10.032101 ms	10.032101 ms
Total					20.032101 ms	20.032101 ms

Table 3. The latency of responding to an error (left controller side), as calculated by OSATE

Model element	Name	Deadline or Connection	Sampling	Flow spec	Additional	Total
thread	control.l.software.partner_comms	0.0 μs	10.0 ms	0.0 μs	10.0 μs	10.0 μs
Connection	partner_comms.partner_status_out → safety_monitor.partner_status	0.0 μs	0.0 μs	0.0 μs	10.0 μs	10.0 μs
thread	control.l.software.safety_monitor:error_flow	10.0 ms	10.0 ms	0.0 μs	10.01 ms	10.01 ms
Connection	safety_monitor.safe_signal → command_proc.safe_signal	0.0 μs	0.0 μs	0.0 μs	10.0 ms	20.01 ms
thread	control.l.software.command_proc:unsafe_flow	10.0 ms	10.0 ms	0.0 μs	20.0 ms	30.01 ms
Connection	command_proc.proc_motion_cmd → motor_ctrl.wheel_speed	0.0 μs	0.0 μs	0.0 μs	20.0 ms	50.01 ms
thread	control.l.software.motor_ctrl:cmd_flow	10.0 ms	10.0 ms	0.0 μs	10.0 ms	60.01 ms
Connection	control.l.software.motor_ctrl.motor_cmd → drive.l.controller.command	64.0 μs	0.0 μs	0.0 μs	10.064 μs	70.074 ms
device	drive.l.controller:cmd_flow	50.0 ms	0.0 μs	50.0 ms	60.064 ms	60.01 ms
Connection	controller.motor_control → motor:control	0.0 μs	0.0 μs	0.0 μs	60.064 ms	120.074 ms
device	drive.l.motor:cmd_flow_sink	0.0 μs	0.0 μs	1.0 μs	60.064 ms	60.01 ms
Total						120.074 ms

The information stored in the AADL model enables many other analyses relevant to the correct design of robots. For example, the specification can be checked for fairness to all entities using a communication bus, based on the rate of message production of each entity. Such analyses depend on tool support; future work should focus on producing analysis tools useful to robot systems.

6 Conclusions

In this work, we have used the AADL formal specification language to specify the design of the redundant control architecture of a safety-monitoring motorised wheelchair. The formal semantics and syntax of AADL shows that the specification is correct.

Using this model, we have formally analysed the control architecture design to indicate that the worst-case latency of response to sensor input and failure is sufficiently low. In both cases, the response time is sufficiently short given the maximum speed of the wheelchair. The dominant factor in safety response speed can be considered the braking speed of the wheelchair, not the control system response time.

References

1. Functional safety of electrical/electronic/programmable electronic safety-related systems. International Electrotechnical Commission (IEC) (2010)
2. Functional safety of electrical/electronic/programmable electronic safety-related systems Part 2: Requirements for electrical/electronic/programmable electronic safety-related systems, ch. 7, p. 40. International Electrotechnical Commission (IEC) (2010)
3. Functional safety of electrical/electronic/programmable electronic safety-related systems Part 3: Software requirements, ch. 7, pp. 35–36. International Electrotechnical Commission (IEC) (2010)
4. Architecture Analysis & Design Language (AADL) (AS5506B). SAE International (2012)
5. Biggs, G., Sakamoto, T., Fujiwara, K., Anada, K.: Experiences with model-centred design methods and tools in safe robotics. In: 2013 IEEE/RSJ International Conference on Intelligent Robots and Systems (IROS), pp. 3915–3922 (November 2013)
6. Feiler, P., Hansson, J.: Flow latency analysis with the Architecture Analysis & Design Language (AADL). Tech. rep., Software Engineering Institute, Carnegie-Mellon University (2008)
7. Feiler, P.H., Gluch, D.P.: Model-Based Engineering with AADL, ch. 15. Addison-Wesley, Westford (2012)
8. Fujiwara, K., Nakabo, Y., Anada, K., Biggs, G., Mizuguchi, D.: The prototype hardware of the dependable robotic cart. In: Proceedings of the 2012 JSME Conference on Robotics and Mechatronics (2012)
9. Topcased, http://www.topcased.org/

Fault Avoidance in Development
of Robot Motion-Control Software
by Modeling the Computation*

Yury Brodskiy, Robert Wilterdink, Stefano Stramigioli, and Jan Broenink

Robotics and Mechatronics, Faculty EEMCS,
University of Twente, The Netherlands
y.brodskiy@me.com,
J.F.Broenink@utwente.nl

Abstract. In this article, we present the process of modeling control algorithms as means to increase reliability of software components. The approach to developing Embedded Control Software (ECS) is tailored to Component-Based Software Development (CBSD). Such tailoring allows to re-use the ECS development process tools in a development process for robotics software. Model-to-text transformation of the ECS design tool is extended to model-to-component transformation suitable for CBSD frameworks. The development process and tools are demonstrated by a use case.

1   Introduction

The quest for safety and autonomy of a robot is extremely complex, and strongly connected to concepts of reliability. Robots are designed to perform a variety of tasks in diversified conditions. However, development of a robotic application is a complex and error-prone process which requires integration of results from many engineering domains (software, mechanical, electrical and control engineering). This is especially important in development of robot motion-control software, as this part of the system is critical for reliability of robots. Thus, it is crucial that fault avoidance techniques are exercised to a full possible extent during development of the software.

Current research in software development for robots is focused on Component-Based Software Development (CBSD) [18,19]. CBSD supports the development and reuse of large-grained pieces of robotics software through component-based software frameworks such as ROS [39], Orocos [20,34], SmartSoft [36,37]. To gain the advantages provided by a component-based software framework, the software has to be structured into independent components. This need for structuring of software has triggered research on the application of Model-Driven Engineering (MDE) techniques to CBSD.

---

* The research leading to these results has received funding from the European Community's Seventh Framework Programme (FP7/2007-2013) under grant agreement no. FP7-ICT-231940-BRICS (Best Practice in Robotics).

D. Brugali et al. (Eds.): SIMPAR 2014, LNAI 8810, pp. 158–169, 2014.

In CBSD, models are used to design and analyze the software architecture [38]. Following the concept of separation of concerns as presented in [21], a software architecture can be described by models formulated in terms of Computation, Composition, Connection [26], Configuration [18] and Coordination [27], referred to as 5C. Composition and Connection indicate the software architecture of the system. Configuration and Coordination describe parametric and discrete states of the system. Computation stands for the actual algorithm implemented in the component, for example of a control law such as a PID controller. Modeling the Computation is not part of the existing CBSD practice.

To make sure that modeling the Computation *becomes* a part of a well-defined development process, we combine two relevant development processes – The Robotic Application development Process (RAP) [29] and the Embedded Control Software (ECS) design trajectory [15,14]. RAP has been proposed by the BRICS project as a result of simultaneously tailoring of over 25 different development processes to the robotics domain and CBSD. The ECS design trajectory represents practices in development of software for embedded applications and explicitly advocates modeling of the algorithm of a software component (controller) [14]. Both development processes use modeling of software to achieve a higher quality product. Nevertheless, these development processes have different perspectives on software modeling. We argue that combining these models results in a uniform description of the software on the modeling level, thus allowing to gain the benefits from both development processes.

Throughout this article, the combination of these two development processes is discussed. Relevant terms used in MDE in application to CBSD are adopted from [21,10]. The dependability related terms are adopted from [1]. The motivation for modeling the Computation to gain software reliability improvement is presented in Section 2. The combination of RAP and ECS design trajectory is discussed in Section 3. The integration of tools used in RAP and the ECS design trajectory is presented in Section 4. The resulting tool-chain is demonstrated by a use case presented in Section 5.

2 Modeling the Computation to Increase Software Dependability

Modeling the Computation is describing the actual algorithm to be implemented. The result of Modeling the Computation is a *computation model*. It represents the mathematical nature of the algorithm. Such model leaves out platform, operating system, framework or programming-language specific elements. A computation model can be constructed based on several different meta-models: transfer functions, logic circuits, Bayesian networks, neural networks, bond graphs.

A computational model serves three purposes:

- A model improves understanding of functioning of the algorithm, thus revealing the points where robustness should be improved.
- A model, supported by simulation tools, can be used to study the behavior of the algorithm, in an attempt to verify its qualities.

– A model can be automatically transformed to a formulation needed for the next step in the development process.

These purposes overlap with means of improving a system's reliability, typical for a development process: fault prevention, fault removal and fault forecasting (Figure 1).

Fault Prevention ⟵⟶ Modeling
Fault Removal ⟵ Code generation
Fault Forecasting ⟶ Simulation

Fig. 1. Mapping of reliability means on purposes of a Computation model

A developer models the Computation to obtain a simplified but competent representation of the algorithm (the model of algorithm). This is achieved by choosing the modeling language that supports an effective and simple representation of the algorithm that is being developed, i.e. the chosen modeling language is more expressive than a general-purpose implementation language. The general-purpose language might obscure the design intent due to a vast number of implementation details, while a model allows to focus on design of the algorithm avoiding implementation issues [38]. The model of algorithm provides a clear expression of the design intent and thus prevents logic faults. It especially concerns the class of development, human-made, deliberate, nonmalicious faults [1] as the trade-offs made at development time are made explicit.

Faults (class of development, human-made, non deliberate, nonmalicious [1]) can be prevented by modeling the Computation with appropriate tool support. The composition rules, defined by the meta-model, can be used to prevent illegal constructs that would result in faults, which are typical unintended actions done by mistake. This enforcement of composition rules on model level also prevents faults occurring due to misunderstanding between collaborating teams [13], which also classify as non-deliberate, human-made faults. Furthermore, appropriate tool support allows to automate the transformation of models to formulations needed for next steps in the development process. This allows reducing significantly the number of human-made faults as the developer is excluded form the transformation process.

Simulation of the algorithm, one of the purposes of modeling the Computation, supports both fault removal and fault forecasting means (Figure 1). This fault removal process is similar to the approach of iteratively refining models, used in the ECS design trajectory [15,14]. In simulation, a designer has full control over the system states, outputs and inputs, thus any situation or behavior can be tested, and the response can be verified. An example of such use of simulations is fault modeling and fault injection [13]. This approach prescribes building a model of faulty behavior in addition to modeling expected behavior. This approach can be used to evaluate performance of the proposed fault-tolerant control. Overall, use of simulateable models simplifies and increases the quality of the fault removal and fault forecasting processes.

3   Modeling the Computation in the Development Process

Modeling of software in a development process can be done from different perspectives (5C as described in [21]), moreover modeling software from each perspective leads to improvement in software quality. Thus by modeling software from all perspectives allows to maximize the benefits from using models in development process. A development process has to indicate at which step each model has to be developed. Furthermore, the steps at which the models are being synchronized and transformed into implementation have to be indicated such that inconsistencies in models are avoided.

The development processes noted above (Section 1) use modeling of software as one of the main activities. Nevertheless, these development processes have different perspectives on software modeling. The goal of combining these development processes is to indicate steps of synchronization and transformation of models into implementation. That would enable modeling software from all perspectives, and development of appropriate tool support as demonstrated later.

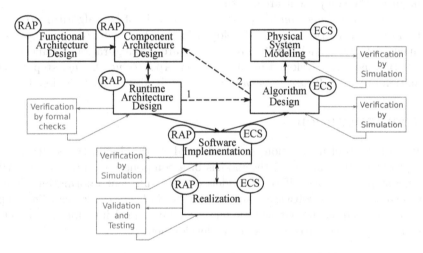

Fig. 2. The proposed ECS trajectory combined with architectural elements form RAP

The updated ECS trajectory (Figure 2) combines the modeling procedures of the ECS trajectory [16] and RAP [29]. Development steps inherited from RAP, indicated with RAP tag, represent the process of modeling the software architecture. Development steps inherited from ECS, indicated with ECS tag, represent the process of modeling the algorithm of the application. Steps, indicated by both tags, are prescribed by both RAP and ECS, and require information about the algorithm and the software architecture. By combining modeling processes of RAP and ECS the information about algorithm and software architecture is captured inform of models before the *Software Implementation* step. These models are complimentary to each other as they contain different type of information about the software system. The combination of these models represents a uniform model of a software component, which covers all 5 aspects of a software system (5C [21]).

To maintain synchronization between models from RAP and ECS two additional interlinks (the dashed lines nr. 1 and nr. 2 (Figure 2)) between architecture design and algorithm design are added. These interlinks indicate information flow during modeling and emphasize the iterative style of model development.

Line nr. 1 (Figure 2) indicates that the constraints imposed by the runtime architecture have to be taken into account during Algorithm design. The analysis of the effects of the run-time architecture on the algorithm performance allows to forecast possible failures and develop algorithms that tolerate these.

Line nr. 2 (Figure 2) indicates that a detailed knowledge about algorithm functioning is required for building the efficient component architecture. For example, a component architecture built without that knowledge might result in unreasonable communication requirements (such extreme band-with or unachievable small latency). Inclusion of component architecture into Algorithm Design step allows to identify these issues at the modeling stage and can lead to restructuring the component architecture.

At the *Software Implementation* step, the models of the algorithm (Computation or Coordination aspects developed in the *Algorithm Design* step) are combined with the model of software architecture (Configuration, Connection, Composition aspects developed in the *Runtime Architecture Design* step). The automation of this *Software Implementation* step is discussed in Section 4.

4   Tool Integration

The goal of the tool integration is, as indicated by the design trajectory (Figure 2), to facilitate combining the models of a component resulted from RAP and ECS steps. Moreover, if these models contain sufficient information about all of the 5 aspects of a software system (5C), the *Software Implementation* step can be automated, such that the models are transformed into forms/artifacts necessary in the consecutive steps of the development process.

Table 1. Tools and their focus in modeling

Configuration & Connection & Composition	Computation & Coordination
BRIDE[9]	MatLAB[30]
SmartSoft[36]	**20-sim[23]**
OpenRTM[33]	LabView[31]
Proteus[35]	OpenModelica[32]
TERRA[3]	Dymola[24]

The development process (Figure 2) can be used with a number of tools that provide similar functionality such as presented in Table 1.

To exemplify the tool integration, the tools BRIDE and 20-sim are used as suggested by the authors of RAP [29] and the ECS design trajectory [15].

The BRIDE toolchain [9] has been developed in the project BRICS to support RAP. It facilitates the design of components and component compositions for robotic application deployment. It offers graphical editors to model components using the BRICS Component Model (BCM) [21], with model-to-model transformations to the software frameworks Orocos RTT [34,22] and ROS [39].

20-sim was developed for the design of mechatronic systems and supports the ECS design trajectory as development methodology. It embodies the concept of concurrent design of mechanical, electrical and control parts of the system. 20-sim provides modeling primitives for designing the Computation. It can be used for both modeling of control algorithms and physical systems behaviour. 20-sim allows a graphical approach to hierarchical structuring of algorithms.

4.1   CBSD- and Computation-Model Integration

The transformation of any Computation meta-model into a component meta-model used by the CBSD tools (like BRIDE) results in a model reduction since the concepts of computation are not supported by such tools. To preserve the computation elements a second artifact is generated – the code (Figure 3). The combination of the generated code and the model completely represent a single component which can be used in the next phase of the development process, i.e. *Realization*.

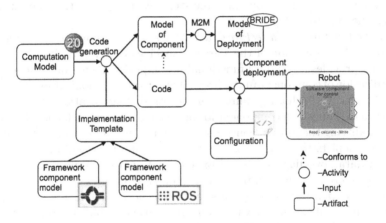

Fig. 3. Model-to-component transformation

The integration between BRIDE and 20-sim is structured as a 2-step process [12]. First 20-sim transforms the Computation model into a code and a model of the component (Figure 3). Second, the model of the component is analysed and, by using predefined rules, a BRIDE model of the component is generated. The newly generated model contains information about the Communication and Configuration (component interface). The Coordination and Computation of the component are only encoded in the component implementation as BRIDE does not offer primitives to describe these concepts.

5   Use Case Application

5.1   BRICkS Stacking Application

The use case is motion control for the KUKA youBot [4,11] mobile manipulator. The resulting set of software components is termed as *motion stack*. These are implemented using the methodology described above. Orocos RTT was used as target component-based software framework.

Based on Figure 2 some of the steps can be performed in parallel. The Physical System Modeling step can be preformed in parallel to the Functional Architecture Design step. The Component Architecture Design, Run-time Architecture Design and Algorithm Design steps have circular dependency, and therefore require an iterative approach. The Software Implementation and Realization steps are preformed sequentially.

The Physical System Modeling step is presented in detail in [25], and a detailed description of the algorithms is presented in [12,10]. The focus of this paper is the architectural design (Section 5.2), the effect of architecture on algorithm (Section 5.3) and automated transformation of the models into components (Section 5.4).

5.2   Architecture Design

The architecture design is done in three steps, each increase the level of detail at which the system is described.

A generic *functional architecture* of a motion stack [12] is presented in Figure 4. The proposed organization of the software specifies the granularity of the algorithms and provides a standard functional decomposition into components. This standardisation of component functions enables further harmonization of the component interfaces, which is a requirement for introducing variation points [17]. As a result, an exchange of a component for one with a different behavior should not require modifying the motion control structure nor any component internals.

Figure 5 depicts the *component-level architecture* of the motion stack in the form of a data-flow diagram, based on its functional decomposition. The presented architecture is an example of a variability solution.

A *run-time architecture* is required to define how components are executed with their time and concurrency relations. A run-time architecture can introduce various effects that will affect the algorithm performance. For example, message passing between components can introduce time delays, or message losses. To verify the algorithm's robustness and tolerance of such effects, the robot model has to include them. Time delay elements (z^{-1}) indicate possible time delays in the signal exchange, that has been used in algorithm verification.

5.3   Algorithm Design

Algorithm Design (Modeling the Computation) goes in parallel with the design of the architecture. The effects that are introduced by the architecture are used to model and identify unexpected behaviours. Knowledge about the algorithm

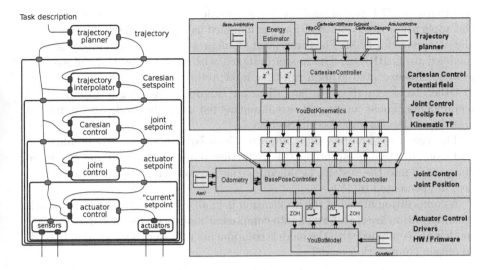

Fig. 4. Conceptual architecture   **Fig. 5.** Architecture of implementation

performance is used to modify the component architecture and generate deployment constraints.

The algorithm design requires a competent model of the system that will be controlled. In the use case, a model developed in [25] was used to verify performance and robustness of the algorithms in a simulation.

The data-flow diagram, shown in Figure 5, has resulted from the architecture design route. Each block of this diagram has to become a software component in the real system and has been filled in with required algorithm according to its task, details of the algorithms are reported in [10].

When the responses of the system meet the task requirements, such model is ready for the Software Implementation step.

5.4   Software Implementation

The parts of the motion stack were implemented as components in the Orocos RTT framework. The data-flow diagram (Figure 5) illustrates the component-level architecture of the motion stack, where blocks in the diagram stand for software components, except z^{-1} which model the effects of communication (latency).

The block at the firmware and drivers level (denoted YouBotModel in Figure 5) implements the communication to the firmware of the youBot actuators and sensors. This component contains operating-system specific and hardware-specific code, and is written in a general purpose language (C++).

The blocks at the "trajectory planner" level of the given application are the Coordination-type components. The Coordination-type components are most efficiently expressed in a FSM, therefore, a DSL for a FSM was used to design the actual trajectory planner components [28]. The existing life-cicle state machine of an Orocos-RTT component has been extended to include states required for the application. The Coordination was modeled using rFSM [28], a textual modeling language for FSM. The component Configuration and Communication were modeled using BRIDE. The model designed with rFSM is part of the working system, it is executed using a run-time interpreter based on Lua.

Other blocks in the data-flow diagram (Figure 5) are 'pure' Computation components. These components are implemented using the model-to-component transformation, as described in Section 4.

The generated component is imported into BRIDE, where Communication and Configuration perspectives can be further refined to connect the generated component into the system. Detailed instructions on using code generation process are presented by [12].

A composition model of the application is finalized using BRIDE. The models of computation are transformed into component models usable by BRIDE. These models are combined with the models components that were developed in BRIDE to obtain composition model.

6   Testing the Methodology

The methodology and the youBot motion stack software, resulting from applying our method, have been tested for reusability and reliability, in three different occasions, namely three BRICS events.

In the first event, the BRICS research Camp 3 [6], the youBot motion stack was used to test re-usability of the components developed using the proposed methodology. The software was provided to students, research camp participants, with only brief explanation of the algorithmic aspects of the system; the Computation and Coordination model were presented. The students have successfully used concepts of modeling of Computation and Coordination to adapt the provided system to their tasks, which demonstrates ease of re-use of the developed components. Two groups of 4 students were using the proposed methodology to modify the provided youBot motion stack using our tool-chain. Moreover, one of the groups modified their own development tools according to our methodology to develop a sequence control for solving their exercises.

In the second event, Automatica 2012 [7], the youBot motion stack was used to test reliability of the components with respect to inter-component communication faults. The algorithms were shown to work with communication over a congested WiFi [12]. The software was subjected to prolonged active use, with frequent interruptions for inspection and parametric changes, which were done for demonstration purposes. The setup was performing flawlessly for the whole week of the trade fair (5 days 8 hours a day). Comparable research software is rarely capable of withstanding such stress testing on first-time use.

At the third event, BRICS research Camp 5 [8] re-usability and reliability of the components were further tested. The software has been given for modification to the BRSU RoboCup@work team, after a brief introduction similar to Research camp 3 student teams. The RoboCup team has successfully modified parts of the motion stack and uses this software for robot control during completions. This also confirms that components developed using the proposed methodology can be easily re-use for different applications with high level of reliability.

The software integration developed in Section 4 is available as open source [40,41] and is being used in other projects of our lab such as for example [5].

7   Conclusions

The combination of both approaches, the CBSD method (RAP) advocated by BRICS and the ECS design trajectory, results in uniform coverage of modeling perspectives (5C) for a software component, and thus results in more reliable robotic components and applications.

The proposed approach contributes to software quality improvement as follows:

- Automated model-to-code transformations reduce faults during implementation of the algorithm by excluding human factor from the process.
- Modeling enables the designer to focus on the chosen aspects of the system (*e.g.* algorithm or architecture), instead of implementation details, and thereby increasing quality of the resulted software.
- Simulation of the algorithm allows to examine hypothetical/dangerous situations using fault modeling techniques, such as sensor failures, which can be used for development of fault tolerance algorithms.

The methodology tests have shown that algorithms verified in simulation have a high success rate on a real setups, which confirms results reported by [14].

To achieve the uniform coverage of modeling perspectives, two different modeling tools had to be used. Each tool focuses on a different engineering role. Two tools were used as an example of the approach, BRIDE and 20-Sim. BRIDE is used to model architecture of the system, and 20-sim is used to model the algorithm.

The presented model-based tool integration shows that tools can easily be combined on the component level. A model-to-model transformation is used to export the component interface of a 20-Sim sub-model to an Orocos-RTT component model. The Orocos-RTT component model is used in BRIDE to design the deployment of a robotic application. The advantage of directly generating the executable component from 20-Sim is that the target component meta-model is not required to support an equivalent Computation meta-model because the algorithm code is directly generated for the target framework. The software integration developed in Section 4 is available as open source code [40,41] and is being used in other projects such as for example [5]. The integration approach is generic such that other tools can be integrated in a similar way.

Future work is further developed the tool-chain getting beyond prototype stage.

The developed tool chain requires creation of separated components for each modeling language being used. The template of Generic Architecture Component

(GAC) presented by [2] demonstrates the need to combine Coordination and Computation primitives in a single component. The tool-chain can be modified to accommodate that requirement.

References

1. Aviezienis, A., Laprie, J.C., Randell, B., Landwehr, C.: Basic Concepts and Taxonomy of Dependable and Secure Computing. IEEE Trans. on Dependable and Secure Computing 1(1), 11–33 (2004)
2. Bezemer, M.M.: Cyber-Physical Systems Software Development. Ph.D. thesis, University of Twente (2013)
3. Bezemer, M.M., Wilterdink, R.J.W., Broenink, J.F.: CSP-Capable Execution Framework. Communicating Process Architectures 68, 157–175 (2011)
4. Bischoff, R., Huggenberger, U., Prassler, E.: KUKA youBot - a mobile manipulator for research and education. In: Proc IEEE Int'l Conf on Robotics and Automation, pp. 1–4 (May 2011)
5. de Boer, H.: Modeling and Control of the Philips Robot Arm. Msc thesis, University of Twente (2012)
6. BRICS: BRICS Research camp 3 (2011),
   http://www.best-of-robotics.org/3rd_researchcamp/MainPage
7. BRICS: BRICS - European Research Project - demonstration booth. 5th International Trade Fair for Automation and Mechatronics (May 2012)
8. BRICS: BRICS Research camp 5 (2012),
   http://www.best-of-robotics.org/5th_researchcamp/MainPage
9. BRICS: BRIDE - the BRIcs Development Environment (January 2013),
   http://www.best-of-robotics.org/bride
10. Brodskiy, Y.: Robust autonomy for interactive robots. University of Twente, Enschede (2014)
11. Brodskiy, Y., Dresscher, D., Stramigioli, S., Broenink, J.F., Yalcin, C.: Design principles, implementation guidelines, evaluation criteria, and use case implementation for robust autonomy. Tech. Rep. D61, The BRICS Project (nr 231940) (January 2011)
12. Brodskiy, Y., Wilterdink, R., Broenink, J.F., Stramigioli, S.: Collection of methods for achieving robust autonomy. Tech. rep. (2013)
13. Broenink, J.F., Fitzgerald, J.F., Gamble, C.J., Ingram, C., Mader, A.H., Marincic, J., Ni, Y., Pierce, K.G., Zhang, X.: D2.3 — Methodological Guidelines 3. Tech. rep., The DESTECS Project (CNECT-ICT-248134) (December 2012)
14. Broenink, J.F., Groothuis, M.A., Visser, P.M., Bezemer, M.M.: Model-Driven Robot-Software Design Using Template-Based Target Descriptions. In: ICRA 2010 Workshop on Innovative Robot Control Architectures for Demanding (Research) Applications, pp. 73–77. IEEE (May 2010)
15. Broenink, J.F., Groothuis, M.A., Visser, P.M., Orlic, B.: A model-driven approach to embedded control system implementation. Control, 137–144 (January 2007)
16. Broenink, J.F., Ni, Y.: Model-driven robot-software design using integrated models and co-simulation. In: Int'l Conf. Embedded Computer Systems, pp. 339–344 (2012)
17. Brugali, D., Gherardi, L., Biziak, A., Luzzana, A., Zakharov, A.: A Reuse-Oriented Development Process for Component-Based Robotic Systems. In: Noda, I., Ando, N., Brugali, D., Kuffner, J.J. (eds.) SIMPAR 2012. LNCS, vol. 7628, pp. 361–374. Springer, Heidelberg (2012)

18. Brugali, D., Scandurra, P.: Component-based Robotic Engineering Part I: Reusable building blocks. Robotics Automation Mag. 16(4), 84–96 (2009)
19. Brugali, D., Shakhimardanov, A.: Component-Based Robotic Engineering (Part II): Systems and models. Robotics Automation Mag. 17(1), 100–112 (2010)
20. Bruyninckx, H.: Open Robot Control Software: the OROCOS project. In: Proc IEEE Int'l Conf on Robotics and Automation, pp. 2523–2528. IEEE (2001)
21. Bruyninckx, H., Hochgeschwender, N., Klotzbucher, M., Soetens, P., Kraetzschmar, G., Brugali, D., Garcia, H., Shakhimardanov, A., Paulus, J., Reckhaus, M., Gherardi, L., Faconti, D.: The BRICS Component Model: a Model-Based Development paradigm for complex robotics software systems. In: Proc of Annual ACM Symposium on Applied Computing, vol. 28, pp. 1758–1764. ACM (2013)
22. Bruyninckx, H., Soetens, P., Koninckx, B.: The real-time motion control core of the Orocos project. In: Proc IEEE Int'l Conf on Robotics and Automation, vol. 2, pp. 2766–2771. IEEE (September 2003)
23. Controllab Products, B.V.: 20-sim (2013), http://www.20sim.com
24. Dassault Systemes AB: Dymola (2013)
25. Dresscher, D., Brodskiy, Y., Breedveld, P., Broenink, J.F.: Modeling of the youBot in a serial link structure using twists and wrenches in a bond graph. In: Proc SIMPAR 2010 Workshop, Darmstadt, pp. 385–400 (2010)
26. Hochgeschwender, N., Gherardi, L., Shakhimardanov, A., Kraetzschmar, G., Brugali, D., Bruyninckx, H.: A Model-based Approach to Software Deployment in Robotics. In: Proc IEEE/RSJ Int'l Conf. on Intelligent Robots and Systems. IEEE/RJS (November 2013)
27. Klotzbucher, M., Biggs, G., Bruyninckx, H.: Pure Coordination using the Coordinator – Configurator Pattern. CoRR abs/1303.0 (2013)
28. Klotzbucher, M., Bruyninckx, H.: A Lightweight Real-Time Executable Finite State Machine Model for Coordination in Robotic Systems. Tech. rep. (2007)
29. Kraetzschmar, G., Shakhimardanov, A., Paulus, J., Hochgeschwender, N., Reckhaus, M.: Deliverable D-2.2: Specifications of Architectures, Modules, Modularity, and Interfaces for the BROCRE Software Platform and Robot Control Architecture Workbench. Tech. rep., BRICS FP7 project deliverable (2010)
30. MathWorks: MatLAB (2013), http://www.mathworks.com
31. National Instruments: LabView (2013)
32. Open Source Open Modelica Consortium: OpenModelica (2013)
33. OpenRTM Project: OpenRTM Project (2013)
34. Orocos Project: Smarter control in robotics & automation (January 2013), http://www.orocos.org
35. Proteus Project: Proteus (2013)
36. Schlegel, C.: SmartSoft: Components and toolchain for robotics (January 2013), http://smart-robotics.sourceforge.net
37. Schlegel, C., Worz, R.: The software framework {SmartSoft} for implementing sensorimotor systems. In: Proc IEEE/RSJ Int'l Conf on Intelligent Robots and Systems, vol. 3, pp. 1610–1616 (1999)
38. Schmidt, D.C.: Model-driven engineering. Computer, 25–31 (2006)
39. Willow Garage: ROS project (January 2013)
40. Wilterdink, R.J.W., Brodskiy, Y., Broenink, J.F.: Eclipse 20-sim update site (February 2013), http://www.ce.utwente.nl/20sim/updates/
41. Wilterdink, R.J.W., Brodskiy, Y., Tadele, T.S., Broenink, J.F.: 20-Sim C-code generation templates and model-to-model transformations (2013), https://git.ce.utwente.nl/20sim

Robotic Engineer's Specifications for a Well-Fitted Model-Driven Control Architecture for Robots

Éric Moliné, Nicolas Morette, Cyril Novales, and Pierre Vieyres

PRISME Laboratory, UPRES n°4229, Université d'Orléans,
63 Av. de Lattre de Tassigny, 18000 Bourges, France
{name.surname}@univ-orleans.fr

Abstract. This paper gives an overview of reflections about more generic robotic architectures models and their associated tools. The objective of our work is not to define a new robot software but rather to specify common robotic requirements for future component-based models. These models could be used as a common-base by the robotic sub-communities whatever the purpose their different robots have been designed for, whatever the targeted hardware, the chosen frameworks or the host operating systems. Even if we are not yet strongly familiar with the specificities of the Model-Driven Architecture (MDA) and with the Domain-Specific Language (DSL), we are self-convinced by the powerful benefits that these two fields could bring to robotics and to robotic architecture models. In this paper, we discuss about the characteristics a robotic architecture model should own to be efficiently designed by software model engineers and easily but efficiently used by robot engineers.

Keywords: Model-Driven Robotic Architecture, Component-based Robot Architecture, Robotics Designer, Robot.

1 Introduction

Being at the crossing point of various research fields, robotics is a fast growing domain that can address lots of applications. At the first ages of the robotics, a single researcher (or engineer) had the capabilities to design a full robotic software architecture well-adapted to a particular purpose. Nowadays, the scale and the scope of robotics have so widely grown that no one can imagine that only one single person may support a large-scale robot architecture design, software development and integration effort. Even if most of the designed robotic architectures of these last decades came from robotics background [1,6,7,9,10,12,14] there is another domain dealing with the general issue of the architecture modeling and that cannot be ignored: the software engineering field. Our starting assumption is that for the design of a new robotic system, the role of each actor shall be clearly identified as well as the efficient tools they will use.

Especially from a robotics business point of view, a full team is required to support large-scale robot architecture design, software development and integration effort. So the key of development success is in the distribution of roles and

D. Brugali et al. (Eds.): SIMPAR 2014, LNAI 8810, pp. 170–181, 2014.

expertise, as it is already done in others domains such as video game. Moreover, as robotic system has to cope with an open-ended surrounding environment, the consequences are that it is impossible for robotic experts to identify all the situations and to code adequate configuration and/or reactions for all of them. As a first analysis of the main roles, we have identified three actors: the robotic expert, the robotic architecture designer and the software model engineer.

The *robotic expert* is the expert in charge of writing and of implementing the algorithms for a given robotic system. The required code can either be a driver-level software, a perception processing algorithm (low-level data processing) or a more abstract reasoning algorithm based on a more complex and abstracted representation of the surrounding environment. The robotic expert provides a strong expertise in his domain, such as 3D perception, navigation, grasping, etc., when implementing specific functions.

The *robotic designer*'s role is to identify functions the designed robotic system must have to fully answer a specific need. He also has to insure that the global behavior of the system takes into account all the bindings between functions. He can be considered as the robotic system integrator or the global architect of the system. Robotic experts and robotic designers are both *roboticians* but in charge of different tasks during the development process.

Finally the last actor is the *software model engineer*. Even if he is not deeply aware of the robotic domain constraints, his added value is to provide the robotic designer with powerful and useful tools well adapted to the definition of a specific robotic model. Figure 1 presents their respective contributions and relationships. Section 2 presents the benefits of software engineering approaches in recent robotics applications and their limitations from a robotic designer's point of view.

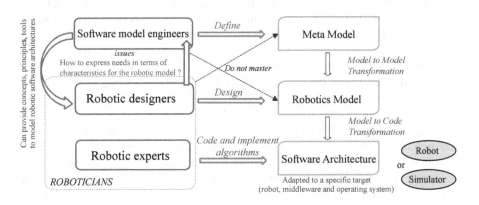

Fig. 1. The interaction scheme among the three robotic identified actors

2   Model-Driven Architectures and Domain-Specific Language

During the development process, software model engineers have the expertise to provide a real benefit to roboticians such as a better software reusability and scalability, whatever the targeted hardware, the chosen frameworks or the robot host operating systems. Recently, model-based approach and domain specific languages have become extensively studied for robotic applications. Recent international conferences reflect this growing popularity, such as Simulation, Modeling, and Programming for Autonomous Robots (SIMPAR) or Domain-Specific Languages and Models for Robotic Systems (DSLROB) that both started in 2009.

Romero-Garcés and al. present [11] how the use of DSL and MDA has improved their component-oriented framework called RoboComp and how they have reduced the number of human-made errors while optimizing the development time. Schlegel and al. propose [13] a model-driven design process that covers all the life cycles of robotic systems from development to deployment through evolution and maintenance. This process starts from the development of a meta-model, with a high level of abstraction to finally end at a completely executable architecture on a specific real-time robot. Here, the different steps are to refine the platform independent model (PIM), where information on the middleware, operating system, programming languages and other properties are unknown, into a platform specific model (PSM) and then into a platform specific implementation (PSI) where robotic experts can write their code. Then the final step consists in the deployment of the components. The Model-Driven Architecture (MDA) methodology allows the developer to automatically refine their models thanks to Model to Model transformations (M2M) or Model to Text transformations (M2T) in order to obtain the source code. With the same objective of improving and facilitating the development of robotic applications, Ortiz and al. created "C-Forge" [8] with its model loader that directly interprets models, while Dhouib and al. introduced a DSL called RobotML (Robotic Modeling Language) [4] which aims robotic designers to specify missions, environments and robot behaviors. RobotML provides a tool chain for robotic systems development that is an extension to the Eclipse-based UML modeling tool Papyrus. The authors report that the use of RoboML allows designers to spend more time on design than on dealing with low level details; moreover, the architecture is made explicit and switching to a new target platform is much easier.

In on hand, even if roboticians should require what they want, they are often not able to express it precisely according to computer sciences. On the others hand, even if they know how quality software systems should be developed in various application domains, software model engineers are not the domains expert and therefore they may misunderstand some of the roboticians' needs and some of specific concepts of robotics are too abstruse for them. The proposed meta-models for a robotic development may use concepts that are useless for roboticians, while forgetting to include useful notions for robotics. Another difficulty comes from technologies, notions and languages used by software model engineers that are too abstruse for roboticians. In the French research project Proteus , RobotML-based model was used but it did not take into account the needs of synchronism between the different components of the architecture. The lack of adequacy between the robotic needs and the software engineering tools drawn from our experience as members of the Proteus[1] project motivated us to draft specifications of a generic robotic model strengthening the bridge between robotics and software engineering. Section 3 presents the main advantages of the most used middlewares and frameworks in robotics.

3   Generic Robotic Model

A first criterion for the generic robotic model is that it has to be a usable and understandable model for robotic designers and engineers. For this reason a component-based model has been chosen, as the notion of components is widely used in robotics [2,3] and enables modularity and reusability needed for efficiency in robotics. Each component has an interface for communication and data exchange with other components and the full interaction of components provides the robotic system with the behaviors or functionality needed to address a specific mission. Orocos[2] is a framework that proposes a complete and reliable solution to address the development of real-time robotic applications. Nevertheless its lack of a suitable GUI to implement the different functions cannot help to clearly identify the role of the robotic designer. Since 2009, a middleware has encountered a quick and wide success in the robotic communities as a large acceptance: the open source robotics platform ROS developed by Willow Garage [10]. ROS is here to route data (called ros topic) from producer components (called here ros node) to consumer components that have subscribed to the needed data. ROS success can be explained by the fact that the philosophy of its designers matches the roboticians' needs: a peer-to-peer communication layer, tools-based, multilingual, thin (reusability) and before all free open-source. Nevertheless, while ROS provides an interesting hardware abstraction, it is not dealing with realtime constraints. Conversely, the ContrACT development environment proposed by LIRMM laboratory[9] is based on an asynchronous supervision process and an applicative real time scheduler that performs a fine grain decomposition of complex synchronous robotic algorithms into individual real-time modules. This approach allows an accurate management of real-time constraints execution and of reactions to constraints violation when problems such as CPU saturation occur.

The notion of component is also strongly linked with the notion of data and data flow, as it is important to define how the components are using information and how they communicate. Widely used solutions to define communication are based on the publisher/subscriber paradigm. Hence, we propose in this paper a specification book from roboticians' requirements. Due to previous discussions in this section, the specifications shall respect the following criteria:

---

[1] http://www.anr-proteus.fr/
[2] http://www.orocos.org/

- being suitable with a component based model,
- having in each component a consumption policy to manage input data,
- having in each component a trigger policy to run code,
- having a markup data policy giving meta data information to the data itself.

4 Specification Book for a Robotic Component-Based Model

Typically, when a robotician describes the component-based control architecture for a robot, these components represent different processes that may run together to perform the targeted application. These components exchange the input/output data by "links" (simulink-like charts). Each component contains a sequential algorithm written in a dedicated language (C++, Python...). Each component produces (or provides) output data, that are required by other component as input data. A virtual "wire" modeling the data flow links the provider-component and the consumer-component. Thus each component presents three parts: one part that receives the data, one part that processes the data, and one part that produces output data. The part that processes the data is typically the algorithm: it uses the received input data and is also triggered by some of these input data. Some of the inputs are stamped as synchronous or asynchronous to manage the policy to run the algorithm. The production of output data is made along the algorithm run. Thus, instead of having a component with input and output ports, we propose to split it in three units: the Input Management Unit (IMU), the Component Core Unit (CCU) and the Ouput Management Unit (OMU), (Fig. 2).

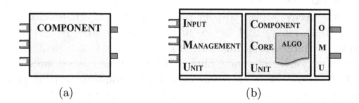

(a)   (b)

Fig. 2. Standard component view (a) and our proposed component model (b)

The CCU contains the algorithm, *i.e.* the code. By definition, the algorithm is sequential and needs input data with its own specified type; it produces data, also with its own specified type. It is written in a language (mainly C/C++). The goal is to keep this code with its own input/output format and its own code lines. It thus becomes reusable in other components in other robotic applications. The IMU performs two tasks: its first task is to receive, to store and to convert input data for the CC Unit. Its second task is to manage the trigger policy of the CCU algorithm. Finally, the task of the OMU is to produce the data to be sent to others components.

4.1   IMU – Collect and Store: Policy of Consumption

The first task of the IMU is to collect the input data: when an input arrives, the IMU stores it in a buffer. The data becomes available to be used by the algorithm of the Component Core Unit (CCU). The CCU can then pick this data to use it in its code. As we assume the components as independent algorithms running in parallel, we must consider that data are produced and consumed at different times. In theory, all algorithms of components can be performed instantaneously, and consume the input data when they are produced. But practically, it is not yet possible: the CPU(s) have time processing limitations, and even when we use a real time OS, all algorithms cannot be performed simultaneously. This implies it cannot be sure that data are consumed by a subscriber component instanta-neously when a provider component produces it. Thus, data must be stored and buffered somewhere between the production time and the consumption time. This task is performed by the IMU. For each input data, the IMU constructs a dedicated buffer with its own policy of consumption.

Classical FIFO and LIFO formalism can be used to extract data from the buffer. FIFO is for "first in / first out" and means that the oldest data which has been inputted in the buffer is the first data to be read. LIFO is for "last in / first out" and means that the last data which has been inputted in the buffer is the data which must be used by the CCU. Once a data has been read -and therefore used by the CCU- there is no longer need to store it in the buffer, thus data is removed. Concerning the LIFO policy of data consumption, a "clear older data" option is also available. Indeed, in some cases it is not useful for the CCU to process previous data as only significant is the last one. Situations like emergency obstacles avoidance only need the latest information from proximetry sensors or obstacles detection components. With the clear older data option activated, once the last data has been read, the entire buffer is emptied.

In this work, we propose a third formalism called CYFO for "Chose Your first Out". It allows defining different sub-policies to subsample data. The underlying idea is that the components are able to choose in the buffer the most appropriate data. Also, as for LIFO, a "clear older data" option is also available for CYFO policy. In some cases only the latest data since a chosen date or a particular event are useful. With the clear older data option activated, once the chosen data has been read, all the older data in the buffer are removed.

The size of the buffer size can be finite by being n time the size of the data; or it can be limitless but this latter case can lead to an infinite loop during running of the component. In most of the cases, the size is chosen according to the frequency of production of data regarding to the frequency of consumption of those data by the CCU. It is quite easy to fill a buffer of a finite size. Data are stocked one after the others as long as the buffer limit is not overpassed. When this occurs, and in order to allow the latest one to be stored, oldest data are removed even if they were not yet processed: this situation if often called *data overflow*.

To specify the "Policy of Consumption" we have design a graphical model (Fig. 3). The buffer is represented as a suite of boxes and their respective labels.

LIFO/FIFO/CYFO over the buffer specify the way the CCU read data stored in the buffer. The box with a number represents the size of the buffer; infinite pattern means no limitation. The box with Clr label -when it exists- specifies that data older than the one read are deleted in LIFO/CYFO buffer.

Fig. 3. Example of Graphical Policy of Consumption. From left to right: Infinite Buffer with FIFO policy; Buffer with LIFO policy, a size of 5 and the clear older data option on; Buffer with CYFO policy and a size of 9.

The IMU performs also the transtyping of the input data in the type of the data needed by the code of the CCU. That allows the use of any algorithm in the CCU without changing the code of this algorithm. The only modification is to add the transtyping of input data inside the IMU; this subpart of the IMU is called the parser.

4.2   IMU – Trigger the CCU: Policy of Triggering

The second task of the IMU allows us to define when data is available for the CCU; or more precisely, when the Component Core Unit can consume an input data. Typically, two methods of consumption are considered:

– When the algorithm needs it, it consumes the data; it extracts data from the input buffer with the previous policy of consumption (LIFO, FIFO, CYFO). This data is consumed as synchronous data.
– When data arrives from the provider component, this triggers the algorithm that begins to run. These data are consumed as asynchronous data.

Distinguish which input data must be synchronous or asynchronous corresponds to the Policy of Triggering of the IMU. By default it is assumed that every input data is synchronous; this means that when the algorithm in the CCU is running, it uses the input data as soon as it needs it. But as CCU is run as a cycle it is important to define when the core begins each cycle. Therefore roboticians need one or more ways to trigger the cycle of an algorithm.

One Data Is Specified as Asynchronous. The process is simple in theory: when an asynchronous Data-i1 is provided, that triggers the CCU and the cycle of the algorithm begins. Unlike standards models (cf. RTMaps [5], Orocos), robotician may need to trigger on another type of event than only one asynchronous data.

Several Data Is Specified as Asynchronous. This asynchronism can be composed with two Boolean operators: OR(+) and AND($\times$).

1. Data-i_1 + Data-i_2: the core is triggered either by Data-i_1, or by Data-i_2. The algorithm starts using the respective data as long as one of the two is updated. The respective other data (Data-i_1 or Data-i_2) thus become synchronous data in this cycle.
2. Data-i_1 × Data-i_2: the core is triggered when the two data have been updated. That means it waits for the second data to start the algorithm.

Lag Operator. $Lag(t, i_1)$ means that the Data-i_1 will be taken into account after a time lag of t milliseconds after its production. **Cycle operator.** Finally, we may have a CCU that is not triggered by an external input. It may be run in a regular cycle, for example every 40 ms (including the process time). $Cycle(t)$ means that the process is trigged every t milliseconds.

Trigger Function and Graphical Representation. We have designed a graphical representation for policy of triggering. Asynchronous input, Lag and Cycle are represented as symbols, laid after the input data buffers (Fig. 4). For the lag symbol, the value inside the box represents the lag-time in milliseconds. For the cycle symbol, the value inside the box represents the cycle-time in milliseconds. The asynchronous function is written in the "Trigger" box, at the bottom of the IMU, with Boolean operators (+ and ×).

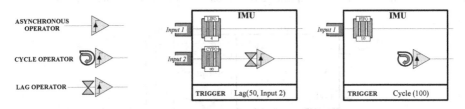

Fig. 4. Graphical policy of triggering. The different operators (left) and some examples.

4.3   CCU: Container for the Algorithm

This Core Unit is the algorithm. It contains the sequential code that may be run in cycle. It got its own inputs and outputs, with its own format. We do not modify this format inside the CCU; the IMU provides the input data in this custom format, assuming the transtyping. The policy of consumption and the policy of triggering are not made inside this unit (but in the IMU also). Thus, the CCU only contains the code of the algorithm, allowing the robotician to use any code previously programmed by him or not.

4.4   OMU: Transtype and Tag the Output Data

The OMU has a simple task: transtype the output data of the CCU algorithm to produce data with the respect of the data-flow protocol (Sect. 5). OMU adds also other fields to the data, such as time, component id, etc. Once again, the algorithm of the CCU is not in charge of this part, and we can use any type of code in a component, the adaptation is made in the OMU. Similarly to the IMU, a parser is also present here to produce output data from the Component Core Unit with the XML formalism.

4.5   The Entire Component: IMU+CCU+OMU

Thus, the component is designed with three units (Fig. 5):

- The Core Component Unit (CCU) contains the algorithm, written with standard code.
- The Input Management Unit (IMU) interfaces the input data for the algorithm, specifying the Consumption Policy and the Trigger Policy.
- The Output Management Unit (OMU) interfaces the output data for the data flow between the components.

With these three units we can discriminate the different functionalities of the component. The algorithm code can be used "as it is" without major modifications. The policies are implemented by the robotician inside the Input Management Unit, separately from the code. The two policies - consumption and trigger - are clearly separated, and graphically represented, without any ambiguity. Moreover, they are linked and dedicated to each component. Most of robotic middleware use the same buffer, in the output data, that implies to link the consumption policy of each component that subscribe to it. In our specification, the storage of data in a buffer is performed by each component in its IMU; it allows each subscriber component to choose its own consumption policy.

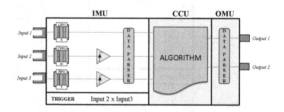

Fig. 5. The component based model with the IM, CC and OM Units

5   Data

As in other component-based models, roboticians may define the data-flow between the components. Although a communication services is also available, ROS middleware provides to the community the major part of its system: ROS topics. The node distribution of consumer/provider of data allows the different threads to communicate on the net substrate, splitting the communication service on one standalone or several distant machines, and allowing heterogeneous software to share data. The ROS-data type predefined all the robotics data, giving de facto standard that was missing previously in the community. But these data, as well defined they can be, are fixed in their type and their composition. A component must wait a data with its fitted type. Robotic data, like in other technical domains, is various and highly dependent of the used hardware and software; the interconnection, and a fortiori data flow in a component-based model, become versatile from one robotic application to another. Then a way to interconnect heterogeneous hardware and software is to include the data description inside the data.

5.1 XML Data

We propose to use markup data, which means that the structure of the data contains meta-information on the data itself. XML markup formalism is a good solution to perform the job: in addition of the value(s) of the data, we can integrate the type(s), the unit(s), the name(s), the provider, the timestamp, ttl, etc to the data itself. All these information, taken into account inside each component IMU, allows the interoperability of components, software and hardware. The IMU of a component can extract from a markup data the good data needed by its CCU. If the provider -and the provided data- changes, robotician just need to add a new transtyping function in the parser subpart of the IMU. To the best of our knowledge, there is no such approach in robotic data modeling. Usually, data is just a collection of bytes with no direct link to physical information and it can be interpreted by the "subscriber" only when it knows what kind of data the "publisher" is sending. Using a XML representation of data means to multiply the weight of a data by a non-negligible coefficient, but the gain for a component-based model of a robot application is very large:

- We intrinsically obtain the afferent information of the data; its unit, its timestamp, its producer, its type, etc.
- All these information are explicitly described, allowing interoperability between data providers and data subscribers. Subscribers can change their data provider without any major correction.
- Explicit xml data description allows sending this data "alone" on a broadcast net, without any interface.
- We do not need an end-to-end link between a data provider component and a data subscriber component. We can use broadcast net substrate for communication.
- We can embed "classical" data by a dedicated parser component to perform inter-connection with other middleware.

Thus, the balance between pro (previously listed gains) and cons (only the size/weight) let us no doubts. The gains will offer advantages and possibilities unknown in traditional models. Process such kind of "heavy" data was solved in the internet communication, and we think that it can be the same in robotics.

5.2 Streamed Data and Shared Data

The data-flow in our model specification uses only streamed data. This kind of data is produced by a component and then sends to others component which needs it; and each component uses this data freely, without modifying the original data. In robotics, we also need shared data: they are usually associated to a notion of "blackboard". The most significant robotic example of a shared data is a map. One or several components can build and modify this shared map, part by part; and several components can read this map. Sending a entire map in streamed data each time a component change a part of it is not feasible as there would be too many data to send. In our model specification, we have not yet integrated shared data. For the moment, we substitute the shared data entity by a component which works as map server: it receives the request to modify or read part of the map by its inputs, and serves the data by its outputs.

6   Discussion and Conclusion

The specifications that we propose to build a model for robot applications design allows the use of the robotician's well-known component based model, with separation of the roles. The robotic designer builds a global architecture with different components and let the robotic expert to fill the cores of these components. The robotic designer manages the data flow and the coordination of the components thanks to their IMU and may plan a general time organization of the whole robotic application. He manages the xml data type, the IMU inputs, the OMU outputs and the trigger of the components. The robotic expert can code the different algorithms of the CCU or can reuse or link existing codes. Thus, he has to manage the component internal parser to fit the input/output data to the code. Of course, a negotiation can be held between two roboticians on the frontiers of their own fields: IMU and OMU. Morevover, when there are more than two actors, the sharing of the work and the coordination become easier; and this graphical representation of a robotic application let all the actors to understand it both in its globality and in its detail.

The specifications of the robotic model are only a graphical representation of components and data. As robotician experts, our goal is to give a pertinent robot description to the software engineering experts in order to produce a MDA. This MDA must be able, at least, to generate an empty skeleton of the architecture in a given robotic middleware (or several), letting robotic experts to fill the CCU with the code of the algorithm, as developed in the proteus project [4].

We do not consider any differences between "structural data" (standard data flow between components) and "organizational data" (data coming from a supervisor to control a component). The use of xml meta-data let the possibility to integrate these two kind of data in the xml-data by adding some markups. When looking at the data xml structure and the way IMU/OMU work, it is close to a broadcast network working: the IMU/OMU work as net-card and data has a net-type structure. As future work, we propose to use an IPv4 or IPv6 for routing of data. Nowadays the technology of these types of net (non-deterministic) enables to work over the Gigabit per second, giving sufficient baud rate for a robotic application. Moreover, the integration of QoS in IPv6 net may guarantee some local determinist behaviors. A specific dynamic data connection between the components was not considered; the fact that during the run, components subscribe or unsubscribe to data (provider). From the "broadcast net" point of view, a "point to point connection" between a data provider component and a data subscriber component does not exist. Due to the local data buffering in each subscriber component IMU, the data provider just has to send its output data to the net substrate. The subscriber components just have to read this data (and store it with their IMU consumption policy): subscriber component becomes de facto no more a subscriber, but a consumer, free to read and use the provided data. As no subscription is needed, the term of subscriber component disappears and is replaced by the term of consumer component. Similarly to a broadcast net, we do not care if there are one more - or one less - system that uses the data.

References

1. Albus, J.: Drcs: A reference model architecture for demo iii. National Institute of Standards and Technology, Gaithersburg, MD, NISTIR 5994 (1997)
2. Brugali, D., Scandurra, P.: Component-based robotic engineering (part i)[tutorial]. IEEE Robotics & Automation Magazine 16(4), 84–96 (2009)
3. Brugali, D., Shakhimardanov, A.: Component-based robotic engineering (part ii). IEEE Robotics & Automation Magazine 17(1), 100–112 (2010)
4. Dhouib, S., Kchir, S., Stinckwich, S., Ziadi, T., Ziane, M.: RobotML, a domain-specific language to design, simulate and deploy robotic applications. In: Noda, I., Ando, N., Brugali, D., Kuffner, J.J. (eds.) SIMPAR 2012. LNCS, vol. 7628, pp. 149–160. Springer, Heidelberg (2012)
5. Dulac, N., Delaunay, C., Michel, G.: Real time, multisensor, advanced prototyping software. In: Third National Workshop on Control Architectures of Robots, Bourges (2008), http://www.bourges.univ-orleans.fr/CAR08
6. Jaulmes, R., Moliné, E.: Hng: A robust architecture for mobile robots systems. In: Bruyninckx, H., Přeučil, L., Kulich, M. (eds.) European Robotics Symposium 2008. STAR, vol. 44, pp. 123–131. Springer, Heidelberg (2008)
7. Joyeux, S., Alami, R., Lacroix, S., Alexandre, Lampe, o.: Simulation in the laas architecture. In: International Conference on Robotics and Automation-Workshop on Software Development in Robotics (2005)
8. Ortiz, F.J., Insaurralde, C.C., Alonso, D., Sánchez, F., Petillot, Y.R.: Model-driven analysis and design for software development of autonomous underwater vehicles. Robotica, 1–20 (2014)
9. Passama, R., Andreu, D., et al.: Contract: a software environment for developing control architecture. In: 6th National Conference on Control Architectures of Robots (2011)
10. Quigley, M., Conley, K., Gerkey, B., Faust, J., Foote, T., Leibs, J., Wheeler, R., Ng, A.Y.: Ros: an open-source robot operating system. In: ICRA Workshop on Open Source Software, vol. 3, p. 5 (2009)
11. Romero-Garcés, A., Manso, L., Gutierez, M.A., Cintas, R., Bustos, P.: Improving the lifecycle of robotics components using domain-specific languages. arXiv preprint arXiv:1301.6022 (2013)
12. Rosenblatt, J.: Damn: A distributed architecture for mobile navigation, in proceedings of the 1995 aaai spring symposium on lessons learned from implemented software architectures for physical agents, h. hexmoor & d. kortenkamp (1995)
13. Schlegel, C., Steck, A., Brugali, D., Knoll, A.: Design abstraction and processes in robotics: From code-driven to model-driven engineering. In: Ando, N., Balakirsky, S., Hemker, T., Reggiani, M., von Stryk, O. (eds.) SIMPAR 2010. LNCS, vol. 6472, pp. 324–335. Springer, Heidelberg (2010)
14. Volpe, R., Nesnas, I., Estlin, T., Mutz, D., Petras, R., Das, H.: The claraty architecture for robotic autonomy. In: IEEE Proceedings on Aerospace Conference, vol. 1, pp. 1–121. IEEE (2001)

High Performance Relaying of `C++11` Objects across Processes and Logic-Labeled Finite-State Machines

Vlad Estivill-Castro, René Hexel, and Carl Lusty

Machine Intelligence and Pattern Analysis Laboratory (MiPal)
Griffith University, Nathan, QLD 4111, Australia

Abstract. We present `gusimplewhiteboard`, a software architecture analogous to `ROS:services` and `ROS:messages`, that enables the construction and extremely efficient inter-process relaying of message-types as `C++11` objects, All `gusimplewhiteboard` objects reside in shared memory. Moreover, our principle is to use idempotent message communication, in direct contrast to previously released platforms for robotic-module communication, that are based on an event-driven subscriber model that queues and multi-threads. We combine this with compiled, time-triggered, logic-labeled finite state machines (*llfsms*) the are executed concurrently, but scheduled sequentially, in an extremely efficient manner, removing all race conditions and requirements for explicit synchronisation. Together, these tools enable effective robotic behaviour design, where arrangements of *llfsms* can be organised as hierarchies of machines and submachines, enabling composition of very complex systems. They have proven to be very powerful for Model-Driven Development, capable of simulation, validation, and formal verification.

1 Introduction

Since its inception, the *blackboard control architecture* [17], has become ubiquitous as a mechanism to integrate cognitive processes, behaviours, and problem-solving. It has also become central to agent architectures and publish/subscribe patterns among the software engineering community. Over and above the publisher/subscriber pattern, a blackboard allows a further level of decoupling by being data-centric (rather than component-centric). The provider may supply information for unknown (possibly inactive) consumers without the need to be aware of a consumer's interface, only the interface to the blackboard is necessary.

From a software architecture perspective, the flexibility of a blackboard is also incorporated into the notion of a broker, enabling a sender to issue what we will refer to as **add_Message**($msg : T$), a non-blocking call that may optionally include additional information, e.g. a sender signature, a timestamp, or an event counter that records the belief the sender has of the currency of the message. There are essentially two modes for retrieving a message.

D. Brugali et al. (Eds.): SIMPAR 2014, LNAI 8810, pp. 182–194, 2014.

subscribe(T, f): The receiver subscribes to messages of a certain *type* T (of an implied *class*) and essentially goes to sleep. Subscription includes the name f of a function. The blackboard will notify the receiver of the message *msg* every time someone posts for the given *class* T by invoking $f(msg)$ (usually queued in a *type* T specific thread). This is typically called PUSH technology.
get_Message(T): The receiver issues a get_message to the blackboard that supplies the latest *msg* received so far for the *type* T. This is usually called PULL.

The *type* identifies the communication channel, and in ROS' PUSH technology is named a ROS::topic. The modules posting (publishing) or getting (subscribing to) messages are called *nodes*. The data structures available for messages (and described in msg files) are restricted to a simplified message description language, because ROS aims at supporting cross-programming-language communication. This architecture is common in robotic systems and other robotic projects have produced similar infrastructures: Carmen (carmen.sf.net), Microsoft Robotics Studio (msdn.microsoft.com/en-us/robotics/), MIRA [6], MOOS (www.robots.ox.ac.uk/~mobile/MOOS/wiki/pmwiki.php), Orca (orca-robotics.sf.net), Orocos (www.orocos.org), Player (playerstage.sf.net), and YARP (http://eris.liralab.it/yarp/).

Such robotic-system architectures organise many modules under different paradigms. One of them is the sense-decide-act cycle. Here, sensors post information onto the blackboard. This information may be processed by decision makers (even as complicated as planners) that then publish commands to actuator modules. The blackboard enables very flexible information processing about the state of the world that is supplied by sensors. For example, if sensors are noisy, then an intermediate *filter* (such as a Kalman filter) can be placed in between the raw posting of the sensor and the decision maker. This mechanism can be extended to a whole pipeline of publishers and subscribers between the sensor data and the final actuators. The features of gusimplewhiteboard include:

1. Completely C++11 and POSIX compliant; thus, platform independent: used on Mac OS X (Mountain Lion), LINUX 13.10, Aldebaran Nao 1.14.3, Webots 7.1, the Raspberry Pi (www.raspberrypi.org), and Lego NXT.
2. Released as a ROS:catkin package (mipal.net.au/downloads.php).
3. Extremely fast performance for add_Message and get_Message, intra-process as well as inter-process.
4. Completely OO-compliant. The classes that can be used are not restricted, the full data-structure mechanisms of C++11 are available.
5. Very clear semantics that removes lots of issues of concurrency control.

2   Challenges of Inter-module Communication

Control modules in charge of robot behaviour rely heavily upon predictable communication latency. Even very standard algorithms in robotics, like the Kalman filter, would be significantly less effective if the time between the reading of an observation and the execution of the filtering step was randomly perturbed. The motion model would not be able to make sufficiently accurate predictions, and the integration of information provided by the next observation with the prediction would be jeopardised. Similarly, issuing commands to actuators heavily depends on the issuer having reasonably accurate information of the position of the actuator at the time of issuing the next command. If sensor information or control commands are unboundedly delayed, the safety of actions can be seriously compromised. Thus, the emergence of compliant actuators is not enough: the software architecture is equally responsible for safe operation.

Delays not only depend on the type of channel used by the blackboard architecture, but also the determinism (or lack thereof) of the concurrency model used. Our software architecture proposes to schedule publishers and subscribers sequentially (see Section 3). In such a model, the use of `subscribe` can be minimised or avoided. The use of PUSH technology (for example ROS) results in the classical *producer-consumer problem* (or *bounded-buffer* problem) of multi-process synchronisation and its associated challenges (e.g. critical sections, and message queues). Throughout, the call-back function f must be fast enough to terminate and be ready to process the next invocation. Deadlocks, live-locks, starvation, or similar concurrency issues can result in catastrophic consequences. But even in the best of scenarios, a traditional, multi-threaded operating system cannot usually guarantee a schedule that will meet deadlines for all tasks; hence, there is simply no guarantee when an specific event will be handled. With this in mind, it is somewhat surprising that the robotics community is adopting this approach by endorsing ROS which for inter-process communciation uses the network stack to relay messages (wiki.ros.org/ROS/TCPROS), and even *nodelets* (that only work within the same process) use a `subscribe` and queuing mechanism. In fact, the issues of using networking infrastructure as the transport layer has prompted some developers to state that ROS was originally intended for a single host, and not necessarily suitable for distributed communication [14]. However, others (`MOOS`, `Microsoft Robotics Studio`, `naoqi` non-local modules, etc.) have also built on top of TCP/IP, nondeterministic, multi-threaded processing and/or event-handling of the underlying operating systems; and thus face the very same challenges.

3   Arrangements of Logic-Labeled Finite-State Machines

We now present `clfsm`, our compiler and scheduler for arrangements of *llfsms*. Since Harel's seminal work [16], finite-state machines (FSMs) have become ubiquitous models of system behaviour. Finite-state machines guide coding and model-based system development [29,30]. Among the software engineering community, FSMs machines are ubiquitous. Studies have demonstrated that, jointly with class-diagrams, state-charts are the top most used UML artefact [7,27]. FSMs are the best understood tool for model-driven development in software engineering [24]. For modelling the behaviour of robots, variants of FSMs have also become fundamental. *Augmented* FSMs are the basis of the subsumption [4] and reactive software architectures [23]. In RoboCup, several teams and their research groups use FSMs to model and implement behaviours [18,22,25,28].

Tools for deploying systems using FSMs include the robotics simulator `Webots` (offering *BotStudio*) [26], *StateWORKS* [30] and *MathWorks*® *StateFlow*, ROS has a tool named `smach` [3] (wiki.ros.org/smach), Qt's *State Machine Framework* (qt-project.org/doc/qt-5/statemachine-api.html) that is based on the W3C's state chart XML (SCXML) (www.w3.org/TR/scxml/), the `rFSM` [18] framework in `Lua`, and the `boost` library `Meta State Machine` and `StateChart` templates.

Key characteristics of `clfsm` include the following.

1. Complete POSIX and C++11 compliance.
2. Open source `catkin ROS` package release (`mipal.net.au/downloads.php`).
3. Transitions are labeled by Boolean expressions (not events), facilitating formal verification and eliminating all need for concerns about event queues.
4. Transition labels are arbitrary C++11 Boolean expressions, enabling reasoning into what may otherwise seem a purely reactive architecture.
5. Handling of machines constructed with states that have UML 2.0 (or SCXML) **OnEntry**, **OnExit**, and **Internal** sections with clear semantics.
6. Guaranteed sequential ringlet schedule for the concurrent execution of FSMs (removing the need for critical sections and synchronisation points).
7. Efficient execution as the entire arrangement runs as compiled code without thread switching.
8. Being agnostic to communication mechanisms between machines, allowing, for example use with ROS:services and ROS:messages – however, we recommend the use of our class-oriented `gusimplewhiteboard`.
9. Mechanisms for sub-machine hierarchies and introspection to implement complex behaviours. FSMs can be suspended, resumed, or restarted, as well as queried as to whether they are running or not.
10. Formal semantics that enables simulation, validation, and formal verification.
11. Associated tools such as (`MiEditLLFSM` and `MiCASE`) that enable rapid development of FSM arrangements.

Some details of these characteristics as well as examples of their use will follow. The corresponding download includes full documentation and examples. Videos illustrating the tools (`youtu.be/gN6rIveCWNk`) and using ROS (`youtu.be/AJYA2hB4i9U`) are available online.

4   The Logic-Labeled Finite-State Machine Model

Each *llfsm* consists of a set S of **states**, and a transition table $T : S \times E \to S$. There is a distinguished state $s_0 \in S$, named the initial state. Our *llfsms* are of the synchronous type [16]. The set E are expressions. This is a very important distinction from all other approaches where *events* label transitions (the dominant UML approach). The use of Boolean expression to label transitions has a series of advantages: it simplifies semantics, facilitates scheduling and handling of concurrency [9,10,12] and enables validation and formal verification [11]. This produces rapid development and simulation of robot behaviours [5].

Since any `C++11` expression can label a transition, we can incorporate reasoning and deliberative architectures in what otherwise would be a reactive architecture. Thus, it is possible to include an entire reasoning system, for example using `Prolog` and invoke it from `C++11` using standard APIs. This approach was used for poker hands [2] and to build a poker playing robot. We have found `DPL`, a common sense non-monotonic logic, very useful for declarative aspects. For example, `DPL` can be used for expressing the soccer off-side rule in a way similar to the original FIFA specification [1], or describing when it is dangerous for an elderly lady to face a stranger [1]. The `C++11` *llfsm* mechanism has been shown to suitably integrate planning incorporating *Planning Domain Definition Language* (PDDL) planners [8]. Fig. 1 illustrates the power of merging reasoning with the `C++11` statements in state activities using a simplified example of a vision pipeline. Here, a blob (of orange pixels) reported by the vision module is analysed for its fitness to correspond to a ball. The `C++11` arithmetic enables the calculation of values such as the ratio of orange pixels to other pixels in the blob. The `DPL` rules determine that blobs whose orange-colour density is not higher than a threshold are not to be considered balls. Other conditions include how close the blob matches a square as opposed to an elongated rectangle[1]. Figure 2 shows a feedback loop control for keeping the ball in sight.

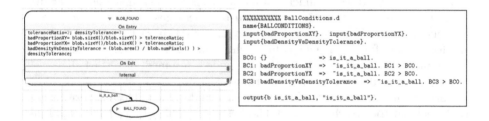

Fig. 1. A state with calculation and a Decisive Plausible Logic (DPL) theory that defines when a blob is a ball

Fig. 2. A simple ball tracker

The semantics for $T(s_i, e_t) = s_j$ is that when the machine is in state $s_i \in S$ and e_t evaluates to true, the machine will move to the state s_j. Without loss of

---

[1] We are thankful to Francisco Martín-Rico from the SPiTeam for this example.

expressivity, the transitions are considered in sequence (as in *MathWorks®* and `StateFlow` with `SymLink`), that is, $T(s_i, e_t) = s_j$ will transition to state s_j if e_t evaluates to true and no prior e_s ($\forall s < t$) evaluates to true in $T(s_i, \cdot)$.

The **OnEntry** section is executed upon arrival from a different state, while actions in the **OnExit** section are executed iff a transition fires. Thus, the actions in these two sections are executed once and only once. The third section (like UML's `do`) is executed only if none of the transitions fires. When the internal actions are completed, the cycle repeats with evaluating the sequence of expressions of the transitions out of the state. One pass over the cycle is a *ringlet*.

Variables and Machine Communication. The compiler is completely agnostic of custom libraries or communication mechanisms. Variables can be created in any C++11 context. Importantly, variables can be created at the state level (*intra-state-variables*), or at the machine level, exclusive to one and only one *llfsm* instance and its states.

Concurrency Model. In one ringlet execution there is only one **read** operation at the beginning, by which a local copy of each external variable is made before the execution of any section or the evaluation of any expression labelling any transition. This read operation is a snapshot phase (similar to `rFSM` evaluation contexts, in order to avoid *open environment* [18] inconsistencies). That is, the execution context of a ringlet for external variables remains the same throughout. At the end of the ringlet, a **write** reflects external variables. While the ringlet dispatcher will ensure ringlet atomicity for concurrent *llfsm*, the snapshot phase will also ensure a consistent view of the world outside the FSM arrangement, such as external events (e.g. new sensor readings). If no transition fires and the internal actions complete, then a new ringlet commences.

An ensemble of *llfsms* is executed in a round-robin fashion from one ringlet of one *llfsm* to the next. Thus, the *llfsm* arrangement is a single sequential execution, executed by one thread. While event-driven execution of ringlets is possible, the evaluation of logic expressions is predominantly state-based. This is also reflected in the convention to use idempotent whiteboard messages for communication. Moreover, time-driven guards such as `after()` and `after_ms()` allow the designation of precise state times and an execution style that follows the principles of the time-triggered architecture [20].

The use of a deterministic schedule for the arrangement brings several advantages over a nondeterministic, multi-threaded approach. From the design point of view, open concurrency (where the management of switches between threads is left to the system) puts an unnecessary cognitive load on the behaviour designer as it opens all sorts of needs for synchronisation, and vigilance of nondeterministic communication delays. Burdens include managing critical sections and fairness as well as avoiding deadlocks, live-locks, and starvation (not to mention the associated complexity of CPU context switch overhead, and other system overhead). Our model enables formal correctness verification of models. Model-checking on concurrent threads, by contrast, quickly becomes infeasible for all but the most trivial tasks, as it must consider the combinatorial explosion of all possible state combinations in the system. For robotic systems and embedded systems where there are strict timing requirements, sequential execution is superior to the multiplication of threads [25]. The models produced with *llfsms* can be verified using public domain model-checking technology (NuSMV) within a matter of seconds [13,5], but using behaviour trees – which spawn parallel threads – requires several days of CPU time [15].

Scalability. Composition of machines is not only essential for abstraction, but it is a very powerful encapsulation mechanism when building complex (deeply nested) state machines. Complex models can be created by composing simple *llfsms* into more complex behaviours, and those in turn, into still more complex behaviours; clfsm supports Brooks' famous subsumption architectures [4], without prescribing strict, hierarchical dependencies. In fact, an entire multi-agent system can be built this way. Here is how the clfsm tool supports subsumption architectures or similar organisations.

Each *llfsm* has a single designated state, the SUSPEND state, that has an (implicit) transition to this state from each of the machine's states. This transition is the first one evaluated in every sequence of outgoing transitions and checks whether the machine shall be suspended. The libclfsm run-time library provides the suspend() function which allows a machine to suspend another. When the token of execution arrives at the machine named in the suspend, the **OnEntry** section of SUSPEND gets executed. Implicit transitions from the SUSPEND state back to the each state also exist that are labelled with the destination state's name. A transition to the previously running state, the *resume state*, gets triggered by the resume() libclfsm call. Alternatively, restart() can be used to unsuspend a machine and restart it from its initial state. Thus, SUSPEND acts like any other state, with exactly the same semantics (e.g. the machine will execute its **Internal** section while suspended). Any state can be designated the SUSPEND state (an empty one is create by clfsm if none exists). Based on this, hierarchical control of machines that, in turn, start other machines, can be achieved by explicitly suspending sub-machines in the **OnEntry** section of SUSPEND (by issuing suspend() calls to all sub-machines).

In addition to controlling the suspension of *llfsms*, libclfsm provides an is_suspended() introspection predicate that can be used as a transition label (or as part of any other Boolean expression in the C++11 code) to detect whether a given machine is suspended or not.

5   The gusimplewhiteboard Implementation

gusimplewhiteboard is a library that implements a decentralised, distributed access pattern without the need to initiate a broker (in ROS, ROS:roscore is a pre-requisite and must be running before any nodes can communicate). To use gusimplewhiteboard, a module simply needs to include the corresponding headers and link against the library. The first module to execute on a host creates the corresponding data structures for the blackboard in shared memory.

For example, to issue a message for debugging purposes, one can use a predefined message type Print. The module must then includes two public files.

```
#include "gugenericwhiteboardobject.h"
#include "guwhiteboardtypelist_generated.h"
```

Then, to add_Message to the blackboard, one declares (in the guWhiteboard name space), a blackboard singleton instance for the object (using a known blackboard type) by appending _t to the type name:

```
Print_t print;
```

Now, we can use a setter (or, for convenience, the overloaded function call operator ()) to actually post a message (a std::string for Print):

```
print("Hello, blackboard");
```

To observe the effects of the module we provide a tool guWhiteboardMonitor to inspect the messages as they are posted to the blackboard[2]. The monitor makes visible the effect of the print by displaying the following output.

```
Type: Print    Value: Hello, blackboard
```

To construct the classes for objects to become known to the blackboard, a default constructor, the assignment operator, and a description() serialisation method that returns a std::string, are required. The header file of newly defined classes must be placed in a well-known directory with some pre-processor directives and the class name must be associated with its type(s) in a well-known file[3]. With this, any module can construct blackboard objects of that class. E.g., a class Ball_Belief could describe the coordinates of the centre of an orange blob (likely to be the ball) in the reference framework of the camera image. The following C++11 code constructs an object of such a class.

```
Ball_Belief a_ball(50,30);
```

The gusimplewhiteboard approach to add_Message comprises two statements, first declaring the handler, then adding the object to the blackboard.

```
Ball_Belief_t wb_ball;    wb_ball.set(a_ball);
```

This is much simpler than the analogous construction of a publisher in ROS (there is no need to explicitly register as a node and obtain a NodeHandle as well as requesting to obtain a ROS:Publisher object).

Introspection. We already mentioned guWhiteboardMonitor, a tool that makes use of description(). Readers familiar with ROS may also be aware of the versatility provided by being able to publish messages of a certain topic onto the communication mechanism through rostopic pub. Our corresponding tool is gusimplewhiteboardposter. This tool is based on the requirement that pre-existing classes, as well as new user-defined classes that want to support introspection, need to implement a method called from_string(). This method, at a minimum, deserialises an instance of the class previously serialised by the description() method (but may include arbitrarily versatile parsing of more user-friendly input strings). It should be noted that this is optional and its implementation only impacts on gusimplewhiteboardposter.

---

[2] This is analogous to ROS's rostopic echo. By default, the guWhiteboardMonitor displays every object posted, but it is possible to specify a type and the effect is analogous to rostopic echo displaying the data published on a ROS:topic.

[3] Again, this is analogous to the ROS construction of a msg description.

Getting Messages from the Blackboard. As discussed before, the preferred approach of our software architecture is a synchronous type of concurrency, analogous to a time-triggered architecture (as opposed to an event-driven architecture). It is well documented in the literature [19,21] that the reliability of time-triggered systems is significantly easier to determine than event-driven systems. Time-triggered systems handle peak-load situations by design. The bandwidth of communications and message rate is constant across low, regular, and peak load situations. Event-driven systems are inherently unpredictable, they can collapse during peak loads or event showers, and no analytical guarantees can be given for their performance in worst-case scenarios.

In a round-robin scheduling of modules interested in a message, a module that has the execution token (the module that has the CPU) can request information from the blackboard. Besides including the corresponding header files for the user-defined class, the actual code to achieve this is also very simple.

```
Ball_Belief_t wb_ball;
Ball_Belief ball = wb_ball.get();    // or alternatively: ball = wb_ball();
```

This PULL approach always retrieves the most recent information, i.e. the last information that was published. For ease of implementation of event-triggered subscribers, `gusimplewhiteboard` provides a class analogous to the PUSH approach, the `whiteboard_watcher`. A module that wishes to become a subscriber carries out a $\text{subscribe}(T, f)$ operation as follows.

```
whiteboard_watcher *watcher;
watcher = new whiteboard_watcher();
SUBSCRIBE(watcher, class T, subscriber_class, subscriber_class::f);
```

The semantics of such a subscription (e.g., the semantics of `ROS:subscriber`) is fixed size queuing followed by the invocation of the callback function *subscriber_class*::f (using `libdispatch`, `https://libdispatch.macosforge.org`). There is limited queuing of messages and, for the reasons outlined earlier, in our own code we deprecate the use of event-triggered queuing in favour of time-triggered handling of idempotent messages.

6   Putting gusimplewhiteboard into Practice

Our `gusimplewhiteboard` has proven a very efficient and effective communication infrastructure of objects defined by fully fleshed C++11 classes. In combination with `clfsm`, they provide a very flexible control architecture [2] that minimises concurrency concerns and has facilitated the rapid development of complex, high-level behaviours through composition of modules and *llfsms*. Moreover, C++11's static type system enables far more secure software development. Libraries and modules have been developed for image processing, sensor noise filtering, localisation and navigation, object tracking, and motor control, for Naos, as well as for the ePuck, and simulators such as `Webots`. Fig. 3 on the next page shows the power of fully C++11 compliant messages with `clfsm`. The two states implement a feedback loop for an ePuck to follow a line. The code in between `#ifdef DEBUG` and `#endif` demonstrates that even pre-processing

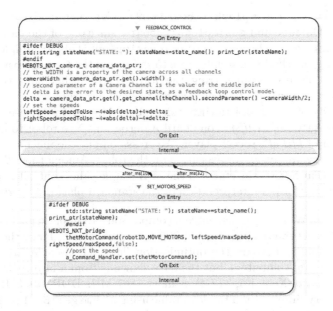

Fig. 3. Two states that use `gusimplewhiteboard` services to perform a feedback loop to control an ePuck that follows coloured lines

directives are handled and thus, debugging and monitoring information can be relayed to the blackboard, and reviewed by `guWhiteboardMonitor`. As per control theory, the sensing and estimation of the discrepancy between the desired system output and the sensor reading is encapsulated in the FEEDBACK state. The statements

```
WEBOTS_NXT_camera_t camera_data_ptr;
cameraWidth = camera_data_ptr.get().width();
```

retrieve the camera object from the blackboard using the `camera_data_ptr` handler for a known message of the `WEBOTS_NXT_camera` class. We can PULL the object and obtain an attribute in one go, e.g. `camera_data_ptr.get().width()`.

```
delta = camera_data_ptr.get().get_channel(theChannel).secondParameter()
      - cameraWidth/2;
```

obtains a sensor message of the `WEBOTS_NXT_bridge` class. This demonstrates the use of sophisticated class composition allowed by C++11 (as opposed to the ROS:msg restrictions). Finally, `delta` stores the measured error, followed by the computation of the desired motor target speeds. The SET_MOTORS_SPEED state simply constructs a local `WEBOTS_NXT_bridge` object and posts it to the whiteboard. You can see a video of this state machine in action at `http://youtu.be/F8K4V78vUbk`

Of course `gusimplewhiteboard` can be considered an alternative to the event-driven blackboard control architectures developed by the robotics community. Our approach aims at establishing components for which formal verification is possible. However, its presentation here is not meant to be a replacement for ROS:roscore, ROS:services, or ROS:nodelets, but a complement.

In fact, we have a gusimplewhiteboard-ROS bridge that enables relaying of data across ROS:core and gusimplewhiteboard: since one of the basic ROS:msg types is String.msg and classes known to gusimplewhiteboard implement the description() method as a serialisation to string and the from_string() methods as a materialisation from a string, the bridge is a publisher/subscriber across ROS:roscore and gusimplewhiteboard that relays messages.

The capacity of clfsm and gusimplewhiteboard in day-to-day use is remarkable. We currently run 27 *llfsms* on board Alderbaran's Nao robot to implement the behaviour of *MiPal*'s soccer player. We cross-compile the machines to native code before they are set-up for execution on the robot. Among those 27, there is one machine that follows the states of the SPL-league game controller, providing an unambiguous, formal interpretation of the standard platform league rules.

Performance. We have implemented a comparison catkin package, benchmarking gusimplewhiteboard posting and ROS topic publishing. Thus, the compiler used is the same and so are the optimisation flags. The benchmark has been tested with several computers, but the data shown is from a late 2013 Mac Pro, 3 GHz 8-Core Intel Xeon E5, 32 GB memory 1867 MHz DDR3 ECC RAM. The data type is very simple, it is a Boolean value using std_msgs::Bool in the case of ROS and the boolean type from C++11 for the gusimplewhiteboard. Larger, more complicated types make ROS even slower. For example, for an add_Message, the gusimplewhiteboard delivers 411,895,543 messages per second while ROS only manages 47,925. Moreover, ROS seems to be affected by kernel and networking constraints, e.g., a bottleneck in the number of messages per second the kernel can push through locally. The delays in ROS have been documented before [6], but our catkin benchmark here shows at least 50 times faster performance (and in the CPUs on board of robots, the gap would be larger).

gusimplewhiteboard		ROSmacports *Hydro*	
get_Message	0.0024 μs	ROS:subscribe()	20.14 μs
add_Message	0.0120 μs	ROS:publish()	20.87 μs

7   Conclusion

The released clfsm ROS package contains simple examples that demonstrate the construction and execution of *llfsms*. Our videos demonstrate an arrangement of 6 *llfsms* that make a Nao avoid obstacles. The tools for building this behaviour were used in a third year undergraduate course and students could construct this behaviour within a single, two hour laboratory session. This provides evidence of the flexibility and rapid prototyping and development that can be achieved with clfsm. The full construction of this behaviour also appears in the download and documentation of the MiEditLLFSM state machine editor. Compositions of machines have also been used to create higher levels of navigation and planning for the ePuck in the Webots simulator (also a student lab session), using a feedback loop control approach to construct a coloured-line follower.

References

1. Billington, D., Estivill-Castro, V., Hexel, R., Rock, A.: Non-monotonic reasoning on board a sony AIBO. In: Lima, P. (ed.) Robotic Soccer, ch.3, pp. 45–70. I-Tech Education and Publishing, Austria (2007)
2. Billington, D., Estivill-Castro, V., Hexel, R., Rock, A.: Architecture for hybrid robotic behavior. In: Corchado, E., Wu, X., Oja, E., Herrero, Á., Baruque, B. (eds.) HAIS 2009. LNCS, vol. 5572, pp. 145–156. Springer, Heidelberg (2009)
3. Bohren, J., Cousins, S.: The SMACH high-level executive [ROS News]. IEEE Robotics & Automation Magazine 17(4), 18–20 (2010)
4. Brooks, R.A.: Intelligence without reason. In: 12th ICJAI 1991, Sydney, pp. 569–595 (1991)
5. Coleman, R., Estivill-Castro, V., Hexel, R., Lusty, C.: Visual-trace simulation of concurrent finite-state machines for validation and model-checking of complex behaviour. In: Noda, I., Ando, N., Brugali, D., Kuffner, J.J. (eds.) SIMPAR 2012. LNCS, vol. 7628, pp. 52–64. Springer, Heidelberg (2012)
6. Einhorn, E., Langner, T., Stricker, R., Martin, C., Gross, H.-M.: MIRA - middleware for robotic applications. In: 2012 IEEE/RSJ IROS, Portugal, pp. 2591–2598 (2012)
7. Erickson, J., Siau, K.: Can UML be simplified? practitioner use of UML in separate domains. In: 12th EMMSAD 2007, vol. 365, pp. 87–96. CEUR (2007)
8. Estivill-Castro, V., Ferrer-Mesters, J.: Path-finding in dynamic environemnts with PDDL-planners. In: 16th Int. Conf. Advanced Robotics (ICAR), Montevideo (2013)
9. Estivill-Castro, V., Hexel, R.: Arrangements of finite-state machines semantics, simulation, and model checking. In: Int. Conf. on Model-Driven Engineering and Software Development MODELSWARD, pp. 182–189. SCITEPRESS, Barceloan (2013)
10. Estivill-Castro, V., Hexel, R.: Module isolation for efficient model checking and its application to FMEA in model-driven engineering. In: 8th ENASE Evaluation of Novel Approaches to Software Engineering, pp. 218–225. INSTCC, Angers (2013)
11. Estivill-Castro, V., Hexel, R.: Correctness by construction with logic-labeled finite-state machines – comparison with Event-B. In: 23rd Australasian Software Engineering Conf., Sydney. IEEE Computer Soc. CPS (2014)
12. Estivill-Castro, V., Hexel, R., Rosenblueth, D.A.: Efficient modelling of embedded software systems and their formal verification. In: 19th Asia-Pacific Software Engineering Conf (APSEC 2012), pp. 428–433. IEEE Computer Soc., CPS (2012)
13. Estivill-Castro, V., Hexel, R., Rosenblueth, D.A.: Failure mode and effects analysis (FMEA) and model-checking of software for embedded systems by sequential scheduling of vectors of logic-labelled finite-state machines. In: 7th Int. IET System Safety Conf., Edinburgh, UK, Paper 3.a.1 (2012)
14. Garber, L.: Robot OS: A new day for robot design. Computer 46(12), 16–20 (2013)
15. Grunske, L., Winter, K., Yatapanage, N., Zafar, S., Lindsay, P.A.: Experience with fault injection experiments for FMEA. Software, Practice and Experience 41(11), 1233–1258 (2011)
16. Harel, D., Naamad, A.: The STATEMATE semantics of statecharts. ACM T. on Software Engineering Methodology 5(4), 293–333 (1996)
17. Hayes-Roth, B.: A blackboard architecture for control. In: Distributed Artificial Intelligence, San Francisco, pp. 505–540 (1988)
18. Klotzbuecher, M.: rFSM v1.0-beta6, http://www.orocos.org/rfsm

19. Kopetz, H.: Should responsive systems be event-triggered or time-triggered? IEICE Transactions on Information and Systems 76(11), 1325 (1993)
20. Kopetz, H., Bauer, G.: The time-triggered architecture. Proc. of the IEEE 91(1), 112–126 (2003)
21. Lamport, L.: Using time instead of timeout for fault-tolerant distributed systems. ACM Transactions on Programming Languages and Systems 6, 254–280 (1984)
22. Lötzsch, M., Bach, J., Burkhard, H.-D., Jüngel, M.: Designing agent behavior with the extensible agent behavior specification language XABSL. In: Polani, D., Browning, B., Bonarini, A., Yoshida, K. (eds.) RoboCup 2003. LNCS (LNAI), vol. 3020, pp. 114–124. Springer, Heidelberg (2004)
23. Mataric, M.J.: The Robotics Primer. MIT Press (2007)
24. Mellor, S.J., Balcer, M.: Executable UML: A foundation for model-driven architecture. Addison-Wesley, Reading (2002)
25. Merz, T., Rudol, P., Wzorek, M.: Control system framework for autonomous robots based on extended state machines. In: ICAS 2006, Silicon Valley, vol. 14 (2006)
26. Michel, O.: Webots: Professional mobile robot simulation. J. Advanced Robotics Systems 1(1), 39–42 (2004)
27. Reggio, G., Leotta, M., Ricca, F., Clerissi, D.: What are the used UML diagrams? a preliminary survey Technical report, Universitá di Genova, Italy (DIBRIS) (1998)
28. Risler, M., von Stryk, O.: Formal behavior specification of multi-robot systems using hierarchical state machines in XABSL. In: AAMAS 2008-Workshop on Formal Models and Methods for Multi-Robot Systems, Estoril (2008)
29. Samek, M.: Practical UML Statecharts in C/C++, 2nd Edition: Event-Driven Programming for Embedded Systems. Newnes (2008)
30. Wagner, F., Schmuki, R., Wagner, T., Wolstenholme, P.: Modeling Software with Finite State Machines: A Practical Approach. CRC Press, NY (2006)

A Survey on Domain-Specific Languages in Robotics

Arne Nordmann[1,2], Nico Hochgeschwender[3], and Sebastian Wrede[1,2]

[1] Cognitive Interaction Technology Excellence Cluster (CITEC), Bielefeld University, Germany
[2] Institute for Robotics and Cognition (CoR-Lab.), Bielefeld University, Germany
[3] Department of Computer Science, Bonn-Rhein-Sieg University, Germany

Abstract. The design, simulation and programming of robotics systems is challenging as expertise from multiple domains needs to be integrated conceptually and technically. Domain-specific modeling promises an efficient and flexible concept for developing robotics applications that copes with this challenge. It allows to raise the level of abstraction through the use of specific concepts that are closer to the respective domain concerns and easier to understand and validate. Furthermore, it focuses on increasing the level of automation, e.g. through code generation, to bridge the gap between the modeling and the implementation levels and to improve the efficiency and quality of the software development process. Within this contribution, we survey the literature available on domain-specific (modeling) languages in robotics required to realize a state-of-the-art real-world example from the RoboCup@Work competition. We classify 41 publications in the field as reference for potential DSL users. Furthermore, we analyze these contributions from a DSL-engineering viewpoint and discuss quantitative and qualitative aspects such as the methods and tools used for DSL implementation as well as their documentation status and platform integration. Finally, we conclude with some recommendations for discussion in the robotics programming and simulation community based on the insights gained with this survey.

1 Introduction

Model-driven and domain specific development methods are recognized to cope with the challenges of building complex heterogeneous systems in domains such as aerospace, telecommunication and automotive [1] which face similarly complex integration and modeling challenges as advanced robotics. In the last years, this approach was actively adapted to the robotics domain to handle the complexity of robotics systems and help with the separation of concerns regarding the *functional architecture* and *software architecture*. One goal is to support the development and ease design space exploration. This requires to support the entire experimental toolchain ranging from purely functional modeling to software architectural and technical aspects such as software deployment.

The purpose of this survey is to report on the state of the art in domain-specific languages in robotics, and provide an overview on sub-domains relevant for programming and simulation of robotics applications that are already supported through domain-specific modeling methods. Similar surveys, yet for a wider scope, have been conducted by Biggs and MacDonald [2] as well as Van Deursen et al. [1]. One targeted audience of this survey is the potential DSL *users*, the domain experts looking for method and tool support in their domain. This survey provides means to assess availability and usability

D. Brugali et al. (Eds.): SIMPAR 2014, LNAI 8810, pp. 195–206, 2014.

of the DSLs to formulate their experimental or system hypotheses and generate reproducible experiments. We also target DSL *developers* and system integrators in robotics,
to provide an overview on the state of the art, common solutions and best practices, and
foster scientific exchange and community building inside the domain.

The paper starts with a short introduction to the core concepts of domain-specific
modeling in Section 2 and defines a minimal set of methodological requirements on
DSL approaches to be included in the systematic review. Subsequently, Section 3 analyses the targeted domain and exemplifies the use of domain-specific modeling techniques
along a reference example from the RoboCup@Work competition. Section 4 explains
how the literature survey was conducted along a defined protocol, while Section 5 classifies and quantitatively assesses the found literature, also providing an overview of
several non-functional aspects. On that basis, Section 6 discusses some of these aspects along key publications and identifies best practices both for DSL engineering
and DSL-related publications and documentation. Section 7 summarizes the survey and
propose recommendations for further community development (exchange among researchers) and discusses requirements for re-use of knowledge provided with domain-
specific models in the area of simulation and programming of robotic applications.

2   Domain-Specific Languages

In order to perform a systematic review on domain-specific modeling for simulation
and programming of robotics applications, a necessary prerequisite is to define what we
consider a domain-specific (modeling) language and what we don't. According to van
Deursen et al. [1], a DSL is defined as a *"programming language or executable specification language that offers, through appropriate notations and abstractions, expressive
power focused on, and usually restricted to, a particular problem domain"*. The abstractions and notations must be *"natural/suitable for the stakeholders who specify that
particular concern"* [3]. These definitions already highlight two fundamental characteristics of well-designed DSLs: their expressive power targeted a specific domain and the
definition of formal notations intuitively understandable for domain experts while being
machine processable, eventually yielding executable models of robotics applications.

Model-driven software development with DSLs aims to extract agreed-upon syntax
and semantics from the problem domain, e.g., by reviewing existing code examples and
APIs, through the analysis of formal descriptions found in the literature or the application of further analysis patterns [4]. Based on the results of these domain analysis
steps, the identified abstractions and desired notations can be realized as a DSL. Instead of hiding the domain concepts in a compilation unit implemented with traditional
programming techniques, the DSL approach provides the specific abstractions at the
model level. In contrast to *General Purpose Languages* (GPL) such as C++, Java, or
Python, DSLs usually contain only a restricted set of notations and abstractions. Compared to *external* DSLs that define their own syntax and semantics, so-called *internal*
DSLs are embedded in extensible general purpose languages such as Lua, Racket or
Ruby. They extend the syntax and potentially the semantics of the host language with
domain-specific notations and abstractions. This adds the expressive power of the DSL

to the GPL. While internal DSLs typically rely on (and are bound to) the execution semantics of their host language, external DSLs are transformed to a format that directly allows execution on a target platform or interpretation, e.g., through a virtual machine.

Similarly, *Domain-specific Modelling Languages* (DSML) that use graphical notations must be differentiated from general purpose modeling languages such as UML or SysML. While it is still possible to add domain-specific abstractions to these languages, e.g. using UML Profiles (cf. MARTE [5] to describe and analyze real-time systems), adding domain-specific notation to graphical modeling languages is much harder.

In order to efficiently implement and apply a DSL approach for the development of robotics systems and to fully exploit its benefits, DS(M)Ls are typically realized in toolchains tailored to model-driven development such as the Eclipse Modelling Project [6]. These so-called *language workbenches* such as MPS [7] offer extensive support for the development of the DSLs themselves and for the actual system modeling tasks performed by a language user. DSLs developed in these environments facilitate the users modeling tasks typically with textual and/or graphical editors with rich code completion and dynamic constraint checking. Furthermore, these environments provide extensions points to plug-in required model-to-model (M2M) and model-to-text (M2T) transformations in order to generate code from system models that integrates with the overall environment used for the development of a robotics application.

The above mentioned aspects comprise fundamental characteristics that need to be addressed in a DSL approach. Hence, the DSL approaches considered in this survey i) must provide a language definition or meta-model, e.g. Ecore or (E)BNF, ii) must be textual (internal or external) or graphical languages, iii) must provide an example of their concrete syntax (notation), iv) should[1] explain how a mapping to a target technology is achieved. While these criteria are formulated from a software engineering perspective, the most important criteria to decide whether a paper or article is included in the systematic review is whether or not it targets a relevant concern in the robotics domain. In order to allow for a more fine-grained mapping of DSL-related publications that conform to the criteria introduced above to the robotics domain the following section identifies a set of relevant sub-domains along a reference example that we consider particularly relevant and mature in the context of simulation and programming of robotics systems.

3   Domain Analysis

To exemplify the domain of this survey we use the Precision Placement Test (PPT) from the RoboCup@Work competition. It is a new competition in RoboCup that targets the use of robots in industrial scenarios where robots cooperate with human workers and machines for complex tasks ranging from manufacturing, assembly, automation, and parts-handling up to general logistics. The PPT exemplifies the complexity and huge variability of competences and capabilities required to develop today's robot applications. We consider this example to represent the current state of the art involving mature robotics disciplines so that we expect to find consolidated knowledge in the

---

[1] This relaxation allows to include purely analytical approaches in the review, which we also consider relevant contributions.

```
Robot Fancy {
RobotBase FancyBase {
    inertia_params { ... }
    children { link1 via jA}
}
link link1 {
    id = 1
    inertia_params {
        mass = 1.0
        CoM = (0.5, .0, .0)
        Ix=0.0025  Iy=0.084 Iz=0.084
        Ixy=0.0  Ixz=0.0 Iyz=0.0
```

(a) PPT platform used in RoboCup@Work   (b) Kinematics DSL example [10]

form of DSLs. In the following we will explain the PPT and also synthesize a core set of subdomains[2] which are relevant in solving the task and later used for classification of the surveyed publications. We are aware that this list is non-conclusive, but focus on these for the sake of brevity.

The main objective of the PPT is to assess the robot's ability to grasp and place objects into object-specific cavities (see Fig. 1a). The objects are taken from a set of (a priori known) standardized industrial objects such as screws, nuts, bolts and profiles. For the test a single robot is placed in front of a service area which stores the objects to be manipulated. The objective is to pick each object and place it in the corresponding cavity. Once the objects are picked up and placed or the time is over the task ends. To simulate and solve the problem one usually first needs to know the $\boxed{\text{Robot Structure}}$ $\bigcirc{1}$ of the target robot platform. This comprises representation of the actual physical realization of robot platforms (e.g., mobile base and manipulator) in terms of their mechanical structure and kinematic as well as dynamic properties. This subdomain roughly corresponds to Part B of Springer Handbook of Robotics (*Robot Structures*). Furthermore, $\boxed{\text{Coordinate Representations and Transformations}}$ $\bigcirc{2}$ between parts of the robot and its environment are required to enable computation of position, force, and velocity of the robot joints. This subdomain roughly corresponds to Part A in the Handbook of Robotics (*Robotics Foundations*). Exemplary DSL representatives for this subdomain are URDF [8] and the work of Frigerio et al. [9], shown in Fig. 1b. In general, the PPT demands advanced $\boxed{\text{Perception}}$ $\bigcirc{3}$ and $\boxed{\text{Reasoning and Planning}}$ $\bigcirc{4}$ abilities, namely to recognize and match objects and the correct cavities. Further, precise $\boxed{\text{Manipulation and Grasping}}$ $\bigcirc{5}$ abilities are required, namely to grasp and place the object in such a manner that it fits into the cavity. These subdomains roughly correspond to Part C (*Sensing and Perception*), Part A Chapter 9 (*AI Reasoning Methods for Robotics*), and Part D Chapter 28 (*Grasping*) in the Handbook of Robotics.

For each sub-task (object/cavity *detection/recognition* and object *manipulation*) there are several options to approach the problem which all require $\boxed{\text{Coordination}}$ $\bigcirc{6}$ primitives such as finite-state machines. For instance, the placement of objects in the cavities can be achieved through first perceiving and computing the position of the cavities and then generating a plan yielding a pose where the object can be dropped in the cavity. A more control-based approach is to compute an approximately position of the cavity

---

[2] Subdomains will be marked in the format $\boxed{\text{Name}}$ $\bigcirc{\#}$ where # is a continuing number.

and then placing the object on the arena and sliding the object into the cavity by means of force-feedback. This approach demands advanced ⎣Motion Control⎦ ⑦ abilities in order to cope with uncertainties in the environment and fulfill constraints such as force-limits which corresponds to roughly to Part A Chapter 7 (*Force Control*) in the Handbook for Robotics. Example DSLs for this task are TFF [11] and iTaSC [12]. The presented capabilities all need to be integrated in an overall ⎣Architecture⎦ ⑧ with ⎣Components⎦ ⑨ as the basic building blocks which are preferable re-usable also for other applications. This domain corresponds roughly to Part A Chapter 8 (*Robotic Systems Architectures and Programming*) in the Handbook of Robotics.

4 Process

The selection of the publications for this survey focused on publications that developed domain-specific languages (DSL) to conceptualize aspects of the introduced domain or support certain research or engineering aspects. To find these, we scanned relevant robotics and software conference proceedings for a set of keywords. For the actual selection process we defined two inclusion criteria (IC) and two exclusion criteria (EC):

Table 1. Inclusion criteria (IC) and exclusion criteria for publications in this survey

IC1	In proceedings of the International Conference on Intelligent Robots and Systems (IROS), International Conference on Robotics and Automation (ICRA), International Conference on Simulation, Modeling, and Programming for Autonomous Robots (SIMPAR), Robotics: Science and Systems Conference (RSS), workshop on Software Development and Integration in Robotics (SDIR) or the workshop on Domain-Specific Languages in Robotics (DSLRob) **and** search matching one of the keywords *"domain-specific language"*, *"domain-specific modeling language"*, *"generative programming"*, *"specification language"*, *"description language"*, or *"code generation"*.
IC2	in proceedings of the Code Generation Conference (CG) and the International Conference on Generative Programming: Concepts & Experiences (GPCE) **and** search matching one of the keywords *"robot"* and *"robotics"*.
EC1	DSL does not model or support aspects of the introduced domain.
EC2	Either is no DSL or publication not complying with our definition from section 2, e.g. notation not documented via grammar or example.

IC1 included 208 publications after removing duplicates, IC2 included additional 2 publications, adding up to a total of 210 publications. We consider all publications from IC1 to pass EC1, as they passed through a review process of robotics conferences. EC2 filtered 169 publications, leading to a total of 41 publications that will be analyzed and discussed in the remainder of this survey.

5 Analysis

This section assesses technical aspects across the publications in this survey. The publications are analyzed along their subdomains according to Section 3 and regarding their temporal distribution as well as their utilized tool or method.

Subdomains. A first analysis we did was grouping DSLs and their publications by common semantics, abstractions and use-cases according to the domain example introduced in Section 3. This is intended to serve as a map for potential DSL users as well as foster discussion and reuse of languages and the underlying models for DSL developers. The

Table 2. Overview of the surveyed DSLs and their subdomains: ■ = in focus, □ = partially

	Subdomain(s)								
	① Struct.	② Transf.	③ Perc.	④ Plan.	⑤ Manip.	⑥ Coord.	⑦ Ctrl.	⑧ Arch.	⑨ Comp.
Muehe2010						□	■		
Akim2010						■			□
Reckhaus2010						■			
Frigerio2011	■	□					■		
Trojanek2011	■					■		■	
Anderson2011	■								
Romero2011									■
Ingles2010						■			
Angerer2012	□					■			
Klotzbuecher2012						■			
Laet2012		■							
Nordmann2012							■	■	□
Buchmann2013	■		□				■		
Hochgeschw2013			■						
Blumenthal2013	■								
Dantam2012						■			
Kilgo2012									■
Dhouib2012						■		■	■
Brugali2012						■		■	■
Vanthienen2013						■			
Klotzbuecher2011						■	■		
Loetzsch2006					■	■			
Steck2011						■			
Anderson2012	□								□
Haas2012						■			
Dai2002						■			
Manikonda1995						■	■		
Kunze2011	■			□					
Kanayama2000		■					■		
Rosa2007									□
Graves1999	■								
Tousignant2012						■			
Murray1992	■						■		
RuggGunn1994					■				
KressGazit2010	□				□	□			
Ljungkrantz2007	■					■			
Thomas2013						■	■		
Ferstenberg1986							■		
Bordignon2010	■								

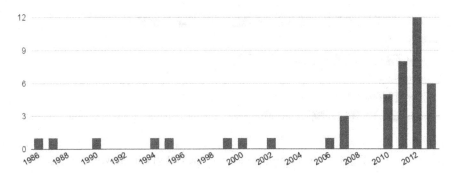

Fig. 2. Temporal distribution of the publications in this survey ranging from 1986 to 2013

categorization is given in Table 2 and references the subdomains introduced in Section 3. The table is an initial version, though, that we intend to update continuously and maintain online[3], enriched with the aspects discussed in the remainder of this survey. The left-most column of Table 2 references this online table, as space constraints unfortunately don't allow citation of all surveyed publications.

The initial grouping by subdomains seems reasonable, as the assignment of most of the DSLs and publications to subdomains was quite straight-forward. However, the number of publications per subdomain varies significantly. Whereas we found no DSLs in the subdomain of Manipulation and Grasping (5), Coordination (6) for example seems to be quite well-covered as over 20 publications entirely or partially belong to this subdomain. The Robot Structure (1) and Motion Control (7) subdomains are also well-covered with roughly 10 publications each. These numbers may indicate how well-explored or even stable a discipline or subdomain is.

Temporal Distribution. Model-driven and domain-specific approaches are on the rise in robotics, we plotted the temporal distribution of the publications in this survey, as shown in Fig. 2. The distribution clearly supports a positive trend of DSLs in robotics respectively their publications, especially since around the year 2010 with several publications per year. This is equivalent to the start of the DSLRob workshop, the numbers, however, clearly exceed the number of DSLRob publications per year, proving that this is also a trend on general robotics conferences.

Methods / Tools. This section analyzes the methods and tools that were used for development of the surveyed DSLs, as far as this is assessable via the publications or referenced documentation. This comprises tool support for developing external DSLs, as well as development of internal DSLs, as shown in Fig. 3.

The majority of DSLs assessed with this survey is realized as an external DSL. Although different tools and methods are being used, Fig. 3 shows that the *Eclipse Modeling Project* [6] (EMP) seems to be quite widely used. It therefore seems to be a good integration point and opportunity for DSL compatibility in this domain. Some publications mentioned the extensive EMP tool-support explicitly as a big advantage of

---

[3] http://cor-lab.org/robotics-dsl-zoo

Fig. 3. Tools and methods used for the DSLs in this survey

developing DSLs inside the Eclipse framework [13, 14], or the possibility of language re-use [15], as approaches within EMP share the same representation (Ecore). 7 publications in this survey developed their DSLs as internal DSL, for example in Lisp [16], and Lua [12]. 7 of the assessed publications developed DSLs and their tool-chain manually and without the aforementioned tool support, e.g. with custom parsers and tools.

6   Discussion

This section highlights different aspects of the surveyed DSLs as well as their publications that we think are important for i) language developers to enable language re-use, interoperability and discussing the core concepts, as well as ii) language users to allow assessing the availability and usability of the DSLs. We show different approaches to extract best practices in terms of documentation, accessibility and evaluation of robotics DSLs to make suggestions to the community. The need for this became clear during analysis of the publications for this survey, as lots of the aspects discussed here were largely undocumented and/or hard to access.

Accessibility and Documentation. An important factor for re-use of DSLs, scientific exchange and community building around DSLs in robotics is their accessibility and documentation. This comprises several factors like technical accessibility (e.g. download of the language or models), licensing, and documentation of the DSL, its usage and execution context. Only a subset of the DSLs in this survey is documented in a way that would allow interfacing with it, e.g. with a documented meta-model [14, 17, 18]. While some publications give hints on the meta-model or show parts of it [19, 13], several publications document their meta-model mostly through exemplary models. Some DSLs are available for download as open-source software [18, 8, 20].

A good way to promote re-use of s DSL is to provide tutorials and examples of its usage, as download together with software frameworks and dependencies (if necessary), as done for example by [21, 8]. Laet et al. propose their semantics for standardization in the context of the robotics engineering task force [22].

Artifacts and Use-Case. To assess the intended use of the DSLs, we looked at the artifacts generated (if any) and the context they are used in. While the DSL can be used to generate visualizations of systems, e.g. the system architecture [23] or platforms [8], the main use-case for DSLs is to generate executable code to perform experiments or provide supporting routines. DSLs within the identified subdomains often cover similar use-cases. The ⎡Robot Structure⎤ ① subdomain for example primarily targets controllers and platform as well as simulation support. Frigerio et al. [18] and Laet et al. [16] target kinematics and dynamics controllers that can be embedded in motion control systems. Bordignon et al. [24] exemplify the usage by generating code to simulate the specified robot platform in a particular simulation framework.

Artifact generation from DSLs becomes especially powerful and suited for re-use if the toolchain supports different M2M and M2T transformations. Either to generate different artifacts like visualization, computational routines and glue code [23], or executable code for different programming languages or software platforms [10, 11, 25].

Evaluation. Evaluation of a DSL-based approach in their intended use-case is not only interesting from a developer's perspective, but also serves as a foundation for a decision from a user's perspective. A number of the surveyed publications evaluated the semantics or the generated artifacts. A surprising yet positive outcome of the analysis was, that quite a number of the DSLs in this domain are evaluated not only in simulation, but on real hardware [26, 14, 18, 13], and even on different platforms [19, 11].

We can roughly differentiate two different kinds of evaluation approaches: qualitative and quantitative evaluation. Qualitative evaluation is often done by conceptual discussions based on examples, e.g. portability of the semantics to different platforms [14, 19, 11]. Laet et al. [21] for example model some typical use-cases and show how common errors can be avoided by using its proposed semantics.

Özgür [27] lists four different quantitative benefits and corresponding metrics, that can be used to evaluate a model-based approach and can serve as a best practice:

1. **Efficiency** can be evaluated in terms of performance and memory utilization. Frigerio et al. [9] for example benchmarked the generated C++ code in its intended use-case, being forward and inverse kinematics and dynamics on different numbers of degrees-of-freedom.
2. **Scalability** in terms of compilation time and system size.
3. **Productivity** in terms of size, effort or number of change requests. Examples are Ringert et. al [28] and Romero-Garces et. al [29]. Both evaluate the usage of a DSL from the developers perspective against classical approaches by means of empirical software engineering. Non-functional aspects they covered comprise time spent for learning of the technologies, effort for fixing bugs, component re-use and complexity of understanding re-used software artifacts. [11] conducted hardware experiments on a PR2 and a KUKA LWR and analyzed the necessary number of lines of code for platform-independent and robot/framework specific code.
4. **Reliability**, e.g. in terms of defects introduced in a period of time.

Platform. An important aspect of the generated artifacts and the model transformations is how tightly they are coupled to a certain platform. "Platform" in this context means the technical execution context, so the software framework, and all additional tools or libraries necessary to use the DSL or the generated artifacts.

First of all we have to differentiate between the DSL being used in a interpretation vs. a generation manner. Interpretation of a DSL is always being tied to a (DSL-specific) interpreter (e.g. [30]). For DSLs that are used in a generation manner, we differentiate between three classes of platform-dependency:

1. Proprietary solutions like *KRL* [31] and *RAPID* [32] that are targeted to a single platform and don't target openness or platform independence at all.
2. Generation of artifacts that are tied to or dependent on a library stack, software framework or runtime environment [13, 17, 33]. Some of the DSLs in this survey target a certain framework or environment, but come with exchangeable generators to explicitly allow re-use of the DSL and its concepts in different frameworks or environments as discussed above. Klotzbücher et al. [11] make the platform explicit, by distinguishing between platform-independent and platform-specific models.
3. Transformation of the DSL code directly to a general purpose language (e.g. Ada [14] or C++ [10]) being the most platform-independent option by reducing platform dependencies to a minimum, which provides clear advantages. It is easier portable, even to embedded systems [14], easier to re-use and eases scientific exchange. It also reduces assumptions about the platform from within the DSL.

DSL Development Process. Mernik et al. [4] discuss that the identification and formalization of domain-specific abstractions is an important decision pattern for DSL development. However, to reuse, refine or to define new abstractions one needs to perform activities known in the area of *knowledge representation* such as domain and problem assessment and expert consultation. Unfortunately, in the assessed papers very little is written about the process *how* the abstractions have been identified, e.g. based on an ontology [25], a formalism [16] or a domain analysis [23]. One reason may be that the DSL developers are very often simultaneously also the DSL users and domain experts. Hence, assessing the domain is performed in an ad-hoc and implicit manner. To bring forward the DSL development in robotics we argue that robotic DSL papers should report also about the process of *how* and on which basis one developed certain domain-specific abstractions.

7 Synopsis

We surveyed the available literature on domain-specific (modeling) languages used for design, simulation and programming of robotics systems. The quantitative analysis supports that DS(M)Ls are a current active research field for simulation and programming of robots, however, compatibility and re-use of different DSLs and approaches is still an issue. Yet the *Eclipse Modeling Project* may serve as an integration platform for DSLs in robotics as it is already widely used. We further discussed, how different approaches to documentation, evaluation and platform-dependency affect the availability and usability of a DSL. We intend this survey to serve the robotics DSL community to foster exchange between DSL developers as well as providing an orientation for potential DSL users. Following the idea of the *EMF Concrete Syntax Zoo*[4] we intend to continuously maintain the survey as an online *Robotics DSL Zoo*[5] and invite the community to provide feedback and contribute. Future iterations of this survey will comprise further conference proceedings and include journal publications.

---

[4] http://www.emftext.org/index.php/EMFText_Concrete_Syntax_Zoo
[5] http://cor-lab.org/robotics-dsl-zoo

Acknowledgement. This work was supported by a grant of the Cluster of Excellence Cognitive Interaction Technology (CITEC) at Bielefeld University. Nico Hochgeschwender received a PhD scholarship from the Graduate Institute of the Bonn-Rhein-Sieg University.

References

[1] van Deursen, A., Klint, P., Visser, J.: Domain-Specific Languages: An Annotated Bibliography. ACM Sigplan Notices (2000)

[2] Biggs, G., MacDonald, B.: A Survey of Robot Programming Systems. In: Australasian Conference on Robotics and Automation (2003)

[3] Völter, M., Benz, S., Dietrich, C., Engelmann, B., Helander, M., Kats, L., Visser, E., Wachsmuth, G.: DSL Engineering Designing, Implementing and Using Domain-Specific Languages (2013)

[4] Mernik, M., Heering, J., Sloane, A.M.: When and how to Develop Domain-Specific Languages. ACM Computing Surveys 37(4), 316–344 (2005)

[5] Gérard, S., Selic, B.: The UML – MARTE Standardized Profile. In: The International Federation of Automatic Control, Seoul, Korea, pp. 6909–6913 (2008)

[6] Gronback, R.C.: Eclipse Modeling Project: A Domain-Specific Language (DSL) Toolkit. Addison-Wesley Professional (2009)

[7] JetBrains. Meta Programming System

[8] Ioan Sucan. Unified Robot Description Format (URDF)

[9] Frigerio, M., Buchli, J., Caldwell, D.G.: Code Generation of Algebraic Quantities for Robot Controllers. In: International Conference on Intelligent Robots and Systems, pp. 2346–2351 (October 2012)

[10] Frigerio, M., Buchli, J., Caldwell, D.G.: A Domain Specific Language for Kinematic Models and Fast Implementations of Robot Dynamics Algorithms. In: Workshop on Domain-Specific Languages and Models for Robotic Systems (2011)

[11] Klotzbücher, M., Smits, R., Bruyninckx, H., De Schutter, J.: Reusable Hybrid Force-Velocity controlled Motion Specifications with executable Domain Specific Languages. In: International Conference on Intelligent Robots and Systems, pp. 4684–4689 (2011)

[12] Vanthienen, D., Klotzbücher, M., De Schutter, J., De Laet, T., Bruyninckx, H.: Rapid application development of constrained-based task modelling and execution using Domain Specific Languages. In: International Conference on Intelligent Robots and Systems (2013)

[13] Angerer, A., Smirra, R., Hoffmann, A., Schierl, A., Vistein, M., Reif, W.: A Graphical Language for Real-Time Critical Robot Commands. In: Workshop on Domain-Specific Languages and Models for Robotic Systems, Tsukuba (2012)

[14] Trojanek, P.: Model-Driven Engineering Approach to Design and Implementation of Robot Control System. In: Workshop on Domain-Specific Languages and Models for Robotic Systems (2011)

[15] Blumenthal, S., Bruyninckx, H.: Towards a Domain Specific Language for a Scene Graph based Robotic World Model. In: Workshop on Domain-Specific Languages and Models for Robotic Systems (2013)

[16] De Laet, T., Schaekers, W., de Greef, J., Bruyninckx, H.: Domain Specific Language for Geometric Relations between Rigid Bodies targeted to Robotic Applications. In: Workshop on Domain-Specific Languages and Models for Robotic Systems (2012)

[17] Thomas, U., Hirzinger, G., Rumpe, B., Schulze, C., Wortmann, A.: A New Skill Based Robot Programming Language Using UML/P Statecharts. In: International Conference on Robotics and Automation (2013)

[18] Frigerio, M., Buchli, J., Caldwell, D.G.: Model based code generation for kinematics and dynamics computations in robot controllers. In: Workshop on Software Development and Integration in Robotics, St. Paul, Minnesota, USA (2012)

[19] Reckhaus, M., Hochgeschwender, N.: A Platform-Independent Programming Environment for Robot Control. In: Workshop on Domain-Specific Languages and Models for Robotic Systems (2010)

[20] Lötzsch, M., Risler, M., Jungel, M.: XABSL – A Pragmatic Approach to Behavior Engineering. In: International Conference on Intelligent Robots and Systems, pp. 5124–5129 (2006)

[21] De Laet, T., Bellens, S., Bruyninckx, H., De Schutter, J.: Geometric Relations between Rigid Bodies (Part 2): From Semantics to Software. IEEE Robotics and Automation Magazine (September 2012)

[22] De Laet, T., Bellens, S., Smits, R., Aertbelien, E., Bruyninckx, H., De Schutter, J.: Geometric Relations between Rigid Bodies (Part 1): Semantics for Standardization. IEEE Robotics and Automation Magazine (June 2012)

[23] Nordmann, A., Wrede, S.: A Domain-Specific Language for Rich Motor Skill Architectures. In: Workshop on Domain-Specific Languages and Models for Robotic Systems, Tsukuba (2012)

[24] Bordignon, M., Schultz, U.P., Stoy, K.: Model-Based Kinematics Generation for Modular Mechatronic Toolkits. In: International Conference on Generative Programming and Component Engineering, p. 157 (2010)

[25] Dhouib, S., Kchir, S., Stinckwich, S., Ziadi, T., Ziane, M.: RobotML, a Domain-Specific Language to Design, Simulate and Deploy Robotic Applications. In: Noda, I., Ando, N., Brugali, D., Kuffner, J.J. (eds.) SIMPAR 2012. LNCS, vol. 7628, pp. 149–160. Springer, Heidelberg (2012)

[26] Thomas, U., Finkemeyer, B., Kröger, T., Wahl, F.M.: Error-Tolerant Execution of Complex Robot Tasks based on Skill Primitives. In: International Conference on Automation and Robotics, Taipei, Taiwan (2003)

[27] Özgür, T.: Comparison of Microsoft DSL Tools and Eclipse Modeling Frameworks for Domain-Specific Modeling in the Context of the Model-Driven Development. Master, Blekinge Institute of Technology (2007)

[28] Ringert, J.O., Rumpe, B., Wortmann, A.: A Case Study on Model-Based Development of Robotic Systems using MontiArc with Embedded Automata. In: Dagstuhl-Workshop MBEES: Modellbasierte Entwicklung eingebetteter Systeme IX (2013)

[29] Romero-Garcés, A., Manso, L.J., Gutierrez, M.A., Cintas, R., Bustos, P.: Improving the Lifecycle of Robotics Components using Domain-Specific Languages. In: Workshop on Domain-Specific Languages and Models for Robotic Systems (2013)

[30] Mühe, H., Angerer, A., Hoffmann, A., Reif, W.: On reverse-engineering the KUKA Robot Language. In: Workshop on Domain-Specific Languages and Models for Robotic Systems (2010)

[31] KUKA System Software 5.5 - Operating and Programming Instructions for System Integrators. Technical report, KUKA Roboter GmbH (2009)

[32] RAPID Overview. Technical report, ABB Robotics Products

[33] Steck, A., Schlegel, C.: SMART TCL: An Execution Language for Conditional Reactive Task Execution in a Three Layer Architecture for Service Robots. In: Int. Workshop on DYnamic languages for RObotic and Sensors systems (DYROS), pp. 274–277 (2010)

Towards Rule-Based Dynamic
Safety Monitoring for Mobile Robots

Sorin Adam[1], Morten Larsen[1], Kjeld Jensen[2], and Ulrik Pagh Schultz[2]

[1] Conpleks ApS, Struer, Denmark
[2] University of Southern Denmark, Odense, Denmark

Abstract. Safety is a key challenge in robotics, in particular for mobile robots operating in an open and unpredictable environment. To address the safety challenge, various software-based approaches have been proposed, but none of them provide a clearly specified and isolated safety layer. In this paper, we propose that safety-critical concerns regarding the robot software be explicitly declared separately from the main program, in terms of externally observable properties of the software. Concretely, we use a Domain-Specific Language (DSL) to declaratively specify a set of safety-related rules that the software must obey, as well as corresponding corrective actions that trigger when rules are violated. Our prototype DSL is integrated with ROS, is shown to be capable of specifying safety-related constraints, and is experimentally demonstrated to enforce safety behaviour in existing robot software. We believe our approach could be extended to other fields to similarly simplify safety certification.

1 Introduction

Safety is a key challenge in robotics, in particular for domains such as precision agriculture where large, mobile robots operate in an open and unpredictable environment [1]. Safety is typically addressed by a combination of physical safety systems [2], the use of a safety-aware control algorithm [3], and the use of a software architecture that maps safety-critical program parts to a specific subsystem [4]. In an effort to address the safety challenge, various software architectures have been suggested for agricultural robotic vehicles [5, 6], but none of them provide specification and isolation of the safety-critical parts of the software. This increases the risk that programming errors will cause violations of those safety properties of the robot that are dependent on the correctness of the software. Moreover, faulty or erratically behaving hardware poses an additional safety risk: software built on implicit assumptions regarding the reliability of the hardware must monitor the system to ensure that these assumptions remain valid, failure to do so may compromise safety.

Mainstream robotic middleware such as Orocos [7] and ROS [8] allows software to be built in terms of reusable and individually tested components that can be deployed in separate execution environments, but do not provide any explicit means of expressing safety-related concerns. Model-driven software development approaches allow controllers to be automatically assembled from well-specified

D. Brugali et al. (Eds.): SIMPAR 2014, LNAI 8810, pp. 207–218, 2014.

components with explicit invariants that can be monitored at runtime, but typically provide a component-centric view that does not address the performance and safety of the system as a whole [9, 10]. Specific components can include invariants that specify assumptions about the hardware, but there is no comprehensive, implementation-independent specification of the hardware platform. In the specific case of safety, we observe that safety concerns may cross-cut the component structure of the system, for example enforcing a stop after a bump sensor has triggered could involve different software components (one for the sensor, one for the motion actuators).

We propose that safety-critical concerns regarding the robot software be explicitly declared separately from the main program, in terms of the overall functionality of the software. Rather than addressing the individual functionality of specific components, we address the functionality of the system as a whole in terms of externally observable properties of individual components, their communication, and the state of the surrounding execution environment.The main contribution of our work is the proposal and proof-of-concept experiments of a simple yet expressive rule-based language for enforcing safety constraints on existing ROS-based software. This paper presents the initial language design and prototype implementation, and experimentally documents the effectiveness of the solution through a series of experiments that test safety-oriented scenarios both involving software and hardware failures.

The rest of this paper is organised as follows: Section 2 discusses robot safety and model-driven software development, after which Section 3 presents our main contribution, Section 4 documents the experimental validation of our approach and discusses limitations, last Section 5 concludes.

2   Robot Safety and Modeling

2.1   Robot Safety

A robot has to be safe and reliable [11]. In the context of our work, *robot safety* concerns all elements of the robot and its immediate environment in which one or more errors may constitute a threat to nearby humans, animals, facilities and the robot itself. Faults in control architectures for mobile robots can be categorised as [12]: Environment (such as unpredictable environmental changes); Environmental Awareness divided into sensing faults (due to sensor or perception algorithm limitations) and action faults (unexpected outcomes of actuations); Autonomous System divided into decision making faults (lack of knowledge leading to inadequate decision making), hardware faults (sensors, actuators, embedded hardware) and software faults (with regards to software design, implementation and runtime execution). From a technical point of view, we aim to provide a system-wide supervision system that dynamically detects software faults; detection of hardware faults is supported to the extent that the fault is detectable from software. In this respect, our approach is similar to Blanke et al, where manually implemented supervision modules are used at different levels to increase safety and reliability in an autonomous robot conducting maintenance tasks in an orchard [13]. In our work, we aim to automatically implement all parts of the supervision infrastructure based on declarative rules, but currently limit the supervision to deal with safety (not reliability). Unlike more general-purpose runtime monitoring systems based on temporal logic, we focus on providing a simple specification language easily accessible to non-experts.

2.2 Commercial Applications and Legal Regulations

We are interested in commercial applications of mobile robots within the agricultural sector. In Europe, from the regulatory point of view, robots are *currently* treated like any other commercial machine and thus have to comply with three European Directives: 2006/95/EC, 2001/95/EC, and 2006/42/EC. One group of the stated requirements concerns safety, usually evaluated by performing a safety risk assessment and reduction by using a standard like ISO 12100:2010. Therefore, the safety risk assessment is the primary source for the safety requirements of the robot. Standards like ISO 13849 provide guidance for establishing safety performance levels (PL) for the safety-related controllers. However, the safety PLs refer only to qualitative aspects of the software development, and are not concerned with quantitative aspects like latency, performance or reaction time. The standards demand, for higher safety PLs, increased software quality, and thus extensive code reviews, testing and documentation, all adding up to the project cost and delaying the release date. Moreover, the safety certification requirements can make the effort of releasing a new revision comparable with that of releasing of a new product.

2.3 Software Safety

Safety-critical software can be implemented in a general-purpose language and then verified automatically, and fault-tolerance can be improved using traditional techniques for software reliability, such as n-version programming [14]. Alternatively, using model-driven software development driven by a metamodel, the software can be specified in a high-level formalism from which an implementation satisfying the required properties can be automatically derived [15, 16]. Formal modeling enables analysis of more abstract properties, such as the safety of a robot, to be formally verified [17]. Automatic generation has the added benefit of accelerating software development [18–20, 10]. In this work we use a simple metamodel to describe existing ROS software, enabling both static analysis of the integrity of the software [21], as well as correctly programming in a high-level domain-specific language that targets this existing software, which is the subject of this paper.

2.4 Analysis

A commonly attributed reason for the popularity of ROS is the large amount of freely available software for the platform, in the form of reusable components (nodes). Indeed, the use of components as reusable building blocks is fundamental to many approaches for model-driven software development for robotics [20, 10]. To ensure correct runtime functionality in a component, its execution can be monitored according to predefined invariants that essentially specify a contract for the dynamic behaviour of the component [9]. In all cases, the required safety-related behaviour may be specific to the application (e.g., the maximal speed at which the robot may move), may concern system-wide properties (e.g., a correlation of sensor values from multiple sensors), and may entail system-level reactions (e.g., an emergency stop of the robot). Since robot safety ultimately is a system-level property, we believe it is essential to enable the programmer to specify safety in terms of the robot software as a whole. Making this safety specification separate from the functionality facilitates verifying that the safety specification conforms to safety requirements, provided we guarantee that the robot software always follows the safety specification. In this paper, we propose to program the functionality-providing part of the software using standard ROS nodes, and to automatically program the safety-enforcing part based on declarative rules.

3   Rule-Based Dynamic Safety Monitoring

We propose a software architecture for implementing the safety-related functionality of the robot software separated from the main functionality, driven by a domain-specific language (DSL) for declaratively specifying the safety requirements. In more detail, safety rules, for example identified when performing the risk assessment, are described at a high level using the Rule-Based Safety Specification (RuBaSS) DSL. RuBaSS provides a simple and declarative syntax, making the task of implementing the safety-related requirements more accessible to robotics experts with a lower degree of software engineering expertise. The risk of errors is reduced, as the RuBaSS declaration drives the automatic generation of all safety-related code. Our approach directly enables an implementation-independent reuse of the safety-related part of a robot controller between different releases, since the RuBaSS declaration does not need to change when the underlying software changes (except that names shared between RuBaSS rules and component interfaces must be kept consistent). Moreover, the infrastructure can be reused in a range of products: the code generator can be directly reused whereas low-level interfaces to sensors and actuators will be specific to each robot. Safety-related customisation for the products is thus mainly achieved at the higher level, using the safety language.

The implementation of the low-level hardware interfacing and the code generation part of RuBaSS is naturally the responsibility of a skilled software development team, this division of roles is a normal consequence of introducing a more structured approach to robotics software development [20]. To further enhance robustness of the safety layer, and hence the overall safety of the robot, development of the code generator and execution supporting platform could be done by separate teams, targeting different programming languages. The decision for

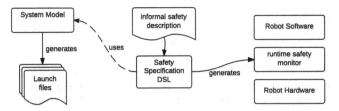

Fig. 1. Process overview

the implementation languages will normally be platform dependent, so different robotics platforms could favour certain languages. For example, for ROS-based robots, the safety-related code generation could target C++ and Python; in this paper, for simplicity we only implement a single prototype based on Python, in the future we expect to also support C++.

3.1   Overview

We consider that safety in robotic systems is a cross-cutting feature that interacts with many different parts of the system, so we propose to specify safety-related concerns in a separate declaratively programmed subsystem. This approach enables runtime isolation of the safety-related part from the rest of the robot application: although not currently implemented, the safety-related constraints can execute in a different context, for example using off-the-shelf virtualisation techniques, or on different hardware. Fig. 1 shows the overall workflow of using RuBaSS. The developer derives a RuBaSS from an informal safety specification and can access information from a system model which provides information on components (topics and nodes), thereby providing static consistency checks of the specification. The RuBaSS compiler generates a runtime safety component which monitors the specified properties of the software system.

The use of a DSL enables the total system cost to be optimised, since the same specification can be automatically redeployed by using different code generators. For example, the safety-related functionality may be executed as a regular ROS node during development, and then during field testing be redeployed to run on a dedicated, high-reliability hardware platform with modest processing power requirements, while the rest of the robot software executes on an inexpensive, less reliable hardware platform. The safety-related language we propose relies on the modularity offered by frameworks like Orocos and ROS, where the software functionality is divided into several intercommunicating parts implemented in dedicated components. We currently only support components that communicate using topic-based publish-subscribe, support for other communication patterns is considered future work. Monitoring of internal component state is not supported, if needed we expect that an approach similar to Lotz et al could be used [9].

```
1  action primitive stop;
2  entity drive_system : encoder_node, actuator_node; {
3    rules: // simple example comprising one actuator
4     actuator_erratic:
5      ((topic /cmd_vel_left.linear.x > 0.02m/s
6         or topic /cmd_vel_left.linear.x < −0.02m/s)
7          and topic /encoder_left.data == 0) for 0.4sec; }
8  if (drive_system.actuator_erratic for 1 sec) then { stop; };
```

Fig. 2. RuBaSS example (prettyprinted): enforcing stop on erratic behaviour

3.2   The Language

A simple example of the RuBaSS language is presented in Fig. 2 (a more extensive set of rules is used for the experiments later in the paper). The listing demonstrates the main features of the language. RuBaSS code is written in a safety description file containing two key parts: entities that group nodes together based on their functionality, and the behaviour section where the safety requirements are described. The safety-related actions the robot can execute can be triggered from the behaviour section; in this example the primitive action stop is declared, a complete set of actions can be imported from a robot-specific library. If the stop action is invoked by the rules, the robot stops (primitive actions are implemented in the underlying robot firmware). The entity section describes the drive_system as being composed of two nodes: the encoder_node and the actuator_node. For this entity only one rule is exemplified: actuator_erratic. This rule collects three different conditions under a common name using logical operators expressed in words. The rule is fulfilled when the actuator is unresponsive. RuBaSS also accepts temporal conditions, e.g., a logical expression is assessed and has to remain true for a continuous period of time. The behavioural section is where robot actions are associated with selected event occurrences. In the example, the actuator is declared to be "erratic" if there is a command and the encoders are not reporting any movement. Since this condition can occur during normal operation, e.g., due to reaction delays, a temporal condition is added specifying that the command and lack of movement must be present for more than 0.4 seconds. In summary, the entity rules define concrete safety-related events, the behavioural part of the specification concerns what action to take when based on combinations of these events.

In general, RuBaSS supports multiple entities and multiple compound rules defined inside every entity. The rules can be constructed around nodes or topics. Nodes can be supervised in terms of liveness, CPU and memory usage, whereas topics can be supervised in terms of publishing frequency and constraints on the data exchanged. The behaviour section associates actions to logical combinations of rules. All conditions, both for rules and behaviours, can be time-quantified using the for operator, and all constants can include physical units; units are currently only for documentation, statically checking their consistency using a component model that annotates physical units to components is future work.

3.3   Target Platform and Code Generation

A proof of concept of RuBaSS, generating Python code, has been implemented. Python has been chosen due to its ease of use and previous experience with Python and ROS; for production code C++ would be a better choice for target language, since it can both execute on a standard laptop and be executed on an embedded system with few resources. (Since having multiple implementations is advantageous for safety-critical systems, the Python-generated code could run on a PC-class controller together with the embedded code on a low-end controller.)

In order to ease the code generation, a Python library implementing classes for representing rules, entities, topic and node monitoring has been developed. A rule object stores the result of each rule evaluation in a timestamped buffer, making the result of the rule accessible for a given time interval. The topic monitoring class also stores the received ROS messages in a timestamped buffer. Each of the classes implement a loop method allowing the rule to be evaluated, and in the case of a topic, the average frequency to be calculated. The loop method is called on each object at a specific interval, currently 0.1 seconds (10 Hz), but can be set as high as the computer performance allows.

The need to access past data of the left hand side of the operator, complicates the generation of the code for the `for` operator. The solution used is to implement a buffering scheme in the rule and topic monitoring classes. However, the expression may be composed of a number of sub-expressions, for which past results should be kept. To solve this problem, we analyse the RuBaSS program before code generation and replace the left-hand side expression of a `for` with a reference to an intermediate rule containing the original left-hand side expression. Each time a rule is evaluated, the timestamped result is stored in a buffer used to remove old rule results outside of the time limit of the `for` expression.

4   Experiments

Experiments have been conducted using two different robots running different software: a physical *Frobit* robot and the standard, simulated iClebo *Kobuki* robot from the ROS distribution. The Frobit [22] is a small, low-cost robot designed for rapid prototyping; it is differentially steered and the low-level interface resembles that of many tracked and wheeled field robots; it is running the standard deployment of the FroboMind ROS-based software framework for field robots [5] on an i3 PC with 3Gb RAM running Ubuntu 12.04. The Kobuki is similar to the Frobit but has a different low-level interface and runs the standard, different and independently developed ROS-based control software, demonstrating the generality of our approach.

The experiments have been conducted using a specially written ROS test node, illustrated in Fig. 3. The node consists of a common part implementing the launch of the test cases and another containing the test-case-specific code for test environment (physical or simulated). For the Frobit, the test node is able to physically interrupt control lines of the wheels encoders and motors

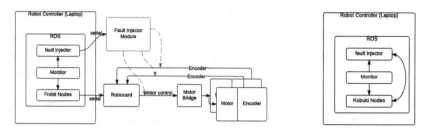

Fig. 3. Robot setup. Frobit hardware setup (left) and Kobuki setup (right).

through an Arduino-type board communicating with the test program via a serial connection. As the Arduino board is able to control the motors, the RuBaSS `stop` command is implemented using this board. For the Kobuki, the velocity commands coming from the robot's controller are altered by the test program to simulate a misbehaviour. In all cases we measure the time between when a fault has been introduced and when the safety-related node sends the stop command. All experiments have been repeated ten times.

A set of safety rules extracted from the risk assessment performed for commercial robots developed at Conpleks[1] have been implemented using the DSL. For the Frobit experiments, RuBaSS was used to implement rules supervising the wheels encoders, and limiting the linear speed of the robot (in total 3 entities and 9 rules). For the Kobuki experiments, the rules enforce a maximum linear and spinning speed for the robot, a maximum processor load for the ROS node controlling the robot, as well as the area the robot is allowed to move in (in total 1 entity and 4 rules).

4.1   Hardware Failure Experiments

For the Frobit, a number of experiments have been performed simulating a single fault or combination of wheels encoders not working or motors misbehaving. In all tests, the robot has been manually controlled using a remote control (a Nintendo Wii game controller) and specific faults, such as an encoder failure, were manually triggered using the test node. The experimental scenarios, implemented in the dedicated ROS test node, were running on the same hardware platform as the rest of the robot.

We tested combinations of the following failures: (1) Left or right wheel encoder not working (denoted E_x): The control line for the left and/or right wheel of the quadrature encoder has been interrupted. (2) Left, right, or both motors running at full speed (denoted M_x): The H-bridge controller of one or both motors have been wired in such a way that the motor has been forced to run at full speed, but the direction of movement (forward or backwards) was still under the control of the robot. (3) Combined simulated faults, with left or right motor full speed and right or left wheel encoder not working.

---

[1] The GrassBots grass-cutting robot [23] and the FIXFeeder mink-feeding robot [24] from Conpleks ApS.

Table 1. Experimental results. All times are in seconds. E indicates encoder failure, M indicates motor speed exceeded, in both cases left or right.

Frobit	Ideal	Avg	SD	Min	Max		Kobuki	Ideal	Avg	SD	Min	Max
E_R	1.40	2.07	0.35	1.41	2.66		Boundary	0.00	0.07	0.02	0.03	0.09
E_L	1.40	1.87	0.24	1.60	2.34		Max speed	1.00	1.23	0.42	0.91	2,00
M_R	0.50	0.82	0.13	0.61	1.02		Max spin	0.70	8.15	1.89	4.66	10.32
M_L	0.50	1.71	0.30	0.92	2.13		*(Exp=0.2)*	0.20	0.17	0.03	0.12	0.21
M_{LR}	0.50	0.86	0.31	0.58	1.56		*(Exp=0.0)*	0.00	0.17	0.04	0.11	0.22
$M_L + E_R$	0.50	0.72	0.10	0.58	0.93		CPU	1.50	1.71	0.14	1.51	1.95
$M_R + E_L$	0.50	0.74	0.18	0.57	1.11							

4.2 Simulated Experiments

Several experiments have been performed using the simulated Kobuki robot: leaving a predefined area, exceeding the linear or spinning speed, and ROS-node CPU overload. All the tests were executed by indicating a target goal for the robot, leaving the planner to decide a route and control the robot. The same dedicated test ROS node has been used as for the Frobit, interfacing to the simulator by having the node monitor and modify the velocity and odometry information exchanged between the simulator and the robot.

We performed the following experiments: *(1) Boundary exceeded:* The robot target position has been set outside the predefined safety area, forcing the controller to violate the safety rules when driving the robot towards the target. The time interval between the moment when the border has been touched by the robot and when the stop command was issued by the safety ROS node has been measured. *(2) Maximum linear or spin speed exceeded:* The velocity commands issued by the controller have been modified by the test node: with every new velocity command received, an increasingly drifting amount has been added to the linear or spin velocity field value of the commands sent to the simulated robot. The test case measured the delay between the moment when the sent velocity command exceeds the maximum allowed linear or spin speed defined by the safety rules and when the stop command have been sent by the safety node. *(3) CPU overload:* The test node simulated a temporary software misbehaviour of one of the ROS nodes by executing a CPU-intensive loop for a determined period of time. The test case measured the time between when the CPU intensive loop was entered and when the safety node issued the stop command.

4.3 Results

The data obtained are shown in Table 1 for both the Frobit and Kobuki experiments. The columns in the table refer to the ideal minimum expected time according to the safety rules (Ideal), average time over the 10 repeated experiments (Avg), standard deviation (SD), minimum (Min) and maximum (Max) reaction time of the safety-related node measured during the experiments. For the Kobuki, the "maximum spinning speed exceeded" experiment has been repeated with the RuBaSS rules reacting to the speed being continuously exceeded for 0.7 seconds, 0.2 seconds and 0 seconds (instant reaction).

4.4 Discussion

All the tests performed were successful: the robot stopped when expected to stop. However, for the Frobit experiments, in the cases of right and left encoder error, the average reaction time was significantly higher than the ideal one. The reason is the way the temporal rule works: the condition has to be true continuously for the specified amount of time. Any change in the monitored values will reset the rule, and thus will delay triggering the action. In case of the wheel encoders, one line of the quadrature encoders was interrupted which generated some noise at the output. Similarly, there is a significant difference in reaction time when the right or left motor was forced to run at full speed. Even though the robot was not able to control the speed of one of the wheels, the rotation direction was still left under the control of the robot. In the left motor running at full speed experiments, the control algorithm of the robot changed the rotation direction of the left wheel several times, inducing a brake effect on the wheel, and delaying the fulfilment of "continuous speed exceeded for 0.4 seconds." In the simulator experiments the minimum measured reaction time is, in some cases, lower than the minimum ideal reaction time; The reason is the lack of real-time in event publishing and event handling, and the unsynchronised messages published by the ROS nodes. Conversely, the results of the tests when maximum spinning speed is exceeded are far from the minimum ideal value. Here, the robot has been instructed to spin at a value different from the one calculated, diverting from the planned route, and triggering the controller error correction mechanisms. The rule used requires the condition to be true continuously for 0.7 seconds, so even if the maximum spinning speed was exceeded momentarily, the triggering condition was not fulfilled as the controller tried to compensate. The recorded time presented in the table includes successful robot controller error corrections, and therefore is much longer that the ideal minimum one. A similar behaviour was seen in the case of the linear speed being exceeded, but at a much lower scale, giving a lower standard deviation. When the reaction time was set to 0.2 seconds, the robot did not have time to react to the introduced spinning error: the topics were publishing new messages every 0.1 seconds (10 Hz), so two consecutive cases of exceeding the maximum spinning were enough to trigger the safety rule. In the case when the safety rule was changed to react to any single case of exceeding the maximum spinning speed, due to the fact that the robot software is not reacting in real-time to the events but with a delay of approximately 0.1 seconds, the end results of the experiment are not significantly different from the case when 0.2 seconds reaction time was tested. The CPU load safety rule implementation detects if ROS nodes running in separate threads are overloaded. The usage of this kind of rule is limited, since the same processor is used for both assessing the rule conditions and running the ROS node code. To address those limitations we plan to monitor a heartbeat signal in the supervised ROS nodes and measure its frequency on another processor [25].

In the experiments only a complete stop action has been used as the reaction to any safety rule violation. That was done for simplicity of the implementation, but is obviously not the best action in all real-life scenarios. An improved fault-handling based on diagnosis and fault isolation will be addressed in a future work together with improving the RuBaSS language to statically detect overlapping safety rules or potential contradictions. We note that for the implementation of safety-related rules using our DSL to take place without modifying the existing source code, we are dependent on the interfaces of the robot (e.g., the exposed interfaces between the different ROS nodes). If the needed information is not available on the exposed interfaces, the appropriate ROS nodes of the robot would have to be modified to publish it.

5 Conclusion

We have shown that it is possible to use RuBaSS to generate the implementation of the safety rules identified during a safety risk assessment, covering both hardware faults (e.g., encoders or motors not working) and misbehaviour of the software controlling the robot (e.g., the robot leaving the designated working area or CPU overload). RuBaSS has a simple syntax, making it easy to express the safety rules, and enabling the generation of runtime safety monitoring code, as our initial proof-of-concepts experiments demonstrate. Moreover, based on our initial experience, we find that addressing safety issues of robots with RuBaSS is efficient and easily customisable, even with partial access to source code. A systematic and realistic validation of RuBaSS is considered future work, we expect that the language, the software architecture and the implementation need to be significantly extended to be useful for realistic scenarios.

References

1. Kohanbash, D., Bergerman, M., Lewis, K.M., Moorehead, S.J.: A safety architecture for autonomous agricultural vehicles. In: American Society of Agricultural and Biological Engineers Annual Meeting (July 2012)
2. Griepentrog, H., Andersen, N., Andersen, J., Blanke, M., Heinemann, O., Madsen, T., Nielsen, J., Pedersen, S., Ravn, O., Wulfsohn, D.L.: Safe and reliable: further development of a field robot. In: Henten, E., Goense, D., Lokhorst, C. (eds.) Precision Agriculture 2009, pp. 857–866. Wageningen Academic Publishers (2009)
3. Bouraine, S., Fraichard, T., Salhi, H.: Provably safe navigation for mobile robots with limited field-of-views in unknown dynamic environments. In: 2012 IEEE International Conference on Robotics and Automation (ICRA), pp. 174–179 (May 2012)
4. Griepentrog, H., Jæger-Hansen, C., Ravn, O., Andersen, N., Andersen, J., Nakanishi, T.: Multilayer controller for field robots - high portability and modularity to ease implementation. Paper presented at LAND.TECHNIK - AgEng 2011 (2012)
5. Jensen, K., Bøgild, A., Nielsen, S., Christiansen, M., Jørgensen, R.: Frobomind, proposing a conceptual architecture for agricultural field robot navigation. Paper presented at CIGR 2012 (2012)
6. Nebot, P., Torres-Sospedra, J., Martnez, R.J.: A new hla-based distributed control architecture for agricultural teams of robots in hybrid applications with real and simulated devices or environments. Sensors 11(4), 4385–4400 (2011)
7. Bruyninckx, H.: Open robot control software: the orocos project. In: IEEE ICRA 2001 Proceedings, vol. 3, pp. 2523–2528 (2001)

8. Quigley, M., Conley, K., Gerkey, B., Faust, J., Foote, T., Leibs, J., Wheeler, R., Ng, A.Y.: Ros: an open-source robot operating system. In: ICRA Workshop on Open Source Software, vol. 3(2) (2009)
9. Lotz, A., Steck, A., Schlegel, C.: Runtime monitoring of robotics software components: Increasing robustness of service robotic systems. In: Proceedings of the 15th International Conference on Advanced Robotics, pp. 285–290. IEEE (2011)
10. Gherardi, L., Brugali, D.: Modeling and reusing robotic software architectures: the hyperflex toolchain. In: IEEE International Conference on Robotics and Automation (ICRA) (to appear, 2014)
11. Dhillon, B.S.: Robot reliability and safety. Springer (1991)
12. Crestani, D., Godary-Dejean, K.: Fault tolerance in control architectures for mobile robots: Fantasy or reality? In: 7th National Conference on Control Architectures of Robots, Nancy, France (2012)
13. Blanke, M., Blas, M.R., Hansen, S., Andersen, J.C., Caponetti, F.: Autonomous robot supervision using fault diagnosis and semantic mapping in an orchard. In: Fault Diagnosis in Robotic and Industrial Systems, pp. 1–22. iConcept Press Ltd. (2012)
14. Powell, D., Arlat, J., Deswarte, Y., Kanoun, K.: Tolerance of design faults. In: Jones, C.B., Lloyd, J.L. (eds.) Dependable and Historic Computing. LNCS, vol. 6875, pp. 428–452. Springer, Heidelberg (2011)
15. Schlegel, C., Steck, A., Brugali, D., Knoll, A.: Design abstraction and processes in robotics: From code-driven to model-driven engineering. In: Ando, N., Balakirsky, S., Hemker, T., Reggiani, M., von Stryk, O. (eds.) SIMPAR 2010. LNCS (LNAI), vol. 6472, pp. 324–335. Springer, Heidelberg (2010)
16. Stahl, T., Völter, M.: Model-Driven Software Development: Technology, Engineering, Management. Wiley (2006)
17. Yakymets, N., Dhouib, S., Jaber, H., Lanusse, A.: Model-driven safety assessment of robotic systems. In: 2013 IEEE/RSJ International Conference on Intelligent Robots and Systems, IROS (2013)
18. Bordignon, M., Stoy, K., Schultz, U.: Generalized programming of modular robots through kinematic configurations. In: Proceedings of IROS 2011: The 2011 IEEE/RSJ International Conference on Intelligent Robots and Systems, pp. 3659–3666 (2011)
19. Schultz, U., Bordignon, M., Stoy, K.: Robust and reversible execution of self-reconfiguration sequences. Robotica 29(1), 35–57 (2011)
20. Steck, A., Lotz, A., Schlegel, C.: Model-driven engineering and run-time model-usage in service robotics. In: Proceedings of Generative Programming and Component-Based Engineering (GPCE). ACM (2011)
21. Larsen, M., Adam, S., Schultz, U., Jørgensen, R.N.: Towards automatic consistency checking of software components in field robotics. In: RHEA 2014: Second International Conference on Robotics and Associated High-technologies and Equipment for Agriculture and Forestry (May 2014)
22. Larsen, L.B., Olsen, K.S., Ahrenkiel, L., Jensen, K.: Extracurricular activities targeted towards increasing the number of engineers working in the field of precision agriculture. In: XXXV CIOSTA & CIGR V Conference, Billund, Denmark (July 2013)
23. Conpleks ApS: Grassbots, https://www.youtube.com/watch?v=KMjEUrB5C5I
24. Conpleks ApS: Fixfeeder, https://www.youtube.com/watch?v=q8h63rYoNQ0
25. Jensen, K., Larsen, M., Nielsen, S.H., Larsen, L.B., Olsen, K.S., Jørgensen, R.N.: Towards an open software platform for field robots in precision agriculture. Robotics 3(2), 207–234 (2014)

A Proposed Software Framework Aimed at Energy-Efficient Autonomous Driving of Electric Vehicles

José-Luis Torres Moreno[1], José-Luis Blanco Claraco[1,*], Mauro Bellone[2],
Francisco Rodrìguez[3], Antonio Gimènez[1], and Giulio Reina[2]

[1] Dept. of Engineering, Universidad of Almería, 04120 Almería, Spain
`jlblanco@ual.es`
[2] Dept. of Engineering for Innovation, Universitá del Salento, 73100 Lecce, Italy
[3] Dept. of Computer Sciences, Universidad of Almería, 04120 Almería, Spain

Abstract. This paper describes the development of an electric car prototype, aimed at autonomous, energy-efficient driving. Starting with an urban electric car, we describe the mechanical and mechatronics add-ons required to automate its driving. In addition, a variety of exteroceptive and proprioceptive sensors have been installed in order to obtain accurate measurements for datasets aimed at characterizing dynamic models of the vehicle, including the complex problem of wheel-soil slippage. Current and voltage are also monitored at key points of the electric power circuits in order to obtain an accurate model of power consumption, with the goal of allowing predictive path planners to trace routes as a trade-off between path length and overall power consumption. In order to handle the required variety of sensors involved in the vehicle, a MOOS-based software architecture has been developed based on distributed nodes that communicate over an onboard local area network. We provide experimental results describing the current stage of development of this platform, where a number of datasets have been already grabbed successfully and initial work on dynamics modeling is being carried on.

Keywords: Autonomous vehicles, Mobile robotics, Software architecture.

1 Introduction

While autonomous driving in realistic situations remains a challenging problem, the DARPA challenge [1] and the Urban Challenge in 2004 and 2007 [2] have clearly shown that such a challenge could reasonably be addressed according to the recent progresses in the field of perception and autonomous navigation for unmanned vehicles. The Carnegie Mellon University *Tartan Racing* team won the urban challenge in 2007 using a hierarchical control system for planning and sensing [3]. The keystone of their winning approach is the convenient combination between on-board mechatronic system and software architecture. Their

---

* Corresponding author.

D. Brugali et al. (Eds.): SIMPAR 2014, LNAI 8810, pp. 219–230, 2014.
© Springer International Publishing Switzerland 2014

vehicle incorporates a variety of lidar, radar and visual sensors to safely navigate urban environments, as well as a software architecture decomposed into five broad areas: mission planning, motion planning, behavior generation, perception and world modeling. Another team, the VisLab group, achieved 15,926 km of autonomous driving in 2010, driving from Parma (Italy) to Shangai (China) using a Piaggio Porter Electric Power van [4,5]. The sophisticated vision system that equips the VisLab's van including cameras and laser scanners allowed the autonomous driving even in critical scenarios and challenging roads [6].

Although autonomous vehicle technology is not completely mature yet, it has been attracting economic and industrial interest for years, and commercial cars include increasing levels of autonomy year after year. On one hand, social implications of such a huge revolution will change our way to see the transportation systems increasing the quality of our life. On the other hand, vehicles will have to be equipped with a large number of sensors that are still expensive and, most importantly, safety and reliability are mandatory, still open requirements.

Current experimental autonomous vehicles require sophisticated control algorithms as well as a large number of sensors, hence the need to employ a number of embedded computers and specific software architectures aimed at distributed sensing and processing capable of real-time performance. A variety of such architectures can be found in the literature and the industry. For example, the MIT DARPA Urban Challenge Team developed a set of libraries and tools for message passing and data marshalling called Lightweight Communications and Marshalling (LMC) [7]. Their work was targeted at real-time systems such as the experimental vehicle employed for the challenge. In such situations, high-bandwidth and low latency are critical issues. Recently, the Robotics Operative System (ROS) [8], a new software architecture for mobile robotics, is getting increasingly popular among research labs and industries. ROS provides both, a middleware for structured communications between processing nodes and a set of ready-to-use software nodes for many specific tasks usually found in robotics.

Our electric car architecture is based on Open Mobile Robot Arquitecture (OpenMORA) [9], originally developed by MAPIR lab, University of Málaga, and at present also co-maintaned by the authors of this work. OpenMORA relies on two open-source frameworks: MOOS [10], and Mobile Robot Programming Toolkit (MRPT) [11]. MOOS is a middleware for distributed robotic architectures based on the publish-subscribe (pub/sub) pattern. It comprises a core C++ library and a set of tools for managing and monitoring so-called *communities* of distributed modules. Key advantages of MOOS against other alternatives are its simplicity and its suitability to attain sub-millisecond round-trip message passing. At the core of MOOS is the idea of a minimalist data-type middleware (i.e. only double numbers and text strings are allowed to be exchanged between modules), hence that transmitting complex data types (e.g. laser scans or images) over MOOS implies custom implementations of data marshalling. For that purpose we use MRPT, which provides data structures for the most common autonomous vehicle sensors along with efficient serialization and deserialization mechanisms. MRPT is also employed for low-level interfacing with most sensors,

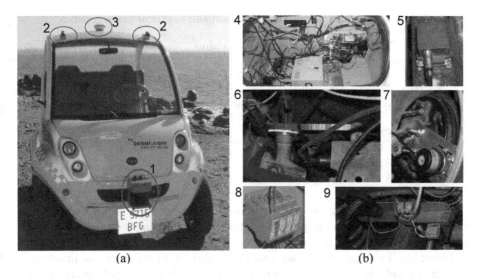

(a)   (b)

Fig. 1. (a) Autonomous car prototype, with visible sensors marked in red, and (b) close-ups of the rest of sensors. Labeled devices are: (1) Sick LMS-200, (2) PGR Flea3 USB3 cameras, (3) GPS antenna, (4) embedded computers in the car trunk, (5) IMU system, (6) steering-wheel actuator and encoder, (7) rear wheels encoders, (8) voltage and (9) current sensors.

performing sequential Monte-Carlo (SMC) vehicle localization [12] and providing autonomous reactive navigation control [13]. Together, MOOS and MRPT have a small footprint and allow modules to be written in C++ and run in a number of platforms and operative systems (i.e. Windows, OSX, GNU/Linux, GNU/kFreeBSD).

The rest of the paper is organized as follows. Section 2 describes our custom autonomous car prototype including its sensors system, then section 3 introduces the proposed software architecture. We finalize with Section 4 providing on-road experiments and drawing some conclusions.

2 Prototype Description

An electric car prototype has been developed at the Automatic, Robotics and Mechatronics (ARM) research group at University of Almería with the ultimate scientific objective of studying novel localization, mapping and energy-efficient path planning techniques. The prototype, presented in Figure 1, consists of a urban electric car that has been adapted for automated control. Table 1 provides a summary of its most relevant mechanical and electric characteristics. The prototype features a 48 volt DC-motor and 8 gel-batteries, selected thinking of the future requirements of energy efficiency. Its batteries system ensures an autonomy of 90 km at a maximum travel speed of about 45 km/h. In its current form, the prototype features both: full manual control, or autonomous mode. For the implementation of such automatic control, the car required the installation

Table 1. Summary of vehicle mechanical and electrical characteristics

Mechanic characteristics	Value
length × width × height	2680 × 1525 × 1780 mm
Track	1830 mm
Front/rear wheelbase	1285/1260 mm
Weight without/with batteries	472/700 kg

Electric characteristics	Value
DC motor XQ 4.3	4.3 kW
Batteries (gel technology)	8 × 6 V −210 Ah
Autonomy	90 km

of a large number of sensors and actuators as well as a computer architecture capable of properly handling all the dataflow in real time (refer to section 3). Figure 2 shows an illustrative scheme of the embedded computers and sensors architecture. Two embedded computers PC1 and PC2 constitute the processing core of the vehicle, gathering information from each sensor and giving control commands to each actuator.

During the prototype construction, the first task carried out was the automation of typically human-actuated signals, namely: steering and throttling. The former was addressed by implementing a so-called steering-by-wire system, which consists of a 12 volt DC-motor coupled to the steering column by means of an electromagnetic clutch. Such system is governed by a custom microcontroller-based steering controller which controls the motor by means of a PWM signal. Furthermore, the controller reads back the angular position of the steering column by means of an incremental optical encoder attached to it. In order to allow recovering the manual steering mode, the controller is capable of uncoupling the motor and the steering column by actuating over the electromechanical clutch.

Regarding the automatic propulsion, we generate a throttle signal equivalent to that one generated at the gas pedal. This is easily achieved by actuating on the propulsion DC-motor controller via an analog signal from the NI-DAQ board connected to PC2. As a way to watch and characterize the power supplied by this motor, we monitor the current and voltages at the rotor, the stator and the main battery terminals. The motor controller allowed manual selecting between forward and reverse drive and also between two working regimes (dubbed "sport" and "economy") by means of switches in the front panel of the vehicle. Now those connections have been replaced by electronics which is controlled via digital outputs from the DAQ system.

Once the problem of automating the vehicle controls is overcome, the rest of sensors aim to different control strategies, state observers, fault-tolerance systems or supervisory tasks. Among the kind of the control tasks which can be performed on the prototype, one can distinguish between low and high level controllers. The mission oriented philosophy of the implemented architecture makes possible to reuse some low-level controllers for higher supervisory tasks as path planning or obstacle avoidance. Some examples of these low-level controllers comprise the cruise control system or the low-level steering controller running on the custom microcontroller-based platform.

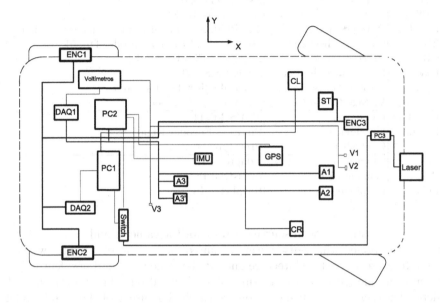

Fig. 2. Hardware equipment lay-out

A description of sensors layout can be found in Figure 2 while their properties are summarized in Table 2. Next, we give further details on the hardware components installed in our prototype:

Computers: *PC1* is the host computer, it features a quad core 2 GHz processor running a 64bit Ubuntu operating system. Its tasks comprise the execution of MOOS core and the acquisition of wheel encoders, the communication with the low-level steering controller and cameras images processing. *PC2* runs Windows 7 operating system and acquires current/voltage signals as well as actuates over the throttle setpoint via a NI-DAQ board as well as the throttling signals. Moreover, this computer is responsible for the management of the GPS device and the IMU.

The single board computer (SBC) *PC3* is a Raspberry Pi connected to the rest of computers in the architecture via Ethernet protocol. It has been prepared to execute several algorithms of control and state observers. Moreover, due to its emplacement in the front part, this is the computer which is connected to the laser scanner. The choice of a SBC for these task is based on the principle of delegating each process to the cheapest (in terms of both, economy and power consumption) hardware platform capable of executing it in a reliable way.

Table 2. List of sensors, I/O devices and computers

Label	Type	Model
IMU	Inertial sensor	Xsens MTI 300
GPS	GPS	Hemisphere R100
ENC1,2	Wheel encoders	2 × Phidgets Optical Rotary Encoder ISC3004
ENC3	Steering-wheel encoder	SICK Optical Rotary Encoder DFS61
CR,L	stereo camera	2 × Flea3 FL3-U3-13E4C-C
Laser	Laser Range Finder	SICK LMS 200
A1,2,3, 3'	Current transducer	4 × Hall-effect LEM sensors
V1,2,3	Voltage transducer	3 × Phoenix Contact
DAQ1	I/O device	NI-USB-6211
DAQ2	I/O device	Phidgets Encoder High-Speed
ST	Controller	Prototype
PC1	Ubuntu O.S.	Adapted PC
PC2	Windows 7 O.S.	Industrial PC
PC3	Raspbian	Raspberry Pi

Since we mostly use open source software for the cameras and vision systems, whereas the pre-existing sensors were acquired on the NI-DAQ board, we have chosen to preserve past architecture and, at the same time, add new features on the car as an independent architecture. This allows also to change every module independently at every advance of our research. The usage of the Windows OS in one of the computers comes after carefully evaluating the support of NI-DAQ C++ libraries under different driver versions and GNU/Linux distributions without finding any with an acceptable level of functionality and reliability.

Sensors: The Xsens MTI-300 *IMU* is connected to PC2 via USB, and collects the vehicle angular position and velocity along with its acceleration on x,y,z axes at a frequency up to 2 kHz. The differential *GPS* R100 by Hemisphere ensures the localization of the vehicle within a tolerance of 2 cm thanks to RTK correction techniques. It is connected to PC2 through two RS-232 ports, for both data communication and correction via 3G Internet access. The SICK LMS *Laser* attached to the front part of the vehicle scans up to 180 degrees at a frequency of 18 Hz and a range of 81 m. A specifically developed controller converts the RS-432 signal to USB aimed to the communications with the PC3. The *ENC1* and *ENC2* Phidgets Optical Rotary Encoder ISC3004 mounted at the rear wheels offer a resolution of 360 pules per revolution (ppr) which allows to implement a low-cost efficient odometry system. However, the *ENC3* encoder attached to the steering column consists of the SICK DFS61 model with a resolution of 10000 ppr since the requirements of precision of the steering angle determination. The *CL* and *CR* PGR Flea3 USB3 cameras attached to the upper front left and right part of the vehicle respectively comprises the computer vision system controlled by PC1 at a frequency up to 80 kHz. Regarding the power consumption of the vehicle, three voltmeters (*V1*, *V2* and *V3*) and ampere-meters (*A1*, *A2* and *A3*) measure the voltage and current in the rotor, the field and the batteries.

Additionally, the ampere-meter A3' detects the sense of the current from the batteries in order to identify when the regenerative braking system is actuating.

I/O Devices: *DAQ1* is a National Instrument USB-6211 acquisition board with 16 analog inputs (16-bit, 250 kS/s), 2 analog outputs (16-bit, 250 kS/s), 4 digital inputs and 4 digital outputs and 2 32-bit counters. It is connected to PC1. On the other hand, *DAQ2* is a Phidgets Encoder HighSpeed 4-Input board which acquires the signals from the encoder of the rear wheels and communicates with the PC2 via USB. Finally, the *ST* device refers to the steering controller box which is connected to the PC1 via USB.

3   The MOOS-Based Software Architecture

This section introduces the MOOS-based [10] distributed software architecture that has been developed for interfacing all vehicle's sensors and actuators. The fundamental processing element in MOOS is a *module*, an independent process that publishes and subscribes to *variables*. Several modules typically subscribe to the same variable whereas one normally finds only one publisher for each variable (although the latter is not a strict rule and the opposite makes sense in some situations), forming processing *pipelines*. A central hub called *MOOSDB* is in charge of assuring that all publishers reach all subscribers, which may be running on different computers across the local network. At present our distributed system comprises two embedded computers and one single-board-computer (SBC) (Raspberry PI-B), all of them interconnected through 1000Mbs Ethernet. Sub-millisecond communication delays and the usage of a local Network Time Protocol (NTP) server assures the accurate synchronization between timestamps of data gathered in different computers, a crucial issue for either grabbing datasets for offline processing or for closing control loops online.

Upon this MOOS middleware, we have designed a set of C++ modules which communicate to each other uniquely by means of message-passing under a pub/sub pattern. As customary in software engineering, our approach comprises a *layered* structure, beginning at the lowest level where modules directly interface hardware, and up to the higher levels where modules become more platform-independent. In fact, our guiding idea is allowing the transparent replacement of all the modules that interface the real vehicle with a physics (multibody dynamics) simulator, thus easing and boosting development of high-level algorithms and controller prototypes. At present such simulator is under development, thus in the following we focus on the specific modules designed for the vehicle prototype.

A sketch of the lower layers of our architecture is provided in Figure 3. Starting our description from the bottom up, we find a first layer containing all physical devices (labeled "hardware" in the figure). Next, we have the two lower layers of the software architecture itself, namely: (i) Drivers layer and (ii) the vehicle-abstraction layer (VAL). In the former layer we find software modules, each one in charge of interfacing a specific device. Modules in this layer are generic and

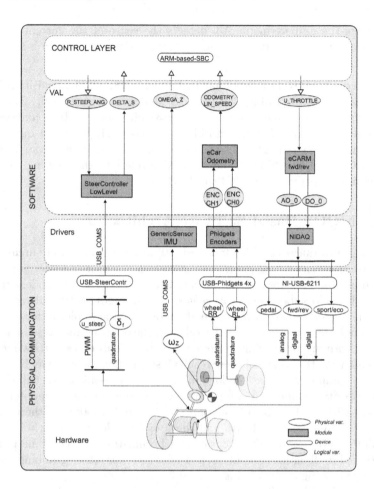

Fig. 3. Layered structure of the proposed software architecture. Refer to section 3 for details.

reusable, in the sense of being agnostic about the semantic or relevance of each sensed or output signal. In our present implementation this layer contains: (i) a module to read from the XSens MT4 Inertial Measuring Unit (IMU) placed at the vehicle center of mass, whose more relevant output for this work is the instantaneous rate of change in yaw (ω_z); (ii) an interface to the two rear wheels quadrature encoders, which ultimately provide wheel odometry (dead reckoning) and the linear and angular velocities of the vehicle (disregarding slippage); and (iii) the interface to a National Instruments DAQ providing several analog and digital inputs and output, from which only the outputs directly related to throttle control are displayed in Figure 3 for conciseness.

Upwards in the architecture we reach the VAL. The goal of this layer is providing a uniform interface (i.e. set of MOOS variables) that isolate the specific vehicle being used from high-level controllers. Therefore, we find two kinds of

Trajectory GPS (m)

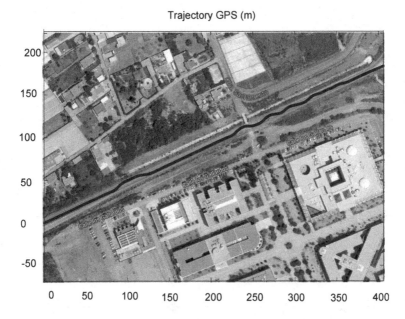

Fig. 4. GPS registered signal

modules in this layer: (i) non-generic hardware drivers (e.g. the "SteerController" module which interfaces our custom microcontroller-based steering wheel controller), whose output have a semantic closely related to the robotic platform, and (ii) converters between generic sensor signals and meaningful variables (e.g. from encoder velocity in ticks per second to vehicle linear velocity).

We decided that the following variables are sufficient for modeling and controlling an Ackermann-like vehicle:

- R_STEER_ANG (Input): Desired reference or setpoint for the steering angle.
- U_THROTTLE (Input): Desired normalized throttle in the range $[-1, 1]$, with negative values implying reverse gear.
- DELTA_S (Output): The actual instantaneous steering angle.
- OMEGA_Z (Output): Instantaneous yaw rate of the vehicle, as measured by the IMU.
- ODOMETRY_LIN_SPEED (Output): Current linear speed of the vehicle, according to rear wheels encoders.

Upon these layers there also exist other high-level modules in charge of, for example, robust vehicle localization and reactive navigation, which lie outside of the scope of the present paper.

4 Preliminary Experimental Results and Discussion

So far, experiments carried out with the proposed prototype consist of grabbing datasets as the car is driven along fixed paths. As an example of such datasets,

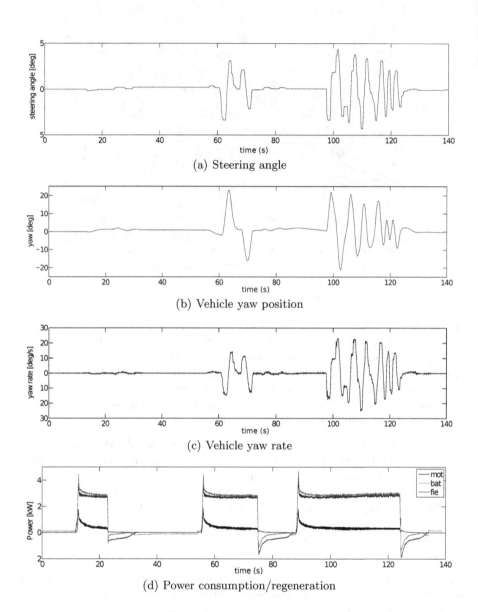

(a) Steering angle

(b) Vehicle yaw position

(c) Vehicle yaw rate

(d) Power consumption/regeneration

Fig. 5. Experimental results

Figure 4 shows the GPS signal regarding one of the paths followed in a particular experiment. This experiment consisted in the drive of the vehicle through a straight road of about 500 m, car speed ranges between 0 and of 10 m/s. The first part of the experiment consists of a straight line maneuver. The vehicle accelerated from a state of repose, and then was stopped again. The second part belongs to a double lane change, which reproduces typical real driving conditions. Finally, a slalom maneuver is performed in the last part of the experiment. Figure 5(a) represents the steering angle as the manual input signal as long as Figures 5(b)-(c) show the vehicle response in terms of its yaw angle and rate respectively. As can be seen, even when the steering angle attends to severe driving conditions as those of the third part of the experiment, the signals from the IMU fit perfectly to such a fast transient response. Regarding the power consumptions Figure 5(d) represents the energy consumption of rotor and field of the motor as well as the power supplied by the batteries. It can be seen the high requirements when the vehicle accelerates from an initial state of repose, whereas some part of the kinetic energy is returned to the batteries when the vehicle decelerates.

To conclude, the experience gained with this work demonstrates that the middleware MOOS, together with the proposed architecture built upon it, perfectly fits the demanding requirements of a distributed control architecture for an electric vehicle. To end this section, a word is in order regarding the several lines of work that remain open at present. One of them consists of contrasting theoretical models for slippage with experimental results, given different kinds of terrain and driving conditions. Another open challenge is exploring robust data fusion techniques to achieve a ground-truth 6D vehicle localization (position and attitude) as it moves at high speed. We are experimenting with fusion of stereo visual odometry, inertial data from the IMU and the wheels encoders. Finally, estimating the state of charge of the vehicle batteries is also a goal related to energy-efficient driving, a process that will require grabbing datasets that include currents, voltages and temperature measurements for the gel batteries. It is clear that all these open fronts deserve much future work after the design and construction of the presented vehicle prototype.

Acknowledgment. This work has been partially funded by the Spanish "Ministerio de Ciencia e Innovación" under the contract "DAVARBOT" (DPI 2011-22513) and the grant program JDC-MICINN 2011, as well as by the Andalusian Regional Government grant programs FPDU 2008 and FPDU 2009, co-funded by the European Union through the European Regional Development Fund (ERDF).

References

1. Thrun, S., et al.: Stanley: The Robot That Won the DARPA Grand Challenge. In: Buehler, M., Iagnemma, K., Singh, S. (eds.) DARPA 2005. STAR, vol. 36, pp. 1–43. Springer, Heidelberg (2007)
2. Leonard, J., How, J., Teller, S., Berger, M., Campbell, S., Fiore, G., Fletcher, L., Frazzoli, E., Huang, A., Karaman, S., et al.: The darpa urban challenge (2009)

3. Urmson, C., Bagnell, J.A., Baker, C.R., Hebert, M., Kelly, A., Rajkumar, R., Rybski, P.E., Scherer, S., Simmons, R., Singh, S., et al.: Tartan racing: A multimodal approach to the darpa urban challenge. Technical Report 967, Robotics Institute (2007)
4. Bertozzi, M., Broggi, A., Cardarelli, E., Fedriga, R.I., Mazzei, L., Porta, P.P.: VIAC Expedition Toward Autonomous Mobility. Robotics and Automation Magazine 18(3), 120–124 (2011) ISSN: 1070-9932
5. Broggi, A., Medici, P., Zani, P., Coati, A., Panciroli, M.: Autonomous vehicles control in the VisLab Intercontinental Autonomous Challenge. Annual Reviews in Control 36(1), 161–171 (2012) ISSN: 1367-5788
6. Broggi, A., Buzzoni, M., Felisa, M., Zani, P.: Stereo obstacle detection in challenging environments: the VIAC experience. In: Procs. IEEE/RSJ Intl. Conf. on Intelligent Robots and Systems, San Francisco, California, USA, pp. 1599–1604 (September 2011)
7. Huang, A., Olson, E., Moore, D.: LCM: Lightweight communications and marshalling. In: Proceedings of the IEEE/RSJ International Conference on Intelligent Robots and Systems (IROS) (October 2010)
8. Quigley, M., Conley, K., Gerkey, B.P., Faust, J., Foote, T., Leibs, J., Wheeler, R., Ng, A.Y.: Ros: an open-source robot operating system. In: ICRA Workshop on Open Source Software (2009)
9. MAPIR lab (University of Málaga), ARM group (University of Almería): Open Mobile Robot Arquitecture (OpenMORA) (June 2014),
   http://sourceforge.net/projects/openmora
10. Newman, P.M.: MOOS-mission orientated operating suite. Technical Report 2299, Massachusetts Institute of Technology (2008)
11. Blanco, J.L., et al.: Mobile Robot Programming Toolkit (MRPT),
   http://www.mrpt.org/
12. Blanco, J.L., González, J., Fernández-Madrigal, J.A.: Optimal filtering for nonparametric observation models: applications to localization and slam. The International Journal of Robotics Research 29(14), 1726–1742 (2010)
13. Blanco, J.L., González-Jiménez, J., Fernández-Madrigal, J.A.: Extending obstacle avoidance methods through multiple parameter-space transformations. Autonomous Robots 24(1) (2008)

Structured Design and Development
of Domain-Specific Languages in Robotics*

Sven Schneider, Nico Hochgeschwender, and Gerhard K. Kraetzschmar

Department of Computer Science, Bonn-Rhein-Sieg University,
Grantham-Allee 20, 53757 Sankt Augustin, Germany
{sven.schneider,nico.hochgeschwender,gerhard.kraetzschmar}@h-brs.de
http://inf.h-brs.de/

Abstract. Robot programming is an interdisciplinary and knowledge-intensive task. All too often, knowledge of the different robotics domains remains implicit. Although, this is slowly changing with the rising interest in explicit knowledge representations through domain-specific languages (DSL), very little is known about the DSL design and development processes themselves. To this end, we present and discuss the reverse-engineered process from the development of our Grasp Domain Definition Language (GDDL), a declarative DSL for the explicit specification of grasping problems. An important finding is that the process comprises similar building blocks as existing software development processes, like the Unified Process.

1 Introduction

Robot programming is a challenging and complex exercise, which is very often prone to errors. We argue, that the main reason for the complexity and difficulty lies in the fact that robot programming is a knowledge-intensive exercise and that this knowledge often remains implicit. For example, to program a robot to grasp an object for the sake of transportation already demands knowledge about many diverse domains, such as the environment where the robot is operating in, the object to be grasped, the robot platform itself and its grasping abilities, and the goals and constraints of the task. Fortunately, the importance of explicit knowledge representations is attracting growing interest from the robotics community. This is important, in order to make robot programs more consistent, deterministic, and reusable. On the one hand, approaches, such as KnowRob [18], are based on ontologies and enable the *sharing* and *reasoning* of knowledge obtained from different sources, to achieve the task at hand. On the other hand, approaches based on the Model-Driven Engineering (MDE) paradigm [16], exploit the knowledge for systematic *software development* and are already adopted by mature domains such as avionics, automotive, and telecommunication. In MDE, the

---

* The authors gratefully acknowledge the on-going support of the Bonn-Aachen International Center for Information Technology. Nico Hochgeschwender received a PhD scholarship by the Graduate Institute of the Bonn-Rhein-Sieg University which is gratefully acknowledged.

D. Brugali et al. (Eds.): SIMPAR 2014, LNAI 8810, pp. 231–242, 2014.

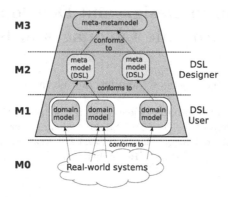

Fig. 1. Diagram of the meta-modeling approach (based on [10], p. 4685)

concept of *meta-modeling* is used, to digest, develop, and consolidate abstractions describing a certain domain. To support this process, MDE introduces several levels of abstractions (see Fig. 1). Ranging from a higher to a lower level of specificity or detail in the knowledge of a domain [4]. Most importantly, on the M2 level, the domain knowledge, in terms of domain concepts with concrete names, relations among each other, and properties are formalized. In the MDE paradigm, an M2 model can be represented by a *domain-specific language (DSL)*, which represents the knowledge of the properties and relationships in the model with a terminology and syntactical constructs that practitioners in the domain are familiar with [4]. In general, the MDE approach is very appealing, as the metamodels of a domain are stable, whereas the concrete domain models can differ a lot. Thus, design and development of software *by* and *for* reuse is enhanced.

Recently, the MDE approach and DSLs have gained popularity in robotics. Several DSLs for different aspects of the robotics domain are available. Ranging from DSLs to express force-velocity controlled robot tasks [10] to coordinate transformations and kinematic structures [8]. However, a sound domain analysis and conceptualization is a necessity, in order to find the *right* abstractions, which suit the domain best and which later form the building blocks of a DSL. Unfortunately, we know very little about the DSL design and development process itself. The vast majority of DSL articles focus on the language itself and not on *how* the DSL has arisen from a domain analysis. We argue that in order to make progress with DSL development in robotics, we need to know what the workflows, activities, and stakeholders of DSL design and development are. In particular, as robotics is an interdisciplinary domain, which contains subdomains which are well consolidated (e.g., math or coordinate representations) and more emerging subdomains such as perception, manipulation, and planning. Answering these questions will eventually help also to identify best practices, development patterns and guidelines which are applicable for future DSL projects in robotics.

In this paper, we present the lessons learned which we gained while designing and developing a DSL called Grasp Domain Definition Language (GDDL) [17]. One major lesson learned is a reverse-engineered process model for the design and development of DSLs in robotics. We present and discuss the process itself and how the process has been applied to the development of GDDL.

2   Overview of GDDL

GDDL is a declarative DSL for specifying grasping knowledge, as well as grasping problems in a grasp planner-independent representation. With this approach, it resembles the Planning Domain Definition Language (PDDL) [9] for automated task planning. GDDL decomposes the overall grasping domain into subdomains for representing *objects*, *hands* and *tasks*. Additionally, a *composition* subdomain enables the specification of grasps as a composite of the previous three subdomains. During the design, two cross-cutting subdomains were identified, namely, the *units* subdomain for specifying physical units and the *geometry* subdomain, which captures the semantics of geometric object relations, such as *position*, *orientation* or *pose*. As the subdomains themselves are not the scope of this paper, we only present excerpts of those subdomains in the DSL development process.

Originally, GDDL was motivated by the problem of data labeling in many existing machine learning approaches for grasping, such as presented in [2]. Instead of labeling a large amount of randomly generated grasps, a domain expert should specify the criteria for a good grasp once. Then, grasps should be labeled automatically based on these specifications. Mernik *et al.* [14] call this approach "task automation". From this initial scope, GDDL developed into a more versatile language, which also covers fields beside pure data labeling. Currently, it allows the explicit and formal specification of grasping knowledge, which enables the verification of user-provided grasp data. Therefore, GDDL can be used as a "front-end" for configuring different grasp planners.

GDDL features a full-fledged integrated development environment (IDE) which is based on the Eclipse Xtext[1] framework. The domain metamodels are specified in the Eclipse Modeling Framework's (EMF)[2] Ecore fromat. Different use cases have been implemented with GDDL, on simulated and real robotic platforms, such as a Care-O-bot 3 with a Schunk Dextrous Hand (SDH) or a KUKA youBot. In our implementation, the GraspIt! [15] simulator was extended to interpret GDDL and plan grasps based on GDDL specifications.

3   DSL Development Process

Following this overview of GDDL, we describe a generic DSL development process, which we reverse-engineered by analyzing the different phases of the GDDL development. For each phase, examples from GDDL are provided.

---

[1] http://www.xtext.org/
[2] http://www.eclipse.org/modeling/emf/

3.1 Process Concepts

The process involves three types of stakeholders, which have different interests in and expectations about the project. Each stakeholder contributes to the development process during different phases.

Domain Experts. They want to solve some problem in their domain and see the potential that a DSL improves the solution or simplifies the task. Thus, they are also the main users of the developed DSL. While the domain experts have a sound understanding of their domain, they are not necessarily software developers. For GDDL, a domain expert is interested in specifying knowledge about manipulation and grasping, so that a robot can apply this knowledge. Often, the understanding of a single domain is not sufficient to solve the problem, as exemplified by the different aspects of manipulation and grasping in the previous section.

Subdomain Experts. They have very good knowledge about a field which is related to the domain experts' problem. Thus, in certain phases, they contribute knowledge about this subdomain to the DSL development. For instance, in robotic grasping, there are researchers with a strong background in evaluating and simulating contacts between objects and fingers, while others focus on the representation of objects, reaching from kinematics to affordances.

DSL Developers. They are the software developers in the process and usually do not have a background in the previous domains. Therefore, they cooperate with the previous two experts, to get an insight into their domains, but also to extract the relevant domain knowledge. The developers then formalize this knowledge into metamodels. Based on these metamodels, they design and implement the DSL tooling.

In the development of GDDL, these roles were taken on by the same person. However, in a more complex project, different and potentially multiple persons represent the stakeholders. The interaction between these stakeholders in different project phases forms the DSL development process, which consists of the following concepts:

Activities represent work that is performed by one or more of the stakeholders to solve a task. Usually, activities require input from previous process phases and produce output for other activities.

Artifacts are the output of an activity. Depending on the activity, artifacts include developed software or textual and graphical documents which describe, for instance, use cases, requirements or reviews. Each artifact is stored in a repository.

Models are a special type of an artifact in the DSL development process, which represents formalized domain knowledge. The MDE paradigm describes one approach to represent models in a hierarchical manner.

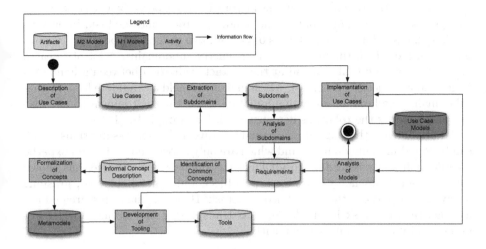

Fig. 2. Diagram of the development process

3.2   Process Flow Phases

Fig. 2 depicts our reverse-engineered DSL development process. In this section we explain and motivate each step in the process along recurring examples from the GDDL development. To this end, we have selected three different subdomains, namely, *a*) the units subdomain, *b*) the geometry subdomain; and *c*) an excerpt from the hand subdomain for representing grasp semantics. The latter assigns semantic properties, like grasp stability or grasp shape, to given hand configurations.

Description of Use Cases. The domain expert describes several applications or use cases which demonstrate *a*) the diversity and variability; and *b*) the commonalities in the domain of his problem. The resulting use cases are stored in a repository for further analysis in the next activity. In GDDL such use cases include rather simple tasks, like grasping an object for transportation or pouring liquid from a glass, to more complex tasks, such as cutting with a knife or spraying liquid with a spray bottle. These tasks are targeted at robots with different hands.

Extraction of Subdomains. In the following activity, the domain expert analyses the use cases, to find groups of common and relevant features: the *subdomains*. The analysis is either guided by the expert's prior domain knowledge or research, for instance, based on existing scientific literature surveys. A decomposition into subdomains allows the domain expert, for example, to easier identify aspects that concern more than one domain. Such aspects are extracted from the special-purpose domains into reusable general-purpose domains. All identified subdomains and associated material are saved in the subdomain repository.

An initial extraction of subdomains in grasping is proposed by Cutkosky in [5]. The proposed subdomains contain the hand, the object and the task. In later iterations and subdomain refinements of GDDL, two general-purpose subdomains have been identified, the units and the geometry subdomains. A lot of research in robotic grasping is also aimed at the contact evaluation between a hand or a finger and an object (see e.g. [3]), which makes this field a candidate for a further subdomain. Similarly, in many manipulation tasks, the environment should also be considered by the robot, as demonstrated, for example by [1].

Additionally, a thorough domain analysis reveals hidden assumptions which can be found in many domains and which are only known to the domain experts. The domain analysis leading to GDDL's metamodels, for instance, has shown that grasping does not just concern an object and a hand. Instead, grasping always has a purpose that is defined in a task. However, many research efforts assume, that the task is simple, such as transporting or holding objects, but don't specify this assumption explicitly.

Analysis of Subdomains. In the next phase, the domain expert in cooperation with the subdomain expert, investigates *each* subdomain in the subdomain repository in more detail. One outcome of this investigation is, that the subdomain extraction was too coarse and further subdomains should be added. This leads to a further iteration of the subdomain extraction activity, now taking into account the refined structure of subdomains. Another possible outcome is a collection of requirements *for each* subdomain based on existing subdomain knowledge or state of the art analysis through scientific literature research.

In grasping and manipulation, two commonly found concepts are *positions* and *orientations* of bodies w.r.t. other bodies. Examples of functional requirements (FR) for the geometry subdomain are:

FR1. The robot shall compute *positions* of a body w.r.t. another body.
FR2. The user shall specify *positions* of a body w.r.t. another body.
FR3. The robot shall efficiently calculate *orientations* between two bodies.
FR4. The user shall naturally specify *orientations* between two bodies.

Similarly, non-functional requirements (NFR) are specified, such as

NFR1. A textual editor shall be provided to the user.
NFR2. The keywords of the language shall be highlighted in the editor.
NFR3. Syntax errors shall be listed in a separate editor window.

Additionally, it was decided, to rely on existing, specialized grasp planners, such as GraspIt! [15], for the hand-object contact evaluation at run-time. Similarly, also the environment should be taken into account only at run-time, by validating, that generated grasps result in collision free motions during grasping.

Identification of Common Concepts. This activity is handled only by the subdomain expert. The subdomain expert investigates the *functional requirements* which he gets from the metamodel requirements repository and derives

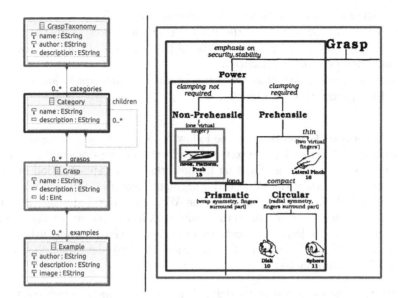

Fig. 3. On the right side, an excerpt of a grasp taxonomy is shown (see [5], p. 273). Different concepts, which are identified in the domain analysis phase, are highlighted by the colored boxes. The left side shows a metamodel for grasp taxonomies, where the concepts are formalized. The grasp taxonomy on the right side conforms to this grasp taxonomy metamodel.

concepts. A concept represents a commonality or category within a domain. After the subdomain expert has identified the concepts, he documents them, so that a common terminology emerges. The resulting informal descriptions are stored in a repository. For each concept, they contain elements such as, a lexicographic explanation or an exemplifying diagram, a graphical or textual ontology which represents the relation to other concepts, a list of known limitations or examples of this concept.

For instance, from the previously-defined functional requirements, the following concepts are derived:

- The *positions* in **FR1** and **FR2** can be represented by the same, common concept, called *PositionVector*.
- The *orientations* in **FR3** and **FR4** should be represented by two different concepts, for instance, *Quaternion* and *RollPitchYawAngle*.

Another example of concept identification is depicted in Fig. 3. It shows a grasp taxonomy which is one approach for representing grasp semantics. On the right side of the figure, different concepts of grasp taxonomies are highlighted. Based on [5], a grasp taxonomy can be described informally as, for instance:

- A grasp taxonomy is a "hierarchical tree of grasps" [5].
- The layers are derived from the influence of the object geometry and the task. Higher layers focus more on the object shape, while lower layers also include detailed task information.
- Known limitations are, that grasp taxonomies are incomplete and often tailored to specific tasks or objects.

Formalization of Concepts. In the following phase, namely the concept formalization, the DSL developer receives the informal descriptions and transforms them to formal metamodels. Existing frameworks for the specification of metamodels are, for instance, the Object Management Group's (OMG) Meta-Object Facility (MOF)[3], the EMF's Ecore or the Web Ontology Language (OWL)[4]. While the DSL developer performs the main work in this phase, he also receives support from the subdomain expert, for example, to clarify ambiguities in the informal descriptions. During the formalization, the DSL developer chooses one of the following approaches:

Definition. New metamodels are defined, if no proper metamodels exist. This will usually be the case for the core metamodels of a domain. In GDDL, this includes the metamodels for describing tasks, objects and hands (beside the kinematics and dynamics description), which were defined from scratch. With the system of units (SI), an informally described metamodel for representing physical units already exists. Based on [7] and the Boost.Units[5] library, a formal units metamodel was defined for GDDL. The left side of Fig. 3 depicts another example of a formal metamodel for grasp taxonomies. This metamodel is derived from the informal concept description of grasp taxonomies.

Refinement. Existing metamodels are refined, in case there are metamodels from related projects which already cover the subdomain partially. In GDDL, the existing, formalized Task-Frame Formalism (TFF) metamodel by Klotzbücher et al. [10] was refined, by extending it with the units metamodel. Similarly, the geometry metamodel, which is formally described in [6], was extracted from the existing C++ implementation and then refined by the units metamodel.

Reuse. If a metamodel for a subdomain already exists, for example, as part of a standard, or from another project, it is reused unchanged. An example of metamodel reuse in GDDL is the Unified Robot Description Format (URDF)[6] for describing kinematic and dynamic properties of robotic hands and objects.

---

[3] http://www.omg.org/spec/MOF/2.0/

[4] http://www.w3.org/TR/owl2-overview/

[5] http://www.boost.org/doc/libs/1_55_0/doc/html/boost_units.html

[6] http://ros.org/wiki/urdf

```
┌─ GDDL Grammar Excerpt ─────────────────────────────────────────┐

Category returns grasp_taxonomy::Category
    : name=ID ':' 'Category' '{'
        ('description' ':' description=STRING)?
        ('identifier' ':' id=INT)?
        (grasps+=Grasp | children+=Category)*
      '}'
    ;
└────────────────────────────────────────────────────────────────┘
```

Fig. 4. Excerpt of GDDL's Xtext grammar for representing a category in a grasp taxonomy. This grammar is aligned with the *Category* concept of the metamodel in Fig. 3, i.e. a category consists of exactly one *name*, an optional *description* and *identifier*, and references any number of *children* categories and *grasps*.

Development of Tooling. Only the DSL developer is responsible for the tooling development. The input to this activity are, on the one hand, the domain metamodels from the metamodel repository and, on the other hand, the non-functional requirements from the metamodel requirements repository. The metamodels form the basis of the textual DSL's grammar or the items visualized in a graphical editor. Based on the non-functional requirements, the type, layout, structure and constraints of the editor are specified. The developed tools, such as the editors for specifying M1 models, and also the application-specific generators for generating M0 representations of the models are stored in the tool repository.

The non-functional requirements **NFR1–NFR3** for GDDL specify that a text editor with syntax highlighting and the possibility to visualize syntax errors should be developed. Due to these (and other) requirements, we chose the Eclipse-based framework Xtext for the editor implementation. Fig. 4 shows an excerpt of GDDL's formal grammar, from which Xtext generates a full-fledged IDE. The grammar is aligned with GDDL's metamodels. In addition to the IDE, the DSL developer of GDDL also implemented an interface for GraspIt!, to interpret GDDL specifications.

Implementation of Use Cases. In this phase, the domain expert and the subdomain expert implement their use cases with the developed tools. The results are M1 use case models which are then either input to *a*) runtime components directly as configuration; or *b*) code generators (which are also part of the tools repository) for generating M0 representations of the models, such as code, deployment or configuration files.

In GDDL, such models describe, for example, specific hands like a SDH or a youBot gripper, objects like a spray bottle, as well as, various tasks from transportation to tool-use. Fig. 5 shows a simple textual model of Cutkosky's grasp

```
  ┌─ Simple Grasp Taxonomy ──────────────────────────────────────────────
  │
  │ cutkosky_taxonomy: GraspTaxonomy by "Mark␣R.␣Cutkosky" {
  │     description: "A␣simple␣grasp␣taxonomy"
  │
  │     power: Category {
  │         description: "emphasis␣on␣security,␣stability"
  │
  │         prehensile: Category {
  │             description: "clamping␣required"
  │
  │             lateral_pinch: Grasp {
  │                 description: "Lateral␣Pinch"
  │                 identifier: 16
  │
  │                 Example {
  │                     author: "Thomas␣Feix"
  │                     description: "Lateral"
  │                     image: "http://grasp.xief.net/images_grasps/i_16_1"
  │             } } } }
  │ }
  └──────────────────────────────────────────────────────────────────────
```

Fig. 5. Example of a grasp taxonomy in GDDL. The specification conforms to GDDL's metamodel which is shown in Fig. 3.

taxonomy (see Fig. 3). The syntax of this excerpt conforms to the previously explained grasp taxonomy grammar, and therefore also to the grasp taxonomy metamodel. When the domain expert provides the implemented use case models to GraspIt!, the simulator plans grasps, which are compliant with the specified models.

Analysis of Models. In the final phase, the domain and subdomain experts investigate the modeled use cases and the created tools. If the models describe the use cases sufficiently well and the experts are satisfied with the tools, the process terminates. Otherwise, deficits, missing functionality or newly found commonalities between the subdomains are identified and serve as input for new metamodel requirements. They are included in the next process iteration.

An example of new functional requirements can be found in the design process of GDDL. Initially, a simple, custom kinematics description format was designed. However, this resulted in additional work for the integration with existing libraries. Consequently, the format was replaced by the existing URDF metamodel in another iteration. An example of other non-functional requirements can be derived by investigating the shown grasp taxonomy model (see Fig. 5). Currently, the grammar is tailored to programmers as it uses a C-like syntax with many braces. Such a representation is not suitable for grasping experts with limited programming experience. Instead, a graphical editor for grasp taxonomies could be a solution for them.

4   Discussion and Related Work

As our DSL development process has been reverse-engineered, a comparison with more traditional and general development processes found in Software and

Systems Engineering is worthwile. Interestingly, the process described here, contains comparable key building blocks and terminology, as the well-known *Unified Process* (UP) [13]. In both cases, the building blocks, such as activities, iterations, stakeholders, and cycles are crucial to describe who, when, and why some activity is performed. In addition, activities such as the creation of use cases is similar to the UP. However, one main difference remains: the major artifacts are metamodels and not executable source code. Therefore, activities like unit testing are not that straightforward to implement in the DSL development process, as comparable techniques, such as model-based testing are not (yet) mature enough. As our process uses established concepts, we argue that it is worthwhile to investigate whether it is possible to model the process itself as it still contains a sufficient amount of domain-specific aspects such as the concrete sequence and type of activities.

Kolovos *et al.* [11] have identified the three stakeholders *a)* the *system/software engineer*, who aligns with the DSL developer in our process and develops the tooling, *b)* the *developer*, who uses the tools to develop M1 models; and *c)* the *customer*, who evaluates the developed M1 models. While only the system/software engineer has an equivalent in our process, the authors also outline an "end-user programming" approach, which combines the developer and the customer. This latter approach has also been identified in our reverse-engineered development process.

Just as in software development, reusability is an important requirement in metamodeling that helps to increase model quality and decrease development time. While some metamodels have been reused or refined in the GDDL development, this often included copying or recreating metamodels from scientific literature. Preferably though, metamodels should be shared in an online metamodel repository from which they can be downloaded easily. This leads to the conclusion, that the robotics DSL community has not progressed so far, that excessive metamodel reuse is possible.

5   Conclusion

In this paper we have presented and exemplified a DSL development process which was reverse-engineered from the development of GDDL, our DSL for explicitly specifying complex robotic grasping tasks. Our process resembles well-known software development processes such as the UP. We plan to apply this process to the development of new DSLs and, while doing so, will also investigate if the process matches DSLs for purposes other than the initial goal of GDDL, i.e. *task automation*. In addition, we plan to investigate the integration of our proposed DSL process model into an overall robot software development process such as the BRICS Robot Application Development Process [12].

References

1. Berenson, D., Diankov, R., Nishiwaki, K., Kagami, S., Kuffner, J.: Grasp planning in complex scenes. In: Proc. IEEE-RAS International Conference on Humanoid Robots (2007)

2. Bohg, J., Welke, K., Lon, B., Do, M., Song, D., Wohlkinger, W., Madry, M., Aldma, A., Przybylski, M., Asfour, T., Mart, H., Kragic, D., Morales, A., Vincze, M.: Task-based grasp adaptation on a humanoid robot. In: 10th IFAC Symposium on Robot Control (2012)

3. Borst, C., Fischer, M., Hirzinger, G.: Grasp planning: How to choose a suitable task wrench space. In: Proc. IEEE International Conference on Robotics and Automation (2004)

4. Bruyninckx, H., Klotzbücher, M., Hochgeschwender, N., Kraetzschmar, G., Gherardi, L., Brugali, D.: The BRICS component model: A model-based development paradigm for complex robotics software systems. In: Proc. ACM Symposium on Applied Computing (2013)

5. Cutkosky, M.R.: On grasp choice, grasp models, and the design of hands for manufacturing tasks. IEEE Transactions on Robotics and Automation 5, 269–279 (1989)

6. De Laet, T., Bellens, S., Smits, R., Aertbelien, E., Bruyninckx, H., De Schutter, J.: Geometric relations between rigid bodies: Semantics for standardization. IEEE Robotics & Automation Magazine 20, 84–93 (2012)

7. Foster, M.P.: Disambiguating the si notation would guarantee its correct parsing. Proceedings of the Royal Society 465, 1227–1229 (2009)

8. Frigerio, M., Buchli, J., Caldwell, D.G.: Code generation of algebraic quantities for robot controllers. In: Proc. IEEE/RSJ International Conference on Intelligent Robots and Systems (2012)

9. Ghallab, M., Knoblock, C., McDermott, D., Ram, A., Veloso, M., Weld, D., Wilkins, D.: PDDL - the planning domain definition language. Tech. rep., Yale Center for Computational Vision and Control (1998)

10. Klotzbücher, M., Smits, R., Bruyninckx, H., De Schutter, J.: Reusable hybrid force-velocity controlled motion specifications with executable domain specific languages. In: Proc. IEEE/RSJ International Conference on Intelligent Robots and Systems (2011)

11. Kolovos, D.S., Paige, R.F., Kelly, T., Polack, F.A.C.: Requirements for domain-specific languages. In: Proc. 1st ECOOP Workshop on Domain-Specific Program Development, DSPD 2006 (2006)

12. Kraetzschmar, G.K., Shakhimardanov, A., Paulus, J., Hochgeschwender, N., Reckhaus, M.: Specifications of architectures, modules, modularity, and interfaces for the brocre software platform and robot control architecture workbench. BRICS project deliverable D2.2 (2010)

13. Kruchten, P.: The Rational Unified Process: An Introduction. Addison-Wesley Professional (2003)

14. Mernik, M., Heering, J., Sloane, A.M.: When and how to develop domain-specific languages. ACM Computing Surveys 37, 316–344 (2005)

15. Miller, A., Allen, P.K.: Graspit!: A versatile simulator for robotic grasping. IEEE Robotics & Automation Magazine 11, 110–122 (2004)

16. Schmidt, D.C.: Guest editor's introduction: Model-driven engineering. Computer 39(2), 25–31 (2006)

17. Schneider, S., Hochgeschwender, N., Kraetzschmar, G.K.: Declarative specification of task-based grasping with constraint validation. In: Proc. IEEE/RSJ International Conference on Intelligent Robots and Systems (to appear, 2014)

18. Tenorth, M., Beetz, M.: Knowrob: A knowledge processing infrastructure for cognition-enabled robots. International Journal of Robotics Research 32, 566–590 (2013)

ROS-I Interface for COMAU Robots

Stefano Michieletto[1], Elisa Tosello[1], Fabrizio Romanelli[2], Valentina Ferrara[2],
and Emanuele Menegatti[1]

[1] Intelligent Autonomous Systems Lab. (IAS-Lab.)
Department of Information Engineering (DEI), University of Padova
Via Gradenigo 6a, 35131 Padova, Italy
{michieletto,toselloe,emg}@dei.unipd.it
http://robotics.dei.unipd.it
[2] Research & Development Group in Motion
and Control of Comau Robotics
Via Rivalta 30, 10095 Grugliasco, Italy
{fabrizio.romanelli,valentina.ferrara}@comau.com
http://www.comau.com

Abstract. The following paper presents the ROS-I interface developed
to control Comau manipulators. Initially, the Comau controller allowed
users to command a real robot thanks to motion primitives formulated
through a Comau motion planning library. Now, either a ROS or a non
ROS -compliant platform can move either a real or a virtual Comau robot
using any motion planning library. Comau modules have been wrapped
within ROS and a virtual model of a Comau robot has been created.
The manufacturer controller has been innovatively used to drive both
the real and the simulated automata.

Keywords: ROS, Industrial, Manipulators, Simulation.

1 Introduction

Nowadays industrial robots have to perform complex tasks at high speeds and
have to be capable of carrying out extremely precise and repeatable operations
in an industrial environment; however, robot manufacturers left their controllers
closed to the user who wants to improve their capabilities and to extend their
computational power. On the other hand, the scientific community asks for a
more open system in order to apply its researches on an industrial product,
and this process must be carried out in a very short period. Moreover industrial robots are designed with several requirements such as industrial standards,
safety regulations, user-friendly interface approach and cost reductions which
are not easy to combine with an open approach. Therefore there is a thriving
research activity on these new topics which involves both industrial robotics and
applications.

There were several attempts to open industrial controller such as in [11]
and [4]. In the late 1991 Comau Robotics began its effort to implement Open
features with the third generation controller (C3G); this was a first experience

D. Brugali et al. (Eds.): SIMPAR 2014, LNAI 8810, pp. 243–254, 2014.

on the open control [5], but later this became the basis for more powerful implementations which gave the possibility to develop the forth generation open controller called C4G Open. This system architecture allowed to give the robot new features and capabilities such as sensory feedback control [9].

The next challenge in industrial robotics was to increase ease of use, flexibility and integrability of the open controller; in this context, Comau saw in the ROS-I project the natural evolution of the Open control, where a standard interface, compliant with industrial use and reliable, was mandatory. Other robot manufactures are involved in the ROS-I program[1]: ABB, Adept, Fanuc, Universal Robot and Motoman. Only Motoman released production ready code. In the other cases the software is not yet production ready code and it has only some levels of unit-testing. For Adept and Fanuc only joint position streaming is supported, with the controller currently overriding commanded velocity with a constant one. Trajectory downloading, velocity or force control are note yet supported. For ABB only trajectory streaming is supported [14]. The Motoman driver controller interface, instead, provides a more high-performance interface for controlling Motoman robots, and it meets qualitative criteria for being used in production systems. The controller plans the movements using an existing ROS-compliant motion planning library: MoveIt[2]. And it provides a low-level control of joint position, velocity, and path timing. Being ROS non real-time, the computational load decreases robot speeds down to 20% and 70% of robot capabilities. Following the Motoman example, this paper presents the ROS-I interface developed to control Comau manipulators. The stack contains:

- ROS nodes implementing the communication with C4G Open (the Comau industrial robot controller);
- the Comau Smart5 SiX robot model in the Universal Robot Description File (URDF[3]) format for the simulated representation of the automata;
- the Open realistic Robot Library (ORL) (the Comau motion planning library).

These tools allow either a ROS or a non ROS -compliant platform to move either a real or a virtual Comau Smart5 SiX robot. Both a position and a velocity controller are supported and motion commands can be issued using both ORL and any other ROS-compliant motion planning library. As above mentioned, other manufactures offer packages suitable only for MoveIt. Moreover, in our case both the real and the simulated automata are driven using C4G Open. Being it real-time, the faithful control of the robot and its 100% speed are guaranteed.

The rest of the paper is organized as follows. In Section 2 existing standard and open architectures will be presented together with an overview of the ROS-Industrial standards. The integration of ROS-I within the Comau C4G Open controller will be discussed in Section 3, followed by the experimental setup and tests of Section 4. Conclusions and future works will be depicted in Section 5.

---

[1] http://rosindustrial.org/

[2] http://moveit.ros.org/

[3] http://wiki.ros.org/urdf

2 Overview

2.1 Open Control Architecture

The Open Robot Controller is a software and hardware control architecture which allows the easy and safe integration of the Robot Control Unit with an external Personal Computer. The integration helps programming the automatized robotic cell and lets the extraction of data from external sensors.

C4G Standard Controller. The standard COMAU C4G controller consists of a modular architecture with three different hierarchical hardware levels (see Figure 1).

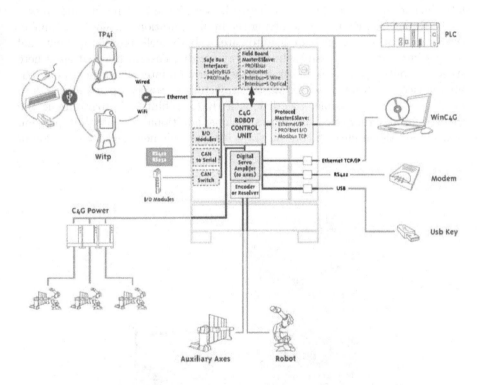

Fig. 1. Standard architecture for the Comau C4G robot controller

The first level is the System Master Processor (SMP+) control board. At this level, all high level processes take place: interpretation of user programs, management of operator interfaces, network communications, trajectory generation, computation of dynamic model and management of assigned tasks, collisions detection, system diagnostics, high hierarchical level centralized adjustment process, axes synchronizing control, management of all I/O devices. The second level is the Model Predictive Control (MPC) board, inside: fine interpolation of the manipulator trajectory, robot position adjustment, real time system diagnostics, master-slave axes management. The lower level is the Digital Signal Processing (DSP) board, inside: control of electric motor currents and torque generation process for individual axes control, power stage management, position sensor and acquisition of motor angular measurements, high speed digital and analogical I/O management. The system architecture is based on a real time communication. It has a frame rate of $1ms$ on an Ethernet network that uses an UDP protocol, between the SMP+ board (client) and the MPC board (server).

Comau C4G Open Controller. The standard C4G controller does not allow sensors and devices connections to the robot. This restriction has been overcome opening the robot controller: a second server process has been inserted introducing an external PC in the network (see Figure 2). The PC adds power to the Robot Control Unit simplifying the implementation of complex manufacturing applications: programming automated robotics cells is easier and external sensors integration is possible. In this way, writing custom applications where standard control processes and trajectory generation interact with external sensors, devices or PCs is feasible. Mixing trajectories between open and standard modalities is also possible, together with the possibility of programming the robot using different open modalities such as: additional and absolute position control, additional current control, trajectory management and modification of

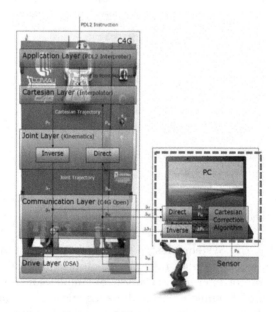

Fig. 2. Open Control architecture for the Comau C4G robot controller

pre-planned trajectory. Different Open architectures have been presented in several European Projects (SME Robot[4] and ARFLEX[5]) to correct a real trajectory using vision systems or to integrate an inertial navigation tool. The C4G Open Control is based on GNU/Linux Operating System and the real-time is achieved by using the Real-Time Application Interface (RTAI) [6] module to extend the standard kernel with real-time capabilities. On the other hand, in order to provide a real-time communication layer, C4G Open architecture uses Real-Time networking (RTnet) [1] stack, an open source hard real-time network protocol compatible with RTAI.

2.2 Open Realistic Robot Library

The Open realistic Robot Library (ORL) has been developed in order to perform operations on a virtual robot without having it. The motivation behind the realization of this library is that C4G Open forces the user to program at a low level in motor round references. The ORL allows the user to program at a high level in order to let him develop custom applications with C4G Open (or C5G Open, if we consider the new controller Comau is developing). The library allows to perform the following operations:

- Initialization of the virtual robot on Linux (complete Comau robot family) starting from a real configuration file
- Computation of Direct and Inverse Kinematics, for each Comau robot
- Error management of position and joint ranges
- Integration of Comau Trajectory Generator and Interpolator
- Computation of the Dynamic Model and Jacobian

All these operations are realistic, i.e. they describe what the robot would do if they were performed via the Comau standard programming language (PDL2) on the real robot. Performing direct/inverse kinematics allows the user to control the real robot workspace in advance (e.g. joint stroke-ends, Cartesian avoided positions). Routines for the direct motor rounds control are included, together with motion functions able to convert and manage degrees or Cartesian references.

2.3 ROS-Industrial

Creating robust and general-purpose robot software is hard. Every task and every environment has its own encoding and there is not a homogeneous solution to all its instances. The Robot Operating System (ROS) [12] is an open-source project that aims to develop a common framework for robotics applications thanks to collaborations among single individuals, laboratories, and institutions. It is a set of tools, libraries, and conventions collected to simplify the creation of complex and robust robot behaviors across a wide variety of robotic platforms. ROS is

---

[4] http://www.smerobot.org/
[5] http://www.arflexproject.eu/

utilized by the research community for service robotics applications, but its technology can be applied to other application areas, including industrial robotics. For this purpose, ROS-Industrial has been developed . It extends ROS capabilities, such as advanced perception and path/grasp planning, enabling industrial robotic applications previously technically infeasible or cost prohibitive. ROS high-level functionalities are combined with the low-level reliability and safety of industrial robot controllers creating a robust, reliable, and hardware-agnostic software.

3   Integration

As already stated, a real time communication channel is necessary to obtain a proper interaction between the Comau C4G controller and the external PC providing additional capabilities. The communication is based on a real time thread providing robot status information from the external PC to the robot controller and viceversa. In this work, we extended the basic real time thread by developing several parallel threads in order to decouple the real time communication process from the data provided in input, to control the robot, and in output, to give back its status. With this aim, existing modules were wrapped in ROS. The current ROS version is used: Hydro. As both the ROS framework and C4G Open support the Ubuntu Linux distribution, its 13.04 version is used, maintaining RTAI and RTnet to satisfy the C4G Open requirements. The wrapper maintains existing features. The user can still

- directly program the robot using the PDL2 language;
- use ORL functions to formulate robot motion primitives that the C4G controller will then convert into the equivalent machine code.

In addition, the user can now impose motion directives in the form of ROS commands: a ROS message with the motion request is sent to the system, ROS redirects the message to the motion library, and the latter answers with a ROS message containing the motion primitives the controller needs to move the robot. ROS integration makes ORL a simple form of the system: the library has to be considered as any other motion planning library and for this reason, at any time the user can replace it with any other ROS compliant motion library, e.g., MoveIt.

A TCP/IP connection was implemented to give non ROS compliant frameworks the possibility to interface to the proposed system. This type of protocol provides reliable, ordered and error-checked delivery of data. The ordered data transfer guarantees the robot to execute the motion primitives in the same order specified by the user. Reliability ensures the retransmission of lost packets and the consequent execution of all motion primitives. As result, the robot will executes all the desired motion commands in the desired order.

Enforcing a robot to directly execute a specific task can be inefficient. The non-tested task can be impracticable: the imposed goal can be unreachable because of the robot joints limits; or it can cause damages: the robot can collide with the surrounding world. For the same reasons, testing an application directly on the real robot can be expensive in terms of time and money. Performing tests in a simulated environment is the solution. A virtual model of a Comau robot was created, its use is guaranteed within any ROS compliant simulator (e.g., Gazebo [8] or VRep [7]); and a plug-in allowing the robot control inside Gazebo was developed.

A description of the process adopted to make the system usable both in the simulated and in the real environment follows.

3.1 Simulation

With the aim of replicating the motion of a Comau robot inside a ROS compliant simulator, a virtual model of a Comau Smart5 Six robot was developed. The virtual representation involves the creation of a package containing the robot meshes and the URDF file describing the geometry, kinematics and dynamics of the robot, such as joints masses and inertial matrices. In order to control the robot virtual model within the Gazebo simulation environment, the following tools have been developed: a plug-in connecting the Comau robot controller to Gazebo, and a wrapper for ORL. The latter ensures the same trajectories interpolation both for the virtual and the real robot, that results in the same robot movements execution both in the virtual and in the real world.

3.2 Real Robot

In order to command the real robot using ROS, the following problem must be faced: the robot communication is hard real-time (it has a frame rate of 2 ms) and ROS is non real-time. A communication node was developed. It includes both a real-time and a normal priority thread. The former establishes the connection between the controller and the real robot. The latter provides the controller with the motion data: if a ROS compliant platform aims at controlling the robot sending it specific motion directives, then the thread will deliver these motion commands to the controller in the form of ROS messages. If a non ROS compliant processor has the same request, the thread will send the motion primitives to the controller in the form of TCP/IP messages. Performed tests show that the proposed structure ensures the absence of robot/controller connection errors and lets the user to control the robot both through a real and a non real-time platform.

The Comau system is now compliant with the current ROS version and lets users to control both a real robot and its simulated counterpart by using the same motion controller. Figure 3 compares the initial and the obtained system.

4 Experiments

The system has been developed in order to fulfill the specifications due to different Robot Learning from Demonstration (RLfD) [3] [2] studies we are conducting

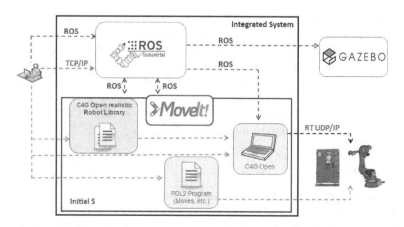

Fig. 3. The developed system including the initial structure (red) and the integration with ROS (blue)

(a) Human demo   (b) Simulated experiment

Fig. 4. The first experiment: use of a position controller

in our laboratory. The adopted RLfD frameworks involve challenging conditions in terms of different tasks, objectives, interpolation algorithms, and motion controllers. These aspects are all crucial in a dynamic industrial environment, in which the aims are heterogeneous and related to the goal to be reached.

In the analysed cases, humans teach to a Comau Smart5 SiX manipulator how to achieve simplified industrial movements. The system is structured as follows: a human performs a task; an RGB-D sensor acquires the scene. A skeleton tracking algorithm extracts the useful information from the acquired data (positions and orientations of skeleton joints). This information is given as input to the motion re-targeting system that remaps the skeleton joints into the manipulator ones. The collected data are used to train a Gaussian Mixture Model (GMM) in order to retrieved a generalize motion trajectory by applying a Gaussian Mixture Regression (GMR). Subsequently, the robot motion controller interprets the generated trajectory to make the manipulator reproduce robot movements

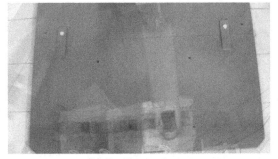

(a) Human demo   (b) Real experiment

Fig. 5. The second experiment: use of a velocity controller

similar to the human ones. Motion commands are imprinted using ROS messages. Experiments were performed both in virtual and real world, and two different scenarios were treated, each one by utilizing different motion planning libraries.

The first scenario consists of the displacement of a piece. A human demonstrator moves a box along a line from the beginning to the end of a 45 cm long table; the manipulator reproduces the same task both in the real world and in simulation (depicted in Figure 4). More details can be found in [10]. The task requires very accurate robot movements, so that the manipulator is controlled by setting joint positions. The interpolation of robot motion is computed by ORL, that offers high reliable functions to command a robot in position. Accuracy and repeatability tests were performed by measuring the different displacements performed on a box. In the real world the robot moves the same box as the actor, and the table is replaced with a white paper sheet situated on the floor. On 25 attempts, the system obtained an average displacement of 54.332 +/- 0.7547667. Instead, in simulation the virtual box has the same characteristics of the real one, while the table is longer and larger in order to avoid singularities when the box reaches the end of the table. In this case, the accuracy is even better with an average of 45.011 +/- 0.402 cm. The simulated replica is then faithful to the real human demonstration and the real robot displacement has a gap of about 10 cm. The alteration is due to the different frictional forces: the material of the support surface used in the real experiment has a friction coefficient lower then that of the tables used for the demonstration and for the simulated representation. Having a lower friction coefficient facilitates displacements. Finally, both the real and the virtual variances are negligible: small existing variations are due to sensors and motors noises or to an imprecise manual positioning of the box at the beginning of every test.

The second scenario simplifies the arrest of a piece before its extraction from the conveyor belt. A subject stops a Lego Mindstorms NXT[6] robot performing a uniform rectilinear motion on a 60 cm long table after 20 s from the motion start. The action can be interpreted as the block of an object after a certain

---

[6] http://www.lego.com/en-us/mindstorms/?domainredir=mindstorms.lego.com

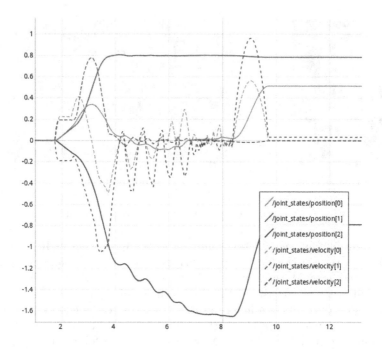

Fig. 6. Robot joint positions and velocities during the second test

event. A velocity controller is required in order to make the robot moving within a certain time interval. A custom interpolator has been used to compute the velocities with respect to the joint positions [13]. It is worth to notice that no other element has been changed in the system. Figure 6 shows positions and velocities of the three joints controlled by our framework during the experiment.

In the real reproduction, a Pioneer[7] robot with a box on its top moves at constant velocity in front of the manipulator robot, the latter has to "stop" the former within a certain period of time blocking the box situated on its top (depicted in Figure 5). In the simulated environment, robot movements are tested and ROS commands are formulated in order to coordinate the start of the two robots. The experiment does not require measurements because precision is not required. The robot stopped the box in time in all the 25 performed trials.

The analysis of the proposed cases shows that the created ROS-I interface is reliable: motion commands are imprinted using ROS messages and robots properly perform the imposed tasks. This means that no message was lost or received in disorder. Robots movements match both in the virtual and in the real world, proving the proper utilize of a unique controller in both realities. Finally, moving the robots using two different motion libraries evinces the versatility of the proposed system by testing different controllers as easily replaceable modules.

---

[7] http://www.mobilerobots.com/ResearchRobots/PioneerP3DX.aspx

Moreover, users are not required to use the Comau motion planning library, but they can use any open-source or customized library.

5   Conclusions

The paper presented the method used to extend the Comau SpA controlling system. The initial system was composed of a robot controller, the C4G Open, and a motion planning library, ORL. The latter was used to send the former the motion commands robots needed to move. The final system preserves these characteristics; in addition, it is ROS-compliant, it lets the user to control both a real robot and its simulated counterpart using the same controller, and it lets him to replace the Comau motion planning library with any library of the same type. To test the system, a Comau Smart5 SiX robot was asked to perform two different tasks, both in simulation and in the real world and both using ROS commands. The former involved the displacement of a static box and required the development of a position controller. The latter considered the capture of a moving object and a velocity controller was used for its attainment. The experiments choice is easily justifiable: it permits to test the system using two types of motion planning libraries. In fact, the position controller requires the sending of position commands to move the robot; ORL includes this function and for this reason it can be used in the experiment. The velocity controller, instead, needs velocity commands. ORL does not includes this function and an ad-hoc motion planning library must be developed and used. Experiments showed that both the real and the virtual robot performed the same movements during the execution of both assignments. This proves that using the same controller in both environments guarantees the same trajectories interpolation. The detected movements precision proves the good functioning of the system itself, the proper development of the ROS-I interface and the possibility to use any type of motion planning library. Having a ROS-I interface makes the Comau system reusable by the entire ROS community, and having a replaceable motion planning library is an essential characteristic to make the system freely accessible and usable not only at an industrial but also at a research level.

The developed code has been released as a Open Source software[8] in order to foster research in the field.

As future work authors aim to extend the implementation to the new Comau motion controller, the C5G Open. In this way, Comau will maintain its ROS compatibility solving existing C4G Open limitations. Developing a ROS-I interface for the C5G Open will lead to an innovative product leader both in the research environment and in the industrial context. Nowadays more and more flexible and smart applications will be able to use it, integrating sensors and complex algorithms.

---

[8] At the moment of writing, the source code is in the develop branch of the following GitHub repositories: `https://github.com/iaslab-unipd/c4g_controller`, `https://github.com/iaslab-unipd/smart5six_description`, `https://github.com/iaslab-unipd/smart5six_gazebo_plugin`

Acknowledgement. This work was funded as part of the research project Fibremap[9] by the European Commission in FP7 ICT under Grant No. 608768.

References

1. Rtnet a flexible hard real-time networking framework. In: 10th IEEE International Conference on Emerging Technologies and Factory Automation, Italy (2005)
2. Argall, B.D., Chernova, S., Veloso, M., Browning, B.: Robotics and autonomous systems. A Survey of Robot Learning from Demonstration 57(5), 469–483 (2009)
3. Billard, A., Calinon, S., Dillmann, R., Schaal, S.: Robot programming by demonstration. In: Siciliano, B., Khatib, O. (eds.) Handbook of Robotics, pp. 1371–1394. Springer, Secaucus (2008)
4. Blomdell, A., Bolmsjo, G., Brogardh, T., Cederberg, P., Isaksson, M., Johansson, R., Haage, M., Nilsson, K., Olsson, M., Olsson, T., Robertsson, A., Wang, J., Department of Automation of Lund University: Extending an industrial robot controller: implementation and applications of a fast open sensor interface. Robotics and Automation Magazine 12 (2005)
5. Dogliani, F., Magnani, G., Sciavicco, L.: An open architecture industrial controller. Newsl. of IEEE Robotics and Automation Soc. 7(3), 19–21 (1993)
6. Dozio, L., Mantegazza, P.: Real time distributed control systems using rtai. In: Sixth IEEE International Symposium on Object-Oriented Real-Time Distributed Computing, Hakodate, Hokkaido, Japan, May 14-16 (2003)
7. Freese, M., Singh, S., Ozaki, F., Matsuhira, N.: Virtual robot experimentation platform V-REP: A versatile 3D robot simulator. In: Ando, N., Balakirsky, S., Hemker, T., Reggiani, M., von Stryk, O. (eds.) SIMPAR 2010. LNCS, vol. 6472, pp. 51–62. Springer, Heidelberg (2010)
8. Koenig, N., Howard, A.: Design and use paradigms for gazebo, an open-source multi-robot simulator. In: Proc. of IEEE/RSJ International Conference on Intelligent Robots and Systems (IROS 2004), pp. 2149–2154 (2004)
9. Lippiello, V., Villani, L., Siciliano, B.: An open architecture for sensory feedback control of a dual-arm industrial robotic cell. Industrial Robot: An International Journal 34(1), 46–53 (2007)
10. Michieletto, S., Chessa, N., Menegatti, M.: Learning how to approach industrial robot tasks from natural demonstrations. In: IEEE Workshop on Advanced Robotics and its Social Impacts (2013)
11. Oonishi, K.: The open manipulator system of the mhi pa-10 robot. In: Proceeding of International Symposium on Robotics (1999)
12. Quigley, M., Gerkey, B., Conley, K., Faust, J., Foote, T., Leibs, J., Berger, E., Wheeler, R., Ng, A.: Ros: an open-source robot operating system (2010)
13. Tosello, E., Michieletto, S., Bisson, A., Pagello, E., Menegatti, E.: A learning from demonstration framework for manipulation tasks. In: 45th International Symposium on Robotics (ISR 2014) and 8th German Conference on Robotics (ROBOTIK 2014) (2014)
14. Venator, E.: Hardware and software architecture of abby: An industrial mobile manipulator. In: 9th IEEE International Conference on Automation Science and Engineering (August 2013)

---

[9] http://fibremap.eu/

Robot Unit Testing*

Andreas Bihlmaier and Heinz Wörn

Institute for Anthropomatics and Robotics (IAR),
Intelligent Process Control and Robotics Lab. (IPR),
Karlsruhe Institute of Technology (KIT),
76131 Karlsruhe, Germany
{andreas.bihlmaier,woern}@kit.edu

Abstract. We introduce Robot Unit Testing (RUT) as a methodology
to bring modern testing methods into robotics. Through RUT the range
of robotics software that can be automatically tested is extended beyond
current practice. A robotics simulator is used to bridge the gap between
well automated tests that only check a robot's software and time consuming, inherently manual tests on robots of alloy and circuits. An in-depth
realization of RUT is shown, which is based on the Robot Operating System (ROS) framework and the Gazebo simulator due to their prominence
in robotics research and inherent suitability for the RUT methodology.

1 Introduction

Software testing, not as merely a good practice, but rather as a software development paradigm, has (re)gained widespread popularity. In particular test-driven
development (TDD) is as a core concept of agile software engineering methods. Regardless of whether TDD provides a benefit compared to other types of
software development processes (cf. [10]), the importance of test coverage for
complex software systems is not called into question. Unit testing together with
integration and regression testing is an enabler for high quality and long-term
supportability of large scale software systems. Therefore, it is hardly surprising
that the Robot Operating System (ROS) relies on and encourages unit, integration and regression testing. To state a few benefits of testing as regarded by the
ROS community[1]: faster incremental code updates, more reliable refactoring,
better code design and prevention of recurring bugs.

However, something crucial is missing from these tests – in ROS and other
robotic frameworks: robots. As we try to show in the following, this does not
have to be the case. Of course, in contrast to the universal Turing machine, there
is (so far) no universal physical machine. Additionally, the physical machine
must be unbreakable or to be exact infinitely many times breakable. In Robot
Unit Testing there is an additional gap between all tests passing and the system
working correctly. If the test coverage of a software is high and all tests pass, one

---

* This research was carried out with the support of the German Research Foundation
(DFG) within project I05, SFB/TRR 125 "Cognition-Guided Surgery".

[1] http://wiki.ros.org/UnitTesting

D. Brugali et al. (Eds.): SIMPAR 2014, LNAI 8810, pp. 255–266, 2014.

is justified to believe the software will work correctly, but it is not guaranteed. The additional gap in RUT stems from an additional artificiality, test data is not real data and simulated robots are not real robots. Yet, if our proposed RUT methodology is implemented there will remain gaps, but the current gaping abyss will narrow.

The following section (Sec. 2) concerns the current best practices in automated software testing. The further text is divided into two major parts, the first one (Sec. 3) details what we mean by Robot Unit Testing, its methodology. The second part (Sec. 4) applies RUT to ROS enabled robots, translates the abstract terminology of the first part into ROS terms, fills in details and provides results. A short summary (Sec. 5) concludes our presentation of RUT.

*depending on purpose

Fig. 1. The real KUKA LWR4+ and its simulated counterpart are clearly distinguishable in this image. They can not be said to be equivalent. However, from the viewpoint of our proposed Robot Unit Testing methodology, they are sufficiently similar in order to avoid breaking one of them by automated breaking of the other one.

2   Automated Software Testing

This section will not mention any manual testing methods, such as program inspection, walkthroughs or reviews. Although we find these to be valuable tools, manual methods are not our concern here. We bring up Robot Unit Testing as a methodology that enables *automated* testing of robots.

In the following short overview of automated testing, we follow the recently updated classic presentation by Myers et al. [8]. Because we do not introduce a new software-only testing methodology, such as the material discussed in this section and due to the limit space, no extensive state of the art for software testing is provided here. The purpose is to shortly introduce the most important aspects and vocabulary of testing (cf. [11]) necessary for the following sections.

First, tests can be distinguished by whether the internal workings of software components are known and exploited for testing. In case they are, one speaks of white box testing. Otherwise, it is called black box testing. Different software metrics apply for the two cases. The most important difference is that white box testing allows to precisely state the statement, condition and other types of coverage about the tested code. The next categorization separates functional from non-functional (e.g. stress) testing. Furthermore, one can distinguish between the scope included in a single test. While unit testing examines small fragments of the system, integration testing pertains to their interaction. The last terminological distinction that has to be introduced concerns the testing purpose. Common purposes include the early detecting of problems, the verification of the API contract and the avoidance of regressions through changes. All these are within reach of robotics research once the RUT methodology is utilized.

Complementary to testing as a technique there are testing methodologies that systematise testing into engineering. The most important methodologies for the paper at hand are test-driven development (TDD) and continuous integration (CI). TDD is about writing tests even before the code that is required to make them succeed [1]. CI is not as clearly defined, but all variants have in common that there must be a high degree of automated software build processes together with extensive test coverage [4].

We conclude this condensed survey of automated software testing methodology with two remarks: First, the testing mindset reckons software development as an iterative process and the test coverage provides the much needed non-formal loop invariant for the iteration. Second, testing is all about greater – justified – confidence in software quality. The following section explains why we deem RUT to be a crucial missing link in current robot software engineering.

3   The RUT Methodology

Sir the Simple Robot

To make the description more vivid, we'll assume a SImple Robot *Sir* made up of a manipulator, its arm, and a camera sensor, its eye. The scenario for the robot is to recognize a certain landmark, the red button, approach the landmark from its surface normal and continue a few millimeters, i.e. press it. Sir's arm can be controlled by specifying a Cartesian pose, which is converted to joint positions. The joint positions are interpolated and finally sent to the black box motor control unit. Sir's eye observes the world as a video stream of two megapixel color images at 30 frames per second seen as originating from a black box. Each image is preprocessed and compared against a database of known objects, if a match is found the object's position is known by Sir.

Requirements I: Robotics Simulator

Robot Unit Testing rests on the assumption that modern real-time robotics simulations are able to substitute real sensors and actuators *sufficiently* well. The plausibility of this assumption now rests on the notion of "sufficient" that we adopt. Sufficient here means that average robots in average environments doing averagely difficult tasks are simulated with an accuracy that makes them succeed or fail with the same average probability as in the real scenario. Here probability does not necessarily have to be interpreted in a frequentist manner, rather it can be seen as a degree of belief (cf. [5]). The point being, if the simulated robot can perform a kind of task reliably, so should the real robot and vice versa. It does not matter whether the simulation is accurate enough to also pass this test for other kinds of tasks. Therefore, no quantitative criterion for geometric, kinematic or dynamic realism has to be met in order to utilize and profit from RUT. We will come back to this point later in the section.

Requirements II: Robot Software

As will be shown, what is important for RUT are well designed robot software architectures. The robot software must permit to reroute the data flow to actuators and from sensors, ideally at several layers of abstraction. It is not strictly necessary, yet clearly preferable, if the rerouting function is available without directly changing the software, i.e. being a runtime instead of compile time option. In our example, the commands to Sir's arm position could be accessed as target pose, target joint position and interpolated joint position. Sir's accessible sensor data would consist of the video stream and the stream of detected object positions. Fortunately, this kind of flexible robot software is not a desirable exception anymore, but rather the state of the art in academia and becoming a standard in industry.

Bringing Things Together: The Big Picture

There are two ideas at the core of the Robot Unit Testing methodology: First, to redirect the actuator and sensor data at the *lowest* feasible level of abstraction to a robotic simulator. Second, to write unit tests that interact with the robot at the *highest* feasible level of abstraction.[2] Fig. 2 shows the general structure of RUT.

Again in the example, Sir is simulated at the level of interpolated joint positions and rendered camera images. In other words the simulator interface receives interpolated joint positions and sends rendered camera images. The unit tests control Sir by Cartesian poses, whose calculation is based on detected object positions.

Get Out of the Rut: Benefits of RUT

Obviously, neither using a robotic simulator nor writing tests are recent inventions in robotics research or software engineering, still thus far their full potential

---

[2] We do not presuppose a layered architecture or any specific architecture for that matter. We use the terms high and low level to refer to the semantic level of data, i.e. in our usage of these terms a Cartesian pose is on a higher level than a vector of joint positions of some kinematic.

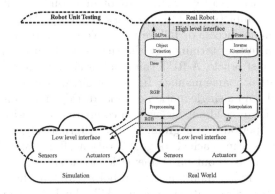

Fig. 2. The figure illustrates how Robot Unit Testing is related to the software and hardware components of the real robot. The shaded area highlights the software components utilized by both the real robot and its unit tests.

lies idle. What we want to contribute to with the notion of Robot Unit Testing is a systematic and sound presentation of a new methodology in robotics research and engineering. Its benefits are a novel level of automated test coverage for robots – as entities of software embedded in sensors and actuators. We propose to *test robots*, not just their isolated (software) components. Once a RUT framework is in place, we expect the same level of quality increase that tightly integrated testing brings to complex software systems (cf. [7]).

To elaborate on the new level of test coverage, we want to point out that *all software components of the real robot* under test besides very low level hardware components take part in RUTs. In case of Sir the tested components include the high level interface code, inverse kinematics, interpolator, image preprocessing and object detection. The only components left untested are the motor controller and camera firmware, which are usually black boxes in the real world, too. This large test coverage does not have to go along with large or complicated RUT code, as will be discussed later on.

Bringing Things Together: The Details

To recapitulate, the interface we write RUTs against is the highest level of abstraction offered by the robot software. The interface to the robotics simulator is the lowest available level of abstraction. RUTs should obey general rules established in the software testing community and conversely avoid its anti-patterns. One anti-pattern is particularly noteworthy: Avoid to build up system state. Each RUT should be executable on its own, not dependent on others and should also not interfere with them. This will be achievable with any robot framework defined as suitable for RUT above. Ideally the tests can be run in parallel by rerouting each test instance to a different robotics simulator instance. If this is not supported, it must only be ensured that the simulators state is completely reset between the sequentially running tests.

RUTs can be written to test a single robot function – our notion of "unit" in robotics – or a complete robot skill or task capability. What the test checks in order to determine success or failure is completely up to the purpose of the particular test. In testing terminology the success or failure condition is often referred to as the test oracle. A RUT can monitor actuator and sensor data in a very close or a rather coarse manner. In case of Sir, we can initialize its arm in a known pose and send a single motion command. Depending on what invariant the test should guarantee about Sir, we can compare each position of each joint in each simulation period to our ground truth. Alternatively, we may only care about whether Sir's arm reached its goal position after a specified amount of time. If the invariant is about Sir's kinematics we would most likely select the former, if we are currently modifying this robot subsystem the latter one seems more useful. To test Sir's button pressing skill, the RUT would initialize an environment with a red button at a known location and execute the skill. Again, depending on the test's purpose, it could suffice to test whether Sir's arm stops in a button press position. The complete RUT would consist of placing Sir and the red button in a known position, starting the skill and monitoring Sir's simulated arm position to check it against the correct final pose. This is everything required to ascertain that no later modification – anywhere in Sir's system – introduces a regression with respect to all involved actuator and sensor systems.

Here the point has come to say more about required simulation realism and accuracy. We only required the simulation to be sufficiently similar for a certain kind of task, so that this task will work similarly well on the real and simulated robot. For the RUT of Sir's button pressing skill two accuracy requirements must be met. Geometrical accuracy on the one hand and visual accuracy on the other hand. Sir's simulated kinematic must be accurate enough for the following to hold: For all relevant button positions the delta between simulated and real final pose is small enough to count as a button press in both cases. An analogous proposition must hold for Sir's visual perception. That is, the simulated scene must – for the relevant button positions – be visually close enough to the real one in order for the button to (wrongly) count as detected in reality and simulation. This vague notion ("relevant positions", "count as") is not a shortcoming of our approach, but part of the RUT methodology. Ground truth is always relative to what we judge to be sufficiently close to our use cases. As robotics simulators become more accurate, the RUT coverage can increase and include cases previously inaccessible to RUT. However, our point is that current simulators are *already* perfectly suited to facilitate RUT now. As long as the RUT methodology is minded, adopting Robot Unit Testing can provide a justified higher level of confidence in the quality of robot software development.

Cost of RUT in Terms of Additional Components and Effort

Talking about benefits of a methodology must be accompanied by elaborating on the costs of adopting it. In the following section, we'll detail element by element what it takes to implement RUT on ROS in terms of components, models and effort. Beforehand, we give a more abstract presentation of the requirements together with a glance to what state of the art robotics frameworks and simulators already provide. The difference between the two is the cost to implement RUT.

Considering Fig. 2, we can discern four necessary elements: Code to implement each test case, simulation models, simulated actuators with an appropriate interface and simulated sensors with an appropriate interface. In the previous subsection, we have already elaborated on the test code. As should be the case in non-robot testing, simple tests only require a few lines of code: Create input data, call the interface with the input data and compare the result with a reference. Since we use the robot's high level interface, the only open question relates to getting the test results. In some cases the result is directly provided by the robot software, e.g. whether Sir sees a certain object. In other cases the result is a state of the simulated world. Fortunately, the simulated world is fully observable from the RUTs point of view – of course not from the simulated robot. Thus, no substantial effort is required to query this world state. Simulation models represent the next element. It can require a substantial amount of work to produce these. Yet, in our experience most of the work is typically already done. Either because the robots are already simulated or at least CAD models are available. Often the CAD models were already created in order to built the robot in the first place. The last two elements, namely simulated actuators and sensors with the appropriate interface, can be dealt with together. All the major robotics simulators such as Gazebo[3], MORSE[4] and V-Rep[5] provide a variety of simulated actuators and sensors. Most actuators and sensors can already be accessed through the standard interface of common robot software frameworks. On the other hand it can take substantial work to remedy a situation, where the simulated item is not available or does not provide the required interface. To summarize, the effort required to adopt RUT is very low if the robot under test is already simulated for other purposes or at least a visualization exists. Otherwise, the effort increases along the dimensions of uncommon actuators and sensors, uncommon robotics simulators and uncommon robot frameworks.

4   RUT for ROS

The Robot Operating System (ROS) [9] is a well known and prevalent framework for modular and distributed robot software. This section describes our implementation of Robot Unit Tests for ROS. There are several open-source robotics simulators with ROS support available. We selected the Gazebo simulator because it seems to be the one currently favored by the ROS community. Furthermore, the simulator used in the DARPA virtual robotics challenge (VRC) is closely based on Gazebo [6]. In the remainder of the section, our goal is to relate everything generally said about methodology to the tangible implementation.

---

[3] http://gazebosim.org/
[4] http://www.openrobots.org/wiki/morse/
[5] http://www.coppeliarobotics.com/

Robots under Test

Our example implementation was done to test the software stack for two lightweight robot arms, the KUKA LWR4+ and the Universal Robots UR5, and their attached sensors. An industrial camera and an endoscope camera together with optics used for minimally invasive surgery (MIS) are mounted to the arms, shown in Fig. 1. To keep the presentation short and concise, the component graph of Sir the SImple Robot used as example in the previous section, has a lot in common with the actual ROS software. Fig. 3 shows the annotated graph of the actual ROS nodes.[6]

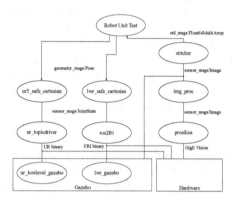

Fig. 3. The extended ROS graph used as example for simple and complex Robot Unit Tests is shown. Edges are annotated with the ROS message types or the protocol passed between the nodes. All solid framed nodes are part of the system independent of whether RUT is integrated.

Initial Effort Required for RUT

All solid framed nodes in Fig. 3 depict software that is required independently of simulation and RUT. Only the Gazebo model plugins for the two robot arms are supplements. In our case, they expose the respective vendor specific binary protocol interface and convert received commands to movements of the Gazebo joints and vice versa.

It is important to understand why we required, according to our RUT methodology, that one should go down to the level of vendor specific binary protocols and when one can and should stay at a higher interface level: Due to our specific demands in surgical robotics, the ros2fri and ur_topicdriver node are our own implementation to ROS-ify the robot arms. Therefore, we wanted the RUTs to include this part of the robot as well – following the RUT rule to test robots, not components. Had our test *purpose* been different, we could have used a generic joint model plugin already provided by Gazebo. In this case there would have been no additional code required to start with RUTs.

---

[6] We assume the reader to be familiar with ROS terminology, otherwise please refer to the above cited reference or http://wiki.ros.org/ROS/Concepts

All nodes required for the industrial camera are provided by the ROS community. We regarded them together with the camera firmware as black boxes outside our test domain. Therefore, the RUT methodology suggests sensor_msgs/Camera as the appropriate interface. This is fortunate because the ROS sensors plugins for Gazebo provide exactly this interface to the simulated camera.

Thus, the only elements missing for RUT are the simulation models for Gazebo. To create these in the form of meshes together with a URDF[7] or SDF[8] description, can take substantial effort. However, since the advent of ROS Industrial[9] the models are already available for a large number of (industrial) robots. This is the case for the UR5. Even if this doesn't apply to a certain robot, such as the LWR4+, there is a good chance that the model must be created anyway. The same model formats are required for visualization with rviz[10]. Making this another case where RUT does not involve additional effort. To sum up, most of the required RUT elements are already available for a robot that is well integrated with ROS. Let's put them to a novel use in RUTs.

A Basic RUT

A basic, yet essential, Robot Unit Test for the robot arms is to test self-collision free reachability of poses. The simulated environment is initialized with a certain robot arm configuration, i.e. world to base transformation and robot joint positions. Referring to the node names in Fig. 3, the test input is a Cartesian pose to the safe_cartesian nodes. The test result consists of two outputs: Detected collisions and the final pose of the simulated robot arm. For poses reachable by the arm, a test counts as successful if and only if no collision occurs and the arm reaches the target pose after a specified amount of time and stops there. For an unreachable pose, we define success as the arm not moving at all. Depending on the context, other definitions are conceivable, such as stopping in the point closest to the target pose that is reachable. Whether a pose should be reachable, i.e. the ground truth, is either tested with the real robot or validated through a human observer. We only test poses – together with environments, whose ground truth has been once verified, either one way or the other, to be correct. All these poses together make up the test data for this particular RUT. As usual in testing, effort and coverage increases with a larger set of test data.

ROS Tools

Before describing a more complex RUT, a note on tool support provided by ROS. Rostest[11] is an extension to ROS launch files, that takes care of starting up all the required nodes together with the simulator. Furthermore, a combination

---

[7] The Unified Robot Description Format, cf. http://wiki.ros.org/urdf

[8] The Simulation Description Format, cf. http://gazebosim.org/sdf.html

[9] http://rosindustrial.org/

[10] http://wiki.ros.org/rviz

[11] http://wiki.ros.org/rostest

of ROS command-line tools started from the launch file, especially rostopic, already provides most of the necessary test infrastructure. We will soon release code to the community that provides a similarly generic interface to check for certain events in the Gazebo simulation, e.g. something reaches a certain pose. Combined, with the include capability of launch files, each RUT only consists of four lines: Include the other launch file to start everything up, parametrize the simulated world, send a target pose, begin checking for success or failure.

An Extended RUT

To show the capabilities of RUT regarding complex tests, a short description about testing a continuous real-time image stitching node [2][3] on the same robots follows. The stitching node only uses the camera video as input because the algorithm trades image processing requirements against movement restrictions. Traditional software-only unit tests and ROS node test are used to ensure some of the image (pre)processing and performance invariants. Nevertheless, ultimately the camera video – the camera being attached to the arm's flange – depends on the arm trajectory. At this point we leave behind the state of the art in testing and enter the new realm of RUT. In the RUT methodology, we now have to consider what deviation from the current result should be brought to our attention through a failed test. The stitching result is a panorama image. Should we compare it to one of a correct run? No, or at least not if we do not want to define a new ground truth for every change in the simulators rendering pipeline.

The question to be answered according to our methodology is: What exactly is the test's *purpose*? It is not to check rendering details of the simulated camera image. Rather, we want to assert the robot's skill (cf. what we said about Sir in the previous section) of continuous stitching. We made sure the task is of a kind, where the simulation is accurate enough. Which means that the rendered camera images provide a sufficiently similar level of detail, e.g. edge and ORB features, to suffice for the robot's skill under test. Having gone through these methodological considerations, a test emerges that is easy to implement and robust to changes we do not care about: An integral part of stitching the images together, is calculating their relative offsets based on extracted features. If the assumptions to do RUT were satisfied in the first place, the offsets will be sufficiently stable and can be used as test oracle. After following through the RUT methodology, we can test all components involved into this non-trivial robot skill by a few lines of code that compare image offsets. The recent effort to create tools that automatically and continously execute ROS tests [12], based on the Jenkins continous intergration server[12], further facilitate adoption by the robotics community.

Results

By now the methodology of Robot Unit Testing as theory and practice should have become clear. Therefore, it is time to evaluate the claimed benefits for

---

[12] http://jenkins-ci.org

robotics research and. robot software development. As it is often the case in software engineering, we provide qualitative results because their quantification would not bring further insight at this point in time. Once we arrived at the mindset behind what is written down in this paper as RUT methodology, we can clearly see the following improvements: Finding more bugs and finding them earlier. Introducing less regressions through code changes, or to be more precise finding regressions before deploying the new version to the real robot and having to hit the emergency stop button. Hence, less testing is required on the real robot, which is inherently manual if one doesn't want to risk breaking it. We can allow us to have greater confidence during development cycles. As long as all RUTs give us green light, we can postpone the manual testing of the new version. On that account we gain development speed – without having to fear that everything fails once we conduct the manual tests.

The proponents of test-driven development make a point that writing software in a way that facilitates testing is a best practice in itself. We affirm their position from our own experience. Previous versions of our ROS interface, consisted of less independent nodes. For example the intermediate nodes in Fig. 3 were integrated with their parent nodes. In terms of functionally the inverse kinematics did not have a public interface to the joint space interpolator. We refactored the nodes because this eased writing RUTs. This only superficially sounds like inverted reasoning. The objective is high quality robot software in order to obtain reliable robots. But in the process of ensuring long-term quality through writing RUTs, the very means tend to further their objective.

5   Conclusions

We presented Robot Unit Testing as a novel methodology based on existing technologies that advances the state of software development for robots. The goal and ultimate purpose is to extend the reach of automated tests beyond software components to whole robots, seen as entities of software embedded in sensors and actuators. Robot unit tests comprise *all* software components of the real robot down to the level selected as simulator interface. As explicitly shown in our RUT implementation for ROS, this level can be as low as vendor specific interfaces. In this case everything above what is a black box in hardware is included in the tests. Implementing the methodology for ROS is not only valuable in itself and to give a more detailed account, but our results also warrant to claim the benefits of RUT. We conclude our presentation of RUT by stating once more that it will make a difference to start doing *continuous, automated testing of robots* instead of robot components.

References

1. Beck, K.: Test-Driven Development By Example. Addison-Wesley, Amsterdam (2002)
2. Bihlmaier, A., Wörn, H.: Automated endoscopic camera guidance: A knowledge-based system towards robot assisted surgery. In: Proceedings for the Joint Conference of ISR 2014 (45th International Symposium on Robotics) Und ROBOTIK 2014 (8th German Conference on Robotics), pp. 617–622 (2014)
3. Bihlmaier, A., Wörn, H.: Ros-based cognitive surgical robotics. In: Workshop Proceedings of 13th Intl. Conf. on Intelligent Autonomous Systems (IAS 2013), pp. 253–255 (2014)
4. Duvall, P.M.: Continuous Integration. Addison-Wesley (2007)
5. Hjek, A.: Interpretations of probability. In: Zalta, E.N. (ed.) The Stanford Encyclopedia of Philosophy. Winter 2012 edition (2012)
6. Levi, N., Kovelman, G., Geynis, A., Sintov, A., Shapiro, A.: The DARPA virtual robotics challenge experience. In: 2013 IEEE International Symposium on Safety, Security, and Rescue Robotics (SSRR), pp. 1–6. IEEE (2013)
7. Lewis, W.E., Dobbs, D., Veerapillai, G.: Software Testing and Continuous Quality Improvement, 3rd edn. CRC Press, Boca Raton (2008)
8. Myers, G.J., Sandler, C., Badgett, T.: The Art of Software Testing, 3rd edn. Wiley and Sons, New Jersey (2011)
9. Quigley, M., Conley, K., Gerkey, B., Faust, J., Foote, T., Leibs, J., Wheeler, R., Ng, A.Y.: ROS: an open-source Robot Operating System. In: ICRA Workshop on Open Source Software, vol. 3 (2009)
10. Rafique, Y., Misic, V.B.: The Effects of Test-Driven Development on External Quality and Productivity: A Meta-Analysis. IEEE Transactions on Software Engineering 39(6), 835–856 (2013)
11. Saha, G.K.: Understanding Software Testing Concepts. Ubiquity, 2:1 (February 2008)
12. Weisshardt, F., Kett, J., de Freitas Oliveira Araujo, T., Bubeck, A., Verl, A.: Enhancing software portability with a testing and evaluation platform. In: Proceedings for the Joint Conference of ISR 2014 (45th International Symposium on Robotics) Und ROBOTIK 2014 (8th German Conference on Robotics), pp. 219–224 (2014)

IMI2S: A Lightweight Framework
for Distributed Computing

Salvatore M. Anzalone, Marie Avril, Hanan Salam, and Mohamed Chetouani

Institut des Systmes Intelligents et de Robotique,
Universit Pierre et Marie Curie
Pyramide, T55/65
CC 173, 4 Place Jussieu
75005 Paris, France

Abstract. An increasing number of applications require the integration of heterogeneous hardware and software components. Due to the
high levels of complexity that such integrations demand, several solution
have been proposed in the state of art of software engineering. This paper introduces the IMI2S framework: a distributed computing software
platform aimed to cope with such levels of complexity by simplifying the
functional decomposition of the problems through the implementation
of highly decoupled, efficient and portable software. We will present the
design issues addressed in the development of the IMI2S framework. We
will show through two case studies its flexibility and its general efficacy.

Keywords: Software frameworks, distributed computing, multimodal
perception, sensor networks, social signal processing, robotics framework.

1 Introduction

Recent years have shown a continuous growth in the number of complex
applications that rely on the processing of huge amount of data perceived
from different sensors. Domotics[9], surveillance systems[2,3], entertainment
appliances[1],medicals[5], robotics[4], are just few examples of applications that
use multimodal sensed data to extract relevant information about the environment and to consequently control specific appliances.

From the point of view of software engineering, the challenges that systems
characterized by high levels of complexity arouse, are many. Heterogeneous systems, that can be directly connected to a single machine or that are actually
spread over the environment through a network, should be able to communicate
in a standardized way, access in a concurrent way to the same data, process it in
real-time using different algorithms, control through a standard interface all the
hardware systems and the algorithms parameters. A framework able to simplify
the management of such complex scenarios is needed.

Several approaches present in the state of art of distributed systems are useful to engage these kind of problems. CORBA[15], "Common Object Request
Broker Architecture", as instance, has been proposed as multi-language and

D. Brugali et al. (Eds.): SIMPAR 2014, LNAI 8810, pp. 267–278, 2014.

multi-platform framework to distribute objects across a network. In its approach, CORBA objects are shared objects that can be referenced by any process active in a network, regardless by the execution host. In this vision a centralized broker process, the CORBA Orb, will maintain the information about them, about their life cycle, their exposed methods and properties. CORBA objects will share their methods through a remote procedures call system, while, through an interface definition language, strong types will assure coherence of data during the communications. While CORBA still remains an important milestone on the development of distribute frameworks, it failed its original mission of becoming a standard due to partial support by programming languages, a steep learning curve, and several design flaws, such as the specific design for low latencies networks, the absence of threading support, the unencrypted traffic subjected to eavesdropping and man-in-the-middle attacks, and other technical issues.

Aside by general purpose frameworks as CORBA or as Microsoft DCOM[10], a strong contribute on distributed computing has been produced by research in signal processing and in robotics. From the point of view of signal processing, such frameworks are useful to create pipelines of algorithms able to extract and fuse between them high level information. Relevant software solutions are NMM[11], "Network Media Manager", proposed by Motama, originally proposed to manage in real-time multimedia streams, or SSI[18], "Social Signal Interpretation", from the University of Augsburg, specifically developed for real-time human behavior analysis. Both frameworks are effective on facilitating and speeding up the development process in case of feed-forward pipelines, however the implementation of feedback mechanisms and signalling results complicated. SSI, in particular, suffers also of high levels of coupling.

In robotics the need of distributed computing has always been an important and still open issue. Such systems require not only feedforward and feed backward streaming mechanism, but also synchronous and asynchronous communication, multi-threading, runtime object inspection and, in the best case, they should allow developers to work with the same tools in both simulated and real environments. Important improvements have been offered by the experiences at the RoboCup[17], in particular by the "Standard Platform League": all the teams worked with the same robotic platform, a team of four Sony Aibo quadruped robots, focusing just on the software aspects. Among the notable solutions proposed, the "GermanTeam" team tried to deal with the software and hardware capabilities of the Aibo platform by building a robust and extensible framework[14]. Algorithms ran sequentially on two parallel processes, one dedicated for actuators control, another one for high level processing, while a third process was responsible for logging, debugging and runtime inspection through the network.

Beside the Robocup systems, another still popular framework is the "Player/ Stage Project" client/server architecture for robot control and simulation[8]. Player acts as an abstraction level to standardize all the robot hardware interfaces while the robot hardware can be real or simulated through Stage.

Moreover, using CORBA as middleware, Orocos[6], "Open Robot Control Software", provides an object oriented infrastructure for modules concurrently running that are able to exchange streamed data through strongly typed ports. Orocos objects share methods, properties, commands and events and, as CORBA objects, can be deployed anywhere in the network. Orocos represents an important attempt to define a standard for robotics platform, but, despite the many efforts this remains a distant goal: the many existent robotics frameworks still remain strictly tighten to their own particular robotic platforms.

In any case, communities of developers are grown up around each framework, sharing code, experiences and a common, long-term vision. The ones built around YARP[12], "Yet Another Robot Platform", and around ROS[13], "Robot Operating System", are just two notable examples of successful communities developing on robotics framework. The YARP framework has been mainly designed as specific platform for the iCub robot. While developed by Willow Garage for their own robotic platforms, ROS always had a more standardizing vocation: now ROS is actually one of the most used frameworks for robotic applications. Both frameworks share a similar centralized name-server, but differ on the communications approaches: while YARP follows the observer pattern, ROS supports both classic remote procedure calls and streaming via "Publisher/Subscriber" pattern.

In this paper we propose the "Interaction, Multimodal Integration and Social Signals" (IMI2S) framework: a new, lightweight framework for distributed computing. All the cited platforms share similar concepts and basic ideas, implemented using slightly different software solutions. IMI2S framework tried to pick the best practices shown by all these previous experiences while considering their main issues. The result is a very thin software layer that allows developer to build highly decoupled, efficient, and portable software. Following, we will show the detail of the design of this framework; some cues related to its implementation; its effectiveness and its flexibility on tackling problems in different scenarios, by presenting its use in two cases of study.

2   System Design

An analysis of the features of the software built upon the existing frameworks shows a large variety of algorithms and application, from robotics control systems to signal processing to multiple sensors information gathering and coordination. However, all these applications share a similar level of high complexity and the similar necessity of a functional decomposition of problems to its basic issues. The IMI2S framework works as useful tool for developers to exploit a functional decomposition of complex problems. Developers will implement complex solutions using simple, small and basic operative units that are able to interact between them. Such basic modules are executed as independent computational units able to solve a particular problem. Input and outputs of different modules are then connected between them in order to exploit the main, complex problem.

270 S.M. Anzalone et al.

The requirements that have been chosen as main features of the presented framework[1] are:

* Modularity: as already stated, the main goal of this framework is to allow developers to easily break complex problems into simpler tasks. This is achieved by introducing the concept of "Module" as independent, low-coupled computational unit that is able to solve a particular problem. Each module is able to communicate with other modules in a network and share its results through a peer to peer approach. A "Publisher/Subscriber" communication pattern assure a low coupling functional design of the modules. No broker or any kind of "central server" solution will be used: the developer will take care of the existence of modules in the network, of connection to correct addresses and of the validation of data exchanged.

* Efficiency: the framework is thin and lightweight, able to support both off-line and real-time data analysis. This essentiality is achieved through low memory usages and simplicity of the framework control algorithms. The efficiency will also be part of the communication layer, that will be characterized by a protocol with low over-heads.

* Portability: particular choice for this framework is its characteristic of interoperability between platforms and languages. Algorithms and data structures used in the framework core are common to many languages, while libraries used are multi-language and multi-platform. Accordingly, the framework is portable among Windows and Unix platforms, and can be implemented in C/C++, Python and Java. Modules built upon the framework core can take advantage of the features coming from the huge amount of existing systems, devices and libraries that belongs to each different platform, while maintaining the ability of communicating each other.

* Maintainability: the functional decomposition proposes the individuation of basic, independent tasks. But as solving basic task, such modules are reusable in different contexts. Moreover, since such modules should be very specialized on solving particular problems, it will be easy to extend them or to test completely overturned algorithms able to solve the same problem. IMI2S framework is also open source: this will facilitate the reviewing process and its update with new features.

* Usability: past experiences, such as CORBA or Microsoft Robotics Studio, shown how a good framework can fail its usage in extensive scales, due to its complexity and the difficulty found on its learning. The framework proposed is easy to learn and thin enough to be easily included in any development processes.

3 System Implementation

The implementation choices of IMI2S framework have been guided by the stated features of modularity, efficiency, portability, maintainability and usability. All

---

[1] Following the standard ISO/IEC 9126 and ISO/IEC 25010:2011.

the implementation issues are similar regardless the language or the operative system in which the platform is implemented. Without losing in generalization, we will refer from here to the implementation issues of such framework using an object oriented language, upon a Unix-like platform. The core subject of the platform is the "Module", the computational unit in which basic tasks are accomplished. This is implemented as a multi-thread process that refers to a "ModuleHandler" object that will maintain all the information related to the module itself, such as its name, its status, its networking connections. Communication between modules is achieved through a "NetworkHandler": here, the 0MQ library has been chosen as convenient multi-platform and multi-language library able to implement all the low level communication related to the Publisher/Subscriber pattern.

According to this pattern, senders publish messages broadcasting the data to all the receivers, if any, connected. Publishers send such messages without any knowledge of the receivers. On the other side, one or more receivers can subscribe to publishers; then they will wait to retrieve message when they will be published. The network handler is able to instantiate and maintain the status of "Publisher" and "Subscriber" objects. Each module is free to instantiate any publisher and any subscriber needed. Publishers objects are used to send messages on demand. Subscribers objects, instead, will create threads that will wait the arrival of new message from publishers; data will be then available through an opportune callback function defined on the instantiation of the subscriber object itself.

Message exchanged between modules use a standard XML format described through a set of XSD schemas. Such XSD schemas are used to validate exchanged data and to generate classes for automatic binding for serialization and deserialization of data. Convenient tools that allow this code synthesization are PyXB[2], Python based implementations, or CodeSynthesis XSD[3], for C/C++ based, platform-independent implementations.

The XSD schemas define a hierarchy of message types. The root this hierarchy is the type "Message", characterized by a timestamp, an index and a state that can be conveniently used by developers. All the data types exchanged between modules inherit their properties from the type Message (see Figure 1). Common message types exchanged are: "Point", defined by a triplet of floats (x, y, z) as a common point in a 3D space; "Euler", defined by a triplet of floats (alpha, beta, gamma) as eulerian angles in a 3D space; "Quaternion", defined by a quadruplet of floats (x, y, z, w) as quaternion angles in a 3D space. Other used message types are: "Pose", defined by a Point schema and an Euler schema; "Matrix", defining a 2D matrix by its columns, its rows, its type (according to the OpenCV matrix types), and its data, encoded in base64 format. Developers can extend the set of known message types by inheriting them from the type "Message" into new XSD schemas.

All the message types have a temporal reference. It is demanded to the developer a wise use of timing for a correct synchronization between the modules.

---

[2] PyXB website: http://pyxb.sourceforge.net/
[3] Code Synthesis XSD website: http://www.codesynthesis.com/products/xsd/

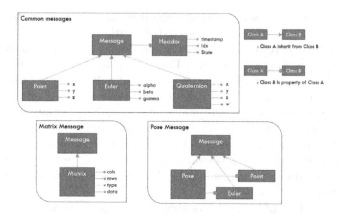

Fig. 1. Hierarchy of commonly used message types described in the XSD schemas

The best approach suggested and used in the IMI2S framework is the synchronization of the hosts in the network with a main time server through the use of the Network Time Protocol. In such way developers are free to use the main clock of each host to obtain a time reference for synchronization issues.

4   Performances and Case Studies

The performances and the limitations of the IMI2S framework have been studied by matching measures related to timings and memory usage with similar measures collected using the ROS framework and the YARP framework. In order to investigate how the behavior of the framework could change in accord to its different implementation and, in particular, with the different libraries used, two version of IMI2S have been developed. These implementation use two different XML libraries for serialization and deserialization of the data, CodeSynthesis XSD and CodeSynthesis XSDe[4]. Results are shown in 2. More in the detail, Figure 2a shows the publishing time, the time employed by the frameworks to create and to send a message through the communication channel, in accord with the size of the data that should be sent. It is possible to see how the performances of IMI2S are strictly dependent by the XML serialization library used. The use of the XSDe library assures a level of performances similar to that produced by the YARP framework, until 4096kBytes of data. Figure 2a shows the interprocess communication latency, the time spent by two processes using the same framework to create, send, receive and deliver a message, in accord with the size of the data sent. Also in this case the implementation of the IMI2S framework through the XSDe library almost matches the performances of YARP, until 2048kBytes of data sent. Figure 2c shows the memory consumption of each framework during the transmission of packets of increasing sizes, from 1kByte to 8192kBytes. The memory usage of the IMI2S framework implemented using the XSDe library has comparable performances to the YARP framework. In all the three

---

[4] Code Synthesis XSDe website: http://www.codesynthesis.com/products/xsde/

cases the ROS framework outperforms both YARP and the XSDe based IMI2S framework, while the XSD based IMI2S system fails all the comparison.

In the next sections we will show the flexibility and the modularity of the IMI2S framework through the presentation of its usage in the context of two human-interaction application scenarios: a cultural study, in which the interaction happens between a human and a virtual agent; a medical study, in which the interaction occurs between two humans. Following, we will present both scenarios and we will show how the IMI2S framework is enough flexible and efficient to successful engage both problems.

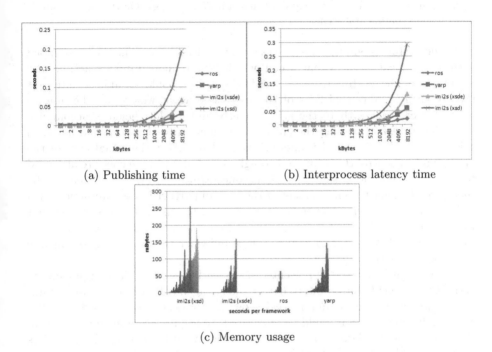

(a) Publishing time   (b) Interprocess latency time

(c) Memory usage

Fig. 2. The performances of the imi2s framework implemented through two XML libraries, matched against Yarp and Ros frameworks

4.1 Human-Agent Interaction

In this case of study the IMI2S framework is applied in the context of the project A1:1 (Avatar one to one scale)[5]. This project focuses on the engagement of people in a museum (Historial de Vende situated at Lucs-sur-Boulogne, France), through the interactions with a virtual, human-sized character. The experimental setup is composed by a big screen in which the avatar acts, some exhibits as focus of attention ("Soldier bending his arc") and the user that interacts with the avatar (see Figure 3).

---

[5] Project A1:1 website: http://projectavatarfr.wordpress.com

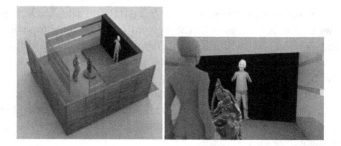

Fig. 3. On the left: the experimental setup of the A1:1 project. On the right: visitor's view in the experimental scene.

To successful accomplish this interaction, the virtual agent should be equipped with communication skills that would permit him to understand the actions and intentions of the visitor. In other words the agent should be able to interpret the verbal and nonverbal cues of the user. The agent would thus be able to properly act/react with/to the user properly and would efficiently accomplish his assigned task of passing the cultural information to the interested users. In this context, the presented framework is used to detect the social cues of the visitor and to control the agent accordingly. In addition, these cues are also used to interpret higher level signals, such as concentration or attention, that will be then fused to infer the engagement of the human partner in the interaction with the avatar[16]. Knowing the engagement level of the user, the avatars behavior would be designed to react consequently, engaging more or less the user in accord to his perceived interest, and finally understand when the user totally disengages from the interaction.

As shown in Figure 4, the presented framework is used to create a pipeline to extract high level features and to detect the engagement level of the users. First of all, the acquisition module is used (now, an RGB-D sensor is used, however other multimodal sensors could be integrated) to acquire the users image, depth, skeleton and audio data in an online interaction with the agent. These outputs are then used by a first low level features extraction set of modules: the proxemics module will generate features such as the distance between the hands; the face tracker that will take as input the RGB image from the kinect module, will calculate the head pose and facial feature points; the speaking activity module that will use as its input the audio messages from the same module, will output the speaking turn taking features; from the skeleton data, the posture module will predict the posture of the user. Moving to higher level modules, in the same chain of processing, the outputs of the first level modules are used to extract information such as the Action units, from face tracking module, and head and body gestures, from the posture module. The emotion, such as happiness with a smile or boring, can be deduced in a third level by the Emotion module as we see from the figure. Finally higher level deductions as concentration and attention are computed from all the output of the lower level modules: higher and lower level feature are fused together to infer the engagement state of the visitor.

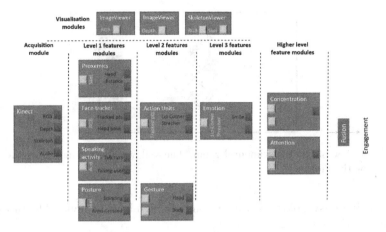

Fig. 4. Use of the presented framework in a human-agent interaction project

4.2   Human-Human Interaction

One of the objectives of the Synchrony, Early Development and Psychopathology (Syned-Psy) project is to characterize synchrony/dys-synchrony in mother infant interaction occurring in situations of severe emotional neglect[6]. Synchrony is defined as a dynamic and reciprocal adaptation of interactive partners behaviors, in a dyadic and temporal point of view. As a matter of fact, in human behavior, early development and infant/caregiver interactions are paradigmatic interactive situation in which synchrony is a key process. In this context, synchrony means that infant and the caregiver have simultane-ous behaviors. It also means that the infant and the caregiver move fluidly from one state to the next. In sum, synchronic maternal behaviors are related to efficient mother infant interactions whereas dyssynchronic ones qualify improper mother infant interactions[7]. As complex phenomenon, synchrony characterization requires the perception and understanding of social and communicative signals (speech, linguistic cues, prosody, gesture, emotions) and also a continuous adaptation. Thus, the IMI2S framework has been used as convenient computational tools to detect and extract significant behaviors in the interactions. Such characterizations will be used and compared with results of traditional psychological analysis to help psychiatrists in their diagnostics and to understand early interactions dynamics. During a visit for a medical monitoring with psychologists, mother and child are invited to play together around a small table with toys. Here, two Microsoft Kinect are placed in a convenient place in front of each participant (see Figure 5). Two computers record data received from Kinects (RGB image, depth image, skeleton and audio data) in order to perform an offline processing.

The IMI2S framework is used to extract high level interactive features, such as engagement from heads distance, joint attention or intrusion from shoulders orientation and hands distance. The definition of these features are determined

---

[6] Syned-Psy Project ANR reference number: ANR-12-SAMA-0006.

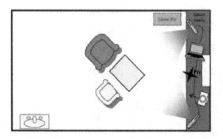

Fig. 5. Top view of the experimental room. The yellow chair is the sit for the child, the green for the mother).

with the help of psychologists, who decompose high level behavioral features into a collection of low level ones.

The modularity of the framework offered the possibility to use solutions that are already developed for A1:1 project. However, compared to the project A1:1, this scenario presents more challenges, since two RGB-D sensors and two users will be studied: data acquired by the these sensors, that are actually placed in two different location of the room, should be roto-translated and merged in order to share a common Cartesian space; then, a similar elaboration performed in the A1:1 project can be carried out for each human partner present in the scene.

Figure 6 presents the pre-processing pipeline for skeleton data coming from the two displaced RGB-D sensors. Skeleton data of mother and child from both sensors is corrected to belong to the same Cartesian space; each skeleton is then labeled, identifying the two users in the scene, the mother and the child. Finally, data is merged in a unique stream, inconsistent skeletons are suppressed (for example if the tracked skeleton is misplaced) and data is smoothed through average filtering. Thanks to this pre-filtering pipeline, the features extraction can be done with the existing modules developed for the A1:1 project.

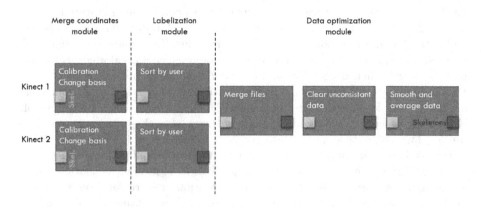

Fig. 6. Use of the presented framework for multi-sensors, multi-users pre-treatment

5   Conclusion and Future Works

In this paper we introduced the IMI2S framework, a distributed computing soft-ware platform designed to support our vision of modularity, efficiency, portability, maintainability and usability. We shown the general efficiency of the framework by presenting how its performances are comparable to the performances of state of art frameworks, such as YARP. We shown also the flexibility that the low coupling of the framework offers by presenting its usage in two different cases of study. Results obtained incite us to pursue our development of the IMI2S framework by adding new functionalities and by promoting the creation of a community around it.

Future works include its usage in other different contexts, such as social signals extraction for autism spectrum disorder assessment, but also for the control of robotic frameworks, such as Aldebarans Nao. Emphasizing on its portability and efficiency characteristics, we plan its implementation also in embedded systems such as Raspberry Pi and Arduino.

Acknowledgments. The work was partially funded by the European Commission, through the Project Michelangelo (FP7-ICT No. 288241), and by French National Agency of Research, through the Projects Syned-Psy (ANR-12-SAMA-0006) and the French National Program "Investissements dAvenir pour le dveloppement de lconomie numrique".

References

1. Anzalone, S.M., Cinquegrani, F., Sorbello, R., Chella, A.: An emotional humanoid partner. In: Linguistic and Cognitive Approaches to Dialog Agents (LaCATODA 2010) at AISB (2010)
2. Anzalone, S.M., Menegatti, E., Pagello, E., Sorbello, R., Yoshikawa, Y., Ishiguro, H.: A multimodal people recognition system for an intelligent environment. In: Pirrone, R., Sorbello, F. (eds.) AI*IA 2011. LNCS, vol. 6934, pp. 451–456. Springer, Heidelberg (2011)
3. Anzalone, S.M., Menegatti, E., Pagello, E., Yoshikawa, Y., Ishiguro, H., Chella, A.: Audio-video people recognition system for an intelligent environment. In: 2011 4th International Conference on Human System Interactions (HSI), pp. 237–244. IEEE (2011)
4. Anzalone, S.M., Yoshikawa, Y., Ishiguro, H., Menegatti, E., Pagello, E., Sorbello, R.: Towards partners profiling in human robot interaction contexts. In: Noda, I., Ando, N., Brugali, D., Kuffner, J.J. (eds.) SIMPAR 2012. LNCS, vol. 7628, pp. 4–15. Springer, Heidelberg (2012)
5. Anzalone, S.M., Tilmont, E., Boucenna, S., Xavier, J., Jouen, A.-L., Bodeau, N., Maharatna, K., Chetouani, M., Cohen, D.: How children with autism spectrum disorder behave and explore the 4-dimensional (spatial 3d+ time) environment during a joint attention induction task with a robot. Research in Autism Spectrum Disorders 8(7), 814–826 (2014)
6. Bruyninckx, H.: Open robot control software: the orocos project. In: Proceedings of 2001 IEEE International Conference on Robotics and Automation, ICRA, vol. 3, pp. 2523–2528. IEEE (2001)

7. Feldman, R.: Parent–infant synchrony biological foundations and developmental outcomes. Current Directions in Psychological Science 16(6), 340–345 (2007)
8. Gerkey, B., Vaughan, R.T., Howard, A.: The player/stage project: Tools for multi-robot and distributed sensor systems. In: Proceedings of the 11th International Conference on Advanced Robotics, vol. 1, pp. 317–323 (2003)
9. Ghidoni, S., Anzalone, S.M., Munaro, M., Michieletto, S., Menegatti, E.: A distributed perception infrastructure for robot assisted living. In: Robotics and Autonomous Systems (2014)
10. Horstmann, M., Kirtland, M.: Dcom architecture. Microsoft Corporation (July 1997)
11. Lohse, M., Repplinger, M., Slusallek, P.: Network-integrated multimedia middleware. Services, and Applications, Department of Computer Science, Saarland University, Germany, Diss. (2005)
12. Metta, G., Fitzpatrick, P., Natale, L.: Yarp: Yet another robot platform. International Journal of Advanced Robotic Systems 3(1) (2006)
13. Quigley, M., Conley, K., Gerkey, B., Faust, J., Foote, T., Leibs, J., Wheeler, R., Ng, A.Y.: Ros: an open-source robot operating system. In: ICRA Workshop on Open Source Software, vol. 3 (2009)
14. Röfer, T., Laue, T., Burkhard, H.D., Hoffmann, J., Jüngel, M., Göhring, D., Lötzsch, M., Düffert, U., Spranger, M., Altmeyer, B., et al.: Germanteam robocup 2004 (2004)
15. Schmidt, D.C., Levine, D.L., Mungee, S.: The design of the tao real-time object request broker. Computer Communications 21(4), 294–324 (1998)
16. Sidner, C.L., Lee, C., Kidd, C.D., Lesh, N., Rich, C.: Explorations in engagement for humans and robots. Artificial Intelligence 166(1), 140–164 (2005)
17. Sorbello, R., Cinquegrani, F., Chella, A., Anzalone, S.M.: A new architecture based on a simulation environment for four legged and humanoid robots. In: 13th IEEE/IFAC International Conference on Methods and Models in Automation and Robotics, MMAR 2007 (2007)
18. Wagner, J., Lingenfelser, F., Baur, T., Damian, I., Kistler, F., André, E.: The social signal interpretation (ssi) framework: multimodal signal processing and recognition in real-time. In: Proceedings of the 21st ACM International Conference on Multimedia, pp. 831–834. ACM (2013)

Are Middlewares Ready
for Multi-robots Systems?

Stefan-Gabriel Chitic, Julien Ponge, and Olivier Simonin

Université de Lyon, INSA-Lyon, CITI-INRIA,
69621, Villeurbanne, France
{stefan.chitic,julien.ponge,olivier.simonin}@insa-lyon.fr

Abstract. Autonomous robot fleets are complex systems that require the interaction and communication between heterogeneous hardware and software. Despite many years of work in robotics, there is still a lack of established software architecture and middleware, in particular for large scale multi-robots systems. Many research teams are still writing specific hardware orientated software that is very tied to a robot. This vision makes sharing modules or extending existing code difficult. A robotic middleware should be designed to abstract the low-level hardware architecture, facilitate communication and integration of new software. In this paper, we present and compare seven existing middlewares capable of being used in multi-robot systems. We also present two dedicated cloud based multi-robots platforms. After this analysis, we discuss why a cloud of robots and not a cloud for robots is more suitable in a fleet context.

Keywords: Multi-robot systems, Middleware, Robotic cloud.

1 Introduction

An autonomous robot fleet refers to multiple robots (two at least) capable of sharing data and performing one or several tasks together. It can also include mobile or fix connected objects and sensors cooperating together to achieve a common goal. A robot is a complex and heterogeneous system that requires communication and interaction between robot components (various sensors, actuators and software components). The research in distributed artificial intelligence has shown that the division of tasks reduces the complexity and the difficulty of a problem, even if this requires coordination mechanisms [8]. The same concept can be applied into the robotic world. There is a great need of having large scale multi-robot systems capable of splitting tasks of a greater problem. There is also a need of information sharing between robots and external objects. The communication inside a fleet can be done using a centralized network infrastructure like WiFi Access Points or in a decentralized architecture using Ad-hoc networks. Robots have a great potential in many new applications as they offer new approaches to problems like surveillance tasks, search and rescue missions in area where personal access may not be possible or hostile, etc.

D. Brugali et al. (Eds.): SIMPAR 2014, LNAI 8810, pp. 279–290, 2014.
© Springer International Publishing Switzerland 2014

Multi robots systems can increase their computation power using external architectures like data-grids [25] or clouds for robots. The main advantage of a cloud of robots is the decreased time of computation as it is parallelized, since the computation is parallelized into a data-center with many CPU working on the same task. This approach has also it's down-side, since each robotic system has to communicate and share data with a centralized system hosted in a data-center using Internet network.

Despite many years of work in robotics, there is still a lack of a software architecture and well-accepted family of middlewares [23]. A family of middlewares is composed of softwares and tools sets that act as an abstraction and integration layer between an network or operating system and applications. The developed software is tied to the architecture and hardware being used. This makes sharing modules and algorithms almost impossible in practice.

However, there is a convergence trend between the robotic and the middleware world, in order to build efficient middleware solutions for robotics. This trend is true with ROS[1] establishes a more typical loosely-coupled, layered software architecture as found in traditional general-purpose software engineering.

A family fo robotic middlewares should manage heterogeneity of the hardware, facilitate the communication inside and outside a robot, improve software quality, reduce time and costs in order to build new applications, allow robots to be self-configuring, self-adaptive and self-optimizing to environnement changes. Combining component and service-oriented programming greatly simplifies the implementation of highly-adaptive, constantly-evolving applications [9]. Robots should be capable of auto-provisioning (auto-discover and self-install of the software modules and libraries used by the other robots in the fleet) and self-profiling.

There already exists middlewares that try to achieve parts of the desired needs. Most of them are designed for single robot contexts and they can also be used in a fleet context, but there also exist new cloud based approaches designed for multi-robot goals. This paper discusses the needs of having a family of middlewares in large scale multi-robot systems and how it facilitates software development. We compare the different existing solutions presenting the advantages and down-sides of the existing middleware based on several criteria that cover the architecture and infrastructure of each framework. We also present two cloud for robots solutions.

The paper is structured as follows: Section 2 defines the challenges a multi-robot middleware encounters. Section 3 describes the existing solutions. Section 4 presents our comparative criteria. Section 5 compares the main solutions based on these challenges. Section 6 presents the existing cloud solutions for robotic fleet and Section 7 synthesizes the analysis of existing solutions. Section 8 concludes the paper.

---

[1] Robot Operating System [22].

2   Challenges for Middleware in Robotic Systems

Why a Middleware for Robotics? Middlewares are important components in the process of developing, deploying and operating software. Nowadays, robots are used in a fleet context, being capable of having a global environment perception and a communication inside the fleet and with external communicating objects like sensors, network and service gateways, mobile devices with wireless capabilities [18]. The robots may be ubiquitous and heterogeneous. All the devices and the robots themselves are made of a diversity of hardware controlled by a variety of software developed in different programming languages using multiple standards and protocols to communicate.

One of the challenges is software modularity as presented in [7]. The robotic applications development need to embrace a more software-oriented modular vision. The development process should be simplified by integrating higher-layers of abstraction with application interfaces (APIs) [18]. Also, the middleware should support plug-and-play mechanism for new developed modules, being capable of hot swapping new packages.

Furthermore, it should be able of sharing modules and knowledge with repositories such as RoboEarth [24] (see section 6).

Infrastructure and Communication. The modules should run on any infrastructure, which implies that the middleware should propose a hardware abstraction layer in order to facilitate the reuse of the modules. The middleware should make the robot aware of its capabilities by automatically discovering the sensors and actuators. Those capabilities should be organized in robotic services that should be broadcast to allow each robot to know what its team members are capable of. This automatic resource and service discovery and configuration mechanisms will increase the potential of each robot. Since the robots can move independently and are dynamic, they need to self-organize[2] inside the fleet in a decentralized network. Moreover, due to the mobility of robots, the fleet can divide itself at a communication layer but keeping the same fleet configuration at an application layer, so the members should self-adapt to the new fleet-configuration [26].

The middleware should provide a system of information sharing and collaboration among all involved components offering communication support and interoperability [4]. It should make this system transparent to the developer by masking the low level communication with a more human-compressible language.

The middleware should also provide collaboration support among the robots making sure that all robots share the same values of shared information. Also it should provide APIs that will make the development of multi-robot collaborating applications easier.

---

[2] A process where some form of global order or coordination between robots arises out of the local interactions between them (e.g. a leader election using a peer to peer biding system).

Down-Sides. Even the most challenging middleware might have problems. As mentioned in [23], the fact of having a hardware abstraction layer hiding the heterogeneity of sensors and actuators has its down-sides. The specificity of sensors, their positions, their limits, their failures and robots shapes increase the complexity of a controlling software. Extrapolating and/or integrating these assumptions makes the middleware more complex and more prone to failures. While in classical cloud environment the network could be considered almost reliable, this is hardly the case in a robotic fleet. The middleware should not try to catch a network failure exception, but instead accept that the network is temporary unreachable and operate in a degraded mode until the network communication is reestablished. The same logic should be applied also in case of hardware failure since robots usually run in hazardous environment.

Taking everything into account, the challenges for a multi-robot middleware are high. There are lots of techniques and research done in cloud middleware that can be applied into a fleet context. However there is a lot of differences between a cloud and a fleet due to mobility and communication limits inside a fleet. Up to now, many attempts into creating a promising middleware for robots have been done.

Next sections will present and compare the most relevant middlewares and cloud platforms for robotic fleets.

3   Existing Middlewares

In this section we are going to present the most used middleware with applicability in a fleet. A complete survey of all the middleware for mono robot is clearly impossible because of the large number of existing middleware and release of new ones. To reduce the number presented in the paper, we first considered their compatibility in a multi-robots environment and the number of citations. Even more, we are not taking into consideration the real time systems, since we believe that hard real time systems need specialized APIs from the hardware layer to dedicated operating system to application layer. Based on our criteria, we have selected seven most used robotics middleware:*Player/Stage, ROS, Miro, MRDS, Marie, Orca* and *Pyro*. We should keep in mind that there are also other available middlewares like: *Claraty, OpenRTMaist* [2], *OPRoS* [10], *Carmen, Orocos* [5], *ERSP, RoboFrame, WURDE, Aseba, Skilligent, SmartSoft, iRobotAware, Yarp, Spica, Babel, DROS, IRSP, K- MIDDLEWARE, OpenRDK, OpenJAUS, ORCCAD, RIK, MRPT, MissionLab, Webots*, etc. Some of these middleware are also compared from mono-robot perspective in the section 4 of [16] and section 2 of [17].

The following summary gives an overview of each selected software including a description of it, the compatible robotic platforms and the most relevant features.

Player/Stage. [14] project is designed to provide an infrastructure, drivers and a collection of dynamically loaded device-shared libraries for robotic applications. It is one of the first middleware that emerged for robotic systems and there are other middlewares that wrap Player. It doesn't consider a robot as a single entity, but instead it treats each device separately, being a repository server for actuators, sensors and robots. The main features of Player are the device repository server, the variety of the programming languages, the socket based transport protocol, modularity and open-source.

The middleware is composed of 2 components: Player and Stage. Player is the middleware itself and Stage is a simulator. The platform that can run the Player/Stage middleware include: MobileRobots, Segway, Acroname, K-Team robots, iRobot's RFLEX-based, Botrics and Evolution Robotics.

ROS. (Robot operating system) [20] is a recent flexible middleware for robot applications. It is a collection of tools, libraries, and conventions that aim at simplifying the task of creating complex and robust robot behavior across a wide variety of robotic platforms. It provides hardware abstraction, device drivers, visualizers, message-passing, package management.

ROS comes with a series of libraries containing often-needed robotic services like SLAM, Autonomous navigation of a Known Map, object follower, etc. ROS is designed to be cross-platform.

The platforms that support ROS include PR2, Turtlebot, Kobuki, Husky and Dr. Robot Jaguar V4 with Manipulator Arm, and more.

Miro. [13] is a distributed, object orientated middleware developed to improve the software development process by increasing the integrability of heterogeneous software, the modularity and the portability of robot applications. It was developed in C++ for Linux based on the *Common Object Request Broker Architecture* (CORBA). This allows cross-platform interoperability making the middleware applicable to a distributed multi-robots context.

The platforms that can support Miro include: iRobot B21, MobilieRobots Pioneer. Miro is very flexible and can easily be extended to support new devices and robot applications.

Microsoft Robotics Developer Studio. (MRDS) [12] is a Windows-based middleware for robot control and simulation from Microsoft.

Visual Programming Language, which is a key component of MRDS, is a graphical development environment that uses a service and activity catalog.

MRDS is aimed at academic, hobbyist and commercial developers, and handles a wide variety of robot hardware like Eddie Robot, ABB Group Robotic, CoroWare CoroBot, Lego Mindstorms NXT, iRobot Create, Parallax Boe-Bot etc.

Marie. (Mobile and Autonomous Robotics Integration Environment) [6] is a middleware designed to allow the integration and distribution of software for robotic systems. It uses the *Adaptive Communication Environment* (ACE) communication framework. The centralized component provided by the middleware called *Mediator Design Pattern* (MDP) allows software components to connect to MARIE.

MARIE can run on MobileRobots Pioneer 2. Its main features is the interoperability and re-usability of robotic software modules.

Orca. [1] is a open-source middleware for developing component-based systems. It provides the mechanics to create building-blocks which can be pieced together to form arbitrarily complex robotic systems.

To implement a distributed component-based system, CORBA was chosen in Orca first version, but was rapidly changed with Ice, a new approach to object-oriented middleware.

The platform that can run the Orca middleware include: MobileRobots, Segway, K-Team robots, iRobot's RFLEX-based, Evolution Robotics.

Pyro. (Python Robotics) [19] goal is "to provide a programming environment for easily exploring advanced topics in artificial intelligence and robotics without having to worry about the low-level details of the underlying hardware a robot programming environment". It wraps Player/Stage middleware so that any component written for this system is also available to Pyro.

There are many libraries for Pyro that provide specific robotic services. The middleware is compatible with MobileRobots Pioneer, Sony Aibo and all robots supported by Player/Stage.

4   Comparative Criteria

We are going to compare the seven robotic frameworks presented above from a software engineering point of view because the middleware concept first emerged from this area and there are lots of knowledge that can be transfered into robotic applications. We have grouped the comparative criteria into two major groups: *Architecture* and *Infrastructure*. Each major group is composed of different criteria relevant to the group.

The *Architecture* evaluates the impact that the framework has over the host operating system and is composed of:

Vendor Locking - the middleware operating system dependence. This criteria expresses the portability of a system across multiple platforms and systems.

Durable Data Storage Services - tools that allow to persist data from sensor and other robots from the fleet. The data persistence layer is important for saving mission results, for experimental data validations, for off-line data processing as well as for sensor data replay in a simulator.

Robustness to Failures - the detection of a software failure, any degraded model to run and the afterwards recovery process. The fact that a middleware is aware of failures is essential for the robotic applications. Furthermore, it is important that robots continue performing their tasks in a degraded mode until the system has recovered form the failure.

The *Infrastructure* evaluates tools and APIs provided by the middleware and is composed of:

Management and Monitoring - tools provided to manage, debug, configure and monitor the middleware components. Since robots are complex devices, it is important to facilitate the supervisor task by offering a complete vision of the sensors, actuators and other components status of each robot.

Multi Robot Coordination Services - tools to make consensus over network shared values, to elect a leader or to assign specific robotic tasks. Inside a robotic fleet, it is important to have management tools to distribute algorithms in order to reduce the complexity of the robotic applications development.

Communication - The communication is very important between different components of a robot in order to allow it to successfully perform its task, as well as inside a fleet in order to allow robots to interact with others.

5   Middleware Comparison

This section analyzes each middleware based on the criteria presented in the above section. Each major group is represented in a separate subsection that includes a table that summaries the subsection. The evaluation is relative to all the middlewares. A **+** represents that all criteria requirements are satisfied, a + represents that most of the requirements are present, a $\sim$ shows the fact that the criteria is partially satisfied and a - represents that criteria is not fullfield.

Table 1. Architecture

Middleware	Vendor locking	Durable data storage services	Robustness to failures
Player/Stage	Linux, Windows	+ (Blackboard)	+
ROS	Repositories: Ubuntu, Debian. From source: generic Linux, Windows, MacOS	**+** (Rosbags)	+
Miro	Linux	$\sim$	+
MRDS	Windows	$\sim$	+
Marie	Linux	$\sim$	+
Orca	Linux	$\sim$	+
Pyro	Linux	$\sim$	- (Neither degraded mode, nor component isolation)

5.1   Architecture

Table 1 summaries the *Architecture* group. It is composed of *Vendor locking*, *Durable data storage services* and *Robustness to failures*.

Vendor Lock-In. Since the robots inside of a fleet can have heterogeneous operating systems, the vendor criteria is very important in the choice of a middleware. Besides *MRDS* which runs only on Windows, the other middleware run on Linux. *Player/Stage* and *ROS* are cross-platform.

Durable Data Storage Services. *ROS* and *Player* are the only middlewares that provide durable data storage services. Topics and service messages can be persisted in rosbags. The other frameworks do not provide any native API to save sensor information.

Robustness to Failures. None of the middlewares have a special dedicated degraded mode and nodes cannot be restarted automatically after failure. Besides *Pyro*, all the middlewares provide component isolation[3]. *ROS* needs an IP address at the initialization to run roscore. Once all the nodes are started, roscore crash won't affect the other nodes.

5.2   Infrastructure

Table 2 summaries the *Infrastructure* criteria. It has the following columns: *Management and monitoring*, *Multi robot coordination services* and *Communication*.

Management and Monitoring. Besides *Miro* and *Orca* which provide neither monitoring nor management interfaces, the rest of the middlewares include graphical monitoring software. *MRDS* uses Visual Studio as IDE. *ROS* has multiple management tools and a QT graphical dashboard monitoring.

Multi Robot Coordination Services. None of the middlewares provide native multi robot coordination services. *Player/Stage* includes third-party coordination algorithms developed for it. *ROS, Miro, MRDS, Orca, Marie* and *Pyro* delegate the coordination services to the application layer.

Communication. Communication between the infrastructure layers in *Player/Stage* and *Pyro* are done using direct socket connections as their primary method of communication. *Miro* data sharing is assigned to CORBA's IIOP. *Marie* uses shared memory and sockets. *MRDS* and *ROS* dispose of high level messaging APIS that support both synchronous and asynchronous communication.

   Based on the above tables, ROS appears to be the most suitable middleware for multi-robot systems, followed by MRDS. Both of them are fulfilling totally or partially almost all the criteria. In the following section, we present another emerging approach, cloud for robots.

---

[3] Component isolation or sand-boxing is a security mechanism for separating running process. The code and data spaces are also separated for each process.

Table 2. Infrastructure

Middleware	Management and monitoring	Multi robot coordination services	Communication
Player/Stage	~	+ (Third-party coordination)	~
ROS	+ (Dashboard and management)	~	+ (Sync. & async.)
Miro	− (None)	~	~
MRDS	+ (Visual Studio plugins)	~	+ (Sync. & async.)
Marie	~	~	~
Orca	− (None)	~	~
Pyro	~	~	~

6 Existing Robotic Cloud Platforms

Besides the middleware orientated vision that has started to grow in the robotics world, another software vision emerges in the robotic fleet context: the robotic cloud. A robotic cloud is mostly formed of robots, communicating objects and other hardware infrastructure elements that share information and resources in a transparent way for the developer. The main advantage besides the information sharing is an increased computation power by parallelizing the processes and a decrease in on board hardware complexity on each robot. We are going to present the two cloud platforms that we are aware of at the moment, DAvinCi [3] and Rapyuta [11]. They are both using ROS middleware.

6.1 DAvinCi

DAvinCi [3] is a framework that provides advantages like scalability, parallelism and sharing infrastructure of a Software as a Service (Saas) cloud platform for robotic services inside a fleet. It can be used in scenarios where there are multiple robots performing in parallel a task. The collected data is merged in a cloud environment and then resent to each robot.

It is based on ROS as messaging middleware on the robotic component of the system and Hadoop [27] cluster for cloud component. The assumption made by the platform is that each robot is WiFi enabled and the infrastructure includes a centralized WiFi access point and a gateway linking the robotic fleet to the cloud services.

We remark the strong dependencies on a pre-existing cloud infrastructure and a centralized WiFi access that reduce the environment applicability of the system, as well as the overhead generated of wrapping ROS binary messages into HTTP requests.

6.2 Rapytua

Rapytua [11] is a open source Platform as a Service(PaaS) that provides a customizable computing cloud based environment. It is also known as "the RoboEarth Cloud Engine" because it facilitates robots access to the RoboEarth [21] knowledge repository.

Rapytua is composed of an elastic computing model that dynamically allocates computing environments for robots. This allows robots to share services and information. The computing environments are implemented using Linux Container. The platform is ROS compatible and it benefits of a well-established ROS protocol, allowing all ROS packages to run directly.

We can note the overhead of using JSON to serialize ROS binary messages and the dependencies on a WiFi centralized access. On the other hand, the platform is not linked to a specific cloud platform which makes the system portable.

7   Discussion

None of the presented middlewares are fully suitable for a large scale multi-robot system. In our opinion, ROS is the emerging middleware with the most potential to evolve into one of the most used framework for robotic fleets. It still needs work since it has no multi-robot coordination system and no automated testing environment, but it has already the advantage of having a large community that develop new packages for it. Another key element of ROS is its communication mechanism. It support both synchronous and asynchronous communications and can easily be customized with new message types. It has a large database of drivers making a very good abstraction of the hardware layer. New modules and packages can be developed and integrated quickly. It is very permissive for the developers allowing them to code in different programming languages.

The advantages of a robotic fleet are the parallelizations of tasks that reduces the time needed to accomplish them, the information sharing and the robustness to failure. If a robot fails during a task, the task can be reassigned to another fleet member [15]. In this context, new distributed software infrastructures are proposed. The concept of cloud for robots is emerging, allowing them to communicate with external cloud infrastructure and deport heavy computing operations as well as allowing them to interact with the Internet of things. The down-side of the existing infrastructure for this new concept is the communication infrastructure that supposes: a centralized WiFi access. This reduces the use cases of robotic fleets that may also be used in uncontrolled environments without a communication infrastructure.

We consider that a fleet of robots can be organized as a cloud of robots and not a cloud for robots. There is a lot of work in multi-robot systems to automatically distribute tasks of a greater problem. Our vision is to bring all the benefits of a cloud environment into the robotic fleet by allowing robots to share information, resources, computation power across heterogeneous devices with different computational power. The robot will correspond to a machine in the cloud. We plan to use ROS and/or MRDS as a communication layer with the robots internal components and research a new middleware overlay, capable of working with other middleware, as well as for fleet management, multi-robot coordination, resource sharing and tasks parallelization.

We need to take into account the problematics of a cloud systems that supposes the communication are always stable and apply them into a unstable communication environment generated by the mobility of robots. The framework should work in both centralized or ad-hoc infrastructure. Furthermore, we need to take into consideration a degraded mode where the robot is isolated from the rest of the fleet in terms of communications and by performing the task independently until meeting its fleet.

8 Conclusion

In this paper, we have presented the challenges that a robotic middleware has to encounter nowadays in a multi-robot system. We surveyed seven classic middleware for robotics and discussed some of the main issues from a software engineering point of view. We have compared their capabilities in term of multi-robot requirements such as communication, cooperation services and robustness. After defining deferent criteria we summarized the advantages and the limitation of each selected middleware. We have identified two middlewares, *ROS* and *MRDS*, as the most adapted for a multi-robot context.

In addition, we have considered two cloud solutions for robotics with their downsides. We propose another vision that consists in defining a cloud of robots and not a cloud for robots. In this perspective, we started to work with ROS which appears in our analysis as the most suitable middleware for robotic fleets.

References

1. Alexei Makarenko, A.B., Kaupp, T.: On the benefits of making robotic software frameworks thin. In: POn the Benefits of Making Robotic Software Frameworks Thin IEEE/RSJ International Conference on Intelligent Robots and Systems (IROS 2007), San Diego CA, USA, October 29-November 02 (2007)
2. Ando, N., Suehiro, T., Kotoku, T.: A software platform for component based RT-system development: OpenRTM-aist. In: Carpin, S., Noda, I., Pagello, E., Reggiani, M., von Stryk, O. (eds.) SIMPAR 2008. LNCS (LNAI), vol. 5325, pp. 87–98. Springer, Heidelberg (2008)
3. Arumugam, R., Enti, V.R., Bingbing, L., Xiaojun, W., Baskaran, K., Kong, F.F., Kumar, A.S., Meng, K.D., Kit, G.W.: Davinci: A cloud computing framework for service robots. In: 2010 IEEE International Conference on Robotics and Automation (ICRA), pp. 3084–3089. IEEE (2010)
4. Biggs, G., Ando, N., Kotoku, T.: Native robot software framework inter-operation. In: Ando, N., Balakirsky, S., Hemker, T., Reggiani, M., von Stryk, O. (eds.) SIMPAR 2010. LNCS, vol. 6472, pp. 180–191. Springer, Heidelberg (2010)
5. Bruyninckx, H.: Simulation, modeling and programming for autonomous robots: The open source perspective. In: Carpin, S., Noda, I., Pagello, E., Reggiani, M., von Stryk, O. (eds.) SIMPAR 2008. LNCS (LNAI), vol. 5325, p. 1. Springer, Heidelberg (2008)
6. Côté, C., Létourneau, D., Rai'evsky, C., Brosseau, Y., Michaud, F.: Using MARIE for mobile robot component development and integration (April 2007)
7. Elkady, A., Sobh, T.: Robotics middleware: A comprehensive literature survey and attribute-based bibliography. Journal of Robotics (2012)

8. Ferber, J.: Multi-Agent Systems. An Introduction to Distributed Artificial Intelligence. Addison Wesley, London (1999)
9. Frénot, S., Le Mouël, F., Ponge, J., Salagnac, G.: Various Extensions for the Ambient OSGi framework. In: Adamus Workshop in ICPS, Berlin, Allemagne (July 2010)
10. Han, S., Sook Kim, M., Park, H.S.: Open software platform for robotic services. IEEE Transactions on Automation Science and Engineering 9(3), 467–481 (2012)
11. Hunziker, D., Gajamohan, M., Waibel, M., D'Andrea, R.: Rapyuta: The roboearth cloud engine. In: Robotics and Automation, ICRA (2013)
12. Johns, K., Taylor, T.: Professional Microsoft Robotics Developer Studio. Wrox Press Ltd., Birmingham (2008)
13. Kraetzschmar, G.K., Utz, H., Sablatnög, S., Enderle, S., Palm, G.: Miro - middleware for cooperative robotics. In: Birk, A., Coradeschi, S., Tadokoro, S. (eds.) RoboCup 2001. LNCS (LNAI), vol. 2377, pp. 411–416. Springer, Heidelberg (2002)
14. Kranz, M., Rusu, R.B., Maldonado, A., Beetz, M., Schmidt, A.: A player/stage system for context-aware intelligent environments (2006)
15. Legras, F., Glad, A., Simonin, O., Charpillet, F.: Authority sharing in a swarm of UAVs: Simulation and experiments with operators. In: Carpin, S., Noda, I., Pagello, E., Reggiani, M., von Stryk, O. (eds.) SIMPAR 2008. LNCS (LNAI), vol. 5325, pp. 293–304. Springer, Heidelberg (2008)
16. Manso, L., Bachiller, P., Bustos, P., Núñez, P., Cintas, R., Calderita, L.: RoboComp: A tool-based robotics framework. In: Ando, N., Balakirsky, S., Hemker, T., Reggiani, M., von Stryk, O. (eds.) SIMPAR 2010. LNCS, vol. 6472, pp. 251–262. Springer, Heidelberg (2010)
17. Martínez, J., Romero-Garcés, A., Manso, L., Bustos, P.: Improving a robotics framework with real-time and high-performance features. In: Ando, N., Balakirsky, S., Hemker, T., Reggiani, M., von Stryk, O. (eds.) SIMPAR 2010. LNCS, vol. 6472, pp. 263–274. Springer, Heidelberg (2010)
18. Mohamed, N., Al-Jaroodi, J., Jawhar, I.: A review of middleware for networked robots. International Journal of Computer Science and Network Security (5) (2009)
19. Pyro. Website (2012), http://pyrorobotics.com/?page=PyroModuleIntroduction/
20. Quigley, M., Conley, K., Gerkey, B., Faust, J., Foote, T., Leibs, J., Wheeler, R., Ng, A.Y.: Ros: an open-source robot operating system. In: ICRA Workshop on Open Source Software, vol. 3 (2009)
21. RobotEarth. A worldwide web for robots (2014), http://roboearth.org/
22. ROS. Robot operating system (2014), http://www.ros.org/
23. Smart, W.D.: Is a common middleware for robotics possible? In: Proceedings of the IROS 2007 Workshop on Measures and Procedures for the Evaluation of Robot Architectures and Middleware. Citeseer (2007)
24. Tenorth, M., Perzylo, A.C., Lafrenz, R., Beetz, M.: The roboearth language: Representing and exchanging knowledge about actions, objects, and environments. In: 2012 IEEE International Conference on Robotics and Automation (ICRA), pp. 1284–1289. IEEE (2012)
25. Torkestani, J.A.: A highly reliable and parallelizable data distribution scheme for data grids. Future Generation Computer Systems 29(2), 509–519 (2013); Special section: Recent advances in e-Science
26. Valle, D., Nuno, E., Basañez, L., Arana-Daniel, N.: Consensus of networks of non-identical robots with flexible joints, variable time-delays and immeasurable velocities. In: IROS, pp. 5878–5883 (2013)
27. Xu, G., Xu, F., Ma, H.: Deploying and researching hadoop in virtual machines (August 2012)

Declarative Specification
of Robot Perception Architectures

Nico Hochgeschwender[1,2], Sven Schneider[1],
Holger Voos[2], and Gerhard K. Kraetzschmar[1]

[1] Bonn-Rhein-Sieg University, Computer Science, Sankt Augustin, Germany
nico.hochgeschwender@h-brs.de
[2] University of Luxembourg, SnT Automation Research Group, Luxembourg

Abstract. Service robots become increasingly capable and deliver a broader spectrum of services which all require a wide range of perceptual capabilities. These capabilities must cope with dynamically changing requirements which make the design and implementation of a robot perception architecture a complex and tedious exercise which is prone to error. We suggest to specify the integral parts of robot perception architectures using explicit models, which allows to easily configure, modify, and validate them. The paper presents the domain-specific language RPSL, some examples of its application, the current state of implementation and some validation experiments.

1   Introduction

Service robots operating in industrial or domestic environments are expected to perform a wide variety of tasks in different places with often widely differing environmental conditions. This poses many challenges for the perception-related parts of the control software (here referred to as **robot perception architecture (RPA)**), which includes recognizing and tracking manipulable and non-manipulable objects, furniture, people, faces, and recognizing gestures, emotions, sounds, and speech.

Designing a single set of perception components that performs all these perceptual tasks simultaneously, robustly, and efficiently would require enormous effort and would result in unmanageable complexity. To meet the challenges of service robotics we need concepts, methods, and tools for designing and developing RPAs in a very flexible manner. Ultimately the robot should be able to adjust to the wide range of situations autonomously (e.g. by dynamically selecting a set of perceptual components into an RPA configuration for a particular task). Fig. 1 illustrates the concept, where the components shown in red compose the RPA configuration active when the pose of a person is required. To do so, explicit knowledge representation about its available perception capabilities/functionalities (as depicted in Fig. 1) are required.

However, many RPA design decisions remain nowadays implicit. These decision concern the robot *platform*, robot's *tasks*, and the *environment* in which the

D. Brugali et al. (Eds.): SIMPAR 2014, LNAI 8810, pp. 291–302, 2014.

robot operates. Some examples include the selection and configuration (e.g. resolution and data frequency) of sensors, the selection and parameterization of filters and feature detectors (see also [1]), and the selection, configuration and/or training of classifiers. Also, the domain experts connect all these perceptual components into a coherent RPA. We argue that implicit design decisions are a major cause for the inflexibility of today's RPAs as if any of the implicit assumptions is changing, the task to adapt the RPA remains challenging and is prone to errors.

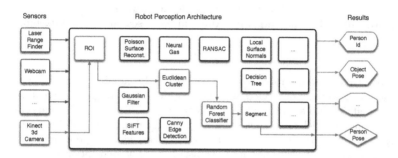

Fig. 1. The design space of Robot Perception Architectures (RPAs) includes the following constituents: *i*) heterogenous sets of sensors (blue boxes), *ii*) processing components (black boxes), *iii*) task-relevant information and knowledge (brown boxes), and *iv*) perception graphs (red visualized path)

Providing RPAs with the aforementioned cabilities requires to model the design decisions in an explicit and computable manner [2]. In the work presented here, the Model-Driven Engineering [2] approach is adopted for the design and development of RPAs as it enables modeling *for* and *by* reuse. More precisely, we introduce a set of meta-models and a corresponding domain-specific language (DSL) which enables the declarative and explicit specification of the integral parts of RPAs (see Sec. 2). We also show how concrete domain models are reused in an architecture facilitating the demand-driven selection and execution of perception graphs stored in a (model) repository (see Sec. 3).

2   RPSL: Robot Perception Specification Language

In the following we introduce the meta-models (abstract syntax) of the RPSL which is a textual domain-specific language (DSL) [2]. The RPSL allows to specify the integral parts of RPAs in an explicit manner. To identify the domain abstractions required to specify RPAs a domain analysis was performed on existing RPAs [3] which have been integrated on various robot platforms. Ranging from people detection, recognition and tracking to object recognition, pose estimation and categorization the assessed functionalities cover a wide range of perceptual capabilities required for today's service robots. Several core domain concepts were identified and described, namely components, algorithms, and perception graphs. These domain concepts correspond roughly to the structural constituents of RPAs as shown in Fig. 1. We also identified conceptual spaces as a cross-cutting domain. We apply a MDE approach using the Eclipse Modeling Framework (EMF)[1]. Each domain is specified in the form of an Ecore model. Based on the Ecore models, we developed a DSL using the Xtext framework[2].

Example: Color-Based Region Growing Segmentation. To exemplify the domain abstractions introduced with RPSL we use a standard segmentation method commonly applied in robotics, namely color-based region growing segmentation [4]. An example of the output of the system is shown in Fig. 2. Here, a scene with industrial objects such as screws and nuts is segmented. We assume the following setup: *i)* A RGB-D camera provides a $3D$ point cloud with RGB information at a resolution of 640×480 pixels. *ii)* Another component implements the color-based region growing segmentation. The component takes the whole point cloud as an input and provides a list of segmented regions, based on a certain configuration such as color range and minimum/maximum number of points per segmented region.

 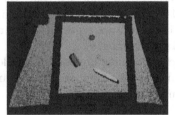

(a) Before Segmentation   (b) After Segmentation

Fig. 2. Example of the color-based region growing segmentation

2.1 Modeling Components

We propose component-based development for RPAs similar to [5]. The core idea is to use components as building blocks and to design RPAs by composing components with clearly defined interfaces. Component-based development fosters structured design and development and is nowadays the predominant software development approach in robotics [6].

The Component Meta-Model (CMM) (see Fig. 3) borrows the core structural elements, such as components and ports, from the BRICS Component Model (BCM) [6] and has been enriched through RPA-specific aspects. The main objective of the CMM is to model Components, the basic building blocks of RPAs. Each Component contains Ports of type InputPort and OutputPort, which serve as endpoints for communication between Components. Comparable

---

[1] http://www.eclipse.org/modeling/emf/
[2] http://www.eclipse.org/Xtext/

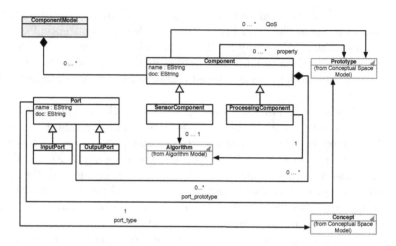

Fig. 3. The Component Meta Model (CMM)

to robot software frameworks such as Orocos RTT and others[3] `Ports` are typed. In RPSL, the type is modeled using the conceptual space meta-model (CSMM) presented in Sec. 2.3. Based on our domain analysis [3] we identified and distinguish between two types of `Components`, namely `SensorComponents` and `ProcessingComponents`.

SensorComponents are used to model sensors (e.g. cameras and laser range finders) and `ProcessingComponents` are used to model purely computational components which implement functionalities such as filters and feature detectors. `ProcessingComponents` link to an `Algorithm` modeled using the algorithm meta-model (see Sec. 2.2). Nowadays, some sensors preprocess data internally (e.g. noise filtering) before the sensor data is delivered. Thus, `SensorComponents` might link to an `Algorithm` as well. Each `Component` has `properties` such as configuration parameters, which are specific to the actual functionality (e.g. the minimum number of points per region for the region-growing segmentation), and `Quality of Service (QoS)` characteristics, such as worst case execution time. Similarly to `Ports`, the `QoS` characteristics and `properties` are modeled using the CSMM. `Components` are the basic first-class primitives in our meta-model. Currently, we do not support composition of components on a CMM level; hierarchies will be introduced later with the Perception Graph Meta-Model (PGMM) (see Sec. 2.4). `Ports` of `Components` are solely intended for data exchange among `Components` and not for configuration concerns (e.g. configuration ports found in other component models [7]). This design decision implies that the domain expert needs to specify all components together with particular configuration values. This approach fosters the modeling of feasible configuration values for components, as the domain expert is led to provide them. This also provides the possibility (if needed at a later stage) to reduce the design space (e.g. through grouping components).

---

[3] See [7] for a discussion on Component Models found in robotics.

2.2   Modeling Algorithms

The main objective of the Algorithm Meta-Model (AMM) (see Fig. 4) is to model *meta-information* about the algorithms which are integrated in components[4].

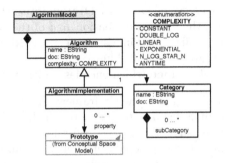

Fig. 4. The Algorithm Meta Model (AMM)

We distinguish between `Algorithm` and `AlgorithmImplementation`, where `AlgorithmImplementation` models a particular implementation of an `Algorithm`. Each `Algorithm` belongs to a `Category` (e.g. filter, feature descriptor) and provides information about its `Complexity`. Grouping algorithms in certain categories is feasible and *best practice*. In fact, every major computer vision and perception library, such as PCL [8] or OpenCV [9], is organized in categories sharing some properties. The distinction in `Algorithm` and `AlgorithmImplementation` is useful because it enables the domain expert to model different implementations of a particular algorithm. The color-based region growing algorithm, for instance, could either be implemented naïvely on the CPU, while another implementation is optimized for GPUs. Both implementations are specializations of the same `Algorithm` (e.g. `RegionGrowing`), but have different `properties` such as precision.

2.3   Modeling Conceptual Spaces

RPAs are producing heterogenous output spanning multiple levels of abstractions and ranging from raw sensor data and subsymbolic representations to symbolic information. The type of output depends on the task of the robot and on other functional components demanding the information. For example, in a pick-and-place scenario a decision making component might be interested in the types/names (symbolic information) of present objects, whereas a grasping component demands information about the pose of an object. Hence, a knowledge representation approach which enables us to model data produced by RPAs

---

[4] Please note, we do not model the algorithms themselves, e.g. in terms of steps and procedures.

on various levels of abstractions is required. In [10], Gärdenfors introduced Conceptual Spaces (CS) as a knowledge representation mechanism, which is used here and extended for RPSL. A CS contains the following constituent parts:

- A **Conceptual Space** is a metric space where **Concepts** are defined as convex regions in a set of domains (e.g. the concept *Color*).
- A **Domain** includes a set of **Domain Dimensions**[5] that form a unit and are measurable (e.g. the domain dimension *Red* of the RGB color model).
- An **Instance** is a specific vector in a space (e.g. the RGB color *red* with the values 255 (red), 0 (green), and 0 (blue)).
- A **Prototype** is an **Instance** which encodes typical values for a **Concept**.

The vector-based representation of the CS framework allows to apply similarity measures such as Euclidian distance to decide to which concept an instance belongs. In [11], Chella *et al.* showed that the CS framework enables the systematic integration of different knowledge representations as required in robotics. Further, the CS representation facilitates computationally efficient implementations based on the vector-based approach.

The Conceptual Space Meta-model (CSMM))(see Fig. 5) is a formalization of the CS framework as an Ecore model. In RPSL its purpose is to model the input and output of computational components of RPAs. Additionally, we use it to model QoS and general properties of Components and Algorithms. The CSMM contains several Concepts, where Concepts may contain subConcepts thereby supporting hierarchical concept structures. For each Domain a DomainDimension is defined. According to Gärdenfors, a DomainDimension is measurable. As RPAs deal with different types of data we introduce four DomainDimensions based on the work of Stevens [12], namely NominalDimension, OrdinalDimension, IntervalDimension, and RatioDimension. Each dimension permits to apply a set of logical and mathematical operators suitable to model different data.

Example: The color-based region growing segmentation component produces a list of regions. For each region the points belonging to it, the number of points, and the average RGB value of the points in the region are stored. We model a region as a Concept named Region referring to three Domains, namely PointCloud, NumberOfPoints, and AvgColor. We now exemplify the AvgColor domain which is decomposed into four DomainDimensions each of them of type IntervalDimension. Three of them are used to model the RGB color model and one for the standard deviation σ of the color distribution of the region. Each IntervalDimension for the RGB color model is equipped with an Interval ranging from 0 to 255 and of type Integer whereas the range for σ is from 0 to 1 and of type Double. Furthermore, a prototype is defined, which declares typical values for each Domain. For instance, depending on the configuration of

---

[5] In [10], a domain dimension is named quality dimension. For the sake of avoiding confusion with the term Quality of Service, we renamed it domain dimension.

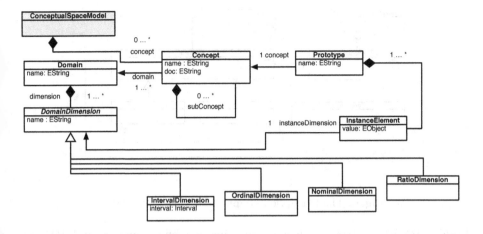

Fig. 5. Excerpt of the Conceptual Space Meta Model (CSMM). For the sake of readability some elements are not shown: the set of mathematical operators applicable on each domain dimension, the `Interval` class for the `IntervalDimension`, and the full set of attributes for each dimension class.

the algorithm the `NumberOfPoints` would be an `IntervalDimension` with an interval from 50 (minimum number of pixels per region) to 10,000.

2.4   Modeling Perception Graphs

The Perception Graph Meta-Model (PGMM) (see Fig. 6) enables the composition of components (see Sec. 2.1) in a directed acyclic graph (DAG) of components. A `PerceptionGraph` (PG) consists of two types of `Elements` (where `Element` refers to exactly one `Component`), namely `Nodes` which have at least one successor and `Leafs` without successor. To explicitly model successors, `Nodes` are connected through `Connections`, which have one `InputPort` and one `OutputPort` and refer to exactly one `Element`. Hence, we ensure that we do not connect two `InputPorts` or `OutputPorts` with each other. The PGMM enables the domain expert to model PGs which can easily be reused. Ranging from simple filtering pipelines to more elaborated PGs with multiple input, output and processing branches.

2.5   Modeling Constraints

Once domain concepts are represented as meta-models, we can also define constraints on concrete domain models conforming to these meta-models. Similarly to [13], we use the Object Constraint Language (OCL)[6] to model two types of constraints, namely atomic and composition constraints. Here, atomic constraints are valid for single meta-models whereas composition constraints appear when we compose meta-models (e.g. CSMM and PGMM in Sec. 2.4).

---

[6] http://www.omg.org/spec/OCL/2.3.1/

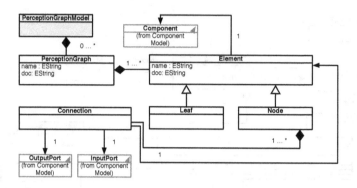

Fig. 6. The Perception Graph Meta Model (PGMM)

Beside atomic constraints, such as ensuring non-empty names and IDs, we check the following composition constraints: *i)* Each `Element` of type `Leaf` in a `PerceptionGraph` refers to a `Component` with at least one `OutputPort`. This ensures that a `PerceptionGraph` always provides an output. *ii)* Each `PerceptionGraph` does not have any directed cycles. This ensures the DAG property.

2.6 Modeling Demand

So far, we have modeled the integral parts of RPAs. To allow for demand-driven selection of PGs, we need abstractions to express demands. For that, we introduce the concept of a `Request`, which encodes an expected piece of information which is to be provided as the output of a `PerceptionGraph`. As inputs and outputs are modeled with the CSMM, a `Request` needs to know which `Concepts` are available in our architecture (see also Fig. 8). We introduce the concept of a `PrototypeRequest`. A `PrototypeRequest` consists of *i)* the prototype, which is a concrete instance of a concept (i.e. all properties have a specific value), *ii)* a distance, which determines how close values must be to the prototype, and *iii)* a distance measure. An example of a `PrototypeRequest` is shown in Fig. 7. The general idea of a `ProtoypeRequest` is that a *client* (the component expressing the demand) defines an expected value for each `DomainDimension` of a `Concept` which is later used to compute the most suitable PG. The suitability is defined by the `Request` in terms of `Similarity` which contains a `Metric` (e.g. a Euclidian distance or Jaccard distance) and a corresponding distance value which is interpreted as the maximally-allowed deviation. Assuming the `Request` can be fulfilled, the *client* expects some sort of data which is specified in the `Data` entry. Here, we support either one sample or a list of samples (in our example a list of Regions).

```
from myconcepts import Region as R

PrototypeRequest segmentedRegions {
 Prototype regionPrototype {
  R.AvgColor.Red = 220
  R.AvgColor.Green = 20
  R.AvgColor.Blue = 60
  // ...
 }

 Similarity similarity {
  Metric m = SIMILARITY_METRIC.EUCLIDIAN_DIST
  Distance  d = 0
 }

 Data data {
  List_of Region
 }
}
```

Fig. 7. An excerpt of a `PrototypeRequest` modeled with the `Request` DSL for the segmentation example

3   RPSL Run Time Environment

To validate the abstractions introduced by the RPSL and to realize the demand-driven selection and execution of previously modeled PGs we implemented the RPSL run time architecture shown in Fig. 8. During design time, a domain expert uses an editor to model concrete domain models of `PerceptionGraphs` using previously modeled `Components` and `Concepts`. The `PerceptionGraphs` and `Concepts` are stored in dedicated repositories which are accessible at run time by the run time architecture, which is bound to receive several requests each of which encodes a demand for a concrete piece of information that can be

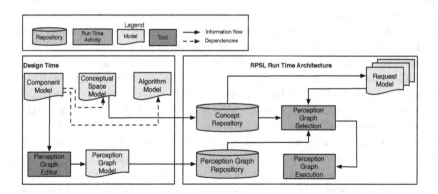

Fig. 8. The RPSL Run Time Architecture

provided by a stored `PerceptionGraph`. This demand is modeled with the abstractions introduced in Sec. 2.6. Based on the request and the models stored in the repositories we need to *select* and *execute* a `PerceptionGraph` (see activities in Fig. 8). Demand-driven selection and execution of perception graphs is beneficial for two reasons: First, it is not necessary anymore to deploy PGs before they are actually required at run time as for many tasks the sequence which PG needs to be active is not known a priori. In particular, for resource-constrained robots (e.g. micro air vehicles) this is advantagous as the use of resources like memory can be optimized. Second, requests are made explicit, which faciliates step-wise development and systematic testing of RPAs.

Algorithm 1. Selection of a perception graph based on a request

---

Input: Request R, set of perception graphs $PG = \{pg_1, pg_2, ..., pg_i\}$
Output: Set of candidates $C = \{\{c_1, c_2, ..., c_i\}$ where $C \subset PG$
    for all Output o_i in PG **do**
      if Concept C_R of R matches the concept C_i of o_i **then**
        if R is of type `PrototypeRequest` and o_i includes `Prototype` p_i **then**
          // Compute similarity dist. with given measure between C_R and p_i
          $d_i \leftarrow R.similarity.m(C_R, p_i)$
          if $d_i <= R.distance$ **then**
            $C \leftarrow C \cup pg_i$

Perception Graph Selection and Execution. To select a PG matching a particular `Request`, we apply Algorithm 1 which iterates over each PG stored in the repository and assesses the outputs it provides. As a result, a `Request` can yield any of the following situations: *i*) no PG matches, *ii*) exactly one PG matches, *iii*) several PGs match. In the case of a `PrototypeRequest`, the PG with the shortest distance is executed.

Implementation and Experiments. The architecture shown in Fig. 8 is work in progress, implemented in Java and Ruby, and will be released soon as open source.[7] For each meta-model presented in Sec. 2, we already provide an Eclipse-based textual editor which enables the specification and storage of domain models. The run time system of the RPSL architecture contains two main modules: PG `selection` and PG `execution`. The `selection` module realizes the platform-independent algorithm described above, whereas the `execution` modules is platform-dependent. The modeled PGs are independent of a particular framework in which the PGs are implemented. For execution of the PGs, the PG primitives are mapped to framework-specific primitives. So far, we have a direct mapping to ROS nodes implementing the PGs, but we plan to realize this step with a Model-2-Model transformation from the PGMM to a framework-specific meta-model. To assess the overall approach, we modeled several PGs ranging from smaller examples such as the different variants of the region growing PG

---

[7] https://github.com/nicoh/RPSL

to more complex PGs, such as combined region of interest, segmentation, and shape-extraction PGs. For each PG we also tested corresponding **Requests**. It is possible to select a PG which matches the **Request** even in a repository which is unstructured (different PGs stored for different purpose).

4   Discussion and Related Work

To the best of our knowledge the presented approach is the first which applies the MDE approach to the design and development of RPAs. Although MDE approaches are becoming popular in robotics, they mainly focus on subdomains such as coordinate representations [14].

The CSMM turned out to be a general-purpose meta-model which is applicable not only to describe the input and output of components but also their properties and QoS characteristics. We intend to consider this information also in the selection process to select the fastest or most reliable PG. To which extend this information will be reflected in the **Request** remains open and will be investigated in ongoing work. To model these *non-functional* properties we will also investigate the meta-models proposed in [15].

Even though with **PrototypeRequests** we can already select PGs we foresee the implementation of different types of **Requests** such as **ConstraintRequests**. Here, a **ConstraintRequest** would define constraints (e.g. inequality constraints such as $>$, $<=$ etc.) on **DomainDimension** which is beneficial when several PGs provide the same concept at their output, but their characteristics differ (e.g. different **Intervals** for the same **DomainDimension**).

To define acceptable names and terms for the **Concepts** is crucial for the usage of the proposed approach. Hence, we will investigate ontologies proposed in other projects such as [16]. In contrast to the work by Moisan *et al.* [1], our approach does not depend on a feature-model representation as it is mainly driven by the integral architectural parts of RPAs.

We also plan to enrich the PG **execution** through deployment models [13] such that PGs can be deployed on platforms which increase the performance.

5   Conclusion

This paper presented the Robot Perception Specification Language (RPSL) which enables the explicit specification of RPAs. We showed how to model and store ready-to-use perception graphs and to efficiently select the most appropriate perception graph at run time.

Acknowledgement. Nico Hochgeschwender is recipient of a PhD scholarship from the Graduate Institute of the Bonn-Rhein-Sieg University, which he gratefully acknowledges.

References

1. Moisan, S., Rigault, J.-P., Acher, M., Collet, P., Lahire, P.: Run time adaptation of video-surveillance systems: A software modeling approach. In: Crowley, J.L., Draper, B., Thonnat, M. (eds.) ICVS 2011. LNCS, vol. 6962, pp. 203–212. Springer, Heidelberg (2011)
2. Schmidt, D.C.: Guest editor's introduction: Model-driven engineering. Computer 39(2), 25–31 (2006)
3. Hochgeschwender, N., Schneider, S., Voos, H., Kraetzschmar, G.K.: Towards a robot perception specification language. In: Proceedings of the 4th International Workshop on Domain-Specific Languages and Models for ROBotic Systems (DSLRob) (2013)
4. Zhan, Q., Liang, Y., Xiao, Y.: Color-based segmentation of point clouds. International Archives of the Photogrammetry, Remote Sensing and Spatial Information Sciences 38, 248–252 (2009)
5. Biggs, G., Ando, N., Kotoku, T.: Rapid data processing pipeline development using openrtm-aist. In: 2011 IEEE/SICE International Symposium on System Integration (SII), pp. 312–317 (2011)
6. Bruyninckx, H., Klotzbücher, M., Hochgeschwender, N., Kraetzschmar, G., Gherardi, L., Brugali, D.: The brics component model: A model-based development paradigm for complex robotics software systems. In: Proceedings of the 28th Annual ACM Symposium on Applied Computing, SAC 2013, pp. 1758–1764. ACM, New York (2013)
7. Shakhimardanov, A., Hochgeschwender, N., Kraetzschmar, G.K.: Component models in robotics software. In: Proceedings of the Workshop on Performance Metrics for Intelligent Systems, Baltimore, USA (2010)
8. Rusu, R.B., Cousins, S.: 3D is here: Point cloud library (pcl). In: Proceedings of the International Conference on Robotics and Automation (ICRA) (2011)
9. Bradski, G.: The OpenCV Library. Dr. Dobb's Journal of Software Tools (2000)
10. Gärdenfors, P.: Conceptual spaces - the geometry of thought. MIT Press (2000)
11. Chella, A., Frixione, M., Gaglio, S.: A cognitive architecture for artificial vision. Artif. Intell. 89(1-2), 73–111 (1997)
12. Stevens, S.S.: On the Theory of Scales of Measurement. Science 103, 677–680 (1946)
13. Hochgeschwender, N., Gherardi, L., Shakhirmardanov, A., Kraetzschmar, G., Brugali, D., Bruyninckx, H.: A model-based approach to software deployment in robotics. In: 2013 IEEE/RSJ International Conference on Intelligent Robots and Systems (IROS), pp. 3907–3914 (November 2013)
14. Nordmann, A., Hochgeschwender, N., Wrede, S.: A survey on domain-specific languages in robotics. In: Brugali, D., Broenink, J., Kroeger, T., MacDonald, B. (eds.) SIMPAR 2014. LNCS (LNAI), vol. 8810, pp. 193–204. Springer, Heidelberg (2014)
15. Ramaswamy, A.K., Monsuez, B., Tapus, A., et al.: Solution space modeling for robotic systems. Journal for Software Engineering Robotics (JOSER) 5(1), 89–96 (2014)
16. Dhouib, S., Kchir, S., Stinckwich, S., Ziadi, T., Ziane, M.: RobotML, a domain-specific language to design, simulate and deploy robotic applications. In: Noda, I., Ando, N., Brugali, D., Kuffner, J.J. (eds.) SIMPAR 2012. LNCS, vol. 7628, pp. 149–160. Springer, Heidelberg (2012)

A Modeling Framework for Software Architecture Specification and Validation

Nicolas Gobillot, Charles Lesire, and David Doose

ONERA, The French Aerospace Lab.,
2 Avenue Edouard Belin, 31055 Toulouse, France
{firstname.lastname}@onera.fr

Abstract. Integrating robotic systems into our everyday life needs that we prove that they will not endanger people, i.e. that they will behave correctly with respect to some safety rules. In this paper, we propose a validation toolchain based on a Domain Specific Language. This DSL allows to model the software architecture of a robot using a component-based approach. From these models, we provide tools to generate deployable components, as well as a two-step validation phase. This validation first performs a real-time analysis of the component architecture, leading to an evaluation of the software architecture schedulability. Then we can check the validity of some behavioral property on the components.

1 Introduction

Nowadays, computer-based systems occupy an increasing place in our everyday or professional life. Robots for instance were absent of our houses in the 80's but today tasks performed by such machines are increasing. In the early days, only simple tasks were given to robots due to different limitations: robots were mechanically limited by their heavy materials, their sensors and actuators were big and inaccurate and their processors were slow (HERO [1] or PUMA[2]). Thanks to miniaturisation, mechanical parts are lighter, electronic circuits are smaller and processors are powerful enough to perform complex tasks (Da Vinci Surgical System[3] or Curiosity[4]). To make these robots usable in our everyday life, we need to ensure that they respect some safety rules, especially regarding their damaging capabilities. Safety has been considered regarding several aspects of robotics:

- *collision avoidance*, adapting the robot movements in presence of obstacles (e.g., [13] generates safe velocity bounds based on environment geometry; [16] conceives a mechanical system able to detect contact at an early stage);
- *human interaction*, where human behaviors are anticipated to avoid collisions while interacting with people (e.g., [23] in manufacturing places, [29] that tracks pedestrian behaviors);

---

[1] http://www.hero-1.com/Broadband/
[2] http://www.digplanet.com/wiki/Programmable_Universal_Machine_for_Assembly
[3] http://www.davincisurgery.com/index.php
[4] http://mars.jpl.nasa.gov/msl/mission/rover/

D. Brugali et al. (Eds.): SIMPAR 2014, LNAI 8810, pp. 303–314, 2014.
© Springer International Publishing Switzerland 2014

- *fault detection and tolerance*, where software/hardware reconfigurations or mode changes are controlled depending on what happens in the environment (e.g., [15] use invariant monitoring and change robot's mode accordingly; [19] uses a hierarchical decomposition of actions to switch between alternatives);
- *controller synthesis*, where the robot behavior is guaranteed by construction of the movement or action policy (e.g., [9] for continuous control of non-linear robots; [20] that verifies an action policy while learning it).

Another specificity in robot development is its fast evolution. This fast evolution leads to short development cycles of several month unlike in aeronautics or in the nuclear field which have development cycles of tenths of years. Due to this we need fast and accurate methods and tools to guarantee that the robots will always have a safe behavior. In order to have fast development cycles, we need to reuse hardware and software parts between robots and design these parts with maximum modularity.

To help the software robot developer, modern designs are made of two parts: a middleware and a component-based architecture. The middleware provides operating system and hardware abstractions. The middleware typically proposes an Application Programming Interface to develop and deploy tasks and threads without taking into account the operating system and thus the hardware specificities. Among robotic-oriented middlewares, we can cite OROCOS [27] as a real-time focused middleware, ROS [21] that provides a large amount of already developed components, and $G^{en}{}_oM3$ [18] that provides a component generator with a component modeling language.

A component-based design pattern allows the software architect to build a robotic architecture by assembling existing software components (see [5,6] for a survey on component-based software engineering in robotics). These software components are made of two parts: their communication interface and their internal behavior. Communications are driven by connecting ports or by service calls between two or more components. The component's behavior is often defined by a state-machine, that allows to define several operational modes, including some degraded mode to be robust to sensor or software failures.

In this paper, we propose an evolution of the Mauve Domain Specific Language (DSL) [17] to specify robotic architectures through an extensive use of models. These models are then used to generate the executable codes run on the real robots. From this DSL, we then provide methods and tools to analyze and check the validity of functional and temporal properties leading to robot safety.

2   Experimental Setup

We will illustrate our approach using a concrete robotic experiment. This case study uses a Pioneer 3-DX robot (P3DX) from Adept Mobile Robots (Fig. 1). The P3DX is a wheeled robot equipped with an internal computer which serves as a controller interface. Its stock capabilities allows it to move around through its wheel speed controller and avoid some obstacles using its sonar range finders.

Its motors are sufficiently powerful to move around outdoors on reasonably rough terrains and its small size allows it to find its way in corridors. Our P3DX platform is equipped with a Hokuyo UTM-30LX laser scanning range finder and an Asus Xtion Pro Live depth and color camera. In this case study, our robot has to navigate safely in unknown and dynamic environments. We then need some navigation functions (including localization and mapping), a path planning algorithm to compute paths to follow, and a control function to follow correctly this path. We also want our robot to detect and track specific objects identified by color patterns.

Fig. 1. The P3DX platform equipped with a Hokuyo laser and a laptop for processing

The objective of this work is to propose first a design process for software architectures of autonomous robots, based on a DSL (section 3), and then to prove some aspects of the robot safety using tools leaning upon this DSL (section 4).

3   The Mauve DSL

This section presents the Mauve DSL for specifying and conceiving software architectures for autonomous robots. This DSL is an extension of [17]. It is based on four layers: *codels*, that correspond to the computational aspects of the software, *components*, that are elementary blocks of the software, *architecture*, where components are instantiated and connected, and *deployment*, where the execution policy of the architecture is defined depending on the target.

3.1   Codels

A *codel* (term taken from [18]) stands for an *elementary code* and represents any computational part of a component. The Mauve DSL does not provide any means to implement the codel (which could be implemented in any language; for code generation and analysis, we only support C and C++). The Mauve DSL provides instead a language for specifying the codels, that will then be called from components. Listing 1.1 shows the specification of codels implementing detection of an object of interest (Detect), and tracking of this object on images (Track). They both take an image as input, and provide the pose of the object.

Code 1.1. Codels from an image detection and tracking algorithm

```
1 codel Detect(img: Img): Pose
2 codel Track(img: Img): Pose
```

3.2   Components

According to [28], *a component is a unit of composition with contractually speci-fied interfaces and explicit context dependencies only. A software component can be deployed independently and is subject to composition by third parties.*

Therefore, in order to help composition and modularity, we decompose the specification of a component into a *shell* (or interfaces) and a *core* (or function-ality). In order to perform some validation of the component and architecture behavior, we also define some contracts that indicate the conditions of use of the component.

Component's Shell. The shell of a component defines its interface, i.e. its inputs and outputs. We propose three types of interfaces: *properties*, which are component parameters, generally set at instantiation or deployment time (e.g., the max velocity of a platform); *data ports*, similar to the *push* pattern of [24], are used to publish data from/to a component; they are typed and oriented; *operations*, similar to the *query* pattern of [24], are used to call functions or send requests to components.

Specifying a shell is then done by listing the properties of a component (with a type and possibly a default value), its ports (with a type and a direction – in or out), and its operations (same way as codel signature). Values of properties, as well as connections of ports and operations, are not done at the moment of specifying a component shell. Instead, they are defined when instantiating and connecting components (*architecture* specification step).

Listing 1.2 shows the shell specification of the detection and tracking compo-nent. It has one property, `cameraType`, used to configure properly the compo-nent, e.g. by mapping the camera type value to resolution and focal length of the sensor. Default value refers to a Asus Xtion depth sensor. The component also has one input port `imgPort` to get an image stream (typically from a sensor component) and one output port *objectPort* exposing the pose of the detected and tracked object.

Code 1.2. Shell of the detection and tracking component

```
1 shell DT_Shell {
2   property cameraType: string default "Xtion"
3   input port imgPort: Img
4   output port objectPort: Pose
5 }
```

Component's Core. The core of a component defines its behavior. It can be described on two ways: first by mapping provided operations to codels, and second, by specifying a state-machine. Using a state-machine representation has some advantages, among which clearly separating the different functionalities of the component, and providing some states to handle errors, then increasing the robustness or reconfiguration skills of the architecture. A state-machine is defined by a set of states and a set of transitions connecting the states. Each state represents a step in the functional behavior. The whole functionality is achieved by a sequence of states connected with transitions. The execution of each state is decomposed into several blocks, following the same approach as in UML state charts for instance:

- entry, defining instructions called only when a state is entered;
- run, called each time a state is active;
- exit, called when a state is exited (through a transition);
- handle, called when no transition is taken;

In each block, it is possible to write some instructions provided by Mauve, such as reading or writing on ports, calling codels, or calling remote operations. In each state, possible transitions are specified by a label, a guard, and a destination state. Listing 1.3 shows the core of the detection and tracking component. Its state machine is made of four states:

- Initialize (line 3), in which some algorithm data structures are prepared;
- Cleanup (line 6), in which data are cleaned;
- Detecting (line 9), in which the input port is read, the detecting algorithm is called, and the resulting pose is published on the output port;
- Tracking (line 18), similar for the tracking algorithm.

Transitions are guarded by events that will come either from the component itself ([pose] on line 16 checks that a pose has been returned by Detect) or triggered from other components.

Code 1.3. State-machine example using the detection and tracking codels

```
1  core DT_Core (DT_Shell) {
2    statemachine {
3      initial state Initialize {
4        transition toDetecting [not initialize] -> Detecting
5      }
6      state Cleanup {
7        transition toInitialize [not cleanup] -> Initialize
8      }
9      state Detecting {
10       run {image = read imgPort}
11       handle {
12         pose = Detect(image);
13         write pose in objectPort
14       }
15       transition toCleanup [cleanup] -> Cleanup
16       transition toTracking [pose] -> Tracking
17     }
18     state Tracking {
19       run {image = read imgPort}
20       handle {
21         pose = Track(image);
22         write pose in objectPort
23       }
24       transition toDetecting [pose] -> Detecting
25     }
26   }
27 }
```

Component's Contracts. Contracts are meant to represent the condition of use of a component, and the result or behavior we could expect when executing this component. The shell of the component already specifies a contract: it declares the inputs needed by the component, and the type of data published by the component. The Mauve DSL provides complementary instructions to specify functional properties of the components. These properties represent an abstraction of the behavior of the component. For instance, the role of the guidance component is to follow a path while avoiding obstacles. For this component the most important feature regarding safety is to avoid collisions. Listing 1.4 shows how this property is expressed as a contract on the guidance component: the robot has to stop (speed command sent on speedPort must be equal to 0) whenever something is detected (read from the scanPort) within a safety distance (defined as a component property).

Code 1.4. Contract on the Guidance component

```
1  shell Guidance_Shell {
2    codel minRange(scan: Scan): double
3    property robotType: string default "unicycle"
4    property safetyMargin: double default 0.5
5    input port scanPort: Scan
6    output port speedPort: Speed
7
8    contract emergencyStop:
9      [minRange(read scanPort) < safetyMargin ⇒ write 0 in speedPort]
```

3.3   Architecture

Creating a functional software layer for autonomous robots settles on reusing and composing basic component blocks. The *architecture* design step consists in instantiating some components (defined using the previous language instructions), and possibly define some properties. Then these components are connected together, specifying the configuration of the communication. For instance, it is where we can specify that a connection between two ports is buffered, and specify the management policy of the buffer (size, circular or not).

We developed a Navigation, Guidance and Control component-based architecture meant to be run on mobile robots [12], that we modified, improved, and adapted to the match the Mauve DSL presented in this paper. It results in the architecture of Fig. 2, made of eight components (drawn as circles): components for sensor (Camera and Laser) and actuator (Robot) interfaces; the Navigation, Guidance and Control components managing movements; a SLAM component to build a map and navigate in it; and finally the Detection and Tracking component.

This architecture is specified using the Mauve DSL. Listing 1.5 shows a piece of the architecture specification where two components are instantiated: camera and detectTrack, and the ports of the two components are connected.

Code 1.5. Part of the architecture specification

```
1  instance camera: Camera {}
2  instance detectTrack: DT_Core {}
3  port camera.imgPort data detectTrack.imgPort
```

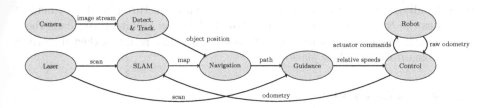

Fig. 2. Simplified component-based architecture running on the robot

3.4 Deployment

The deployment is the target-specific part of a real-time software development. It will map the components and architecture specification to the final target (environment, platform) in order to be executed. The deployment is decomposed into several layers: the *hardware*, also called target, corresponds to the actual platform used for experiments, i.e. sensors, computer units, etc. Using the Mauve DSL, architecture components properties can be set to indicate which platform is used, e.g., by defining the device port on which the camera is connected; the *middleware* is a layer over the operating system providing a set of features that makes development easier. For the moment, the only supported middleware is Orocos [27], and therefore we do not provide any mean to choose the middleware.

In order to be able to analyze the deployed architecture, and more specifically its real-time characteristics, we impose that each component is mapped to at most one thread. When deploying the components, we then associate to each component an activity indicating the execution behavior of the component. This activity allows to define the period of the component, its priority, and its deadline. These properties will then be mapped to Orocos components activities, resulting in properties of the corresponding OS threads. We can also set the affinity of a component, i.e. the core on which the component will run if executing on a multi-core platform.

Listing 1.6 shows a part of a deployment where the `robot` component has a period and a deadline of 100ms, a priority of 0. Furthermore, we can specify the execution time of codels (codel `command` takes 16ms to execute), used for real-time analysis (see section 4.1).

Code 1.6. Part of a deployment specification

```
1 deployment {
2    command = 16..16
3    activity robot {
4       priority = 0
5       period   = 100
6       deadline = 100
7    }
```

3.5 Execution

Along with the Mauve DSL, we provide a code generation toolchain that, for each Mauve component, generates the code of an Orocos component linked with the corresponding codels library; and for each Mauve architecture plus deployment, generates the code of an Orocos script that deploys the architecture (loads the components, instantiate them, connects them, ...) The result is then directly executable on the specified platform.

3.6 Why a New DSL?

A lot of software modeling DSLs for robotics can be found in the literature. In [14] the robot's software architecture is modeled in three main layers: the *functional architecture*, the *component architecture* and the *runtime architecture*. The *functional architecture* expresses the functionality needed in an architecture. The *component architecture* details the software implementation of the architecture's functionality. Lastly the *runtime architecture* defines the deployment of the components on the robot's operating system. This framework also generates *roslaunch* files for ROS [21]. [10] uses an UML-based language called RoBoTML, based on an ontology to reuse as much as possible robotic knowledge. This knowledge is split into five packages: *robotic system, system environment, data types, robotic mission* and *platform*. Afterwards the robotic architecture is defined using the RoBoTML packages, and it is possible to generate executable code for several robotic middlewares, among which is Orocos. V^3CMM [1] separates the robotic architecture in three abstraction levels: *Computation Independent Models, Platform-Independent Models* and *Platform-Specific Models*. Once the architecture is set-up, a model-to-model transformation is used to provide UML models, and then executable code through a model-to-text transformation to the Ada 2005 programming language. In this paper, we have described the Mauve DSL. Mauve relies on more or less the same concepts than other DSLs. The aim of Mauve is to not only provide architectural abstraction, simple software design and code generation but also to systematically perform validation and analysis based on these models. It hence seemed difficult to reuse an existing DSL, as we needed to specify new concepts (or to prevent the use of existing concepts).

Two major works are using DSLs for architecture specification along with a validation process: SmartSoft [25] models the architecture and the components through model layers. It provides real-time specific parameters to allow a static analysis of the architecture through CHEDDAR [26]. Regarding the real-time analysis, we propose to reason on the component models to have a more accurate estimation of architecture schedulability. Moreover, we are concerned with other analysis than just real-time analysis. BIP [2] is a modeling language that comes with safety properties and deadlock freedom analysis tools. The safety properties ensure that no unexpected behavior will ever happen thanks to global state exploration. The deadlock analysis goes through a structural analysis to guarantee the software will keep its nominal execution. The major drawback of using this paradigm is that generated code is tied to their own execution engine (behaving as a scheduler), and real-time analysis is not dealt with.

4 Validation Tools

The main objective of our work is to perform some validation of the executed software architecture for an autonomous robot. We therefore lean upon the modeling framework presented above in order to reason on the architecture behavior. Regarding the presented experimental case study, it is for instance important for the P3DX robot to ensure that it will not collide with any object in the environment. Proving this safety constraint relies on several concerns: we first need to prove that a logical property is true, by reasoning on the contracts provided by the components. Second, we need to check that all component will be able to execute in time. This last property is called schedulability.

4.1 Real-Time Analysis

The aim of the real-time analysis is to *a priori* check the schedulability of the architecture on a specific system, before deploying it on the real system. Usually the schedulability of a system is defined by the schedulability of all the tasks involved in the system. We do not detail in this paper all the models and computations for the analysis to happen, as it is a bit out of the scope of the paper, but we give a brief explanation of the whole process.

When specifying the deployment of the architecture using the Mauve DSL, we map components to real-time tasks on the system, with tasks parameters such as period, deadline, and priority. Classical schedulability methods directly use these parameters, along with an estimation of the computation time of each task, to compute the Worst Case Response Time (WCRT) of a task. If the WCRT of a task is lesser than its period, the task is said schedulable.

We have adapted this process to use models of components, in order to perform a more accurate computation of the WCRT. We transform component models into Periodic State-Machines (PSM), on which each transition is labeled with the time taken to go from one state to another, computed from the state blocks, the execution times of codels, and the interactions between components (e.g., when a component calls an operation on another component). The execution time of each codel is obtained using Worst Case Execution Times (WCET) analysis. We tried two approaches depending on the codels: a static analysis, using Otawa [22], where the binary code is directly analyzed to estimate the number of cycles a function will take to execute; and a statistical analysis based on execution runs of the component. For now we made only basic statistics to deduce an experimental WCET, but we are currently working on using extreme-value theory to have a mathematically sound estimation (with a given probability) of the WCET. We then modified the classical WCRT computation algorithm to take into account tasks state-machines (PSMs) and component interactions. It results in a new evaluation, called WCRT+, which is still pessimistic (hence safe) but more accurate than the classical approach.

Table 1 presents the results of the schedulability analysis of our robotic architecture. The lower the priority value, the higher the priority of the component. The WCET value corresponds to the WCET of the most time-consuming transition of the PSM. The WCRT and WCRT+ columns are respectively the "classical" and our state-machine based evaluations. The WCRT+ computation method proves the schedulability of the architecture whereas the typical method indicates the `Navigation` component may not be schedulable.

Table 1. Real-time characteristics of the architecture's components

component	priority	WCET	WCRT	WCRT+	deadline
Robot	0	16	16	16	100
Control	1	3	19	19	100
Guidance	2	12	31	31	100
Laser	3	22	53	53	150
SLAM	4	30	83	83	150
Camera	5	10	93	93	250
Detection and Tracking	6	30	237	237	250
Navigation	7	30	**338**	**297**	**300**

4.2   Checking Behavioral Properties

Previous section shows how we used the component and architecture models to accurately compute the deadline (and the schedulability) of the deployed components. Enforcing these deadlines is needed for a good behavior of the robot. However it is not sufficient to guarantee the correctness of this behavior. In this section, we propose to analyze the correctness of this behavior by studying the evolution of the components (and their state machines) along the time.

For the moment, the properties that we are able to manage rely on observation points: we can specify instructions or states on which we want to elaborate a property. For instance, we can express, using these observation points, that a component will eventually enter in state A, or that when component *guid* enters state *running*, then component *control* will eventually enter state *running* before 10 time units (see listing 1.7).

Code 1.7. Specification of a property

```
1 property latency = guid.running leadsto control.running within [0, 10]
2 assert latency
```

Formally, these properties are expressed using a temporal logic that accepts Dwyer's patterns [11] extended with timed data. Verifying such properties is quite complex in general, as we must analyze both the control flow of the architecture but also the interactions between components (leading to task preemption). We then developed a specific validation process that directly uses temporal information coming from the real-time analysis presented in section 4.1. For that, the Mauve model of the components and architecture, along with the properties we want to analyze, are transformed into Timed Petri Nets using the RT-Fiacre language [3]. The resulting model is then analyzed using Tina [4], which either validates the property or provides a counter example as a timed execution of the system.

5   Conclusion and Perspectives

In this paper, we have presented a robotic architecture modeling framework based on the Mauve DSL. It allows to model robotic software architectures from the algorithms to a real-time deployment thanks to four layers: the *codels* specification, the *component* modes, the specification of the *architecture* and, finally, the *deployment*. From these models, Mauve is able to generate C++ executable code designed for Orocos-RTT [27]. Along with the Mauve DSL, we have provided tools to first analyze the real-time correctness of the architecture, and second to check the validity of some behavioral properties.

For future developments, we plan to improve the validation toolchain by analyzing not only behavioral properties but also properties that contain data, such as the contract defined in listing 1.4. To do that, we will rely on well known tools for codel analysis, such as Frama-C [8] and Coccinelle [7]. Finally, we plan to apply our design and validation process to other kind of robots, like hybrid leg-wheel robots and quadcopters.

References

1. Alonso, D., Vicente-chicote, C., Ortiz, F., Pastor, J., Alvarez, B.: V3CMM: a 3-View Component Meta-Model for Model-Driven Robotic Software Development. Journal of Software Engineering for Robotics (JOSER) 1, 3–17 (2010)
2. Basu, A., Gallien, M., Lesire, C., Nguyen, T.H., Bensalem, S., Ingrand, F., Sifakis, J.: Incremental Component-Based Construction and Verification of a Robotic System. In: ECAI, Patras, Greece (2008)
3. Berthomieu, B., Bodeveix, J., Farail, P., Filali, M., Garavel, H., Gaufillet, P., Lang, F., Vernadat, F.: Fiacre: an intermediate language for model verification in the TOPCASED environment. In: Embedded Real Time Software and Systems (ERTSS), Toulouse, France (2008)
4. Berthomieu, B., Vernadat, F.: Time Petri Nets Analysis with TINA. In: Int. Conf. on Quantitative Evaluation of Systems (QEST), Riverside, CA, USA (2006)
5. Brugali, D., Scandurra, P.: Component-Based Robotic Engineering. Part I: Reusable Building Blocks. IEEE Robotics and Automation Magazine 16(4) (2009)
6. Brugali, D., Shakhimardanov, A.: Component-Based Robotic Engineering. Part II: Systems and Models. IEEE Robotics and Automation Magazine 17(1) (2010)
7. Brunel, J., Doligez, D., Hansen, R.R., Lawall, J.L., Muller, G.: A foundation for flow-based program matching using temporal logic and model checking. In: ACM Symposium on Principles of Programming Languages, Savannah, GA, USA (2009)
8. Cuoq, P., Kirchner, F., Kosmatov, N., Prevosto, V., Signoles, J., Yakobowski, B.: Frama-C, A Software Analysis Perspective. In: Eleftherakis, G., Hinchey, M., Holcombe, M. (eds.) SEFM 2012. LNCS, vol. 7504, pp. 233–247. Springer, Heidelberg (2012)
9. DeCastro, J.A., Kress-Gazit, H.: Guaranteeing reactive high-level behaviors for robots with complex dynamics. In: IROS, Tokyo, Japan (2013)
10. Dhouib, S., Kchir, S., Stinckwich, S., Ziadi, T., Ziane, M.: RobotML, a Domain-Specific Language to Design, Simulate and Deploy Robotic Applications. In: Noda, I., Ando, N., Brugali, D., Kuffner, J.J. (eds.) SIMPAR 2012. LNCS, vol. 7628, pp. 149–160. Springer, Heidelberg (2012)

11. Dwyer, M.B., Avrunin, G.S., Corbett, J.C.: Patterns in property specifications for finite-state verification. In: Software Engineering, Los Angeles, CA, USA (1999)
12. Gobillot, N., Lesire, C., Doose, D.: A Component-Based Navigation-Guidance-Control Architecture for Mobile Robots. In: ICRA – SDIR Workshop, Karlsruhe, Germany (2013)
13. Haddadin, S., Khoury, A., Rokahr, T., Parusel, S., Burgkart, R., Bicchi, A., Albu-Schaffer, A.: A truly safely moving robot has to know what injury it may cause. In: IROS, Vila Moura, Portugal (2012)
14. Hochgeschwender, N., Gherardi, L., Shakhirmardanov, A., Kraetzschmar, G.K., Brugali, D., Bruyninckx, H.: A model-based approach to software deployment in robotics. In: IROS, Tokyo, Japan (2013)
15. Jiang, H., Elbaum, S., Detweiler, C.: Reducing failure rates of robotic systems though inferred invariants monitoring. In: IROS, Tokyo, Japan (2013)
16. Lens, T., von Stryk, O.: Investigation of safety in human-robot-interaction for a series elastic, tendon-driven robot arm. In: IROS, Vila Moura, Portugal (2012)
17. Lesire, C., Doose, D., Cassé, H.: MAUVE: a Component-based Modeling Framework for Real-time Analysis of Robotic Applications. In: ICRA – SDIR Workshop, Saint-Paul, MN, USA (2012)
18. Mallet, A., Pasteur, C., Herrb, M.: GenoM3: Building middleware-independent robotic components. In: ICRA, Anchorage, AK, USA (2010)
19. Nakamura, A., Nagata, K., Harada, K., Yamanobe, N., Tsuji, T., Foissotte, T., Kawai, Y.: Error recovery using task stratification and error classification for manipulation robots in various fields. In: IROS, Tokyo, Japan (2013)
20. Pathak, S., Pulina, L., Metta, G., Tacchella, A.: Ensuring safety of policies learned by reinforcement: Reaching objects in the presence of obstacles with the iCub. In: IROS, Tokyo, Japan (2013)
21. Quigley, M., Conley, K., Gerkey, B., Faust, J., Foote, T., Leibs, J., Wheeler, R., Ng, A.: ROS: an open-source Robot Operating System. In: ICRA Workshop on Open Source Software, Kobe, Japan (2009)
22. Rochange, C., Sainrat, P.: OTAWA: An Open Toolbox for Adaptive WCET Analysis. In: IFIP Workshop on Software Technologies for Future Embedded and Ubiquitous Systems (SEUS), Waidhofen, Austria, pp. 35–46 (2010)
23. Rybski, P., Anderson-Sprecher, P., Huber, D., Niessl, C., Simmons, R.: Sensor fusion for human safety in industrial workcells. In: IROS, Vila Moura, Portugal (2012)
24. Schlegel, C.: Communication Patterns as Key Towards Component-Based Robotics. International Journal of Advanced Robotic Systems 3(1) (2006)
25. Schlegel, C., Steck, A., Brugali, D., Knoll, A.: Design Abstraction and Processes in Robotics: From Code-Driven to Model-Driven Engineering. In: Ando, N., Balakirsky, S., Hemker, T., Reggiani, M., von Stryk, O. (eds.) SIMPAR 2010. LNCS, vol. 6472, pp. 324–335. Springer, Heidelberg (2010)
26. Singhoff, F., Legrand, J., Nana, L., Marcé, L.: Cheddar: a flexible real time scheduling framework. ACM SIGAda Ada Letters 24, 1–8 (2004)
27. Soetens, P., Bruyninckx, H.: Realtime hybrid task-based control for robots and machine tools. In: ICRA, Barcelona, Spain (2005)
28. Szyperski, C.: Component Software: Beyond Object-Oriented Programming. Addison-Wesley, Reading (2002)
29. Tamura, Y., Le, P.D., Hitomi, K., Chandrasiri, N.P., Bando, T., Yamashita, A., Asama, H.: Development of pedestrian behavior model taking account of intention. In: IROS, Vila Moura, Portugal (2012)

Reverse Engineering of Middleware
for Verification of Robot Control Architectures

Ali Khalili[1,2], Lorenzo Natale[2], and Armando Tacchella[1]

[1] DIBRIS, Università degli Studi di Genova
Via Opera Pia 13, 16145 Genova, Italy
Ali.Khalili@edu.unige.it, Armando.Tacchella@unige.it
[2] iCub Facility, Istituto Italiano di Tecnologia (IIT)
Via Morego, 30, 16163 Genova, Italy
Lorenzo.Natale@iit.it

Abstract. We consider the problem of automating the verification of distributed control software relying on publish-subscribe middleware. In this scenario, the main challenge is that software correctness depends intrinsically on correct usage of middleware components, but structured models of such components might not be available for analysis, e.g., because they are too large and complex to be described precisely in a cost-effective way. To overcome this problem, we propose to identify abstract models of middleware as finite-state automata, and then to perform verification on the combined middleware and control software models. Both steps are carried out in a computer-assisted way using state-of-the-art techniques in automata-based identification and verification. Our main contribution is to show that the combination of identification and verification is feasible and useful when considering typical issues that arise in the implementation of distributed control software.

1 Introduction

Publish-subscribe middleware such as ROS [15] and YARP [6] are becoming increasingly common in control architectures of modern robots. The main advantage of using middleware is that control modules can communicate seamlessly among each other and with device-specific APIs, possibly across different computing platforms. While operational scenarios for autonomous robots are becoming increasingly complex — see, e.g., the DARPA robotics challenge [13] — the issue of dependability at all levels of a robot's architecture is getting more attention. In particular, if robots must be operated safely, control architectures must be verified against various requirements, which include also software specific properties, like deadlock or race avoidance. However, the task of verifying control software built on top of some middleware cannot be accomplished unless a precise model of the middleware is available, because a seemingly correct control code can easily lead the robot to unwanted states if middleware primitives are misused. An example of such case is when a sender assumes buffered communication to a receiver, but the channel is configured without buffering; if

D. Brugali et al. (Eds.): SIMPAR 2014, LNAI 8810, pp. 315–326, 2014.

the sender expects acknowledgment for every message, but some message is lost, then a deadlock condition may ensue.

Insofar a component of a control architecture is assigned precise semantics, formal correctness verification is made possible, and many control software fallacies can be spotted at design time. However, developing a formal model can be difficult for large and complex middleware like ROS or YARP. A viable solution to this problem is to adopt automata-based *identification* techniques – see, e.g., [16] for a comprehensive list of references. The key idea is that the internal structure of a middleware component can be inferred by analyzing its interactions with an embedding context. Identification algorithms supply the component with suitable input test patterns to populate a "conjecture" automaton by observing the corresponding outputs; then, they check whether the conjecture is behaviorally equivalent to the actual component. When such an abstract model of the original component is obtained, it can be used as a stub to verify software components relying on it. This is where automata-based *verification* enters the scene. Given the inferred models of middleware components, and a model of the control software relying on them, Model Checking [14,4] techniques provide an automated way to check behavioral properties about the composition of the models. In this way, confidence in a correct implementation of the overall control architecture is increased, and problems can be spotted before they cause expensive or even dangerous failures during robot's operation.

To demonstrate the effectiveness of our approach, we considered some relatively simple, yet significant, examples of control code built on top of YARP [6]. Our choice is dictated by several reasons, including a deep knowledge of the platform, and a fairly large installed base due to the adoption of YARP as the standard middleware of the humanoid iCub [12]. Moreover, YARP is a publish-subscribe architecture quite similar to other middleware widely used in the robotics community such as ROS. From the implementation point of view, YARP is a set of libraries written in C++ consisting of more than 150K lines of code. The purpose of YARP is to support modularity by abstracting algorithms and the interface to the hardware and operating systems. YARP abstractions are defined in terms of protocols. One of the main features of YARP is to support inter-process communication using a "port" abstraction. Our case studies focus mostly on the identification of various concrete mechanisms underlying this abstraction, e.g., buffered vs. non-buffered ports, and then to check control code relying on such implementations. Practical identification of different kinds of abstract models of YARP ports is enabled by our tool AIDE (Automata IDentification Engine)[1]. Model checking the composition of control code and middleware is accomplished with the state-of-the-art tool SPIN [8]. The results obtained combining AIDE and SPIN, albeit still preliminary, show that our approach is promising for the identification and verification of control-intensive parts of the code, i.e., those parts where the complexity of the code raises from control flow rather than data manipulation.

---

[1] AIDE, developed in C#, is an open-source software: `http://aide.codeplex.com`

The remainder of this paper is organized as follows. In Section 2, a short summary of background and the related works will be provided. Section 3 introduces and motivates our YARP-based case studies. Section 4 presents our experiments on identification and verification. Finally, some concluding remarks and possible directions of future works are given in Section 5.

2   Background

We define an *interface automaton* (IA) as a quintuple $P = (I, O, Q, q_0, \rightarrow)$ where I is a set of *input actions*, O is a set of *output actions*, Q is a set of states, $q_0 \in Q$ is the *initial state* of the system, $\rightarrow \subset Q \times (I \cup O) \times Q$ is the *transition relation*, and the sets O, I and Q are finite, non-empty and mutually disjoint. Our definition of IA is the same given in [1], which does not take into account the possibility of formalizing hidden actions. Since we wish to infer IAs as models of middleware components, we can neglect such actions without losing generality in our context. The set of all actions $A = I \cup O$ is the *action signature* of the automaton. Given a state $q \in Q$ and an action $a \in A$, we define the *next state function* $\delta : Q \rightarrow 2^Q$ as $\delta(q, a) = \{q' | q \xrightarrow{a} q'\}$, where we write $q \xrightarrow{a} q'$ to denote that $(q, a, q') \in \rightarrow$. An action $a \in A$ is *enabled* in a state $q \in Q$ if there exists some $q' \in Q$ such that $q \xrightarrow{a} q'$, i.e., $|\delta(q, a)| \geq 1$. A state $q \in Q$ wherein all inputs are enabled is *input-enabled*, and so is an automaton wherein all states are input-enabled. An input-enabled IA is also known as *I/O automaton* [11]. Given a state $q \in Q$, the set $out(q) \subseteq Q$ of *observable actions* is the set of all actions $a \in O$ where a is enabled in q. If $out(q) = \emptyset$, then q is called *suspended* or *quiescent*. According to [5], an *execution fragment* of the automaton is a finite alternating sequence of states and actions $u_0, a_0, u_1, \ldots, u_n$ such that $u_i \in Q$, $a_i \in A$ and $u_i \xrightarrow{a_i} u_{i+1}$ for all $0 \leq i < n$.

Automata-Based Inference. Automata-based identification (also, automata learning) can be divided into two wide categories, i.e., passive and active learning. In *passive learning*, there is no control over the observations received to learn the model. In *active learning*, the target system can be experimented with, and experimental results are collected to learn a model. Whenever applicable, active learning is to be preferred because it is computationally more efficient than passive learning – see [9] for details. Furthermore, active learning is not affected by a potential lack of relevant observations because it can always query for them. However, active learning requires that the target system is available for controlled experimentation, i.e., it cannot be performed while the target is executing. The basic abstraction in active learning as introduced by Angluin in [2], is the concept of *Minimally Adequate Teacher* (MAT). In our case, it is assumed that a MAT exists and it can answer two types of questions, namely *output queries* and *equivalence queries*. An output query amounts to ask the MAT about the output over a given input string, whereas equivalence queries amount to compare a *conjecture* about the abstract model of a system with the system itself. The result of equivalence queries is positive if the model and the system are behaviorally equivalent, and it is a *counterexample* in the symmetric difference of the relations computed by the two automata, otherwise. In practice, since the system is unknown, equivalence queries must be approximated by, e.g., model-based testing. Our tool AIDE is a collection of learning algorithms for several abstract models, including IAs. In particular, we use the Mealy machine inference algorithm L_M^+ [16] together with the approach presented in [1] to identify IAs. This model of identification is particularly suited in contexts where the behavior of the system is jointly determined by its internal structure, and by the inputs received from the environment – also called *tester*.

Formal Verification. Automata-based verification — see, e.g., [3] — encompasses a broad set of algorithms and related tools, whose purpose is to verify behavioral properties of systems represented as automata. In particular, we consider algorithms and tools for Model Checking [14,4]. The basic idea behind automata-based verification technique is to exhaustively and automatically check whether a given system model meets a given specification. In this approach, a property is specified usually in terms of some temporal logic, and the system is given as some kind of automaton. In this work, we use SPIN [8], a generic verification system that supports design and verification of asynchronous process systems. In SPIN, the models are specified in a language called PROMELA (PROcess MEta LAnguage), and correctness claims can be specified in the syntax of standard linear temporal logic (LTL). Several optimization techniques, including partial order reduction, state compression and bit-state hashing are developed to improve performance of verification in SPIN. Details on the encoding of IA into SPIN are given in Section 4. Here, we give a short overview on how verification works in SPIN and similar tools. In SPIN, the global behavior of a concurrent system is obtained by computing an asynchronous interleaving product of automata, where each automaton corresponds to a single process. This means that, in principle, SPIN considers every possible interleaving of the atomic actions which every process is composed of. Technically, such product is often referred to as the state space or *reachability graph* of the system. To perform verification, SPIN considers claims specified as temporal formulas. Typical claims include, e.g., safety claims like "some property is always/never true", or liveness claims like "every request will be acknowledged". Claims are converted into Büchi automata, a kind of finite state automata whose acceptance condition is suitable also for infinite words. The (synchronous) product of automata claims and the automaton representing the global state space is again a Büchi automaton. If the language accepted by this automaton is empty, this means that the original claim is not satisfied for the given system. In other case, it contains precisely those behaviors which satisfy the original formula. Actually, the reachability graph is not computed up front because, if n is the number of state variables, the computation would be exponential in n. Rather, the composition of the two automata is performed "on the fly", starting from the initial set of states of the system, and then considering the reachable ones given the process descriptions and the potential interleaving. SPIN terminates either by proving that some (undesirable) behavior is impossible or by providing a counterexample match.

```
1: Initialize buffered ports Q₁ and Q₂
2: Connect Q₁ to Q₁'
3: while true do
4:     for i = 1 to N do
5:         Write message m to Q₁
6:     end for
7:     Read message from Q₂
8: end while
```

```
1: Initialize buffered ports Q₁' and Q₂'
2: Set the reading mode of Q₁' as strict
3: Connect Q₂' to Q₂
4: while true do
5:     for i = 1 to N do
6:         Read message m from Q₁'
7:     end for
8:     Create a message and write it to Q₂'
9: end while
```

Fig. 1. Case study 1: An example code *Planner* (left) and *Controller* (right)

3 Case Studies

Our motivation for this work is to to enable verification techniques for robot control software which uses middleware modules. In this section, we introduce two case studies. We focus on variations of the well-known producer-consumer paradigm. The reason is that similar situations are commonly found in robotic applications where loosely coupled modules are interconnected through publish-subscribe middleware and run concurrently.

Case Study 1. We consider two software components that exchange messages with loose synchronization. A practical example is a *Planner* (P1) that generates a set of N via points for a *Controller* (P2). The latter takes responsibility to execute each requests, in a variable amount of time. The *Planner* does not wait for execution of the individual commands but rather sends all N messages to the *Controller* and then waits for a synchronization packet that signals the termination of the whole sequence. In a publish-subscribe architecture this can be achieved using two channels. The *Planner* uses the first channel (between Q_1 and Q_1') to send via points to the *Controller*, then waits for a message that acknowledges execution of the sequence from the *Controller* through the second channel (between Q_2 and Q_2'). Since there is no synchronization, the buffering policy in the connections can affect the correct behavior of the system. In this application, the programmer assumes that connections are configured to queue at least N messages. This may or may be not true in YARP where, by default, connections are configured to *drop* messages to reduce communication latencies[2]. The programmer therefore must override the default configuration of the connections to ensure that messages are queued and never dropped. Pseudo code for this scenario is given in Figure 1. Given this code, we can see that, if messages are dropped in the connections, a deadlock occurs. In practice, the robot may not only fail to follow the desired trajectory, but due to interpolation in the *Controller*, it may even end up in unsafe configurations.

Case Study 2. In publish-subscribe architectures, sensory information and commands travel on distinct channels. It is therefore common for components to receive information from multiple sources and synchronize their activities on

---

[2] This policy may seem counter-intuitive but it is fundamental for closed-loop control.

```
1: P1
2: Initialize buffered ports Q₁
3: Connect Q₁ to Q′₁
4: for i = 1 to N₁ do
5:     //Do the job
6:     Send message m to Q₁
7: end for
1: P2
2: Initialize buffered ports Q₂
3: Connect Q₂ to Q′₂
4: for i = 1 to N₂ do
5:     //Do the job
6:     Send message m to Q₂
7: end for
```

```
1: P3
2: Initialize buffered ports Q′₁ and Q′₂
3: Set the reading mode of Q′₁ and Q′₂ as strict
4: for i = 1 to N₃ do
5:     Read message m₁ to Q′₁
6:     Read message m₂ to Q′₂
7:     //Do the job
8: end for
```

Fig. 2. Case study 2: An example of two producers (P_1 and P_2) and one consumer (P_3) which are using YARP buffered port for their communication

data received from such connections. In this scenario, the consumer receives data from two producers. A practical example is a grasping application. Here the *Tracker* ($P1$) identifies the 3D position of the object in the work space (for example using stereo vision in the form of (x, y, z)). This information reaches the *Controller* ($P2$) through the connection between Q_1 and Q'_1 which in turn computes the torque commands to the motors. Another component ($P3$) reads sensory data from a Force/Torque sensor placed in the kinematic chain, and publishes it on a separate channel. The *Controller* relies on this information to detect collisions and control the force exerted at the end-effector (connection between Q_2 and Q'_2). The programmer of the *Controller* must decide how to read data from both connections. The crucial point is that these connections can become inactive. These might happen when no valid target is detected by the *Tracker*, or in situation where the *Tracker* was closed by the user or died unexpectedly. By default, YARP defines that readers wait for data on a port (blocking behavior). This allows tight synchronization and reduces latencies. An inexperienced programmer may read data from both channels using the default mode introducing an unexpected deadlock when *Tracker* does not produce data. The pseudo-code of this scenario is presented in Figure 2. The connection between $P1$ and $P2$ to $P3$ is implemented using buffered ports with strict mode. To simulate the behavior where one of the producers stops sending data we added a counter N_i to the main loop of each process. We verify the effects of different relative values of N_i on the overall behavior.

In both the case studies describe above, we consider a combination of identification and verification to be detailed in Section 4. However, we would like to point out that identification alone is often useful to strengthen middleware, by helping the discovery of corner bugs that are elusive in common usage patterns. Out of many identification experiments that we conducted with YARP in our preliminary work, we show in Figure 3 the result of one which turned out as a report in the YARP bug-tracking system. In this example, we consider applying an interrupt method on a port. Interrupting a port is supposed to unblock any blocked thread waiting for the port. The model in Figure 3 is the one identified

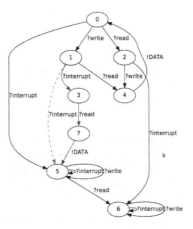

Fig. 3. The identified model of a port with one reader, one writer, and one thread which interrupts the write port. The expected model would feature the dotted transition — from state 1 into state 5 — but the actual model identified by AIDE and implemented in YARP has the solid ones instead. Transitions labeled with "?" and "!" represent input and output actions, respectively.

by AIDE for one port reader, one port writer, and a thread which interrupts the writing port. The model shows that interrupting a write port has been implemented so that it unblocks future writes, but it waits for completion of the current one, which was not the expected behavior. Indeed, this specific behavior was not documented, and never occurred in YARP practical applications, so it went unnoticed so far.

4   Experiments

Considering YARP port components as the system under learning (SUL) to be modeled as IA, we use AIDE to identify abstract models with different parameters. The configuration of components in the inference procedure is presented in Figure 4. As we mentioned in Section 2, the basic inference algorithm is L_M^+ [16], and it is implemented in the module "MM Learning Algorithm" where "MM" stands for "Mealy Machine". The algorithm relies on a software component, called "MM Oracle" in Figure 4, whose task is to approximate the behavior of a MAT on a real system. Together, these two modules are the core of a Mealy machine inference program — "MM Learner" in Figure 4. Since we wish to identify YARP models as IAs, we connect a further component — "IA Translator" in Figure 4 — which implements the approach presented in [1] to identify IAs on top of a Mealy machine learning algorithm. All these modules are part of AIDE, and they collectively perform the task of "IA learner". The "System Wrapper" component (in C++) bridges between the abstract alphabet on the learner side, and the concrete alphabet of the SUL. It manages different threads,

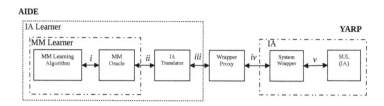

Fig. 4. Components of the learning procedure. The connections are (i) queries asked to the MAT (MM Oracle), (ii) bi-directional translation of interface automata and Mealy machines, (iii) actions and events of the system, (iv) the TCP connection to remote system-wrapper, (v) the abstraction/concretization made by the system wrapper.

handles the method calls in each thread, and the abstraction of messages — "*bottles*" in YARP terminology. To connect the wrapper to AIDE, we built a "Wrapper Proxy" which uses TCP/IP connections to facilitate identifying systems remotely, possibly across different computing architectures.

4.1   Identification of Ports in YARP

Configuration of Ports. Considering a port connection, we examine different parameters which affect its behavior. In the case of a (standard) YARP port in a scenario with one sender and one receiver, the type of communication is of a "send/reply" type, wherein the sender and the receiver are tightly coupled. In the case of buffered ports, the sender and the receiver enjoy more decoupling, in the sense that YARP takes care of the lifetime of the objects being transmitted through the port and it makes a pool of them, growing upon need. By default, a buffered port keeps the most recent message only. Therefore, messages that come in between two successive calls to read, might be dropped. If the so called "strict" mode is enabled, YARP will keep all received messages — like a FIFO buffer. Notice that, in this mode, the state space of the abstract automaton would be infinite. Therefore, to learn this model with AIDE, we limit the system to send no more than N packets, i.e., we assume that the buffer will not exceed the maximum size of N messages. In addition to a standard "Read" method which exists in normal ports, a *non-blocking read* feature is also available in buffered ports. Identification results for ports in various configurations are presented in Table 1 (top)[3]. We have also extended the alphabet of buffered ports to include non-blocking reading from the port for both strict and non-strict mode of reading — these two experiments are presented with an "*" in Table 1. The reported measures include number of states $|Q|$ and transitions $|T|$ of the identified model, number of output ("#MM") and equivalence ("#EQ") queries in the learning algorithm, number of experiments on the SUL, and total time spent on learning. The behavior of a normal port is similar to a non-strict buffered port. In

---

[3] All the experiments in this Section have been carried out on a Sony Vaio laptop with Core2Duo 2.26GHz CPU and 4GB of RAM on Ubuntu 12.04.

Table 1. The result of inference for different models in YARP port component (top), and inference for different maximum size of buffer (N) in YARP buffered port (bottom). In the topmost table, for buffered ports, we consider $N = 3$.

Model	$\|Q\|$	$\|T\|$	#MM	#EQ	#Experiments	Time (s×1000)
port	4	5	18	1	33	0.6
buffered port (non-strict)	4	6	35	2	50	1.0
buffered port (strict)	8	11	132	4	180	2.0
buffered port (non-strict)*	4	8	63	2	114	2.5
buffered port (strict)*	8	16	224	4	323	12.0

Size	$\|Q\|$	$\|T\|$	#MM	#EQ	#Experiments	Time (s×1000)
1	4	5	18	1	32	1.0
2	6	8	54	3	86	2.1
3	8	11	132	4	180	2.0
4	10	14	225	6	260	10.0
5	12	17	504	7	396	17.0
6	14	20	987	8	531	31.0

normal ports, both reading from port and writing to it are blocking, whereas in non-strict buffered port, writing is not a blocking primitive: if the buffer is not empty, the second write will overwrite the previous message. In buffered ports with strict mode enabled, writing to the port is non-blocking, but the difference compared to non-strict mode is that the buffer does not drop older packets and it acts as a first-in-first-out buffer. In this case, the state space of the model would be infinite, and thus the buffer should be limited to a maximum size for finite state identification to work. These behavioral differences account for the different number of states and transitions in the identified models, as reported in Table 1. We have also considered the effects of increasing the maximum buffer size (N) in buffered ports when the reading mode is set to be strict. These results are shown in Table 1 (bottom). For $N = 1$, the observed model is the same as normal ports, and by increasing the size, the size of the model grows gradually. Notice that, if $e(N)$ denotes the number of experiments as a function of buffer size N, then we see that $e(N)$ grows more than proportionally with n. The CPU time spent for identification grows even faster due to some overheads in our current implementation. In particular, the capability of resetting the SUL is required by the identification algorithm. In our case, resetting the SUL includes releasing all the resources of the system, i.e., ports and threads working with them, and initializing the system again. This operation is performed in the system wrapper, and, in all our experiments, more than 95% of the total identification time is spent to reset the SUL. We expect that working on this bottleneck should enable us to experiment with larger buffer sizes, and also to infer a more accurate growth estimate for $e(n)$. Another issue which might affect the efficiency is the TCP/IP connection through the Wrapper Proxy, whereas calling YARP functions directly in AIDE would slightly decrease the identification time.

Technical Remarks. Since the inferred models are deterministic, identical queries should produce the same answer. Therefore, we can cache the queries to avoid expensive repetitions. This is done by storing a tree of execution traces which can be exploited to avoid an experiment on a system whenever the corresponding query is a prefix of another one which has been already executed. In our implementation, the cache query is used as a filter between the MAT and the SUL, which makes it transparent from the MAT's point of view. Our reports above include only the actual number of queries on the system. Furthermore, in all of our experiments, less than 0.5% of the identification time was spent in the learning algorithm. The most time-consuming parts are network communication, system reset, and thread management. As we have mentioned above, one reason for such inefficiencies is that the wrapper uses several delays to make sure it is obtaining the correct result, since obtaining even one wrong observation in the output or equivalence queries would result in failing to learn a correct model.

4.2   Verification

The conversion of IAs inferred by AIDE into a PROMELA model is accomplished as follows. Every model is translated into one process type which communicates with two unbuffered channels — to simulate synchronous communication. These are *InChannel* and *OutChannel*, and their task is to receive input actions from environment, and emit output events correspondingly. To make the composition flexible, the input and output channels are the parameters of the process type. At any time, the next state is determined by the received input action (or the emitted event) and all the transitions are performed as atomic actions. In addition to PROMELA, AIDE is able to export inferred automata in DOT graph format, C++ and the input language of other model checkers. The model of programs which use the ports are translated into automata as well. Here, the translation is manual, but in principle, it could be done in an automated fashion. Finally, the composition of the inferred model with the code model is done automatically by SPIN.

Case Study 1. The results of verification, including the number of generated states by the model checker, the consumed memory, time and result of verification, are reported in Table 2 (top). Considering the identified model of a buffered port with non-strict mode of reading, SPIN finds a deadlock in the model after exploring 39 states, although the whole state space has about 16K states. In fact the problem arises if the client sends packets too quickly through a YARP port configured for non-strict mode. In this case, there is a concrete chance that the server misses some of the packets, and a deadlock occurs. For strict mode, we consider a specific size of buffer N, namely $N = 1$ and $N = 6$.

Case Study 2. As before, we perform verification for buffered port with strict mode of reading. The results are presented in Table 2 (bottom). We examined different values for N_1, N_2 and N_3 and the size of buffer. As shown in the Table, when $N1 = N2 = N3$ all processes finish successfully. But if either $N1$ or $N2$

Table 2. Results of SPIN for the first case study (top) and second case study (bottom). In the topmost table, for buffered port, non-strict mode of reading and strict mode of reading for ($N = 1$ and $N = 6$). In the bottommost table, different N_i's and size of buffer. The last row is the result of model checking with non-blocking read from Q'_1.

Model	#States	Memory(MB)	Time(s)	Conclusion
Buffered Port (non-strict)	38	128	0.01	deadlock
Buffered Port (strict, $N = 1$)	15K	129	0.04	OK
Buffered Port (strict, $N = 6$)	42K	132	0.09	OK

N_1	N_2	N_3	$Size$	#States	Time(s)	Memory(MB)	Conclusion
100	100	100	1	8K	0.02	129	OK
90	100	100	1	790	0.01	128	deadlock
100	100	100	6	128K	0.33	140	OK
90	100	100	6	1930	0.02	128	deadlock
200	200	200	6	519K	3.29	176	OK
180	200	200	6	3820	0.04	129	deadlock
90*	100	100	6	19M	91.00	1300	OK

are less than $N3$, P_3 will be stuck as expected. Indeed, in situations where P_1 may finish sooner than P_3, the solution would be to change reading from Q'_1 (line 5 in Figure 2) to a non-blocking read. Using the corresponding model and the maximum buffer size of 6, SPIN can prove the non-existence of deadlock in 91 CPU seconds — last row of Table 2 (bottom).

5 Conclusion

In this paper, we show how to exploit automata-based inference and verification techniques to identify port components of YARP middleware, and to verify control software build on top of them. Since YARP is the middleware of choice in the humanoid iCub, AIDE can enable the adoption of precise techniques for testing and verification of relevant components in iCub's control architecture.

To the best of our knowledge, this is the first time that a combination of identification and verification techniques is applied successfully in robotics. Similar contributions appeared in a series of works by Doron Peled and others — see, e.g., [7] for the most recent work — with hardware verification as the main target. However, our approach is more general since it decouples identification techniques from verification techniques, and it enables the combination of different flavors of such techniques.

Considering the current limitations of our work, we see (non)determinism and scalability as the two main issues. As for nondeterminism, it is well known that middleware can respond in different ways according to external events which are never completely under control. The algorithms that we have considered here assume that the middleware is behaving deterministically, which might turn out to be an unrealistic assumption. However, in a recent contribution [10], we have shown how to deal with nondeterminism when learning Mealy machines, and we expect to be able to extend this result also to IAs. Scaling to more complex components is a challenge for our future research agenda. In spite of harsh computational-complexity results, both identification and verification tools have a record of success stories in dealing with industrial-sized systems. Furthermore, AIDE already enables developers to check their code against common errors such as, e.g., incorrect port flagging, and it has also been useful in supplying YARP creators with corner bugs that helped them to improve some basic functionality of platform. We expect that improving the bottlenecks due to resetting the system, i.e., managing ports and related threads in the system wrapper, will improve the capacity of our techniques.

References

1. Aarts, F., Vaandrager, F.: Learning I/O automata. In: Gastin, P., Laroussinie, F. (eds.) CONCUR 2010. LNCS, vol. 6269, pp. 71–85. Springer, Heidelberg (2010)
2. Angluin, D.: Learning regular sets from queries and counterexamples. Information and Computation 75(2), 87–106 (1987)
3. Baier, C., Katoen, J.: Principles of model checking. MIT Press, Cambridge (2008)
4. Clarke, E., Emerson, E., Sistla, A.: Automatic verification of finite-state concurrent systems using temporal logic specifications. ACM Transactions on Programming Languages and Systems (TOPLAS) 8(2), 263 (1986)
5. De Alfaro, L., Henzinger, T.: Interface automata. ACM SIGSOFT Software Engineering Notes 26(5), 109–120 (2001)
6. Fitzpatrick, P., Metta, G., Natale, L.: Towards long-lived robot genes. Robotics and Autonomous Systems 56(1), 29–45 (2008)
7. Groce, A., Peled, D., Yannakakis, M.: Adaptive model checking. Logic Journal of IGPL 14(5), 729–744 (2006)
8. Holzmann, G.J.: The SPIN model checker: Primer and reference manual, vol. 1003. Addison-Wesley, Reading (2004)
9. Kearns, M., Vazirani, U.: An introduction to computational learning theory. MIT Press (1994)
10. Khalili, A., Tacchella, A.: Learning nondeterministic mealy machines. In: Proceedings of the 12th International Conference on Grammatical Inference (ICGI) (to appear, 2014)
11. Lynch, N.A., Tuttle, M.R.: Hierarchical correctness proofs for distributed algorithms. In: Proceedings of the Sixth Annual ACM Symposium on Principles of Distributed Computing, pp. 137–151. ACM (1987)
12. Metta, G., Natale, L., Nori, F., Sandini, G., Vernon, D., Fadiga, L., von Hofsten, C., Rosander, K., Lopes, M., Santos-Victor, J., et al.: The iCub Humanoid Robot: An Open-Systems Platform for Research in Cognitive Development. Neural Networks: The Official Journal of the International Neural Network Society (2010)
13. Pratt, G., Manzo, J.: The DARPA Robotics Challenge [Competitions]. IEEE Robotics & Automation Magazine 20(2), 10–12 (2013)
14. Queille, J., Sifakis, J.: Specification and verification of concurrent systems in CESAR. In: Dezani-Ciancaglini, M., Montanari, U. (eds.) Programming 1982. LNCS, vol. 137, pp. 337–351. Springer, Heidelberg (1982)
15. Quigley, M., Conley, K., Gerkey, B., Faust, J., Foote, T., Leibs, J., Wheeler, R., Ng, A.Y.: ROS: an open-source Robot Operating System. In: ICRA Workshop on Open Source Software, vol. 3 (2009)
16. Shahbaz, M.: Reverse Engineering Enhanced State Models of Black Box Software Components to Support Integration Testing. Ph.D. thesis, Institut Polytechnique de Grenoble, Grenoble, France (2008)

An Extensible Software Architecture
for Composing Motion and Task Planners

Zakary Littlefield*, Athanasios Krontiris, Andrew Kimmel, Andrew Dobson,
Rahul Shome, and Kostas E. Bekris

Computer Science Department, Rutgers University, Piscataway, NJ 08554, USA
kostas.bekris@cs.rutgers.edu

Abstract. This paper describes a software infrastructure for developing and composing task and motion planners. The functionality of motion planners is well defined and they provide a basic primitive on top of which it is possible to develop planners for addressing higher level tasks. It is more challenging, however, to identify a common interface for task planners, given the variety of challenges that they can be used for. The proposed software platform follows a hierarchical, object-oriented structure and identifies key abstractions that help in integrating new task planners with popular sampling-based motion planners. Examples of use cases that can be implemented within this common software framework include robotics applications such as planning among dynamic obstacles, object manipulation and rearrangement, as well as decentralized motion coordination. The described platform has been used to plan for a Baxter robot rearranging similar objects in an environment in an efficient way.

1 Introduction and Related Work

The basic motion planning problem for kinematic systems is a traditional, well studied problem in robotics, for which a variety of solutions have been proposed, many of them based on sampling-based algorithms [1]. Such algorithms have also been extended in the context of planning with significant dynamics, planning for high-dimensional challenges involving kinematic chains, or planning under uncertainty. The maturity of the motion planning field also led to the development of software platforms that facilitate the use of such state-of-the-art solutions in different application domains [2, 3, 4, 5].

One of the most interesting challenges, however, relates to integrating such motion planners with task planning, i.e., the high-level reasoning for completing tasks that requires symbolic, combinatorial or discrete planning. Integrating task and motion planning is receiving increasing attention in the related literature recently [6, 7, 8, 9]. The architecture proposed in this paper focuses on providing a reusable, extensible software platform for integrating task with motion planners. The focus is mostly on providing the communication primitives for composing motion planning primitives.

Some examples that relate to this objective include the following:

- *Manipulation:* Multi-modal motion planning [10, 11] and rearrangement of obstacles in the environment [12].

* Zakary Littlefield's work was supported by a NASA Space Technology Research Fellowship. Any conclusions expressed here are of the authors and do not reflect the sponsors' views.

D. Brugali et al. (Eds.): SIMPAR 2014, LNAI 8810, pp. 327–339, 2014.

- *State × Time Planning:* Planning among dynamic obstacles [13]; Sensor-based task planning [14, 15]; Exploration and coverage of an environment [16].
- *Multi-agent Challenges:* Motion coordination [17, 18]; Adversarial challenges, such as pursuit-evasion [19].
- *Task Sequencing:* Multi-goal challenges, including Traveling Salesman Problems and switching goals [20].

There are also many challenges that might involve multiple aspects of the above tasks. For instance, a scenario where multiple manipulators are operating in the same workspace and need to coordinate in order to relocate a large object may require many levels of reasoning. Rather than having users write a single, highly complex task planner to achieve this, it is desirable to allow the composition of task planners instead out of individual modules, allowing for reuse of existing task planning capabilities.

The goal of the proposed infrastructure is to provide a straightforward framework for integrating task and motion planners so that they can be used across multiple application domains. In such a framework, motion planners can be freely exchanged without affecting task-level reasoning, and task planners can be composed in a general, hierarchical manner to solve complex challenges.

While having such a unified structure for task planning is desirable, it is also inherently challenging, primarily because task planning is application specific and there is such a wide variety of application domains. Creating an interface for task planning which can be used for all conceivable applications is infeasible; however, composing task planners in a hierarchical fashion allows for a simple, generalizable interface. This work utilizes abstractions referred to as task specifications and queries to facilitate this interface.

The proposed software infrastructure, referred to as PRACSYS is an extension of a previous effort by the authors [21]. In the previous version, the focus was on the introduction of controllers and planners. In this version, integrating planners to solve task planning challenges is the main objective. This has distinctive characteristics in comparison to related software efforts, while at the same time it can be integrated with many of them. PRACSYS offers a robust infrastructure for task planning, as well as a control framework unavailable in other motion planning platforms, such as the Open Motion Planning Library (OMPL) [2] and MoveIt! [5]. Other packages such as Gazebo [22] offer simulation capabilities, but they do not offer the planning capabilities of PRACSYS. The Reflexxes motion library [23] also focuses on control, generating trajectories in real-time while integrating sensing information, but does not focus on longer-horizon planning components. PRACSYS also supports planning over controllers, due to its unique architecture, which is not afforded by the aforementioned packages.

2   General Architecture of PRACSYS

PRACSYS consists of several different components, which operate as different processes and are responsible for different aspects of the overall infrastructure. The Robot Operating System (ROS) is the middle-ware that allows for the different components to communicate with each other through message passing, loads the necessary input parameters and provides compatibility with other software packages [24]. The overall architecture of PRACSYS is shown in Figure 1.

The simulation node performs the simulation of the physical world, including obstacles, and receives sensing data. It is able to detect whether undesirable collisions occur for different states of the simulated world. Furthermore, it provides a hierarchical tree of control systems, which simulate both the physical robots and other moving systems in the world as well as controllers that operate over them. This hierarchy supports the construction and composition of low-level controllers to perform control, as detailed in the authors' previous work [21]. The purpose of controllers is to perform reactive control given access to the state of the systems under them in the hierarchy and potential access to sensing data. At the lower level of the simulation hierarchy, there are always physical "plants", i.e., robots that receive controls and update their state accordingly. In situations that the software infrastructure is not used to directly plan for a physical system, the simulation module takes the role of the ground-truth model of the world. Through message passing, this module can transmit the ground-truth state of the simulated world to the other models of PRACSYS, such as the sensing and the planning nodes.

The planning node is responsible for performing the high-level logic of task and motion planning, which is discussed in detail in this paper. The planning node uses an internal representation of the world called a "world model", which internally performs simulation in order to achieve longer-horizon planning, in contrast to the short-horizon controllers of the simulation node. It receives the true state of the world from either a ground

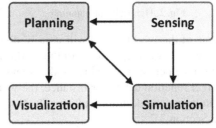

Fig. 1. The major inter-node interactions in PRACSYS

truth simulation node or from the sensing node. The sensing node can either simulate a sensor given information from the simulation node or it can directly communicate with a real world sensor to generate the corresponding data.

The communication in PRACSYS facilitates the interactions between the nodes. The simulation node is often responsible for publishing ground truth information for planning and sensing purposes, as well as for visualizing the world. The planning node sends computed trajectories and planning structures to visualization, and forwards plans to simulation for execution. The visualization node provides a user interface to validate results and allows for interactive applications. PRACSYS can run with or without a visualization node. PRACSYS also contains a set of core functions which resides in a *utilities* package, which is used by all of the nodes.

3 Integration of Motion and Task Planners

The planning node is designed to easily compose planners in a hierarchical fashion. At the top of the hierarchy lies the *planning application*, which can access *task planners*. Task planners address specific high-level tasks and can internally call other task planners. *Motion planners* exist at the lowest level of the hierarchy and have a specific interface. Both task and motion planners are extensions of abstract planners and both have access to *planning modules*, which correspond to useful primitives, such as sampling of states and controls, as well as steering functions. Planners and modules can access the *world model*, which encapsulates the control systems operating in the world.

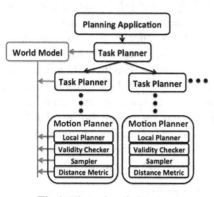

Fig. 2. Hierarchy of planning

The interactions between the different classes of the `planning` node are illustrated in Figure 2. The arrows in the figure imply that the class from where the arrow originates has access to and calls functions of the class the arrow points towards. Task planners can be composed to perform more complex tasks; for instance, a navigation task and manipulation task can be used by a higher-level task planner to perform a retrieval task using a mobile manipulator. The leaves of the planning hierarchy are always motion planners, which actually select the controls that the underlying control systems of the world model will use. To do so, they make use of the planning modules, which provide them access to the world model, which is detailed in Section 3.1. The interface between planning modules and task planners with the world model are via direct function calls. For instance, the world model can be queried to check if a state results in an undesirable collision. It also provides access to sensing, which is described in Section 3.2.

The planners interface one with another through the use of *task specifications* and *queries*, both detailed in Section 3.3. Specifications are used to inform lower-level planners what are the parameters of the task to be solved. Two planners can be stacked one on top of the other, only if the lower level one addresses task specifications requested by the higher level one. For example, motion planning specifications are of a specific type and inform a motion planner what low-level modules to use when building the planning data structure (e.g., a roadmap or a tree), and identify a stopping criterion. Queries are similarly passed from higher-level to lower-level planners. The latter are responsible to fill the query with the requested information and return it to the higher-level planner. For example, a motion planning query contains a start state-goal state pair, and the motion planner is responsible for returning the feasible trajectory and plan which brings the system from the start to the goal.

3.1   World Model and Simulator

In order to properly perform planning, the evolution of the environment and the control systems in it need to be modeled. This is encompassed by the *world model* abstraction. The *world model* includes an internal simulator, which can be structured to model the controllers and underlying dynamics of agents. The simulators employed by the world model are the same found in the `simulation` node. This internal simulator provides the capability of collision checking and potentially simulating complex physical phenomena through the use of the Bullet physics engine [25].

The *world model* abstraction allows for the definition of a *state space* and a *control space* used by the planning process. The *state space* represents the necessary information in order to fully specify a snapshot of the world in terms of the relevant kinematic and dynamic parameters of the involved moving or movable systems. The *control space* provides the input to the simulator that allows it to modify the state over time. These abstractions provide the ability to store states and controls so that the world model can be placed into a desired configuration from a planner or a planning module.

These definitions also allow diverse options for task planners to create different *planning contexts* for the motion planners to plan in. A *planning context* consists of different divisions of the underlying simulator's *state* and *control space*, and is comprised of three subspaces: a *planning space*, *object space*, and *inactive space* as shown in Figure 3. The *planning space* is the subset of a space that a motion planner would plan over, such as the state space of a robot manipulator. The *object space* consists of all systems that are not directly "controlled" by the planner, but still are considered for collisions and may move during the simulation. A task planner can change the state of such systems

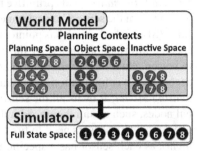

Fig. 3. An example of different planning contexts that can be created. Each planning context consists of a *planning space*, *object space*, and an *inactive space*. Each of these spaces has a different meaning to the task planners in PRACSYS.

(e.g., when an object is grasped and moves according to the motions of a manipulator) and inform the *world model*, or they can have their own controllers that handle their evolution over time (e.g., in the case of dynamic obstacles). Finally, the *inactive space* consists of all the systems that may be present in the simulation but are not considered by the planning process. These may be used by other motion planners in the task planning hierarchy.

In most situations, these spaces are direct subsets of the full state space. Nevertheless, the true planning space may be difficult for motion planners to directly work with. Consider the case of physically simulated systems, where a car-like robot is composed of a chassis and four wheels. In the physics engine, 60 DOFs will be needed to keep track of the parameters of the involved 5 rigid bodies. Nevertheless, most planners would operate over a lower-dimensional projection of that planning space. In these situations, an *embedded space* can be used. This space transforms a higher dimensional space into a lower dimensional given a proper mapping function.

3.2 Integration of Sensing with Planning

Sensing is an important aspect of the PRACSYS framework, and for many applications it plays a vital role in determining the planning contexts, e.g., when a robot uses a sensor to detect the other moving systems in the scene. The sensing framework is comprised of a set of extendable primitives, through which a wide variety of sensing contexts is supported. An example of sensing primitives, along with an example interaction with the simulation node, is shown in Figure 4. The primitives are as follows:

- *Sensors:* They perceive the state of the world. Sensors can either be simulated, such as detecting the configurations or geometries of objects in the simulation, or they can represent actual physical sensors, such as a RGB-D camera generating point cloud data. This is possible through the use of the ROS architecture, since a "sensor" class can simply use external communication through ROS topics and services to query its physical counterparts. A sensor has an individual update frequency, which represents how often it measures the world, and consequently updating its representation.
- *Sensing Information:* This primitive represents how a controller uses the information derived from the sensors' measurements. A controller may have one or more Sensing Infos (SI), each of which has pointers to individual sensors, which it uses to construct specific information for use by the controller. For example, a controller might need to reason about the proximity of other objects in the world, and thus would need to access both a configuration sensor and a geometry sensor to build such information.
- *Sensing Model:* It owns all the sensors and manages the interactions between external nodes, such as simulation, with the other sensing primitives. It is responsible for checking when sensors need to fire (which corresponds to sensors taking a measurement), as each sensor has a specific firing frequency, as well as checking how often each SI calculates new information.

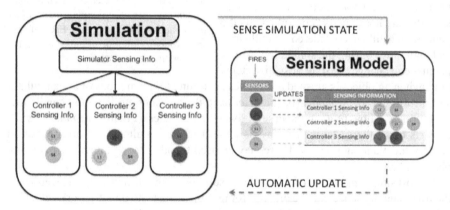

Fig. 4. An example sensing framework which interacts with the simulation node. Each controller in the simulation has sensing information, with the simulator owning a concatenation of all controller's sensing information. The simulation informs the sensing model that it has a new simulation state, with which the model fires any sensors that are ready to measure. The simulation is automatically updated by any new sensor readings in the corresponding sensing infos.

Sensing is seamlessly integrated into planning through the use of the world model, which owns a simulation tree and thus inherently can update SIs after calling the sensing model. Planning contexts, which determine which parts of the simulation tree are active, also determine which SIs are actively updating. Since the sensing model must be informed that it is time to sense, task planners have full control over the information that sensing reasons over, as well as how to use the information obtained from sensing.

3.3   Queries and Specifications

This section describes the task specifications and queries that are used as the interface between task planners and motion planners. Specifications describe the problem that a planner lower in the hierarchy needs to solve. Queries give the initial and final conditions of the problem and will be returned with the answer constructed by the planner below. Figure 5 depicts these exchanges between the planners through appropriate interface.

The higher level planner, a task planner, builds a problem specification for the lower level planner, which can be either a task or a motion planner. The problem specification contains information that a planner needs in order to set up and solve a problem, which generally allows some preprocessing to occur. The information that is given in the specification by the higher level planner has to match with the information that is expected by the lower level planner. The problem specification may define different modules, such as local planners, validity checkers, samplers, distance metrics and/or stopping criteria. These modules are mandatory when the planner below is a motion planner and the corresponding problem specification is called a motion planning specification. Depending upon the application, a motion planner can receive additional information like seed states for the search structure it maintains, commonly a tree or a graph in the case of sampling-based motion planning.

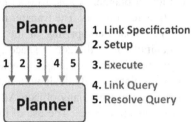

Fig. 5. The interface between planners in the planner hierarchy. First, a planner must receive a planning specification from its parent planner (1). Then, the planner can setup its internal data structures using that specification (2). Finally, after allowing the planner execution time (3), queries can be linked and resolved (4,5).

Once a problem has been already set up according to the problem specification, a query is the request made to a planner to solve a specific instance of that problem. The query is the last interface between the planners in the different levels. A typical query includes the initial and the final configuration for the problem instance. If the planner below is also a task planner, then the query passed to this task planner might be used to construct a new query for underlying planners. In the case of a motion planning query, the query contains the initial state of the system and the goal state(s) that the system has to reach. It then returns the path (sequence of states) and the plan (sequence of controls) that will bring the system to the goal. Similar to problem specifications, the information contained in the query has to correspond to what the lower level planner expects.

4   Use-Cases

4.1   Rearrangement Using Baxter

One important property of this framework is the ability to stack planners in order to reuse them (both task and motion planners). The rearrangement manipulation framework, uses a stack of two task planners and two motion planners (Figure 7). In this problem a robotic arm is used to rearrange geometrically similar and interchangeable objects. The following bottom-up description showcases the reusability of the components.

The problem of moving a manipulator can be solved using a motion planner (e.g. PRM*). A typical motion planner builds a data structure (e.g., a graph) and then computes a path on this data structure to connect the start to the goal configuration. The motion planner is able to plan either for transit or transfer motions. The transfer motion planner plans in a space comprising of the state space of the manipulator as the active space and the object it is grasping as the object space, whereas the transit motion planner only deals with the manipulator, which is not grasping any object. All other objects form the inactive space. The use of the two motion planners is shown in Figure 7. The framework can specify the different state spaces by using the planning context, explained earlier in the paper (Fig. 3). The calls to the two motion planners differ because

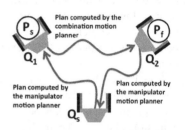

Fig. 6. Each motion of the manipulator (blue arrows) correspond to a plan computed by a motion planner. The compilation of these individual steps result to move an object to a different pose.

of the different planning modules that are defined in the corresponding specifications. A manipulation task planner can utilize these motion planners in order to solve a higher level task, which is to use a manipulator to move an object from an initial pose to a final pose. Nevertheless, in order to achieve this task, the planner needs to solve the transit to the first pose, transfer to the second pose with the object in hand and transit back to a safe position (Fig. 6). The problem specification for this planner will have information about the modules that can be used, the stopping criteria for the algorithm, extra information that the manipulator needs to be able to grasp the objects, but most importantly the different planning contexts that the planner needs for the completion of the task. The query for the manipulation planner will request for a path and a plan that will move an object from an initial pose to a target pose. The manipulation task planner given the information from its input problem specification can build the problem specifications for the motion planners.

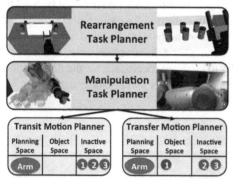

Fig. 7. The hierarchy of planners used in the rearrangement problem

The high level task is the rearrangement of multiple objects using the manipulator. The manipulator task planner resides under the rearrangement task planner (Figure 7). After setting up the problem specification of the manipulation task planner, the rearrangement task planner can request from the manipulation task planner the computed plan for moving the object from one pose to another. The query comprises of the initial pose of an object as the start state and the final pose of that

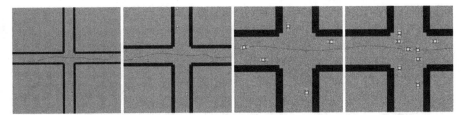

Fig. 8. Snapshots of the dynamic obstacle use case executing the plan found by the motion planner. The problem is to move from the leftmost lane and pass the car in front of it. The screen shots are progressively zoomed in toward the intersection where many cars are entering at the same time. The path of the selected car is shown in the image.

object as the goal state of the problem. The rearrangement task planner reasons about moving objects between different poses in order to solve the rearrangement problem. This higher level task planner combines all the plans that will rearrange the objects from the initial to the final arrangement. The final plan can be transmitted using ROS messages to a real system, such as Baxter, in order to execute it.

4.2 Planning among Dynamic Obstacles

One of the main uses for the world model abstraction is using controllers in the planning loop. In this use case, the behavior of dynamic obstacles is defined through the use of a controller. Then, the goal is to find a motion plan for a simple car-like system among these moving obstacles. Here, a simple kinematic model is used to simulate cars moving in straight lines, but can be modeled more accurately given more complex controllers.

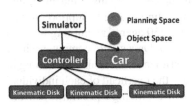

Fig. 9. The world model structure for this example. The car's state space is the only part considered for the planning space, while all of the dynamic obstacles are considered objects that the controller handles, but the motion planner doesn't need to know about.

Figure 9 details the organization of the world model into its planning space and object space. Since the motion planner doesn't need to explicitly model the movement of the moving obstacles, they can be considered for collisions only, and the controller will control the evolution of their states. There is no need to include an inactive space for this task because there is only one planning context that needs to be considered, and the task is a simple motion planning problem. The only requirement for this planning context is that the state of these obstacles is stored during the motion planner's execution. This is done by using a simple embedded space, which for correctness maintains the full state of the world model's internal simulator, but hides it from the motion planner.

The choice of the controller for the obstacles is arbitrary in this setup. Anything that understands how to control the moving obstacles can be placed here, thereby allowing many different behaviors to be modeled. For this experiment, the controllers for the dynamic obstacles are known apriori, therefore the true controller exists in both the ground-truth simulation and the planning's world model.

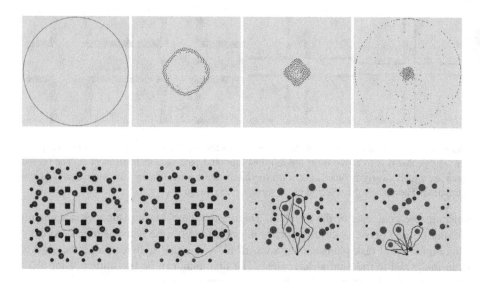

Fig. 10. (Top Row) Snapshots of the local scalability experiment running 250 agents using sensing and local collision avoidance techniques. (Bottom Row) Snapshots of decentralized multi-agent coordination experiments in two different environments.

4.3   Decentralized Multi-robot Coordination

Scalability is an important requirement, and PRACSYS aims towards this along two directions: (a) the number of agents that can be modeled on a single machine, and (b) the number of communicating processes the architecture is able to support. To test the local scalability of PRACSYS, an experiment with 250 agents attempting to swap places with one another was used, as shown in Figure 10. On a single computer with a 3.1 GHz Intel i3 processor and 8GB of RAM, this experiment was capable of running in real time at 50 frames-per-second, which also includes the overhead of each individual robot running a local collision avoidance technique while utilizing a proximity sensor.

Given this collision avoidance capability, a decentralized multi-robot coordination challenge was constructed, which utilized every component of PRACSYS. The challenge involved multiple robots moving in highly-constraining scenarios with each agent attempting to reach some goal location. This required each robot to operate in a replanning framework, where each agent individually sensed its environment and queried its own planning node to recompute a solution path every 0.5 seconds. The overall structure of the experiment is shown in Figure 11. Beginning at the simulation node, a hierarchical system tree was used, where one branch consisted of: *consumer controller* over a *velocity obstacle controller* over a holonomic *disk plant*. The consumer controller translates the trajectories from planning into relevant controls for the velocity obstacle controller [26], which generates collision-free controls. For some time t during the experiment, each disk agent sends an update of the simulation state to planning - this involved the agent utilizing sensing, along with generating a query asking planning to compute a solution trajectory to some goal location. While the planning node answers this new query, the robot begins executing its trajectory at t to reach a state at $t + 1$.

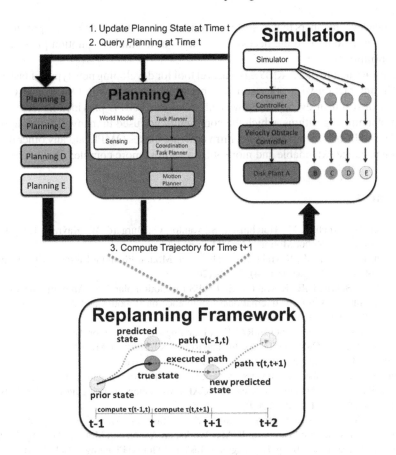

Fig. 11. The interaction between planning and simulation for a decentralized, multi-agent robot coordination challenge

Each robot runs its own individual planning node, where: given an updated state of the world (i.e., through sensing on simulation) at some time t, the task planner generates an appropriate *planning context* to represent the *world model*, and uses the *sensing information* to construct a *planning query* containing the proximity information of other agents (i.e., the sensed agents' positions and velocities). This query informs the motion coordination task planner (MCTP) which parts of the environment were heavily congested. The MCTP then uses the trajectory at t and simulates where the robot would end up at $t + 1$. It uses this newly predicted state, changes the motion planner's *problem specification* so as to compute a trajectory from $t + 1$ to $t + 2$ that would minimize conflicts with other robots. Once such a solution trajectory is computed by the motion planner, this trajectory is sent back to the simulation side via a ROS topic.

5 Discussion

This paper describes a software infrastructure for integrating task and motion planners. By taking advantage of the hierarchical nature of real-world tasks, the creation of hierarchical task planners makes software construction natural. PRACSYS provides this infrastructure, along with the necessary modules of a simulator, motion planners, and sensing primitives.

The infrastructure of PRACSYS is a useful tool for developing new types of task planners. The interaction with other software packages, such as with OMPL and Gazebo [2, 22], can result in even more powerful solutions. OMPL provides many different motion planning algorithms, which the community has used in many different applications. The addition of a task planning infrastructure makes OMPL and any other motion planning package extendable and more able to address more complex challenges.

References

[1] Choset, H., Lynch, K.M., Hutchinson, S., Kantor, G., Burgard, W., Kavraki, L.E., Thrun, S.: Principles of Robot Motion. The MIT Press (2005)

[2] Şucan, I.A., Moll, M., Kavraki, L.E.: The Open Motion Planning Library. IEEE Robotics and Automation Magazine 19(4), 72–82 (2012)

[3] Plaku, E., Bekris, K.E., Kavraki, L.E.: OOPS for motion planning: An online open-source programming system. In: International Conference on Robotics and Automation (ICRA), Rome, Italy, pp. 3711–3716 (2007)

[4] Diankov, R., Kuffner, J.J.: OpenRAVE: A Planning Architecture for Autonomous Robotics. Technical report, CMU-RI-TR-08-34, The Robotics Institute, CMU (2008)

[5] Sucan, I., Chitta, S.: MoveIt! http://moveit.ros.org

[6] Hauser, K., Latombe, J.C.: Integrating task and PRM motion planning: Dealing with many infeasible motion planning queries. In: ICAPS Workshop on Bridging the Gap Between Task and Motion Planning (2009)

[7] Koenig, S.: Creating a Uniform Framework for Task and Motion Planning: A Case for Incremental Heuristic Search. In: ICAPS Works. on Action and Motion Planning (2010)

[8] Lozano-Perez, T., Kaebling, L.: Integrated Task and Motion Planning in Belief Space (2013)

[9] Nedunuri, S., Prabhu, S., Moll, M., Chaudhuri, S., Kavraki, L.E.: SMT-Based Synthesis of Integrated Task and Motion Plans for Mobile Manipulation. In: ICRA (2014)

[10] Hauser, K., Ng-Thow-Hing, V.: Randomized Multi-Modal Motion Planning for a Humanoid Robot Manipulation Task. IJRR (2011)

[11] Kaelbling, L., Lozano-Pérez, T.: Integrated Robot Task and Motion Planning in the Now. CSAIL Technical Report (2012)

[12] Stilman, M., Kuffner, J.J.: Planning Among Movable Obstacles with Artificial Constraints. In: WAFR (2006)

[13] Ayan, N.F., Kuter, U., Yaman, F., Goldman, R.P.: HOTRiDE: Hierarchical ordered task replanning in dynamic environments. In: ICAPS Workshop on Planning and Plan Execution for Real-World Systems (2007)

[14] Gaschler, A., Petrick, R.P., Kröger, T., Knoll, A., Khatib, O.: Robot task planning with contingencies for run-time sensing. In: ICRA Workshop on Combining Task and Motion Planning (2013)

[15] Olawsky, D., Krebsbach, K., Gini, M.: An analysis of sensor-based task planning. Technical report (1995)

[16] Bhattacharya, S., Michael, N., Kumar, V.: Distributed coverage and exploration in unknown non-convex environments. In: Martinoli, A., Mondada, F., Correll, N., Mermoud, G., Egerstedt, M., Hsieh, M.A., Parker, L.E., Støy, K. (eds.) Distributed Autonomous Robotic Systems. STAR, vol. 83, pp. 61–75. Springer, Heidelberg (2013)

[17] Bekris, K.E., Tsianos, K.I., Kavraki, L.E.: Safe and distributed kinodynamic replanning for vehicular networks. Mobile Networks and Applications 14(3), 292–308 (2009)
[18] Marino, A., Parker, L.E., Antonelli, G., Caccavale, F.: A decentralized architecture for multi-robot systems based on the null-space-behavioral control with application to multi-robot border patrolling. Journal of Intelligent & Robotic Systems 71(3-4), 423–444 (2013)
[19] Stiffler, N.M., O'Kane, J.M.: A Sampling Based Algorithm for Multi-Robot Visibility-Based Pursuit-Evasion. In: IEEE Intl. Conf. on Intelligent Robots and Systems (2014)
[20] Saha, M., Sanchez-Ante, G., Latombe, J.C., Roughgarden, T.: Planning multi-goal tours for robot arms. Int. J. Robotics Research 25(3), 207–223 (2006)
[21] Kimmel, A., Dobson, A., Littlefield, Z., Krontiris, A., Marble, J., Bekris, K.E.: PRACSYS: An Extensible Architecture for Composing Motion Controllers and Planners. In: Noda, I., Ando, N., Brugali, D., Kuffner, J.J. (eds.) SIMPAR 2012. LNCS, vol. 7628, pp. 137–148. Springer, Heidelberg (2012)
[22] Koenig, N., Hsu, J., Dolha, M.: Willow Garage, Gazebo: http://gazebosim.org/
[23] Kröger, T.: Opening the door to new sensor-based robot applications—The Reflexxes Motion Libraries. In: ICRA (2011)
[24] Willow Garage, Robot Operating System (ROS), http://www.ros.org/wiki/
[25] Bullet Physics Engine, http://bulletphysics.org
[26] van den Berg, J., Lin, M., Manocha, D.: Reciprocal Velocity Obstacles for Real-Time Multi-Agent Navigation. In: IEEE ICRA (2008)

A Component-Based Meta-Model and Framework in the Model Driven Toolchain C-Forge⋆

Francisco J. Ortiz, Diego Alonso, Francisca Rosique, Francisco Sánchez-Ledesma, and Juan A. Pastor

Division of Systems and Electronic Engineering (DSIE)
Universidad Politécnica de Cartagena, Campus Muralla del Mar, 30202, Spain
francisco.ortiz@upct.es

Abstract. This paper describes a Component-Based Meta-Model (WCOMM) and framework (FraCC) as part of a complete Model-Driven Software Development process and toolchain: C-Forge. The approach given in the design of WCOMM and FraCC is presented highlighting the differences with other similar approaches. To illustrate the use of C-Forge, the development of a control architecture for the robots in project MISSION is presented.

Keywords: MDSD, component-based robotic framework, toolchain.

1 Introduction and Motivation

Component Based Software Engineering (CBSE) [1] paradigm is promoting in robotics the encapsulation of proven solutions into reusable building blocks, considering components as something beyond a compiled module or library. However, many times, the lack of support for development of components and their integration into the global robotic system has limited its adoption. Robotic software is no longer constructed from scratch, but rather there are a number of specialized software toolkits, libraries, middleware and frameworks that provide developers with different levels of support and infrastructure for the development, maintenance and execution of robotics applications. However, the higher the supporting infrastructure, the deeper the knowledge of the software and its configuration details the developers must have. On the other hand, most of these solutions do not define a clear and well-supported development process that combines generation and evolution of software code and evaluation of requirements, including early model analysis.

Beyond the success of libraries and robotic middleware, recent works [2,3] and specialized workshops (SIMPAR, SDIR, MORSE) illustrate a clear interest to formalize the software development process for robotics by providing developers with model-driven and component-based designs processes supported by toolchains. The Model-Driven Software Development (MDSD) [4] paradigm raises the level of abstraction of the development process by allowing domain experts to express domain concepts in their designs. Thus, the complexity of middleware, frameworks or any other

---

⋆ This work has been partially supported by the Region of Murcia's Government Project MISSION-SICUVA (ref. 15374/PI/10) Spanish CICYT project ViSel-TR (ref. TIN2012-39279) and the Spanish MEC FPU Program (grant AP2009-5083).

D. Brugali et al. (Eds.): SIMPAR 2014, LNAI 8810, pp. 340–351, 2014.

software artefacts can be hidden by carefully choosing the correct abstractions. These models are independent of the implementation technologies, so that best software engineering practices (including early validation and verification activities) can be feasibly applied. Model-driven technologies also provide support for automatically transforming models [5] into other representations, either models or text (normally source code). For these benefits, the robotics community is increasingly interested in MDSD and highlights the need of formal models that allow developers the reuse of designs and architectural elements independently of the implementation platform, as well as the toolchains that support the generation and validation of models and code [6].

The main contributions of this paper are (1) the description of a component-based framework, FraCC, with a White Box Component Meta Model (WCOMM) and a toolchain, C-Forge, that makes possible to integrate it in an MDSD development process, (2) the description of the features that distinguish our proposal from other similar approaches, and (3) the application of C-Forge to a case study to illustrate, the benefits of combining MDSD and CBSE in a toolchain. The case study considers the development of the control software of several autonomous vehicles developed in the context of the national project MISSION.

There is a particular focus on illustrating the main differences of our approach compared with others similar in the literature, in particular: (1) the proposal of WCOMM as white-box components with explicit behaviour and activities (2) the ability to express at model level orthogonality and concurrent behavior of the component (3) the direct execution of models linked to source code thanks to a FraCC model loader (4) the deployment of WCOMM and FraCC models with a flexible assignation of concurrent tasks to threads and processes. FraCC take into account non-functional aspects of the design such as task scheduling, concurrency management, and distributed communication. Among other advantages, this enables FraCC to carry out schedulability analysis.

Section 2 presents an overview of the C-Forge toolchain. Section 3 reviews key CBSE and MDSD aspects of current development technologies for robotics compared to those proposed by our approach. Section 4 discusses details of the MDSD process the C-Forge applied to the MISSION case of study. The last Section presents conclusions and future research directions.

2   Overview of C-Forge Toolchain

C-Forge is a toolchain built on top of the Eclipse IDE and its MDSD plug-ins Xtext, GMF and Epsilon. It provides full support for the development of component-based software applications, from modelling to execution. C-Forge integrates two main elements (shown in Fig. 1): (1) a White-box COmponent MetaModel (WCOMM), which embodies a component model for describing component-based applications, and (2) a C++ framework, entitled FraCC, that provides the required run-time support for executing WCOMM models with different deployment configurations. It also provides three model transformations (A, B and C in Fig. 1). Transformations (A) and (B) generate the artefacts FraCC needs to execute a WCOMM application (mainly, C++ templates for user code and a deployment model that describes how the application is executed, see Section 2.2). One of the main characteristics of our approach is that, thanks to the modelling primitives provided by WCOMM and the way FraCC organises and executes WCOMM components, the user has full control over the concurrency characteristics of the application (mainly, number of threads, their computational load and timing properties, see Section 2.2). Model transformation (C) exploits this feature to generate an analysis file for the Cheddar schedulability analysis tool [7], so that the user can check whether the final application will meet its real-time requirements.

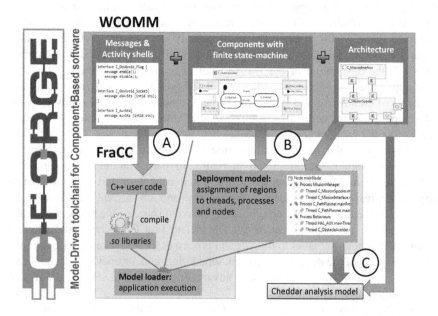

Fig. 1. The C-Forge development process

2.1   The White-Box Component Meta-Model (WCOMM)

WCOMM components are modelled as white-boxes. That is, the user models both the component structure (the component boundary, its ports, message types, etc.) and its behaviour (mainly, how the component react to the messages it receives from other components or from the results of internal computations). Components are connected by linking compatible ports, i.e., ports that receive messages sent by the port they are connected to, and vice-versa, though WCOMM allows connecting ports that can receive more messages than those that are sent by the port they are connected to. According to OMG's MARTE specification [8], WCOMM ports can be classified as flow-oriented, non-atomic (messages can have parameters of any type), bi-directional, and behavioural (messages can fire events in the component FSM) ports. Messages are asynchronous no-reply, which makes possible to support any communication scheme and assures a low coupling between components. The structural view of the application architecture is modelled as a set of components and the connections through their ports.

Component reactive behaviour is modelled in WCOMM by means of a Finite-State Machine (FSM) with hierarchical and orthogonal regions, inspired by those defined in UML 2. Orthogonal regions are a powerful modelling concept, allowing the users to model potentially concurrent parts of the component behaviour (which can be sequentially or concurrently executed by FraCC). Transitions are triggered by events, which can be produced by both message reception and internal computation. States in WCOMM can contain one activity shell, which is a wrapper of the concrete algorithm that will be executed when the state becomes the region's active state. These shells only define the messages the activity receives and sends to other activities or ports. The algorithmic code will be implemented by the user in further steps. Messages serve not only as the mechanism to share information among components, but also as links between the structure and behaviour parts of a component. When an activity is added to a state, the user can decide whether it will be periodic or sporadic.

The C-Forge support for WCOMM is composed of three tools (see WCOMM box in Fig. 1): (i) A textual editor for modelling data-types, messages and activity shells; (ii) A graphical tool for modelling simple components (structure and behaviour); (iii) A graphical tool to define complex components, e.g., the structural view of an application architecture as a set of connected components. The modelling of applications is a pure CBSE process at this stage. Therefore, the user does not have to know the implementation details of the platform that will ultimately support the execution.

2.2   The FraCC Framework

FraCC is a C++ framework that provides the required run-time support for executing WCOMM components. We say "execute" because, unlike other approaches, we do not generate implementation code, but rather FraCC provides a model loader that directly loads WCOMM models and according to them instantiates FraCC classes. Two additional artefacts are needed to complete application execution: the C++ code of the algorithms embedded in WCOMM activities, and a description of how FraCC must execute the components' regions. C++ code templates, where the user must add the application-specific code, are generated from WCOMM activities by a model transformation (A in Fig. 1). The user code is then compiled into a dynamic library and loaded by the model loader when needed. FraCC imposes some restrictions to the code contained in an activity, e.g., infinite loops are forbidden, and activities cannot spawn threads or create mutexes. Thus, the approach provides a clear separation of concerns, differentiating component modelling from activities implementation.

FraCC allows developers to explicitly control the concurrency of the application, and to perform a schedulability analysis by using a deployment model, generated by a model transformation (B in Fig. 1) from WCOMM models. This transformation generates a default deployment that can be modified through a C-Forge tool. This model enables users to distribute the application in threads, processes and nodes, by assigning components to processes and regions to threads. Any assignment is possible (for instance, assigning regions of different components to the same thread) as long as all component regions are assigned to threads of the same process. Regions are, therefore, the corner stone of the approach, connecting both tools: they model part of the component behaviour in WCOMM, and are the unit of workload assignment in FraCC. Regarding the communication mechanism, FraCC uses POSIX message queues when regions are assigned to processes residing in the same node, and communication software otherwise.

A model transformation (C in Fig. 1) generates a file for the Cheddar schedulability analysis tool [7] from the WCOMM and deployments models [9]. Appropriate changes can then be made to the applications models based on the analysis outcomes. FraCC deployment model therefore provides a clear separation between architecture and execution, allowing user to define and test different execution schemes for the same application architecture.

3   Differentiating Aspects of C-Forge Toolchain

This section describes the main innovative features of C-Forge, WCOMM and FraCC compared to some of the most referenced methodologies for robotics software engineering. Table 1 shows the considered component-based toolchains, classifying them into two main groups depending on whether they are supported by MDSD technologies. As stated in [2], ROS[1] and YARP[2] could not be considered in a strict sense component-based frameworks, since they lack an explicit component model, but they have been included ass they are widely used in robotics. General purpose distribution middleware is also included in Table 1.

Table 1. Classification of component-based toolchains and middleware technologies

		MDSD Toolchain				Other tool support		
Robotic Component Based Software	Tool support	C-Forge	SmartSoft	BRICS	RobotML	RTMaps	OPROS	- no -
	Component Model	WCOMM	SmartSoft	BCM	RobotML	RTMaps	OPROS	ORCA
	MD transfor. → Execution framework	FraCC	SmartSoft	OROCOS		RTMaps	OPROS	ORCA
Robotic Middleware	Tool support				ROS			
	No tool supp.				YARP			
Middleware	Distribution	ACE / TAO	omniORB					ICE

Solid arrows in Table 1 represent model transformations that generate the implementation code in each toolchain. The input of each transformation is an application described in terms of the component model. The output is executable code for the execution framework targeted by the toolchain. Though input models are independent of the implementation technologies, in practice, the development

---

[1] ROS homepage: http://www.ros.org
[2] YARP homepage: http://eris.liralab.it/yarp/

of transformations is an intensive work and most MDSD-toolchains choose a single implementation technology. RobotML and BCM (BRICS Component Model) are examples of how the same component based application can target different frameworks. There is a plus sign between FraCC and WCOMM expressing a key point of our approach: we do not use transformations to generate executable code, but instead FraCC loads directly WCOMM models to instantiate its classes accordingly and links the activity shells to user code corresponding to activities implementation. This makes possible the reconfiguration of the application at execution time.

Although WCOMM, Smartsoft and RobotML do not transform directly to ROS, they all have gateways to ROS modules. Dotted arrows indicate that an execution framework uses a general purpose communication middleware.

[10] offers an exhaustive survey on existing component models in robotics software frameworks. In order to let the reader know how WCOMM+FraCC incorporate features considered in this survey we summarized it in Table 2 considering only the execution frameworks and including (1) three new component models (FraCC, Smartsoft and RTMaps[3]), and (2) new features related to concurrency and real-time support, which are inherent to robotic applications.

Table 2. Comparative of component models primitives in execution frameworks. The darker the cell, the lower the compliance with the property.

	FraCC	SmartSoft	OROCOS	RTMaps	OPROS	ORCA	ROS
Type of Comp. Ports	Data / implicit behaviour	Data	Data / Event / Config.	Data	Data / Event / Method	~ Data Publ. / Subscribe	~ Data Publ. / Subscribe
Type of Comp. Intface	~ Behaviour msgs	Services req/reply	Services req/reply	NO	~ Method Port (cli/ser)	Publish / Subscribe	Services req/reply
Data Types support	YES (typed msgs)	YES (comm.object)	YES (standard)	YES (ROS-like)	NO	YES (BROS guide)	YES (robot specific)
Connector / Connection	NO / YES	NO / YES	YES / YES	NO / YES	NO / YES	NO / NO	NO / NO
Internal Life Cycle FSM	3 states	3 states	9 states	- Info not available -	6 states	2 states	NO
Funct. Algorithm	User defined	NO	User defined	NO	NO	3 states	NO
Deployment of the comp.	Flexible Depl. and threading	Smart tasks	periodic / non period. activity	Own control of threads	NO	Thread by MiddW ICE	NO
Concurrency & RT	Concurrency + RT	RT	RT	RT	NO	NO	NO

---

[3] RTMAPS homepage: http://www.intempora.com/

Component, Connectors, Interfaces and Data Types

At the component level, WCOMM allows designing separately the entire structure and behaviour of components, as well as the defining types of activities (activity shells) that can be assigned to states and linked to user code. This inclusion of activities as part of the model is not considered in other approaches. These aspects favour that the structure and the reactive behaviour of the components as well as the algorithms executed by them can evolve separately.

Most component models differentiate data ports from service ports or interfaces, while WCOMM defines a single port type. Each component can interpret the same message as mere data or as a service request depending on its FSM. The semantics of communications between WCOMM components is, by default, asynchronous no-reply, because it makes no assumptions about the behaviour of other components. Other communication semantics, such as synchronous reply, can be implemented in the FSM. We think that the asynchronous approach provides independence of execution and favours the low coupling between components, although it could introduce additional complexity in the FSM when synchronous reply semantics is needed.

Regarding component's execution model, BCM comprises three FSMs: (1) the life cycle FSM, which defines the different stages from the creation to the finalization of the component, is present in all component-based approaches; (2) the functional algorithm FSM, to specify the behaviour/algorithm of a component (WCOMM components are white-boxes with explicit behaviour expression; and (3) the interface FSM, which defines constraints on the execution order of the operations specified by the interface. These constraints are implicit in the functional FSM of WCOMM components.

Concurrency, Component Deployment and Real Time Issues

One of the most differentiating aspects of our approach in our opinion is the concurrency management and flexible deployment of the application. By means of the orthogonal regions, it is possible to define potential internal concurrency in the WCOMM components (see Fig. 4 in Section 4.4). The transformation that generates the deployment model hides all the distribution complexity to application developers. The deployment model allows distributing the execution of the orthogonal regions in different threads. This allows grouping the activities performed by different components according to their timing requirements, since regions of different components can be assigned to the same thread. The tool chain hides all the complexity of creating and managing processes and threads, as well as their synchronization and communications mechanisms, but at the same tame allows developers to define their number, the activities that they should execute and their periods of execution.

Regarding real-time issues, the application timing requirements can be explicitly defined in the WCOMM models at the level of activity. The FraCC design and the way the regions are mapped to threads allow a model transformation to generate a schedulability analysis file for the Cheddar tool to verify that the considered deployment meets the deadlines. We measure the execution time of the activities in a isolation, and then use this data in conjunction with the deployment model, the information of the operating system scheduler and the information of the framework behavior to generate a schedulability analysis model that serves as input to the Cheddar analyzer. If a deployment is not schedulable, the developer can modify it. If no deployment is schedulable, the developer can: (1) modify the application architecture, and (2) change the algorithms implementations.

4 Applied Design Process with C-Forge for Robotic Applications

4.1 The Robotic Platforms in Project MISSION

C-Forge has been used to develop the robotic control software in the project "Comprehensive framework for software development of autonomous underwater vehicles based on models, components and frameworks (MISSION)". This project started from a previously developed Remote Operated underwater Vehicle. To ease the testing of the functionality, we used two terrestrial vehicles with the same hardware that the AUV. Fig. 2 shows the common hardware architecture for all the robots: (a) the NI LabVIEW Robotics Starter Kit, DaNI, (b) a robotized golf cart, VEGO, developed by the authors in a previous project and (c) the underwater vehicle. As can be seen in Fig. 2, the CompactRIO executes low level control routines and sensor acquisition, while higher level control tasks have been implemented using C-Forge to run in an on-board embedded PC with a wireless internet link to the remote HMI.

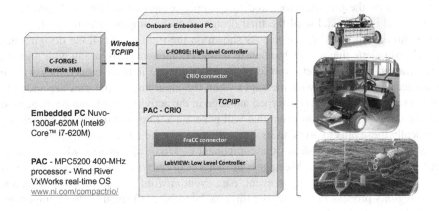

Fig. 2. Common hardware architecture

Fig. 3 shows a three-tier component-oriented architecture modelled with a graphical tool included in C-Forge. A top layer for mission planning communicates with the central execution component (*C_MissionSequencer*) which sequences the tasks to the lower tracking and obstacle avoidance layer in contact with the CRIO connector. This architectural diagram is a computational model itself that can be refined, executed and transformed into other models (e.g., analysis models), or to executable code. Due to space limitations and the focus of the conference, this article gives more importance to the explanation of how to use C-Forge to develop a robotics application rather than the detailed explanation of the application itself. A closer look for another underwater vehicle development can be found in a recent publication [9].

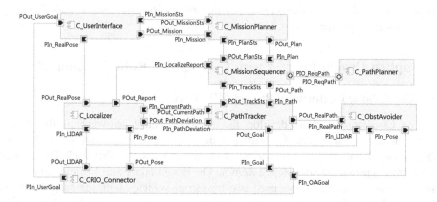

Fig. 3. General component-oriented architecture for robots in MISSION

4.2   The Design of Simple Components

Each component in Fig. 3 is a WCOMM simple component with its behaviour defined by means of a FSM including orthogonal regions when needed, and the activity shell for each state (Fig. 4). Application data types and messages are specified by using a textual tool along with the graphical tool to define simple components. The whole process is iterative and incremental until the final design of each component is reached, with a clear definition of ports' messages. As shown on the right of Fig. 4, the designer has a graphical palette that allows him/her to define component ports, along with regions, states, transitions, events, etc. In this phase, the ports are initially empty, they will be completed in accordance with messages when the input and output pins are added to activities. Each pin represents a typed message in the activity, which can be associated with data in ports or with an event that will generate a transition in a FSM. By joining graphically these pins to ports, messages will appear in the corresponding port.

As an example, Fig. 4 shows the component *C_MissionSequencer* which contains three concurrent regions. Messages in ports can provide the components with information but also generate an event, e.g., event *misEnd* in the port *POut_PlanSts*. These regions process in parallel the three tasks to be performed by the component: (1) *R_ProcessingCmds* processes the mission commands and reports arriving from *C_MissionPlanner* and *C_Localizer*. It also reports states of lower layers; (2) *R_MissionSequencer* interprets and sequences the execution of every task included in the mission, e.g. requiring a new path plan to *C_PathPlanner*; (3) *R_MotionMonitor* monitors the current movement of the vehicle, in normal or in emergency states. Once the models of all simple components are completed, the application model itself is refined to include them, as shown in Fig. 3.

4.3   Detailed Implementation and Flexible Deployment with FraCC

Once finished the WCOMM model, according to the workflow of Fig. 1, the user executes the model to text transformation (A) to generate the C++ skeletons of the

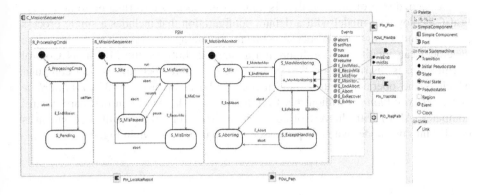

Fig. 4. Design of the *C_MissionSequencer* component. Graphical links from Pin to Port messages are displayed only when editing the state, the rest remain hidden.

software code corresponding to the "shell" of the activities (including the access code to input and output messages and events). The developer fills in methods *init()*, *onEntry()*, *onExit()*, *doCode()* (see Fig. 5), using methods *get_XX()* and *set_XX()* to access the information in input and output pins. The method *doCode()* is executed while the FSM is in the state associated to the activity. It represents a step of the executed algorithm.

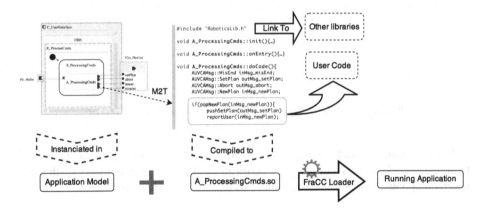

Fig. 5. Code excerpt for activity *A_ProcessingCmds*. The skeleton of the class where the user adds the code is generated by the model-to-text transformation (A) in Fig. 1.

Fig. 5 exemplifies how the developer codifies the *A_ProcessCmds* algorithm. The definition of *AUVCAMsgs* is automatically generated by the toolchain. Once completed, the code is compiled as dynamic libraries. These libraries can independently evolve since they are linked to the model (not embedded in it). This separation of concerns provides great flexibility since the code and the models can be maintained separately.

The second step of the workflow is a model-to-model transformation to obtain the FraCC deployment model with a default configuration that includes a single process per node and a single thread per component containing the component regions. The developer can modify this configuration as needed. Initially, the MISSION Control Architecture is distributed on two computers: (1) a tele-operation station computer which is the operator control unit (including the components *C_MissionInterface* and *C_MissionPlanner* without hard RT requirements), and (2) an on-board control computer (AUV) with the rest of components. Therefore, the default deployment is divided into two nodes with one processor in each one, as shown in Fig. 6.

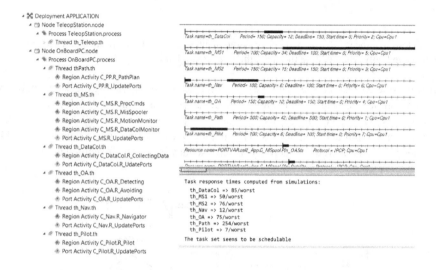

Fig. 6. Deployment model and schedulability analysis with Cheddar

Finally, from this default deployment, an automatic transformation generates a temporal model to carry out an early verification of the RT requirements of the on-board components by using Cheddar analysis tool. For a detailed discussion, see [9].

5   Conclusions and Future Work

In this paper we have presented a description of C-Forge: a model-driven and component-oriented toolchain. The explanation of the design process has been illustrated with its application to the development of control software for different autonomous mobile robots of the national project MISSION. Compared to other toolchains, the main innovating aspects could be summarized as:

– WCOMM components are white-boxes with explicit support to define potential concurrency inside components at the model level. The behaviour of the component is modelled by FSM but with the novelty of including an activity inside each state to model the shell of an algorithm, which will be developed by the user in further steps, allowing to evolve independently. Communication among components is performed by typed asynchronous no-reply messages through compatible ports, thus assuring a low coupling among components.

- The run-time support for executing WCOMM components is provided by the C++ framework FraCC, which includes a model loader that directly interprets WCOMM models and execute applications by loading the previously compiled activities code.
- FraCC have been designed to provide the user with explicit control over application concurrency, in terms of both the number of threads and their temporal characteristics, so that compliance with them can be verified.
- The separation between architecture and deployment enables application developers to generate, analyze and test various deployment scenarios without changing the component definitions and the structural view of the application architecture.

Future investigation will include the RT analysis of the execution of tasks from additional AUV capabilities required by other missions. A study on potential combinations of deployment configurations will also be considered in order to analyse resource management in AUV systems.

References

1. Crnkovic, I., Sentilles, S., Vulgarakis, A., Chaudron, M.R.V.: A classification framework for software component models. IEEE Trans. Software Eng. 37(5), 593–615 (2011)
2. Schlegel, C., Steck, A., Lotz, A.: Model-driven software development in robotics: communication patterns as key for a robotics component model. In: Introduction to Modern Robotics, pp. 119–150. iConcept Press (2012)
3. Dhouib, S., Kchir, S., Stinckwich, S., Ziadi, T., Ziane, M.: RobotML, a domain-specific language to design, simulate and deploy robotic applications. In: Noda, I., Ando, N., Brugali, D., Kuffner, J.J. (eds.) SIMPAR 2012. LNCS, vol. 7628, pp. 149–160. Springer, Heidelberg (2012)
4. Bézivin, J.: On the unification power of models. Journal of Systems and Software 4(2), 171–188 (2005)
5. Mens, T., van Gorp, P.: A taxonomy of model transformation. Electronic Notes in Theoretical Computer Science 152, 125–142 (2006)
6. Bruyninckx, H., Hochgeschwender, N., Gherardi, L., Klotzbücher, M., Kraetzschmar, G., Brugali, D.: The brics component model: A model-based development paradigm for complex robotics software systems. In: Proc. of the 28th Annual ACM Symposium on Applied Computing, pp. 1758–1764. ACM Press (2013)
7. Singhoff, F., Plantec, A., Dissaux, P., Legrand, J.: Investigating the usability of real-time scheduling theory with the cheddar project. Journal of Real Time Systems 43(3), 259–295 (2009)
8. OMG_MARTE. Uml profile for marte: Modeling and analysis of real-time embedded systems v1.1 (2011)
9. Ortiz, F., Insaurralde, C., Alonso, D., Sánchez, F., Petillot, Y.: Model-driven analysis and design for software development of autonomous underwater vehicles. In: Robotica, pp. 1–20 (April 2014)
10. Shakhimardanov, A., Hochgeschwender, N., Kraetzschmar, G.: Component models in robotics software. In: Proc. of the Performance Metrics for Intelligent Systems Workshop, PerMIS 2010 (2010)

Merging Partially Consistent Maps

Taigo Maria Bonanni, Giorgio Grisetti, and Luca Iocchi

Dept. of Computer, Control and Management Engineering
Sapienza University of Rome
Via Ariosto 25, 00185, Rome, Italy
{bonanni,grisetti,iocchi}@dis.uniroma1.it

Abstract. Learning maps from sensor data has been addressed since more than two decades by Simultaneous Localization and Mapping (SLAM) systems. Modern state-of-the-art SLAM approaches exhibit excellent performances and are able to cope with environments having the scale of a city. Usually these methods are entailed for on-line operation, requiring the data to be acquired in a single run, which is not always easy to obtain. To gather a single consistent map of a large environment we therefore integrate data acquired in multiple runs. A possible solution to this problem consists in merging different submaps. The literature proposes several approaches for map merging, however very few of them are able to operate with local maps affected by inconsistencies. These methods seek to find the global arrangement of a set of rigid bodies, that maximizes some overlapping criterion. In this paper, we present an off-line technique for merging maps affected by residual errors into a single consistent global map. Our method can be applied in combination with existing map merging approaches, since it requires an initial guess to operate. However, once this initial guess is provided, our method is able to substantially lessen the residual error in the final map. We validated our approach on both real world and simulated datasets to refine solutions of traditional map merging approaches.

1 Introduction

To autonomously execute complex tasks such as object delivery, house cleaning, etc., mobile robots need to know their operating environment. This is usually addressed by the Simultaneous Localization and Mapping (SLAM) problem, that provides an estimate of the map and of the robot trajectory based on the robot measurements.

SLAM has been object of research for more than two decades, and effective solutions are available [21],[18],[9],[22],[16],[19]. The most common sensor used to build robotic maps is the laser scanner, and existing approaches can effectively be used to construct maps.

Regardless the technique employed, unless one uses some sort of absolute sensor like a GPS, even the most effective methods might fail when the environment size becomes too big. Acquiring data for SLAM is an error-prone procedure that requires attention to obtain satisfying results. Often the operator forgets to visit

D. Brugali et al. (Eds.): SIMPAR 2014, LNAI 8810, pp. 352–363, 2014.

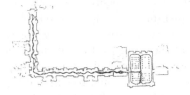

(a) Consistent SLAM result of a first mapping session

(b) Consistent SLAM result of a second mapping round

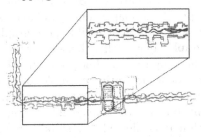

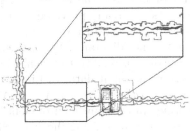

(c) Standard map merging approach on rigid bodies

(d) Our map merging approach based on deformable bodies

Fig. 1. Motivating example of our approach. *a)*, *b)* are the input graphs. The global map shown in *c)* is affected by inconsistencies that are corrected by our algorithm, as shown in *d)*.

certain locations during data acquisition, or makes mistakes that challenge the SLAM engine he is using (e.g. in a VisualSLAM session one might enter in a room with poor light conditions).

Furthermore, typical SLAM systems require to operate on data gathered in a single session. In other words they require a continuous trajectory to produce a consistent map. If the environment changes, a new map needs to be computed from new data. This results in the need of performing tedious and error prone data acquisition sessions, each time the environment changes. A branch of literature addresses this problem by employing a team of robots, instead of a single one, thus addressing the multi-robot SLAM problem. Alternatively one might merge different local maps, acquired at different points in time. If the sole aim is to get the map, the latter approach has obvious advantages, since it requires less resources. Furthermore, in case the environment changes, new data have to be acquired only in the changed portion, and be subsequently integrated in the global map, after removing the outdated local map.

In this paper, we present a novel approach for merging partially consistent maps. Typical map merging methods regard the maps as rigid bodies. A solution for map merging is a set of rigid transformations between the maps that maximizes their consistent overlap. This has the obvious limitation of not dealing with noise that might affect the local maps, and result in artifacts. This error is always present and comes from the process used to estimate the input maps. Conversely, our method operates on maps that are regarded as network of springs and masses. We reduce the problem of merging two maps to the problem of deforming two networks onto each other so that the residual energy of the system is minimal. This corresponds to finding the configuration of the nodes in the two networks that best preserves the original layout of the input maps. Notice that the algorithm presented in this work is orthogonal to existing map merging methods, and can be used to refine their solutions when the input maps are affected by substantial error.

In case one uses the well known graph-based formulation of SLAM [8], such a network is already provided as a pose graph. If the map is only available as an occupancy grid or an image, we detail how to obtain a feasible pose graph using Voronoi diagrams. By operating on graphs, our method benefits from a reduced dimensionality, thus achieving efficient computation while preserving the details of the input data. In Figure 1 we provide a motivating example for our work. Fig, 1*a)* and 1*b)* are the SLAM results of two different mapping session, performed in the same environment. We want to merge these maps into a single one, possibly minimizing the error. Since each map is affected by residual errors, combining them through a single rigid transformation propagates the error in the global map, as shown in Fig. 1*c)*. Instead, our approach, illustrated in Fig. 1*d)*, can achieve the goal by deforming the maps onto each other. This has the dual effect of increasing the global consistency and of providing a consistent map for navigation.

2   Related Work

State-of-the-art solutions to map merging are based on image registration techniques. The partial maps are regarded as tiles of an image that should be composed to form the global map. Erinc *et al.*, [7], present an anytime merging technique based on appearance maps, exploiting image similarity to find candidates. Other approaches, [20], [5], are based on the spectral analysis of the Hough transforms of the maps to merge. These methods aim at finding the position of each local map with respect to the frame of the global map. A shortcoming of this class of algorithms is their sensitivity to errors in the local maps. When these local maps are subject to deformations, a set of pure rigid transformations is not sufficient to compute a globally consistent map. Our method is orthogonal to these approaches. In our current implementation we did not focus on providing an initial alignment between the maps. This task can be solved by using one of the methods above. Conversely, our approach seeks to maximize the consistency of partially aligned maps, by warping them onto each other.

Map merging has been addressed also in the context of multi-robot SLAM. Léon *et al.* proposed an approach based on particle filters. Their SLAM system merges the maps of different robots by using the map estimated by one robot as a measurement in the filter of another robot. Carlone *et al.*, [4], present an approach using an estimation kernel to compute the relative transformation among robots, without any a-priori knowledge. Leung *et al.*, in [15], presented a decentralized and distributed algorithm for cooperative SLAM, based on a set of rules for the interchange of information. Cunningham *et al.*, in [6], presented an approach called Decentralized Data Fusion (DDF) for the generation of a common map called *condensed map* built after the marginalization of shared landmarks. Lazaro *et al.*, [14], presented a multi-robot SLAM approach based on condensed measurements for the exchange of information among robots. These methods are designed to operate within a full SLAM pipeline which requires to cope with on-line aspects and to deal with communication issues. In the context of multi-agent systems, Jennings *et al.* [12] presented a distributed mapping approach that relies on an approximation of generalized Voronoi graphs, built during the mapping procedure, and a simple distance-based metric for matching portions of graph. Topological approaches address the problem framing it as a graph isomorphism, where one wants to find the set of equivalences between nodes and edges of different subgraphs [3]. Along this line of research, Huang *et al.* [11], presented an approach merging topological maps inspired to maximal common subgraph problem. After building an initial set of matching hypotheses among vertices of the graphs, these hypotheses are then discarded or confirmed considering geometric features of the environment. These methods, however require a symbolic representation of the map, which is not provided by common SLAM engines.

In summary, existing map merging methods aim at getting a global alignment between local maps, but they are highly sensitive to noise in the input. Multi robot SLAM systems are able to deal with this problem, but they are rather complex and, in order to operate correctly, they require the data to be acquired at the same time. In this paper we present an approach to generate a globally consistent map out of noisy local maps.

3   Graph-Based Map Merging

Our approach is an off-line procedure for merging partially consistent local maps having a limited overlap. The most suitable representation for our purpose is to model the maps using graphs of measurements, as in the graph-based SLAM formalization [8]. To align the maps into a globally consistent one, we iteratively deform one of them onto the other, connecting robot poses, which belong to different graphs, if the observations made at these nodes are similar.

The remainder of this section is organized as follows. In Section 3.1, we detail our formalization of maps as deformable bodies. Since graphs of measurements from SLAM are not always available, we propose a method for the extraction of deformable networks out of occupancy grid maps in Section 3.2. Subsequently, in Section 3.3, we address how the inter-graph data association is carried out.

3.1   Map Representation

According to the graph-based SLAM formalization, we represent a deformable map as a graph of the form: $\mathcal{G} = \langle \mathcal{X}, \mathcal{C} \rangle$. Each node $\mathbf{x} \in \mathcal{X}$ is associated to a robot pose in the environment. Each edge $e = \langle \mathbf{x}_i, \mathbf{x}_j \rangle \in \mathcal{C}$ expresses spatial relationships among poses, either from the robot motion or by correlating similar observations of the environment. Since the nodes of this graph are robot poses, they are also called *pose graphs*.

The energy or log likelihood of a configuration of nodes can be formulated as follows. Let $\mathbf{x} = (\mathbf{x}_1, \ldots, \mathbf{x}_n)^T$ be a vector of poses, where $\mathbf{x}_i$ describes the pose of node i. Let $\mathbf{z}_{ij}$ and $\mathbf{\Omega}_{ij}$ be respectively the mean and the information matrix of an edge between the node i and the node j. In energetic terms, $\mathbf{z}_{ij}$ can be seen as equilibrium point of a spring with stiffness $\mathbf{\Omega}_{ij}$ connecting the masses located at $\mathbf{x}_i$ and $\mathbf{x}_j$. If this edge represents a virtual measurement, its equilibrium point is the transformation that makes the observation acquired from i maximally overlap with the observation acquired from j. Let $\hat{\mathbf{z}}_{ij}(\mathbf{x}_i, \mathbf{x}_j)$ be the relative transformation between the two nodes. For a given configuration the energy l_{ij} of a measurement $\mathbf{z}_{ij}$ is therefore

$$l_{ij} \propto [\mathbf{z}_{ij} - \hat{\mathbf{z}}_{ij}(\mathbf{x}_i, \mathbf{x}_j)]^T \mathbf{\Omega}_{ij} [\mathbf{z}_{ij} - \hat{\mathbf{z}}_{ij}(\mathbf{x}_i, \mathbf{x}_j)]. \tag{1}$$

Let $\mathbf{e}(\mathbf{x}_i, \mathbf{x}_j, \mathbf{z}_{ij})$ be a function that computes the distance from the two poses to the equilibrium point. For simplicity of notation, we will encode the indices of the measurement in the indices of the error function

$$\mathbf{e}_{ij}(\mathbf{x}_i, \mathbf{x}_j) = \mathbf{z}_{ij} - \hat{\mathbf{z}}_{ij}(\mathbf{x}_i, \mathbf{x}_j). \tag{2}$$

Minimizing the energy of the graph consists in finding the configuration of the nodes $\mathbf{x}^*$ that minimizes the energy of all the edges

$$\mathbf{F}(\mathbf{x}) = \sum_{\langle i,j \rangle \in \mathcal{C}} \mathbf{e}_{ij}^T \mathbf{\Omega}_{ij} \mathbf{e}_{ij}, \tag{3}$$

thus, it seeks to solve the following equation:

$$\mathbf{x}^* = \operatorname*{argmin}_{\mathbf{x}} \mathbf{F}(\mathbf{x}). \tag{4}$$

A graph-based SLAM engine will already provide a graph in a minimal energy configuration. However, when merging two graphs, the individual solutions might not be globally optimal due to the addition of constraints between different graphs. Thus, to find the most likely configuration, we need to compute a new assignment of poses that minimizes the following equation:

$$\mathbf{F}(\mathcal{X}) = \sum_{\langle i,j \rangle \in \mathcal{C}_1} \mathbf{e}_{ij}^T \mathbf{\Omega}_{ij} \mathbf{e}_{ij} + \sum_{\langle i,j \rangle \in \mathcal{C}_2} \mathbf{e}_{ij}^T \mathbf{\Omega}_{ij} \mathbf{e}_{ij} + \sum_{\langle i,j \rangle \in \mathcal{C}_{12}} \mathbf{e}_{ij}^T \mathbf{\Omega}_{ij} \mathbf{e}_{ij} \tag{5}$$

Here $\mathcal{C}_1$ and $\mathcal{C}_2$ are respectively the edges in the first and the second graphs, while $\mathcal{C}_{12}$ are the edges connecting the first and the second graph. To solve this problem we use the open source **g2o** optimization package [13]. The effects of potential outliers is reduced by using Dynamic Covariance Scaling [1] to lessen the contribution of edges that disagree with their neighbors.

3.2   Obtaining the Representation from Grid Maps

If we have only sets of grid maps, we can still generate the required pose graphs, complete of measurements, by using Voronoi diagrams. The Voronoi diagram can be straightforwardly extracted as the locus of points in the free space that are equidistant from at least two occupied cells in the map. On grid maps, the Voronoi diagram provides also a good estimate of the topology of the environment and a plausible trajectory for the robot. The pose graph is computed sampling points of the diagram and correlating nearby nodes according to its connectivity. Finally, the observations are obtained by ray-tracing the obstacles of the grid map to the sampled poses, simulating the behavior of a laser scanner. The typical output of the procedure is shown in Figure 2.

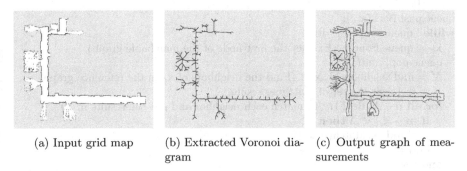

(a) Input grid map   (b) Extracted Voronoi diagram   (c) Output graph of measurements

Fig. 2. Extracting the Voronoi Diagram out of an input grid map, we are able to generate a graph of measurements compliant with our graph matcher

3.3   Data Association among Partially Consistent Maps

In this section we describe our graph-merging procedure. The input of our algorithm are two graphs $\mathcal{G}_r$ and $\mathcal{G}_m$, respectively the *reference graph* and the *matchable graph*. The output is a set of edges $\mathcal{M}$ connecting vertices of $\mathcal{G}_r$ to vertices of $\mathcal{G}_m$. We assume that the two graphs have been partially overlayed in a region around an initial node $\mathbf{x}_r$ of the matchable graph. We progressively deform the matchable graph, towards the reference, according to a breadth first visit. Each time we expand a node $\mathbf{x}_c$ in the current graph, we seek for neighbors in the reference and we attempt to match the observations through a data association routine. If the results of the observation matching are satisfactory, we initialize the position of the expanded node according to the one provided by the matching procedure. This will make the two corresponding observations in the two different maps overlapping, and we add the corresponding edge to $\mathcal{M}$.

Subsequently, we schedule for expansion all the neighbors of $\mathbf{x}_c$ in $\mathcal{G}_m$, and we set their position based on the newly computed position of $\mathbf{x}_c$ and the connecting edge. The pseudo-code for this procedure is shown in Algorithm 1.

Notice that the algorithm is independent from the sensor used. The only requirement is to provide a function *tryMatch*($\mathbf{n}, \mathbf{x}_c$) that attempts to register the observation made from two nodes, and if found, returns the corresponding transformation. In our current implementation the function *tryMatch*($\mathbf{n}, \mathbf{x}_c$) is implemented by a scan-matching routine.

Algorithm 1. Graph Merge

Require: $\mathcal{G}_r$: reference graph, $\mathcal{G}_m$: current graph, $\mathbf{x}_m$: initial vertex in $\mathcal{G}_m$, Δ: minimum distance for matching, *minScore*: minimum score to accept a match.
Ensure: $\mathcal{M}$: edges connecting vertices of $\mathcal{G}_r$ to vertices of $\mathcal{G}_m$.

$\mathcal{M} := \emptyset$; {Initialize the output set of measurements}
$\mathbf{x}_m$.setParent($\mathbf{x}_m$);
queue.pushBack($\mathbf{x}_m$);
while ! queue.empty() **do**
  $\mathbf{x}_c$ = queue.front(); {Extract the first node of the matchable graph}
  queue.popFront();
  $\mathcal{N}$ = findNeighbors($\mathcal{G}_r$,$\mathbf{x}_c$); {Find the neighbors of $\mathbf{x}_c$ in the reference graph}
  $S := \emptyset$; {clear the set of matching results}
  for all $\mathbf{n} \in \mathcal{N}$ **do** {Try to match each neighbor and put the results in S}
    if $|\mathbf{n} - \mathbf{x}_c| < \Delta$ **then**
      S.add(tryMatch($\mathbf{n}, \mathbf{x}_c$));
    end if
  end for
  s = bestMatch(S); {Pick up the best match}
  if s.score() > *minScore* **then**
    $\mathcal{M}$.add(edge($\mathbf{x}_c$, $\mathbf{n}$, s.transform())); {Create a new edge and add it to $\mathcal{M}$}
    $\mathbf{x}_c$ = $\mathbf{n} \oplus s$.transform(); {Initialize $\mathbf{x}_c$ applying the transform of s to $\mathbf{n}$}
  end if
  for all $\mathbf{x}_n \in$ neighborsOf($\mathbf{x}_c$) **do**
    if $\mathbf{x}_n$.parent() == null; **then**
      $\mathbf{x}_n$.setParent($\mathbf{x}_c$);
      e = edgeBetween($\mathbf{x}_c$, $\mathbf{x}_n$);
      $\mathbf{x}_n$ = $\mathbf{x}_c \oplus e$.transform();
      queue.pushBack($\mathbf{x}_n$);
    end if
  end for
end while

---

4   Experiments

We evaluated our approach on real and simulated robot systems, and through synthetic experiments. Experiments with raw real data show the applicability of our system to a practical scenario, while synthetic experiments characterize the performance of our method with varying parameters.

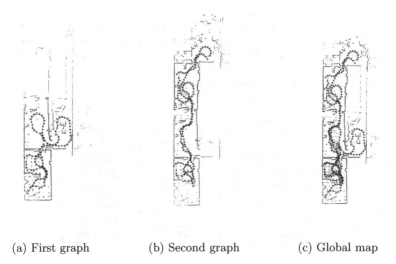

(a) First graph   (b) Second graph   (c) Global map

Fig. 3. This figure illustrates the behavior of our algorithm on the Bremen University dataset. *a)*, *b)* are the input pose graphs, representing different portions of the same environment. *c)* shows the merged pose graph.

4.1 Raw Data Experiments

Our scenario consists in a mobile robot equipped with a laser range finder and a test environment. We acquired the datasets in different, but partially overlapping, portions of the environment. We processed each dataset with a graph-based SLAM engine to obtain the corresponding pose graph. We then compute two solutions, one obtained using our approach, and another derived via a gradient descent algorithm. Finally, the computed solutions are compared evaluating their entropy, [2]. To analyze the behavior of the algorithm when working on grid maps, obtainable using also non graph-based SLAM engines like GMapping [9], we computed an occupancy grid map out of each pose graph. From each grid map, we recompute a pose graph as described in Section 3.2, and we seed them as input to our algorithm.

We conducted the experiments above using a real robot in our building (Dis-Basement). In addition, we used some public datasets [10] to generate realistic maps. We then used the Stage simulator to record multiple datasets of the same environment. Table 1 summarizes the results of our experiments, while Figure 3 shows a typical result. In all cases we analyzed the final solution of our system provided a lower entropy than the baseline, thus a more consistent map.

4.2 Synthetic Experiments

We found that the dominant aspect influencing the behavior of our system is the error affecting the local maps solutions. To quantify this effect, we generated a set of synthetic pose graphs of a robot moving in a Manhattan world. We generated edges between nearby poses and we corrupted them with Gaussian

Table 1. Analysis of the entropy of reconstructed global maps. We compare the result of a gradient descent-based technique, second column, against the approach presented in this paper, third column. In bold, we highlight the best result, for each dataset used for the validation.

A more detailed description, together with the datasets, can be found at:
www.dis.uniroma1.it/~bonanni/datasets

Dataset	Single Rigid Transformation	Graph-Based Map Merging
Dis-Basement-Small	2039.99	**1538.54**
Dis-Basement-Big-Real	2144.23	**2090.17**
Dis-Basement-Big-Voronoi	4059.91	**3856.92**
Dis-F1-Real	5639.96	**5528.97**
Dis-F1-Voronoi	5928.52	**5778.84**
UBremen-Real	3436.44	**3308.56**

Table 2. Analysis of the absolute trajectory error at increasing levels of gaussian noise. For the translational error, we perturbed both the x, and y axes. In bold, we highlight the best result, at the given noise configuration. Our approach, fourth column, offers better performance with respect to the alignment obtained by a single rigid transformation, third column.

Translational error $[x, y]$ (m)	Rotational error (deg)	Rigid Transformation ATE	Deformable Bodies ATE
[0.05, 0.01]	2	469.074	**10.2425**
[0.1, 0.01]	2	721.868	**42.5413**
[0.15, 0.01]	2	719.509	**150.515**
[0.2, 0.01]	2	877.672	**243.552**
[0.25, 0.01]	2	989.12	**523.802**
[0.05, 0.02]	2	402.974	**9.49795**
[0.1, 0.02]	2	682.997	**32.4582**
[0.15, 0.02]	2	893.562	**62.5047**
[0.2, 0.02]	2	1029.25	**296.88**
[0.25, 0.02]	2	1130.6	**394.299**
[0.05, 0.03]	2	336.44	**10.4215**
[0.1, 0.03]	2	593.754	**30.4705**
[0.15, 0.03]	2	825.884	**59.5759**
[0.2, 0.03]	2	1058.69	**310.821**
[0.25, 0.03]	2	1329.29	**421.79**

noise. The noise in the edges models the errors in the matching procedure used by a SLAM algorithm, and affects the final solution. Given two partial pose graphs, we compute the ideal merged graph by adding all the edges between nearby nodes in the two input graphs and we optimize the final result. This result is the best we can do with the noisy input data, and serves us as a baseline. The ideal edges are computed from the ground truth accessible by the simulator.

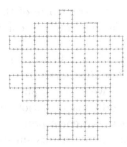

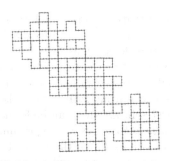

(a) Reference trajectory without noise

(b) Matchable trajectory without noise

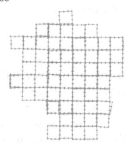

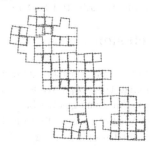

(c) Reference trajectory with noise

(d) Matchable trajectory with noise

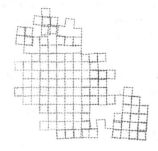

(e) Standard map merging approach

(f) Our approach based on deformable bodies

Fig. 4. This figure shows a synthetic experiment where we evaluate our approach on a simulated Manhattan world. *a)*, *b)* show the ground truth trajectories of the robot. *c)*, *d)* show the outcome of a graph-based SLAM algorithm on these trajectories. The residual error results in inconsistencies. *e)*, *f)* show the result of a standard map merging procedure that just overlays the maps with a single transformation and of our approach.

Figure 4 shows the typical pose graphs used in these experiments. In addition to the sensor noise, we also characterized the potential failures of the matching routine used in the *tryMatch()* function of Algorithm 1. The chances of success of a scan matcher depend mostly on how good is the initial guess. We simulated a scan matcher, by implementing a *tryMatch()* function that, having access to the ground truth, reports a solution only if the relative transform of the nodes passed as argument is close to the ground truth. Furthermore, we corrupt the resulting transformations, by adding Gaussian noise.

We evaluate the quality of the solution of the graph matching by measuring the *Absolute Trajectory Error* (ATE), [23], between the ideal solution and the one computed by our algorithm. For sake of comparison, we also compute the ATE of the best solution that can be found by a single rigid transformation, by using the *Iterative Closest Point* algorithm, ICP, [17], between corresponding nodes. In all cases the ATE of the merged map using our approach was substantially smaller than the baseline obtained by rigid body transformation. As expected, the quality of the solution decreases as the error residual increases, and the estimate is mostly affected by the rotational part of the error.

5 Conclusion

In this paper we presented a generic approach to merge maps described as pose graphs. In case the maps are available as grid maps we provided a technique to extract plausible pose graphs based on Voronoi diagrams. Our method is able to cope with residual errors affecting the input maps, and to remove the artifacts that a standard map merging method leaves in. We validated our approach on real world datasets, and we characterized its sensibility to the noise in the input solutions by simulation, although a more detailed evaluation and a more precise comparison with other existing methods is in progress. Future work is mainly focused at extending the approach to the 3D case, since it represents the new horizon of different modern SLAM techniques.

Acknowledgments. This work has partly been supported by the European Commission under FP7-600890-ROVINA.

References

1. Agarwal, P., Tipaldi, G.D., Spinello, L., Stachniss, C., Burgard, W.: Robust map optimization using dynamic covariance scaling. In: Proceedings of the IEEE International Conference on Robotics and Automation (ICRA) (May 2013)
2. Blanco, J.L., Fernández-Madrigal, J.A., Gonzalez, J.: An entropy-based measurement of certainty in rao-blackwellized particle filter mapping. In: 2006 IEEE/RSJ International Conference on Intelligent Robots and Systems, pp. 3550–3555. IEEE (2006)
3. Bunke, H.: Graph matching: Theoretical foundations, algorithms, and applications. In: Proc. Vision Interface, vol. 2000, pp. 82–88 (2000)
4. Carlone, L., Ng, M.K., Du, J., Bona, B., Indri, M.: Rao-blackwellized particle filters multi robot slam with unknown initial correspondences and limited communication. In: 2010 IEEE International Conference on Robotics and Automation (ICRA), pp. 243–249. IEEE (2010)
5. Carpin, S.: Fast and accurate map merging for multi-robot systems. Autonomous Robots 25(3), 305–316 (2008)

6. Cunningham, A., Paluri, M., Dellaert, F.: Ddf-sam: Fully distributed slam using constrained factor graphs. In: 2010 IEEE/RSJ International Conference on Intelligent Robots and Systems (IROS), pp. 3025–3030. IEEE (2010)

7. Erinc, G., Carpin, S.: Anytime merging of appearance-based maps. Autonomous Robots 36(3), 241–256 (2014)

8. Grisetti, G., Kümmerle, R., Stachniss, C., Burgard, W.: A tutorial on graph-based slam. Magazine on Intelligent Transportation Systems 2(4), 31–43 (2010)

9. Grisetti, G., Stachniss, C., Burgard, W.: Improved techniques for grid mapping with rao-blackwellized particle filters. IEEE Trans. on Robotics 23(1), 34–46 (2007)

10. Howard, A., Roy, N.: The robotics data set repository, Radish (2003), http://radish.sourceforge.net/

11. Huang, W.H., Beevers, K.R.: Topological map merging. The International Journal of Robotics Research 24(8), 601–613 (2005)

12. Jennings, J., Kirkwood-Watts, C., Tanis, C.: Distributed map-making and navigation in dynamic environments. In: Proceedings of the IEEE/RSJ International Conference on Intelligent Robots and Systems, vol. 3, pp. 1695–1701. IEEE (1998)

13. Kümmerle, R., Grisetti, G., Strasdat, H., Konolige, K., Burgard, W.: g2o: A general framework for graph optimization. In: Proc. of the IEEE Int. Conf. on Robotics & Automation (ICRA) (2011)

14. Lazaro, M., Paz, L., Piniés, P., Castellanos, J., Grisetti, G.: Multi-robot slam using condensed measurements. In: 2013 IEEE/RSJ International Conference on Intelligent Robots and Systems (IROS), pp. 1069–1076. IEEE (2013)

15. Leung, K.Y.K., Barfoot, T.D., Liu, H.H.: Distributed and decentralized cooperative simultaneous localization and mapping for dynamic and sparse robot networks. In: 2011 IEEE International Conference on Robotics and Automation (ICRA), pp. 3841–3847. IEEE (2011)

16. Lu, F., Milios, E.: Globally consistent range scan alignment for environment mapping. Autonomous Robots 4, 333–349 (1997)

17. Lu, F., Milios, E.: Robot pose estimation in unknown environments by matching 2D range scans. Journal of Intelligent and Robotic Systems 18(3), 249–275 (1997)

18. Montemerlo, M., Thrun, S., Koller, D., Wegbreit, B.: FastSLAM: A factored solution to simultaneous localization and mapping. In: Proc. of the National Conference on Artificial Intelligence (AAAI), Edmonton, Canada, pp. 593–598 (2002)

19. Olson, E., Leonard, J., Teller, S.: Fast iterative optimization of pose graphs with poor initial estimates. In: Proc. of the IEEE Int. Conf. on Robotics & Automation (ICRA), pp. 2262–2269 (2006)

20. Saeedi, S., Paull, L., Trentini, M., Seto, M., Li, H.: Map merging using hough peak matching. In: 2012 IEEE/RSJ International Conference on Intelligent Robots and Systems (IROS), pp. 4683–4688. IEEE (2012)

21. Smith, R., Self, M., Cheeseman, P.: Estimating uncertain spatial realtionships in robotics. In: Cox, I., Wilfong, G. (eds.) Autonomous Robot Vehicles, pp. 167–193. Springer (1990)

22. Thrun, S., Liu, Y., Koller, D., Ng, A., Ghahramani, Z., Durrant-Whyte, H.: Simultaneous localization and mapping with sparse extended information filters. Int. Journal of Robotics Research 23(7/8), 693–716 (2004)

23. Wulf, O., Nuchter, A., Hertzberg, J., Wagner, B.: Ground truth evaluation of large urban 6d slam. In: IEEE/RSJ International Conference on Intelligent Robots and Systems, IROS 2007, pp. 650–657. IEEE (2007)

Lower Limb Stiffness Estimation during Running: The Effect of Using Kinematic Constraints in Muscle Force Optimization Algorithms

Roberto Bortoletto[1], Enrico Pagello[1], and Davide Piovesan[2]

[1] Intelligent Autonomous Systems Laboratory (IAS-Lab.), University of Padua, Department of Information Engineering, Via G. Gradenigo 6/b, 35131 Padova, Italy
{roberto.bortoletto,epv}@dei.unipd.it
[2] Biomedical Program, Mechanical Engineering Department, Gannon University, 109 University Square, PMB #3251, Erie, PA 16541, USA
piovesan001@gannon.edu

Abstract. The focus of this paper is on the effect of muscle force optimization algorithms on the human lower limb stiffness estimation. By using a forward dynamic neuromusculoskeletal model coupled with a muscle short-range stiffness model we computed the human joint stiffness of the lower limb during running. The joint stiffness values are calculated using two different muscle force optimization procedures, namely: Toque-based and Torque/Kinematic-based algorithm. A comparison between the processed EMG signal and the corresponding estimated muscle forces with the two optimization algorithms is provided. We found that the two stiffness estimates are strongly influenced by the adopted algorithm. We observed different magnitude and timing of both the estimated muscle forces and joint stiffness time profile with respect to each gait phase, as function of the optimization algorithm used.

Keywords: joint stiffness, muscle force, optimization algorithms.

1 Introduction

During the last two decades the interest in understanding the physiological basis of human and animal movement has resulted in an extensive range of experiments. The study of human movement has been improved through the introduction of muscle-driven dynamic simulations. This approach includes mathematical models of muscle activation and contraction dynamics and allows for the calculation of muscle forces, fiber lengths, and other parameters that cannot be easily measured in-vivo. Muscle-driven simulations have been used in a wide variety of applications, including the analysis of human walking [1–3], running [4], and pathological gait [5]. Biomechanical models have been used in several studies to predict the muscle forces and joint torques along with human body motion. One of the first muscle's mathematical models was proposed by Hill [6]. Gordon et al. [7] refined such model by incorporating the dependence between changes in muscle force as function of muscle lengths and contraction speeds. Zajac extended

D. Brugali et al. (Eds.): SIMPAR 2014, LNAI 8810, pp. 364–375, 2014.

the Hill's model introducing a muscle-tendon model [8], which is known as Hill-type muscle force model. The prediction of muscle force can be also calculated independently from a model by means of optimization algorithms. Such algorithms are usually based on a cost function that depends directly on a physical parameters such as force variance, energy, muscle stress, to name a few [9–11]. When accomplishing a task, that require both the following of a trajectory and the exertion of a force, humans need to modulate not only the generated muscle forces, but also the corresponding limb stiffness. During unimpaired gait, depending on the terrain, one might either walk in a relaxed manner or stiffen up to increase stability. Several studies have been proposed to estimate the hip [12], knee [13, 14] and ankle [15] joint stiffness to characterize the mechanical properties of the whole limb [16–18]. Moreover, a preliminary study about the incidence of the adopted muscle-tendon model on the joint stiffness estimation has been proposed in [19].

This paper targets two main research topics: the use of forward dynamic neuromusculoskeletal modeling to estimate muscle forces, joint moments, and joint kinematics from biological signal, and the use of muscle short-range stiffness to estimate human lower limb joint stiffness. In particular, the aim of this study is to evaluate how the adoption of different muscle force optimization algorithms, based on the inclusion or exclusion of kinematic constraints, affects the lower limb stiffness estimation during running.

2 Methods

In this study we performed a series of simulations that coupled a 3D human musculoskeletal model of the lower limb with a model of muscle stiffness, to estimate leg's joint stiffness during running. The algorithm to compute joint stiffness is dependent on the value of the computed muscle force. We compared the stiffness values obtained in simulation using two different muscle force optimization procedures, that we call *Torque-based Muscle Force computation* and *Torque/Kinematic-based Muscle Force computation*. The musculoskeletal model that we used is freely available with the OpenSim[1] platform. It includes seven body segments for each leg: pelvis, femur, patella, tibia-fibula, talus, foot, and toes. Each foot includes the calcaneus, navicular, cuboid, cuneiformis, and metatarsal. Each arm is represented by humerus, ulna, radius, and hand. The joint definitions are derived by [20, 21] and the anthropometry by [22]. The physiological parameters of muscles are in accordance to mean values reported in [23]. 92 muscle-tendon actuators represent the main muscle groups: 43 for each leg, and 6 lumbar muscles. The arm joints are actuated by ideal torque motors. The experimental dataset used here is freely available within the *"Muscle function of overground running across a range of speeds"*[2] section of the SimTk.org[3]. The website is a public repository for data, models, and computational tools related

---

[1] OpenSim Project Overview: https://simtk.org/home/opensim
[2] Project's page: https://simtk.org/home/runningspeeds
[3] Repository's home page: https://simtk.org/xml/index.xml

to physics-based simulation of biological systems. These data were originally collected with the purpose to better understand how the leg muscles coordinate motion of the body segments during running. A detailed description of the adopted experimental protocol is available in [24]. We considered the Electromyographic (EMG), Motion Capture (MC) and Ground Reaction Forces (GRFs) data referred to a male subject (age, 19 years; mass, 75.9 Kg; height, 1.82 m; leg length, 1.00 m) that at the time of testing were not suffering from any musculoskeletal injury likely to adversely affect their sprinting ability. Among the data we considered a medium-paced running speed at 5.20 ms^{-1}. The raw data, available in .c3d format[4], were processed in Matlab to extract the information relative to the kinematic, the GRFs and the EMG signals of the subject. The kinematic and GRFs data were used in OpenSim to scale the musculoskeletal model to the anthropometry of the real subject, and to compute the joint angle values by solving the Inverse Kinematics (IK) problem. Then, using the Residual Reduction Algorithm[5] (RRA) we optimized the model adjusting the mass distribution and joint kinematics to make them consistent with GRFs. The next step was to solve the Inverse Dynamics (ID) problem to compute the joint torques. At this point, the force generated by each muscle was estimated by adopting the two optimization techniques: *Torque-based Muscle Force computation* (subsection 2.1) and *Torque/Kinematic-based Muscle Force computation* (subsection 2.2), which do not involve the use of a specific muscle model, but only information about the Maximum Isometric Force (MIF) exertable by each muscle. The waveforms of the EMG signals were used to highlight the similarities and differences between the obtained estimates, compared with the experimental data.

2.1   Torque-Based Muscle Force Computation

The *Torque-based Muscle Force computation* procedure is based on the use of an optimization which estimates the distribution of muscle forces for a specific set of joint torques. The cost function is the sum of the squared muscle forces (Eq.1), expressed as a fraction of the MIF for each muscle. A set of constraints was considered such that the resulting muscle forces summed to the specific joint torque (Eq.2), and muscle forces were positive and less than or equal to the achievable MIF (Eq.3).

$$u = \min \sum_{i=1}^{M} \left(\frac{F_{m,i}}{F_{m,i}^0} \right)^2 \tag{1}$$

$$\tau_j = \sum_{i=1}^{M} r_{ij} \times F_{m,i} \quad i = 1, 2, ..., M; \quad j = 1, 2, ..., N \tag{2}$$

$$0 \le F_{m,i} \le F_{m,i}^0 \tag{3}$$

---

[4] C3D File Format Specification: http://www.c3d.org

[5] http://simtk-confluence.stanford.edu:8080/display/OpenSim/How+RRA+Works

where $F_{m,i}$ is the muscle force of the i-th muscle and $F^0_{m,i}$ is the corresponding MIF, r_{ij} is the posture-dependent moment arm for the i-th muscle relative to the j-th joint, and τ_j is the torque about the j-th joint. The sum over M elements corresponds to the number of muscle-tendon actuator crossing the hip, knee and ankle joint in the model. N is the number of Degrees of Freedom (DOFs). The data related to $F^0_{m,i}$, r_{ij}, and τ_j were taken from the musculoskeletal model and from the simulation executed within OpenSim. In which the ID problem was solved taking into account the GRFs. Given these data as input and minimizing the cost function with respect to the constraints we obtained the corresponding muscle forces $F_{m,i}$. The *Torque-based Muscle Force computation* procedure was performed in Matlab environment.

2.2   Torque/Kinematic-Based Muscle Force Computation

The *Torque/Kinematic-based Muscle Force computation* algorithm represents the procedure available within OpenSim to compute the muscle excitation and the corresponding muscle force. It is based on the use of the Computed Muscle Control (CMC) tool [25]. We extracted the information related to the muscle force by executing the CMC in order to compute the muscle excitation levels that drives the generalized coordinates of the dynamic musculoskeletal model towards the desired trajectory. The available implementation is based on the combination of Proportional-Derivative (PD) control and Static Optimization (SO) that allow to conduct a standard forward dynamic simulation. A detailed description of the CMC tool operating principles is available in [26]. We report here only the main concepts with particular reference to the computation of the muscle forces. In this study, the SO toolbox is used by CMC to resolve the net joint torques and moments into individual muscle forces subject to the following muscle activation-to-force condition:

$$\sum_{i=1}^{M} a_{m,i} F^0_{m,i} r_{ij} = \tau_j \quad \forall j \tag{4}$$

where M is the number of muscles, $a_{m,i}$ is the activation level ($0 < a_{m,i} \leq 1$), $F^0_{m,i}$ is the MIF, and r_{ij} is the moment arm of the i-th muscle about the j-th joint. τ_j is the joint torque acting about the j-th joint. In CMC, an objective function J combines the sum of squared muscle activations augmented by a set of equality constraints ($C_j = 0$) that requires the desired accelerations to be achieved within the tolerance set for the optimizer (Eq.5).

$$J = \sum_{i=1}^{M} (a_{m,i})^2 \,; \qquad C_j = \ddot{q}^*_j - \ddot{q}_j \quad \forall j \tag{5}$$

where M is the number of muscles and $a_{m,i}$ is the activation level ($0 < a_{m,i} \leq 1$). This setup is equivalent to having an ideal force generators in which the model accelerations $\ddot{q}_j$ are driven toward the desired accelerations $\ddot{q}^*_j$, where q_j

respresents the j-th model coordinate. The desired accelerations are computed using the following PD control law:

$$\ddot{q}^*(t+T) = \ddot{q}_{exp}(t+T) + k_v[\dot{q}_{exp}(t) - \dot{q}(t)] + k_p[q_{exp}(t) - q(t)] \qquad (6)$$

where q_{exp} are the experimentally-derived coordinates, $\ddot{q}^*$ are the desired accelerations, and q are the model coordinates. $k_v = 30$ and $k_p = 900$ are the feedback gains on velocity and position errors, which were experimentally set.

It is worth noting that, by assuming $0 \le F_{m,i} \le F^0_{m,i}$ in *Torque-based Muscle Force computation* and $0 < a_{m,i} \le 1$ in *Torque/Kinematic-based Muscle Force computation*, then Eq.4 is equivalent to Eq.2, and Eq.5 is equivalent to Eq.1. This because, the ratio $F_{m,i}/F^0_{m,i}$ always varies between 0 and 1. On the other hand, the introduction of the kinematic constraints ($C_j = \ddot{q}^*_j - \ddot{q}_j \quad \forall j$) in Eq.5, encompassing the coordinate accelerations, significantly diversifies the two approaches considered here. This is especially true since we are analyzing dynamic movement such as running in its different phases and not simply static poses.

2.3   Stiffness Estimation

The adopted muscle model is known in literature as *Thelen2003Muscle* [27], which is the name of its implementation within the OpenSim. The model is based on the Hill-type muscle model, which represents a muscle-tendon unit through three elements: a contractile element (CE), a parallel element (PE), and a series element (SE). While CE is responsible for the active force, PE accounts for the muscle passive behavior and SE represents the tendon. *Thelen2003Muscle* is a parametric-based implementation capable of representing the muscle mechanical response by considering the following physiological parameters: MIF, Optimal Muscle Fiber Length (OMFL), Tendon Slack Length (TSL), Maximum Contraction Velocity (MCV), and Pennation Angle (PA). Given the normalized muscle force obtained either within CMC or with our dedicated algorithm, the muscle fiber length was estimated by means of Force-Length relationship for each muscle embedded in the OpenSim's Muscle model. The force-length curves modeled the effects of active/passive muscle components. In particular, the active force-length curve was described using natural cubic splines [8], while the passive force-length curve was described using exponential functions [27]. The tendon length was estimated by subtracting the fiber length to the whole-muscle length derived from the path geometry and joint angles within the simulation.

Finally, the short-range muscle stiffness was estimated using the model developed by Cui et al. [28], and already adopted by Perreault et al. [29] for the estimation of the endpoint stiffness of the human arm. The model assumes that the short-range stiffness of a muscle-tendon unit, K_{mt} (Eq.7), results from the stiffness of the muscle fibers, K_m, in series with the stiffness of the tendon, K_t.

$$K_{mt} = \frac{K_m K_t}{K_m + K_t} \qquad (7)$$

K_m is a function of the muscle force F_m and OMFL l^m_0, up to a dimensionless scaling constant. K_t is defined by the ratio between the tendon force and the tendon elongation, which is given by the difference between the tendon length l_t and the TSL l_s^t. By using the estimated muscle forces and the muscle short-range stiffness, we computed the corresponding joint stiffness taking into account the kinematic relationship between changes in joint angles and changes in muscle-tendon length (Eq.8).

$$K_j = J^T \tilde{K}_{mt} J + \frac{\partial J^T}{\partial \theta} \tilde{F}_m \qquad (8)$$

where J is the Jacobian matrix relating changes in muscle joint angles to changes in muscle length, $\tilde{K}_{mt}$ is a diagonal matrix with the stiffness for each muscle in the model, $\tilde{F}_m$ is the vector of muscle forces, and θ is the vector of joint angles. The partial derivative of the Jacobian matrix with respect to joint angles accounts for how angle dependent changes in muscle moment arms influence joint stiffness. It is worth noting that K_j is a 3×3 matrix in which the diagonal elements represent the hip, knee and ankle joint stiffness, while the other elements represent the stiffness relationship existing between hip and knee, hip and ankle, knee and ankle. In particular, not having tri-articular muscles, in this study the hip-ankle stiffness relationship is zero. A comparison between the obtained joint stiffness using the two different muscle force optimization algorithms has been considered to show how the choice of a specific algorithm, for the estimation of force, affects the result we get in the computation of stiffness.

3 Results

The set of results, provided here, shows significant differences in the muscle force estimates obtained by adopting either the *Torque-based Muscle Force computation* or the *Torque/Kinematic-based Muscle Force computation* procedure. A first evaluation has been done by performing a cross-correlation analysis between muscle forces estimated with both *Torque-based Muscle Force computation* and *Torque/Kinematic-based Muscle Force computation* procedures, and the processed EMG signal (Fig. 1). The obtained cross-correlation sequences were normalized so that the autocorrelations at zero lag were identically 1.0. The results show that, for the muscles most involved in the analyzed movement (i.e. Gastrocnemius, Vasti, Rectus Femoris and Bicep Femoris), the cross-correlation related to the *Torque-based Muscle Force computation* is higher than that obtained for the *Torque/Kinematic-based Muscle Force computation* procedure.

Fig. 2 shows a comparison between the processed EMG signal of such representative muscles and their estimated forces. It is clear that most of the time the *Torque-based Muscle Force computation* (blue line) tracks EMG signal better than the *Torque/Kinematic-based Muscle Force computation* (green line), which gives large forces also when there is not EMG signal. This makes the latter less likely to be appropriate. During the optimization stage, through which the muscle force is computed, it may also happen that a high value of the EMG signal does not correspond to an equally high developed muscle force (Fig. 2, Right Rectus Femoris). This behavior may be due to a configuration of the muscle for which, despite the activation level, the fibers length is either very

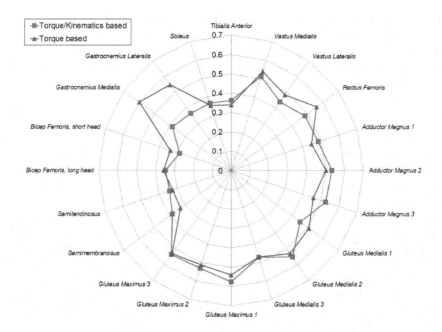

Fig. 1. Maximum values of the cross-correlation functions computed between muscle forces estimated with both *Torque-based Muscle Force computation* and *Torque/Kinematic-based Muscle Force computation* procedures, and the processed EMG signal

stretched or very contracted and does not allow the generation of an appropriate force with respect to the OMFL. Recall that the MIF is generated only at the OMFL. Future study should take into consideration methods to estimate muscle forces that better track the corresponding EMG profiles. Corresponding differences also arise in the stiffness values obtained by adopting either *Torque-based Muscle Force computation* or *Torque/Kinematic-based Muscle Force computation* procedure. As depicted in Fig.3 there is a misalignment of the peaks of the stiffness time profiles with respect to the different phases of movement. We can notice a delay between the instants in which the foot impacts the ground and the instant in which the stiffness peaks generated by either approach occurs. Notice that *Torque/Kinematic-based Muscle Force computation* has an average delay of 112 ms compared to the 82 ms of *Torque-based Muscle Force computation*. Furthermore, the former produces stiffness peaks with a much larger amplitude compared to the latter. The stiffness peaks for both knee and ankle occurs almost synchronously within each model. Furthermore, we can notice that the width of stiffness peaks are different between algorithms. For example, the graph of the knee stiffness shows that the knee is contracted for a longer time in the *Torque/Kinematic-based Muscle Force computation*. The ratio of hip/knee stiffness at the peak is different for the two approaches: 1.28 (*Torque-based Muscle Force computation*), 1.86 (*Torque/Kinematic-based Muscle Force computation*).

The second ratio is bigger indicating a predominancy of hip stiffness over the other joints. Similar considerations hold true for the left lower limb joints.

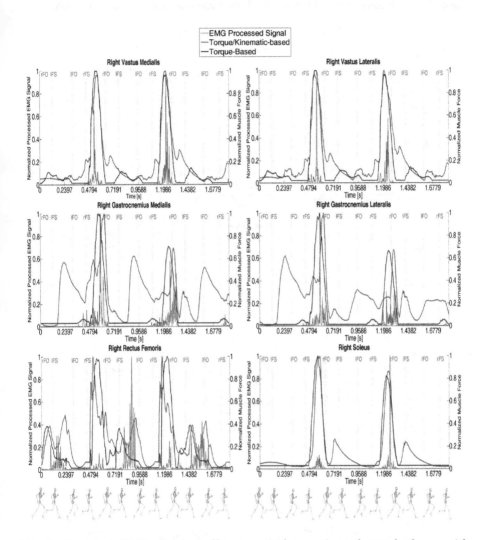

Fig. 2. Processed EMG signal profiles compared to estimated muscle forces with *Torque-based Muscle Force computation* and *Torque/Kinematic-based Muscle Force computation* procedures. The labels stand for Left Foot-Off (lFO), Left Foot-Strike (lFS), Right Foot-Off (rFO), and Right Foot-Strike (rFS).

The inter-joint stiffness estimated in this work for each combination of two joints was found to be symmetric. Furthermore the inter-joint stiffness between hip and ankle was negligible. Thus, only two inter-joint stiffness time profiles are shown in Fig. 4. These results are an indication that all the algorithms were implemented properly. Indeed, since the stiffness is a positive definite tensor it is expected to be simmetric. Moreover, due to the absence of tri-articular muscles connecting the ilium with the foot the hip-ankle component must be zero.

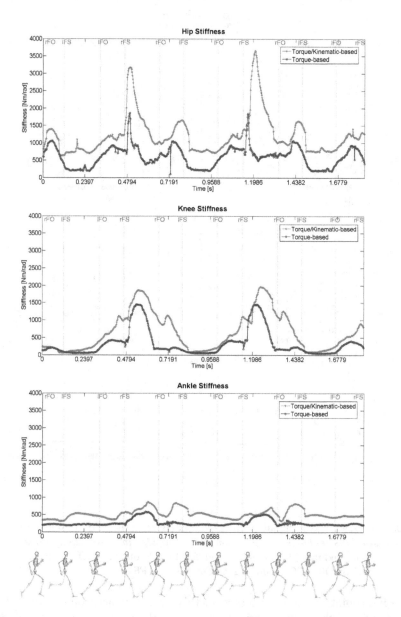

Fig. 3. Right Lower Limb Joint Stiffness estimated values: Hip, Knee, and Ankle. The x-axis reports the time-samples, while y-axis expresses the joint stiffness [Nm/rad]. The labels stand for Left Foot-Off (lFO), Left Foot-Strike (lFS), Right Foot-Off (rFO), and Right Foot-Strike (rFS).

The inter-joint stiffness is not negligible for the pair ankle-knee and knee-hip. However, the magnitude of these stiffness time-profiles is smaller than those proper of the joints.

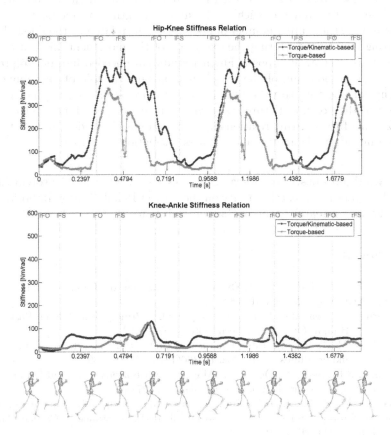

Fig. 4. Right Lower Limb Intra-Joint Stiffness estimated values: Hip-Knee Stiffness Relation, and Knee-Ankle Stiffness Relation. The x-axis reports the time-samples, while y-axis expresses the intra-joint stiffness [Nm/rad]. The labels stand for Left Foot-Off (lFO), Left Foot-Strike (lFS), Right Foot-Off (rFO), and Right Foot-Strike (rFS).

4   Conclusions

In this paper, two different whole-muscle force optimization algorithms are utilized to estimate the lower limb muscle-tendon forces and the corresponding joint stiffness during the running of an unimpaired individuals. It is important to note that the purpose of this study was not to determine which algorithm is better for the estimation of muscle forces, but the goal was to determine how different algorithms may affect the estimation of joint stiffness. Indeed, results show that the choice of the optimization algorithm influences the estimation of the muscle-tendon stiffness and of the corresponding joint stiffness. The adopted modeling and simulation techniques highlight how it is possible to estimate the joint stiffness decomposing the computation into two stages, where the assumption of a muscle-tendon model is actually required only in the computation of the geometrical parameters such as the muscle lengths and moment arms. At the same time, there are a number of open questions related to the possibility of estimating the stiffness during the execution of the movement and not only in relation to particular limb poses. Further studies are needed in order to provide a more precise modeling of the muscle-tendon unit capable of describing how the behavior and the parameterization of the muscle-tendon unit changes as a function of the posture. Future research will focus on providing a better characterization of the existing relationships between muscle models, muscle-tendon force optimization algorithms and stiffness estimation procedures.

Acknowledgements. This research has been supported by Consorzio Ethics through a grant for research activity on the project Rehabilitation Robotics, and by the Faculty research grant at Gannon University.

References

1. Anderson, F.C., Pandy, M.G.: Dynamic Optimization of Human Walking. ASME J. Biomech. Eng. 123(5), 381–390
2. Ackerman, M., van der Bogert, A.J.: Optimality Principles for Model-Based Prediction of Human Gait. J. Biomech. 43(6), 1055–1060
3. Arnold, E.M., Delp, S.L.: Fibre Operating Lengths of Human Lower Limb Muscle During Walking. Philos. T. R. Soc. B. 366(1570), 1530–1539
4. Hamner, S.R., Seth, A., Delp, S.L.: Muscle Contributions to Propulsion and Support During Running. J. Biomech. 43(14), 2709–2716
5. Steele, K.M., Seth, A., Hicks, J.L., Schwartz, M.S., Delp, S.L.: Muscle Contributions to Support and Progression During Single-Limb Stance in Crouch Gait. J. Biomech. 43(11), 2099–2105
6. Hill, A.V.: The Heat of Shortening and the Dynamic Constants of Muscle. Proc. R. Soc. Lond. B (1938)
7. Gordon, A.M., Huxley, A.F., Julian, F.J.: The variation in isometric tension with sarcomere length in vertebrate muscle fibres. J. of Phys. 184, 170–192 (1966)
8. Zajac, F.E.: Muscle and tendon: properties, models, scaling, and application to biomechanics and motor contro. Crit. Rev. Biomed. Eng. 17, 359–411 (1989)
9. Anderson, F.C., Pandy, M.G.: Static and dynamic optimization solutions for gait are pratically equivalent. J. Biomech. 34(2), 153–161 (2001)
10. Erdemir, A., McLean, S., Herzog, W., van den Bogert, A.J.: Model-based estimation of muscle forces exerted during movements. Clinical Biomechanics 22, 131–154 (2007)
11. Monaco, V., Coscia, M., Micera, S.: Cost function tuning improves muscle force estimation computed by static optimization during walking. In: Conf. Proc. IEEE Eng. Med. Biol. Soc. (2011)
12. Shamaei, K., Sawicki, G.S., Dollar, A.M.: Estimation of Quasi-Stiffness of the Human Hip in the Stance Phase of Walking. PloS One 8(12) (2013)

13. Pfeifer, S., Vallery, H., Hardegger, M., Riener, R., Perreault, E.J.: Model-based estimation of knee stiffness. IEEE Trans. on Bio-medical Engineering 59(9), 2604–2615 (2012)
14. Shamaei, K., Sawicki, G.S., Dollar, A.M.: Estimation of quasi-stiffness of the human knee in the stance phase of walking. PloS One 8(3) (2013)
15. Shamaei, K., Sawicki, G.S., Dollar, A.M.: Estimation of quasi-stiffness and propulsive work of the human ankle in the stance phase of walking. PloS One 8(3) (2013)
16. Piovesan, D., Pierobon, A., DiZio, P., Lackner, J.R.: Experimental Measure of Arm Stiffness During Single Reaching Movements with a Time-Frequency Analysis. J. Neurophysiol. 110(10), 2484–2496 (2013)
17. Piovesan, D., Casadio, M., Morasso, P., Giannoni, P.: Arm stiffness during assisted movements following stroke: the influence of visual feedback and training. IEEE Trans. Neural Syst. Rehabil. Eng. 21(3), 454–465 (2013)
18. Piovesan, D., Pierobon, A., DiZio, P., Lackner, J.R.: Measuring Multi-Joint Stiffness during Single Movements: Numerical Validation of a Novel Time-Frequency Approach. PLoS ONE 7(3), e33086 (2012)
19. Bortoletto, R., Pagello, E., Piovesan, D.: How different human muscle models affect the estimation of lower limb joint stiffness during running. Accepted for publication in Proc. of Workshop on Neuro-Robotics for Patient-Specific Rehabilitation, July 18 (2014), IAS-13 Conf., Padua, July 15-19 (2014)
20. Yamaguchi, G.T., Zajac, F.E.: A planar model of the knee joint to characterize the knee extensor mechanism. J. Biomech. 22, 1–10 (1989)
21. Delp, S.L., Loan, J.P., Hoy, M.G., Zajac, F.E., Topp, E.L., Rosen, J.M.: An Interactive Graphics-Based Model of the Lower Extremity to Study Orthopaedic Surgical Procedures. IEEE Trans. Biomed. Eng. 37(8), 757–767
22. Anderson, F.C., Pandy, M.G.: A Dynamic Optimization Solution for Vertical Jumping in Three Dimensions. Comput. Methods Biomech. Biomed. Engin. 2(3), 201–231 (1999)
23. Ward, S.R., Eng, C.M., Smallwood, L.H., Lieber, R.L.: Are current measurements of lower extremity muscle architecture accurate? Clin. Orthop. Relat. Res. 467, 1074–1082 (2009)
24. Dorn, T.W., Schache, A.G., Pandy, M.G.: Muscular startegy shift in human running: dependence of running speed on hip and ankle muscle performance. The J. of Exp. Biol. 215, 1944–1956 (2012)
25. Thelen, D.G., Anderson, F.C., Delp, S.L.: Generating dynamic simulations of movement using computed muscle control. J. of Biomec. 36, 321–328 (2003)
26. Thelen, D.G., Anderson, F.C.: Using computed muscle control to generate forward dynamic simulations of human walking from experimental data. J. Biomech. 39(6), 1107–1115 (2006)
27. Thelen, D.G.: Adjustment of Muscle Mechanics Model Parameters to Simulate Dynamic Contractions in Older Adults. J. Biomech. Eng. 125(1), 70 (2003)
28. Cui, L., Perreault, E.J., Maas, H., Sandercock, T.G.: Modeling short-range stiffness of feline lower hindlimb muscles. J. Biomech. 41, 1945–1952 (2008)
29. Hu, X., Murray, W.M., Perreault, E.J.: Muscle short-range stiffness can be used to estimate the endpoint stiffness of the human arm. Journal of Neurophysiology 105(4), 1633–1641 (2011)

On the Benefits of Component-Defined Real-Time Visualization of Robotics Software

Max Reichardt, Gregor Zolynski, Michael Arndt, and Karsten Berns

Robotics Research Lab., Department of Computer Science,
University of Kaiserslautern, Gottlieb-Daimler-Straße,
67663 Kaiserslautern, Germany
{reichardt,zolynski,arndt,berns}@cs.uni-kl.de
http://rrlab.cs.uni-kl.de

Abstract. The idea of component-defined visualization is introduced and benefits for different challenges in robotics software development are discussed – including system maintenance, component integration, and identification of critical behavior or malfunction. Design considerations for integration in state-of-the-art robotic software frameworks are presented – with an open source implementation for the FINROC framework as a proof-of-concept. Its use in two very different autonomous systems is illustrated. Experiments with these systems indicate that the proposed approach has in fact relevant advantages.

Keywords: Autonomous mobile robots, Framework design, Programming environments, Software visualization, System maintenance.

1 The Idea of Component-Defined Visualization

In the domain of process automation, visualization of system components on possibly large control panels has a long tradition. Subsystem state is displayed in a dedicated and intuitive way. An operator can identify critical situations and failures at a glance. Advantages are so significant that considerable resources are invested in this area.

Related to this idea, we propose an increased level of integrated component visualization in tools and frameworks for development of complex robot control software. We claim and show that this helps to cope with some of the major challenges in robotics software development.

Robot control systems are typically constructed from a set of interconnected components based on some robotic framework, toolkit, or middleware.[1] Many frameworks include tools to visualize connected components as a graph. In our research on large behavior-based networks with possibly many hundreds of nodes, a tool extension that visualizes the behavior meta signals in real-time [6] has proven valuable over many years. In particular, it helps understanding how a network of such components behaves and interacts. Usefulness of a suitable visualization is, however, not limited to behavior components. There are two approaches to visualize further types:

---

[1] For simplicity, the term "framework" will be used in the remainder of this document.

D. Brugali et al. (Eds.): SIMPAR 2014, LNAI 8810, pp. 376–387, 2014.

1. Tools "know" how to visualize all relevant components (*tool-defined*)
2. Components specify how they are visualized (*component-defined*)

The component-defined approach was chosen, as it has the advantages of lower coupling and increased flexibility, since all the components' internal data is accessible. The basic idea is the following: *Each component provides a visualization that should – as tellingly as possible – illustrate its current state and what it is doing.* This can be, for instance, displayed as a kind of animated thumbnail in the component graph. The idea is somewhat related to the concept of a *toString()* method that provides a suitable string representation for any relevant object.

1.1   Related Challenges in Robotics Software Development

Maintaining robotics software of considerable complexity is an important topic in industry and research groups. At university groups, keeping systems maintainable across multiple generations of PhD students is a major challenge. To make matters worse, spending time on software quality is typically not rewarded – as long as systems run sufficiently robust and efficient for experiments. At our lab, the larger projects' source trees consist of roughly 0.5 million SLOC[2] developed in-house and up to around 1600 components. Due to the complexity, it is often tempting to take rash decisions on rebuilding major parts of existing systems or to abandon them completely. We believe that the proposed idea of consequent component-defined visualization can make a noticeable difference in this regard. As we show in Chap. 5, it helps developers to explain what an unfamiliar system is doing – and why.

Finding bugs in robot control systems and increasing their robustness is another laborious activity. Even with well-tested components, problems can occur under specific environmental conditions or when components are reused across many projects and updates alter their behavior in a subtle way. Brugali et al. [3] discuss many challenges with respect to software reuse in robotics. Similar to the visualization in the domain of process automation, we believe that a dedicated visualization of each component supports identifying critical and faulty behavior – in single components as well as their integration and interaction. Again, experiments in Chap. 5 support this hypothesis. The advantages are likely largest when integrating components developed by third parties – due to the system integrator's more limited knowledge about their precise behavior. The visualization can be a supplement to their documentation and diagnostics interfaces.

1.2   Other Benefits and Possible Drawbacks

A factor not to be underestimated, is the potential increase of aesthetics in tool support. In our experience, this has an impact on developers' attitudes towards a framework and the interest in trying things out. In live demonstrations of a robot, showing the fully animated component network on a big screen arguably looks impressive and simplifies explaining.

---

[2] *Physical Source Lines of Code* as generated using David A. Wheeler's 'SLOCCount'.

If a framework provides support for constructing and connecting components at runtime, the effect of each change is immediately visible to the developer. If the visualization is furthermore provided by ordinary data ports (or topics), a framework's existing mechanisms can be used to record it to hard disk. This is a powerful combination for testing and debugging. Apart from that, components' visualizations can often be reused in dedicated graphical user interfaces.

The most obvious drawback with this approach is the development overhead for implementing a suitable visualization for individual components. Notably, several of our existing components were already creating visualization output before. In addition, visualization functionality can often be reused.

Another possible drawback is the runtime overhead that the visualization causes. As computational efficiency is a critical factor especially for mobile systems, it is important to retain the possibility to deactivate all visualization-related functionality. Apart from that, an efficient implementation is desirable.

2   Related Work

In the vast majority of software frameworks for robotics, applications are constructed from reusable components. Well-known solutions include ROS [7], Orocos [11], and OpenRTM-aist [1] – with tools such as *rxgraph* or *RtcLink* for visualization of connected components in a graph. In addition, it is often possible to display and modify component properties, parameters, or the current port values. We provide an overview on the state of the art in framework design in [8]. To our knowledge, no framework currently supports component-defined real-time visualization in its component model or tooling that visualizes the component graph. There are several solutions, though, that visualize component meta-information. Lotz et al., for instance, propose runtime monitoring of components [5]. Component status can be obtained from dedicated *diagnose ports* and is visualized e.g. via traffic lights.

Collet and MacDonald present a generic tool-defined visualization approach focussed on augmented reality [4]. Benefits for debugging systems are highlighted and evaluated. Discussions include a systematic requirements analysis.

Some authors propose visual programming in order to ease development especially for non-programmers. Well-known approaches include LEGO NXT-G, the Visual Programming Language (VPL) in Microsoft Robotics Developer Studio[3] and more general tools such as MatLab/Simulink and LabView. To our knowledge, none of these solutions employs this kind of visualization approach.

Looking outside the domain of robotics, procedural graphics generators such as Nodewerk and NeoTextureEdit[4] greatly benefit from online visualization of the effect network configuration. They were one of the inspirations that led to the development a similar visualization mode for our tools.

---

[3] http://www.microsoft.com/robotics/

[4] http://nodewerk.com/ and http://neotextureedit.sourceforge.net/

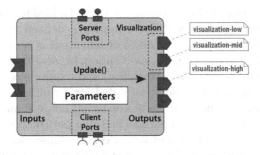

Fig. 1. Basic component model with optional, dedicated visualization outputs. Visualization information can be attached to any output – e.g. using tags.

3 Design Considerations

We target a simple design requiring only minor changes to current frameworks. Visualizations of components can be fairly complex (e.g. if images or maps are involved), thus costly to transfer and process. High update rates are desirable nevertheless – even for many connected tools. Considering these requirements, publishing visualization data using the publisher/subscriber pattern used in data ports of most frameworks was chosen – a simple and scalable solution. A client/server solution polling visualization data may be more flexible, but it is more complex to implement and typically causes more overhead and delay.

Apart from that, tools may display visualizations in different sizes – e.g. almost fullscreen on mouse-over. Always transferring maximum details would waste resources. Therefore, components must be able to provide visualization data in different levels of detail – corresponding to the displayed size. How many levels of detail should be supported is a tradeoff between many factors including simplicity, flexibility, and efficiency. We opted for three: *Low*, *Medium*, and *High*.

Furthermore, a decision on the visualization data format is required. Bitmaps and vector graphics are generic and universal choices. Supporting both is advantageous. Dedicated data types increase efficiency – e.g. for point clouds this can be relevant. If the same data types are allowed that components also use for publishing their data, a components' visualization data might actually be identical to one of its existing outputs. For example, the high-detail visualization of a camera component can actually be its full-resolution image output. In cases like these, it saves resources to use existing output ports for visualization instead of creating new ones. The option to define a default viewport is advantageous in this context, as visualization size might be too small to clearly display all of the data. If a framework allows to assign custom tags or annotations to outputs, an implementation can be very simple – even with dynamic component interfaces. For example, outputs could be tagged with [*visualization-low*], [*visualization-mid*], and [*visualization-high*]. Notably, a framework does not need to be adapted for this step – only components (add tags) and relevant tools.

In other cases, new ports for visualization need to be added. In order not to clutter a component's existing interfaces with ports only needed for visualization, they are created as dedicated visualization ports and added to a separate interface (see Fig. 1). As mentioned in Sect. 1.2, component-defined visualization causes computational overhead and an option to deactivate it is considered important. Using preprocessor directives is not a good option, because they clutter code with #ifdefs (detrimental to e.g. maintainability) and require recompilation to activate – e.g. for debugging. Therefore, we opted for a runtime option that specifies whether visualization ports are to be created. If not, computational overhead is minimal – typically one additional if-condition per component. Notably, the runtime option can easily be turned into a compile-time constant. If dedicated visualization is only generated and published if ports are actually connected, computational overhead is also minimal as long as there are no subscribers. This, however, requires a framework that provides this information.

Finally, extensibility is an important factor to keep in mind. In the proposed design, components can easily provide additional static information via tags or annotations – e.g. visualization shape or layout. Further outputs are also viable.

4   Implementation

We created an implementation of this design for the FINROC framework [9], which our research group and partners employ in a range of autonomous systems – such as offroad vehicles, indoor vehicles, climbing robots, and a humanoid – notably including commercial systems available for purchase.[5] FINROC's key features include a slim and highly modular framework core as well as a zero-copy, lock-free, real-time transport for intra-process communication. It can run on platforms without an operating system. Intra-process runtime construction, support for multiple component models, composite components, dynamic component interfaces, and good integrability with solutions based on other frameworks or standards are further notable features. Our implementation can be downloaded from http://www.finroc.org/ and is part of the FINROC 14.08 stable release.

Notably, less than 50 SLOC in FINROC's tComponent base class are sufficient to add convenient support for component-based visualization:

1. An enumeration for the available levels of detail
2. A method SetVisualizationPort to tag outputs to be used for visualization
3. A port wrapper class tVisualizationOutput for dedicated visualization outputs – together with a runtime parameter that determines whether visualization ports are created

Recurring, reusable visualization functionality – e.g. plotting signals, creating thumbnails – is placed in a separate library rrlib_component_visualization.

In order to display component-defined real-time visualization in the component graph, a new view *Component Visualization* was added to the FINSTRUCT tool (see Fig. 2). It is a subclass of the standard component graph view and retains the functionality to add, connect, and remove components at application runtime – as well as expanding composite components. Visualization size

---

[5] See e.g. http://robotmakers.de/en/references/

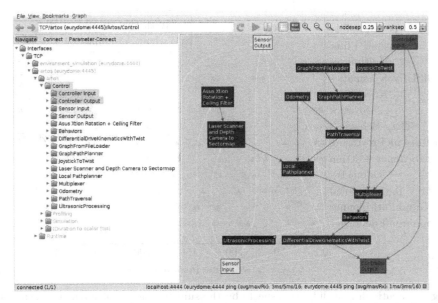

Fig. 2. FINSTRUCT: Application visualization, inspection, and construction. On the right, the component graph of ARTOS' control group is shown.

can be adjusted and a suitable level of detail is chosen automatically. Currently, any data type implementing FINROC's "Paintable" interface can be used for visualization. Colors of nodes and background can be adjusted.

5 Applications and Experiments

In order to evalute the proposed approach, experiments with subsystems of two autonomous mobile systems were conducted: the indoor robot ARTOS [2] and the bucket excavator THOR [10]. Fig. 2 shows the component graph of ARTOS' control group, which is responsible for sensor processing and navigation. Fig. 6 shows the same graph with component-defined visualization enabled. Fig. 7 contains both variants for THOR's perception subsystem for trailer detection.

5.1 Mobile Robot Control Analysis

During this experiment, the subject group of twelve people was presented the main control group of ARTOS in a controlled simulation environment. All participants used the FINSTRUCT tool to explore the system. Half of the group (six people) had the new visualization feature enabled, i.e. they could directly see the visualized state of the components.

The subjects were given the following task while being recorded on camera: "Please look at the robot control group and *describe* what you see and what you *think* the purpose of the components is." The statements and the time they took

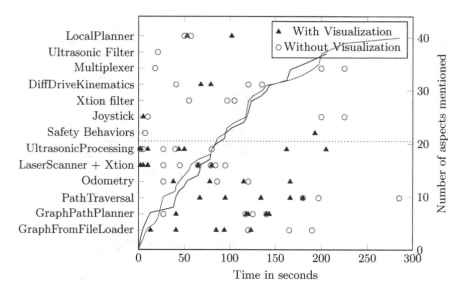

Fig. 3. Mentioning of different aspects by the subjects and total number of aspects named over time

to answer of the subjects were manifold. All mentioned aspects of the control system were collected. For evaluation, they were plotted in a scatterplot (see the left axis of Figure 3) against the time of mentioning by the probands, regardless of the correctness of the explained purposes. On the right axis the cumulative total number of mentioned aspects (of all probands) is plotted (both groups had the same size, so no normalization needed to be applied to the data).

Two interesting findings can be deduced from this plot. First, the presence of visualization does *not* seem to influence the total number of aspects mentioned. Both cumulative graphs have roughly the same shape and slope. As the probands just had to *mention* and not correctly explain the exact internal workings of the components, this observation is not further surprising.

Second, the visualization does seem to influence the perception of the components, as the answers show a difference in *what* the subjects are mentioning and describing *first*. In the graph, the lower six aspects are the ones that have been visualized in this experiment (divided by the thin dashed line). It can be clearly seen by the distribution of points that these aspects are mentioned early if the visualization is activated. On the other hand, the non-visualized aspects (upper six rows) are more likely to be mentioned early when no visualization is active. This arouses the suspicion that visualized components draw much attention towards them and away from non-visualized components that may of course nevertheless be important. When designing visualizations for components this psychological aspect should be taken into account.

In the second part of the experiment (after having described the purpose of the components), a hardware failure (a broken ultrasonic sensor returning a short value) was simulated and the subjects were asked to find out why the

Proband	Vis.	Time (m:s)
1	–	4:35
2	✓	0:03
3	–	4:04
4	✓	0:08
5	–	3:10
6	✓	0:51
7	–	– [6]
8	✓	0:27
9	✓	1:25
10	✓	0:26
11	–	3:18
12	–	4:50

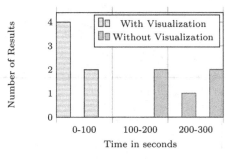

(a) Problem solving durations   (b) Times to find the failure in the system

Fig. 4. Results of the second part of the experiment

robot ceased moving (they were able to interactively control the robot in the simulation environment and were told that there is a "hardware" problem in the simulated hardware). The time the probands took to find the correct cause was recorded and is depicted in Fig. 4.

Analyzing the results, it can be clearly seen that in this scenario, the visualization can drastically reduce the time to find the failed ultrasonic sensor. One may argue that this is an artificial scenario. However, a similar problem was recently encountered with the real ARTOS. Sensors receiving no echo in a new environment, erroneously returned small instead of large distances. Now, with component-based visualization such a failure could be detected faster.

5.2 Understanding Unknown Systems

In this experiment, the participants were shown a part of THOR's perception group. They were asked a series of questions related to a few of the components.

1. What are the inputs of the **Point Cloud Collector**?
2. What is the input and the function of **Height Analysis**?
3. What are the inputs and the function of **Height Difference**?
4. What is the function of **Thresholded Difference**?
5. What is the function of **Grown Difference**?
6. What are the inputs and the outputs of **Steep/Flat Splitter**?
7. What is the purpose of the processing chain from *2* to *6*?
8. What are the outputs of **Heightmap Max/Min (flat)**?

Again, the subjects were divided into two groups – only one using the component visualization view. Both test groups consisted of persons of varying familiarity with FINROC. Some of them immediately knew how to obtain the necessary information. Others needed more time to navigate their way through the tool. Each person was asked the questions listed above, one by one, ensuring the correct answer was given before the next question came up.

In Fig. 5, each line stands for one experiment, showing the answered questions vs. time taken. The graphs for the two groups are separated into positive

---

[6] The participant did not find the cause after five minutes.

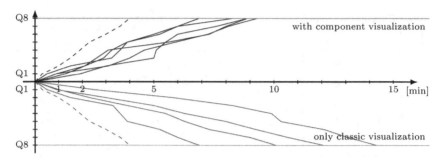

Fig. 5. Time taken to answer the questions

and negative y direction. The dashed lines show the "optimum" time, where we just read the questions and the explanations aloud. The results indicate that answering the questions using component visualization yields a consistent (generally quicker) timing between subjects of differing competency, whereas using the classic visualization the time needed varies greatly.

5.3   Computational Overhead

The computational overhead introduced with component-defined visualization was measured in the two presented systems. As can be seen in Table 1, overhead is not measurable when visualization outputs are present, but not connected. When visualization is active, resource consumption increases only slightly.

Table 1. Measurement of Computational Overhead

Visualization	THOR Control			ARTOS Control		
	absent	disconnected	connected	absent	disconnected	connected
CPU	201.0%	201.0%	201.0%	80.0%	80.0%	83.0%
Memory	784.9 MB	785.5 MB	794.7 MB	32.7 MB	32.7 MB	33 MB
Cycle time	84 ms	84 ms	90 ms	16 ms	16 ms	17 ms

6   Conclusion, Discussion, and Outlook

Overall, we see component-defined visualization as one of many promising measures to increase software quality of robotic components and systems – arguably with a relevant impact on maintainability. The experiments indicate that the proposed software visualization approach can help to understand unknown systems. Furthermore, there are bugs that can be found quicker than without. The approach can be realized efficiently with minimal changes to an existing framework – with negligible computational overhead.

Whether to add visualization support to individual components is always a tradeoff between implementation effort and benefits. Notably, we found bugs in existing components doing this. Especially for very generic components, it can be hard to come up with a suitable visualization though.

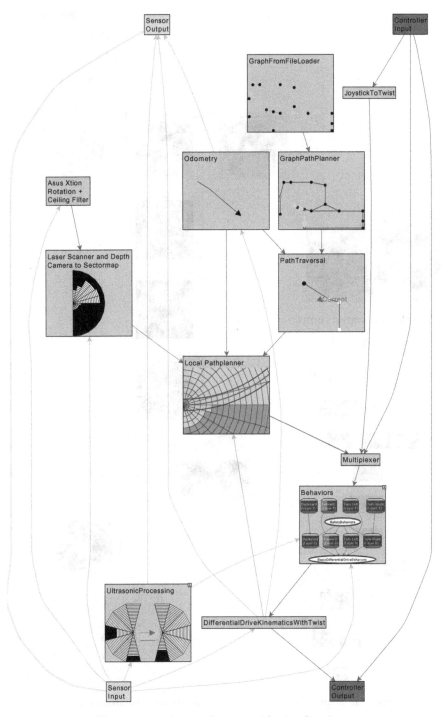

Fig. 6. ARTOS' control group with visualization

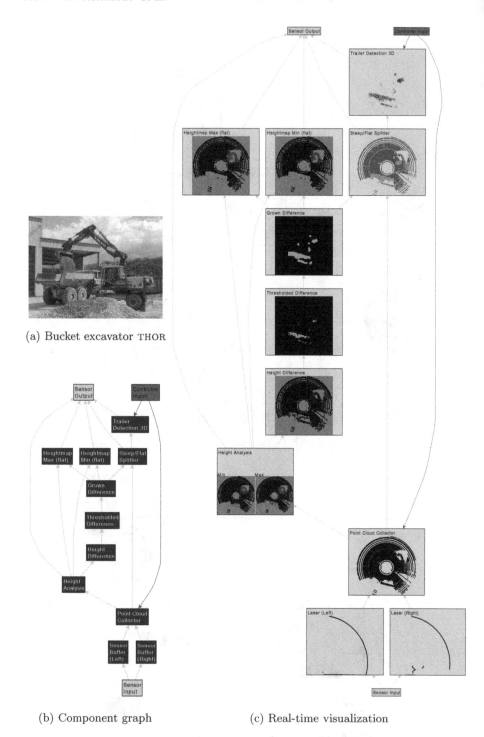

(a) Bucket excavator THOR

(b) Component graph

(c) Real-time visualization

Fig. 7. Trailer detection in the excavator's perception group

Combining component-defined visualization with existing tool-defined approaches is a promising area for future work. Furthermore, experiments with more participants will lead to additional insights. Technically, tools with interactive component visualization views are desirable – allowing e.g. transformations or to hide elements. As visualizations vary in complexity, displaying all components in the same size is not optimal. Components could provide hints on a suitable size. In the current implementation, visualizing many components at high frame rates may require considerable network bandwidth. Data compression – e.g. video codecs for bitmaps – can improve this significantly.

Acknowledgments. Funding by the German Ministry of Education and Research (grant 01IC12S01W, project SINNODIUM) is gratefully acknowledged. We thank our colleagues and students for participating in the experiments.

References

1. Ando, N., Suehiro, T., Kotoku, T.: A software platform for component based RT-system development: OpenRTM-aist. In: Carpin, S., Noda, I., Pagello, E., Reggiani, M., von Stryk, O. (eds.) SIMPAR 2008. LNCS (LNAI), vol. 5325, pp. 87–98. Springer, Heidelberg (2008)
2. Armbrust, C., Koch, J., Stocker, U., Berns, K.: Mobile robot navigation support in living environments. In: 20. Fachgespräch Autonome Mobile Systeme (AMS), pp. 341–346. Springer, Kaiserslautern (2007)
3. Brugali, D., Scandurra, P.: Component-based robotic engineering part i: Reusable building blocks. IEEE Robotics Automation Magazine 16(4), 84–96 (2009)
4. Collett, T.H.J., MacDonald, B.A.: An augmented reality debugging system for mobile robot software engineers. Journal of Software Engineering for Robotics (JOSER) 1(1), 18–32 (2010)
5. Lotz, A., Steck, A., Schlegel, C.: Runtime monitoring of robotics software components: Increasing robustness of service robotic systems. In: 15th International Conference on Advanced Robotics (ICAR 2011), Tallinn, pp. 285–290 (2011)
6. Proetzsch, M., Luksch, T., Berns, K.: Development of complex robotic systems using the behavior-based control architecture iB2C. Robotics and Autonomous Systems 58(1), 46–67 (2010), doi:10.1016/j.robot.2009.07.027
7. Quigley, M., Conley, K., Gerkey, B.P., Faust, J., Foote, T., Leibs, J., Wheeler, R., Ng, A.Y.: ROS: an open-source robot operating system. In: ICRA Workshop on Open Source Software in Robotics, Kobe, Japan (2009)
8. Reichardt, M., Föhst, T., Berns, K.: Design principles in robot control frameworks. In: Horbach, M. (ed.) Informatik 2013. Lecture Notes in Informatics (LNI), pp. 2765–2779. GI, Koblenz (2013)
9. Reichardt, M., Föhst, T., Berns, K.: On software quality-motivated design of a real-time framework for complex robot control systems. Electronic Communications of the EASST Software Quality and Maintainability (60) (2013)
10. Schmidt, D., Proetzsch, M., Berns, K.: Simulation and control of an autonomous bucket excavator for landscaping tasks. In: IEEE International Conference on Robotics and Automation (ICRA), Anchorage, pp. 5108–5113 (2010)
11. Soetens, P.: A Software Framework for Real-Time and Distributed Robot and Machine Control. Ph.D. thesis, Department of Mechanical Engineering, Katholieke Universiteit Leuven, Belgium (2006)

A Primate-Inspired Autonomous Navigation Algorithm Using the Cognitive Mechanism of Mental Rotation

Michael J. Pettinati and Ronald C. Arkin

Georgia Institute of Technology, College of Computing, Atlanta, GA, 30332, USA
mpettinati3@gatech.edu, arkin@cc.gatech.edu

Abstract. Though significant progress on autonomous navigation has been made, the natural world offers interesting examples of navigational techniques that are worth exploring and understanding. The cognitive mechanism of mental rotation has been revealed in numerous cognitive and neuroscientific experiments; its reason for existence and evolution, however, has yet to be thoroughly understood. It is speculated that this mechanism may assist primates in navigation. This paper explores how mental rotation can be used in navigation by developing an autonomous robotic navigation algorithm that draws inspiration from the mechanism. This algorithm was tested on a robot tasked with navigating to a specified goal location contained within the agent's initial view. The testing suggests that mental rotation can be used as an asset in navigation.

Keywords: mental rotation, robotic navigation, mental imagery.

1 Introduction

Autonomous navigation is a problem with a set of robust and efficient solutions [1,2]. The fact that these solutions are sufficient for many applications does not imply that autonomous navigation is a domain where no further progress needs to be made. The natural world offers interesting examples of alternative navigational techniques that are worth taking the time to understand and may offer insights that supplement or enhance existing algorithms.

Evolution has fashioned primates into adept and efficient navigators [3,4]. The ability of nonhuman primates (and human children) to use mapping is limited, therefore, other mechanisms must have evolved in primates to allow for successful navigation [5]. Many studies have identified the mechanism of mental rotation, an ability that allows primates to "envision" a reorientation of an object/scene [6,7,8]. There has been speculation that this mechanism contributes in some way to the navigational capabilities of primates, but there have been few studies conducted to verify these speculations.

The goal of this ONR-funded project is to understand what mental rotations might contribute to the ability of primates to navigate by implementing an autonomous navigation algorithm that draws inspiration from the ability of mental rotations, incorporating this algorithm into our existing robotic specification software, *MissionLab* [9]. In theory, given the view of a scene from a goal

D. Brugali et al. (Eds.): SIMPAR 2014, LNAI 8810, pp. 388–399, 2014.

location and a view of the scene from the robot's current location, an agent can use "mental" rotations to visualize the current view at a three-dimensional orientation that is aligned with its goal's three-dimensional orientation. This view will allow the agent to accurately assess the translational and rotational offset between the current position and goal position.

It is posited that this research could provide the foundation for a navigation algorithm that supports advice giving in robotic navigation. If an agent did not "know" its goal view a priori, something/someone external to the agent could provide a high level description of its goal by relating its relative position and orientation to known objects in the scene. The agent could then use these objects to define the scene and travel appropriately using the biologically-inspired algorithm introduced below. For example, if an agent had to fetch something from a file cabinet in an office within an office building, it might have a map to the office, but it might not know the precise layout of every office in the building. If the agent knew what a file cabinet looks like, upon arriving at the office, it could identify the file system (if there are multiple, one could be specified to the agent) and navigate to the appropriate position relative to the file cabinet using an algorithm like the one described here to carry out its task.

2   Related Work

Research has shown that although human children and nonhuman primates are robust navigators, they do not use maps or precise distances to navigate to a location [3,5]. It is suggested that they instead use mental transformations to overcome changes in perspective and to make general assessments about the direction in which they must move to reach a certain location. Research by Kosslyn et. al. [10] affords more concrete evidence for the use of mental images in humans through neuroimaging studies.

Hutcheson and Wedell [11] discuss how, when humans are immersed in an environment and navigating to a certain location, they tend to use these qualitative, abstract representations to navigate as opposed to using more precise distances or explicit directions; Menzel et al. [4] observed a similar tactic with a nonhuman primate. The Bonobo being observed had to travel from a start location to a designated goal; it did not take a rigid trajectory but varied its path [4]. Starting position did not affect its ability to successfully navigate, implying it possesses the ability to mentally encode the "entire spatial layout" of the area, and can mentally manipulate this encoding to localize itself and travel appropriately [5].

Mental rotation must be differentiated from the cognitive process of perspective-taking spatial abilities and visual servoing or homing techniques. Hegarty and Waller [12] show an explicit distinction between cases where an observer is mentally manipulating a scene or scene object to view it differently and cases where the observer is mentally viewing the scene from a different viewpoint. They [12] state that humans may use both of these skills, but most people have a strong preference for one or the other. As expressed by Arkin [13], visual servoing is distinct from the navigational approach described here in that the visual approach described in this paper is a more deliberative approach. Our approach, described in more detail below, will derive the appropriate navigation direction using abstract representations of the scene rather than working with image features. The three-dimensional, structured representations of the scenes used by our algorithm allow for correspondence between elements of like form in the different scenes (models of identifiable objects or object parts) as opposed to corresponding image features. In the context of advice-giving, full object recognition and semantic labeling will be required.

The evidence presented above has made a case that primates can maintain abstract mental images and manipulate these representations. The navigation approach introduced below has an agent rotating a "mental" visual representation of an object in order to inform its motion. It has also been theorized that mental rotation could be accomplished through the manipulation of propositional logic statements [13], which has received less support than the visual analog approach. We use the visual analog approach.

Stein [14] presents the idea of a robotic system using "mental" simulation in order to guide itself toward a goal location. Stein's [14] system, MetaToto, used an extended simulation where the agent would "imagine" what its sensors would experience at various locations on a floor plan and build a world model. This project is not as deliberative as MetaToto. This work explores a biologically-inspired, semi-reactive navigation algorithm that makes use of a process inspired by mental rotation to continually inform/update the movement of the robotic agent.

3   Navigation Algorithm

3.1   Algorithm Formation

This lab has previously developed a navigational procedure that explored the mechanism of mental rotation [13,15,16]. This system used depth information in order to construct occupancy grids that represented the current view of the scene and the goal view of the scene. Figure 1 shows a view for the robotic agent, the depth image capturing that view, as well as the occupancy grid that was generated from that depth information. The points composing the generated occupancy grids had discrete states of occupied or unoccupied, projecting the scene onto the two dimensional depth and width space.

At the outset of its mission, the agent generated the occupancy grid given the depth image for both its goal and its current location. The agent used a discrete number of "mental" transformations on the current occupancy grid in an attempt to match it to the goal occupancy grid. The correspondence between the two occupancy grids was scored for each transformation. A motion vector was derived from the transformation that resulted in the closest correspondence between the two occupancy grids [13,15]. After the robot had moved a short, specified distance, it would capture the depth information at its new current location, generate the occupancy grid representation at this new location, and repeat the process until the occupancy grids sufficiently corresponded without requiring "mental" transformations[1]. This algorithm had the depth imagery projected onto the ground plane, which is not biologically plausible. To be biologically plausible, the algorithm must work directly within the view of the scene [16].

The neuroscience literature discussing mental rotation is often focused on the rotation of simple objects, not entire scenes. The work done by Aretz and Wickens [6] and by Bläsing et. al. [7] each note a certain amount of fragility in the mechanism of mental rotation. The work presented by Khooshabeh and Hegarty [8] found that in order to overcome this fragility many humans will segment a scene/complex object into distinct parts and mentally rotate these parts individually. This paper's navigation algorithm begins by segmenting the view into discrete planar segments that can be acted on individually.

3.2   Segmentation Algorithm

An overview of the segmentation algorithm used in navigation is presented here; for more depth on its theory, see Erdogan et. al. [17] and Srinivasan and Dellaert [18]. The segmentation algorithm takes as its input RGBD images; these images are captured via the Microsoft Kinect. To begin, these images are smoothed using a bilateral, edge-preserving filter. In order to decrease the size of the algorithm's search space when labeling planar segments, the pixels composing the images are grouped into related, atomic regions known as superpixels. Pixels are uniquely assigned to a superpixel; the pixels are grouped into superpixels based on three different factors: spatial proximity, color, and disparity. The result of performing this "oversegmentation" on the goal views of the two different scenes introduced below are shown as part of Figure 2. The noisiness of the oversegmentations seen is largely due to the limited smoothing of the input RGBD images from the Kinect. The neighborhood in which the bilateral filter smoothed was restricted to allow for the agent's direction to be updated more regularly. As long as the segment(s) the agent is using for navigation is/are consistently recovered, the surrounding noise can be ignored successfully.

Once the oversegmentation has completed, the superpixels are grouped probabilistically using the Rao-Blackwellized Markov Chain Monte Carlo (MCMC) algorithm presented by Srinivasan and Dellaert [18]. Each segmentation consists of a set of planar segments where each planar segment is a set of superpixels. There are eight hundred segmentations generated by the algorithm, and the most commonly occurring segmentation is returned as the three-dimensional representation of the view. The chosen segmentations for the two tested goal views are shown in Figure 2.

---

[1] A video demonstrating these results is available at:
http://www.cc.gatech.edu/ai/robot-lab/brc/movies/brc_video.mp4

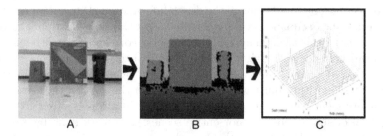

Fig. 1. A) The image of the scene. B) The depth image captured at that view. C) The occupancy grid generated from the depth information.

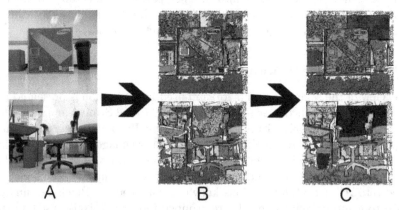

Fig. 2. A) View of scene at goal location for both tested scenes. B) Oversegmentation of goal image for both tested scenes. C) Final segmentation of goal image for both tested scenes. The first test scene appears in the top row. The bottom row contains the second test scene.

3.3 Navigation Algorithm

A high level overview of the navigation algorithm appears in Figure 3. The algorithm is provided with a conception (RGBD image) of the goal. The algorithm immediately captures an RGBD image of its current view using an onboard Microsoft Kinect. It is able to generate a probable planar segmentation, similar to those seen in Figure 2, for both the goal view and the current view using the segmentation algorithm described above. The algorithm must now match segments in the goal view with the corresponding segments in the current view to try to align them using a process inspired by mental rotation. The two views have different segment sets and many of the segments are inconsequential to the scene; therefore, the segments that truly define the scene such as the box in the first scene's goal view or the white board in the second scene's goal view must be identified as segments that the algorithm will use to move the agent to the goal. Ultimately, this process will be automated, however, currently in this bootstrap phase a human user identifies the segments "key" to the goal view and the corresponding segments in the initial current view. After this bootstrap step is complete, the agent navigates to its target goal location autonomously. A human hand-matching the "key" segments for the agent is a shortcoming of this algorithm; however, the bootstrap step will be a focal point of the research moving forward. In the context of advice-giving, something external to the agent will still be identifying what is "key" to the agent for navigation (though not identifying it in either scene). The agent will have to be given or generate a model of the object(s) described by the person assisting it and identify and match these objects for itself in the starting view and goal view.

Immediately following this bootstrap step, the algorithm considers each pair of corresponding segments in turn. It computes the average normal vector for the planar segment in both images. The estimated average normal vector for each plane segment is computed by estimating the normal at each pixel in the given segment using PCL's normal estimation [19] and averaging each pixel normal in the segment. The algorithm attempts a discrete number of rotations to align the current normal vector with the goal normal vector. In a process attempting to mimic mental rotation, the normal vector of the current segment is gradually rotated around each of the three axes. After each rotation, the inner product between the current view segment's normal vector and the goal view segment's normal vector is computed. The maximum value of this computation corresponds to the mental rotation that most closely aligns the orientation of the current view and goal view. The algorithm estimates the offset of the segment in the current view from its position in the goal by using the mental rotation (i.e. using the rotation matrix that aligned the normal vectors) to "visualize" the segment at the same orientation as the goal and determine the three-dimensional spatial distance between the center point of the segment in the goal view and the rotated center point of the segment in the current view. The algorithm makes this assessment for each of the corresponding planes designated as "key" in the scene and finds the average rotation and average estimated offset.

Due to the limited field of view of the Microsoft Kinect, the algorithm is not going to simply send the agent in the direction of the goal. If the agent is oriented and does not simply have to move in depth to reach the goal, the algorithm recommends the agent moves left/right (whichever direction is advised by the comparison stage) as quickly (as much) as possible to avoid being turned away from the segments later in the navigation when they can be more easily lost from view. If the agent is not oriented with its goal view orientation, then the algorithm will orient the agent to avoid losing segments in the periphery of the agent's view. These decisions assumed the agent could "see" all segments used to navigate when oriented at the start and goal locations. After making this assessment, the algorithm sends the angle that points the agent in the appropriate direction. A depth difference between the goal view and current view is also sent.

Once the robot begins to move, the system captures its new current view and uses the segmentation algorithm described above. As Arkin [20] suggests, finding the segments that correspond in the goal view and this new current view is a less complex problem than the bootstrap step. This feedforward step uses information about the robot's motion, the robot's speed and the angle just given to the system, as well as information about the positions of "key" segments in the previous current view to find a correspondence between the segments in the new current view and the goal view. The navigation algorithm considers each segment in the new current view and attempts to inversely map these segments to the previous current view based on the speed of the robot and its most recent direction to see if the segments fall within regions occupied by "key" segments in the previous current view. To limit the number of segments considered, the algorithm only considers segments that are approximately at the estimated depth of the matching segment. After the segments in the new current view that correspond to "key" segments in the goal view have been identified, the algorithm uses the process inspired by mental rotations to make an assessment about the agent's orientation and the appropriate direction in which it should move. This process is going to continue until the agent reaches the depth of the goal location. The navigation concludes at the goal depth because the agent cannot turn ninety degrees without losing the segment(s) being used for navigation.

Data: RBGD goal image
begin

                     Bootstrap Step

    capture first current view RGBD image
    perform planar segmentation on start view and goal view
    identify goal view segments and **match** them to corresponding start view segments
    for *each key segment* **do**
        estimate rotation between segment in current view and segment in goal view
        get approximate offset between current view segment and goal view segment
    end
    compute average rotation and offset between current view segments and goal view segments
    send appropriate motion vector to robotic agent
end
begin

                     Feedforward Step

    while *true* **do**
        capture new current image
        match key segments in new current to those in goal
        for *each key segment* **do**
            estimate rotation between segment in current view and segment in goal view
            get approximate offset between current view segment and goal view segment
        end
        if *at goal depth* **then**
            send angle to orient the agent/zero goal depth
            kill/stop the agent
        end
        send appropriate motion vector to robotic agent
    end
end

Fig. 3. Overview of navigation algorithm

4   Results/Analysis

The algorithm was tested on a Pioneer 2-DX robotic platform. The testing was designed to demonstrate the ability of the algorithm to guide the robotic agent from a variety of starting locations and orientations to a specified goal location and orientation. The successful navigation of a robotic agent using this algorithm would lend support to the idea that mental rotation can serve primates in navigation, and it would provide a foundation for the referenced advice-giving algorithm.

Two different scenes were tested (Figure 2A). Thirty trials were run on each scene. There were three, ten trial experiments conducted for each scene. Each of the ten trial experiments was run with the robotic agent starting at a certain location and orientation and navigating toward the goal location defined for that scene. A trial was only deemed successful if the agent was within 0.5m of the goal location, and the difference between the agent's final orientation and the goal orientation was no more than 10°. The distance from the goal location was measured from the robot center to the goal location. Due to the limited range of the Kinect, trials were restricted to situations where the agent's starting locations were 4.5m from the scene or less. Because the segmentation algorithm extracted planar segments, each trial included at least one planar element that was "key" to the scene to ensure reliable segmentation so the average normal vector would accurately represent orientation.

Figure 4 shows the finite state acceptor (FSA) defined for the robotic agent in *MissionLab*. The robot's behaviors/states are the circular symbols and the triggers for these behaviors are rectangles. In this mission, the agent stops (*MENTA-LALIGNED* is true) when the navigation algorithm indicates that the agent is oriented and an acceptable depth difference has been reached; the robotic agent has reached the goal location at this point. The *MoveMentalDirection* behavior is triggered whenever the agent still has to travel to reach its goal; the behavior uses the heading computed by the navigation algorithm to move in the appropriate direction toward the goal. The *OrientAtGoalDepth* behavior is triggered when the agent cannot translate without going beyond the goal yet still must orient itself properly.

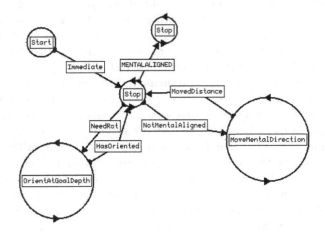

Fig. 4. FSA for robotic agent

4.1   Original Scene Revisited

The first test scene (Figure 2A) contains 3 different objects: a television box, an overturned crate, and a trash barrel. The front of the box was identified as the "key" planar segment that the agent used to navigate in all trials. The depth of this surface was uniform, 2.0m. The agent was pointed directly at the center of the box when the goal RGBD goal image was captured. The results for the thirty trials run at this scene are summarized in Table 1 below. The horizontal displacement is negative if the robot stopped to the goal's left and positive to the right. The difference in depth from the goal was positive if the agent went beyond the goal and negative if the agent stopped before the goal. The rotational offset is positive if the agent finished oriented to the right of the goal orientation.

Table 1. Results: Scene 1. Location: (horizontal, depth). Location 1: (0.5, -2.0), oriented; Location 2: (-0.75, -2.5), oriented; Location 3: (-0.25, -2.0), rotated 20° to the left. Trials where the algorithm failed to navigate using segments contained within the scene have been excluded from the average computations.

Location	Success Percentage	Avg. Rotational Offset from Goal Orientation	Avg. Depth from Goal		Avg. Horizontal Displacement from Goal		Avg. Distance From Goal	
Location 1 (avg. out of 9 trials)	70%	7° ± 4.74°	13.08cm	±	16.49cm	±	21.96cm	±
			8.25cm		8.25cm		8.25cm	
Location 2 (avg. out of 8 trials)	70%	1.38° ± 7.48°	12.21cm	±	-6.63cm	±	22.65cm	±
			10.09cm		15.44cm		4.47cm	
Location 3	90%	6.8° ± 4.66°	8.65cm	±	-4.18cm	±	13.48cm	±
			10.83cm		7.83cm		9.44cm	

The agent successfully navigated toward and stopped (approximately) at the goal in 77% of trials for the original scene. When the algorithm accurately kept track of the segment corresponding to the television box for the extent of the trial, however, the agent successfully attained the goal in 92% of trials (23/25 cases). This consistency shows that, when an agent can accurately track an object, it is using to navigate, mental rotation can effectively be used to aid in navigation. The feedforward step of the algorithm can be attributed, at least in part, to 71% (5/7 cases) of failure in the first test scene.

The feedforward step of the navigation algorithm failed to identify a matching segment contained within the scene, for at least a portion of the trial, in 10.0% of all cases during the testing of the first scene. The algorithm found no matching segment in one case and human intervention was required to stop the agent. The matching segment was not found because it was not contained within the depth range considered by the feedforward step of the algorithm. The estimation of where the segment should appear in depth was inaccurate. In the other cases, the depth at which the algorithm was looking for the box segment was again incorrect and an incorrect segment, not related to the scene, was matched with the box. The robotic agent navigated away from the goal entirely, treating this improper segment as the segment corresponding to the box.

All of the initial RGBD image captures during the testing of this scene occurred at or beyond 4m. The box was located 2m beyond the goal location, and the agent had to travel at least 2m in depth to reach the goal. This distance is at the edge of the range that the Kinect can be depended upon to accurately assess depth.

The notion that the noise from the Kinect poses an issue is supported by the 6.7% of cases where the algorithm failed to align the agent's orientation to its goal orientation due to incorrectly matching the box segment with another segment contained within the goal view. In one case, superpixels from the background and foreground merged with the "key" objects in the scene causing a misidentification to occur. In the other case, an early misidentification took the agent off course. Though the algorithm correctly identified the box in its next iteration and kept track of the box throughout the rest of the trial, the agent was unable to recover and the trial resulted in failure.

In the two cases (6.7% of all cases) where the agent did not "succeed", as defined above, and the feedforward step cannot be attributed to the failure, the agent stopped within 0.5m of the goal location. The agent failed during these two trials because it did not appropriately orient itself at the conclusion of the trial even though the algorithm had instructed it to do so. The algorithm should capture a final image to ensure that the agent has oriented itself.

4.2   More Complex Scene

The goal view of the second tested scene is shown as part of Figure 2A. This second round of testing was meant to reveal more about the capabilities of the navigation algorithm itself by placing the agent at starting positions where the Kinect would provide less noisy RGBD images. In this complex environment, there were numerous objects that were decidedly non-planar meaning that the segmentation could not be trusted to be consistent. There were planar objects at varying depths in the background of the scene. The segment the agent used to navigate, the whiteboard, was partially obscured by chair arms, and it was not at a constant depth. At the goal, the whiteboard was not entirely contained within the agent's view, while the starting location was always far enough back for the agent to be able to view the whiteboard in its entirety. The results for all three locations are summarized in Table 2, which is shown below.

The results of these thirty trials support the notion that mental rotation can be used for navigation. The agent succeeded in 90% of trials (27/30 cases) for this scene compared to 76.67% of trials (23/30 cases) in the other scene. This is likely due to the fact that the robot started closer to the scene and noise from the Kinect did not play a role. The feedforward step only failed once out of the thirty trials. In this one case, the feedforward step identified a segment composed of the floor directly below the whiteboard and the small barrel to the side of the whiteboard as the whiteboard segment. The agent failed to come within 0.5m of the goal in the second scene twice (in 6.67% of all trials). In these two trials, the agent failed to orient itself when it first began to move (though the algorithm accurately assessed the angle it needed to turn to align). It oriented itself with the next update, but the agent was unable to move quickly enough to the left or right without losing track of the segment being used to navigate to reach the goal location. Ultimately, in order to overcome the Kinect's limited field of view, different hardware will have to be used, or the algorithm will have to incorporate a memory that "remembers" the segment's position, even if it is not within view, so it can be identified when the agent needs to confirm its relative position.

Table 2. Results: Scene 2. Location: (horizontal, depth). Location 1: (0.5, -1.5), rotated 10° to the right; Location 2: (-0.75, -1.75), rotated 15° to the right; Location 3: (0.0, -2.25), oriented.

Location	Success Percentage	Avg. Rotational Offset from Goal Orientation	Avg. Depth from Goal		Avg. Horizontal Displacement from Goal		Avg. Distance From Goal	
Location 1	80%	-1.5° ± 6.09°	4.34cm	± 11.74cm	34.19cm	± 10.19cm	36.6cm	± 9.47cm
Location 2	90%	-1.4° ± 5.41°	16.89cm	± 14.03cm	-30.47cm	± 12.45cm	37.73cm	± 11.93cm
Location 3	100%	-0.4° ± 4.65°	13.26cm	± 10.03cm	9.7cm	± 15.48cm	21.09cm	± 12.86cm

5   Conclusions and Future Work

This paper has shown how a process inspired by the cognitive mechanism of mental rotation, a mechanism shown to be present in higher order primates, can be successfully incorporated into an autonomous robotic navigation algorithm. The algorithm introduced allowed the robotic agent to navigate in an informed way toward a goal location without doing any explicit planning. Navigation during almost all trials in which the agent was able to keep track of the segment it was using to navigate was sufficiently robust. Shortcomings in the feedforward aspect of the algorithm can likely be addressed by designing a more computationally efficient algorithm that is able to update more often and able to better smooth noisy input images. Future work also includes using an algorithm like the one described here in the context of advice giving. An agent can be informed to recognize particular objects and can be directed relative to these objects. Once the objects in the scene are recognized a procedure like the one described above can be used to successfully navigate. The process inspired by mental rotation will require rotating the entire object and using correpsondence between object features to assess orientation alignment rather than using normal vectors.

The navigation tasks presented above were simple in nature and had to be largely restricted due to the limitations of the Microsoft Kinect as a sensor. The navigation algorithm has been enhanced since these trials to allow for multi-waypoint navigation where waypoints were composed of multiple "key" segments. Though not yet rigorously tested, there have been successful demonstrations of this algorithm on the Pioneer 2-DX robotic platform. This improvement allows for testing in more complex, real-world environments; it helps to overcome the depth measurement limitations of the Microsoft Kinect.

Acknowledgments. The Office of Naval Research, under grant 00014-11-1-0593, supported this research. The authors would also like to thank Professor Frank Dellaert and Natesh Srinivasan for their contributions to this project.

References

1. Thrun, S., Burgard, W., Fox, D.: Probabilistic Robotics. MIT Press, Cambridge (2005)
2. Arkin, R.C.: Behavior-based Robotics. MIT Press, Cambridge (1998)
3. Menzel Jr., E.W., Menzel, C.R.: Do Primates Plan Routes? Simple Detour Problems Reconsidered (2007)
4. Menzel, C.R., Savage-Rumbaugh, E.S., Menzel Jr., E.W.: Bonobo (Pan paniscus) spatial memory and communication in a 20-hectare forest. International Journal of Primatology 23(3), 601–619 (2002)
5. Lourenco, S.F., Huttenlocher, J.: Using geometry to specify location: implications for spatial coding in children and nonhuman animals. Psycholog. Res. 71(3), 252–264 (2007)
6. Aretz, A.J., Wickens, C.D.: The mental rotation of map displays. Human Performance 5(4), 303–328 (1992)
7. Bläsing, B., de Castro Campos, M., Schack, T., Brugger, P.: Mental rotation of primate hands: human-likeness and thumb saliency. Experiment. Brain Res. 221(1), 93–105 (2012)
8. Khooshabeh, P., Hegarty, M.: Representations of Shape during Mental Rotation. In: AAAI Spring Symposium: Cognitive Shape Processing (March 2010)
9. MacKenzie, D., Arkin, R.C., Cameron, J.: Multiagent Mission Specification and Execution. Autonomous Robotics 4(1), 29–57 (1997)
10. Kosslyn, S.M., Thompson, W.L., Ganis, G.: The case for mental imagery. Oxford University Press (2006)
11. Hutcheson, A.T., Wedell, D.H.: From maps to navigation: The role of cues in finding locations in a virtual environment. Memory & Cognition 40(6), 946–957 (2012)
12. Hegarty, M., Waller, D.: A dissociation between mental rotation and perspective-taking spatial abilities. Intelligence 32(2), 175–191 (2004)
13. Arkin, R.C.: The Role of Mental Rotations in Primate-inspired Robot Navigation. Cognitive Processing 13(1), 83–87 (2012)
14. Stein, L.A.: Imagination and situated cognition. Journal of Experimental &Theoretical Artificial Intelligence 6(4), 393–407 (1994)
15. Arkin, R.C., Dellaert, F., Devassy, J.: Primate-inspired Mental Rotations: Implications for Robot Control. In: Proc. IEEE International Conf. on Robotic sand Biomimetics (2012)
16. Arkin, R.C., Dellaert, F., Srinivasan, N., Kerwin, R.: Primate-inspired vehicle navigation using optic flow and mental rotations. In: SPIE Defense, Security, and Sensing, p. 87560M. International Society for Optics and Photonics (May 2013)
17. Erdogan, C., Paluri, M., & Dellaert, F.: Planar segmentation of RGBD images using fast linear fitting and markov chain monte carlo. In: 2012 Ninth Conference on Computer and Robot Vision (CRV), pp. 32–39. IEEE (May 2012).
18. Srinivasan, N., Dellaert, F.: A Rao-Blackwellized MCMC Algorithm for Recovering Piecewise Planar 3D model from Multiple View RGBD Images. To Appear IEEE International Conference on Image Processing (October 2014)
19. PCL: Normal Estimation Using Integral Images, http://pointclouds.org/documentation/tutorials/normal_estimatio_using_integral_images.php
20. Arkin, R.C.: Towards cosmopolitan robots: Intelligent navigation in extended man-made environments. Doctoral Dissertation. Univ. of Massachusetts, Amherst, pp. 178–216 (1987)

The Cognitive Interaction Toolkit – Improving Reproducibility of Robotic Systems Experiments

Florian Lier[1], Johannes Wienke[1,2], Arne Nordmann[1,2], Sven Wachsmuth[1],
and Sebastian Wrede[1,2]

[1] Cognitive Interaction Technology, Center of Excellence
[2] Research Institute for Cognition and Robotics, CoR-Lab.
Bielefeld University, Bielefeld, Germany
{flier,jwienke,anordman,swachsmu,swrede}@techfak.uni-bielefeld.de
http://www.cit-ec.org,http://www.cor-lab.de

Abstract. Research on robot systems either integrating a large number of capabilities in a single architecture or displaying outstanding performance in a single domain achieved considerable progress over the last years. Results are typically validated through experimental evaluation or demonstrated live, e.g., at robotics competitions. While common robot hardware, simulation and programming platforms yield an improved basis, many of the described experiments still cannot be reproduced easily by interested researchers to confirm the reported findings. We consider this a critical challenge for experimental robotics. Hence, we address this problem with a novel process which facilitates the reproduction of robotics experiments. We identify major obstacles to experiment replication and introduce an integrated approach that allows (i) aggregation and discovery of required research artifacts, (ii) automated software build and deployment, as well as (iii) experiment description, repeatable execution and evaluation. We explain the usage of the introduced process along an exemplary robotics experiment and discuss our approach in the context of current ecosystems for robot programming and simulation.

Keywords: Software Engineering, Experimental Robotics, Development Process, Semantic Web, Continuous Integration, Software Deployment.

1 Introduction

Research on autonomous robots and human-robot interaction with systems that integrate a large number of skills in a single architecture achieved considerable progress over the last years. Reported research results are typically validated through experimental evaluation or demonstrated live at robotics competitions such as the DARPA Robotics Competition, RoboCup or RockIn. Given the complexity of these systems, many of the described experiments cannot easily be reproduced by interested researchers to confirm the reported findings [3]. We consider this a critical shortcoming of research in robotics since replicable experiments are considered good experimental practice in many other research disciplines. Despite this observation, robotics has already made significant progress

D. Brugali et al. (Eds.): SIMPAR 2014, LNAI 8810, pp. 400–411, 2014.
© Springer International Publishing Switzerland 2014

towards better reproducibility [3]. This trend can mainly be attributed to the following developments. Firstly, diverse "off-the-shelf" robots have become available that ideally only need to be unboxed and powered-on, e.g., the PeopleBot [1], PR2 [6], NAO [9], or iCub [13]. These are often available in simulation. Secondly, there are open source and community-driven software ecosystems, established frameworks and libraries available, such as ROS [14], OPRoS [10] or Orocos [5] which support researchers by providing sophisticated software building blocks. Lastly, dedicated activities towards systematic benchmarking of robotic systems have been carried out in terms of toolkits for benchmarking and publicly available data sets, e.g. the Rawseeds Project [4].

From our point of view, these are promising developments that foster reproducibility in terms of hardware as well as software aspects. However, besides these initiatives, there are also more fundamental methodological issues that prevent reproducibility of robotic system experiments. For instance, Amigoni et al. [2] already point out deficiencies in experimental methodology. This includes the frequently neglected impact on experiments caused by the relationship between individual components and the whole system, as well as the way how publications need to be written in order to improve reproducibility. We identified the four following *issues* that are critical with respect to sustainable reproducibility of robotic system experiments:

i) *Information Retrieval and Aggregation:* Publications and associated artifacts relevant for reproduction (software components, data sets, documentation and related publications) are often distributed over different locations, like digital libraries or diverse websites. Hence, already the discovery, identification and aggregation of all required artifacts is difficult. Furthermore, this kind of information is typically not available in a machine interpretable representation.

ii) *Semantic Relationships:* Often, crucial relationships between artifacts are unknown or underspecified, e.g.: which specific *versions* (master or 1.33.7) of software components in combination with which data set, hardware or experiment variant was in use for a particular study?

iii) *Software Deployment:* Most current systems are realized using a component-based architecture [15,10,7,17] and usually not all components are written in the same language. Consequently, they do not make use of the same build infrastructure[1], binary deployment mechanism, and execution environment. Therefore, it is an inherently complex and labor-intensive task to build and distribute a system in order to reproduce experimental results. This becomes even more complex when experiments require software artifacts from more than one ecosystem because there is usually no cross-ecosystem integration model.

iv) *Experiment Testing, Execution and Evaluation:* Advanced robotics experiments require significant efforts spent on system development, integration testing, execution, evaluation and preservation of results. This is particular costly if many of these tasks are carried out manually, which is intriguing,

---

[1] CMake, Catkin, setuptools, ant, maven, etc.

as established methods from software engineering are available to automate these tasks, e.g., based on the continuous integration (CI) paradigm. To the best of our knowledge, so far, these techniques were not widely adopted by the general community for the iterative design, automated execution and ensured repeatability of robotics experiments.

To tackle these issues we introduce an approach for reproducible robotics experimentation based on an integrated software toolchain for system developers and experiment designers. Currently, it supports (robotics) software and simulation environments while physical robots/entities will be introduced in later versions. This toolchain is described in Section 2 and combines state of the art technologies like web-based catalogs and continuous integration methods into a consistent process that facilitates the reproduction process of robotic systems and experiments. After describing the toolchain, we will briefly outline the replication process for a simulation experiment in Section 3 and conclude with a discussion of well-known robotics ecosystems with regard to their support for reproducible experimentation in Section 4.

2   The CITk Toolchain: Concepts and Components

In order to address the aforementioned issues of current robotics research, we have developed an integrated toolchain which accompanies the complete development, reproduction and modification process of robotics systems: the Cognitive Interaction Toolkit (CITk). The CITk consists of a set of software tools which are connected by an underlying software development and reproduction process. This process defines how users interact with our toolchain and has been inspired by current best practices from research and development, especially in robotics. Hence, it ties together existing tools and concepts in an integrated fashion. The general starting point for new users is a web-based catalog. It enables them to browse and search for software components or complete systems and their related artifacts like publications and provides them with the necessary information for the reproduction of these systems. Hence, it addresses the information retrieval and aggregation requirement (i) by means of semantic relationships between the different constituting parts of a complete system and its reproduction process (issue ii). From this catalog, a user who wants to reproduce a system, is directed

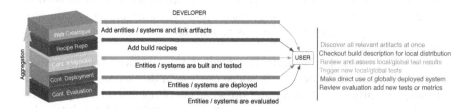

Fig. 1. Cognitive Interaction Toolkit: toolchain and developer workflow

towards a build infrastructure which allows to consistently and conveniently reproduce a system based on the CI methodology. Here, we have developed a new, build system independent, solution to easily bootstrap systems based on a CI server by using a generator approach, which reduces the required knowledge and manual work to a minimum (cf. issue iii). Finally, after deploying a system as a software distribution, the web catalog informs the user about tests and experiments that have been performed with the system. A novel state-machine-based testing tool enables users to consistently reproduce these experiments, thereby resolving issue iv. Throughout the whole process, the web catalog forms a central information point for the user. Moreover, tools included in the CITk process are connected with this catalog to either retrieve the required information or push them back in case a system has been modified or even newly created. This fact is visualized in Figure 1. In the following subsections we will describe the fundamental building blocks of the CITk in detail.

2.1 Information Aggregation and Retrieval

In order to realize a web-based catalog which allows convenient information retrieval, we implemented the data model depicted in Figure 2 by extending the Content Management System *Drupal*[2]. Since Drupal already supports the concept of entities, we were able to translate our data model into so-called Drupal *nodes*. A Drupal node provides a container for diverse attributes which are named fields. Fields eventually contain the actual content of a node, such as title, content authors, links to other nodes, files, or text fields (e.g. version). We implemented all required node types according to our data model within the catalog. An exemplary node type for a *component* can be visited here `https://toolkit.cit-ec.uni-bielefeld.de/node/238`. Each component, as well as other node types, assembles basic meta information about the represented entities, such as repository location, wiki pages, component maintainer etc. Moreover, related nodes are linked to the component. For instance a corresponding

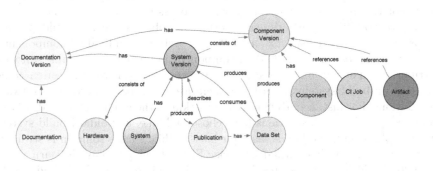

Fig. 2. Cognitive Interaction Toolkit: conceptual data model

---

[2] `https://drupal.org`

publication, version number, component releases, systems, or data sets. Finally, nodes and their fields are semantically enriched to increase machine interpretability by attaching RDF terms to them, e.g., from DOAP[3] and Dublin Core.

Links between different node types form aggregations of nodes. A prominent example of a node aggregation is the system version type which corresponds to a software distribution for a system to reproduce. Here, a system version node assembles *required components*, interrelated experiments (cf. Section 2.3), manuals, how-tos, and of course data sets and publications. In order to prevent redundant labor with respect to user provided content, most of the catalog's content is imported from the entities' origin locations. Thus, we import required information about a publication by using the Mendeley API and the PUB MODS [18] interface for instance. A user only needs to provide a URL pointing to his/her publication and a corresponding node is created automatically. The same strategy is used to add artifact and build job nodes, here the Jenkins REST-like[4] API is utilized. Besides manual creation/import of entries, content can also be added by using the catalog's REST API and client application[5]. In parallel to the import features, catalog content can be either rendered as HTML including RDFa, pure RDF or JSON to improve automated harvesting and interpretation by search engines or client applications. In a first user-study [11] we demonstrated that our approach of referencing/importing existing sources delivers benefits of re-using data and is perceived as efficient. Furthermore, the web catalog is perceived as useful to help researchers to accomplish their individual goals by providing information in this manner. The overall required effort for importing, respectively adding artifacts, was considered low. The *beta* version of the catalog is publicly available at `https://toolkit.cit-ec.uni-bielefeld.de`.

2.2 Automated Build and Deployment

While the data model of the web-based catalog already describes the composition of system components, it lacks information on how to technically reproduce a referenced version of a system and its components, e.g. by deploying and executing it. For this purpose, a controlled build process is essential to achieve re-use and reproducability of experimental setups in robotics. Such a build process comprises two distinct aspects: *a)* the build system of individual components, and *b)* the composition of individual component builds into deployable software distributions. For the first aspect, existing ecosystems in robotics often come with custom build systems in order to facilitate the aspect of creating software distributions. For instance, ROS provides Catkin as the build system and NAOqi promotes qiBuild. Both solutions have chosen CMake, a standard build system for cross-platform C++ builds, as their basis. While such a solution is straightforward, it comes with several drawbacks: First, developers have to learn a new technology, which sometimes results in refusal to integrate at all. Second, established build systems, especially for other languages than C++, are locked out.

---

[3] `https://github.com/edumbill/doap`
[4] `https://wiki.jenkins-ci.org/display/JENKINS/Remote+access+API`
[5] `http://opensource.cit-ec.de/projects/citk`

```
{
  "name":      "openrave",
  "templates": [ "cor-lab", "cmake-cpp" ],
  "variables": {
    "description":  "Open Robotics Automation Virtual Environment...",
    "keywords":     [ "library", "robotics", "simulation" ],
    "repository":   "https://github.com/rdiankov/openrave.git",
    "branches":     [ "master", "latest_stable" ],
    "git.wipe-out-workspace?": false,
  }
}
```

Fig. 3. Recipe for the OpenRAVE [8] toolkit component. Required fields are component name, the project templates (specifying to use a CMake build system in this case), references to the available code branches as well as a URL to the source code repository. Further fields can be used to augment the automatic dependency analysis or customize the build process.

And third, software components developed with such a tailored build system are heavily locked into a specific environment, which prevents the use outside of this environment.

For the aspect of composing software distribution, existing solutions like Catkin, in an abstract view, act as a build script that respects the dependencies of the individual software components by building them in the correct order. While this is sufficient to deploy a software distribution and manually re-trigger the installation of certain components, it does not automatically facilitate the ongoing system development process. For this use case, CI with its emphasis on incremental development and automated testing and reporting is an established technology. However, CI is usually maintained in parallel to the distribution deployment process and as a consequence, build instructions are duplicated between these two distinct processes. Moreover, consistently maintaining a large number of jobs for CI servers that manage a complete software distributions is a complex task that requires a considerable amount of knowledge.

CITk addresses the aforementioned issues by applying a generator-based solution. A newly implemented generator uses minimalistic descriptions of the different software components that belong to a distribution and generates jobs for a CI server, Jenkins in our case. From the descriptions (which augment the data model, cf. Figure 3 for an example) and an automatic repository analysis the dependencies and required build steps are derived. Afterwards, the CI server jobs are generated along user-defined build templates and uploaded to a Jenkins instance. Since templates can be added on the fly, new build systems can be added easily without restricting component developers to certain choices. Moreover, different jobs for either deploying a distribution or supporting the ongoing development can be automatically generated from the same knowledge base, preventing the aforementioned duplication of knowledge. The generated jobs and distributions are optionally synchronized back to the web catalog. Since setting up an appropriate Jenkins server with the required plugins takes some time, we provide pre-packaged installations for new users. As a result, we can use an established technology like the CI server for deploying complete software

systems without knowledge duplication, which results in an improved maintainability. Operating system (OS) dependencies like Debian packages are currently
aggregated manually for specific OS distributions. In the future, we will evaluate
how to include them in the model to improve consistency and posisiblities for
automation.

2.3 Experiment Execution and Evaluation

Besides gathering information about a system and deploying it, a successful reproduction and interaction with the system also includes repeating tests and
experiments. This is necessary to ensure the intended responses of complex interactive systems that operate autonomously. It is well-known that sound experiments imply a well-defined experimental protocol. Unfortunately, experiment
execution and testing are mostly carried out manually and are thus infrequent
and prone to user induced errors. This is especially the case because test setups
are usually complicated and require a high level of technical understanding from
the operator.

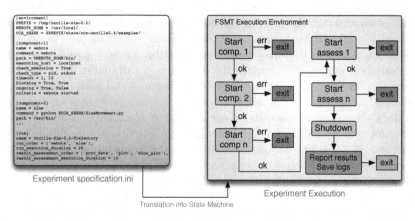

Fig. 4. Simplified conceptual overview of FSMT

Thus, we suggest to convey the concept of an experiment protocol to the orchestration of software components involved in an experiment and to execute,
test and evaluate software intensive experiments in an automated manner. For
this purpose, we introduce **F**inite **S**tate **M**achine **B**ased **T**esting (FSMT)[6], a
software tool that implements the aforementioned suggestions based on finite
state machines that defines the experiment execution. FSMT [12] supports automated bootstrapping, evaluation and shutdown of a software system used in
an experiment. In order to realize this, it provides definition of environment
variables, executable and parameter specification, hierarchical state-based invocation of components, and status (health) checks. A FSMT experiment specification includes three mandatory blocks: environment description, component

---

[6] http://opensource.cit-ec.de/projects/fsmt

definition and the run and assessment state (cf. Figure 4). In the *[environment]* block an experimenter may assign experiment-specific values to variables, these are appended to the existing set of environment variables. Components are specified in *[component-*]* blocks. Here, paths, executables (scripts), and status check conditions are defined, e.g., whether the PID of a specific process is present within a given time frame. Furthermore, FSMT may check the stdout and stderr of components for a given prompt, again, within a specified time frame. Based on the result of multiple status checks, FSMT will block further execution of the state machine or, in case a criterion is not satisfied, stop the experiment to prevent subsequent failures. In the *[run]* state, the actual experiment is conducted, which means that all required components of a system are running (verified) and data is recorded. The recorded data may consist of system specific containers, such as a rosbag[7] or component logs that are recorded for all components by FSMT. In the assessment state, the recorded data is evaluated by assessment components. Here, experimenters may provide scripts or binaries to evaluate data gathered in each run or trial, e.g., plot specified data points. The presented formalization of an experiment protocol allows to consistently reproduce test results in an automated fashion. This makes it a perfect candidate for CI and enables inexperienced experimenters to run tests and experiments consistently. Currently, FSMT supports sequential as well as parallel execution/evaluation of components. However, since it is based on a generic state-machine based execution environment (SCXML), additional conditions like *retrying or looping* are planned as well as distributed execution.

3   Use-Case: System and Experiment Reproduction

After describing the overall structure and components of the CITk approach, we will now outline a typical use case in order to demonstrate the steps required to reproduce a system that has been modeled in the catalog. The reader is encouraged to follow these steps on his/her own Linux computer. In our example, a user wants to reproduce experiments with the Oncilla quadruped robot [16] in a simulation environment. The first step for the user is to browse our online catalog and to load the page describing the system, which is https://toolkit.cit-ec.uni-bielefeld.de/systems/oncilla-quadruped-simulation. This page contains a general description of the system as well as a set of links to specific versions of the system. The user will continue to the version he/she wants to reproduce (0.2 in our case) to get details about the included software components as well as required dependencies for the Linux computer. Hence, the first step is to install the required dependencies using the package management tool of the Linux distribution[8]. Afterwards, he/she follows the link to the build generator recipes comprising the system and downloads the required recipes. In order to generate CI server jobs from the recipes a Jenkins installation as well as our generator are

---

[7] http://wiki.ros.org/rosbag

[8] We use as many standard software components from recent Linux distributions as possible.

required. Download instructions for a pre-packaged environment are included on the website and the user follows these instructions to install the environment on his/her computer. After starting the local Jenkins instance, the generator needs to be invoked to configure the CI server with the jobs for the distribution. The last step is to start the installation process and to open the web page of the local Jenkins instance and to start the orchestration job for the distribution. After this job has finished, the system is reproduced on the user's computer.

Now, the user can focus on reproducing the experiments that have been defined for and deployed with the system. These experiments are available as configuration files for the FSMT testing framework. FSMT and the configurations have just been installed as parts of the software distribution for the system. The web catalog for the system version lists the available experiments and each experiment comes with a description of how to execute it. In our case this is merely a command line to launch FSMT. The user executes the described commands and FSMT reports the results through a report (xunit for instance) and the process return code. After the experiment has been executed successfully, the resulting output, e.g., in form of a plot, can be found on the user's computer (as well as all required logs and data files). Besides the FSMT report, the generated plot can be compared to a reference plot from the catalog entry of the experiment. If everything worked correctly, the system is reproduced on the user's computer and he/she can start to modify it according to his/her needs or define new experiments based on the existing system.

4   Related Work and Discussion

In order to relate our approach to exiting work, we will quantitatively examine the prominent ROS and iCub ecosystems with respect to support for system *reproducibility* based on the four issues we have identified in the introduction: i) information retrieval and aggregation, ii) semantic relationships, iii) software deployment, and iv) experiment testing, execution and evaluation. In the **iCub** ecosystem, a wiki[9] is the primary source of information. The wiki *lists* different kinds of information, such as links to user manuals, source code repositories, papers, related (software) projects and summer schools. The main types of artifacts are iCub modules, applications and tutorials. The corresponding documentation is automatically parsed from source code (Doxygen). However, there are no explicit descriptions of existing "demo" systems (versions respectively) as a whole and their included components. Subsequently, system artifact aggregation and interlinking is not provided. Nevertheless, existing iCub applications and modules are assembled and well documented. The iCub ecosystem can be either built from source or by using pre-built binaries for Debian/Ubuntu Linux distributions and Windows. This means that systems are implicitly modeled by package dependency resolution. Furthermore, a central CI server[10] provides an overview of

---

[9] http://eris.liralab.it/wiki/Main_Page
[10] http://dashboard.icub.org/

the current state of iCub related software. The build system for the iCub ecosystem is based on CMake. With respect to system experiments, the wiki features an example of checking whether a system installation has been successful or not, which can be valued as a basic system experiment. In this example, multiple iCub components are started manually and a provided data set can be replayed. However, based on the example documentation it remains unclear how to assess the outcome of the system installation check. Additionally, there is no support for automated execution or evaluation.

In the **ROS** ecosystem, a wiki[11] is also the main source of information. It contains structured information about installation, tutorials, distributions, robots, packages, libraries, papers, books, events and more. While there are no explicit system descriptions, ROS features system distributions including a set of versioned ROS stacks. Therefore, systems are also implicitly modeled as stacks or meta packages. Fortunately, ROS provides extra wiki sites for a few publications that aggregate source code, data sets and usage examples (for a specific distribution) to reproduce the results published in the attached papers. Furthermore, there are wiki pages per distribution, stack and (meta) package, i.e., for pr2_common[12]. These pages contain basic information, e.g., maintainer, license, website, source code location and links to related/included packages. Basic interlinks between artifacts, i.e., stacks, related packages, dependencies, documentation and source code locations are supported (cf. http://wiki.ros.org/turtlesim) — semantic linking is currently not supported. In recent versions, ROS introduced its own new build system called Catkin that is based on CMake. By using Catkin, developers can easily setup and deploy their own ROS components and even add them to a ROS distribution. ROS also provides a CI build farm to which developer packages can be added via ROS-bloom[13], a release automation tool. In order to start ROS-based systems automatically, ROS features roslaunch, a tool for launching multiple ROS nodes locally and remotely. In a roslaunch file, rostests can be integrated. Therefore, ROS features a mechanism to automatically start and test a stack or package. Explicit experiment descriptions are currently not present in the ROS ecosystem.

In general it appears to be a good practice to publish information about robotics software and the corresponding ecosystem on a structured website. Unfortunately, the assembled information is often not complete with respect to system reproducibility due to a lack of explicit system descriptions, aggregation of all necessary artifacts and the specification of an experimental procedure in both examined ecosystems. Since ROS already features websites which assemble at least source code and data sets for a specific publication, we are confident that this way of information provision is beneficial. However, semantic linking and thus machine interpretability of artifacts is broadly neglected in the examined ecosystems. Systems and system versions are modeled implicitly, but are not visible/marked as such on the websites. Moreover, systems are not associated

---

[11] http://wiki.ros.org/
[12] http://wiki.ros.org/pr2_common
[13] http://wiki.ros.org/bloom

with an experiment protocol or course of action. Not surprisingly, CI plays an important role in both ecosystems but is not considered for local usage, e.g., for decentralized development, testing and distribution. In case of ROS this means that a developer must comply to the ROS release cycle time and server capacity. However, the sponsorship of an automated build infrastructure and tools to automatically create build jobs (cf. ROS-bloom and Section 2.2) reduces the amount of expert knowledge and is thus also considered beneficial. In contrast to our approach, ROS and iCub distributions can be installed via source builds (*not recommended* as stated in the ROS wiki) but also via binary distributions that simplify and speed up installation time. On the other hand, binary packages often raise typical issues such as requiring root permissions for installation, the install prefix is fixed and creating binary packages for diverse operating systems and flavors is a huge effort. With respect to build systems both ecosystems are based on CMake, which facilitates cross-platform compatibility, but also, in contrast to CITk, restricts the number of integrable third-party build tools. This is especially crucial because robotic systems/experiments often incorporate artifacts from more than one ecosystem. Finally, experiment specification, orchestration, automated execution and evaluation is not supported by either ROS or the iCub infrastructure.

5 Conclusion

We introduced an approach for reproducible robotics experimentation based on an integrated software toolchain for system developers and experimenters. It combines state-of-the-art technologies into a consistent process that facilitates the reproduction of robotic systems and experiments. We briefly outlined the replication process for a simulation experiment and discussed the benefits of the approach in comparison to well-known robotics ecosystems and their support for reproducible experimentation. Future work will focus on providing the complete toolchain as open source to the community, extending the build generation with classical continuous integration and deployment features for local development and extension towards modeling hardware components and versions as part of a system description.

Acknowledgements. This research and development project is funded as part of the Center of Excellence Cognitive Interaction Technology (CITEC) at Bielefeld University and by the German Federal Ministry of Education and Research (BMBF) within the Leading-Edge Cluster Competition "it's OWL" (intelligent technical systems OstWestfalenLippe) and managed by the Project Management Agency Karlsruhe (PTKA).

References

1. PeopleBot datasheet, http://www.mobilerobots.com/Libraries/Downloads/PeopleBot-PPLB-RevA.sflb.ashx (visited: May 19, 2014)
2. Amigoni, F., Reggiani, M., Schiaffonati, V.: An insightful comparison between experiments in mobile robotics and in science. Autonomous Robots 27(4), 313–325 (2009)

3. Amigoni, F., Schiaffonati, V., Verdicchio, M.: Good experimental methodologies for autonomous robotics: From theory to practice. In: Amigoni, F., Schiaffonati, V. (eds.) Methods and Experimental Techniques in Computer Engineering. Springer Briefs in Applied Sciences and Technology, pp. 37–53. Springer International Publishing (2014)

4. Bonarini, A., et al.: RAWSEEDS: Robotics advancement through web-publishing of sensorial and elaborated extensive data sets. In: IROS 2006 Workshop on Benchmarks in Robotics Research, vol. 6 (2006)

5. Bruyninckx, H.: Open robot control software: the orocos project. In: Proceedings of IEEE International Conference on Robotics and Automation, ICRA, vol. 3, pp. 2523–2528. IEEE (2001)

6. Cousins, S.: ROS on the PR2 [ROS Topics]. IEEE Robotics Automation Magazine 17(3), 23–25 (2010)

7. Cousins, S., Gerkey, B., Conley, K.: Sharing software with ros [ROS Topics]. Robotics & Automation Magazine 17(2), 12–14 (2010)

8. Diankov, R.: Automated Construction of Robotic Manipulation Programs. PhD thesis, Carnegie Mellon University, Robotics Institute (August 2010)

9. Gouaillier, D., et al.: Mechatronic design of NAO humanoid. In: Proc. Int. Conf. on Robotics and Automation, pp. 769–774 (2009)

10. Jang, C., et al.: OPRoS: A new component-based robot software platform. ETRI Journal 32(5), 646–656 (2010)

11. Lier, F., et al.: Facilitating research cooperation through linking and sharing of heterogenous research artifacts. In: Proc. 8th Int. Conf. on Semantic Systems, pp. 157–164. ACM (2012)

12. Lier, F., Lütkebohle, I., Wachsmuth, S.: Towards automated execution and evaluation of simulated prototype HRI experiments. In: Proc. 2014 ACM/IEEE Int. Conf. on Human-robot Interaction, pp. 230–231. ACM (2014)

13. Metta, G., et al.: The iCub humanoid robot: An open platform for research in embodied cognition. In: Proc. 8th Workshop on Performance Metrics for Intelligent Systems, pp. 50–56. ACM, New York (2008)

14. Quigley, M., et al.: ROS: an open-source robot operating system. In: ICRA Workshop on Open Source Software, vol. 3 (2009)

15. Soetens, P.: A software framework for real-time and distributed robot and machine control. PhD thesis, Katholieke Universiteit Leuven, Faculteit Ingenieurswetenschappen, Departement Werktuigkunde (2006)

16. Sproewitz, A., et al.: Oncilla robot, a light-weight bio-inspired quadruped robot for fast locomotion in rough terrain. In: Symposium on Adaptive Motion of Animals and Machines, pp. 63–64 (2011)

17. Wienke, J., Wrede, S.: A middleware for collaborative research in experimental robotics. In: 2011 IEEE/SICE Int. Symposium on System Integration, Kyoto, Japan. IEEE (2011)

18. Wiljes, C., Jahn, N., Lier, F., Paul-Stueve, T., Vompras, J., Pietsch, C., Cimiano, P.: Towards linked research data: An institutional approach. In: 3rd Workshop on Semantic Publishing, vol. 994, pp. 27–38 (2013)

Enhancing Humanoids' Walking Skills through Morphogenesis Evolution Method

Nicolas Jouandeau[1] and Vincent Hugel[2]

[1] LIASD, Paris 8 University, France
n@ai.univ-paris8.fr
[2] Robotics Department, Toulon-Var University, France
vincent.hugel@univ-tln.fr

Abstract. This paper presents an evolution method used to modify the morphology of humanoids to make them more efficient in a specific direction of walking. Starting from the NAO's model used in the 3D Simulation Soccer League, the walking specializations are based on 5 to 8 parameters that are being evolved. A black-box optimization process is run and guided by a decision-making function that defines the outcome of the humanoid evolution process. The simulation results lead to four optimized morphological profiles, each of them specialized for either forward, or lateral, or diagonal walk, or in-place turn respectively. These results could be used to build heterogeneous humanoids inside a team of soccer players.

1 Introduction

The tuning of gait parameters thanks to automatic procedure has been widely studied. Mimicking humans and using machine learning algorithms are the most common ways to tune walking parameters. Starting from a set of parameters, short modifications are applied iteratively to improve the set of parameters, according to a fitness function. Hebbel et al. [1] successfully used different Evolution Strategies to design a fast forward walker. Following the process of mutation/selection, they proposed solutions to avoid local optima by only selecting children that differ from their parents and to explore more evolution branches over developing multiple parents. Niehaus et al. [2] used Particle Swarm Optimization to design an omni-directional walk. The omni-directional property is synthesized into five walking direction sets. As the gait is modelled with a 14 parameter set, the robot uses parameter values that are defined for the synthesized walking direction. Different speeds result from this approach. Moving left, backward and diagonally forward are equivalent. Compared to these first three directions, moving diagonally backward is slower and moving straight forward is faster. MacAlpine and Stone [3] proposed the use of a uniform-velocity omni-directional walk. The optimization process is achieved with Covariance Matrix Adaptation Evolution Strategy [4] that is able to adapt the next generation according to previous generations' results. The evaluation of walking parameter sets is guided by goToTarget trials, that consist of a sequence of moves to

D. Brugali et al. (Eds.): SIMPAR 2014, LNAI 8810, pp. 412–423, 2014.
© Springer International Publishing Switzerland 2014

different targets along different directions. Travelled distance, spent time and number of falls are taken into account to define a reward of the tested 14 parameters. To keep the advantage provided by fast forward walking and accurate positioning in the field, they added a Sprint parameter set and a Positioning parameter set. Results are developed over 5 reward policies that produce different forward/backward/sideways walking speeds. Farchy *et al.* [5] introduced Grounded Simulation Learning to reduce the gap between simulation and real application in humanoid walking optimization. The simulation process includes simulation server modification to fit simulation and application results, although models are slightly different. Simulation tests use the original NAO version and application tests use the last NAO version with longer legs.

The different techniques in the related work listed above lead to significant results on skill design optimization. However most of the optimization techniques depend on the optimization problem itself. As we look for a single uniform optimization technique without any preliminary step of parameters definition, particle swarm optimization techniques were discarded due to the definition of population size and selection operator that clearly influence the optimization effectiveness and thus require more optimization iterations. Previous work on learning methods also proposed to change reward weights over time to reduce the number of optimization iterations. As we study multiple skill optimization with different metrics, learning methods were also discarded. Therefore the main contribution of this paper is to present a unified humanoid enhancement process through an evolution method that is defined as generic, so that it allows enhancing different skills for different moves using different morphological models.

Jouandeau and Hugel [6] introduced an optimization process that is applied to both morphological characteristics and walking parameters [7,8]. They improved the forward walking speed by tuning 2 morphological and 3 functional parameters using the Confident Local OPtimization [9] (CLOP) process. Two policies were finally proposed to define a best-first agent and a best-average agent. Results showed improvements of the morphological model as the optimization process produced faster humanoid walkers, with more realistic, safe and precise walk. The authors also used the same optimization framework to increase kicking skills of humanoids [10]. For a kick move, they applied a skill optimization process to different subsets of parameters of kicking parameters. Results shows that sequential sub-process optimization can lead to better results.

The developments described in this paper extend the above concept of simultaneous tuning of leg morphology and walking parameters to build humanoids with enhanced walking skills in a specific direction. 5 to 8 parameters are being evolved to optimize 4 different walking specializations, that are forward walk, lateral walk, diagonal walk, and in-place turns.

This paper is organized as follows. Section 2 describes the walking gaits that were used for the proposed approach. Section 3 describes the proposed optimization process according to four desired walking specializations. The process produces simultaneous evolution of morphological parameters and walking parameters to enhance walking skills. Section 4 describes and discusses the obtained results. Section 5 concludes.

2 Walking Gaits

In this study walking gaits were based on the Zero Moment Point (ZMP) technique [11] applied to the 3D-LIP model [12] that is represented by a single inverted pendulum with a massless telescopic leg that connects the supporting foot and the Center Of Mass (COM) of the entire robot. The height of the COM is kept constant, and there is no torque between the ground and the supporting foot. The robot is assumed to walk on a horizontal plane, with alternating single support phases. The double support phase is thus instantaneous.

The equations that govern the relationship between the position (x_G, y_G, z_G) of the COM and the ZMP – named P^* – are given by [12]:

$$\ddot{x}_G = \frac{g}{z_G}(x_G - x_{P*}) \tag{1}$$

$$\ddot{y}_G = \frac{g}{z_G}(y_G - y_{P*}) \tag{2}$$

where g is the gravity.

In our approach the ZMP is kept fixed for each single support phase. This leads to a hyperbolic shape of the COM trajectory for each step, also called *walking primitive*:

$$x_G(t) = (x_G^{i(n)} - x_{P*})\cosh(t/T_C)$$
$$+ T_C \dot{x}_G^{i(n)} \sinh(t/T_C) + x_{P*} \tag{3}$$

$$\dot{x}_G(t) = (x_G^{i(n)} - x_{P*})\sinh(t/T_C)/T_C$$
$$+ \dot{x}_G^{i(n)} \cosh(t/T_C) \tag{4}$$

where n is the step number, $x_G^{i(n)}$ and $\dot{x}_G^{i(n)}$ are respectively the COM initial x-position and the COM initial x-velocity of step n, and $T_C = \sqrt{\frac{z_G}{g}}$. The same holds for $y_G(t)$ and $\dot{y}_G(t)$.

3 Gait and Morphological Optimizations

This section presents the evolution process proposed to improve displacement capabilities of humanoids. The optimization process modifies the morphological characteristics and the walking parameters. It is applied to 4 typical moves: forward translation, lateral translation, diagonal translation, and rotation, to create players with self-adapted morphologies. This section also details different scoring functions for these moves.

3.1 Evolution Process

Using the black box optimizer CLOP, the evolution process is run with a list of input parameters, minimum and maximum values for each parameter and a pick-out function to qualify results. The set $\mathcal{L}$ defines input parameters with their minimum and maximum values. During the evolution process, results are collected in the history set $\mathcal{H}$. For each evolution iteration, a new set of parameter values are chosen from $\mathcal{L}$ according to $\mathcal{H}$. Each evolution iteration is processed over 10 trials, to produce average evaluation values. At the end of each evolution iteration, the fitness function pickOut states if the result is better, equivalent or worse than the best known result. Then parameters converge to best evolution values. This evolution process is presented in Alg. 1. It can be applied to different types T that defines the content of all sets.

Algorithm 1. evolution $< T >(n, \mathcal{L},$ pickOut$)$

1: $(\nu', \mathcal{H}) \leftarrow (\emptyset, \emptyset)$
2: **for** $i = 0$ to n **do**
3:    $p \leftarrow$ newParams $< T >(\mathcal{H}, \mathcal{L})$
4:    $(\nu) \leftarrow$ multipleTrials $< T >(p)$
5:    $(\nu', h) \leftarrow$ pickOut $< T >(\nu, \nu')$
6:    insert $< T >((p\ , h), \mathcal{H})$
7: **end for**
8: **return** paramsFrom $< T >(\nu')$

The pickOut function returns three possible values that correspond to better, equivalent and worse results. At each iteration, a new set of parameters p is chosen. ν' stands for best acceptable results. Each CLOP iteration implies that a new tuple (p,h) is inserted in $\mathcal{H}$. If n is too small, ν' could remain empty, which means that no solution is found over n iterations. As presented in Alg. 1 line 1, the process is started from scratch. At the end, the best parameters that correspond to the results ν' are returned.

3.2 Evaluation of Evolution

A list of constant values are required for the evaluation of the evolution. The $SUCCESS\_RATE$ (that is equal to 0.75) defines the rate of trials achieved without falling. The XY_RATIO (that is equal to 0.1) represents the maximal lateral drift allowed, and YX_RATIO (that is equal to 0.1) the maximal longitudinal drift allowed. The $DIAG\_RATIO$ (that is equal to 1.1) qualifies the maximal drift allowed in a diagonal move between longitudinal and lateral distances travelled. α and β (that are equal to 3 and 1) are introduced to compare averages related to the normal distributions used in the process. γ (that is equal to 0.7) is a ratio to compare standard deviations and to quantify stability.

Our evolution process for humanoids is based on the optimization of 4 types T that correspond to 4 different basic moves : 3 translations and 1 rotation. For

---

Algorithm 2. pickOut $< T >((s, m, \sigma), (s', m', \sigma'))$

1: **if** $s < SUCCESS\_RATE$ **then return** $REJECT$;
2: **if** $type = FORWARD$ **then**
3:     **if** $m_y/m_x > XY\_RATIO$ **then return** $REJECT$;
4:     **return** translationPickOut $(m, \sigma_x, m', \sigma'_x)$;
5: **end if**
6: **if** $type = LATERAL$ **then**
7:     **if** $m_x/m_y > YX\_RATIO$ **then return** $REJECT$;
8:     **return** translationPickOut $(m, \sigma_y, m', \sigma'_y)$;
9: **end if**
10: **if** $type = DIAGONAL$ **then**
11:     **if** $m_y/m_x > DIAG\_RATIO$ **or** $m_x/m_y > DIAG\_RATIO$ **then**
12:       **return** $REJECT$;
13:     **end if**
14:     $e \leftarrow$ sqrt $(\sigma_x + \sigma_y)$
15:     $e' \leftarrow$ sqrt $(\sigma'_x + \sigma'_y)$
16:     **return** translationPickOut (m, e, m', e');
17: **end if**
18: **if** $type = ROTATION$ **then**
19:     **if** $(m_x^2 + m_y^2) > MAX$ **then return** $REJECT$;
20:     **if** $optimize\_accuracy$ **then return** RPO_accuracy $(target, m, \sigma, m', \sigma')$;
21:     **if** $optimize\_time$ **then return** RPO_time (m, σ, m', σ');
22: **end if**

---

each move, $< T >$ defines $type$ value (used in Alg. 2 lines 4, 10, 16 and 24) and eventually a $target$ value (used in Alg. 2 line 29 specially in an accuracy test). The 3 translations are selected among the 8 discrete walking directions : moving along the longitudinal axis (forward and backward), moving sideways (right or left) and moving diagonally (forward or backward, left or right). Since backward walking patterns are not frequently used, only the 5 forward translational moves, namely left, diagonal left, forward, diagonal right and right, were selected for the process. The rotation move is a self-rotating move on the spot. Each translation-move optimization is based on a single policy. Because the default rotation that was tuned manually is already effective – fast, large steps and no fall –, it appears to be close to its optimum parameter values. This is the reason why the optimization process for rotation moves is associated with two possible policies, the first policy fosters better accuracy, and the second policy fosters reduced execution time.

The main core of the evaluation function is presented in Alg. 2. Inside each set ν from Alg. 1 :

- the subset m defines average values of longitudinal step length, lateral step length, turning step angle and execution time.
- the subset σ defines standard deviations values related to the average values.
- the subset s defines the success rate of the experiments.

Therefore, ν (respect. ν') set in Alg. 1 is replaced with its subsets (s,m,σ) (respect. (s',m',σ') in Alg .2).

The evaluation function is used for all moves, calling a more specialized subfunction if preliminary tests are passed successfully. First of all, as tested in Alg. 2 line 1, a miminum success rate s is needed. Therefore, depending on the type of move, the function checks :

- The lateral drift while translating forward, in Alg. 2 line 3.
- The longitudinal drift while translating sideways, in Alg. 2 line 7.
- The shift between translation axes while translating in diagonal, in Alg. 2 line 11.
- The drift while self rotating on the spot, in Alg. 2 line 19.

For the evaluation of translations the same `translationPickOut` function is called with the same average results – named m and m' – but with different criteria:

- Translating forward uses σ_x and σ'_x that define the standard deviations of forward translation on the x-axis, in Alg. 2 line 4.
- Translating sideways uses σ_y and σ'_y that define the standard deviations of sideways translation on the y-axis, in Alg. 2 line 8.
- Translating in diagonal uses distances – named e and e' – that define the standard deviations of the achieved distance, in Alg. 2 line 16.

As rotation is already very effective, the optimization of rotation moves in Alg. 2 is associated with two possible policies, the one fostering accuracy (line 20) or the other one reduced execution time (line 21). Accuracy optimization is achieved according to a specific *target* that defines the desired rotation angle. Details of the respective evaluation functions are explained in the next section.

3.3   Specialized Evaluations

Specialized evaluations regroup: The translation evaluation function, detailed in Alg. 3 ; The rotation evaluation function that checks the resulting accuracy, detailed in Alg. 4 ; The rotation evaluation function that checks the resulting speed, detailed in Alg. 5.

Algorithm 3. `translationPickOut` (m, e, m', e')

1: **if** $m' == UNDEFINED$ **then return** $ACCEPT$;
2: $d \leftarrow$ sqrt ($m_x^2 + m_y^2$);
3: $d' \leftarrow$ sqrt ($m_x'^2 + m_y'^2$);
4: **if** $d < d' - \alpha e'$ **then return** $REJECT$;
5: **if** $d < d' - \beta e'$ **then return** $EQUIVALENT$;
6: **if** $e < \gamma e'$ **then return** $ACCEPT$;
7: **if** $d < d'$ **then return** $EQUIVALENT$;
8: **return** $ACCEPT$;

All these evaluation functions make use of the three constant values α, β and γ: α is the nearness factor: if the new result is not close enough to the best known result, parameters are considered to lead to a worst instead of a best known result ; β is the equivalence factor: the test is similar to the nearness factor test with a different threshold. The result is now $EQUIVALENT$ with this factor whereas it is $REJECT$ with α. Because we compare averages and standard deviations resulting from two experiments, it is logical to ensure that $\beta < \alpha$; γ is the width factor: if the new result is more stable, then it is better.

Algorithm 4. RPO_accuracy $(target, m, \sigma, m', \sigma')$

1: **if** $m' == UNDEFINED$ **then return** $ACCEPT$;
2: **if** $| m_\theta - target | > | m'_\theta - target | + \alpha\sigma'_\theta$ **then return** $REJECT$;
3: **if** $| m_\theta - target | < | m'_\theta - target | - \beta\sigma'_\theta$ **then return** $EQUIVALENT$;
4: **if** $\sigma_\theta < \gamma\sigma'_\theta$ **then return** $ACCEPT$;
5: **if** $| m_\theta - target | > | m'_\theta - target |$ **then return** $EQUIVALENT$;
6: **return** $ACCEPT$;

As these functions are iteratively used, the constant values contribute to the convergence speed of the evolution.

Algorithm 5. RPO_time (m, σ, m', σ')

1: **if** $m' == UNDEFINED$ **then return** $ACCEPT$;
2: **if** $m_{time} < m'_{time} - \alpha\sigma'_{time}$ **then return** $REJECT$;
3: **if** $m_{time} < m'_{time} - \beta\sigma'_{time}$ **then return** $EQUIVALENT$;
4: **if** $\sigma_{time} < \gamma\sigma'_{time}$ **then return** $ACCEPT$;
5: **if** $m_{time} < m'_{time}$ **then return** $EQUIVALENT$;
6: **return** $ACCEPT$;

3.4   Parameters Influence and Trials

The optimization process can be seen as a nature-inspired growth since it makes morphological parameters of the legs and locomotion parameters evolve simultaneously. The first column of Tab. 1 and Tab.2 contains the morphological leg parameters and the walking parameters with upper/lower bounds.

The morphological leg parameters are listed first in these two tables. These parameters are related to the morphology of the leg:

– $ThighRelHip2\_Z$ stands for the semi-length of the femur. The change of this parameter value changes the cural index of the leg, which is the ratio of the tibia length with the femur length. The cural index is one of the key parameters in human morphology since it is useful for the comparison of the different bipeds that colonized the Earth since the appearance of the first hominids. The tibia length is kept fixed.

– $Hip1RelTorso\_X$ is the half length between hips. This parameter can be tuned to build a larger or a narrower pelvis for the humanoid robot. A larger pelvis can increase the reachable space of the legs below the trunk and reduce collisions between legs. This parameter is expected to influence the quality of the walking patterns that involve sideways moves.

– $ratio\_flexion$ is the leg flexion ratio, which is defined as the ratio of the hip height from the ground over the total length of the leg when stretched. A change of the flexion ratio has an influence on the way the robot walks, $i.e$ with knees more or less flexed.

The walking parameters are listed below the morphological parameters in Tab. 1 and Tab.2. The walking parameters can be varied to tune the walking skills of the robot in order to get a quick and well-balanced gait:

– $offset\_MidAnkles\_2\_Torso\_I$ stands for the horizontal distance between the middle of the ankles and the torso center. This parameter allows to balance the weight of the torso with respect to the flexed legs. The COM is considered to be fixed with respect to the torso, and its coordinates inside the torso coordinate frame are calculated automatically in the standing position as a function of the morphological parameters. This is an usual approximation in the case of the LIP-3D model.

– $height\_lift$ is the maximal height of leg lift-off.

– $xlength\_step\_max$ is the maximal forward step length.

– $ylength\_step\_max$ is the maximal sideways step length.

– $theta\_step\_max$ is the maximal turning step angle.

– $dist\_between\_feet\_p\_points$ is the distance between ankles in the rest position. This distance can be adjusted for the robot to walk with the feet more or less apart from each other. This walking parameter is expected to be influenced by the pelvis size.

4 Experiments and Results

The simulation software is composed of 5 different parts, i.e. $rcssserver3d$ [13,14], the client agent $rcssagent3d$-$like$, a coach (that is responsible for starting trial), the CLOP framework [9] and utilities that link everything.

Table 1 indicates the parameters that were used for each walking gait optimization. Table 2 contains the optimized parameters resulting from each of the 5 experiments (that were run according to the 5 evaluation functions) :

– Moving straight ahead, called $Fwd.$ trial.

– Moving sideways , called $Lat.$ trial.

– Moving diagonally forward, called $Diag.$ trial.

– Rotating accurately, called $Rot.$ trial with $Opt.1$ on $Accuracy$ parameters.

– Rotating fast, called $Rot.$ trial with $Opt.1$ on $Time$ parameters.

Table 3 contains the evaluation values, namely s, m_{time}, m_x, m_y, m_θ and the related deviations σ_x, σ_y and σ_θ for each experiment.

Tables 2 and 3 recall the default values of the parameters before optimization. These default values are related to the walking gaits that were tuned manually using expert's knowledge. The default values are useful to be compared to the optimized values obtained.

All experiments change morphological parameters and technical skills simultaneously to fit morphology and walking parameters to maximize values while minimizing other shifting values. As we aim at building a best-first agent, we only use the *Opt.1* policy [6], that defines the best last trial of the evaluation function. Each optimization is achieved with 500 CLOP iterations. Each CLOP iteration is performed over 10 trials. Final results are also calculated over 10 trials.

According to the results listed in Tab. 3 :

- While moving forward straight ahead : *Fwd. Opt.1* morphology is 1.62 times faster than the *Dflt* one (from ratio of m_x values in Tab. 3). *Fwd. Opt.1* morphology is 1.29 times more stable than the *Dflt* one (see parameter s in Tab. 3).
- While rotating : *Rot. Opt.1 on Accuracy* morphology is 3.44 times slower than the *Dflt* one (from ratio of m_{time} values in Tab. 3). *Rot. Opt.1 on Time* morphology is equivalent to the *Dflt* one (similar values for m_{time} in Tab. 3).
- While moving sideways : *Lat. Opt.1* morphology is 1.78 times faster than the *Dflt* one (from ratio of m_y values in Tab. 3).
- While moving on diagonal : *Diag. Opt.1* morphology is 1.51 times faster than the *Dflt* one (from ratio of m_x and m_y values in Tab. 3).

Table 1. All parameters bounds and trial policies

Bounds and trials	Min	Max	Fwd.	Rot.	Lat.	Diag.
Morphological parameters :						
$ThighRelHip2\_Z$	-0.09	-0.02	X	X	X	X
$Hip1RelTorso\_X$	-0.01	-0.10	X	X	X	X
$ratio\_flexion$	0.60	0.95	X	X	X	X
Walking skills parameters :						
$offset\_MidAnkles\_2\_Torso\_I$	0.001	0.030	X	X	X	X
$height\_lift$	0.025	0.080	X	X	X	X
$xlength\_step\_max$	0.020	0.150	X			X
$ylength\_step\_max$	0.020	0.150			X	X
$theta\_step\_max$	0.020	0.785		X		
$dist\_between\_feet\_p\_points$	0.020	0.200		X	X	X

Table 3 shows that the new two rotation morphologies (*Rot. Opt.1 on Accuracy* and *Rot. Opt.1 on Time*) are not better than the *Dflt* one. This results is not surprising because the rotation gait was carefully designed in the original morphology as explained in section 2, and because the rotation gait is less sensitive to dynamical effects along the longitudinal direction that is more prone to falling. Therefore none of these new rotation morphologies were selected. the heterogeneous team. The three remaining morphologies (Fig. 1) present interesting

Table 2. Resulting parameter values

Trial Parameters	Dflt	Fwd. Opt.1	Rot. Opt.1 on Accuracy	Rot. Opt.1 on Time	Lat. Opt.1	Diag. Opt.1
Morphological parameters :						
$ThighRelHip2\_Z$	-0.040	-0.079	-0.082	0.080	-0.061	-0.065
$Hip1RelTorso\_X$	-0.055	-0.022	-0.096	-0.058	-0.083	-0.062
$ratio\_flexion$	0.728	0.902	0.657	0.775	0.809	0.857
Walking skills parameters :						
$offset\_MidAnkles\_2\_Torso\_I$	0.011	0.020	0.006	0.024	0.013	0.009
$height\_lift$	0.030	0.063	0.066	0.069	0.044	0.036
$xlength\_step\_max$	0.080	0.125				0.050
$ylength\_step\_max$	0.060				0.121	0.094
$theta\_step\_max$	1.047		0.205	0.757		
$dist\_between\_feet\_p\_points$	0.110		0.079	0.027	0.123	0.146

Table 3. Results for each trial

Trial Param.	Fwd. Dflt	Fwd. Opt.1	Rot. Dflt	Rot. Opt.1 on Accuracy	Rot. Opt.1 on Time	Lat. Dflt	Lat. Opt.1	Diag. Dflt	Diag. Opt.1
s	0.70	0.90	1.00	1.00	1.00	1.00	1.00	1.00	1.00
m_{time}				2.807	9.643	3.058			
m_x	4.422	**7.168**	0.018	0.023	0.012	0.084	0.078	1.840	**2.843**
m_y	0.304	0.553	0.041	0.053	0.025	2.021	**3.588**	1.942	**2.860**
m_θ	0.123	0.187	5.973	6.161	6.030	0.062	0.060	0.083	0.248
σ_x	0.046	0.075	0.010	0.023	0.015	0.031	0.048	0.064	0.250
σ_y	0.234	0.534	0.032	0.036	0.015	0.053	0.046	0.106	0.287
σ_θ	0.066	0.173	0.068	0.125	0.159	0.021	0.048	0.047	0.131

Table 4. Results of 3 parameter sets for each trial

Trials Param.	Fwd. Fwd.	Fwd. Rot.*	Fwd. Lat.	Fwd. Dgn.	Lat. Fwd.	Lat. Rot.*	Lat. Lat.	Lat. Dgn.	Diag. Fwd.	Diag. Rot.*	Diag. Lat.	Diag. Dgn.
s	0.90	1.00	1.00	1.00	1.00	1.00	1.00		1.00	1.00	1.00	1.00
m_{time}		1.339				1.380				1.398		
m_x	**7.168**	0.035	0.428	1.091	4.737	0.045	0.078	2.423	2.918	0.026	0.418	**2.843**
m_y	0.553	0.042	1.961	2.465	0.540	0.049	**3.588**	2.634	0.201	0.053	3.023	**2.860**
m_θ	0.187	2.232	0.397	0.747	0.270	1.789	0.060	0.119	0.112	2.182	0.237	0.248
σ_{time}		0.001				0.003				0.001		
σ_x	0.075	0.020	0.071	0.046	0.094	0.014	0.048	0.155	0.033	0.015	0.144	0.250
σ_y	0.534	0.033	0.067	0.053	0.407	0.029	0.046	0.158	0.074	0.039	0.054	0.287
σ_θ	0.173	0.003	0.052	0.028	0.236	0.010	0.048	0.072	0.064	0.004	0.009	0.131

Fig. 1. *Fwd.*, *Diag.* and *Lateral* morphologies

properties because they enhance the displacement capabilities, either forward, sideways or diagonally (see m_x and m_y values in bold font in Tab. 3).

However it is necessary to check that each of the three selected morphologies is still compatible with the walking gaits in the other directions, i.e. other than the *enhanced* direction. Table 4 summarizes such results. It shows that the three optimized morphologies are compatible with the gaits in the other directions. In the checking experiments the angle in the rotation gait was limited to $2\pi/3$. In addition since the lateral morphology increased the lateral step up to the maximal bound, it was necessary to limit the diagonal step to maintain the foot trajectory inside the working volume of the leg. Therefore the diagonal step was limited to $0.08m$.

If we observe the values of the morphological parameters listed in Tab. 2, we can notice that the *Lat.* and *Diag.* morphologies have a wider pelvis compared to the *Dflt* morphology and the *Fwd. Opt.1* morphology (see $Hip1RelTorso\_X$ parameter). The pelvis is even wider in the *Lat.* morphology to enable a larger sideways step, i.e. $0.121m$ compared to $0.94m$ with the *Diag.* values. In addition we can notice that all three morphologies have longer thighs (see $ThighRelHip2\_Z$ parameter), and that the flexion ratio is also larger, which means that all new robots will walk in a more high-legged way. This way of walking reminds the human walk where legs get stretched and flexed alternately. The third observation concerns the height of foot lift off. This height is reduced for the *Lat.* and the *Diag.* morphologies. Actually it was noticed that the lateral walk was more sensitive to lift-off height. This is due to ground impacts of the swinging leg that cause oscillations of the torso in the frontal plane, and these oscillations can be dangerous and make the robot fall if the amplitude increases too much. The reduction of the lift-off height is useful to prevent leg impacts from triggering undesired oscillations.

Thanks to this study it is possible to build a new team with heterogeneous players where:

- Strikers built on the *Fwd.* parameter set could be both faster sprinters and nicely reactive due to their fast rotation speed.
- Midfields built on the *Diag.* parameter set could be good at breaking opponents attack.
- Defenders and goalie built on the *Lat.* parameter set) could be good at intercepting the ball or the opponent trajectory.

The next developments will aim at testing teams of heterogeneous soccer players during soccer game plays.

5   Conclusion

We introduced an optimization process that is especially designed for the simultaneous evolution of humanoids' morphological characteristics and walking parameters. The optimization process is essentially guided by a fitness function that distinguishes among better, equivalent and worse results. Three morphological profiles have been produced to create three agents that appear to be more effective than the previous agents that were tuned manually by expert users. Actually the process leads to morphologies well suited for forward walk, lateral walk and diagonal walk. This process will be applied to the building of a heterogeneous humanoid team with new models designed according to specific skills.

References

1. Hebbel, M., Kosse, R., Nistico, W.: Modeling and Learning Walking Gaits of Biped Robots. In: IEEE-RAS Int. Conf. on Humanoid Robots 2013, 1st Workshop on Humanoid Soccer Robots, HSR 2006
2. Niehaus, C., Röfer, T., Laue, T.: Gait Optimization on a Humanoid Robot using Particle Swarm Optimization. In: Second Workshop on Humanoid Soccer Robots, IEEE-RAS 7th Int. Conf. on Humanoid Robots, HSR 2007 (2007)
3. MacAlpine, P., Stone, P.: Using Dynamic Rewards to Learn a Fully Holonomic Bipedal Walk. In: Adaptive Learning Agents Workshop (ALA 2012) (2012)
4. Hansen, N.: The CMA Evolution Strategy: A Tutorial (2011), https://www.lri.fr/~hansen/cmatutorial.pdf
5. Farchy, A., Barrett, S., MacAlpine, P., Stone, P.: Humanoid Robots Learning to Walk Faster: From the Real World to Simulation and Back. In: Int. Conf. on Autonomous Agents and Multiagent Systems (AAMAS 2013) (2013)
6. Jouandeau, N., Hugel, V.: Simultaneous evolution of leg morphology and walking skills to build the best humanoid walker. In: IEEE-RAS Int. Conf. on Humanoid Robots 2013, 8th Workshop on Humanoid Soccer Robots, HSR 2013 (2013)
7. Hugel, V., Jouandeau, N.: Walking Patterns for Real Time Path Planning Simulation of Humanoids. In: 21st IEEE Int. Symposium on Robot and Human Interactive Communication (IEEE RO-MAN 2012) (2012)
8. Hugel, V., Jouandeau, N.: Automatic generation of humanoid s geometric model parameters. In: 17th Annual RoboCup Int. Symposium (RCUP 2013) (2013)
9. Coulom, R.: CLOP: Confident Local Optimization for Noisy Black-Box Parameter Tuning. In: van den Herik, H.J., Plaat, A. (eds.) ACG 2011. LNCS, vol. 7168, pp. 146–157. Springer, Heidelberg (2012)
10. Jouandeau, N., Hugel, V.: Optimization of Parametrised Kicking Motion for Humanoid Soccer Player. In: IEEE-RAS Int. Conf. on Autonomous Robot Systems and Competitions (ICARSC 2014) (2014)
11. Vukobratovic, M., Borovac, B.: Zero-moment point - thirty five years of its life. Int. J. of Humanoid Robotics 1(1), 157–173 (2004)
12. Kajita, S.: Humanoid Robot, Ohmsha Ltd., 3-1 Kanda Nishikicho, Chiyodaku, Tokyo, Japan (2005)
13. Obst, O., Rollmann, M.: Spark – A Generic Simulator for Physical Multi-agent Simulations. In: Lindemann, G., Denzinger, J., Timm, I.J., Unland, R. (eds.) MATES 2004. LNCS (LNAI), vol. 3187, pp. 243–257. Springer, Heidelberg (2004)
14. SimSpark, a generic physical multiagent simulator system for agents in three-dimensional environments, http://simspark.sourceforge.net/

Stability Analysis of Densest Packing
of Objects Using Partial Order Representation
of Feasible Procedural Sequences

Hiromu Onda

Intelligent Systems Research Institute,
National Institute of Advanced Industrial Science and Technology (AIST),
AIST Tsukuba Central 2, 305-8568, Japan
onda@ni.aist.go.jp

Abstract. This paper examines the process involved in separately packing goods of several kinds into a container. During such a process, the volume of each kind of good ("block") must be optimized to minimize container size. For this optimization, densest packing procedures can be used to determine the feasibility of packing by a robot. This paper analyzes packing procedures generated automatically using partial order representation of feasible procedures, which determines stable and feasible procedures by considering that process planning affects the stability, contact forces, and torques of the target packing pattern and its transient piles.

1 Introduction

This paper analyzes feasible procedural order and stability of densest packing of cylindrical objects. Discrete geometry algorithms and results are applied to the planning and packing procedure for goods of several kinds into a box in robotics, as in, for example, packing for home delivery.

Automation of packing for the distribution of goods in logistics is an attractive but challenging problem for robotics. In packing for home delivery, ordered goods of several kinds are packed separately into separate areas in a container (Fig. 1) [1]. Because container sizes are generally fixed, the size of the box chosen is approximated according to the volume of ordered goods. For example, the container boxes used for delivery by SG Holdings [2], a Japanese logistics company, are of five different size types, with different costs according to the type. The types are 60 size, 80 size, 100 size, 140 size, and 160 size. In actuality, "60 size" signifies a box with a total dimension (length, width, and height) of up to 60 cm. It can accommodate a weight of up to 2kg. The company provides boxes for each type: a 100 size box is 32 cm in length, 43 cm in width, and 25 cm in height. To minimize the box size, the volume of goods of each kind ("block") should be optimized. Minimization of the "block" into which objects are packed is a densest packing problem, which has been studied in discrete geometry and operations research.

D. Brugali et al. (Eds.): SIMPAR 2014, LNAI 8810, pp. 424–437, 2014.

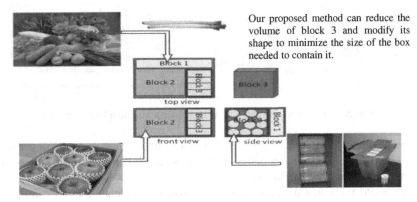

Our proposed method can reduce the volume of block 3 and modify its shape to minimize the size of the box needed to contain it.

Fig. 1. Packing for home delivery

This problem predominantly incorporates object geometry [3, 4]. However, packing procedures and stability have to be considered in order to determine the feasibility of packing by a robot.

In an earlier study [12], packing procedures were generated automatically, and a feasibility check in the form of dynamic simulations, which considered robot load capacity, arrangement of "blocks," and packing procedures, was conducted to assess pattern stability. This type of procedure differs from the conventional densest packing problem.

In packing or piling processes, some transient patterns may be unstable and unfeasible when obtained using certain procedures; therefore, procedures should be chosen and planned carefully. Although [12] addressed the densest packing of objects applied to robotics, and pointed out its importance, the subject was insufficiently handled.

The phenomenon can be found even in some simple packing scenarios. Its causes include construction history and history effect, which are well known in Physics, where the effect of forces and torques on a pile and its consequent stability has been analyzed [5]. In robotics, this "history effect" in packing and piling has not been addressed adequately despite its importance in planning the packing and piling order. For example, one might assume that cylinders are stacked in piles via a procedural sequence such as that depicted in Fig. 2. Because step 6 is omitted in this figure it is not known which cylinder 4 or 7, was chosen in step 6. However, different procedural sequences result in different forces and torques on the pile. The value of r_L in the pile, the reaction force from the left wall of the container to the pile, is not determined uniquely by equations because of friction.

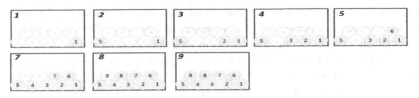

Fig. 2. Example of a procedural sequence

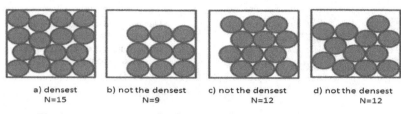

Fig. 3. Densest packing and simple strategy packing in a fixed size box

This phenomenon is analyzed in Section 4. The italic numbers to the upper-left of the figure denote the ordinal numbers of the procedural sequence. Here, the packing pattern of nine circles is carried out in nine steps.

One would think that dynamic simulation would easily enable us to simulate and estimate the stability mentioned above, because it is useful and powerful today. In our case, however, it would only provide a small amount of useful information if the geometry of the objects is not carefully approximated and if contact detection between them is not addressed sufficiently and appropriately. Cylinders are usually approximated as prisms in ordinary dynamics simulation engines. This means that the circles are approximated by polygons in a cross section. If circles in a pile have no stable state, but polygons in a pile might. Therefore, such dynamic simulation is not directly applicable and might even be considered careless if used for stability analysis.

Ordinary dynamics simulators such as ODE [6], Bullet[6], and OpenHRP [7] that approximate cylindrical surfaces using polyhedral surfaces or triangular patches are not useful for the analyses described herein without certain special care because oscillating phenomena can occur even under circumstances in which the cylinder should be rolling in one direction. Moreover, a result stating that a pile is stable might be given even when the pile is actually unstable and incapable of maintaining the state. Following derivation of an analytic solution from equations, this paper gives a range of solutions for stability analysis.

Two main cases in which the procedural sequence affects the stability of a transient pile or the target packing pattern are reported in this paper. The two cases are as follows:

A carefully chosen procedure can construct a stable pile if every variable (reaction force and friction force) is within its permissible range (Case A).

Different procedures can be used to construct the "same" stable pile having different forces and torques under certain conditions. (Case B).

This paper addresses the problem of stability depending on selected procedures, and the method used to determine an appropriate procedural sequence. Two representative cases are described in Section 2. The packing problem for stability presented herein is formulated in Section 3 and the effect of the applied procedural sequence and the positioning of the robot on stability analyzed. The results of a simulation conducted as a feasibility check are presented in Section 4.

One contribution of this paper is that it shows the importance of process planning in terms of how it affects the stability and feasibility of construction of transient piles of a target packing pattern. A "history effect" persists in a transient pile. This effect must be addressed in process planning for packing. Another contribution is a procedural sequences analytical algorithm for stable construction. By appropriately considering the stability and feasibility of transient packing processes using symbolic computation, feasible procedural sequences can be planned more precisely and subtly, even under varied specifications and conditions.

1.1   Densest Packing and Related Work

One might regard the difference between optimal packing and conventional packing as small and a maximum of one unit at best. Unfortunately, the difference may not be negligible. For example, 15 cylinders can be packed into a box using the solution for the corresponding densest packing problem. If the box is packed with cylinders conventionally, 9–12 cylinders (Figs. 3(b)–3(d)) can be contained in it. However, more efficient packing can be realized if densest packing is utilized and the performance of applicable technologies incorporated. Packing problems are a class of optimization problems. Several papers in the field of robotics incorporate such studies. Kawakami et al. attempted 3D bin packing using a genetic algorithm [8], which corresponds to sub-problem A in Section 2 of this paper.

The densest packing problem has been examined in many studies [3, 4, 9–11] in the field of discrete geometry and operations research. One earlier study [12] dealt with the densest packing of objects applied to robotics and the importance of physical properties such as robot load capacity, arrangement of "blocks," and packing procedures.

Using the formulation of conventional packing problems directly to actualize packing by a robot is difficult because the actual packing process is too complicated and difficult to solve in limited time. Appropriate abstractions of this problem according to practical requirements are required. Motion planning, though useful, occasionally takes too much time. Task planning identifies promising plans as candidates in its abstraction level. Like motion planning, dynamic simulation takes too much time and so it is better applied to appropriately reduce the number of candidates identified by a task planner. Consequently, more realistic and appropriate abstracted formulations are necessary. In this paper, suction pads and a vacuum gripper are assumed to be used because of ease of gripping from the top of the object by suction without considering a space for the gripper's fingers [12].

2   Cases in Which Procedural Sequence Affects Stability

Our method can enable appropriate selection of procedural sequences such that objects are positioned accurately and the pile is stable. For instance, a particular procedural sequence makes a pattern stable and maintains variables in a permissible range, but another procedural sequence may render it unstable and put some variables out of the range.

Merely selecting an acceptable procedural sequence can result in changes in pile stability from a stable one (Fig. 4(a) for critical static friction coefficient μ) to an unstable one (Fig. 4(b) for critical μ; a fourth circle is added, creating instability).

In another case (Case B), the same pile may have a different stability depending on the selected procedural sequence.

Let us look at the simple pile construction example shown in Fig. 5. Respective circles are labeled b–j, contacts between circles are labeled 1–16, and contacts between circles and walls are labeled w1–w4, with L and R. For clarity, labels w1–w4, with L and R on the left side of the figure are not shown. A normal component of reaction force from the floor is shown as rwj (j = 1, 2, 3, 4); fwj (j = 1, 2, 3, 4) is the friction force from the floor. In addition, integer i is the index number of circle–circle contact, ri is a normal component of reaction force, fi denotes a friction force, and mg represents the weight of a circle.

The right side of the figure shows the equilibrium conditions of the forces acting on *circle g*. For clarity, tangential friction forces are not shown. For example, f8, f14, fw1, and f_L should be included, but they are omitted from the right side of the figure. Using equilibrium conditions, the permissible range of variables is calculable. The permissible range of F_L in the pile in Fig. 5 is calculable as Eq. A, as described in Section 4.

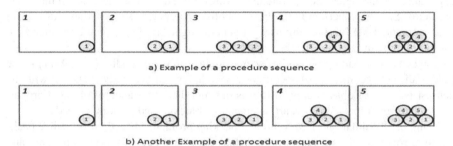

a) Example of a procedure sequence

b) Another Example of a procedure sequence

Fig. 4. Example of procedural sequences

If an appropriate procedural sequence is selected in Case A, then all variables can be made within the permissible range for equilibrium conditions (Case A definition). When a target packing pattern or a transient pile pattern is given, all the procedural sequences for stable construction of the pattern are calculated using a possible subset of all procedures. For Case A, an appropriate procedural sequence can be selected from the possible subset of all procedural sequences.

Equations for equilibrium conditions are constructed and parameterized for all selected possible procedures by using "S-chain." Using these equations, the stability of a pile realized by the procedures can be estimated if parameters such as the cylinder mass and friction coefficients are changed.

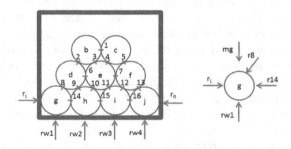

Fig. 5. Example of a pile

Following this *analytic model*, i.e., if a set of equations for equilibrium conditions for the target packing pattern or the transient pile patterns is prepared manually in advance, the stability condition presented above, which depends on procedural sequences, is calculable and can be checked automatically.

3   Packing Procedure Dependency

3.1   Formalizing the Packing Problem

This section presents an overview of packing tasks to realize a target pattern using *skill primitives* for automated packing of objects by robots. For automated packing, it is necessary to plan the target pattern of packed objects, plan packing processes and motions, and program manipulation skill primitives to be realized by robots [12].

We first plan a target pattern of packed objects, in which we consider specifications of how the packing should be done. For example, if the densest packing of objects into a given container or region should be done, then the main specification will be that the densest pattern of objects be planned.

Next, we plan object packing processes, in which we decide which objects should be selected and where they should be positioned. Although this process depends on the robot used to do the packing, it is important to devise a packing process method that is as independent of the robot as possible because calculating motion planning is computationally expensive. Furthermore, these requirements must be addressed during planning because packing specifications sometimes present conflicting requirements.

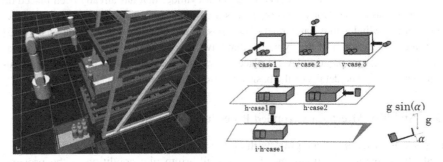

Fig. 6. Example of packing environment

We also require skill primitives to accomplish the packing. These skill primitives are used in accordance with the result of this process planning: a sequence of these primitives. The environment outlined for our scenario is depicted in Fig. 6 (left-side) [13]. Objects are packed in a certain section in a container. In this case, the container is placed at a flow rack, which is often tilted for ease of access to each object in the container. When dealing with different arrangements for identical blocks, different packing problems are solved with respect to the direction of gravity. There are therefore horizontal cases, vertical cases, and intermediate cases: horizontal cases include h-case1 and h-case2; vertical cases include v-case1, v-case2, and v-case3;

intermediate cases include i-h-case1, i-h-case2, i-v-case1, i-v-case2, and i-v-case3. The respective cases are portrayed in Fig. 6 (right-side). If the container is placed at a tilted flow rack, it is i-h-case1, which approximately corresponds to v-case1 under smaller gravity. The intermediate cases were not examined in the previous study reported in [12]. We assume positioning uncertainty δ (approximately 3 mm, uniform distribution) from the sensing of the cylinder position using a vision sensor and control error of positioning using a manipulator [14].

3.2   Applying Solutions to Densest Packing Problems

Packing procedures include basic operations [12] using constraints from the walls and floor, as described below (Fig. 7). A sequence of these basic operations BO1–BO3 enables a robot to position cylinders in precise locations by selection and placement.

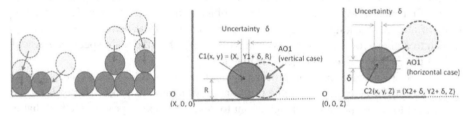

Fig. 7. Basic operations and Auxiliary operation AO1(gravity is (0, 0, -g))

[BO1] places a cylinder in a corner between a wall and the floor. [BO2h] places a cylinder on the floor so that it is touched by another cylinder that has already been placed on the floor by basic operations. [BO2v] places a cylinder on a wall so that it is in contact with another cylinder that has already been positioned there by basic operations. [BO3] places a cylinder on top of the cylinders that have already been placed using basic operations. The auxiliary operation [AO1] places a cylinder within the assumed robot positioning uncertainty δ. The details of the basic operations can be found in [12].

3.3   Stability Affected by Applied Procedural Sequence

In a packing process against gravity, the force and torques in each proceeding process is calculated using the equations of each equilibrium pile condition at the process. Following this formalization, using a computer algebra system called *maxima* [15], the following solutions are obtained ($\mu = 0$ is assumed in this result of the example (Fig. 5)):

$$r1 = r2 = r3 = r4 = r8 = r11 = \frac{mg}{\sqrt{3}}$$

$$r5 = r6 = 0$$

$$r7 = r9 = r10 = r12 = \frac{2mg}{\sqrt{3}}$$

$$r13 = r15 = r_R - \frac{mg}{\sqrt{3}}$$

$$r14 = r_R - \frac{\sqrt{3}mg}{2}$$

$$f_i = 0, (i = 1, \ldots, N)$$

$$rw1 = rw4 = 2mg, rw2 = rw3 = \frac{5}{2}mg$$

$$fwj = 0, (j = 1, \ldots, 4)$$

$$r_L = r_R$$

The static friction coefficient μ is a parameter that indicates whether the pile is stable or unstable. The critical condition of μ is the μ that transforms the solution of equations from an *emptyset* (no solution) to a certain solution.

Given the target of a packing pattern or a pile, we address scenarios in which solutions exist for a given pattern of procedural sequences and others in which no solution exists. We address the problem of finding appropriate procedural sequences by which stable target patterns can be achieved.

4   Simulation and Results

In this section, we apply the algorithm to a problem. More specifically, we use the pattern presented in Fig. 8 as input to the algorithm and obtain the resulting procedural sequence found as output. This section also explains the dependence of the stability of a transient pile or a target pattern on the procedural sequence in a packing task. Figs. 8(a) and 8(b) present different stability states in transient piles. The stability of each state is calculable using the equilibrium equations.

The contact forces and torques are not uniquely determined if the friction coefficient is not zero or if the history of packing affects the stability.

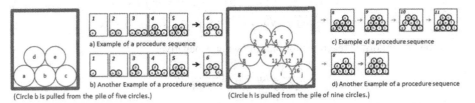

Fig. 8. Example of piles

4.1   Pile Stability of Example

Here, a *pile* is defined as a pattern in a packing process under gravity and *pile stability* is defined as the stability of that pattern under gravity (e.g., vertical or intermediate case in Fig. 6). In this section, pile stability is considered because stability is a problem in actual tasks. Two piles, one stacked using procedural sequence a), Pile A, and the other procedural sequence b), Pile B, are presented in Fig. 8. Pile B fails at the third step in the procedural sequence if the friction coefficient is smaller than $(2 - \sqrt{3})mg$. The notation is similar to that in Fig. 5. In this case, the procedural sequence by the algorithm in this paper is output, which is the procedural sequence in Fig. 8(a).

4.2   Different Stable States of Another Example

Two piles, one stacked using a different procedural sequence c), Pile C, and another using procedural sequence d), Pile D, are presented in Fig. 8 (right-side). In the figure, the procedural sequence of Pile C from steps 1–7 is the same as the sequence of Pile D from steps 1–7. Piles C and D have different stable states. Cylinder h is pulled from the pile in Fig. 5. The pile at step 10 in Pile C is tolerant and stable if cylinder h is pulled under the following condition. The notation is similar to that in Fig. 5. Cylinder h is pulled in the state of the tenth state of the procedural sequence in Fig. 8 (right-side). Therefore, the following equations hold:

$$r9 = r10 = r14 = r15 = rw2 = 0$$
$$f9 = f10 = f14 = f15 = fw2 = 0$$

The problem is one of assessment of the stability of the eleventh state of procedural sequences c) and the ninth state of procedural sequences d). The solution can be estimated by comparing the difference of the two states of the two procedural sequences. Forces and torques in Piles C and D differ. To reduce the algebraic complexity, we assume that the circle–floor and circle–wall contact are smooth. For this pile we assume that it has been built in such a fashion that the normal and frictional forces at contact points one and seven vanish, as

$$r1 = f1 = r7 = f7 = 0$$

The forces and torques of Pile C at the tenth step are as follows:

$$r2 = r3 = \frac{mg}{2\sqrt{3}} + r_L, \quad r4 = r5 = \frac{\sqrt{3}mg}{2} + \frac{3}{2}r_L, \quad r6 = \frac{5mg}{2\sqrt{3}} - r_L$$
$$r8 = 2r_L, \quad r11 = \frac{5\sqrt{3}mg}{2} - \frac{5}{2}r_L, r12 = \frac{10mg}{\sqrt{3}} - \frac{11}{2}r_L$$
$$r13 = -\frac{13mg}{2\sqrt{3}} + 5r_L, \quad r16 = \frac{mg}{\sqrt{3}}, \quad rw1 = mg + \sqrt{3}r_L$$
$$rw3 = \frac{17}{2}mg - 3\sqrt{3}r_L, \quad rw4 = -\frac{3}{2}mg + 2\sqrt{3}r_L, \quad r_L = r_R$$

None of the normal reactions for the following is negative:

$$\frac{13}{10\sqrt{3}}mg \leq r_L \leq \frac{20}{11\sqrt{3}}mg$$

However, outside of this range, one normal reaction is negative at least. Therefore the system has physical equilibrium states only if force r_R satisfies the inequalities. (In fact, our calculations indicate that one of the results in the work by Grindlay and Opie [5] is in error.) In the eleventh step of procedural sequences c), cylinder h is returned to the same position. The forces and torques are the same as the ones in the tenth step. The forces and torques differ from those in the ninth step of procedural sequences d).

4.3   Algorithm for Determining Procedural Sequence

An algorithm is used to determine the procedural sequence. The circles in the target packing pattern are labeled 1–N and the algorithm determines the circle labeled k to be put on the current pile and added to the *RESULT* sequences from the feasible candidates. If the last circle of the pile can be put on the current pile, then the *RESULT* sequences are output as results.

Algorithm: Determining appropriate procedures for constructing a stable pattern

Input:

Position of the centers of circles of the target pattern of N cylinders:

$(Xi, Yi), i = 1, ..., N$

List of N cylinders: *item-list*

Position and orientation of the block (rectangular parallelepiped area in the container) into which the cylinders are placed: (Xb, Yb, Zb, Rb, Yb, Pb)

Block shape (length of each edges of the block): (Lx, Ly, Lz)

Access direction: z is the default value.

Output:

RESULT: (pj$_1$, ..., p j$_N$), a sequence of procedures

Iterative process:

for *item* **in** *item-list* **do**

if root-p(*item, conditions-list*) **then** append(*item, root-item-list*)

else if s-chain(*item, conditions-list*) **then** append(*item, s-chain-item-list*)

else return(ERROR)

S-Chain = create-S-chain (root-item-list, s-chain-item-list, conditions-list)

if FeasibilityCheck(S-Chain) then

   Append(RESULTLIST, SP) ; append SP to RESULTLIST if SP is feasible

end

def FeasibilityCheck (seq)

begin

   for i *from* 1 to (length of seq)

      if FourierElim(Equations[TransientPattern]) *then*

         T

         else NIL

end

Algorithm: create-S-chain (root-item-list, s-chain-item-list, conditions-list);

calculate the subset (S-chain) of all the (candidates of) sequences of procedures for constructing a "stable" pattern

Input:

Positions of the centers of circles of the target pattern of N cylinders:

$(Xi, Yi), i = 1, ..., N$

Position and orientation of the block (rectangular parallelepiped area in the container) into which the cylinders are put: (Xb, Yb, Zb, Rb, Yb, Pb)

Block shape (length of each edges of the block): (Lx, Ly, Lz)

Access direction: z is the default value.

The S-chain definition (Necessary and sufficient conditions to be S-chain): conditions-list = (condition1, condition2, ..., condition Ns)

Output:

s-chain-item-list: S-chain, all the (candidates of) sequences of procedures for constructing a "stable" pattern. This "stability" is defined in the S-chain definition.

Iterative process:

for *item* **in** *item-list* **do**

if root-p(*item, conditions-list*) **then** append(*item, root-item-list*)

else if s-chain(*item, conditions-list*) **then** append(*item, s-chain-item-list*)

else return(ERROR)

return s-chain-item-list

end

FourierElim is similarly defined as a function of maxima, which solves nonlinear inequalities using a Fourier–Motzkin elimination algorithm and a preprocessor that converts some nonlinear inequalities that involve the absolute value, minimum, and maximum functions into linear equations. Additionally, the preprocessor handles some expressions that are products or quotients of linear terms [15].

4.4   S-chain

The S-chain is introduced for two reasons. One reason is that some data structures and tools for management of transient patterns of pattern and procedure order are needed for the analysis herein. The other reason is to reduce the input dataset. If the input dataset is not reduced, i.e., it generates every permutation of N, which is of factorial complexity, the complexity of this algorithm would be prohibitively large. It would make the algorithm infeasible even for moderate sizes of N. For example, even in a small $n = 8$ case, the permutation of $n = 8$ is large, i.e., it is $8! = 40320$. The maxima program is too slow to run 40320 times. S-chain, "support" of which is defined for intermediate case (i-v-case1), has only 32 candidates—significantly less than 40320.

The definition of S-chain is as follows:

Let A denote the set of n items, each of which has its index $i_j \in N, j = 1, \dots, n$.

$$A = \{a(i_1), \dots, a(i_n)\}$$

The S-chain is a family of subsets of A such that all elements are "supported" according to a certain definition of "support." For example, assume that the definition of "support in horizontal case" is such that a circle is designated as a supported circle when it has contact with more than two of {the root circles, walls, or supported circles}. If the centers of three circles, one of which is supported and two of which are supporting, are approximately on the same line, this support is not good support. Therefore such support is excluded from the S-chain by a certain threshold. Figure 9(a) presents an example of an S-chain ($n = 8$, horizontal case, 1088 candidates of procedural sequences. The maxima program is not needed in horizontal cases.). Although it may be difficult to see the details in the figure because of its size, the shape of the graph and its complexity are obvious. Each node of the graph in Fig. 9(a) is a "supported" subset of A. Directly above each node has just one more element (i.e., a cylindrical object) than those of the node below it. These nodes are linked if newly added cylindrical objects are "supported" by any part of the remainder of the cylindrical objects. The top of the nodes denotes the target pattern, which is a subset and includes all eight cylindrical objects as its elements. Each node at the bottom denotes a subset that includes only each root cylinder, which corresponds to a root circle in 2D. In this case, the root circles are four circles at the four corners of the container.

The S-chain has a partial order defined in the natural way because it is represented by a family of subsets. This partial order representation of S-chain can effectively be used to analyze the order of procedures from every subset that include only a corresponding "root circle" to the target pattern and transient patterns.

As another example, assume that the definition of "support in intermediate case" is designated as a supported circle when the circle is in contact with more than two of {root circles, walls, or supported circles}. These are candidates of a stably supported circle pattern if the center of the supported circle is horizontally between the centers of supporting circles and vertically above the centers of those. Figure 9(b) presents an example of the S-chain (n = 8, intermediate case, 32 candidates of procedural sequences). Each node of the graph in Fig. 9(b) is a "supported" subset of A. Directly above each node has just one more element (i.e., a cylindrical object) than those of the node below it. These nodes are linked if newly added cylindrical objects are "supported" by any part of the remainder of the cylindrical objects. The top of the nodes denotes the target pattern, which is a subset and includes all the cylindrical objects as its elements. In this case it is {a1, a2, b1, c1, c2, d1, d2, d3}. Each node at the bottom denotes a subset that includes only each root. In this case, these are {a1} and {a2}, which are the two circles at the bottom corners. An example of S-chain is {{a1}, {a1, a2}, {a1, a2, b1}, {a1, a2, b1, c1}, {a1, a2, b1, c1, d1}, {a1, a2, b1, c1, c2, d1}, {a1, a2, b1, c1, c2, d1, d2}, {a1, a2, b1, c1, c2, d1, d2, d3}}, which is shown also in Fig. 9(b).

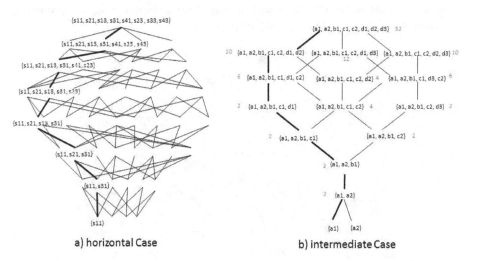

a) horizontal Case   b) intermediate Case

Fig. 9. Example of S-Chain

5   Conclusions

This paper analyzed the procedural sequence and stability of a target packing pattern and its transient piles. Further, it introduced a calculation method for procedural sequence candidates. In order to broaden the application to robotics the results of discrete geometry and OR, these should be considered. Cases in which different procedural sequences affect the stability of the given target packing pattern and its transient piles were described. The problem of determining the appropriate sequence in such a scenario was also addressed.

We presented a rather simple case (in which contact points are easily determined; all cosine and sine values appearing in the equations are equal to 1/2, $\sqrt{3}/2$, 0, or 1) for clarity of description. Application to a more general case is not very complicated because the circle center positions are calculated in advance. The contact points between circles and the normal components' direction of reaction forces can be determined readily from the position data. Fig. 10 presents optimal patterns of the densest circle packing from $n = 1$ to $n = 30$. Therefore, contact points between the circles and their sine and cosine of the equations of the more general pattern are calculable using the position data of circle centers of the more general pattern. These equations are resolved by maxima in the same manner as that described herein.

We assume cylindrical or approximately cylindrical objects. Although this assumption might be regarded as overly strong, it is not a bad idea to assume that packing objects are cylindrical or rectangular parallelepiped because it is a common practice to wrap fragile objects and general shaped objects in cushioning wrap or paper to prevent their breakage or damage, or to put these objects into a small box to stabilize them in a container, thereby strengthening the container structure (e.g., apples in the box in Fig. 1). Differently sized cylinders, objects with more general shapes, and three dimensional packing will be dealt with in future work. In this case, an appropriate definition for "support" of S-chain will be important.

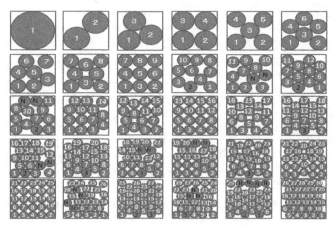

(n=1–30, in vertical case 2a-2) in [20]

Fig. 10. Patterns of 30 densest packing procedures

Acknowledgements. This work was supported by JSPS KAKENHI Grant Number 24500248.

References

1. http://www.oisix.com/ (in Japanese), http://www.daichi.or.jp (in Japanese)
2. http://www.sagawa-exp.co.jp/service/material/box/ (in Japanese)
3. Dowsland, K.A., Dowsland, W.B.: Packing problems. European Journal of Operational Research 56(1), 2–14 (1992)
4. Castillo, I., Kampas, F.J., Pinte, J.D.: Solving circle packing problems by global optimization: Numerical results and industrial applications. European Journal of Operational Research 191, 786–802 (2008)
5. Grindlay, J., Opie, A.H.: Contact force distribution in a pile of rigid disks. Physical Review E 51(1), 718–723 (1995)
6. ODE: Open Dynamics Engine, http://ode.org/, Bullet Physics Engine: http://bulletphysics.org/wordpress/
7. Kanehiro, F., Hirukawa, H., Kajita, S.: OpenHRP: Open Architecture Humanoid Robotics Platform. International Journal of Robotics Research 23(2), 155–165 (2004)
8. Kawakami, T., Minagawa, M., Kakazu, Y.: Auto Tuning of 3-D Packing Rules Using Genetic Algorithms. In: Proc of Int. Workshop. on Intelligent Robots and Systems (IROS 1991), pp. 1319–1324 (1991)
9. Specht, E.: Packomania, http://www.packomania.com
10. Birgin, E.G., Martınez, J., Ronconi, D.: Optimizing the packing of cylinders into a rectangular container: A nonlinear approach. European Journal of Operational Research 160, 19–33 (2005)
11. Lopez, C.O., Beasley, J.E.: A heuristic for the circle packing problem with a variety of containers. European Journal of Operational Research 214, 512–525 (2011)
12. Onda, H.: Formulation of packing problem applying densest packing algorithms to planning of packing for robot. In: Proc. of IECON 2012, pp. 2693–2700 (2012)
13. Onda, H., Harada, K., Yoshimi, T., et al.: Specification, planning and manipulation for packing by robot. In: Proc. of RSJ 2012 (2012) (in Japanese)
14. Hasegawa, T., Suehiro, T., Takase, K.: A model-based manipulation system with skill-based execution. IEEE Trans. on RA 8(5), 535–944 (1992)
15. Maxima 5.30.0 manual, http://maxima.sourceforge.net/docs/manual

Team Size Optimization
for Multi-robot Exploration

Zhi Yan, Luc Fabresse, Jannik Laval, and Noury Bouraqadi

Ecole des Mines de Douai,
59508 Douai, France
{firstname.lastname}@mines-douai.fr

Abstract. This paper analyzes and discusses the problem of optimizing the size of a team of robots for multi-robot exploration. We are concerned with the number of robots for a given exploration task that minimizes both exploration time and cost. Minimizing time means that the exploration should be done as fast as possible. Minimizing cost means that the number of robots and their energy consumption should be as low as possible. To solve this problem, we report in this paper, on a series of exploration simulations based on ROS and MORSE using a cluster of computers. The simulated code is exactly the same as that which would run on the actual robots. Such a simulation infrastructure is crucial to "quickly" execute experiments with different parameters such as the number of robots or their initial positions.

Keywords: Multi-robot systems, exploration, simulation, ROS, MORSE.

1 Introduction

The problem of multi-robot exploration is a primary research topic within multi-robot systems. It requires a group of robots to explore an unknown environment in cooperation, and usually also needs the construction of a map of this environment.

In recent years, the manufacturing of the robot has been considerably developed. Therefore, finding a suitable robot team size for exploration missions becomes a meaningful question. For example, in case of an earthquake, robots can help rescuers to evaluate the damage to the interior of a building. In this case, it is important to do this evaluation as quickly as possible. Consequently, a multi-robot system is a solution. The question is how many robots do we need in such system. Having only a few robots will require a long exploration time and the risk of failure is important: if one robot stops its exploration, a large part of the system is impacted. If rescuers deploy many robots, the system's robustness is increased, but the robots may take too much time to explore because they have to avoid a lot of other teammate robots.

In this paper, we address the issue of team size optimization using realistic simulations based on the robotic middleware ROS (Robot Operating System) [8] and the 3D simulator MORSE [4]. We show how to determine the optimal size

D. Brugali et al. (Eds.): SIMPAR 2014, LNAI 8810, pp. 438–449, 2014.

of a team of robots in order to complete an exploration mission in the shortest time possible and with the lowest cost. We consider two metrics to measure the optimal size of the robot team:

- The time metric. It is the total time required to complete an exploration mission.
- The cost metric. It is the sum of energy consumed by all robots in the team.

The remainder of the paper is organized as follows: Section 2 describes an overview of related work; Section 3 describes our multi-robot exploration system; Section 4 describes our evaluation metrics to the team size optimization problem. Section 5 describes the experimental results obtained with our system. We discuss this work in Section 6, and conclude the paper with Section 7.

2 Related Work

Yamauchi [10] introduced an approach for robotic exploration based on the concept of frontiers. In this approach, a robot can build a grid map with information obtained from laser and sonar sensors, detect the frontier which is the region on the boundary between open space and unexplored space in the map, then navigate to the nearest accessible frontier. By using the proposed approach, a Nomad 200 mobile robot was able to map the open spaces quickly, mapping an environment with 45 feet long and 25 feet wide in about half an hour.

Yamauchi [11] then extended this frontier-based approach to multi-robot systems. He constructed a decentralized system in which each robot has its own global grid map representing its knowledge about the environment. Whenever a robot arrives at a new frontier, it constructs a local grid map representing its current surroundings. This local map is integrated with the robot's global map, and also broadcasted to all of the other robots. Then each robot integrates the local map received from its teammates with its global map. This strategy requires robots to know their relative positions at the beginning of exploration, and use dead reckoning alone for position estimation so as to properly blend the local map and the global map. A limitation of the proposed approach is that robots may waste time by navigating to the same frontier since there is no coordination.

Burgard et al. [2] designed a coordination component based on the approach of Yamauchi. This component applies a probabilistic method which takes the cost of reaching a frontier and its utility into account simultaneously. The cost is given by the distance of traveling to a frontier (by using a value iteration algorithm) and the utility is given by the size of the unexplored area that a robot can cover from this frontier using its sensors. Whenever a frontier is assigned to a robot, the utility of the visible unexplored area of this frontier is reduced to all its teammates, making all other robots explore different areas. Their experimental results show that the coordinated robots can accomplish an exploration task significantly faster than uncoordinated robots.

Howard [5] described a multi-robot simultaneous localization and mapping (SLAM) approach by using a particle filter. The proposed approach is able to handle the case in which the initial position of robots are unknown. They start mapping with only one robot (whose initial pose is arbitrary) and wait until this first robot encounters other robots before incorporating their data into the global map.

Stachniss [9] presented their work on collaborative mapping with teams of mobile robots. Their multi-robot mapping system needs to place the robots in nearby locations. Robots also need to know the relative initial poses of their team members. During exploration, robots within communication range can exchange maps. We have implemented this solution in our simulated multi-robot mapping system.

Lass *et al.* [6] surveyed several evaluation metrics for multi-agent systems. They classified the metrics along two axes: the effectiveness or performance of metrics and the types of data they represent. Measures of effectiveness quantify the system's ability to complete its task in a given environment, while measures of performance are quantitative mesures of some secondary performance characteristics, usually being resource consumption of the system, such as bandwidth usage, energy consumption, communication range or task runtime.

3   Multi-robot Exploration System

Our robots rely on laser sensing for both localization and mapping. We use the ROS (Robot Operating System) middleware for communication both between control software and simulated robots. We also use ROS for inter-robot communication and more specifically for map sharing.

3.1   Single-Robot Setup

The main functions are achieved by the following packages:

- *gmapping*: This package is provided by ROS, which realizes the function of laser-based SLAM. It is used for mobile robot localization. Specifically, it sends pose data to the *explore* package.
- *explore*: The original package is provided by ROS which realizes the frontier-based exploration approach. It has been modified by our research team to be compatible with multi-robot systems. Specifically, a subscriber has been added to receive the map generated from the *map_fusion* package, so as to update the robot's current exploration map.
- *map_fusion*: This package is realized by our research team, which merges multiple exploration maps by considering the relative initial position of the robots, then transfers the fused map to the *explore* package.
- *move_base*: This package is provided by ROS, which navigates the robot to a goal location.

The relationships between the packages are illustrated in Figure 1.

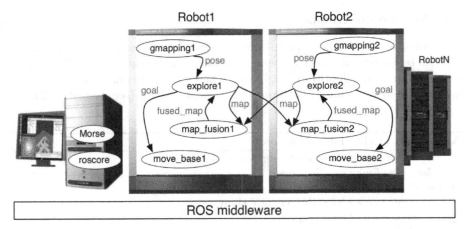

Fig. 1. Our distributed multi-robot exploration system relies on the ROS middleware and the MORSE 3D simulator. Each robot is simulated by a computer that runs 4 ROS nodes.

3.2   Multi-robot Communication

After preparing a single robot with exploration capabilities, the next problem we had to solve is the communication in our multi-robot system. Our current exploration system is a decentralized one, in which each robot can make its own decisions according to the local information with limited communication. In order to cooperate, we introduce some level of communication between neighboring robots [12]. To simulate network range, we introduce a discovery algorithm based on distance between simulated robots. Algorithm 1 illustrates our connection establishment process for $robot_i$.

Algorithm 1. Communication Connection for $robot_i$

1: Querying all published ROS topics
2: Subscribing to robot pose topics
3: **if** $\exists robot_j \in$ exploration team : $distBetween(robot_j - robot_i) < max\_comm\_distance$ **then**
4:    Establishing connection with $robot_j$
5: **end if**

In order to have a quite realistic simulation at least regarding the scale factors, we set a value that indicates the maximum communication distance (i.e. $max\_comm\_distance$) for our multi-robot system, but the impact of obstacles on communication is currently ignored. Moreover, to calculate the distance between two robots, we supposed that the relative initial positions of robots are known.

3.3 Multi-robot Mapping

Each robot in our simulated multi-robot system needs to exchange the grid map with its teammates in order to perform exploration mission cooperatively. Our current map fusion algorithm is lightweight and straightforward, by still supposing that the relative initial positions of robots are known (see Algorithm 2).

Algorithm 2. Map Fusion for $robot_i$

1: $\delta \leftarrow (robot_i.init\_pose - robot_j.init\_pose) \times map\_scale$
2: $robot_i.fused\_map \leftarrow robot_i.map$
3: **for all** $grid$ in $robot_i.fused\_map$ **do**
4:    **if** $grid = NO\_INFORMATION$ **then**
5:        $grid \leftarrow robot_j.map_{grid.pose+\delta}$
6:    **end if**
7: **end for**

3.4 Multi-robot Motion Planning

In our current implementation, map exchange is the only cooperative task done by the robot team. Each robot decides autonomously where to go based on its own grid map. Once the robot has updated its current map, it will select the nearest frontier and move towards it. This solution is not optimal, because different robots may go to explore the same frontier, resulting into redundant and useless exploration and possibly obstructing pathways.

Figure 2 shows three Pioneer 3-DX robots equipped with a SICK LMS500 laser scanner during an exploration mission. The left half of the figure is derived from the 3D simulator MORSE, and the right half is derived from the 3D visualization tool RVIZ [1].

4 Evaluation Metrics

Our goal is to find the optimum size of a robot team (denoted by n) for the purpose of exploring a given terrain. Optimization targets identify the shortest exploration time (denoted by $time$) and the lowest energy cost (denoted by $cost$). The cost refers to the total of energy consumed by a robotic team to perform an exploration mission. We supposed that the energy consumption is proportional to the distance traveled of all the robots in the team. For example, a team of two robots that move forward 10 meters each, consumes 20 units of energy.

$$cost(n) = \sum_{i=1}^{n}(distanceTraveled(robot_i)) \tag{1}$$

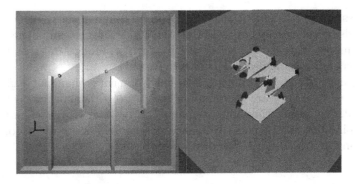

Fig. 2. Three Pioneer 3-DX robots explore an unknown environment cooperatively. In the right part of the figure: the map shown results from fusing local maps provided by three robots; the green arrow indicates the exploration goal (a frontier); the blue arrows indicates the potential exploration targets (frontiers); and the red sphere indicates the loop closure.

Due to the complexity of multi-robot exploration problem, the time and energy cost of a fleet of robots depend not only on the number of robots n, but it is also influenced by several other parameters:

- Robot characteristics. Absolute performances (e.g. exploration time) vary depending on these characteristics. More importantly, repeatability of experiments depends on the homogeneity of used robots. A fleet built out of heterogeneous robots with different capabilities, may lead to very different results from a test run to the others for various reasons such as simply the relative position of robots. This is why we prefer using a homogeneous robot team.
- Terrain properties. These include:
  - Terrain size. More robots are required to quickly explore a large area than a smaller one.
  - Obstacles density and shapes. In an environment with many obstacles, there is less space to explore. On the other hand, navigation may be more complicated, especially with concave obstacles where deadlocks can occur or when multiple robots are located in the same area.
  - Landforms. The exploration of a large single area takes probably less time than an environment that is decomposed into a number of open areas, but connected with narrow corridors. In the latter, it is likely that robots might obstruct one another.
- Robot initial positions. Depending on the environment and obstacles, location of robots at start up, the exploration runtime and/or the energy consumption may be significantly impacted.
- Coordination strategies. For a given set up (terrain, robotic fleet, and initial conditions), results may significantly vary depending on the implemented coordination strategies. As a result, the optimal size of the fleet can be used as an objective value to compare different coordination solutions.

– Wireless range. Cooperation often requires communication which in turn depends on the wireless range. While the wireless range can impact a team's performance, this can be mitigated by path planning strategies that take into account robotic network connectivity [3,7].
– Dynamicity of the environment. If the environment is changing (e.g. building collapses) or if they are other mobile entities (e.g. human rescuers or other robots), exploration time and associated costs can vary for different test runs. Path planning and obstacle avoidance strategies interfere with coordination resulting in an NP-hard optimization problem.

5   Experiments

5.1   Simulation Infrastructure

For our experiments we used the 3D robotics simulator MORSE. Our simulations are run on a cluster computer that copes with the important amount of computations required for the multi-robot 3D simulation. The cluster consists of 70 computing nodes and a master node (entry point). Each computing node contains multiple processors varying from 8 to 12, and RAM varying from 16 Go to 48 Go.

This configuration gives us the possibility to launch the robots simultaneously, but each robot has an initialization phase that takes a different amount of time. It means that the robots start the exploration at different moments, as in actual multi-robot systems where robots are turned on by human operators.

5.2   Setup

As explained in the previous section, the multi-robot exploration is complex due to the number of parameters to be considered. In the following experiment, we decided to fix several parameters and focus our question on the optimal number of robots needed to explore an environment.

Regarding robots characteristics, we work with a homogeneous fleet of robots. We used simulated Pioneer 3-DX robots equipped with a SICK LMS500 laser scanner providing 180 sample points with 180 degrees field of view and a maximum range of 30 meters. The maximal speed of the robot is fixed to 1.2 meter per second and 5.24 radians per second. The odometry is considered as perfect. The robots exchange the exploration map once every 5 seconds and the maximal distance for communication is fixed to 200 meters. This distance value is to avoid the problem of communication between the robots which is not the topic of this paper.

The simulation terrain is an enclosed space, manually generated in Blender (the 3D engine for MORSE). It is 80 meters long and 80 meters wide, and contains several fixed obstacles (a maze-like space, see Figure 3). The distance between walls (or width of corridors) is fixed to 8 meters. Besides, the environment is static, meaning that the exploration robots are the only mobile entities.

For measuring the duration and the energy consumption, we run simulations until the full terrain is covered. Actually, we have considered that the exploration is finished when 99% of the map is discovered.

5.3 Robot Initial Positions

We run three series of simulation each corresponding to an experiment with specific initial positions for the robots. Figure 3 shows the initial position for the three experiments.

Experiment A: Blind exploration without any prior knowledge on the terrain. The robots are placed along a vertical line starting from the top left corner of the terrain to the bottom left corner. The first robot is placed on the top left corner, then the other robots are placed every 4 meters from the previous one. We run simulations in this experiment with fleet sizes ranging from 1 robot, and up to 14 robots.

Experiment B: Exploration with knowledge of maze entry points (1 robot/entry point). The robots are placed at the entry points of the maze terrain. One simulation is run with 2 robots, one robot on top left corner and one on bottom left corner. The second simulation is run with 3 robots, the third robot is placed on the middle left border, at a maze entry point.

Experiment C: Exploration with knowledge of maze entry points (2 robots/entry point). The robots are placed at the same entry points like in the second experiment, but we placed 2 robots at each position. It means that we run simulations with 4 and 6 robots.

5.4 Results and Interpretation

Figure 4 shows the results of our simulation experiments with different sizes of robot teams. We performed 5 runs for each team size, and display the median value of these 5 runs. The figure contains two sets of experimental data corresponding to the exploration time and the exploration cost. The abscissa in the plot denotes the team size, and the ordinate denotes the time (exploration duration) or the cost (total energy consumption).

From the figure we can see that, in general, the more robots in a team the less exploration time is needed, while the changes in the exploration cost is slightly more complex. But it does not mean the more the number of robots, the better. The best results occur here with 12 robots. The exploration time and cost are both minimized with a fleet size of 12 robots.

With the simple share of maps, exploration time and cost are highly dependent on the initial positions of the robots. To verify this hypothesis, we conducted 2 additional experiments (i.e. experiments B and C). In Figure 4, the results of experiment B are shown by red diamonds and the results of experiment C are indicated by blue triangles. Obviously, with some knowledge of the terrain, one

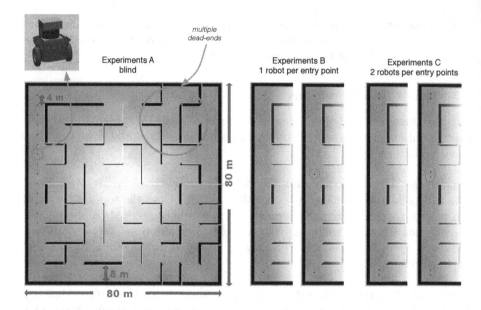

Fig. 3. Simulated environment (a maze-like space) and simulated Pioneer 3-DX robot equipped with a SICK LMS500 laser scanner in the simulator MORSE. The figures show the initial robot pose in the 3 different experiments A, B and C.

can choose better initial positions for the robots. As a result, exploration time and cost are significantly decreased with respect to the experiment A.

In our experiments there was no cooperation between robots, except exchanging maps. Thus, robots might block the path of each other during exploration, and waste time by replanning their own local paths. This results in a longer exploration time and increased exploration cost when robots are too close to each other as in experiment A.

Moreover, the terrain properties are also an important factors affecting the experimental results. Our simulated environment is quite large and complex: it contains a significant number of dead ends. Typically in the top right corner of the maze (Figure 3), the robots need more time to plan their trajectories than in other areas of the terrain. We can suspect that the total time and cost are also bound to the terrain properties.

6   Discussion and Future Work

This work was started by considering the parameter of the number of robots, and subsequently the parameter of initial positions of robots was also considered. The other variables are fixed to ensure that they do not interfere in the experiment. We consider five main variables that should be discussed and integrated for future work.

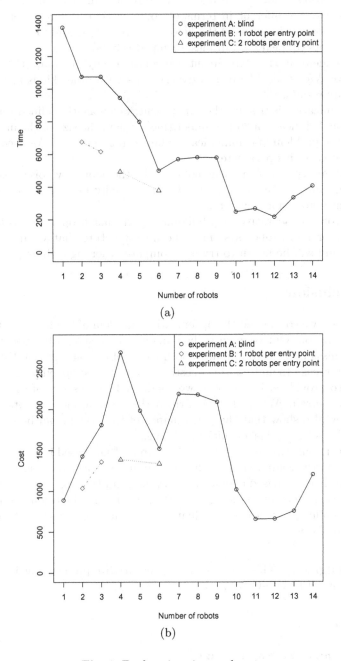

Fig. 4. Exploration time and cost

- Robot characteristics: we consider in this paper only one kind of robot and that all robots have the same characteristics. In realistic situations, the robots may be different in terms of configuration (different version of the same robot), or in terms of the kind (an exploration could be executed well with robots coupled with drones, or biped robots).
- Environment: in this experiment, we consider only one map, that is a kind of maze. We would like to run experiments with other kinds of terrains to compare results.
- Communication issues: for the experiment, we explicitly defined the communication distance to a large number (higher than the size of the map), which avoid the problem of communication between two robots. We need in future work to vary this parameter.
- The odometry precision: we do not consider the odometry noise in this paper. We will integrate it in future work. This usually needs more complex and efficient map fusion algorithms.
- Multi-robot cooperative map building algorithms: cooperation is highly desirable for multi-robot systems. The infrastructure that we have built for this study will be useful to try and compare other algorithms.

7   Conclusions

In this paper, we considered the optimization problem of the fleet size for multi-robot exploration. Our concern is, how many robots should be used for an exploration mission, so as to minimize both the exploration duration time and its cost. It is not easy to address this question due to the complexity of multi-robot systems. To provide a first answer, we conducted three series of simulations in a maze-like terrain. While they confirmed that adding more robots is usually better, they also show that the performance of the system can be significantly improved by selecting better initial positions.

To perform our experiments, we had set up an ROS-based infrastructure that runs on a cluster computer. It includes several essential nodes such as SLAM, map fusion, frontier-based exploration and motion planning. We plan to extend this infrastructure by introducing support for coordinated motion planning. Our goal is to build a test bed for evaluating different coordination algorithms in different conditions.

Acknowledgment. This work is part of the SUCRé project that is supported by Région Nord Pas-de-Calais.

References

1. rviz, http://wiki.ros.org/rviz/
2. Burgard, W., Moors, M., Fox, D., Simmons, R.G., Thrun, S.: Collaborative multi-robot exploration. In: Proc. IEEE ICRA 2000, San Francisco, CA, USA, pp. 476–481 (April 2000)

3. Doniec, A., Bouraqadi, N., Defoort, M., Le, V.T., Stinckwich, S.: Distributed constraint reasoning applied to multi-robot exploration. In: Proceedings of ICTAI 2009, 21st IEEE International Conference on Tools with Artificial Intelligence, pp. 159–166 (2009)
4. Echeverria, G., Lemaignan, S., Degroote, A., Lacroix, S., Karg, M., Koch, P., Lesire, C., Stinckwich, S.: Simulating complex robotic scenarios with MORSE. In: Noda, I., Ando, N., Brugali, D., Kuffner, J.J. (eds.) SIMPAR 2012. LNCS, vol. 7628, pp. 197–208. Springer, Heidelberg (2012), http://morse.openrobots.org
5. Howard, A.: Multi-robot simultaneous localization and mapping using particle filters. The International Journal of Robotics Research 25, 1243–1256 (2006)
6. Lass, R.N., Sultanik, E.A., Regli, W.C.: Metrics for multiagent systems. In: Performance Evaluation and Benchmarking of Intelligent Systems, pp. 1–19. Springer (2009)
7. Le, V.T., Bouraqadi, N., Stinckwich, S., Moraru, V., Doniec, A.: Making networked robot connectivity-aware. In: Proceedings of ICRA (International Conference on Robotics and Automation), Kobe, Japan (May 2009)
8. Quigley, M., Gerkey, B., Conley, K., Faust, J., Foote, T., Leibs, J., Berger, E., Wheeler, R., Ng, A.: ROS: an open-source robot operating system. In: Proc. IEEE ICRA 2009 Workshop on Open Source Software, Kobe, Japan (May 2009)
9. Stachniss, C.: Robotic Mapping and Exploration. Springer (2009)
10. Yamauchi, B.: A frontier-based approach for autonomous exploration. In: Proc. IEEE CIRA 1997, Monterey, CA, USA, pp. 146–151 (July 1997)
11. Yamauchi, B.: Frontier-based exploration using multiple robots. In: Proc. ACM Agents 1998, St. Paul, MN, USA, pp. 47–53 (May 1998)
12. Yan, Z., Jouandeau, N., Cherif, A.A.: A survey and analysis of multi-robot coordination. International Journal of Advanced Robotic Systems 10 (December 2013)

Automatic Evaluation of Task-Focused Parallel Jaw Gripper Design

Adam Wolniakowski[1], Konstantsin Miatliuk[1], Norbert Krüger[2],
and Jimmy Alison Rytz[2]

[1] Automation and Robotics Deptartment, Bialystok University of Technology, Poland
dagothar@gmail.com, k.miatliuk@pb.edu.pl
[2] The Maersk Mc-Kinney Moller Institute, Faculty of Engineering,
University of Southern Denmark, Denmark
{jimali,norbert}@mmmi.sdu.dk

Abstract. In this paper, we suggest *gripper quality metrics* that indicate the performance of a gripper given an object CAD model and a task description. Those, we argue, can be used in the design and selection of an appropriate gripper when the task is known. We present three different gripper metrics that to some degree build on existing grasp quality metrics and demonstrate these on a selection of parallel jaw grippers. We furthermore demonstrate the performance of the metrics in three different industrial task contexts.

1 Introduction

The successful execution of grasping in a robotics system is essential in industrial applications where grasp failure can result in anything from an expensive reduction in throughput to destruction of parts or invaluable fabrication hardware. With the gripper being the only workpiece that physically interacts with the environment, it is obvious that its design characteristics are of influence to successful grasping.

Moreover, robot systems that rely on sensors for object detection and pose estimation introduce increased uncertainties in the system, that will influence grasp success and thereby add additional demands to the robustness of the gripper design.

The design of a gripper includes the selection of the proper gripper kinematics and dynamics. Several of the relevant parameters are depicted in Fig. 1, where a parallel jaw kinematic structure is used. Designing a gripper from scratch is a time-consuming mechanical task and everything but the gripper jaw design are in practice determined by the selection of an off-the-shelf gripper product from one of many companies.

The gripper jaw design is important, since the jaws are the parts of the gripper that are in contact with graspable objects. Several gripper design guidelines [4,3] and papers on gripper design optimization [20,2] have been written to ease, or to better understand how to design a good gripper for a given object and task. However, gripper jaw design remains a cumbersome experts task, that requires special engineering knowledge and often several iterations between designer and floor operator are required to reach a good design.

Hence, a tool for automatically computing optimal gripper designs will be of a huge value to the industrial world of automation, essentially saving weeks of experts work

D. Brugali et al. (Eds.): SIMPAR 2014, LNAI 8810, pp. 450–461, 2014.

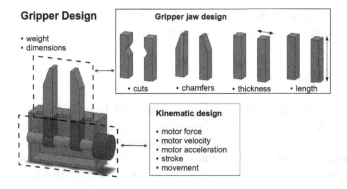

Fig. 1. A limited parameterization of a gripper design. The kinematic design (to the left) is typically determined from off-the-shelf products whereas the gripper jaw design (to the right) is custom designed to allow better grasping of one or multiple specific objects.

whenever a new part needs to be automatically handled. Such a technology may ideally increase flexibility in automation and change the hesitation that todays small and medium sized enterprises have toward automation.

In this paper, we take a step toward automatic gripper design by introducing three statistical gripper metrics for evaluating gripper performance. These metrics express different properties of a gripper such as how often it succeeds in grasping (success probability), from how many directions a gripper may successfully grasp an object (coverage) and how firmly the gripper holds the object (wrench). These properties have different relevance in different contexts and the relative weighting of these three metrics therefore needs to be chosen context specific. For example, when grasping objects placed unstructured in a box, it is important to be able to grasp from many different direction due to collisions with environment. Or when moving with high accelerations the object should be firmly grasped by the gripper.

Our method evaluates gripper designs by using a combination of existing design guidelines and advances within grasp quality metrics [17,12]. We present gripper metrics that can be automatically computed in a dynamic simulator and used during the selection of a specific gripper design. Most gripper designs from simple parallel jaw grippers to advanced dexterous hands can be evaluated in a dynamic grasp simulator. However, in this work we have focused on parallel jaw grippers since they are widely applied in industrial applications.

In this paper, our contributions are:

- a gripper metric which is based on success probability and dynamic grasp simulation.
- a method for including environmental context into the gripper evaluation.
- a method to include existing grasp quality metrics into the gripper evaluation.

In the next section, Sect. 2 we present related work in the areas of automated gripper design computation, gripper design evaluation and grasp quality metrics. Sect. 3 presents an overview of our method based on gripper quality metrics and our experimental evaluation of it. The gripper quality metrics are then described in more detail in

Sect. 4 and our method is then evaluated and discussed on a selection of gripper designs in Sect. 5. Finally we conclude the paper in Sect. 6.

2 Related Work

The difficulty of designing robot grippers has motivated the formulation of several gripper design guidelines [4,3,13]. One of the difficulties implied in these works is that design objectives may conflict, e.g., having a design which is both light and rigid. The design objectives include amongst others: *small gripper footprint, exterior and interior chamfering, small weight, secure grasping, small finger length, avoiding tool changes and aligning grasped objects.*

Furthermore, reviews on the gripper design problem are presented in [2,1]. In [2] a general overview of early gripper designs and control are presented, whereas grippers designed specifically for handling fruits where presented in [1].

In this work, we present a method for evaluation of a specific gripper parameterization which compared to previous approaches is not as fast to compute but instead much more generic, accurate and enables inclusion of context. This is mainly achieved by relying on evaluating grasps using a dynamics based grasp simulator. Such a tool can easily include large parts of the task context in the evaluation of the gripper, which more accurately captures the actual task in which the gripper is to be used. Furthermore, the accuracy over kinematic simulations are also gained due to increased modeling parameters such as friction and motor control.

Early work on the evaluation of gripper mechanism was based on Merit Indexes that described the mechanical effectiveness (Grasp Index G.I.) of a gripper [6] and the Capability Index (C.I.), the latter describing the capability of a gripper in relation to the object dimensions. In [14] these Merit indexes are used in the optimization of the kinematic design of a gripper. The Merit indexes are fast to compute but they are limited to kinematic evaluation and cannot distinguish between changes in the gripper jaw surface.

Changing the surface of gripper jaws can improve how well a gripper aligns objects during grasping. Aligning objects enables more secure grasps but also enables more accurate placement. Gripper jaw design for object alignment was investigated in [20,21,19,8]. In [19] they define a modular gripper surface based on trapezoidal segments for which they present an algorithm that can optimize the gripper design such that a specific alignment of the object is obtained when it is grasped from the top. The work in [8] presents a semi-automatic design of gripper jaws for aligning objects and additionally demonstrates that the jaws can be accurately tested in a dynamic simulation.

Another use of dynamic simulation was presented in [5], where the kinematic design of an under–actuated 2 finger gripper was optimized by first generating a database of grasps using simulation with a fully actuated gripper, which secondly was used to optimize the under–actuated gripper such that it would be able to execute the same grasps as defined in the grasp database. Our use of simulation is a bit similar, however, we define statistical gripper metrics that are computed based on generated grasp databases which then can be used to compare the performance between grippers.

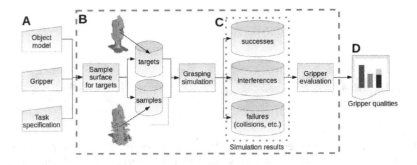

Fig. 2. Computation of gripper quality metrics

To summarize, our work defines suitable gripper qualities based on evaluating grasp qualities over a set of feasible grasps. Compared to previous work, we pursue a statistical approach relying heavily on dynamic simulation, grasp quality metrics and we include contextual information in the evaluation of the gripper. The inclusion of context was demonstrated to be of importance in [15] when evaluating grasp quality. For computing optimal gripper designs, we believe that context is equally important and therefore our method also relies on a description of the context – namely the task specification.

3   System Overview

In this section, we present an overview of our method that is used to compute the quality of a robotic gripper. The method relies on dynamic grasp simulation to evaluate grasps using a specific gripper design.

The method is depicted in Fig. 2, where the inputs to our method (encapsulated in Fig. 2B) are an object model, a gripper design and a task specification.

- The object model consists of a CAD model with associated dynamic properties such as friction, center of mass and inertia.
- The gripper design consists of a collection of CAD models of the gripper, together with the gripper kinematics and dynamics: max gripping force, max gripper velocity, surface friction, inertia and center of mass.
- The task specification defines the actual grasping scenario. This includes the local environment model and an approach direction (see Fig. 3).

The first step in our method (see Fig. 2B) is to compute a database of grasp targets that to a reasonable resolution covers all possible grasps of the object within the task specification. This computation is essentially a sample based grasp planner that, in our case of parallel jaw grippers, base the sampling on nearly parallel surfaces. However, we want to stress that the metrics we propose are generic and can also be applied to other grippers, only the initial sampling strategy would need to be adapted to a novel gripper. The grasp planner used in this work is based on finding near parallel surface

Fig. 3. Scenes used for gripper evaluation. These are in order: a) the belt picking scene with a rotor cap object, b) the belt picking scene with a Dolt object, c) the table picking scene with a cylindrical object. The arrows present the gripper approach direction defined in the task description.

patches, please see [12] for further details. The grasp target sampling generates two databases: *targets* and *samples*. The grasps in the samples-database are the ideal parallel gripper grasps which only need two nearly parallel surfaces to make a grasp. The targets-database is a subset of the samples-database, such that any grasp pose from the samples database are added to the target database only if the gripper can be placed in the grasping pose without being in collision with the object.

The databases are filtered which serves both as downsampling and as rough unbiasing in $SE3^1$.

The next step is to further validate all filtered grasp targets and quantify their grasp quality. The validation is performed in simulation using RobWork [10], where the object is grasped from each grasp target in the filtered database. The simulation includes the static environment described in the task specification. A grasp is deemed successful, if the following conditions are met after the simulated grasp has been executed:

1. the object remains in the gripper with wrench quality exceeding a specified lower limit w_{min},
2. no collisions with fixed obstacles in the scene occurred,
3. the interference (i.e. a measure of negative interaction of gripper with the environment, explained below) at the end of the experiment does not exceed a specified interference limit i_{max}.

The wrench quality represents the robustness of specific grasp, and it is introduced in more detail in Sect. 4.3.

The interference is introduced as a measure of unwanted gripper interaction with movable objects in the scene (e.g. neighbours of the target objects). Interference is calculated as a total sum of differences between the poses of all movable objects from before (P_{start}) and after (P_{end}) grasping:

$$I = \sum_{i=0}^{nobjects} |P_{end} - P_{start}| \tag{1}$$

---

[1] 3-dimensional Special Euclidean group representing translation and rotation.

Successful grasps are added to the *successes* database. If a grasp failed due to interference limit violation (the third condition), then it is added to the *interferences* database. Otherwise, the grasp become part of the *failures* database.

A small fraction of simulations becomes unstable due to limitations of the physical engine. The results of these simulations are discarded. Typically, failures happen in no more than 10% of simulations.

The gripper quality metrics are computed after performing all grasp simulations, based on the numerical results of the simulations and the populations of the databases: *successes, interferences* and *failures*. The sizes of the results databases are denoted as $N_{successes}$, $N_{interferences}$ and $N_{failures}$, respectively.

The output (see Fig. 2D) are three continuous values that each describe a gripper quality: *success probability, coverage* and *average wrench space*. *Success probability* is a measure that captures the average probability of successfully grasping the object from the grasping space, constrained by the task specification. The *coverage metric* evaluates how large the success space is compared to using a conceptual idea of an *ideal* gripper. The *ideal* gripper is an infinitely thin (and thus not generating collisions) gripper that is able to grasp successfully at every nearly parallel surface patch pairs on the object surface. The ideal gripper therefore acts as a hypothesis for defining the possible grasping space which can then be compared to the actual success grasp space to define coverage.

A large coverage is especially interesting for tasks where possible collisions with the surroundings may reduce the number of executable grasps, e.g., in bin picking – in which objects are placed in an extremely unstructured environment, randomly oriented and blocking and obstructing each other, thus requiring a large versatility in possible approaches. Finally, the wrench space metric captures the average force closure of the successful grasp space. For each of the grippers, we are interested in obtaining a selection of few good grasps (in terms of robustness) from multitude of those that were generated. Thus, additionally the average wrench quality is computed for the top 20% best grasps (best in terms of wrench space measurement).

4   Gripper Quality Metrics

In this section, we describe how the three gripper quality metrics are defined and how we calculate these based on the output of the grasp target sampling and the dynamic simulation. It should be noted that these three measures evaluate different characteristics of the gripper performance which we later will demonstrate in Sect. 5.1. As said already above, the relative importance of these characteristics is context– and task–dependent.

4.1   Success Ratio

This metric should capture the overall success ratio of grasps in the *targets* database for the specified task context. The actual success ratio naturally depends on which grasps are selected for execution in the real world scenario. However, as an approximation, the overall success rate of all the simulated grasps is sufficient.

The success rate S is evaluated directly in a dynamic grasp simulation, where the static environment and the interference objects are included. The success ratio is then calculated as $S = \frac{N_{successes}}{N_{filteredtargets}}$, where $N_{successes}$ is the number of successfully executed grasps from the filtered targets database and $N_{filteredtargets}$ is the number of grasps in the filtered grasp database.

4.2 Coverage Index

The coverage metric should measure from how many different directions an object can be grasped. The need for this metric originates from identifying the possibility that a few very high quality grasps might not be sufficient to compute grasps in highly cluttered scenes, simply because objects in the environment may collide with the gripper and thereby strongly limit the successful grasp space. In general, a gripper with a high coverage is very maneuverable within the task constraints which may enable a higher real success rate and faster execution.

The coverage evaluation is based on comparing the grasp success space of the actual gripper with the grasp success space of an abstract, infinitely thin and unbreakable gripper. Such an *ideal* gripper only requires two nearly parallel surfaces on opposite sides of the object to perform a successful grasp.

The coverage is computed as the ratio between the number of possible grasps of the specific gripper and the number of possible grasps of the *ideal* gripper. Since we assume linear correlation between number of grasps and grasp volume due to the un-biasing of the filtering approach, we may infer that the coverage ratio defines the size of the grasp success space relative to the ideally possible success space. The complete success space is only dependent on the object and not the gripper, thereby enabling comparison across grippers.

Thus, coverage is calculated as $C = \frac{N_{gripper}}{N_{ideal}} = \frac{N_{successes} + N_{interferences}}{N_{filteredsamples}}$. Notice that $N_{filteredsamples}$ represents the un-biased (filtered) grasp space of the ideal gripper. The $N_{gripper}$ define all successful grasp targets when not considering failures due to inference.

4.3 Wrench Index

The wrench index should capture the overall quality of all successfully executed grasps. Where the quality reflects the size of the minimum wrench that can make a specific grasp fail.

We use the Grasp Wrench Space (GWS) measure which was originally introduced in [9]. The GWS measure calculate the minimum wrench w_i that is able to disturb a grasp. Hence, larger w_i makes a better grasp. Please see [12] for more details on the implementation.

The wrench index is, in the context of the gripper quality, given as the average wrench of all successful grasps performed by the gripper. It is common for a gripper to have a small number of exceptionally high quality grasps at specific parts of the object, while the remaining grasps have much lower quality. Hence, an average quality over all sucessful grasps might not be sufficient to distinguish between grippers. To better

	a)	b)	c)	d)	e)	f)	g)
	standard	chamfered	flat	square	std. w/ cut.	chf. w/ cut.	clumsy
dimensions	100x20x25	100x20x25	100x25x5	100x10x10	100x20x25	100x20x25	100x20x50
chamfering	–	25x45°	–	–	–	25x45°	–
cutout	–	–	–	–	10x120°	10x120°	–
force	50 N	50 N	50 N	50 N	50 N	50 N	50 N

Fig. 4. Selected gripper designs used for evaluation. These are in order: a) standard gripper, b) chamfered gripper, c) flat gripper, d) square gripper, e) standard gripper with cutout, f) chamfered gripper with cutout, g) clumsy gripper. Dimensions are presented in millimeters.

evaluate a selection of few good grasps generated for the gripper, the average wrench of the top 20% (by wrench measure) of successful grasps is also calculated and provided as an additional result.

The obtained wrench metric values are denoted as W for the average wrench of the successful grasps, and W_{20} for the average wrench of top 20% grasps. The wrench metrics is calculated as the sum of the wrench of all successfully executed grasps divided by the number of successful grasps.

5   Experiments

In this section, we present our experimental results that demonstrate our quality metric on 8 different grippers in 3 different scene contexts. All experiments have been computed in the dynamic simulator RobWork [10].

We first introduce the experimental setup in Sect. 5.1, namely the grippers, the scenes used and their properties. Then we present the computed gripper qualities for each gripper-scene pair in Sect. 5.2 and finally, in Sect. 5.3, we demonstrate how repetitive computations of the metrics behave.

5.1   Experimental Setup

The experimental setup consists of three scenes with a predefined direction of grasp approach (see Fig. 3), and a set of parallel jaw grippers with several hand-designed jaw shapes (see Fig. 4).

For each of the {scene, gripper} combinations, 10 experiments were performed, each with $N = 10000$ grasp targets to sample. The number of actually simulated grasp targets is reduced to around 1000 due to the grasp filtering in the sampling process.

Scenes. The scenes used in the experimental setup are presented in Fig. 3. Three different objects were chosen for the picking task, two objects from industrial applications, i.e. the rotor cap and the Dolt object (top and middle row in Fig. 3). The cylindrical object (bottom row in Fig. 3) was picked to include a simple primitive shape. All of the objects are defined to weigh 1 kg, and the surfaces were assigned the friction properties of plastic.

In both the rotor cap and the Dolt object picking scenarios, three objects are placed in a line on a flat belt surface, 75 mm from one another. The target is the object in the middle, and grasps are performed from one of the sides of the belt, with 45 degrees allowed deviation from that direction.

In the table picking scene, nine cylinders are placed on a 3x3 square grid with 75 mm cell size. The target is the cylinder in the middle, and grasps are performed from the top, with 45 degrees allowed deviation from vertical (see Fig. 3). For all the scenes, the gravitational acceleration was defined to $9.81 m/s^2$.

Grippers. Seven different grippers are used in the experimental evaluation, see Fig. 4. The grippers have been selected such that they include commonly encountered features eg. chamfering and presence of cutout.

Each of the grippers has a parallel-jaw kinematic structure with both fingers coupled to a single Degree of Freedom (DoF). Hence, fingers cannot move independently. For all the grippers, the maximum opening distance between the jaws was set to 10 cm. The grippers are presumed to use the same gripper actuation mechanism, thus for all the designs the maximum closing force was defined to be 50 N. The fingers were defined to be made of plastic for the purposes of friction in the simulation.

5.2   Gripper Evaluations

The gripper evaluations were performed for all scenes and grippers introduced in Sect. 5.1. The results of the experiments for each of the {scene, gripper} combinations were averaged and are presented in Fig. 5 for Rotor cap scene, Dolt object scene, and cylindrical object scene.

Bars in the upper part of the figure present the different gripper metrics: success ratio S, coverage C, average wrench W and top wrench W_{20}. All quality visualizations (the bars) have been scaled relative to the best quality in the same particular experiment e.g. all experiments on a single scene but with varying grippers. Top wrench W_{20} is presented as a light-blue bar overlaying the average wrench W bar in deep blue. Numerical data is presented in the tables in the bottom part of each figure.

As expected the best gripper design vary strongly depending on both the scene and the task context.

For the **rotor cap** picking scene (see Fig. 5A), the *flat* gripper (Fig. 5A-c), performs best in success ratio and coverage. It is surpassed however by a *chamfered cut* (Fig. 5A-f) gripper in terms of average and top wrench index, which is expected due to the cut. The *flat* gripper provides the smallest footprint which makes it possible to easily avoid collisions and interference, and yet the contact surface is still big enough to retain the object robustly.

In the **Dolt** object picking scene (see Fig. 5B), the best results were achieved with the *square* gripper (Fig. 5B-d), which offers the highest coverage and success ratios. The small gripper frame provides high maneuverability and allows to exploit the existence

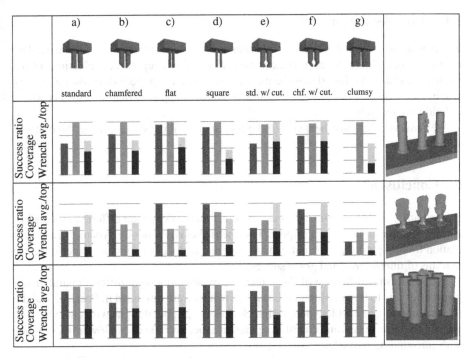

Fig. 5. The results of evaluation for gripper designs a-g for the scenes A-C

of the Dolt object features, i.e. cuts on the side, for better grasping. The second best gripper design was the *chamfered cut* gripper (Fig. 5B-f), with slightly lower success and coverage, but providing much higher top wrench, due to presence of cutout which improves secure grasps on the object.

The **cylinder** picking scene (see Fig. 5C) provides an unique challenge by putting the target object in a confined space between neighboring objects. Grasping from the top only exposes a small percent of the surface of the object. This also voids the benefit of having a prismatic cutout in the gripper, as for the vertical direction of approach, the cutouts are not aligned with the cylindrical object. The contact area for grippers with cutouts is thus effectively smaller, which becomes apparent in the average wrench score for those grippers. The best gripper designs for the cylinder scene were the *flat* (Fig. 5C-c) and *square* (Fig. 5C-d) designs, both with a small foot-print, and for this specific task they both provide a virtually identical contact surface area.

In general it can be noted that the presence of chamfers is reflected effectively in the success level for the gripper. Moreover, as expected, the coverage score of the gripper is greatly influenced by the gripper footprint and the overall gripper dimensions. Wrench index reflects both the contact surface area, and the force closure ability of the gripper's shape.

5.3 Metric Separability

It is crucial that the quality metrics are independent and that they are not influenced by the sampling and filtering approaches. We performed five repetitive evaluations of the quality measures and found that the metrics are clustered in the 3 dimensional quality space with largest variations in coverage. It was also apparent that the clusters where individually separable.

We observed the same behavior of the repetitive quality evaluations on the dolt and cylinder scenes.

6 Conclusion

In this paper, we have presented three statistical metrics covering different aspects important for the evaluation of a gripper. This metric heavily relies on dynamic grasp simulation for computing grasp quality and for dynamically evaluating grasp performance in terms of interference and grasp success.

We demonstrated the use of these metrics, by applying eight different parallel jaw gripper designs to three different scenes. The results were discussed in Sect. 5.2 and the metrics tend to agree with expert design choices eg. gripper designs with cuts will provide more stable grasps and chamfering increase success ratio due to lower interference with surrounding obstacles.

We also demonstrated that the three metrics are independent and we performed repetitive calculations to show that the random and biased sampling does not significantly influence the outcome of the quality measures.

In future work, we will investigate how to use our gripper quality metrics to automatically compute the best possible gripper design for a given task – utilizing, for example, a gradient descent method in the gripper quality space obtained by combining proposed metrics into an objective function. We will also apply our method to a larger variety of kinematic designs and finally we will extend on the concept of the task specification.

Acknowledgments. The research leading to these results has received funding from the European Community's Seventh Framework Programme FP7/2007-2013 (Programme and Theme: ICT-2011.2.1, Cognitive Systems and Robotics) under grant agreement no. 600578, ACAT.

The research has furthermore received founding from the Danish Council for Strategic Research under the grant agreement no. 12-131860, CARMEN.

References

1. Blanes, C., Mellado, M., Ortiz, C., Valera, A.: Review. Technologies for robot grippers in pick and place operations for fresh fruits and vegetables. Spanish Journal of Agricultural Research 9(4), 1130–1141 (2011)
2. Boubekri, N., Chakraborty, P.: Robotic grasping: gripper designs, control methods and grasp configurations – a review of research. Integrated Manufacturing Systems 13(7), 520–531 (2002)

3. Causey, G.: Guidelines for the design of robotic gripping systems. Assembly Automation 23(1), 18–28 (2003)
4. Causey, G.C., Quinn, R.D.: Gripper design guidelines for modular manufacturing. In: Proceedings of 1998 IEEE International Conference on Robotics and Automation, vol. 2, pp. 1453–1458. IEEE (1998)
5. Ciocarlie, M., Allen, P.: Data-driven optimization for underactuated robotic hands. In: 2010 IEEE International Conference on Robotics and Automation (ICRA), pp. 1292–1299. IEEE (2010)
6. Cuadrado, J., Naya, M.A., Ceccarelli, M., Carbone, G.: An optimum design procedure for two-finger grippers: a case of study. IFToMM Electronic Journal of Computational Kinematics 15403(1), 2002 (2002)
7. Ellekilde, L.-P., Jørgensen, J.A., Kraft, D., Krüger, N., Piater, J., Petersen, H.G.: Applying a learning framework for improving success rates in industrial bin picking. In: Proceedings of the International Conference on Intelligent Robots and Systems (IROS), pp. 1–8 (2012)
8. Ellekilde, L.-P., Petersen, H.G.: Design and test of object aligning grippers for industrial applications. In: 2006 IEEE/RSJ International Conference on Intelligent Robots and Systems, pp. 5165–5170. IEEE (2006)
9. Ferrari, C., Canny, J.: Planning optimal grasps. In: IEEE International Conference on Robotics and Automation (ICRA) (May 1992)
10. Jorgensen, J.A., Ellekilde, L.-P., Petersen, H.G.: RobWorkSim - an open simulator for sensor based grasping. In: Proceedings of Joint 41st International Symposium on Robotics (ISR 2010), Munich, pp. 1–8 (2010)
11. Jørgensen, J.A., Petersen, H.G.: Grasp synthesis for dextrous hands optimised for tactile manipulation. In: Proceedings for the Joint Conference of ISR 2010, pp. 1–6. VDE-Verlag (June 2010)
12. Kraft, D., Ellekilde, L.-P., Jørgensen, J.A.: Automatic grasp generation and improvement for industrial bin-picking. In: Röhrbein, F., Veiga, G., Natale, C. (eds.) Gearing Up and Accelerating Cross-Fertilization between Academic and Industrial Robotics Research in Europe, 2nd edn. STAR, vol. 94, pp. 155–176. Springer, Heidelberg (2014)
13. Krenich, S.: Multicriteria design optimization of robot gripper mechanisms. Solid Mechanics and Its Applications, vol. 117, pp. 207–218. Springer, Netherlands (2004)
14. Lanni, C., Ceccarelli, M.: An optimization problem algorithm for kinematic design of mechanisms for two-finger grippers. Open Mechanical Engineering Journal 3, 49–62 (2009)
15. Rytz, J.A., Ellekilde, L.-P., Kraft, D., Petersen, H.G., Krüger, N.: On transferability of grasp-affordances in data-driven grasping. In: Proceedings of the RAAD 2013 22nd International Workshop on Robotics in Alpe-Adria-Danube Region (August 2013)
16. Stulp, F., Theodorou, E., Buchli, J., Schaal, S.: Learning to grasp under uncertainty. In: IEEE International Conference on Robotics and Automation (ICRA), pp. 5703–5708 (2011)
17. Suárez, R., Roa, M., Cornella, J.: Grasp quality measures. Technical report, Technical University of Catalonia (2006)
18. Weisz, J., Allen, P.K.: Pose error robust grasping from contact wrench space metrics. In: IEEE International Conference on Robotics and Automation (ICRA), pp. 557–562. IEEE (2012)
19. Zhang, M.T., Goldberg, K.: Designing robot grippers: optimal edge contacts for part alignment. Robotica 25(03), 341 (2006)
20. Zhang, T.: Optimal Design of Self-aligning Robot Gripper Jaws. PhD thesis, AAI3044755 (2001)
21. Zhang, T., Cheung, L., Goldberg, K.: Shape tolerance for robot gripper jaws. In: IROS, pp. 1782–1787 (2001)

Automatic Verification
of Autonomous Robot Missions

Matthew O'Brien[1], Ronald C. Arkin[1] Dagan Harrington[2], Damian Lyons[2],
and Shu Jiang[1]

[1] School of Interactive Computing, Georgia Tech, Atlanta, GA 30332, USA
{mjobrien,arkin,sjiang}@gatech.edu
[2] Computer & Information Science, Fordham University, Bronx, NY 10458, USA
{dharrington5,dlyons}@fordham.edu

Abstract. Before autonomous robotics can be used for dangerous or
critical missions, performance guarantees should be made available. This
paper overviews a software system for the verification of behavior-based
controllers in context of chosen hardware and environmental models.
Robotic controllers are automatically translated to a process algebra.
The system comprising both the robot and the environment are then
evaluated by VIPARS, a verification software module in development,
and compared to specific performance criteria. The user is returned a
probability that the performance criteria will hold in the uncertainty of
real-world conditions. Experimental results demonstrate accurate verification for a mission related to the search for a biohazard.

Keywords: mobile robots, formal verification, performance guarantees,
automatic translation.

1 Introduction

Mission assurance by providing formal methods for assessing performance guarantees is a well identified need and crucial area of research for autonomy. This is
essential in missions that must get the job done right the first time where there is
no tolerance for failure. We have been focusing in particular on addressing search
and remediation tasks for countering Weapons of Mass Destruction (C-WMD),
e.g., biological, chemical, radiological or nuclear agents that might be posed by
terrorist activities.

A variety of methods, historically based on model checking (e.g., [4],[9]) have
been developed for robot performance guarantees and synthesizing provably correct controllers that have met with some success. But there remain problems
associated with the scalability of these methods and their utility in continuous valued domains, typical of robotic sensing and actuation [10]. Our research,
conducted for the Defense Threat Reduction Agency (DTRA), takes a different
approach, utilizing process algebras as the basis for the representation as opposed
to the temporal logics so often used in model checking. We feel this provides a
better match for the requirements of real-time autonomy, and have had success

D. Brugali et al. (Eds.): SIMPAR 2014, LNAI 8810, pp. 462–473, 2014.

in its application on a range of robotic missions: single robot waypoint [11], multi-robot bounding overwatch [14] and search and explore [7].

To accomplish this we have had to bridge the gap from automatically generated robot control software that is represented in the Configuration Network Language (CNL), a component of the MissionLab Mission Specification System used in our research [18]. This CNL code must then be processed by our verification module (VIPARS Verification in Process Algebra for Robot Schemas) to yield the performance guarantees and predictions necessary for informing the operator regarding the likelihood of success of her mission. Thus CNL must be translated to PARS (Process Algebra for Robot Schemas). Until now this translation has been performed manually, but as described in this paper this central task linking the control software to the verification module is now automatically translated, providing end-to-end operational capability. This paper describes how that transformation has been implemented and tested.

2 Related Work

Formal verification of systems is critical when failure creates a high cost, such as life or death scenarios. A variety of software validation techniques have been developed for applications from airplanes to medical devices. If the use of robots is to expand to similarly critical applications, verification techniques must be developed to meet this challenge. The embodied nature of robot software brings several additional complications. The real world is dynamic, unstructured, and continuous; making modeling difficult. In addition, information about the world provided by sensors is incomplete and noisy. The problem of adapting verification techniques for this domain has been approached in several ways.

One of the main methods of software verification is model checking [6],[19]. In model checking, the system is represented as a finite state automaton and formal specification in a modal logic. All states are explored and compared against the formal specifications or properties. The continuous nature of a robots workspace creates a state space far too large for traditional methods. This is commonly referred to as state explosion, and is a major focus of research in model checking. One technique applied to this problem is symmetry reduction. By determining symmetries, the number of states that must be checked can be reduced. Under ideal conditions, significant reductions can be made. Identifying symmetries may be a difficult task however, and is often dependent on the programming language used [19].

An alternative approach is to synthesize a valid controller given a robot model and a set of specifications. Linear temporal logic (LTL), or a restricted subset of LTL, GR(1), has been used to represent specifications in a way that allows for automatic generation of controllers [4],[9]. Effective motion planning has been demonstrated with this technique. Like model checking, these LTL based controller synthesis techniques can suffer from state explosion under certain circumstances. In addition, it is not clear if LTL techniques can extend to more sophisticated missions outside the realm of motion planning.

This paper presents yet another approach to verification. Process algebras (PA) model parallel or distributed systems and reason about their properties through algebraic techniques [3]. While originally developed for software systems, applications range from robotics to biology [8],[5]. Process Algebra for Robot Schemas (PARS) is a specification language capable of representing software, hardware, and the environment as interacting processes [10]. The following sections overview the software system in development to utilize PARS, the methods of verification, and results from physical implementation.

3   Methods

3.1   System Overview

In the complete robot mission design system, an operator specifies the robot controller in MissionLab. This controller is compiled first into configuration network language (CNL), an internal language of MissionLab. This CNL code is then translated to PARS. The operator also specifies models of the robot and environment, as well as desired performance criteria. VIPARS evaluates the complete system and returns the results to the operator, creating a feedback loop. If performance is unacceptable the operator refines his or her design. This may entail revising the controller or selecting new hardware for implementation. Once the criteria are satisfied, MissionLab creates an executable for the selected platform. Figure 1 shows an overview of this architecture.

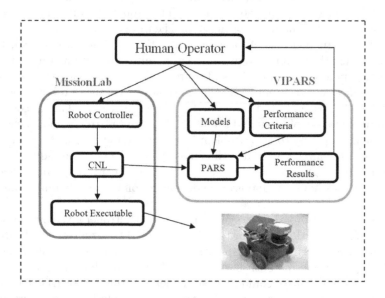

Fig. 1. Overview of system archiecture

3.2   MissionLab and CNL

MissionLab is a software package developed in the GT Mobile Robotics Lab. MissionLab allows users to design missions and robotic controllers graphically, allowing for quick implementation of control schemes without the need for programming experience or concern with low-level details. It incorporates simulation of missions as well as the ability to compile controllers for execution on hardware. The Configuration Network Language (CNL) is one representation of robotic controllers used in MissionLab. CNL is a superset of C++ developed to separate a behaviors implementation from its integration with other behaviors [16].

In CNL, all behaviors for any robotic controller are specified as assemblages of more primitive nodes. Currently, all implemented behaviors are schema-based, from the AuRA architecture [1]. Any node may have a variety of inputs, but only a single output. Primitive nodes only take input from sensors. Assemblages of these nodes are constructed by feeding the output of these primitives into new nodes. Through various arbitration schemes, a single output command is determined and sent to the robot for execution. The implementation of a CNL nodes internal processing is done via traditional C++. See Figure 2 for an example network.

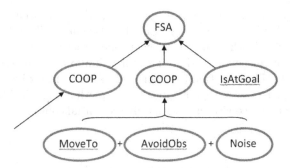

Fig. 2. Part of a CNL node network. Nodes, such as MoveTo, take input from more primitive nodes. The node COOP performs vector summation from all of its inputs, creating a new behavior. The node IsAtGoal is a trigger, tracking conditions to change states. The Finite State Automaton (FSA) selects the output of one behavior for execution on the robot.

3.3   PARS

Process algebras are specification languages that allow for formal verification of concurrent systems. Process Algebra for Robot Schemas (PARS) is a language developed to adapt these techniques to robotic systems [10]. PARS is capable of representing a robotic controller, hardware, the environment, and the interactions between them. A process P is called with initial parameters u1,u2,,un, resulting values v1,v2,,vq, input ports i1,i2,,im, and output ports o1,o2,,op.

$$P\langle u_1, u_2, , u_n\rangle(i_1, i_2, , i_m)(o_1, o_2, , o_p)\langle v_1, v_2, , v_q\rangle \tag{1}$$

Table 1. The basic PARS processes

Process	Stop Condition	Abort Condition
$Delay\langle t\rangle$	After time t	If forced by #
$Ran\langle d\rangle\langle v\rangle$	Returns random sample v from a distribution d	If forced by #
$In\langle p\rangle\langle v\rangle, Out\langle p, v\rangle$	Performs input and output of value v on port p	If forced by #
$Cond\langle op, a, b\rangle$	$a = b, a \neq b, a > b, etc\ldots$	Otherwise

All PARS processes are formed by composition of several basic processes shown in Table 1. This is achieved by three operators. The sequential/conditional operator (;) allows the next process to start if the first process stops, but not if it aborts. For example, a simple process may take in a value on one port, and afterwards output this value on a second port.

$$Pass = In\langle port1\rangle\langle value\rangle; Out\langle port2\rangle\langle value\rangle \tag{2}$$

In addition the concurrent composition (|) and the disabling composition (#) operators allow for processes to run simultaneously. The disabling composition will abort all other processes when one process terminates (stops or aborts). The concurrent composition operator will allow all processes to terminate independently. This notation is sufficient to build complex behaviors via assemblages of simpler processes, analogous to the methodology in MissionLab. A simple example mission constructed with only sequential composition is shown in Figure 3.

```
Mission<w,i> = Goto<w(i)> ; Neq<i,n> ; Mission<w,i+1>
Goto<a> = TurnTo<a> ; MoveTo<a>
MoveTo<g> = In<p><r> ; Neq<r,g> ; Out<v,u(g−r)> ; MoveTo<g>
TurnTo<g> = In<p><r> ; Out<h,d(g−r)>
```

Fig. 3. Simple PARS Mission

A final critical ability for PARS is looping. Tail-recursion, a process calling itself at the end of its execution, is the method chosen. The Mission process in Figure 3 provides an example of tail-recursion. The restriction of all processes to tail-recursion can allow for more efficient verification (see Section 3.5).

3.4   Translation

The automation of the translation of a robot controller into PARS is a critical step to creating a usable software system. By automating the translation of a robot controller to PARS, and incorporating the VIPARS verification module into MissionLab, a nave user could leverage the formal verification techniques in the field. In addition to improving usability, automation ensures the accuracy and reliability of the final translation. Translation can be a challenging problem. In a model-checking approach the first step is the translation of the program to be verified into a transition system, the formal structure in which verification occurs. However, this translation into a transition system is one of the key points at which state-space explosion can occur [2].

Two sets of lexes (lexical analyzers) and grammars are required to parse a CNL file. The first set is for the CNL code; which defines the CNL network and structures a nodes definition. The final set parses the C++ code inside a node definition. This is only required for the switch statement inside the FSA node. Therefore a subset of the C++ grammar, along with some unique tokens, is adequate. The common compilation tools Flex and Bison were used to produce the final scanner and parser.

MissionLab is a behavior-based programming environment where users create complex actions from a library of primitive nodes. A matching library of PARS implementations was created. The translator inputs the PARS definition of any node used by the robot controller into the final PARS file. These processes are later called inside the Mission process in a similar manner to how functions are defined and called in programming languages.

The heart of the translation from CNL to PARS is the creation of the Mission process. PARS code matching the structure of the FSA must be created. This structure can be, in general, any finite state automaton. A PARS implementation of a switch statement was created to represent any mission. However, many missions are linear in nature, and the more complex Mission process structure is not required. By checking certain properties of the triggers in the FSA node, the translation software can determine if a mission is linear, and select the appropriate Mission process design. An example linear mission structure in PARS is below in Figure 4. This structure was utilized for the experimental verification described in section 4.

```
Mission (cPOS)(cVEL)  =    Behavior1 (cPOS)(cVEL)          |
                 Trigger1  ;  Behavior2 (cPOS)(cVEL)       |
                 Trigger2  ;  Behavior3 (cPOS)(cVEL)       |
                 Trigger3  ;  Behavior4 (cPOS)(cVEL)       .
```

Fig. 4. Linear mission process

This initial mission structure is a high level representation of the controller. As discussed before, in MissionLab the highest-level behaviors are assemblages of more primitive nodes. The PARS processes representing lower-level CNL nodes must be created as well. Before the translation software creates a process for a high level behavior in PARS, any additional primitive processes required are created first. For some CNL nodes, this is hardcoded, while for others the number and type of input nodes can vary. The PARS operators needed to coordinate these new processes are also created at this time. As each process calls for the creation of lower level processes, the node network is traversed from top to bottom, creating PARS code that accurately matches the original node network defined in CNL. Figure 5 provides a simple demonstration of this process.

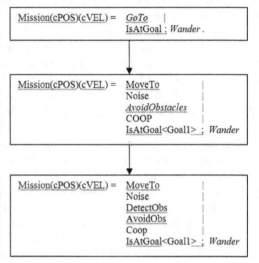

Phase 1: The high level mission structure is created. GoTo and Wander are behaviors that must be decomposed into individual PARS processes. The trigger IsAtGoal is a single process.

Mission(cPOS)(cVEL) =   GoTo |
                        IsAtGoal ; *Wander* .

Phase 2: The GoTo behavior is broken into the primitive processes that compose it, and a process COOP that performs the vector summation of their outputs. AvoidObstacles must be further decomposed.

Mission(cPOS)(cVEL) =   MoveTo |
                        Noise |
                        AvoidObstacles |
                        COOP |
                        IsAtGoal<Goal1> ; *Wander*

Phase 3: The AvoidObstacles behavior is comprised of one process, DetectObs, that manages sensing obstacles, and a second process, AvoidObs, that creates a movement vector away from obstacles. The original GoTo behavior has now been completely specified by PARS processes, and the translator can move to the next behavior.

Mission(cPOS)(cVEL) =   MoveTo |
                        Noise |
                        DetectObs |
                        AvoidObs |
                        Coop |
                        IsAtGoal<Goal1> ; *Wander*

Fig. 5. Initial steps taken to create the complete controller from the PARS implementation of a simple mission FSA. In this example all new processes are executed with concurrent composition, but in general any PARS operators can be selected.

3.5   VIPARS and Validation

The entire system to be verified by VIPARS can be expressed, generally, as:

$$SYS = Env\langle initparams\rangle(vel)(pos)|Mission\langle initparams\rangle(pos)(vel). \quad (3)$$

Which is the concurrent, communicating composition of any number of Controllers (i.e., Mission) and Environment models (i.e., Env). The SYS process in (3) represents a very simplistic situation where the Mission process takes as input a position and outputs a velocity. The Environment process (which currently includes the robot hardware) concurrently inputs a velocity and outputs a position. A simple environment process is broken down in equation (4) to provide an example. Initially, three processes run in parallel. $At\langle r\rangle$ represents the current robot position r in VIPARS. $Odo\langle r \rangle$ represents the odometry sensor, which repeatedly transmits current location information with a normal sensor noise distribution Φ. The $Delay\langle t \rangle$ process ends this group after time t. After words the current velocity, from port v, is combined with the actuator's normal noise distribution Θ to update the robots position. While this is a simple kinematic model, more complex models can include dynamics, battery life, or other properties of the hardware and real world.

$$Env = (Delay\langle t \rangle \# Odo\langle r \rangle \# At\langle r \rangle); Ran\langle \Theta \rangle \langle z \rangle; In\langle v \rangle \langle u \rangle; Env\langle r + (u+z)t \rangle \quad (4)$$

$$Odo = Ran\langle \Phi \rangle \langle e \rangle; Out\langle p, r + e \rangle; \langle r \rangle Odo\langle r \rangle \quad (5)$$

Recall that the robot program must operate and interact with a continuous, unstructured and dynamic environment. This effectively rules out a purely state-based method for verification, such as model checking, where the well-known state-space explosion problem leads to intractable state graphs. We leverage the reactive, recurrent nature of behavior-based robot programs (a behavior-based robot will continually respond to a fixed set of affordances in the environment) to isolate regularities in the combined state-space of Env and Mission. This regularity allows verification to be carried out in a very efficient manner. To make clear the method by which we extract and analyze these periodic regularities in the state-space, first recall that PARS supports iteration in the form of tail-recursion (TR):

$$T\langle v \rangle \langle ... \rangle = P\langle v \rangle \langle u \rangle; T\langle ... \rangle \langle f(v, u) \rangle. \quad (6)$$

The process T in (6) is TR iff its body, P, is a sequential composition of non-recursive processes. In standard TR fashion, input parameters (v) are transformed by some function f, for each successive execution of the process. In [15], we developed an interleaving theorem, a relation between parallel and sequential operations in a process algebraic framework, which allows us to express a parallel, communicating composition of TR processes as a single TR process:

$$SYS = P_1 | P_2 | \ldots | P_m = S(P_1, P_2, \ldots, P_m); SYS \quad (7)$$

where $S(P_1, P_2, \ldots, P_m)$ is the System Period process that is constructed from an analysis of the scope and communication structure of component processes in Sys. This allows us to recast the analysis of the recurrent system to the analysis of some sequential ordering (using a Maximum Likelihood approach in the case that SYS contains processes with probabilistic behavior) period processes $S(P_1, P_2, \ldots, P_m)$.

Once the periodic nature of the concurrent system is determined, VIPARS produces a set of equations called flow-functions by analyzing the port connectivity and TR-transformations of variables for each $P_i \in S(P_1, P_2, \ldots, P_m)$. These flow-functions relate values in the network of the kth time step to values in the network of the (k+1)th time step [12]. The flow functions are used to build a Dynamic Bayesian Network (DBN), and verification is carried out by applying a filtering algorithm to the DBN and monitoring for achievement of the performance specification. For a more detailed discussion on this verification process, the authors recommend [14].

The VIPARS system computes within the network of flow-functions and assesses whether performance criteria are met, given the environment model(s) and controller(s) provided by the operator [13]. The VIPARS verification module provides output in the form of: (1) A Boolean answer of whether the performance criteria are met, and (2) detailed output that allows for iterative refinement of the controller. The environment models can be culled from libraries of robot and sensor models. The current work of automatic translation drastically reduces the need for operator intervention in the MissionLab + VIPARS verification system.

4 Validation

To evaluate the verification, experimental results from a physical implementation are compared to the predicted (verification) results from VIPARS. The metric used for comparison is the success rate of a mission. The general procedure, given a mission, is to first develop an appropriate controller in MissionLab. This controller will both be compiled to a hardware executable for the robot, and translated into PARS for verification. Appropriate models of the chosen hardware platform are imported to the VIPARS system. Performance criteria (such as a time limit and spatial accuracy) are selected and given to VIPARS as well. Results from the VIPARS verification and the physical experiment are compared.

A mission related to the search for a biohazard has been selected. This missions were previously verified with manual CNL to PARS translations in [7]. Here, we reproduce those results using automatic translations. A Pioneer 3-AT was the chosen hardware platform.

4.1 The Search Mission

This mission simulates the search for a target, in this case a potential biological weapon. The controller used is shown in Figure 6. The robot explores until the target is found. A camera was used for detection of the target and a SICK laser scanner for obstacle detection and avoidance. In this test, the target was represented as an orange bucket. Once detected, the robot moves to the target and stops. No counter-measure actions were simulated. This provides the opportunity to test random search behavior as well as object detection within the framework of VIPARS. A time limit of 60 seconds to locate the target was chosen as the performance criteria.

The mission was executed on a physical system 106 times. Due to the randomized search pattern, a large number of trials were used to yield accurate results. Failures occurred when the search pattern did not explore near the target within the time limit.

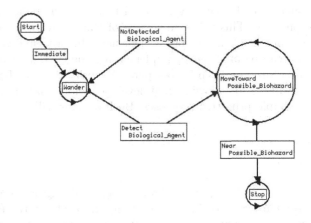

Fig. 6. MissionLab controller for the search mission, shown as it is displayed in the Cfgedit graphical programming tool

4.2 Results

The primary method of validation is the comparison between empirical success probabilities and the predicted success probabilities. Table 2 lists the results for the mission. While the original manual translation showed strong results, 85% versus 83% success rate, the new results still showed qualitative improvement, matching the experimental validation at 83%.

Assuming the null hypothesis is that the probability of success is actually 85%, and the alternative hypothesis that it is smaller, one can use a z-statistic proportion test and calculate a value of $z = 0.58$, and $P(Z < z) = 0.28\%$. Therefore we cannot claim that the improvements are statistically significant, even though the prediction is more accurate. We can conclude that the validity and significance of the VIPARS performance guarantee, originally demonstrated in [7], still holds.

Table 2. Final probability results for the mission

Mission	Total Runs	Experimental P(Success)	VIPARS Manual P(Success)	VIPARS Auto P(Success)
Explore	106	83%	85%	83%

The automatic translation produced exactly the same PARS structure for this mission as the manual translation. However, the verification results reported here differ slightly. The most important contribution to this difference is that the automatic translation used a set of PARS processes built to more directly model the CNL nodes than processes used in the manual translation. The quality of the verification therefore depends on the accuracy with which the PARS primitives model their corresponding CNL nodes.

Selecting a small set of relatively low-level behaviors simplifies the reliance on this correspondence. This takes advantage of the behavior-based controller design. Simple nodes in CNL can be implemented directly in PARS, and the complex behavior can be modeled by implementing the CNL network structure in PARS. An alternate approach is to separately verify these PARS processes. This has the advantage of allowing high-level behaviors that may not easily decompose into simple primitive processes. Both options will be considered in ongoing work.

5   Conclusion

The system described in this paper allows a user to design a robot controller graphically, select hardware for implementation, and evaluate the effectiveness of the system in a chosen environment against specific performance criteria. This information can be used in multiple ways: to refine controller design, to evaluate hardware choices, and to inform the operators decision to execute the mission.

Experimental results were used to validate the verification software. The correspondence between empirical and predicted success probabilities was shown to be very accurate. In addition, these predictions were made with automatically generated PARS files; removing the need for any manual translation.

Some readers may observe that with appropriate models of a robot and the environment, one could run randomized simulations to achieve similar probabilistic results. This would be analogous to sample-based planning, but for verification. The method described in this paper is, in contrast, deterministic and returns complete results (such as the probability of being at any location) without multiple executions of the mission. For many classes of problems, this will more accurate and efficient.

The research presented is being extended in several directions to better test the capabilities and limits of the VIPARS system. Development and testing for multi-agent teams, both homogeneous and heterogeneous, has begun. Testing with two Pioneer 3-ATs has been performed, and future plans include introducing a quad-rotor into the team. SLAM will be utilized in the future to verify with more recent navigation techniques. Finally, the translation software and VIPARS system will be fully incorporated into MissionLab. User studies will be performed to demonstrate that with this system, a nave user can leverage the formal verification tools when designing a mission [18].

Acknowledgments. This research is supported by the Defense Threat Reduction Agency, Basic Research Award #HDTRA1-11-1-0038.

References

1. Arkin, R., Balch, T.: AuRA: Principles and practice in review. Journal of Experimental & Theoretical Artificial Intelligence 9(2-3), 175–189 (1997)
2. Baeir, C., Katoen, J.: Introduction to Model Checking. MIT Press, Cambridge (2008)

3. Baeten, J.: A brief history of process algebra. Theoretical Computer Science 335, 131–146 (2005)
4. Belta, C.: Synthesis of provably-correct control and communication strategies for distributed mobile systems. In: ICRA Workshop on Formal Methods, Anchorage, Alaska (2010)
5. Guerriero, M.L., Heath, J.K., Priami, C.: An automated translation from a narrative language for biological modelling into process algebra. In: Calder, M., Gilmore, S. (eds.) CMSB 2007. LNCS (LNBI), vol. 4695, pp. 136–151. Springer, Heidelberg (2007)
6. Jhala, R., Majumdar, R.: Software Model Checking. ACM Computing Surveys 41(4), 21, 53 (2009)
7. Jiang, S., Arkin, R., Lyons, D., Liu, T.-M., Harrington, D.: Performance guarantees for C-WMD robot missions. In: 2013 IEEE International Symposium on Safety, Security, and Rescue Robotics (SSRR), pp. 1–8 (2013)
8. Karaman, S., Rasmussen, S., Kingston, D., Frazzoli, E.: Specification and planning of UAV missions: a Process Algebra approach. In: American Control Conference, St. Louis, MO, June 10-12 (2009)
9. Kress-Gazit, H., Fainekos, G.E., Pappas, G.: Temporal-Logic-Based Reactive Mission and Motion Planning. IEEE Transactions on Robotics 25(6), 1370–1381 (2009)
10. Lyons, D., Arkin, R.: Towards performance guarantees for emergent behavior. In: IEEE International Conference on Robotics and Automation, vol. 4, pp. 4153–4158 (2004)
11. Lyons, D., Arkin, R., Nirmal, P., Jiang, S., Liu, T.-M., Deeb, J.: Getting it right the first time: Robot mission guarantees in the presence of uncertainty. In: Intelligent Robots and Systems (IROS), pp. 5292–5299 (2013)
12. Lyons, D., Arkin, R., Jiang, S., Liu, T.-L., Nirmal, P., Deeb, J.: Performance Verification for behavior-based Robot Missions. In: AAMAS ARMS 2013 Workshop on Autonomous Robotics and Multirobot Systems, St. Paul, MN (May 2013)
13. Lyons, D., Arkin, R., Jiang, S., Nirmal, P., Liu, T.-L.: A Software Tool for the Design of Critical Robot Missions with Performance Guarantees. In: Conf. on Systems Engineering Research (CSER 2013), Atlanta, GA (March 2013)
14. Lyons, D., Arkin, R., Jiang, S., Harrington, D., Liu, T.-L.: Verifying and Validating Multirobot Missions (submitted, 2014), Available via GT Mobile Robot Lab http://www.cc.gatech.edu/ai/robot-lab/online-publications/ GIRTFT_IROS_2014_v5.pdf (accessed June 10, 2014)
15. Lyons, D., Arkin, R., Nirmal, P., Jiang, S.: Designing Autonomous Robot Missions with Performance Guarantees'. In: IEEE/RSJ International Conference on Intelligent Robots and Systems (IROS), Algarve, PT (2012)
16. MacKenzie, D.: The configuration network language user manual. In: Georgia Tech Mobile Robot Lab (1996), http://www.cc.gatech.edu/aimosaic/robot-lab/ research/MissionLab/mlab_manual-7.0.pdf (accessed June 10, 2014)
17. MacKenzie, D., Arkin, R., Cameron, J.: Multiagent mission specification and execution. Autonomous Robots 4(1), 29–52 (1997)
18. MacKenzie, D., Arkin, R.: Evaluating the Usability of Robot Programming Toolsets. International Journal of Robotics Research 4(7), 381–401 (1998)
19. Simmons, R., Pecheur, C., Srinivasan, G.: Towards automatic verification of autonomous systems. In: IEEE/RSJ International Conference on Intelligent Robots and Systems, vol. 2, pp. 1410–1415 (2000)
20. Ding, X.C., Kloetzer, M., Chen, Y., Belta, C.: Automatic Deployment of Robotic Teams. IEEE Robotics & Automation Magazine 18(3), 75–86 (2011)

Probabilistic 2D Acoustic Source Localization Using Direction of Arrivals in Robot Sensor Networks

Riccardo Levorato and Enrico Pagello

University of Padua, Department of Information Engineering (DEI), IAS-Lab.
Via Ognissanti 72, I-35131 Padova, Italy
{riccardo.levorato,enrico.pagello}@dei.unipd.it
http://robotics.dei.unipd.it

Abstract. This paper explores the 2D Audio Localization using only the Direction of Arrivals (DOAs) of a fixed acoustic source coming from an audio sensors network and proposes a new method for estimating the position of the source using a Gaussian Probability over DOA approach (G-DOA) in the 2D space. This new method was thought for Robotic purposes and introduces a new perspective of the Audio-Video synergy using Video Sensor Localization in the environment for extrinsic Audio Sensor Calibration. Our approach achieves more precise solutions using more sensors and shows better results compared to the analytic Weighted Least Square method (WLS-DOA). Test results using Microsoft Kinect as DOA-sensors within the ROS framework show that the algorithm is robust, modular and can be easily used for robot applications.

Keywords: Acustic Source Localization (ASL), Direction Of Arrival (DOA), Multi-Sensor Network, Robot Audition, Kinect, ROS.

1 Introduction and State of the Art

Sound spectrum analysis is a very important skill for those who live in an environment in which all the noises are helpful for enhancing the knowledge of what happens in the surroundings. One of the most important acoustic skills is the Acoustic Source Localization (ASL). Mammals, for example, have only two hears that physically permit to estimate only the DOA of an acoustic source using interaural time differences and interaural level differences. However, this method is not always correct because it can be ambiguous (i.e. Cone of Confusion). Fortunately this problem can be solved only by tilting the head, moving the pinnas or the whole body [1]. Estimating the distance of the acoustic source requires further skills that take in consideration also sound reflections and echoes (i.e. bats echolocation) [2].

In the acoustic field, a DOA sensor consists of an array of at least two microphones. Common tested acoustic sources are speakers [3], gun shots and human screams [4], clap hands, and so on. There are various techniques for calculating the DOA of an acoustic source such as Angle of Arrival (AoA), Time Difference

D. Brugali et al. (Eds.): SIMPAR 2014, LNAI 8810, pp. 474–485, 2014.
© Springer International Publishing Switzerland 2014

of Arrival (TDOA), Frequency Difference of Arrival (FDOA), and other similar techniques [5][6]. Recently there was an increasing use of sensors networks, that can share audio and video data in a cooperative way, achieving more precise knowledge of the environment. In an Audio Sensor Network (ASN), by knowing the position and pose of each DOA sensor, it is possible to better estimate the position of the acoustic source by sharing and synchronizing the DOA estimations [3][7][8]. In 2D space, ASL with only two DOA sensors is trivial because it is possible to estimate the position of the acoustic source by the simple intersection of two lines, which can give either one solution (the intersection point) or no solution (two parallel lines). Problems arise when there are more than two DOA sensors: each of them has an error prone estimation of the DOA of the acoustic source and most of the times the intersection of all the lines doesn't exist. A method that takes in consideration all DOA estimations from all DOA sensors will give a better estimation of the acoustic source because it will take in consideration the informations coming from all sensors.

In the state of the art there are a lot of works that deal with audio localization [3-11]. Many of them focuses on various techniques that use all the signals coming from all the microphones and try to localize sources fusing all data. In a robotic environment, this approach is not applicable because it is difficult to convey all audio signals in an unique CPU for making all calculations and, over all, synchronize all audio signals in time [9]. Furthermore, the big amount of audio data travelling over the network could create a bottleneck effect and create latency for other important shared data. To solve this problems, a smart approach can be the one that elaborates groups of consistent data, shares the obtained partial results and finally fuses them. In this way each group of microphones in a DOA sensor can estimate the DOA of the acoustic source respectively to its position. Knowing the position of all DOA sensors, it is possible to fuse data into a general reference system and use a convenient method to find an estimation of the source position. This approach was thought to fit with mobile robots with microphones on board that will have to estimate their position with a Simultaneous localization and mapping (SLAM) technique.

Following this topic, Hawkes et Al. [10] proposed an analytic Weighted Least Square method (WLS-DOA) that minimizes the distance of the estimated point to the estimated DOA line and achieves good results in 3D space. In his Phd thesis, Pertilä [5] also focused on DOA-Based Localization and introduced a new approach that tries to eliminate the sensors with bad acoustic DOA estimations starting from the WLS-DOA method of [10].

Although it was shown that this method performed better than WLS-DOA in outlier situations, we found that it is error prone, because in some situations it can discard the DOA sensors that are better than others. A proof of the fail of this method can be easily given if we consider the example in Fig. 1: we can see that the Robust DOA-Based Localization solution (in magenta) is very far from the real one (in blue). On the other hand the WLS-DOA (in green) and our G-DOA approach (in red) solutions are closer to the real solution. This is due to the fact that the DOA estimations of sensors s_1, s_2 and s_3 intersect very close to each other (near the R-DOA solution), not considering that only sensors s_1 and s_5 are the only good estimations and the others s_2, s_3 and s_4 are outliers. The main key of this problem is because it is not advisable to discard any of the sensors because the real position of the source is unknown and it is not possible to detect which DOA sensors are outliers if they have the same probability error to be outliers. Furthermore, the simple WLS-DOA approach can also lead to errors because a WLS-DOA estimation is considered as a line without a precise direction. As an example, in Fig. 1, even if sensor s_2 DOA estimation is pointing towards the south-east, the WLS-DOA approach considers also the northwest direction (and in fact R-DOA fails also for this reason).

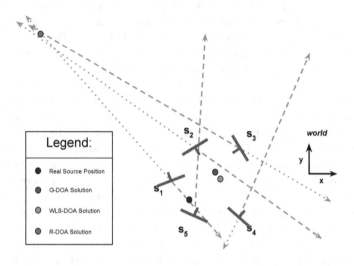

Fig. 1. Robust DOA-Based Localization Failure Example

In our approach we use all the DOA sensors and propose a novel approach that is based on the probability error over the angle of the DOA estimation. The difference with WLS-DOA approach is that G-DOA will minimize the angle (instead of the distance) of the estimated point to the estimated DOA. This new approach is not affected by the angle ambiguity problems of the WLS-DOA approach. Another contribute of this paper is a new concept of Audio-Video data fusion. More specifically, Audio Localization will be strictly correlated to Video Calibration: working with mobile robots it would be very hard to calibrate at each instant the relative position of all microphones of all moving robots with non-invasive techniques (i.e. using an acoustic high-frequency periodic signal as audio reference). For this reason, using SLAM techniques and knowing the relative position of the microphones with respect to the 'visual' sensors, will help robots to share also audio informations. The paper is structured as follows: firstly in section 2 the DOA-Based Localization problem is formalized; new approach details are shown in section 3. Sections 4 and 5 deal with the validation and its respective results. Finally the results are commented and discussed and the conclusions are presented with an anticipation of the future work.

2   DOA-Based Localization Problem

Let S be a set of DOA sensors, with $|S| = N_s \geq 1$. In this scope, a DOA sensor $s \in S$ consists in a microphones array able to compute and estimate the DOA of a generic acoustic source r with respect to the intrinsic reference system of s. Let $\mathbf{s}_k^p = [s_k^x, s_k^y]^T \in \mathbb{R}^2$ and $s_k^o \in (-\pi, \pi]$ represent respectively the 2D position and orientation of kth sensor, $k \in [1, N_s]$, with respect to the 2D Cartesian reference system ($world$). A DOA estimation from s_k is an angle $\alpha_k \in (-\pi, \pi]$ radians. The problem consists in finding the best estimation of the acoustic source position $\mathbf{r} = [r^x, r^y]^T \in \mathbb{R}^2$ assuming that all $\mathbf{s}_k^p$ and s_k^o are known a $priori$ and all α_k are estimated using an arbitrary DOA estimation method (Fig. 2).

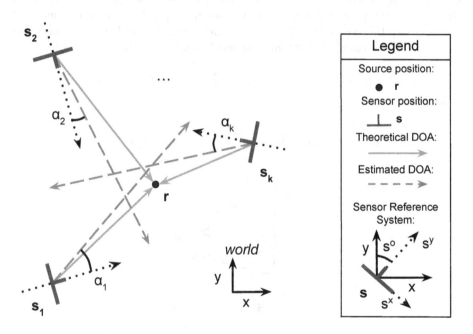

Fig. 2. DOA - Based Localization Problem

For simplicity, the following assumptions are considered:

- all sensors are connected together within a network and can share data;
- all DOA estimations are synchronized in time;
- there is only one fixed (not moving) acoustic source at time;
- the precision of all α_k estimations depends only on the accuracy of each DOA sensor and on the DOA estimation methods used;
- echoes and sound reflection effects are not considered.

3   Gaussian Probability over DOA Approach

Each real DOA estimation α_k has an intrinsic error that depends mainly on the accuracy of the kth sensor. This error can be modelled as a Gaussian probability error in the angle domain with zero mean and variance σ_k using only values in the range $\phi \in [-\pi, \pi]$. The angular probability sensor model $\mathcal{M}_k$ is defined as follows:

$$\mathcal{M}_k \sim \mathcal{N}(0, \sigma_k)_{[-\pi,\pi]} = \frac{1}{\sigma_k \sqrt{2\pi}} e^{-\frac{\phi^2}{2\sigma_k^2}} \quad , \quad \phi \in (-\pi, \pi] \tag{1}$$

At this step it is needed a change of domain from the angular domain to the Cartesian coordinate system $G = (n \times n) \in \mathbb{Z}^2$. G can be thought as a spatial 2D grid with a fixed spatial *range* [m] and a fixed precision parameter *prec* [m] such that $n = range/prec$. For each generic point $\mathbf{q} = [q^x, q^y]^T \in G$ it is calculated the angle $\beta_k^{\mathbf{q}}$ that considers $\mathbf{s}_k^x$ as vertex and it is included between a first line that passes through $\mathbf{s}_k^p$ and $\mathbf{q}$ and a second line given by the axis s_k^y (Fig. 3):

$$\beta_k^{\mathbf{q}} = atan2(q^y - s_k^y, q^x - s_k^x) - s_k^o \quad , \quad \mathbf{q} \in G \wedge k \in [1, N_s] \tag{2}$$

with:

$$atan2(y, x) = 2 \arctan \frac{\sqrt{x^2 + y^2} - x}{y} \quad , \quad atan2(y, x) \in (-\pi, \pi] \tag{3}$$

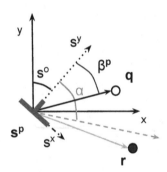

Fig. 3. Representation of all considered angles in a DOA sensor

The probability $\mathcal{G}_k(\mathbf{q})$ for each point $\mathbf{q}$ in the grid G is given by evaluating each angle $\beta_k^{\mathbf{q}}$ in the angular probability sensor model $\mathcal{M}_k$ with respect to the DOA estimation α_k:

$$\mathcal{G}_k(\mathbf{q}) = \mathcal{M}_k(\beta_k^{\mathbf{q}} - \alpha_k) = \frac{1}{\sigma_k \sqrt{2\pi}} e^{-\frac{(\beta_k^{\mathbf{q}} - \alpha_k)^2}{2\sigma_k^2}} \quad , \quad \mathbf{q} \in G \wedge k \in [1, N_s] \tag{4}$$

All results of operations among angles in Eq. (2) and Eq. (4) take a value in the range $(-\pi, \pi]$. The graphical representation of a single DOA sensor estimation probability over the Cartesian plane can be seen in Fig. 4.(a) where red and blue regions have higher and lower likelihoods respectively. At this point all the $\mathcal{G}_k(\mathbf{q})$ are multiplied point-wise obtaining the multiplication of all the probabilities of all sensors $\mathcal{G}(\mathbf{q})$ in the 2D space domain (Fig. 4.(b)).

$$\mathcal{G}(\mathbf{q}) = \prod_{k=1}^{Ns} \mathcal{G}_k(\mathbf{q}) = \prod_{k=1}^{Ns} \left[\frac{1}{\sigma_k \sqrt{2\pi}} e^{-\frac{(atan2(q^y - s_k^y, q^x - s_k^x) - s_k^o - \alpha_k)^2}{2\sigma_k^2}} \right], \mathbf{q} \in G \quad (5)$$

In Eq. (5) it is used the product instead of the sum for the fact that if the likelihoods from different DOA sensors are independent, the intersection of sets equals their product, as stated in [5].

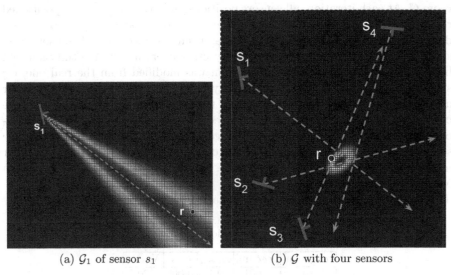

(a) $\mathcal{G}_1$ of sensor s_1 (b) $\mathcal{G}$ with four sensors

Fig. 4. $\mathcal{G}$ over G. Red and blue regions have higher and lower likelihood respectively.

Finally, the point in G with the maximum value of $\mathcal{G}$ is the estimation of the solution $\hat{\mathbf{r}} \in G$ with the proposed Gaussian Probability over DOA approach:

$$\hat{\mathbf{r}} = \underset{G}{\operatorname{argmax}} \, \mathcal{G} \quad (6)$$

It is worth noting that even though the probability axiom $P(\Omega) = 1$ is no longer satisfied in Eq. (1), the omission of this axiom will not compromise the correctness of the procedure. Dealing with multiplication (and not with sums) of probabilities (Eq. (5)), all unused values can be omitted because are not useful and because multiplication of numbers $\in [0, 1]$ still takes a value $\in [0, 1]$. On the other hand it is important to set *a priori* experimental validated variances σ_k in order to represent correctly each angular probability sensor model $\mathcal{M}_k$. The algorithm has always a computational complexity of $\Theta(n^2)$.

4   Validation

The localization performance metric used is the Distance Error (DE) that is distance between the estimated source and the real source positions in meters. The validation is divided in two parts: the first part deals with a general simulation of the DOA-Based problem which aim is the investigation of the properties of the presented approach. The second part is the real test part that is also accompanied by a simulation test to validate the simulation tool.

4.1   Simulation

Simulation was an helpful tool to compare the localization performances of our approach to the traditional Weighted Least Square method (WLS-DOA) [10]. The simulation scenarios consisted in groups of N_s DOA sensors in a virtual room G. At each iteration, all sensors positions and orientations were positioned randomly in G. All tests had only one acoustic source at time positioned randomly in G too. For all simulations it has been assumed that all sensors were similar so they had the same probability error over the DOA estimation and hence same σ_{k_sim}. Each DOA estimation was modified from the real one, for simulation purposes, using the probability model $\mathcal{M}_k$ with the fixed σ_{k_sim} for all k. The simulation was repeated t_{sim} times for each group of sensors. The cardinality of the sensor group was varied in the range $[3, N_{s\_max}]$. As previously said, the case with $Ns = 2$ was not considered for the two reasons that the solution is the trivial intersection of the only two existing DOAs and all other methods give reasonably the same result. Simulation code was implemented in MATLAB.
The simulation parameters used for validation are listed in Tab. 1:

Table 1. Simulation Parameters

range [m]	prec [m]	σ_{k_sim}	t_{sim}	N_{s_max}
10	0.001	0.1	10000	20

The validation metrics calculated for all $N_s \in [3, N_{s\_max}]$ for both G-DOA and WLS-DOA approaches were the following:

- mean value of all DEs;
- variance value of all DEs;
- min and maximum value of all DEs;

Finally it was calculated the difference between the mean value of all DEs $\forall N_s \in [3, N_{s\_max}]$ for further investigating the difference between the two approaches.

4.2   Real Test

We also tested the algorithms in a small real environment. We used three Microsoft Kinect[1] as DOA-sensors. Microsoft Kinect has one RGB-camera, a 3D depth sensor and four microphones positioned as shown in Fig. 5. Each DOA estimation came from $HARK$ software[2] developed in ROS[3] with an error of $\pm 0,0873$ [rad] $= 5°$ [11]. For the sensor calibration, we used the ROS software developed in our laboratory[4] [12] that helped us to easily calibrate and find the extrinsic parameters among Kinect RGB-cameras. Starting from this calibration, we translated each RGB-camera reference point to the reference point of the DOA estimation given by $HARK$ with respect to the $world$. The reference point of the DOA estimation given by $HARK$ is exactly the center point over the x axis of the Kinect as it is shown in Tab. 2. Since Kinect microphones are all positioned in a line, DOAs can only be estimated in the plane xz as a rotation over the y axis. Real tests code was implemented in C++ under ROS.

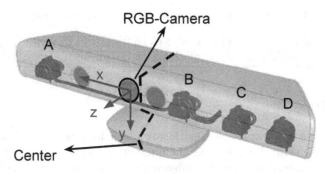

Fig. 5. Kinect sensors - Microphones (A-D) and RGB-camera - positions in 3D. Kinect RGB Reference System is shown with red arrows. The black dashed line represents the center of the Kinect with respect to the x.

Table 2. Kinect sensors - Microphones (A-D) and RGB-camera - positions over x axis

Mic A [m]	RGB Sensor [m]	Center [m]	Mic B [m]	Mic C [m]	Mic D [m]
-0.1150	-0.0140	0	0.0350	0.0750	0.1150

The real test consisted in setting three Kinects in a line with the positions and orientations shown in Tab. 3 and clapping hands in different positions. A total of twenty different positions with $r^x \in [-1,1]$, $r^y \in [0.5,2]$ and a step of 0.5 [m] are visible in Fig. 8. We used $\sigma_k = 0.1$ $\forall k \in [1,3]$. Another simulation was done using the same parameters used in the real test in order to compare the results.

---

[1] http://www.xbox.com/kinect

[2] http://winnie.kuis.kyoto-u.ac.jp/HARK

[3] http://www.ros.org

[4] https://github.com/iaslab-unipd/multisensor_calibration

Table 3. Sensors positions and orientations in real test

Sensor Type	k	s_k^x [m]	s_k^y [m]	s_k^o [rad]
Kinect	1	-1.05296	0.897504	0
Kinect	2	0	0	0
Kinect	3	0.0314011	0.0343866	0

The parameters for the G-DOA simulation are listed in Tab. 4 and the number of samples collected for each test number is shown in Tab. 5.

Table 4. Simulation Parameters for Comparison with real test

$range$ [m]	$prec$ [m]	σ_k	t_{sim}	N_{s_max}
10	0.01	0.1	1000	3

Table 5. Number of samples for each real test position

Test Number	1	2	3	4	5	6	7	8	9	10	11	12	13	14	15	16	17	18	19	20
Number of samples	25	19	23	24	19	25	29	23	37	31	40	29	34	36	43	54	38	54	59	53

5   Results

In Fig. 6.(a) we see that G-DOA performs better in mean than WLS-DOA approach and the error diminishes as the number of sensors grows in the environment. Furthermore, observing the difference of results of the two methods as the number of the DOA sensors augments (in dashed blue), it is possible to see that there is an almost constant difference that is about 10 cm. On the other hand, the WLS-DOA variance performs better than G-DOA variance (Fig. 6.(b)). This fact can be explained looking to Fig. 6.(c-d): G-DOA maximum DEs are higher than WLS-DOA ones but its minimum DEs are lower. This means that G-DOA has an higher accuracy but lower precision with respect to WLS-DOA.

Looking to real tests results and its related simulation results shown in Fig. 7.(a-b) it is possible to see that G-DOA performs always better than WLS-DOA both in mean and in variance and that real results does not differ so much to the ones of its relative simulation. This can be addressed to the fact that in this specific case there are only three sensors and in the simulation results of Fig. 6.(a-d) G-DOA performed always better than WLS-DOA in the case $N_s = 3$. It is evident that errors becomes bigger as the distance between the acoustic source and the sensors grows both in real and in simulation. This is visible looking at results of Test Numbers [1, 5, 11, 16, 20] in Fig. 7 and 8 that correspond to lateral positions in G. This phenomenon reflects the fact that the distance between the real DOA and a position $\mathbf{q}$ increases as $\mathbf{q}$ moves away from the vertex of a fixed angle (Fig. 4.(a)). Finally, from the simulation and real test results in Fig. 7(a-b) we can say that simulation was a reliable and useful tool that helped a lot in investigating and stress the properties of both approaches.

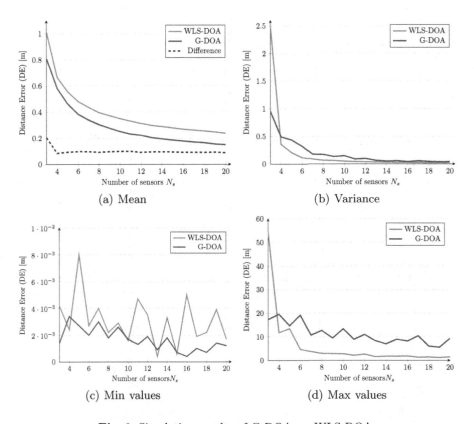

(a) Mean

(b) Variance

(c) Min values

(d) Max values

Fig. 6. Simulation results of G-DOA vs. WLS-DOA

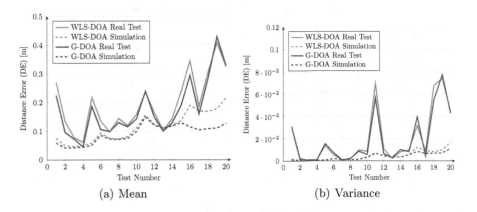

(a) Mean

(b) Variance

Fig. 7. Real test results of G-DOA vs. WLS-DOA

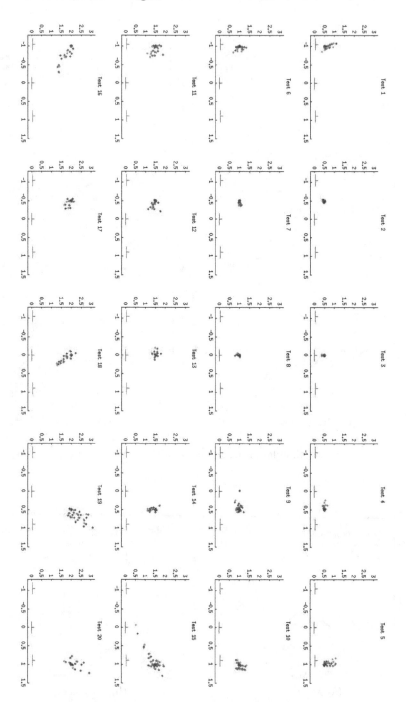

Fig. 8. Real Tests results. WLD-DOA and G-DOA position estimations are in green and red respectively. Source and sensors positions are in blue and red respectively. The axis represents are consistent to the *world* and their scale is measured in meters.

6   Conclusions and Future Work

In this paper we proposed a new method for Audio Source Localization (ASL) using a Gaussian probability over DOA (G-DOA). Video calibration for microphones arrays calibration is also a new *ad hoc* approach for calibrating microphones arrays in a robotic environment. We tested it both in simulation and real environments and showed that G-DOA performs better than WLS-DOA. Further work will focus on speeding up the G-DOA algorithm that takes the most of the time in the product of Eq. (5) in order to expand it to the 3D space.

Acknowledgements. This research has been supported by Telecom Italia S.p.A. with the grant "Service Robotics".

References

1. Wallach, H.: The role of head movements and vestibular and visual cues in sound localization. Journal of Experimental Psychology 27, 339–368 (1940)
2. Griffin, D.R.: Listening in the dark: the acoustic orientation of bats and men. Yale University Press (1958)
3. Omologo, M., De Mori, R.: Acoustic Transduction. In: Spoken Dialogue with Computers. Academic Press (1998)
4. Valenzise, G., Gerosa, L., Tagliasacchi, M., Antonacci, E., Sarti, A.: Scream and gunshot detection and localization for audio-surveillance systems. In: IEEE Conference on Advanced Video and Signal Based Surveillance, AVSS 2007, pp. 21–26 (September 2007)
5. Pertilä, P.: Acoustic Source Localization in a Room Environment and at Moderate Distances - [PhD Thesis]. Tampere University of Technology (2009)
6. Salvati, D.: Acoustic Source Localization Using Microphone Arrays - PhD Thesis. Department of Mathematics and Computer Science - University of Udine (2012)
7. Aarabi, P.: The fusion of distributed microphone arrays for sound localization. EURASIP Journal on Advances in Signal Processing (2003)
8. Di Biase, J.H., Silverman, H.F., Brandstein, M.: Robust localization in reverberant rooms. In: Microphone Arrays: Signal Processing Techniques and Applications. Springer (2001)
9. Ward, D.B., Lehmann, E.A., Williamson, R.C.: Particle filtering algorithms for tracking an acoustic source in a reverberant environment. IEEE Transactions on Speech and Audio Processing 11(6), 826–836
10. Hawkes, M., Nehorai, A.: Wideband source localization using a distributed acoustic vector-sensor array. IEEE Trans. Sig. Proc. 51, 1479–1491 (2003)
11. Nakadai, K., Takahashi, T., Okuno, H.G., Nakajima, H., Hasegawa, Y., Tsujino, H.: Design and implementation of robot audition system "hark" – open source software for listening to three simultaneous speakers. Advanced Robotics 24(5-6), 739–761 (2010)
12. Basso, F., Levorato, R.: Online calibration for networks of cameras and depth sensors. In: OMNIVIS: The 12th Workshop on Non-classical Cameras, Camera Networks and Omnidirectional Vision - 2014 IEEE International Conference on Robotics and Automation (ICRA 2014) (2014)

Control and Omni-directional Locomotion of a Crawling Quadruped

Douwe Dresscher, Michiel van der Coelen, Jan Broenink, and Stefano Stramigioli

Robotics and Mechatronics, Faculty EEMCS,
University of Twente, 7500 AE Enschede, Netherlands
D.Dresscher@ieee.org, J.F.Broenink@utwente.nl

Abstract. Traversing unstructured environments, (statically stable) legged robots could be applied effectively but, they face two main problems: the *high complexity* of the system and the *low speed of locomotion*. To address the complexity of the controller, we apply a control layer that abstracts the legged robot to an omni-directional moving mass. In this control scheme, we apply the gait generator as proposed by Estremera and de Santos. We present theory to determine the theoretically maximum achievable velocity of a quadruped and compare the (omni-directional) maximum velocity of the selected gait generator with this optimum to validate its performance. For our use case the theoretically maximum achievable velocity is $1\ ms^{-1}$; in simulations we achieve a velocity for straight movement of maximum $0.75\ ms^{-1}$. Normal turns with a radius larger than $0.45\ m$ are possible at a velocity of at least $0.1\ ms^{-1}$; the performance of crab turns is too unpredictable to be useful. The gait generator as proposed by Estremera and de Santos is partially capable of supporting omni-directional movement at satisfactory velocities.

1 Introduction

Traversing unstructured environments, (statically stable) legged robots can be superior to their wheeled and tracked counterparts. However, so far only few have made it to practical applications.

Two main problems that have prevented statically stable legged locomotion from being applied effectively are: the *high* complexity of the system and the *low* speed of locomotion [3,6].

To limit the mechanical complexity of the system, we assume a quadrupedal robot: four is the minimum amount of legs required for statically stable locomotion [4]. To address the complexity of the controller, we present a control scheme where we apply separation of concerns to reduce the complexity. Our approach is a port-based approach which provides a control layer that abstracts the legged robot to an omni-directional moving mass (an admittance) as shown in Fig. 1. By applying a force to the abstracted robot, the resulting velocity of the robot can be controlled (for instance with an impedance controller [1,7]) as shown in

D. Brugali et al. (Eds.): SIMPAR 2014, LNAI 8810, pp. 486–497, 2014.

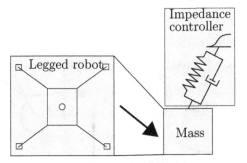

Fig. 1. Abstraction of a legged robot to an omni-directional moving mass that can then, for instance, be controlled by an impedance controller

Fig. 1. This scheme requires a gait controller that ensures that the legs move to support the motion of the robot.

The gait generator as proposed by Estremera and de Santos [2] is capable of generating a gait based on the omni-directional velocity of the robot body and is, for this reason, particularly suitable to be used in the proposed control scheme.

In addition, we present theory to determine the theoretically maximum achievable velocity of a quadruped and compare the speed performance of the selected gait generator with this optimum to validate its performance.

This paper is structured as follows: in Sec. 2, the use case for supporting the theory and evaluating the performance of the gait generator is described. In Sec. 3, the proposed controller structure is presented and explained, including a summary of the gait generator. In Sec. 4, we present theory on the maximum velocity of a quadruped and treat how this applies to the use case. In Sec. 5, the speed performance of the simulated gait generator is presented. In Sec. 6, the simulation results are compared with the theoretical optima and in Sec. 7, conclusions are drawn.

2 Use Case

In this work, we employ a use case to clarify theory and evaluate the speed performance of the gait generator. The use case is a quadrupedal robot of which a top view is shown in Fig. 2a and the legs have a configuration as shown in Fig. 2b. The workspace of a leg in the x-y plane is called the *reachable area* (also shown in Fig. 2a).

Throughout this work, we assume that the mass of the legs is negligible compared to the mass of the base. To account for possibly destabilising effects caused by unmodelled behaviour, a safety margin is used. This safety margin is shown as a circle round the Center of Mass (CoM) in Fig. 2a.

For simplicity reasons, a rectangular motion profile is assumed for a step from a starting foothold to a target foothold, P, as shown in Fig. 3. The ground

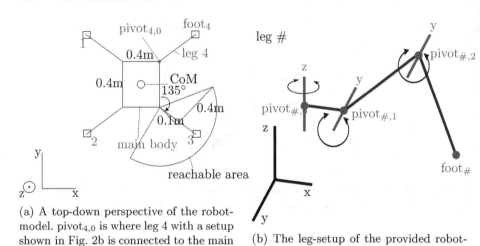

(a) A top-down perspective of the robot-model. pivot$_{4,0}$ is where leg 4 with a setup shown in Fig. 2b is connected to the main body. CoM refers to the center of mass of the robot.

(b) The leg-setup of the provided robot-model. There are three degrees of freedom. n denotes the leg-number [1..4].

Fig. 2. The robot model

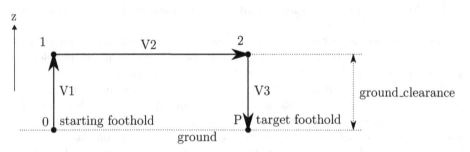

Fig. 3. A step profile. A foot is lifted from point 0 to point 1 with speed V1. The speed between point 1 and 2 is V2. The landing from point 2 to the final foothold P is done at speed V3.

clearance is assumed to be 0.1 m and the velocity at which a leg moves (V1=V2= V3 in Fig. 3) 5 ms^{-1}.

3   Controller Structure: Separation of Concerns

As stated in Sec. 1, we use our controller structure to create a layer that abstracts the legged robot to an omni-directional moving mass. To achieve this several facilities are required as is also shown in Fig. 4:

1. The force that has to be exerted on the robot body needs to be translated to forces that are to be exerted by the legs. (Generalised inverse Jacobian relations)

2. A controller to control the feet over a step trajectory when required (Feet controllers)
3. The step trajectory needs to be generated (Feet trajectory generators)
4. The legs need to be moved such that the movement of the robot body is supported. (Gait generator)
5. Forces to be exerted by the legs need to be translated to forces to be exterted in the joints (Jacobian relations)

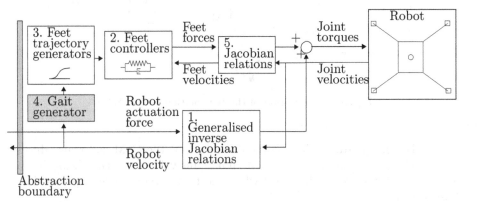

Fig. 4. The abstraction layer with its components

In this work, we assume the feet controllers and feet trajectory generators to be straightforward, and thus we focus on the gait generator.

3.1 Gait Generator

In this Section, we give a short summary of the gait generator.

Two Basic Notions. Two basic notions are used in the summary of the gait generator: the "Kinematic Margin" and the "Transfer Distance".

The Kinematic margin (KM) refers to the distance the CoM can travel in its forward direction until a specific leg is at its physical limit [5]. It is a scalar value that can be visually represented by a line with a length of KM in the direction opposite to the CoM movement and starting at the foot as is shown in Fig. 5. During movement of the CoM, the foot of a leg is assumed to stay in the same location while the rest of the leg moves with the CoM.

The kinematic margin is dependent on the reachable area that is defined by the limits of the leg. The reachable area for the robot model as described in Sec. 2 is shown in Fig. 5. The CoM moves in the direction of the CoM velocity, which causes the reachable area to translate in the same way. After KM meters, the foot will transition out of the reachable area. A minimum value for KM, KM_{min}, is used to denote the smallest kinematic margin among all legs.

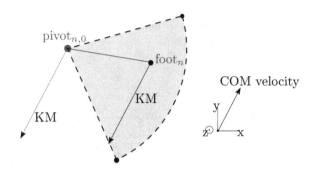

Fig. 5. Visualization of the Kinematic margin (KM)

The Transfer Distance, TD, is the distance that the CoM will travel during the transfer of the foot to P [2]. The minimum value for TD, TD_{min}, is the distance that the CoM will travel when the foot is only moved up and down (also see Fig. 3).

State Machine. The gait generator is built around a state machine as shown in Fig. 6 where, during normal operation, three states (S0, wait; S1, Calculate and; S2, Transfer) are executed sequentially based on three conditions (T01, The next leg can be lifted; T12, Foothold selection successful and; T20, leg transfer complete).

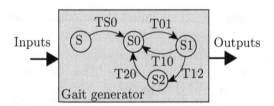

Fig. 6. The main gait-generator state-machine

The output of the gait generator is a leg index for a leg that should be moved and the position where the foot should be placed, the inputs are:

– the location of all feet.
– the location and velocity of the center of mass projection on the xy-plane.

– an indication that the current transfer of a leg has finished.

The three states - S0, S1 and S2 - will now be discussed in detail.

State 0: Wait This is the starting state for the state-machine. All feet are on the ground. A check is made for the ability to lift a leg with stability. A leg is selected based on an order of leg preference:

Order of leg preference = [Priority leg, lowest KM, ..., highest KM]

Here, the first entry is a preferred leg to be transferred that has been determined in the previous state 1. After this, all legs are prioritised based on their kinematic margin: the leg that will reach its kinematic limit sooner has a higher priority.

When the leg preference is determined, the highest priority leg is tested for its ability to be lifted based on the following rule: When the leg is lifted, the center of mass needs to be supported by the other three legs.

When the velocity and forward direction of the vehicle are constant, it is possible to generate a wave gait. A wave gait has superior stability properties [4] and is therefore desirable. In the case of a constant velocity and forward direction of the vehicle, only the highest priority leg is considered for lifting to enforce a wave gait. If the velocity *has* changes, the other legs are considered for lifting in sequence of priority.

The selected leg is named "LT" (Leg to be Transferred). When LT can be lifted with stability - T01 - the state machine transitions to state 1.

State 1: Calculate In this state the next position for the leg to be transferred is calculated. To find a suitable foothold position, several areas are iteratively combined. These areas are named O, D, A, B and C and they are combined (Fig. 7) as follows: First, area O and D are combined.

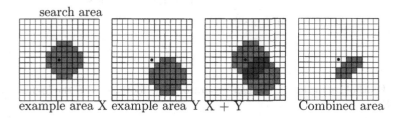

search area

example area X   example area Y   X + Y   Combined area

Fig. 7. An example of combining two limiting areas for the footholds named X and Y. The resulting Combined area on the far right shows the collection of all footholds that appear in X as well as Y.

Area O makes sure that placing the leg LT at P does not restrict the next step to be smaller than the current. Area O also takes care that the foothold P is in the workspace of the leg. It can be interpreted as: After placing the foot of LT at P, it should have a KM which is at least TP higher than KM_{min}. Area D can be interpreted as: the footholds that can be reached while the CoM is still in the current support pattern. This condition has to be met in order for the robot to remain stable during the transition of the leg.

If this results in valid footholds, an NLT (Next Leg to be Transferred) is selected based on the following priority:

$$\text{NLT preference} = \left[\text{Next leg in wave gait, lowest KM,} \dots, \text{highest KM}\right]$$

and areas A, B and C are applied. Area A is used to evaluate if leg NLT can be moved if leg LT is placed at position P. Area A can be interpreted as: The point where LT can be placed such that the CoM can travel at least TD_{min} in distance before it either exits the support patters or leg LT reaches its kinematic limit. Area B can be interpreted as follows: it consists of the points P, where can LT can be placed such that the next leg to be transferred, NLT, can be lifted before any of the legs reach their kinematic limit. When a wave-gait leg order is used, knowledge is available about the next three (and further) legs that will be lifted. Area C consist of the points where LT can be placed such that there is enough space for three following feet to be moved.

If this does *not* result in valid footholds, the next leg in the priority sequence is selected as NLT and the step is repeated. If it *does* result in valid footholds, the algorithm can proceed.

Often, more than one suitable foothold is available after combining the areas. To select a foothold from this set of suitable footholds, a criterion can be used. For this work, we use a simple criterion namely: The maximum kinematic margin of the leg (Fig. 8).

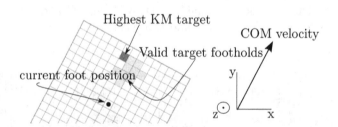

Fig. 8. Foothold selection in the gait generator. The foothold with the highest KM is selected.

If state 1 successfully selects a suitable foothold - T12 -, the state machine goes to state 2. In the case that state 1 fails to find a suitable foothold - T10 - , the state machine returns to state 0.

State 2: Transfer In this state the leg is moved to the target position and the state machine wait until the transition is completed. When the transition is completed, the state machine goes to state 0.

4   Locomotion Speed

In this section, we treat a theory on the theoretically maximum achievable locomotion speed of a crawling quadruped (straight movement only). For this theory,
we assume that a crawl gait is used (LF-RR-RF-LR, [4]).

Ideally, a quadruped is designed such that the rear leg that is maximally
moved forward can reach the same position as the corresponding front leg that
is maximally moved backward. When this is the case, we get consecutive support
patterns as shown in Fig. 9. In this image, l is the maximum step size of a leg.

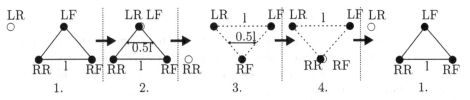

Fig. 9. Consecutive support patterns for a crawl gait when a rear leg, maximally
moved forward, can reach a front leg, maximally moved backward. The black filled
circles indicate support legs and the white filled circles indicate the leg that is going
to make the next step. The black triangles indicate the current support pattern.

Assuming that the CoM travels through the center of the support patterns,
in a straight line, two legs have to be moved while the CoM travels $0.5l$ meters.
This results in a maximum velocity of the CoM of:

$$V_{max} = \frac{l}{4 * t_{step}} \tag{1}$$

Where V_{max} is the maximum velocity of the CoM, l is the maximum step size
and t_{step} is the time it takes to make a step of length l.

It is important to realise that the body of the robot moves when a step is
made. For this reason, the actual size of a step is equal to the distance that the
body travelled plus the distance that the foot travelled with respect to the body:

$$l = l_{step} + t_{step} * V_{max} \tag{2}$$

such that, the actual maximum CoM velocity becomes:

$$V_{max} = \frac{l_{step}}{3 * t_{step}} \tag{3}$$

In reality, a rear leg that is maximally moved forward often can *not* reach the
same position as the corresponding front leg that is maximally moved backward.
This is also the case for our use case. This results in consecutive support patterns
as shown in Fig. 10. In this image, l is the maximum step size of a leg, d is the

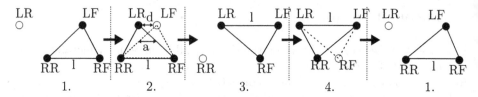

Fig. 10. Consecutive support patterns for a crawl gait when a rear leg, maximally moved forward, can not reach a front leg, maximally moved backward, by a distance d. The black filled circles indicate support legs and the white filled circles indicate the leg that is going to make the next step. The black triangles indicate the current support pattern.

distance between a rear leg's foremost position and a front leg's rearmost position and a is the distance that the CoM can travel while two legs are moved.

The distance a is shorter than $0.5 * l$, namely: $a = 0.5 * (l - d)$. This results in a maximum velocity of:

$$V_{max} = \frac{l - a}{4 * t_{step}} = \frac{l_{step} - a}{3 * t_{step}} \tag{4}$$

For our use case we have:

- $l_{step} = 0.51\ m$
- $t_{step} = 0.14\ s$
- $a = 0.08\ m$

such that we can theoretically achieve a locomotion velocity of:

$$V_{max} = \frac{l_{step} - a}{3 * t_{step}} = \frac{0.51 - 0.08}{3 * 0.14} = 1\ ms^{-1} \tag{5}$$

5   Simulation Results

In this section, we present the simulation results of the locomotion velocity with the simulated gait generator. To simulate the gait generator, a simplified robot model and controller structure are assumed. First of all, we assume that the robot is moving with a fixed velocity and that the "feet trajectory generators" and "Feet controllers" control the feet to move from their starting position to a desired foothold P in $t_{step} = (l_{step} + 0.2)/5$ (see also Sec. 2) where l_{step} is the size of the step. With these assumptions, the controlled system reduces to Fig. 11. To test the maximum velocity of the gait generator for omni-directional movement, simulation runs of 25 s were done to verify stability of the gait for:

1. Straight movement with various crab angles (Fig. 12a).
2. Turning movement, normal and crab-like with various turning radii (Fig. 12b and Fig. 12c).

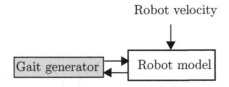

Fig. 11. An overview of the simplified system

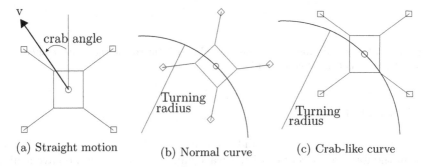

(a) Straight motion   (b) Normal curve   (c) Crab-like curve

Fig. 12. Motion types that are used to test the maximum velocity of the gait generator for omni-directional movement

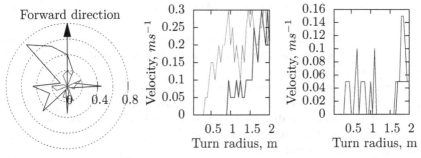

(a) Straight motion under various crab angles   (b) Normal turn with various radii.   (c) Crab turn with various radii.

Fig. 13. Simulation results with wave gait (blue) and with random gait (red)

The simulation results are shown in Fig. 13.

Since the simulation does not include any dynamic effects, no safety margin was used on the CoM location (Sec. 2). Doing so is expected to give the best performance: it is expected that including a safety margin causes a more conservative, and thus slower, gait to be generated. Furthermore, the starting position of the CoM in the support patters was moved 0.1 m to the rear as shown in Fig. 14. This is expected to cause the direction-dependent performance in the velocity of the gait.

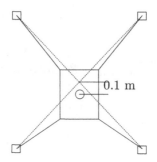

Fig. 14. In the simulations, the CoM was placed 0.1m to the rear with respect to the support patterns (initial condition)

6   Evaluation

In theory, we showed that we could achieve a velocity of 1 ms^{-1} for straight motion in the forward direction, with a wave gait. In simulations we have achieved velocities up to 0.75 ms^{-1} (Fig. 13a) with a wave gait, but not in the forward direction. In the forward direction we achieved 0.4 ms^{-1} (Fig. 13a). These results are in the same range as the results of Estremera and de Santos [2] for straight motion and 40% and 75%, respectively of the theoretically maximum achievable velocity.

It is shown in the simulations that, for straight motion, the overall velocity with a wave gait is significantly better than with a random gait, the latter showing a poor performance.

For strait motion we see a dependency on the crab angle, as expected. The high maximum velocity when moving at a crab angle of $\pi/4$ is curious. We noticed that the initial conditions have a significant effect on the ability of the gait generator to start a gait; we expect that this high velocity is due to a "lucky coincidence" of initial conditions.

The simulations show stable results for making a normal turn at a velocity of at least 0.1 ms^{-1} at a radius of more than 0.45 m (Fig. 13b). The performance for crab turns is too unpredictable to be useful (Fig. 13c). For turns, the performance of the wave gait is significantly worse than the random gait.

7   Conclusions

In this work, we have presented a controller structure in which we applied separation of concerns to address the complexity. In this controller we apply the gait generator of Estremera and de Santos [2]. We have presented theory on the maximum achievable velocity with a statically stable crawl gait and tested the maximum velocity of the gait generator for omni-directional movement resulting in 75% of the theoretical maximum.

The performance of the gait generator is strongly dependent on the crab angle. The highest performance is achieved at a crab angle of $\pi/4$.

Normal turns at low velocities are possible but crab turns show poor performance. The gait generator is partially capable of supporting omni-directional movement at satisfying velocities.

We want to apply the results of this paper in the control strategy by restricting the motion of the robot to velocities where the gait generator has a good performance. Furthermore, future work includes synthesis of the other components in the control strategy and experiments on a quadruped setup.

References

1. Arevalo, J.C., Garcia, E.: Impedance control for legged robots: An insight into the concepts involved (2012)
2. Estremera, J., de Santos, P.G.: Generating continuous free crab gaits for quadruped robots on irregular terrain. IEEE Transactions on Robotics 21(6), 1067–1076 (2005)
3. Hardarson, F.: Locomotion for difficult terrain. Tech. rep., Royal Institute of Technology, Stockholm (1997)
4. McGhee, R.B., Frank, A.A.: On the stability properties of quadruped creeping gaits. Mathematical Biosciences 3, 331–351 (1968)
5. McGhee, R.B., Iswandhi, G.I.: Adaptive locomotion of a multilegged robot over rough terrain. IEEE Transactions on Systems, Man and Cybernetics 9(4), 176–182 (1979)
6. Seeni, A., Schafer, B., Rebe, B.: Robot Mobility Concepts for Extraterrestrial Surface Exploration. Tech. rep., Institue of Robotics and Mechatronics, International space university, Wesseling, Illkirch Graffenstaden (2008)
7. Yoneda, K., Iiyama, H., Hirose, S.: Sky-hook suspension control of a quadruped walking vehicle. In: Proceedings of the 1994 IEEE International Conference on Robotics and Automation, pp. 999–1004. IEEE (1994)

Embodiment Sensing for Self-generated Zigzag Turning Algorithm Using Vision-Based Plume Diffusion

Jouh Yeong Chew, Takumi Yoshihara, and Daisuke Kurabayashi

Department of Mechanical and Control Engineering, Tokyo Institute of Technology,
2-12-1 Ookayama, Meguro-ku, 152-8552 Tokyo, Japan
{jychew,y.takumi,dkura}@irs.ctrl.titech.ac.jp

Abstract. Biomimetic Chemical Plume Tracing (CPT) problem is complex because it couples nonlinearity of biological systems with uncertainty of time-varying plume diffusion. A vision-based simulator is proposed to decouple these difficulties to facilitate multiple runs under controlled environment. This enables identification of efficient biological CPT algorithm. The simulator is used to simulate Embodiment Sensing (ES), i.e. sensing using physical attributes of animals. Wings and antennae of silk moth are used for ES, and evaluated for CPT using vision-based simulator. Results suggest (1) vision-based plume field mimics actual plume diffusion in terms intermittency, and (2) similar performance as that for surge-cast algorithm. The contribution is two-fold, (1) vision-based plume diffusion simulator decouples uncertainty of plume diffusion from nonlinearity of biological system to facilitate biomimetic CPT study, and (2) feasibility of using physical attributes of silk moth to achieve good CPT performance.

Keywords: Embodiment sensing, Bilateral sensing, Chemical plume tracing, Surge-cast, Vision-based plume diffusion.

1 Introduction

Efficient Chemical Plume Tracing (CPT) is important in search and rescue, security and safety operations by tracing and locating the source [1,2]. Research is ongoing with numerous methods being proposed for CPT. Amongst these, are methods using gas sensor networks [3], distributed robotics [4], fluid dynamics [5], and biomimetic algorithms [6,7,8,9,10,11,12]. CPT solutions based on biological systems are well-received because animals exhibit excellent olfaction as natural instinct. For example, foraging by ants [6] and mating by silk moths [7,8],[12,13].

However, most of these methods achieved limited performance. Previous studies reported the mediocre efficiency of the chemotaxis algorithm in identifying the plume source [10], and a separate study suggested the need to improve time and distance to target [13]. These limitations are reasonable due to the complex and intermittent nature of plume diffusion [11],[14]. In addition, there are limited details on how animals achieve efficient CPT in turbulent and time-varying environment because of the nonlinearity of biological systems [12].

D. Brugali et al. (Eds.): SIMPAR 2014, LNAI 8810, pp. 498–508, 2014.
© Springer International Publishing Switzerland 2014

Thus, it seems reasonable to solve the two difficulties independently. However, plume diffusion models are coupled with CPT algorithm in some of the previous studies, such as in infotaxis [9]. Other studies model the randomness of plume diffusion and use it for comparing different CPT algorithms [15]. This restricts performance in actual plume field, which is time-varying and provides ambiguity in identifying biological CPT algorithm, raising doubts on smooth shifting to real applications. This is one of the reasons some studies use experimental robotics to evaluate CPT algorithms [11],[16]. However, experimental robotics may not be the best choice when considering time and cost because large amount of data is required for correctly evaluating biological CPT behavior in a controlled environment.

A method to (1) decouple nonlinearity of biological systems from uncertainty of plume diffusion, and (2) facilitate multiple runs under controlled environment is desired to correctly identify the biological CPT algorithm. This paper proposes a novel method to achieve these functionalities. Biological CPT algorithm is evaluated through simulation using actual plume diffusion in laminar flow, which is recorded from a wind tunnel and processed using simple image processing methods to retain mass concentration gradient of its diffused particles. The simulator is used to realize Embodiment Sensing (ES) for silk moth's CPT, where its antennae and wings are used for detecting chemical particles. This is unlike casting, surge-cast and surge-spiral algorithms [11],[16] that use corrective algorithms with wind direction sensor.

There are numerous contributions from this proposal: (1) vision processing methods are used to retain intermittent diffusion of actual plume, which facilitates independent evaluation of biological CPT behavior, (2) it is possible to conduct multiple trials under similar environment with minimal cost and time compared to experimental robotics, (3) the difference in between simulation and real time experiment is minimized, allowing smooth shifting from simulations to real time applications, and (4) it is feasible to use ES to realize good result that is similar to previous algorithms.

2 Time-Variant Plume Diffusion Based on Image Subtraction

Study on CPT is not easy because its navigation path is dependent on intermittent [9] and highly time-variant [15] plume diffusion, which indirectly represents its target. The localized and random behavior of the plume presents additional uncertainty in the effort to decipher biological CPT algorithm. In this paper, vision processing method is used to obtain actual plume diffusion for the simulation platform to independently evaluate biological CPT behavior of the silk moth. This method reduces difference between actual and simulated plume and allows better observation on biological CPT behavior.

However, vision processing to detect plume diffusion is also not easy. This is primarily because of the translucent nature of plume. Although non-translucent plume can be used to represent plume diffusion, it is neither a trivial task to obtain infinitesimal pixels that represent mass concentration of diffused plume particles in the time domain. In addition, use of filters and morphological operations, has to be careful selected to retain these values. Thus, image subtraction method is used to extract actual plume diffusion. In short, it serves as foreground detector to detect time-variant plume and is advantageous compared to other foreground detectors because it extracts translucent plume and its infinitesimal pixels using minimum filters. This is feasible because the camera is stationary in a controlled environment, where only the plume travels.

Results are obtained by processing plume diffusion video offline. The primary reason is to use the same diffusion to investigate different CPT state variables of the moth. It is possible to conduct the procedure online because a region of interest (ROI) can be used to reduce the area for processing. Figure 1(a) shows one of the frames obtained from the video before the plume starts, i.e. $t = 0$ [s]. The resolution is 720x1280 pixels with an ROI of 200x800 pixels. Figure 1(b) shows experimental setup of the simple wind tunnel. Downwind speed in the x-axis is controlled by adjusting speed of the ventilator fan. Stimulus air inlet is controlled by a solenoid valve using parameters in Fig.1(c), i.e. activation duration d, and activation frequency f. An overhead camera captures the environment of the wind tunnel. Both are connected to a computer.

Plume source is fixed at ROI(100,1) and video sampling rate is 30 [fps], yielding $dt = 1/30$ [s] between each frame. The other parameters are (a) stimulus frequency, $f = 2$ [Hz], (b) ratio of pixel to millimeter, $scale = 1$, (c) $u = 0.625$ [m/s], and the plume is produced by titanium tetrachloride ($TiCl_4$) because of its opaqueness which enables visible plume diffusion. Algorithm 1 is used to process frames recorded from the setup to represent time-variant plume diffusion at i^{th} time-step as DF_i in the simulator. Basically, this section minimizes plume diffusion difference between simulator and actual environment. Next, it is feasible to decipher biological CPT algorithm.

Algorithm 1. Extraction of plume diffusion field based on image subtraction method

1. Mass concentration of diffused plume particles at i^{th} time step is represented by 8-bit unsigned integers of grayscale image pixels with resolution (jxk)
2. Region where plume travels is an ROI measuring (pxq), where $p \in j$ and $q \in k$
3. g frames at $t = 0$ [s] are averaged as the reference frame, $\hat{f}_0 = {}^1/_g \sum_{i=1}^g f_0^i$
4. Frame at i^{th} time step is grabbed from the video and represented as f_i
5. Corresponding plume diffusion at i^{th} time step is given by $df_i = f_i - \hat{f}_0$
6. "Open" morphological operation removes salt and pepper noise in df_i. The set operation $DF_i = (df_i \ominus B) \oplus B$ [17], B is the disk-shaped structuring element.

3   Embodiment Sensing for CPT

Male silk moth exhibits efficient CPT for mating and thus, is a suitable subject of study. It does not exhibit voluntary motion and is elicited by pheromone that is released by conspecific female. This provides clear relationship between olfactory input and behavioral output [12]. In previous studies [11],[15], experiments were conducted in wind tunnel to evaluate the performance of different CPT algorithms, i.e. surge-cast, surge-spiral and casting. Wind direction sensor was used to check the direction of wind when the plume is lost. However, from the perspective of embodiment intelligence, it is reasonable to use silk moth's physical features in Fig.1(d) to achieve efficient CPT. There are two distinctive features, i.e. antennae and wings, and their roles on CPT performance are evaluated using the simulator. This argument is further strengthen by the recent study [7], which suggested moth uses bilateral olfaction for navigation.

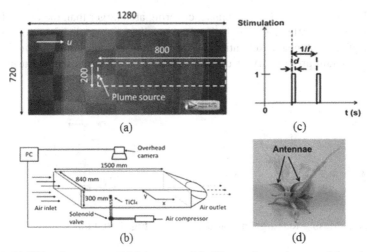

Fig. 1. (a) Video frame at $t = 0$ [s] (not to scale), (b) experimental setup of the wind tunnel, (c) parameters of stimulus input, and (d) distinctive features of silk moth

A separate study suggested the pair of wings is used for "sniffing" [18]. In the next subsections, these features are added to the simulation model for further investigation.

3.1   Antennae for Bilateral Sensing

This section proposes CPT algorithm using bilateral sensing. Binary plume information is used to obtain preliminary observation of its role. It is possible to extend the idea for gradient based bilateral sensing because plume diffusion field processed by Algorithm 1, represents particle mass concentration as 8-bit unsigned integers of each pixel for future work. The Self-generated Zigzag Turning (SZT) CPT behavior [8], which consists of sequential surge-zigzag-loop locomotion is slightly modified in this study. A small change in heading angle is added during surge and the modified SZT is referred to as MSZT in this paper. Figure 2 illustrates different cases of stimulation, where (a) and (c) represents states when either left or right antenna is stimulated. Stimulation of both antennae is represented by (b). This idea is supported by [12], where an inverse model is used to detect stimulus input timing based on locomotion data. The surge motion is trained using locomotion data with angular velocity smaller than 0.20 [rad/s]. The system achieved estimation accuracy higher than 70% that justifies the proposal.

3.2   Wings for "Sniffing"

It is worthy to note silk moths flap their wings and yet, they do not fly when stimulated. [18] suggested that this behavior is part of CPT sensing, where flapping wings create air velocity that is approximately 15 times higher than its walking speed to carry pheromone from anterior to posterior. The decreasing pheromone interception rate due to higher air velocity, is overwhelmed by higher number of pheromone carried to antennae per unit time. This enables moth to sample a larger area than the width of its antennae. This study considers the "sniffing" effect and proposes stimulation method as in Fig.3. The moth is stimulated by left and right ROI, which together, forms a cone-shaped region in front of the antennae, covering area larger than the one in Fig.2 to create the "sniffing" effect. The angle ϕ represents diverging angle of the cone and L is the width of the antennae. Activation of each region is represented by its binary information to obtain preliminary results and gradient-based activation is feasible for future work.

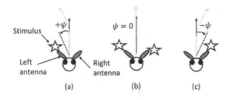
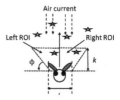

Fig. 2. Bilateral sensing for surge motion to realize ES

Fig. 3. ROI for "sniffing"

4   Simulation and Experimental Design

Subsection 4.1 discusses the MSZT algorithm. Settings of the simulation environment and the physical agent for experiment, is discussed in 4.2 and 4.3, respectively.

4.1   Modified Self-generated Zigzag Turning Algorithm

The proposed algorithm combines ES with MSZT behavior. When ROI of the physical agent is elicited by pheromone particles as in Fig.3, it moves straight with the ψ angle, depending on bilateral stimulation shown in Fig.2. As in Fig.4, this state continues for 0.5 [s], followed by zigzag turning, where the first, second and third turn takes 1.2, 1.9 and 2.1 [s], respectively. The final state loops for 360^0 until a new source is found. If the moth is elicited during this sequence, it will reset the behavior. The algorithm uses no additional sensor such as the wind direction sensor, and no corrective algorithms to reacquire the plume. The primary objective is to investigate feasibility of silk moth's embodiment intelligence for sensing and CPT. At this moment, CPT study focuses on plume tracking, notwithstanding source declaration and plume searching. This also allows comparison with [11] that has the similar focus.

4.2   Simulation Platform

Simulation of ES with MSZT algorithm in vision-based plume field is discussed in this section. Simulation environment is illustrated in Fig.5. At i^{th} time step, DF_i is superposed on navigation field F. Origin starts at top left corner, based on coordinate system of plume image. Plume source is fixed at F(200,200), where F(200,200) = ROI(100,1) and travels downwind to the right. Figure 5 is the simulation frame at $t = 0$ [s]. However, plume diffusion over n time steps, i.e. $S = \sum_{i=1}^{n} DF_i$ for $n = 1000$ [s] and $f = 1$ [Hz], is included for illustration and elaboration. Based on S in Fig.5, it is worthy to note, (1) decreasing gradient, (2) intermittent plume, at downwind position, which is consistent with the description by previous studies [11],[14]. There was turbulence at downwind position that is close to the outlet. This is reasonable due to the simple design of the wind tunnel, and is acceptable because it reflects the similarity of vision-based plume with the actual plume diffusion.

Initial agent position is F(200,1000), which is in the plume because this study focuses on plume tracking behavior. At this stage, plume search is excluded to eliminate high variance which could arise from randomized search techniques [11]. This provides clear results for ES in vision-based plume. Source declaration is done when the agent navigates close to the plume source, i.e. within radius r. Despite using ideal source declaration, integrity of simulation results for plume tracking is not affected. MSZT algorithm is simulated in three different vision-based plume diffusion fields. They are created using different f and determines amount of stimulus in the navigation path. Thus, it is possible to ascertain the performance of ES in challenging environments, i.e. when f is low or when there is less amount of stimulus on the way to plume source. Results for $\psi = \pm 5.0$ [°], L=20.0 [mm], and $\phi = 45.0$ [°], are shown in section 5.

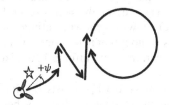

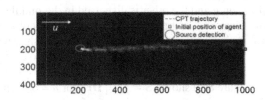

Fig. 4. MSZT   **Fig. 5.** Simulation environment

4.3   Design of Physical Agent

Simulation results are verified by localization of physical agent using same parameters in the same wind tunnel. CPT robot is modified from e-puck EPFL education robot and ethanol (C_2H_6O) is used as chemical source. Figure 6(a) shows the robot with two Catalytic Combustion gas sensors, which are activated by C_2H_6O. They are manufactured and sold by New Cosmos Electric Co. Ltd. The differential-driven robot corresponds to the CPT behavior of the silk moth. Design to enable bilateral sensing and "sniffing" is shown in Fig.6(b), which corresponds to highlighted area in Fig.6(a). Sensors are placed in two individual tubes with ventilation fans at the end of each. Air is drawn from robot's anterior to posterior at higher velocity, which is consistent with [18]. Higher velocity carries more chemical particles per unit time to the sensors. This effect is similar to enlarged ROI in Fig.3 and localization results are shown in section 5.

5   Results and Discussion

Section 5.1 discusses validity of vision-based plume diffusion and its efficiency for representing actual plume diffusion. 5.2 focuses on simulation and experiment results of proposed algorithm. 5.3 discusses results in 5.2 compared to previous study.

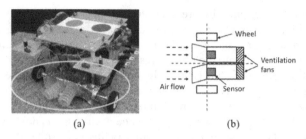

(a)   (b)

Fig. 6. (a) CPT robot, and (b) design for ES

5.1   Vision-Based Plume Diffusion

These parameters are used to obtain plume diffusion from wind tunnel. Original resolution, i.e. $(jxk) = (720x1280)$, is reduced to $(pxq) = (200x800)$, and $g = 10$. Figure 7(a) shows grayscale image after step 1-2 of Algorithm 1 prior to stimulus input, i.e. f_0. (b) shows f_{20} for $f=2$ [Hz]. Two localized plumes are highlighted. One is concentrated near the source and the other is dispersed in the middle. (c) and (d) are the same except that the former is in grayscale and the latter in color. (c) shows pixels with infinitesimal values in highlighted area. These pixels are shown as contour plot in (d) and compared to (b). Both (b) and (d) seem to correspond to each other, implying infinitesimal pixels belong to diffused plume.

Figure 8(a) shows $\mathbf{S} = \sum_{i=1}^{n} \mathbf{DF}_i$ for $n = 60$, which suggests $\mathbf{DF}_i$ consists of salt and pepper noise. (b) shows image after "open" operation. Despite significantly better results, there are some white dots. This is acceptable to avoid eroding infinitesimal pixels that represent mass concentration of diffused plume particles. Results suggest plume diffusion can be represented by 8-bit unsigned integers. This representation is significant for infinitesimal mass concentration when plume diffuses and its translucency increases in time domain, as in Fig.7. In short, it is feasible to use Algorithm 1 to obtain time-varying plume diffusion that is almost similar to captured image for simulating biological CPT behavior. This reduces uncertainty of time-varying plume diffusion and allows smooth shifting from simulation to real applications.

5.2   Simulation and Experiment of Single Source Localization

This subsection shows simulation and experiment results for single source localization using proposed algorithm. Agent's velocity is fixed at 30 [mm/s] and parameters in section 4.2 are used to navigate to the source, where $r = 20$ [mm]. Three varying vision-based plume diffusion environments are used, i.e. continuous stimulus input, $f = 2$ [Hz], and $f = 1$ [Hz]. This evaluates performance of proposed algorithm in challenging environments when amount of stimulus in navigation path varies with f. Five trials are run for each condition for simulations and experiments. Results are summarized in Fig.9.

The evaluation parameters are, (1) success rate, (2) time from initial position to plume source T, and (3) distance overhead D, which is ratio of traveled distance over upwind distance [11]. Evaluation of D reflects CPT efficiency and allows comparison with previous study. When the agent did not successfully reach the plume source within 1000 [s], T and D are N/A. Fig.9(a) shows success rate of simulation and experiment

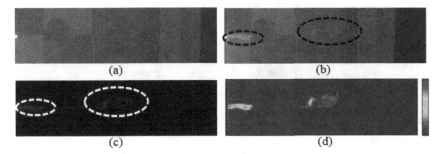

Fig. 7. (a) ROI of f_0 prior to stimulus input, (b) f_{20}, and DF_{20} for (c) grayscale (d) color plot

Fig. 8. S when $n = 60$, (a) no morphological operation, and (b) with "open" operation

results. Similarly, T and D is given in (b) and (c), respectively. Each cluster of bars consists of three components, which represent results for different stimulus input environment, i.e. continuous, 2 [Hz], and 1 [Hz].

Success rate, T, and D for different stimulus input environment show similar pattern, where it performs the best for continuous, and followed by 2 [Hz] and 1 [Hz]. This pattern is reasonable, considering amount of stimulus present in the wind tunnel. As in the case of 1 [Hz], which is considered the extreme case in this paper, lower amount of stimulus in the environment increases probability of agent losing the plume. It is worth noting that the proposed algorithm does not consider any corrective algorithm and additional sensors to reacquire the plume because the objective is to evaluate plume tracking ability of ES. Despite that, performance for continuous and 2 [Hz] in both simulations and experiments is good. Next, this result is compared with those in previous study, i.e. surge-cast algorithm, to evaluate the feasibility of CPT based on ES.

5.3   Discussion

Section 5.1 suggests vision-based plume diffusion from Algorithm 1 mimics actual diffusion in terms of gradient and plume intermittency at downwind position. This is consistent with previous studies [11],[14]. It is also able to detect infinitesimal pixels that represent mass concentration of diffused plumes. Vision-based plume diffusion model decouples nonlinearity of biological systems from uncertainty of plume diffusion and facilitates multiple runs under controlled environment to identify effect of ES for CPT. This minimizes uncertainty of plume diffusion compared to actual environment and allows smooth shifting from simulation to real application.

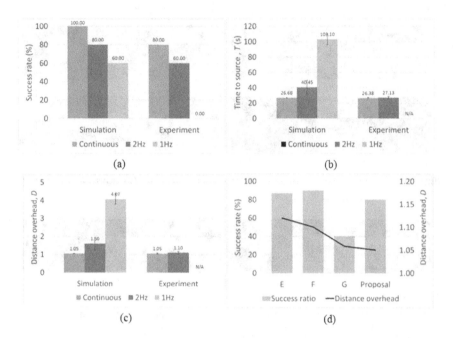

Fig. 9. (a) Success rate, (b) T, (c) D, for simulations and experiments, and (d) Comparison of proposed algorithm with surge-cast algorithm

It is worth looking into the cause of significant difference between simulation and experiment, i.e. 60% against 0% in Fig.9(a). This is caused by downwind airflow during localization experiment, which is not considered when modeling the "sniffing" feature. If agent's heading is in crosswind direction, chemical particles are carried by stronger downwind airflow. However, if agent's heading is in the upwind direction, it is easier to draw in chemical particles, and ventilation effect is boosted by downwind airflow that is in the same direction, thus increasing effectiveness of drawing in more chemical particles. This is evident when T and D in Fig.9(b) and (c) shows only slightly better performance for continuous compared to 2 [Hz] in experiments.

Comparison of proposed algorithm with previous CPT algorithms [11] is possible using success rate and D. Localization results for surge-cast algorithm, which performed the best in [11], is reproduced in Fig.9(d). Success rate on left axis is represented by bars and D on right axis is represented by line. Cases E, F, and G are results for surge-cast algorithm when agent travels different crosswind distance to reacquire plume using wind direction sensor [11]. The last case represents experiment result of using continuous stimulus input, as in Fig.9(a) to (c). This is similar to stimulus input in [11].

Results suggest success rate of proposed algorithm is close to that of E and F. In terms of D, proposed algorithm performed better. In general, results in Fig.9(d) suggest similar performance when compared with surge-cast algorithm. However, it is worth noting this is achieved using only ES with MSZT algorithm. There is no corrective algorithm and wind direction sensor to reacquire the plume. Thus, preliminary results of ES suggest its feasibility for improving CPT algorithms. In short, reliability of vision-based plume diffusion model and its advantages is discussed in the first paragraph of this subsection. Then, comparison is made to determine feasibility of ES for CPT relative to previous algorithms.

6 Conclusion

Vision-based plume diffusion model provides a platform to experiment with different CPT parameters to decipher biological CPT algorithm. This method is promising because it retains infinitesimal mass concentration of diffused particles. Preliminary simulation and experiment results suggest its potential for improving CPT performance. Similar performance as those of other algorithms, i.e. surge-cast, casting, and surge-spiral, are achieved. For future work, it is practical to further confirm results using extensive experiments, improve the "sniffing" design, and investigate the use of plume diffusion gradient to realize efficient biological CPT.

Acknowledgements. The authors would like to thank Professor Ryohei Kanzaki for allowing access to the wind tunnel in his laboratory for recording plume diffusion videos. This study was partially supported by Grants-in-Aid for Scientific Research, MEXT Japan [25420212].

References

1. Settles, G.S.: Sniffers: Fluid dynamic sampling for olfactory trace detection in nature and homeland security. J. Fluids Eng. 127, 189–218 (2005)
2. Ishida, H., Nakamoto, T., Moriizumi, T., Kikas, T., Janata, J.: Plume-tracking robots: A new application of chemical sensors. Biological Bulletin 200, 222–226 (2001)
3. Trincavelli, M., Coradeschi, S., Loutfi, A.: Classification of odors with mobile robots based on transient response. In: IEEE/RSJ Int. Conf. Intelligent Robots and Systems, pp. 4110–4115. IEEE Press, New York (2008)
4. Liu, Z.Z.: Odor source localization using multiple plume-tracking mobile robots. Ph.D dissertation, Dept. Mech. Eng., Univ. Adelaide, Australia (2010)
5. Zarzhitsky, D., Spears, D., Thayer, D., Spears, W.: Agent-based chemical plume tracing using fluid dynamics. In: Hinchey, M.G., Rash, J.L., Truszkowski, W.F., Rouff, C.A. (eds.) FAABS 2004. LNCS (LNAI), vol. 3228, pp. 146–160. Springer, Heidelberg (2005)
6. Meng, Q.H., Yang, W.X., Wang, Y., Li, F., Zeng, M.: Adapting an ant colony metaphor for multi-robot chemical plume tracing. Sensors 12, 4737–4763 (2012)
7. Ando, N., Emoto, S., Kanzaki, R.: Odor-tracking capability of a silkmoth driving a mobile robot with turning bias and time delay. Bioinspir. Biomim. 8, 1–14 (2013)
8. Kanzaki, R., Sugi, N., Shibuya, T.: Self-generated zigzag turning of Bombyx Mori males during pheromone-mediated upwind walking. Zool. Sci. 9, 515–527 (1992)
9. Vergassola, M., Villermaux, E., Shraiman, B.I.: 'Infotaxis' as a strategy for searching without gradients. Nature 445, 406–409 (2007)
10. Russell, R.A., Bab-Hadiashar, A., Shepherd, R.L., Wallace, G.G.: A comparison of reactive robot chemotaxis algorithms. Robotics and Autonomous Systems 45, 83–97 (2003)

11. Lochmatter, T., Martinoli, A.: Tracking odor plumes in a laminar wind field with bio-inspired algorithms. In: Khatib, O., Kumar, V., Pappas, G.J. (eds.) Experimental Robotics. STAR, vol. 54, pp. 473–482. Springer, Heidelberg (2009)

12. Chew, J.Y., Kurabayashi, D.: Quantitative analysis of the silk moth's chemical plume tracing locomotion using a hierarchical classification method. J. Bionic Eng. 2, 268–281 (2014)

13. Li, W., Farrell, J.A., Pang, S., Arrieta, R.M.: Moth-inspired chemical plume tracing on an autonomous underwater vehicle. IEEE Transactions on Robotics 22, 292–307 (2006)

14. Pang, S., Farrell, J.A.: Chemical Plume Source Localization. IEEE Transactions on Systems, Man, and Cybernetics, Part B: Cybernetics 36, 1068–1080 (2006)

15. Li, J.G., Yang, J., Cui, S.G., Geng, L.H.: Speed limitation of a mobile robot and methodology of tracing odor plume in airflow environments. Procedia Eng. 15, 1041–1045 (2011)

16. Harvey, D.J., Lu, T.F., Keller, M.A.: Comparing insect-inspired chemical plume tracking algorithms using a mobile robot. IEEE Trans. Robot. 24, 307–317 (2008)

17. Serra, J.: Image analysis and mathematical morphology. Academic Press, USA (1983)

18. Loudon, C., Koehl, M.A.R.: Sniffing by a silkworm moth: wing fanning enhances air penetration through and pheromone interception by antennae. Journal of Experimental Biology 203, 2977–2990 (2000)

Handling of Asynchronous Data Flow
in Robot Perception Subsystems

Maciej Stefańczyk and Tomasz Kornuta

Warsaw University of Technology, Institute of Control and Computation Eng.
Nowowiejska 15/19 00-665 Warsaw, Poland
{M.Stefanczyk,T.Kornuta}@ia.pw.edu.pl

Abstract. Robot perception subsystems typically form complex networks, with boxes representing computations and arrows presenting the exchanged data. Taking into account that data acquired from robot sensors may arrive with different frequencies, as well as that computations may by performed on different processor cores, a problem of handling of asynchronous data flows appears. Hence appropriate tools facilitating the implementation are highly demanded. In this article we propose a solution to the aforementioned problem, enabling the activation of a conditional behaviour of a given computational block, depending on the presence of data in its input buffers. Theoretical considerations led to the implementation of these mechanisms in a component-oriented framework for development of robot perception subsystems: DisCODe. Operation of the solution was verified on an exemplary perception subsystem using RGB-D camera.

Keywords: robot, perception, component, framework, DisCODe, asynchronous data flow.

1 Introduction

1.1 Motivation of the Work

Service robots are designed to work in human-oriented environment. To cope with unstructured and dynamic nature of such an environment, the robots must be equipped with a multitude of sensors and modules able to aggregate and process the received data. Those measurements can be acquired from diverse sensors, typically having different work-cycles. Such an example is the fusion of data acquired from an RGB-D camera and a laser range finder, as described in [1]. Besides that, the data processing and aggregation might consist of several complex procedures, executed in an appropriate order. This is especially visible in the case of machine vision-based perception subsystems. Additionally, in order to fulfil the real-time requirements and to make implementation easier and more modular, it is a common practice to use multi-threading. Those facts imply that the data processing and aggregation typically form quite complex graphs. Hence mechanisms for the implementation of computational blocks, facilitating the synchronization of asynchronously incoming data, are highly desirable.

D. Brugali et al. (Eds.): SIMPAR 2014, LNAI 8810, pp. 509–520, 2014.

1.2   Article Structure

The article is structured as follows. Section 2 describes the problem of handling of asynchronous data flow and presents how the state-of-the-art robotic frameworks cope with it. In section 3 we present the proposed solution and put the emphasis on data synchronisation and selection of proper activation function according to available (fresh) data. Next we present the DisCODe framework followed by description of examples validating our approach. Article ends with conclusions and future work plans presented in section 4.

2   Problem Formulation

2.1   Asynchronous Data Flow Handling

Aggregation of sensory data requires a series of computations, sometimes very complex. That is why decomposition of whole process into smaller, easier to define and implement blocks is necessary. Apart from mere definition of those blocks, one has to define connections between them to pass data. Whole perception process can be thus presented as a graph, in which nodes represent computational blocks and data flow between them is presented with arcs. Denoting set of computational blocks as B and connections between them as C, perception task T is defined as:

$$T = \langle B, C, f \rangle, \text{ where } C \subset B \times B \text{ and } f : C \to \mathbb{N}, \tag{1}$$

where f determines the multiplicity of connections between given two blocks. Figure 1 shows exemplary processing pipeline. Particular blocks and connections are denoted with indices.

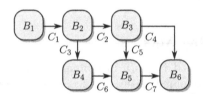

Fig. 1. Exemplary computational flow

There can be two buffer types defined for each j-th computational block B_j: input $_xB_j$ and output $_yB_j$. Additionally, each block can have internal buffer (memory) $_mB_j$ for storing data during processing. Computational block operation in i-th step can be defined in a form of transition function f_j, which, based on data read from input and internal buffers, computes the result and stores it in output buffers and/or updates the internal memory (fig. 2):

$$\left[_mB_j^{i+1}, \, _yB_j^{i+1} \right] := f_j \left(_mB_j^i, \, _xB_j^i \right). \tag{2}$$

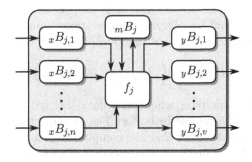

Fig. 2. General structure of j-th computational block

The presence of multiple input buffers of a given computational block imposes that it might possess different working modes, depending on the data available. Hence decomposition of transition function into set of simpler functions, activated in a case when required data is present, can greatly improve description of variant system behaviours. Subset $_xB_{j,\kappa} = \left[_xB_{j,k[1]}, _xB_{j,k[2]}, \ldots\right]$ denotes a subset of input buffers from the set $_xB_j$, consisting of buffers that must contain (fresh) data required for the correct evaluation of k-th variant of transition function. Analogically, $_yB_{j,\kappa}$ denotes a subset of output buffers $_yB_j$ which values will be computed by k-th function. This leads to following definition of k-th variant transition function (fig. 3):

$$\left[_mB_j^{i+1}, _yB_{j,\kappa}^{i+1}\right] := f_{j,k}\left(_mB_j^i, _xB_{j,\kappa}^i\right), \quad k = 1, \ldots, n_{f_j}, \tag{3}$$

where n_{f_j} is the number of variant functions of j-th computational block.

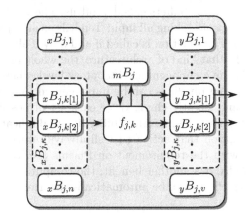

Fig. 3. The structure of j-th computational block with k-th variant transition function dependent elements highlighted

When variant functions are defined, next step is to define their activation condition. Assuming, that for carrying computations input buffers must contain data, activation condition of variant function (3) can be defined as a predicate:

$$P^i_{j,k}\left(xB^i_{j,\kappa}\right) = \exists\left(xB^i_{j,k[1]}\right) \wedge \exists\left(xB^i_{j,k[2]}\right) \wedge \ldots, \tag{4}$$

where $\exists$ operator returns true, when fresh data (i.e. not used in evaluation of any other function) is available in buffer. The aforementioned condition (4) is necessary for determination whether the computation can be performed or not, but does not indicate the order of the execution of variant functions in the case when more than one of them can be activated. We describe the possible solutions of the stated problem in the selected state-of-the-art robotic frameworks in the following section.

2.2 Related Work

Orocos. In OROCOS (Open RObot COntrol Software) [2], there are no specialized methods aiding variant data processing, i.e. the programmer on his own is responsible for creation of the proper mechanisms of queueing and for calling the required transition functions. State of input buffers can be checked using either callback functions connected with new data arriving to buffer, or inside *updateHook()* method, which is called in every execution loop of a component. The biggest problem is to differentiate between data in ports used in the same *updateHook()* or in previous component step, which is sometimes useful. It is not possible to fully remove data from buffer without extending Orocos mechanisms.

Ecto. In Ecto framework [3] the basic processing unit is called Cell. Each Cell has a set of input and output buffers called Tendrils. The whole cell is equivalent to single transition function, taking all input Tendrils as an input, and producing output on all outputs. The function is called if and only if all of the input buffers are filled with data. In that kind of architecture, the whole problem described in this article is moved from component level to a task level, where some alternative variants of the processing pipelines can be implemented. As a result some Cells must be duplicated and slightly changed for each set of possible input buffers, which could result in poor code maintainability due to duplication. On the other hand, such an assumption that activated Cell always returns data on every of its output together with the requirement on Plasms (i.e. tasks in Ecto) being directed, acyclic graphs, has another benefit: the computation order of all Cells constituting the given Plasm can be automatically determined once, at the start of the system.

ROS. Robot Operating System (ROS) [4] offers more advanced synchronisation mechanisms for calling transition functions for handling data incoming to a given processing block (called Node) through communication channels (Topics). In ROS it is possible to define a single callback function, dependent on multiple topics, which will be activated when messages in associated topics will fulfil the particular requirements. Those rules of activation can be set manually by programmer; however, there are also two predefined conditions: the function is called if all received messages have exactly the same timestamp, or when it differs at most by a defined interval. However, the order of execution in the case of several processing modes (transition functions) is undefined. And even more – it is not possible to simply check whether data from the message passed to a function was already used in any other function during same processing step. This behaviour significantly hinders the implementation of alternative processing pipelines in ROS.

3   Proposed Solution

3.1   DisCODe Framework

The core of DisCODe framework (Distributed Component Oriented Data Processing) was written in C++, and its implementation utilizes mostly three main paradigms: component-oriented programming [5], reflection [6] and generic programming [7]. Combination of aforementioned paradigms resulted in creation of mechanisms allowing to decompose virtually any perception process into directed graph of independent, but cooperating, components. Components are grouped into separate component libraries (DCL – DisCODe Component Library), each connected with some specific subset of sensory data processing. Mechanisms of loading components, passing data between them, executing actions and managing execution threads are provided by framework, along with additional tools prepared to speed up creation process of new components and libraries and, also, manage running perception tasks and dynamically change their properties.

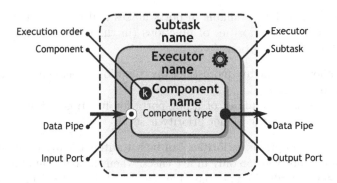

Fig. 4. Graphical representation of the major elements of the DisCODe task

As it was mentioned before, steps of perception tasks are implemented as separate components, managed by various execution threads (called executors) and communicating with each other via data streams. Fig. 4 introduces the graphical notation corresponding to those elements. Such a decomposition simplifies task parallelization, which could e.g. speed up the whole process. There are, however, no mechanisms enabling automatic decomposition into processing threads. Hence the user must explicitly define (in task definition file) number of threads and assign components executed in them. Above executors, in task hierarchy, there are subtasks. It is a mechanism for organization and managing execution threads, which allows to start and stop groups of components, thus effectively change processing pipeline at runtime. It enables robot control subsystem to change behaviours of perception subsystem according to current needs.

3.2   Transition Function Activation

Every component can possess a set of input data ports (to receive data) and output ports (to send processing results). Actual processing is done inside transition functions (fig. 5), which takes selected input ports as an arguments and produces values for output ports. Activation of selected function depends on data availability in input ports and function priority.

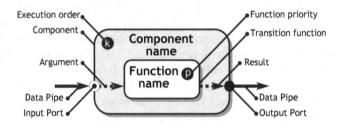

Fig. 5. Major elements of the DisCODe component

It is possible, that data available in ports makes multiple functions possible to activate, that is why priorities of functions (in the context of components) were set, with some assumptions:

- it is not allowed to define more than one function dependent on the same subset of input ports,
- priority depends on number of input ports for function – the more ports function depends on the higher priority is set.

Based on those assumptions, priorities can be set automatically in many cases, requiring manual intervention only in few cases, when the same number of input ports is used across multiple functions. This can be achieved by defining relative priorities during component definition. At this point, with functions sorted by priorities, operation of the component can be presented as an automation, in which activation conditions are checked until one method is activated. In most of the cases, function will consume data from input ports, thus disabling them from further checking in other functions. There is, however, possibility to define function dependent on some port, which doesn't use those data, just taking some action when it is available. In this case, data is still available in port, allowing other functions depending on this port to be activated during the same component processing loop. If there are no more functions ready to be activated, execution thread moves to next component or suspends until new data is available (if there are no components to be activated).

Whole process described earlier abstracts from all aspects of scheduling on OS level. To prevent starvation (known problem in multi-threaded software) during single processing loop in component each function is tried once to activate (in order depending on priorities), and after checking all functions system moves to another component. There is, however, no automatic mechanism for scheduling components inside single execution thread. Task of proper ordering (defined in task file) lies on the user completely.

3.3   Example: Multimodal Segmentation

As an example of task, in which aforementioned approach is used, we present multimodal segmentation of dense depth maps with associated color information [8]. The aim of this task is to segment objects in image composed from multiple pictures, aligned with each other, e.g. RGB image, depth map, normal map. The necessity of using multiple criterions for assigning points to clusters is clearly visible on fig. 6. Using only colour will make it impossible to differentiate white objects lying on paper, using only depth will make it hard to distinguish between objects lying one on top of another, and using only normal direction as a discriminator would result in merging objects with same direction of walls, but placed far from each other.

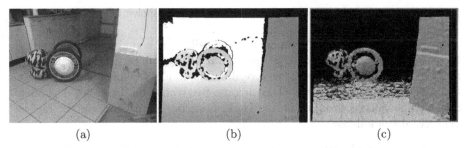

(a)   (b)   (c)

Fig. 6. Sample input images for multimodal segmentation: (a) RGB image (b) depth map (c) normal map

Our point similarity function (5) has four parameters, defining how close each of components has to be in both pixels, T_C, T_D and T_N, where C stands for normalized RGB color, D for depth and N for normal vector, respectively:

$$S(p_x, p_y) = \text{FUN} \left(\frac{d_C(p_x, p_y)}{T_C}, \frac{d_D(p_x, p_y)}{T_D}, \frac{d_N(p_x, p_y)}{T_N} \right) \tag{5}$$

The final value can be calculated by substituting FUN with either *sum* or *max* function, each giving slightly different results. Distances are calculated by associated *d* functions. Color comparison is done by calculating Euclidean distance between the normalized RGB values (i.e. R/L, G/L, B/L, where L means luminance) of both points, and T_C is the maximum allowed difference. The position distance of points is calculated also as an Euclidean distance between their 3D coordinates, and T_D is expressed in meters. Normal vectors are compared by angle between them, with T_N being maximum allowed angle deviation.

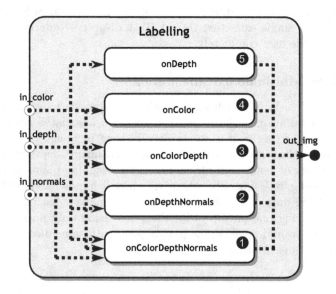

Fig. 7. Structure of the Labelling component

In presented task, main component responsible for actual labelling of points to cluster them into segments, is called **Labelling**. Its structure is shown on fig. 7. Three main input ports receive different modalities of processed image: RGB, depth and normal map. There are also five transition functions, dependent on different subsets of input ports. Those functions, in order from the highest priority, are as follows:

- **processColorDepthNormals** – all modalities are available, thus we use most advanced labelling technique,
- **processColorDepth** – normal map is unavailable, for example standard input from Kinect,
- **processDepthNormals** – no RGB image is unavailable, for example scans from tilting laser with computed normal vectors,
- **processColor** – only RGB image is available, processing falls back to standard color image labelling,
- **processDepth** – only depth image is available, processing works as depth discontinuity detector.

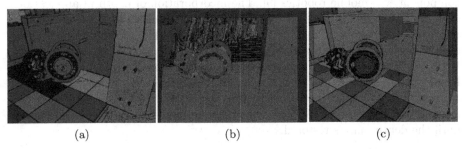

(a)   (b)   (c)

Fig. 8. Sample output images with labels for multimodal segmentation: (a) only color image is available (b) only depth images are available (c) color, depth and normal maps available

Cases with normal image available without depth image are left, because every time, if we have normals computed, those are based on depth image, thus depth would be also available.

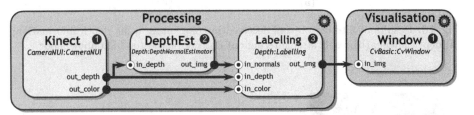

Fig. 9. Task responsible for display of point clouds acquired from the Kinect sensor

All functions of presented component produce the same type of output – image with pixels colored according to labels for every pixel. This image is then used as an input in actual segmentation, which produces a set of segments extracted from input data based on given labels. Figure 8 presents sample results for different inputs available (thus different functions were called). It is worth noting, that functions in presented component are designed in a way, that only one at a time can be called and there is no possibility of producing output image more than once, as it could badly influence further processing (many differently labelled images available at the same time). Structure of whole segmentation task is presented on fig. 9. Color image aquired by Kinect camera is directly passed to Labelling component, depth image is passed to both Labelling and DepthEst, which estimates normal vectors, passed as third input to Labelling. Labelled image is then simply displayed.

3.4 Robotic Applications

The presented above task is rather simple and was created only as an example use case for Labelling component. A proper, more complex application of this component was mobile robotics [9]. The incorporation of depth in applications such as detection of objects for automated cleaning tasks gave good results and improved overall robotic task performance for example by locating unreachable objects without the need of driving near them (fig. 10). The advantage of utilization of the developed mechanisms for automatic mode (transition function-based) switching was that when the depth information was not available (even temporary, due to e.g. improper lighting conditions) the whole task switched automatically into standard, color based mode, and the continued recognition until the depth map is restored.

(a)   (b)

Fig. 10. Results of filtering objects detected in color image using depth information; (a) depth image, (b) result after filtering out objects placed too high above floor

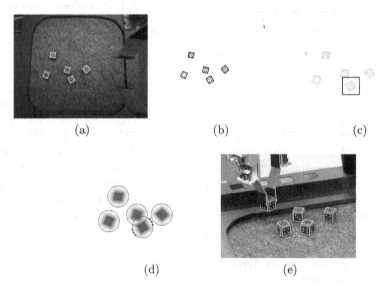

(a)   (b)   (c)

(d)   (e)

Fig. 11. Selection of the dice to be acquired: (a) image retrieved from the camera, (b) image with the contours extracted, (c) selection of the dice, (d) determination of the possible grasping poses, (e) the gripper holding the acquired dice

Besides that, DisCODe, playing the role of a vision subsystem of MRROC++ based controllers [10,11], has been successfully used in a number of robotic systems. Worth noting examples include: a robot playing a game of dice (where the DisCODe-based vision subsystem was responsible for the analysis of the game state as well as for the localization of dices for their subsequent grasping, as presented in fig. 11), construction of desired structures out of a set of bricks or a system proactively recognizing operator hand postures [12] (fig. 12).

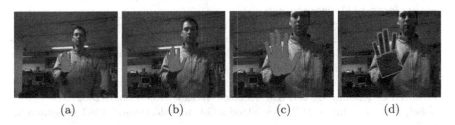

(a)   (b)   (c)   (d)

Fig. 12. Stages of the active hand pose recognition: (a-c) approach the hand-like object, (d) pose identification

4   Conclusion

The article focused on data processing in complex systems, such as robots perception subsystems. We proposed to decompose the processing pipelines into a network of computational blocks and indicated a problem of variant data processing appearing in the case of asynchronously incoming data. Based on the short survey of state-of-the-art robotic frameworks we proposed a solution implemented in the DisCODe framework. The developed solution was successfully utilized in several perception subsystems, however, in this paper we focused on one of them: multimodal segmentation of RGB-D images.

It is worth noting that prioritization is not the only possible mechanism for selection of transition functions based on data availability in buffers. In particular, we also considered an approach in which user would have to define the full automata describing functions called for every possible combination of data presence/absence in all buffers. It would be, however, rather cumbersome. For the component with five inputs, functions should be assigned to each of the $2^5 = 32$ combinations. In the case of automatic prioritization, user has to resolve manually only few ambiguities (the same number of buffers as input to function).

Acknowledgments. Authors acknowledge the support of National Science Centre, Poland via the grant number DEC-2012/05/D/ST6/03097. The authors would like to thank to Tomek Pokorski and Kasia Wasak for their help and the permission to use the images taken during the execution of the selected robotic applications using DisCODe framework.

References

1. Stefańczyk, M., Banachowicz, K., Walęcki, M., Winiarski, T.: 3D camera and lidar utilization for mobile robot navigation. Journal of Automation Mobile Robotics and Intelligent Systems 7(4), 27–33 (2013)
2. Bruyninckx, H.: The real-time motion control core of the OROCOS project. In: Proceedings of the IEEE International Conference on Robotics and Automation, pp. 2766–2771. IEEE (September 2003)
3. Willow Garage: Website of the Ecto framework for perception (2011), http://ecto.willowgarage.com
4. Quigley, M., Gerkey, B., Conley, K., Faust, J., Foote, T., Leibs, J., Berger, E., Wheeler, R., Ng, A.: ROS: An open-source Robot Operating System. In: Proceedings of the Open-Source Software Workshop at the International Conference on Robotics and Automation, ICRA (2009)
5. Szyperski, C., Gruntz, D., Murer, S.: Component Software: Beyond Object-Oriented Programming, 2nd edn. Addison-Wesley Professional (2002)
6. Sobel, J.M., Friedman, D.P.: An introduction to reflection-oriented programming (1996)
7. Alexandrescu, A.: Modern C++ Design: Generic Programming and Design Patterns Applied. Addison-Wesley Professional (2001)
8. Stefańczyk, M., Kasprzak, W.: Multimodal segmentation of dense depth maps and associated color information. In: Bolc, L., Tadeusiewicz, R., Chmielewski, L.J., Wojciechowski, K. (eds.) ICCVG 2012. LNCS, vol. 7594, pp. 626–632. Springer, Heidelberg (2012)
9. Stefańczyk, M., Bojar, K., Kasprzak, W.: Utilization of depth and color information in mobile robotics. In: Burduk, R., Jackowski, K., Kurzynski, M., Wozniak, M., Zolnierek, A. (eds.) CORES 2013. AISC, vol. 226, pp. 845–854. Springer, Heidelberg (2013)
10. Zieliński, C., Szynkiewicz, W., Winiarski, T., Staniak, M., Czajewski, W., Kornuta, T.: Rubik's cube as a benchmark validating MRROC++ as an implementation tool for service robot control systems. Industrial Robot: An International Journal 34(5), 368–375 (2007)
11. Zieliński, C., Winiarski, T.: Motion generation in the MRROC++ robot programming framework. International Journal of Robotics Research 29(4), 386–413 (2010)
12. Kornuta, T., Zieliński, C.: Behavior-based control system of a robot actively recognizing hand postures. In: 15th IEEE International Conference on Advanced Robotics, ICAR, pp. 265–270 (June 2011)

Design of a Healthcare Sensor Managing System for Vital Sign Measuring Devices

Min Ho Lee, Ho Seok Ahn, Kevin Wang, and Bruce A. Macdonald

Department of Electrical and Computer Engineering,
CARES, University of Auckland, Auckland, New Zealand
mlee242@aucklanduni.ac.nz,
{hs.ahn,kevin.wang,b.macdonald}@auckland.ac.nz

Abstract. In this paper, we present a healthcare sensor managing system that manages healthcare sensor devices in a distributed environment. It is an independent system, but can cooperate by wireless communication with client systems, such as robots and smart phones. We have designed five key concepts of our sensor managing system including plug and play, status managing, scheduling of requests, expandability, and compatibility. We have developed a sensor managing system based on our design concepts, and applied this system to a healthcare application. It consists of three parts: a healthcare robot system, a sensor manager system, and sensor device systems. It can be applied in various use case scenarios for heterogeneous devices, between single and multiple clients. To verify the efficiency of our system, we report functionality experiments focusing on each of the five key concepts.

Keywords: Healthcare robot system, vital sign measuring system, sensor managing system, healthcare robot, caring of older adults, health condition management.

1 Introduction

The global population of older adults is on the rise in many parts of the world [1]. Many researchers are developing healthcare technologies to address this increasing need to support people. Wearable physiological monitoring systems monitor the health status of the human user who wears the system, for example, AMON, and CodeBlue [2-3]. Most of these systems use wireless sensor networks, and some health monitoring systems are already commercialized, but have not been applied to robot systems. Robots are also being included in healthcare system design. Some robot systems help people with physical aspects of healthcare, for example RIMAN helps nurses or family members to lift patients safely [4]. Some robots are used for helping people with dementia [5] and autism [6], and some robots have the role of doctors or nurses under remote teleoperation by the doctor or nurse [7-8].

In our previous work, we have developed a homecare service robot that includes a medication reminding function for the elderly and a caregiver robot which guides how to measure vital signs, illustrated in Fig. 1 [9-11, 25]. We undertook clinical trials in

D. Brugali et al. (Eds.): SIMPAR 2014, LNAI 8810, pp. 521–532, 2014.
© Springer International Publishing Switzerland 2014

real environments, such as hospitals, rest homes, and a retirement village [11-13, 26-28]. In our study, we found that robots are effective for giving healthcare service to the elderly although the acceptance of robot's reactions is different for cultural background, gender, age, and job [14-17]. Moreover our healthcare robot and applications are helpful to older adults. Especially, medication schedule reminding helps older adults to take medicine on time, which is important for maintaining their health. Measuring vital signs also helps people to manage their health conditions in their homes.

Our healthcare robot carries some healthcare sensor devices which measure essential vital signs data such as blood pressure, blood oxygen, and pulse rate. But there are some limitations to using healthcare sensor devices, for example, a healthcare robot cannot carry large and heavy healthcare sensor devices and may not be able to supply enough power to operate healthcare sensor devices. To solve these problems, we designed and developed an independent sensor managing system, which manages all healthcare sensor devices without any wired connection to the healthcare robot system. The sensor managing system is an independent system including functions such as checking status of all devices, detecting and registering new devices, and scheduling of requests. The healthcare robot is an assistant for human users and sends the requests of human users to the sensor managing system through wireless communication. Then, the sensor managing system controls the appropriate healthcare sensor device by checking the status, sending commands, and receiving data. We can easily add or remove various healthcare sensor devices without considering the healthcare robot. It can also be operated by other client systems such as smart phones or tablets.

This paper is organized as follows. In Section 2, we introduce the design of a sensor managing system. In Section 3, we explain the implementation of our healthcare sensor managing system. In Section 4, we present experiments and evaluations. Finally, we conclude this paper in Section 5.

Fig. 1. A human user measures his vital signs using the healthcare sensor managing system with the guidance of a healthcare robot. The measured vital sign data is sent to a medical server via the healthcare robot and caregivers can check the health condition by observing the data.

2   Design of Sensor Managing System

2.1   Key Concepts

The main focus of our design is to create a generic sensor managing system for various sensor devices in a distributed environment. The sensor managing system is able to dynamically identify and classify the type of sensor devices. For this, our design includes the following functions.

1) *Plug and Play*: When a sensor device is newly connected, the sensor managing system should recognize the new connection, and make it available for using without additional set up procedures by users. It is a general plug and play function supported by modern operating systems, such as Microsoft Windows [18].

2) *Status Managing*: When sensor devices have been registered by the sensor managing system, the sensor managing system periodically checks and keeps track of the status of all sensor devices, which are connected within the network, without the intervention of human users.

3) *Scheduling of Requests*: The system should be able to dynamically allocate services of available devices to the users of the system, at appropriate measurement times. It also supports access of services from multiple clients and schedules the services according to requests.

4) *Expandability*: The system should be able to manage various devices of different combinations; multiple heterogeneous typed devices, and different devices of the same type.

5) *Compatibility*: The use of the sensor managing system should not be specific to a single platform but rather should function with devices and clients of all platforms by considering healthcare standards for EHR (electronic health records) such as HL7 [19].

2.2   System Architecture

Fig. 2 shows the sensor managing system that consists of three sub-systems each of which function in a distributed system: client systems, a sensor manager system, and sensor device systems. The user interacts with a client system to use and control the sensor device systems. Then, the client system sends requests to the sensor manager system using the predefined Application Program Interface (API), which is supported by the sensor manager system. The sensor manager system has the list of available devices, maintained by periodically polling for devices, and sends the requests from the clients to the appropriate sensor device.

The client system has the role of channeling between the user application and the sensor manager system, and service robots and tablets can be used as the client systems. Therefore, the client system should have interaction functions including input and output methods as well as communication functions for sending the requests from human users to the sensor manager system and obtaining the results. The main communication between the client system and the sensor manager system requires working consistently across multiple platforms, so we use web sockets [20], which provide full duplex communication over a single TCP connection and allow the client to be independent of any platform, making it scalable. Then the client system makes a request call for services using APIs via the sensor manager system. In the communication, data security is not considered at this moment, but we have a plan to use https or encryption in the near future.

The sensor manager system manages the status of each connected device. The sensor manager system uses Robotics Operating System (ROS), which is a well-known robotic framework includes various communication methods as well as intelligent packages for robot, as the underlying method of communication between each component because it is simply adapted on embedded Linux system as well as qualified in various systems [21]. ROS communication can work in two ways; by either setting up publisher and subscriber objects, or by creating a service object where clients can make a service call to the server object. The manager module of the sensor manager system manages various types of sensor devices by keeping track of run-time status of devices that have been registered. It also tracks the connection status of each device.

The ROS bridge layer [22] in the sensor manager system acts as the bridge between the web communications and ROS environment through web sockets, allowing our sensor management system to interact with the client systems of various platforms, which can function in both local and distributed environments. Likewise the option of using a web socket implementation is not only restricted to the client, but also can be applied to implementation of the sensor device component as well. The sensor device system handles the device driver logic of the sensor device, on extracting the low level data from the sensor devices. The port scanner module allows plug and play features by recognizing devices connected to the port. To communicate with the sensor manager system, the sensor device system uses the Message Handling module which is based on using ROS service calls.

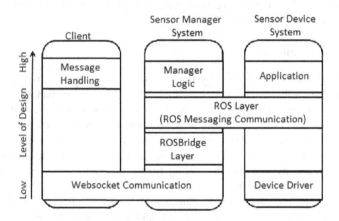

Fig. 2. System architecture of the sensor managing system, and its components. The client is the user defined application to communicate with the system. The sensor manager keeps track of statuses of various devices and the sensor device contains the device logic to extract the raw data.

The APIs are called by the clients to the sensor manager system to control the sensor devices. The APIs are designed for two purposes; to manage the acquisition of devices and to control devices. For acquisition, either a Request (or Terminate) call is issued to allocate (or deallocate) the sensor device to the client. Once a successful allocation has been made, the sensor manager returns the details of the allocated device. The selection process can be classified by stating the details of the device which are defined by message types. Firstly in order to request a device, the user must specify the type field to declare which type of sensor they want. Then the manager tries to find the best matching solution based on other fields such as the bid field which specifies the device id.

3   Healthcare Sensor Managing System

3.1   Overall System

We have implemented a healthcare sensor managing system based on our sensor manager architecture, which is introduced in Section 2. We use a mobile service robot as a client system, and it interacts with human users by speaking and displaying information on a touch screen. We developed the sensor manager system and the sensor device systems using real healthcare sensor devices, which are used in healthcare environments.

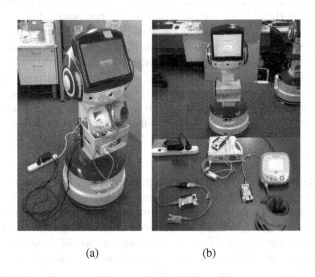

(a)   (b)

Fig. 3. HealthBot systems. (a) Previous HealthBot, which carries vital signs measurement devices on its tray. Power cables for vital sign measurement devices are connected. (b) New version of HealthBot, which uses the healthcare sensor managing system. These devices are controlled by the requests from the healthcare robot through wireless communication.

Fig. 3(a) shows our previous healthcare robot system, HealthBots, a kiosk type robot, which is currently used in the Gore family doctor's practice in the South Island of New Zealand. This system works well, as we found in our previous trials [11-13], but has some limitations. It carries healthcare sensor devices and connects them directly to the HealthBot. It is useful to patients who have some difficulty moving since it carries the healthcare sensor devices to them, but there are limitations to this movement due to the power cables to supply power to the healthcare sensor devices. While these issues can be resolved by providing onboard power, this solution must be applied for each vital signs device.

Fig. 3(b) shows our new healthcare robot system with the sensor managing system. It is the same robot as our previous work, but does not carry any healthcare sensor devices on the robot. Instead, HealthBot communicates with the sensor managing system to measure and obtain the vital signs of human users. In this system, we can use a wider variety of healthcare sensor devices, such as height and weight measurement devices, which are large and heavy to carry. The measured results are recorded by our medical server system, RoboGen. Then, users and family members as well as clinicians including doctors, nurses, and psychologists can access the user data and monitor the health condition of human users easily through the RoboGen webpage.

3.2   Client Systems

We used the same HealthBot shown in Fig. 3 as the client system of the healthcare sensor managing system. HealthBot is a kiosk type mobile robot, powered by a 24V Li-Polymer battery, and consists of a camera, a Pan-Tilt enabled touch screen, speakers, microphones, ultrasonic sensors, bumper sensors, a laser scanner and two single board computers. User responses were received via the touch screen and HealthBot responds to participants with synthesized speech, visual output on the screen, and movements. HealthBot's synthetic speech is generated through a diphone concatenation type synthesis implemented with Festival speech synthesis system [23] and used a New Zealand accented diphone voice developed at the University of Auckland [24].

3.3   Sensor Manager System

The main role of the sensor manager system is managing the status of the healthcare sensor devices, and scheduling the requests from the HealthBot. We chose a BeagleBone system in a ROS environment for the embedded platform because it is an effective prototype development platform able to run an operating system and ROS. The sensor manager system runs the ROS-master, ROS-bridge, and the manager module of the system. ROS-master maps names and low level registration such as IP address and host to each component in the ROS environment, tracking publishers/subscribers and services. ROS-bridge converts the ROS messages to web socket messages in JSON format (and vice-versa) to establish communication between manager and the client. The manager module keeps track of all the devices in a tree-map structure by first classifying them into different sensor types and then by IDs. The sensor manager system can be placed anywhere that provides access to the network, or can be carried on the HealthBot.

3.4   Sensor Device System

The main role of the sensor device systems is controlling healthcare devices according to the requests from the sensor manager. We measure three kinds of vital sign from three types of measurement devices shown in Fig. 3(b). TABLE 1 shows the devices used in our system. Each of the different types of vital sign measurement device provides the results of a different context, where the PulseCor BP device returns diastolic, systolic and heart rate measurements, while the Masimo SPO2 device returns the oxygen saturation rate in the blood and the heart rate. The OxySmart SPO2 device is portable as well as inexpensive, so it is useful for an individual house environment. Each vital sign measurement device is connected to the BeagleBone sensor device system. The sensor device system can be placed anywhere available to access the network.

Table 1. Specification of Vital Sign Measurement Devices

Name of device	Measurable vital signs		
	Blood Pressure	Blood Oxygen	Pulse rate
PulseCor BP	O	-	O
Masimo SPO2	-	O	O
OxySmart SPO2	-	O	O

4   Experiments and Evaluations

4.1   Experimental Environment and Scenario

In the experiments, we applied the proposed healthcare sensor managing system to the HealthBot system shown in Fig. 3(b), and evaluated the performance of the key functionalities developed in Section 3. We monitored the procedure of each device measurement test, and measured the latency, then compared the results with our previous system. TABLE 2 shows the specifications of the HealthBot computer used for processing, and BeagleBone, which is used for the healthcare sensor managing system. The BeagleBone has a much lower specification than the computer in the HealthBot, but it is enough to process the managing function.

Table 2. Specification of Experimental Platforms

Category	HealthBot	BeagleBone
Processor (CPU)	Intel Core2 Duo 2.4GHz	ARM Cortex A8 720MHz
Memory (RAM)	1.95GB	256MB
Operating System	MS Windows XP Professional	Angstrom Linux v2012.05

4.2   Experimental Results and Evaluations

4.2.1   Plug and Play

Fig. 4 shows the procedure of plug and play for sensor devices in the healthcare sensor managing system. The plug and play function was developed by scanning ttyUSB interfaces of the sensor device system. When a healthcare sensor device is connected to the sensor device system, the sensor device system recognizes the new connection, and reports it to the sensor manager system. Then, the sensor manager system classifies the device by type, and registers the device on the available list. Finally, the sensor manager system sends the feedback including the service ID of the sensor device to the sensor device system.

We measured the latency of the plug and play process over 5 iterations shown in TABLE 3. It took less than 3 seconds on average over 5 iterations for the whole procedure on three sensor devices. More specifically it took about 1 second (about 35% of the whole latency) for the system processing, and it is quite fast in the embedded system comparing with our previous system, which uses the HealthBot system that took approximately 1.5 seconds on average over 5 iterations without wireless latency. This is mainly because it is dependent on the BeagleBone board's ability to detect the tty interface rather than being dependent on the devices so the time of detection shouldn't differ from device to device.

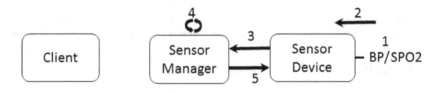

Fig. 4. The sequence of the plug and play process. 1) New connection of sensor device. 2) Recognizing new connection. 3) Reporting new connection. 4) Registering new sensor device. 5) Returning of feedback.

Table 3. Latency of Plug And Play (average over 5 iterations)

Sensor Devices	Whole	System	Wireless
PulseCor BP	2.97	0.91	2.06
Masimo SPO2	2.80	0.90	1.90
OxySmart SPO2	2.68	1.05	1.63

4.2.2   Status Managing

Fig. 5 shows the procedure for managing status of sensor devices, which are on the available list. It is a periodic routine procedure of the sensor manager system. The sensor manager system sends a status checking request to the sensor device system, like a ping. Then the sensor device system checks the status of the connected sensor device, whether it is active or not, and reports the status of the sensor device to the sensor manager system. The sensor manager system repeats this procedure every 10 seconds as well as when the operation request is received.

TABLE 4 shows the latency of the status managing process over 5 iterations. It took about 2 seconds on average over 5 iterations for the whole procedure on three sensor devices. We can see that the latency from these status managing is almost purely wireless latency. The total latency is smaller than the previous result as the response message (step #2 of Fig. 4) is just a simple ACK message, which doesn't require much computation. The latency is mainly due to wireless communication, which is over 99% of the whole latency. Similar results were shown for all devices as the procedure of the status managing function is independent of devices themselves.

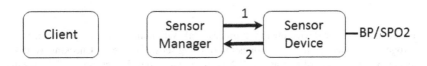

Fig. 5. The sequence of the status managing process. 1) Sending status checking request periodically. 2) Responding the status checking request.

Table 4. Latency of Status Managing (average over 5 iterations)

Sensor Devices	Whole	System	Wireless
PulseCor BP	2.013	0.003	2.01
Masimo SPO2	1.773	0.003	1.77
OxySmart SPO2	1.525	0.005	1.52

4.2.3   Device Operation

Fig. 6 shows the procedure of the device operation function. When the client system requests using a sensor device, the sensor manager allocates the device to the client by checking the availability of the devices, and sends the operating request to the sensor device system. If there is no available sensor device on the list, the sensor manager system reports to the client system that there is no available device. When the sensor device system gets the request, it measures the vital signs of the human user, and returns the results to the sensor manager system. Finally, the sensor manager reports the results to the client.

TABLE 5 shows the latency of the device operation process over 5 iterations. The device time, which includes initialization and measurement of vital signs, is different for sensor devices, and it is over 50% of the whole latency. It took less than 0.1 second for the system processing, and about 2 seconds for wireless communication similar to other experiments. It is reasonable latency for measuring vital sign data, compared to our previous system.

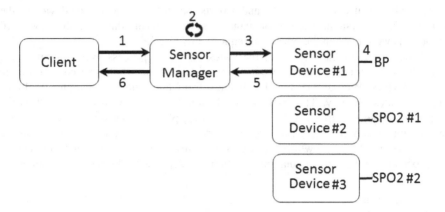

Fig. 6. The sequence of the device operation process. (a) With homogeneous typed devices. (b) With heterogeneous typed devices. 1) Requesting of using sensor device. 2) Checking available sensor device. 3) Requesting of operation. 4) Measuring vital sign. 5) Returning of the results. 6) Reporting the results.

Table 5. Latency of Device Operation (average over 5 iterations)

Sensor Devices	Whole	System	Wireless	Device
PulseCor BP	55.05	0.04	2.01	53
Masimo SPO2	4.06	0.03	2.03	2
OxySmart SPO2	50.1	0.05	1.96	3

5   Conclusions

We have designed a sensor managing system architecture and implemented the design for a healthcare sensor managing system, for the HealthBots. The main purpose of designing the new sensor managing system is separating the sensor system from the HealthBot, physically, electrically, and in terms of software components. The sensor managing system is an independent system, and communicates with not only the robot, but also any systems connected within the network. In addition, the sensor device system can be placed anywhere accessible to the network. For these purposes, we designed the sensor managing system by considering five key concepts: plug and play, status managing, scheduling of requests, expandability, and compatibility.

We developed the healthcare managing system based on the designed architecture, and applied it to HealthBots, which is the healthcare robot system developed by the CARES (Center for Automation and Robotics Engineering Science) in the University of Auckland. We used three kinds of vital sign measuring devices to measure blood pressure, pulse rate and blood oxygen saturation, which are essential health information for healthcare. We monitored the procedure of each function, and measured the latency to compare it with our previous system. From the experiment results, we verified the efficiency of the sensor managing system. Some issues should be improved in our future work; especially we should reduce the latency for wireless communication. In addition, our sensor managing system is designed for supporting a multi-client environment, and this aspect should be evaluated in the future. We will show our sensor manager system can be applied to a tablet without the robot system in the future.

References

1. United Nations, World population aging, United Nations Publications, New York (2002)
2. Anliker, U., Ward, J.A., Lukowicz, P., Tröster, G., Dolveck, F., Baer, M., Keita, F., Schenker, E., Catarsi, F., Coluccini, L., Belardinelli, A., Shklarski, D., Alon, M., Hirt, E., Schmid, R., Vuskovic, M.: AMON: A wearable multiparameter medical monitoring and alert system. IEEE Transactions on Information Technology in Biomedicine 8(4), 415–427 (2004)
3. Shnayder, V., Chen, B., Lorincz, K., Fulford Jones, T.R.F., Welsh, M.: Sensor networks for medical care. Division Eng. Appl. Sci. Harvard Univ., Cambridge, MA, Tech. Rep. TR-08–05 (2005)
4. Mukai, T., Onishi, M., Odashima, T., Hirano, S., Luo, Z.: Development of the tactile sensor system of a human–interactive robot 'RI-MAN'. IEEE Transactions on Robotics 24(2), 505–512 (2008)
5. Wada, K., Shibata, T., Musha, T., Kimura, S.: Robot therapy for elders affected by dementia. IEEE Engineering in Medicine and Biology Magazine 27(4), 53–60 (2008)
6. Cabibihan, J.-J., Javed, H., Ang Jr., M., Aljunied, S.M.: Why Robots? A Survey on the Roles and Benefits of Social Robots in the Therapy of Children with Autism. International Journal of Social Robotics 5, 593–618 (2013)
7. Iftikhar, M., Mariappan, M.: Otorob (Ortho Robot) with Docmata (Doctor's Eye): Role of Remote Presence in Developing Countries. In: International Conference on Advances in Human-oriented and Personalized Mechanisms, Technologies, and Services, pp. 51–56 (2009)
8. Ito, K., Sugano, S., Iwata, H.: Development of attachable tele-echography robot by a bystander at injury scene. In: International Conference on Mechatronics and Automation, pp. 1270–1275 (2010)
9. Datta, C., Yang, H.Y., Kuo, I.-H., Broadbent, E., MacDonald, B.A.: Software platform design for personal service robots in healthcare. In: IEEE International Conference on Robotics, Automation and Mechatronics, pp. 156–161 (2013)
10. Datta, C., Yang, H.Y., Tiwari, P., MacDonald, B.A.: A Healthcare Robot for Monitoring Adverse Drug Reactions in Older People. In: International Conference on Ubiquitous Robots and Ambient Intelligence, pp. 10–11 (2012)
11. Jayawardena, C., Kuo, I., Datta, C., Stafford, R.Q., Broadbent, E., MacDonald, B.A.: Design, implementation and field tests of a socially assistive robot for the elderly: HealthBot Version 2. In: International Conference on Biomedical Robotics and Biomechatronics, pp. 1837–1842 (2012)
12. Stafford, R.Q., MacDonald, B.A., Jayawardena, C., Wegner, D.M., Broadbent, E.: Does the Robot Have a Mind? Mind Perception and Attitudes Towards Robots Predict Use of an Eldercare Robot. International Journal of Social Robotics 6(1), 17–32 (2014)

13. Kuo, I.H., Rabindran, J.M., Broadbent, E., Lee, Y.I., Kerse, N., Stafford, R.M.Q., MacDonald, B.A.: Age and gender factors in user acceptance of healthcare robots. In: International Symposium on Robot and Human Interactive Communication, pp. 214–219 (2009)

14. Ahn, H.S., Choi, J.Y.: Can We Teach What Emotions a Robot should Express? In: IEEE International Conference on Intelligent Robots and Systems, pp. 1407–1412 (2012)

15. Ahn, H.S., Lee, D.-W., Choi, D., Lee, D.-Y., Hur, M., Lee, H.: Uses of Facial Expressions of Android Head System according to Gender and Age. In: IEEE International Conference on Systems, Man, and Cybernetics, pp. 2300–2305 (2012)

16. Ahn, H.S., Lee, D.-W., Choi, D., Lee, D.-Y., Hur, M., Lee, H.: Appropriate Emotions for Facial Expressions of 33-DOFs Android Head EveR-4 H33. In: IEEE International Symposium on Robot and Human Interactive Communication, pp. 1115–1120 (2012)

17. Ahn, H.S., Lee, D.-W., Choi, D., Lee, D.-Y., Hur, M., Lee, H.: Difference of Efficiency in Human-Robot Interaction According to Condition of Experimental Environment. In: Ge, S.S., Khatib, O., Cabibihan, J.-J., Simmons, R., Williams, M.-A. (eds.) ICSR 2012. LNCS, vol. 7621, pp. 219–227. Springer, Heidelberg (2012)

18. Ahn, H.S., Baek, Y.M., Sa, I.-K., Na, J.H., Kang, W.-S., Choi, J.Y.: Design of Reconfigurable Heterogeneous Modular Architecture for Service Robot. In: IEEE International Conference on Intelligent Robots and Systems, pp. 1313–1318 (2008)

19. http://www.hl7.org.nz/about

20. Peter, L., Greco, F.: Html5 web sockets: A quantum leap in scalability for the web. SOA World Magazine (2010)

21. Quigley, M., et al.: ROS: An open-source Robot Operating System. In: ICRA Workshop on Open Source Software (2009)

22. Crick, C., Jay, G., Osentoski, S., Pitzer, B., Jenkins, O.C.: Rosbridge: Ros for non-ros users. In: International Symposium on Robotics Research (2011)

23. Black, A.W., Taylor, P., Caley, R.: The festival speech synthesis system (2012), http://www.cstr.ed.ac.uk/projects/festival

24. Watson, C.I., Teutenberg, J., Thompson, L., Roehling, S., Igic, A.: How to build a New Zealand voice. In: Proceedings of the New Zealand Linguistic Society Conference (2009)

25. Ahn, H.S., Kuo, I.-H., Datta, C., Stafford, R., Kerse, N., Peri, K., Broadbent, E.L., MacDonald, B.A.: Design of a Kiosk Type Healthcare Robot System for Older People in Private and Public Places. In: Brugali, D., Broenink, J., Kroeger, T., MacDonald, B. (eds.) SIMPAR 2014. LNCS (LNAI), vol. 8810, pp. 578–589. Springer, Heidelberg (2014)

26. Broadbent, E., Tamagawa, R., Kerse, N., Knock, B., Patience, A., MacDonald, B.: Retirement home staff and residents' preferences for healthcare robots. In: IEEE International Symposium on Robot and Human Interactive Communication (ROMAN 2009), pp. 645–650 (2009)

27. Ahn, H.S., Santos, M.P.G., Wadhwa, C., MacDonald, B.A.: Development of Brain Training Games for a Healthcare Service Robot for Older People. In: International Conference on Social Robotics, pp. 1–11 (2014)

28. Stafford, R.Q., Broadbent, E., Jayawardena, C., Unger, U., Kuo, I.H., Igic, A., Wong, R., Kerse, N., Watson, C., MacDonald, B.A.: Improved robot attitudes and emotions at a retirement home after meeting a robot. In: IEEE International Symposium on Robot and Human Interactive Communication, pp. 82–87 (2010)

Kinesthetic Teaching in Assembly Operations – A User Study

Arne Muxfeldt, Jan-Henrik Kluth, and Daniel Kubus

Institut für Robotik und Prozessinformatik,
Technische Universität Braunschweig, Germany
{amu,jkl,dku}@rob.cs.tu-bs.de
http://www.rob.cs.tu-bs.de/

Abstract. Kinesthetic teaching is a commonly employed method for programming robots using the *Programming by Demonstration* (PbD) paradigm. It is widely regarded as an intuitive approach to robot programming, which can be performed by shop-floor workers. Much research in this area has focused on pick-and-place tasks while demanding assembly tasks have received less attention so far. Nonetheless, in various contributions kinesthetic teaching is utilized to gain insight into human assembly strategies by deriving trajectories, mating forces, etc. To evaluate the discrepancies between kinesthetic teaching and manual assembly in the context of industrial assembly tasks, we conducted a user study with 78 participants featuring four different tasks. Our results confirm the ease of learning attributed to kinesthetic teaching but also suggest that trying to transfer human assembly strategies using this method may suffer from a substantial flaw.

Keywords: User study, kinesthetic teaching, programming by demonstration, physical human-robot interaction, assembly tasks, robot programming.

1 Introduction

The increase in life expectancy among European populations, also known as the Ageing of Europe, requires to adapt industrial production environments to the ageing workforce. This process involves a higher degree of automation as well as robot assistance functions for non-ergonomic tasks. Welding and painting, for example, are already highly automated in the automotive industry. In contrast, demanding assembly tasks, which involve - for instance - snap fitting or tight tolerances, are mainly performed manually today. Many of these tasks, however, demand high mating forces or require postures that prove harmful to health in the long run. Therefore, assistive robots relieving workers from these wearisome tasks are required. To facilitate programming and utilize process knowledge of shop-floor workers, PbD is often used with assistive robots. Similar considerations apply to robots processing small lot sizes in small and medium enterprises. The PbD paradigm includes a multitude of different approaches [2], e.g., approaches relying on motion capturing techniques or kinesthetic teaching. The

D. Brugali et al. (Eds.): SIMPAR 2014, LNAI 8810, pp. 533–544, 2014.
© Springer International Publishing Switzerland 2014

latter method is based on human workers guiding the robot by physical contact [1].

Kinesthetic teaching is said to be an intuitive approach to robot programming that can be learned easily by shop-floor workers. However, little information quantifying this aspect can be found in the literature.

Several approaches apply kinesthetic teaching to extract and transfer human assembly strategies to robots. However, there is no justification that the assembly strategies and parameters extracted from kinesthetic teaching will correspond to the strategies and parameters employed in manual assembly. Compared to manual assembly, the reduced tactile feedback as well as the occurring inertia and friction when guiding the robot suggest that there will in fact be significant discrepancies regarding assembly strategies and parameters. If so, the idea of extracting human assembly strategies by kinesthetic teaching should be re-evaluated.

To shed some more light on the latter surmise as well as the claimed ease of learning, we performed a user study with 78 participants and four different assembly tasks. We focus on the duration of an assembly operation as our key performance measure. In particular, we consider the following four hypotheses:

1. **Learning Effect by Repeated Execution:** Executing a task or several tasks that resemble each other repeatedly reduces the required time significantly.
2. **Manual Assembly Performance Cannot Be Achieved by Kinesthetic Teaching:** The duration for completing a task required in manual assembly cannot be achieved when guiding the robot.
3. **Performance in an Assembly Task Depends on Personal Attributes:** The required time varies with age, spatial sense, previous knowledge and personal attitude towards technical devices.
4. **Correlation between Performance in Manual Assembly and Kinesthetic Teaching:** Participants performing well in manual assembly will also perform well in the kinesthetic teaching trials.

The remainder of this paper is organized as follows: First, we describe related work regarding the application and evaluation of kinesthetic teaching approaches. In Sect. 3 we describe our setup and outline the user study, including the definition of a performance measure based on the duration of the experiment. Subsequently, we present our results in Sect. 4. More detailed results can be found in [11]. Finally, we conclude the paper in Sect. 5.

2   Related Work

PbD is widely used, especially for programming robots with redundant kinematics. Argall et al. composed a survey of various methods in PbD [2]. Especially kinesthetic teaching has been used for many different purposes. Kormushev et al. used kinesthetic teaching to teach different positions and an additional haptic device to teach forces [7]. In contrast Delson et al. used the taught positions and forces to automatically generate a program for a robot. Their approach was to remove irrelevant parts of the taught trajectory by checking whether each part is in a specified range of acceptable forces and trajectories [5].

More frequently than in industrial robotics, PbD is used in the domain of humanoid robots because it seems logical and intuitive to transfer human motions to humanoid robots. Billard et al. used kinesthetic teaching to speed up the learning process of a humanoid. Furthermore, teaching is regarded as a user friendly human-robot-interface [3]. Schou et al. showed the influence of kinesthetic teaching onto industrial robotics. They used kinesthetic teaching in combination with task level programming to create a helpful tool for production floor operators [13].

To our knowledge no user study focusing explicitly on the differences between manual assembly operations and operations in a kinesthetic teaching process has been conducted so far. Wrede et al. performed a study to compare a form of assisted kinesthetic teaching to an unassisted case for a redundant robot. They also introduced a new human-robot-interface based on kinesthetic teaching and machine learning [14]. Pais et al. presented another user study in the context of PbD. Their focus was to evaluate the user friendliness of a tactile user interface but they did not consider the influence of their interface on the interaction with the robot [12].

Our findings suggest that both motions and parameters derived by kinesthetic teaching will differ significantly from those found in manual operations - which has been overlooked by the previously mentioned studies and approaches.

A possible alternative to prevent potential distortions is to use motion capturing instead of kinesthetic teaching like Dillmann et al. did [6]. But motion capturing is a costly process and might fail for typical industrial assembly tasks where occlusions and clutter occur frequently [10].

3   Experimental Setup

In the following section we describe our setup including the used parts, sensors and the robot. Afterwards we outline our design of the study including composition, questionnaire and participants. Finally, we introduce a performance measurement based on contact phases.

Hardware. In Fig. 1 and Fig. 2 the experimental setup is shown. The robot (2), specifically a KUKA Lightweight Robot (LWR IV+) [4], was mounted upside down to minimize interference. All assembly tasks were executed on a basis platform (5) on top of a JR3 50M31A-I25 force torque sensor (1). Below the platform an overload protection device (6) is visible which was used to prevent potential damages due to sensor overload.

Using the force torque sensor, it was possible to capture forces and torques for all assembly methods. During the usage of the robot, the end effector pose was additionally acquired directly via the KUKA Fast Research Interface. An optical tracking system (3), the Polaris Accedo by Northern Digital Inc., was used to capture the pose during executing tasks in combination with the handle (see

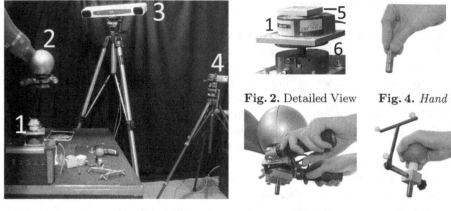

Fig. 2. Detailed View   Fig. 4. *Hand*

Fig. 1. The experimental setup   Fig. 3. *Robot*   Fig. 5. *Handle*

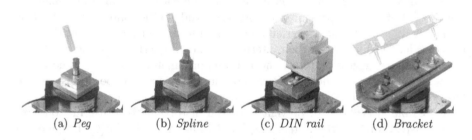

(a) *Peg*   (b) *Spline*   (c) *DIN rail*   (d) *Bracket*

Fig. 6. The four assembly tasks

paragraph Assembly Methods). Both sources were transformed into a common coordinate system. Additionally, the participants were recorded on video with a camera (4) during the entire experiment. The whole setup was surrounded by a black curtain in order to generate reproducible environment settings with minimal disturbance from outside for each participant.

Assembly Task. The study is based on four assembly tasks which are: to insert a peg into a hole (in the following addressed as *Peg*), to insert a spline shaft into a base (*Spline*), to mount a clip with a socket on a DIN rail (*DIN rail*) and to assemble a mounting bracket to the associated base (*Bracket*). Pictures of all tasks are given in Fig. 6 and detailed engineering drawings of all used parts can be found in the technical report [11].

Assembly Methods. In order to perform the assembly tasks, three different methods (*Robot, Hand* and *Handle*), which are presented in Fig. 3 to Fig. 5, were used. For the first method the assembly part was attached to the robot, which was controlled in a gravity compensation mode. This mode does not compensate inertia and friction completely. The robot was equipped with two handles at the end effector enabling full control of orientation and position by a human operator. The second method was using the hand directly, also referred to as manual assembly. For the third method the assembly part was attached to a handle. This method was supposed to be an intermediate method which allows limited tactile feedback in the assembly but less interference from inertia or damping than a robot. Neglecting inertia and friction, the methods *Handle* and *Robot* differ merely with respect to their interface (two handed vs. one handed).

Order of Experiments. To detect learning effects, different combinations and orders of assembly tasks and methods were performed. To avoid an exponential blow-up, the possible permutations had to be limited. The tasks (*Peg*, *Spline*, *DIN rail*, *Bracket*) were performed in the mentioned and reversed order. For the assembly methods, two orders (*Hand, Robot, Handle*) and (*Robot, Hand, Handle*) were investigated. Each participant performed only one of these combinations. For each task the participants cycled through the different methods before switching the task. The term *experiment* is used for a specific combination of method and task like *Robot/Peg*. Each of the twelve experiments was performed five times in a row by each participant.

Participants. The total number of participants is 78. Two thirds of them are between 14 and 39, and the remaining third between 44 and 71 years old. 38 are female, 40 male. Nearly half of the participants are university graduates or students. We cannot assume that these participants describe a representative sample of the population.

Contact Phases. We employ the length of the contact time per experiment to classify the performance of an assembly operation. The detection of the initial contact and the loss of contact are based on the measured force values. If the measured force is above the sensor noise level for at least 0.1 seconds it is assumed that the current state is in contact. No contact is assumed if the measured force is in the range of the sensor noise for at least 1.0 seconds. These values are based on observations using the video recordings and a frequency analysis of participant motion (see Sect. 4). The goal of this definition is to distinguish between a deliberate loss of contact and a loss because of external factors like a rebound of the assembly part on the surface. Using this definition of a *contact phase* up to 97% of the experiments had one single contact phase. This means, after establishing initial contact, the participants rarely lost contact deliberately to retry the whole process.

4   Results

Boxplot Visualization. In the following presentation of the results, box plots are used. If the data points followed a Gaussian distribution, the dotted lines would cover 99.3% of the samples [9]. However, our data is not always distributed

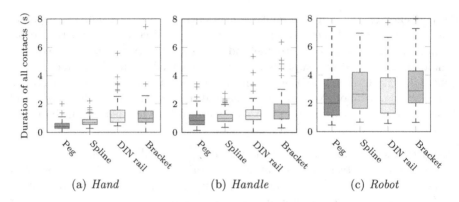

(a) *Hand*   (b) *Handle*   (c) *Robot*

Fig. 7. Duration of contact in the fifth trial for each combination of assembly method and task

normally. If not mentioned otherwise, the number of data points in each box corresponds to 78 – the number of participants. Plots are scaled such that the dotted lines are always visible, but not necessarily every outlier.

Complexity of Assembly Tasks. For each of the combinations of our four assembly tasks with the three methods (experiment), we evaluate the total contact duration. In Fig. 7 the results of the last of five trials are visualized. In Fig. 7(a) and Fig. 7(b), it can be seen that the four assembly tasks have roughly an increasing duration from task *Peg* to the task *Bracket*. This progression suggests that the difficulty of the tasks also increases in that order.

When using the robot, the contact duration is longer and more scattered compared to using the hand or the handle. This observation suggests that the parameters of the assembly strategy using the robot differ from the natural strategy. There is also a significant difference in the order of complexity in the assembly tasks *Spline* and *DIN rail*. This might be due to the increased lever when using the robot.

Learning Effect. Regarding the learning effect by repeating the same experiment, there is a distinctive decrease in duration from the first to the second trial. The following trials only improve the duration by a small amount. Fig. 8 shows the relative duration of the second to the fifth trial of the task *Peg*. For each participant, the durations of the last four trials are divided by the duration of the first trial yielding a contact duration normalized to the first trial. For example, a participant who requires six seconds in the first trial and only three seconds in the second trial would score 0.5 in the second trial. Using this figure the individual relative changes can be identified. The largest relative improvement occurs in the method *Robot* where the median improves by about 43%. The improvement from the first to the second execution in the method *Hand* is only about

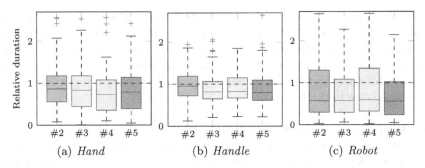

(a) *Hand*   (b) *Handle*   (c) *Robot*

Fig. 8. Relative duration (to first trial) of contact phases for assembly task *Peg*

23%. These observations confirm the ease of the learning attributed to kinesthetic teaching.

Note that due to the relative visualization, the variance in the first trial is set to zero but is still included because the relative durations of the following trials show higher variances accordingly. The other assembly tasks exhibit a similar development and are omitted due to space restrictions.

Figure 9 shows the results for the experiment *Robot/Peg* of only that half of the participants who started with the peg task. This subset is further divided into two groups with about 20 persons: A group who used the robot first (Fig. 9(c) & (d)) and a group who performed manual assembly first (Fig. 9(a) & (b)). Consequently, this experiment was the first one for participants in (c) & (d) and the second one for participants in (a) & (b) (following their experiment *Hand/Peg*).

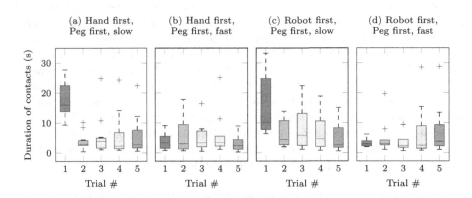

Fig. 9. Experiment *Robot/Peg*: Comparison of the development of 'fast' and 'slow' participants and influence of method order

Both of these groups are further divided into the 50% fastest (Fig. 9(b) & (d)) and the remaining (Fig. 9(a) & (c)) group, according to their result in the first trial of the experiment *Robot/Peg*. Therefore, each box in the plots is comprised of 10-12 data points, meaning participants.

It is interesting to see that the median duration in the last trial of all four groups is similar (2.7 s, 2.4 s, 2.6 s, 3.8 s) compared to the standard deviation. This means that after five trials of the experiment *Robot/Peg* members of each group can achieve a similar result (regarding duration) even if they did not have previous knowledge of the task (group that used the robot first) or had shown bad performance in the first trial.

Statistical Tests. As mentioned in the introduction it was expected that the results of the experiments would depend on the one hand on individual attributes like technical affinity and spatial sense, and on the other hand on demographic data like age. This data was acquired by using a questionnaire which contains standardized questions to measure the self-assessed technical affinity and images of 3d-tasks for the spatial sense. Statistical tests are used to test correlations between all recorded attributes.

We cannot apply standard ANOVA as the random variables are not distributed normally. However, we can use the Kruskal–Wallis one-way analysis of variance - a nonparametric version of ANOVA, which does not rely on the normal distribution assumption [8]. The test checks the null hypothesis that two or more sets of samples are from the same distribution. The alternative hypothesis is that not all samples are from the same distribution.

In our case, we use the contact duration, the average mating force, and the length of the assembly path as samples. The partition into groups is based on various factors including technical affinity, spatial sense, age, education, and other demographic parameters. The tests are conducted on data of individual experiments (like the experiment *Robot/Peg*) because as already shown the results are different for each combination. The test results show no general conclusive dependency on any of the tested group partitions. Several tests reject the null hypothesis at a 5% significance level but these rejections only occur in single experiments. Therefore, no significant general influential factors can be found.

As an example, the influence of spatial sense on the contact duration is visualized in Fig. 10. Depicted is the cumulative relative frequency that a member of a group has successfully finished the task after the given time. The three groups are created based on the individual spatial sense score and are approximately equal in size. In the left case of that figure (experiment *Robot/Peg*), the Kruskal–Wallis test does not result in a significant rejection of the null hypothesis, in the right case it is rejected at the 5% significance level, meaning that the samples are not drawn from the same distribution.

Correlation between the Assembly Methods *Hand* and *Robot*. To verify the hypothesis that participants showing good results in the *Hand* experiments also achieve good results in the *Robot* experiments, the participants are divided into two groups. For each participant and for each assembly task, the median duration of their five *Hand* trials is calculated. Then the median of these medians is taken as the separator between the two groups. Note that these two groups contain no information about the order of assembly tasks or methods.

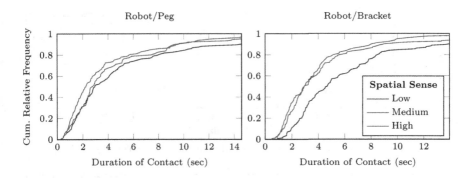

Fig. 10. Probability of being below a certain contact duration based on spatial sense classifications of the participants

Looking at the two groups and comparing the median contact duration of the *Robot* experiments, only in the task *Bracket* there is a significant difference between the groups, meaning that persons who complete *Hand* trials faster are not in general faster in completing *Robot* experiments. The results of the Kruskal-Wallis tests are $p = 0.5$ (*Peg*), $p = 0.2$ (*Spline*), $p = 0.6$ (*DIN rail*) and $p = 0.05$ (*Bracket*). Apart from the bracket, all cases suggest that the division of the groups is not significant at a 5% level, meaning that there is in general no conclusive evidence for a correlation between the contact duration in *Hand* and *Robot* experiments.

Differences between Assembly Methods. In order to compare different assembly methods, force torque data is used since only this type of data was recorded for all assembly methods. Comparing the applied forces reveals significantly different distributions. In Fig. 11(a) the relative frequencies of forces for the task *Peg* executed with each method are shown. Each line represents a sum of histograms from all relevant trials in which the forces were normalized to the maximum force applied by each participant (over all three methods). Additionally, the bin counts of each of these histograms were normalized with respect to the duration of the corresponding trial to ensure equal influence of each trial.

The first major difference is the measured maximum force. Using the robot, higher mating forces were applied to the parts compared to the methods *Hand* and *Handle*. This might be due to physical effects like the higher inertia and friction loss in the robot joints. However, the method *Handle* shows a similar, but less pronounced, behavior which indicates that the decreased tactile feedback has a dominant influence. Other possible factors are the different points of force application and the deteriorated vision due to the robot. The different shapes of the distributions are another striking difference. For the methods *Hand* and *Handle* the distributions decrease monotonically whereas the method *Robot* has a long phase of nearly constant relative frequency after an initial drop.

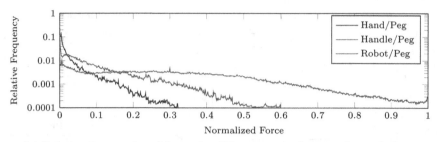

(a) Relative frequencies of forces for different methods executing task *Peg*

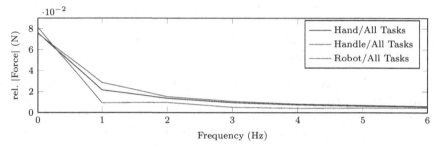

(b) Force amplitude spectrum during participants motion

Fig. 11. Comparison of different assembly methods

For each assembly method, the force data of all participants and all experiments is used to perform a Fast Fourier Transform (FFT). Figure 11(b) shows the mean of all FFTs per assembly method. Before the mean is calculated, the amplitude of each FFT is normalized by using the integral of the corresponding FFT. Without this normalization, participants who mainly use high forces would have a greater influence on the final shape. The steady force component of the method *Robot* is the highest and the corresponding plot has the steepest downward slope. This might be due to the high inertia of the robot and the friction losses in the robot joints resulting in a mechanical low-pass. In contrast to the method *Robot* the shapes of the methods *Hand* and *Handle* are similar in shape. One interesting detail is that the shape of the method *Handle* is a bit higher than the shape of the method *Hand*, except for very low frequencies.

5   Summary and Conclusion

Revisiting our hypotheses from the introduction, we would like to summarize important findings of the study. Substantial evidence for rapid learning effects could be found confirming the ease of learning attributed to kinesthetic teaching. Surprisingly, neither a general correlation between the performance in manual assembly and in kinesthetic teaching nor a clear dependency on personal attributes could be observed.

A learning effect exists, especially regarding the first and the second execution. The effect is larger in the experiments involving the robot. More complex assembly tasks could require more repetitions. A learning effect also occurs when executing the same assembly task by different assembly methods. Participants who assemble manually before guiding the robot perform better in their first robot trial concerning the same task. However, this performance gain decreases gradually and cannot be observed in the final trial. After several repetitions of a specific task, participants achieve similar performance. This observation indicates that kinesthetic teaching is a suitable method for programming robots by shop-floor workers.

Solving an assembly task manually results overwhelmingly often in the best performance regarding required contact duration and applied forces. The relative complexity difference between tasks observed in manual assembly cannot generally be transferred to kinesthetic teaching.

There was no conclusive evidence that the performance in an assembly task depends on personal attributes in general. Merely a slight dependence on spatial sense could be found.

Participants who show good performance in manual assembly do not necessarily perform well when guiding the robot. No general statistical evidence for a correlation between the performance in kinesthetic teaching and in manual assembly could be observed.

Furthermore, our study suggests that human assembly strategies cannot be extracted easily via kinesthetic teaching. Comparing manual assembly with kinesthetic teaching, substantial differences in required contact duration, applied forces, and movement frequencies can be observed. Thus, deriving human assembly strategies by kinesthetic teaching is likely to yield significantly distorted results. To extract and transfer human assembly strategies to robots using kinesthetic teaching, the effects caused by the reduced tactile information as well as the inertia and friction losses of the robot have to be considered to quantify their influence.

Currently, we are deriving assembly strategies based on the data recorded during this user study. By comparing the strategies derived from manual assembly with those from kinesthetic teaching, the observation that kinesthetic teaching is not a viable option to transfer human assembly strategies to robots will be supported. Moreover, the comparison will give important clues on how guiding the robot influences and alters assembly strategies found in manual assembly.

References

1. Akgun, B., Cakmak, M., Yoo, J.W., Thomaz, A.L.: Trajectories and keyframes for kinesthetic teaching: A human-robot interaction perspective. In: Proceedings of the Seventh Annual ACM/IEEE International Conference on Human-Robot Interaction, HRI 2012, pp. 391–398. ACM, New York (2012)
2. Argall, B.D., Chernova, S., Veloso, M., Browning, B.: A survey of robot learning from demonstration. Robotics and Autonomous Systems 57(5), 469–483 (2009)
3. Billard, A., Calinon, S., Dillmann, R., Schaal, S.: Robot programming by demonstration. In: Siciliano, B., Khatib, O. (eds.) Springer Handbook of Robotics, pp. 1371–1394. Springer, Heidelberg (2008)

4. Bischoff, R., Kurth, J., Schreiber, G., Koeppe, R., Albu-Schäffer, A., Beyer, A., Eiberger, O., Haddadin, S., Stemmer, A., Grunwald, G., et al.: The kuka-dlr lightweight robot arm-a new reference platform for robotics research and manufacturing. In: 2010 41st International Symposium on Robotics (ISR) and 2010 6th German Conference on Robotics (ROBOTIK), pp. 1–8. VDE (2010)
5. Delson, N., West, H.: Robot programming by human demonstration: adaptation and inconsistency in constrained motion. In: Proceedings of the 1996 IEEE International Conference on Robotics and Automation, vol. 1, pp. 30–36 (1996)
6. Dillmann, R., Asfour, T., Do, M., Jäkel, R., Kasper, A., Azad, P., Ude, A., Schmidt-Rohr, S., Lösch, M.: Advances in robot programming by demonstration. KI - Künstliche Intelligenz 24(4), 295–303 (2010)
7. Kormushev, P., Calinon, S., Caldwell, D.G.: Imitation Learning of Positional and Force Skills Demonstrated via Kinesthetic Teaching and Haptic Input. Advanced Robotics 25(5), 581–603 (2011)
8. Kruskal, W.H., Wallis, W.A.: Use of ranks in one-criterion variance analysis. Journal of the American statistical Association 47(260), 583–621 (1952)
9. MathWorks: Matlab Documentation - Boxplot (2014), http://www.mathworks.de/de/help/stats/boxplot.html (accessed July 22, 2014)
10. Moeslund, T.B., Hilton, A., Krüger, V.: A survey of advances in vision-based human motion capture and analysis. Computer Vision and Image Understanding 104(2-3), 90–126 (2006), special Issue on Modeling People: Vision-based understanding of a person's shape, appearance, movement and behaviour
11. Muxfeldt, A., Kluth, J.H.: User study on different assembly tasks. Tech. Rep. 07-14-1, Technische Universität Braunschweig, Institut für Robotik und Prozessinformatik (2014), http://www.rob.cs.tu-bs.de/content/03-research/01-projects/69-userstudy/TechnicalReport.pdf
12. Pais, L., Billard, A.: Tactile interface user-friendliness evaluated in the context of robot programming by demonstration. In: HRI Workshop on Advances in Tactile Sensing and Touch Based Human-robot Interaction (2012)
13. Schou, C., Damgaard, J., Bogh, S., Madsen, O.: Human-robot interface for instructing industrial tasks using kinesthetic teaching. In: 2013 44th International Symposium on Robotics (ISR), pp. 1–6 (October 2013)
14. Wrede, S., Emmerich, C., Grünberg, R., Nordmann, A., Swadzba, A., Steil, J.J.: A user study on kinesthetic teaching of redundant robots in task and configuration space. Journal of Human-Robot Interaction 2(Special Issue: HRI System Studies), 56–81 (2013)

A Constraint Based Motion Optimization System for Quality Inspection Process Improvement*

Nicolò Boscolo[1], Elisa Tosello[2], Stefano Tonello[1], Matteo Finotto[1],
Roberto Bortoletto[2], and Emanuele Menegatti[2]

[1] IT+Robotics Srl, Strada Prima 11, 35129 Padova, Italy
{nicolo.boscolo,stefano.tonello,matteo.finotto}@it-robotics.it
[2] Intelligent Autonomous Systems Laboratory,
University of Padova, via Gradenigo 6a, 35131 Padova, Italy
{elisa.tosello,emg,bortolet}@dei.unipd.it

Abstract. This paper presents a motion optimization system for an industrial quality inspection process where a vision device coupled with a manipulator robot arm is able to perform quality and completeness inspection on a complex solid part. In order to be deployed in an industrial production plant, the proposed system has been engineered and integrated as a module of an offline simulator, called WorkCellSimulator, conceived to simulate robot tasks in industrial environments. The novelty of the paper concerns the introduction of time constraints into the motion planning algorithms. Then, these algorithms have been deeply integrated with artificial intelligence techniques in order to optimize the inspection cycle time. This integration makes the application suitable for time-constrained processes like, e.g., autonomous industrial painting or autonomous thermo-graphic detection of cracks in metallic and composite materials.

1 Introduction

A manufactured product must adhere to a defined set of quality criteria. It must be designed and built according to safety standards specified in the purchasing documentation, and it has to be free of defects and non-conformities. Quality control (QC) [8] is a procedure intended to ensure the observation of these requirements. In order to implement an effective QC program, an enterprise must first decide which specific standards the product must meet; then the sequence/type of QC actions must be determined, for instance the visual inspection to detect defects, such as cracks or surface blemishes. Typically, companies that engage in quality inspection have a team of workers who focus on inspecting products. Some studies show that manual inspection faces numerous problems [2]: human experts require intensive training, and even between well-trained individuals, results tend to be observer-dependent. [6], [10], and [12] state that the accuracy of human visual inspection declines with dull, endlessly routine jobs, that means a 100% quality assurance is often unfeasible. Inspection tasks can be dangerous other than difficult: workers may be required to handle materials hazardous. For example, detection of cracks in metallic and composite parts in the automotive and aircraft industry

* This research has been funded by the European Unions 7th Framework (FP7/2007-2013) under grant agreement No. 284607, *Thermobot*[1] project.

D. Brugali et al. (Eds.): SIMPAR 2014, LNAI 8810, pp. 545–553, 2014.

requires magnetic particle inspection: an ecologically undesirable and injurious to human health. Automated visual inspection is an alternative. Automation leads to several advantages [5], including:

- Freeing humans from a dull and routine;
- Saving human labor costs;
- Performing inspection in unfavorable environments;
- Reducing demand for highly skilled human inspectors;
- Matching high-speed production with high-speed inspection.

In order to maximize the aforementioned benefits, experts have to select the automated strategy that better affect the performance of production processes in terms of production cost, cycle time, and production quality. The choice can be complicated because these impacts vary from one inspection strategy to another. Thus, simulation can be used to compare different strategies and select the most appropriate one [7].

In this paper, a motion optimization system for an industrial quality inspection process is presented. A robot with a vision system on its end-effector has to fully examine a complex solid part, e.g., for detecting cracks. Employing an automated inspection system is useful if the robot correctly inspects the part performing a time-saving coverage path. The novelty of the paper is the use of a minimum path covering algorithm able to comply with time constraints.

In this way, even time limited industrial quality inspection processes can be analyzed; e.g., in the autonomous thermo-graphic detection of cracks, a manipulator robot coupled with a thermo-camera inspects a 3D component.

In order to save time during the inspection strategy setup, the authors decided to simulate the process. With this aim, the proposed system has been engineered and integrated as a module of an offline simulator, called WorkCellSimulator [11]. The software, developed by IT+Robotics, is able to simulate robots tasks in industrial environments allowing the definition of specific automated cells for customized production processes, the robot off-line programming, the examination of robots and work cell machineries proper functioning, and the plan transfer into the real world. For a correct product inspection, WorkCellSimulator enables the user to reproduce the scene and to select the inspection points over the product. The system checks the points validity: every point must be collision free and reachable by the robot. Points not satisfying the requirements are removed and the remaining ones are ordered to form the minimum coverage path the robot will follow during the inspection.

The remainder of the paper is organized as follows: Section 2 contains an overview of the WorkCellSimulator planning procedure, exposing the adopted approaches for the path and motion planning, the collision avoidance and the ATSP[1] algorithm used to sort the inspection zones and to obtain the minimum coverage path. Section 3 reports the experiments performed on a practical case: the thermo-graphic detection of cracks, and Section 4 concludes the paper and outlines the future work.

---

[1] Asymmetric Travelling Salesman Problem.

2   Proposed Architecture

Given a 3D model of the inspected product, WorkCellSimulator guides the user from the definition of the workcell (robot and other components) to the selection of set of the visually inspected zones over the product. Then, the simulation core computes a sub-optimal valid path which takes in account the time constraints extracted from the defined zones. In a second stage, the simulator solves the motion planning problem related to the path generated in the previous step. Concluding, the motions are translated in the robot controller language and sent to the machine.

2.1   Data Workflow

When the 3D model of the product is imported, an oriented point cloud is created. This redundant set of points will represent the feasible robot positions where the robot is able to acquire images which will be used for cover the desired inspection with the selected camera device. The points set is redundant in order to take more acquisitions of the same surface. Each point is composed of three translations (X, Y, Z) (in millimetres) and three rotations (R_x, R_y, R_z) (in radians) representing the coordinates of the robot end-effector taking the product as the reference system. The simulator core verifies each point: points can be valid (i.e. reachable and not colliding), not reachable (robot joints limits do not let the robot reaching the point) or colliding (if the robot reaches the point, it will collide with the surrounding world). In the last two cases, they are discarded from the trajectory and only the remaining points are exploited to plan the path.

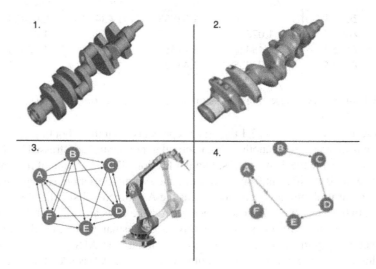

Fig. 1. System workflow overview. In (1) the product is imported and divided in zones (2). Then in (3-4), the motion planner coupled with the ATSP solver will compute the path.

Usually the product is not completely inspected, only the most relevant and sensible parts are checked. For this reason the system permits to the user to select and group in zones the points over the product. Each zone represents a space region to inspect. As in the case of crankshaft, usually the zones are not placed one next to another. Then, the robot needs to compute some extra movements to reach one zone from another. These transitional movements increase the time of the inspection critically if not well managed. The times required for moving from one zone to another can change if the zones ordering change. Subsequently, the simulator attempts to reduce these times modeling them as a feature to be optimized. Inside the simulator the problem is treated as a complete graph. Formalizing, the nodes represent the zones and the edges are weighted with the time required by the robot to drive between a couple of zones. Using the motion planning module, the simulator will compute the time cost to go from one zone to another, the edge cost. The graph is used as input for the ATSP solver, which will generate a time-saving sequence to cover all the inspection zones.

2.2   ATSP Solver and Heuristics

The solver used in this work is the Concorde TSP solver one of the most advanced and fastest TSP solvers using branch-and-cut where the Chained Lin-Kernighan [3] heuristic has been implemented and used in the described application. The Concorde TSP Solver is written in the ANSI C programming language and has been used to obtain the optimal solutions to the full set of 110 TSPLIB [9] instances, the largest having 85,900 cities.

	Zone 1	Zone 2	Zone 3	Zone 4
Zone 1	0	1,02835	1,43427	1,02835
Zone 2	1,02835	0	1,75662	1,43427
Zone 3	1,43427	1,51386	0	1,02835
Zone 4	1,02835	1,43427	1,02835	0

Fig. 2. Costs matrix representing the robot time needed to travel from one zone to another

As described in Subsection 2.1 the graph represents what the robot trajectory time is in moving from one zone to another. The manipulator dynamics are stressed by different and not manageable mechanic actors, like the friction. Then, the time of moving from zone A to zone B is different from performing the symmetric action (see Figure 2). For this reason our problem has been modeled as the Asymmetric TSP where each pair of nodes has two edges connecting each other where edge costs are different. Despite this, the Concorde is coded for the symmetric traveling salesman problem (TSP) and some related network optimization problems. To reformulate the ATSP as a TSP, for each zone a dummy zone (e.g, for Zone A a dummy zone Zone A*) is added. Between each zone and its corresponding dummy zone a negative or very small distance with cheap value is used. This ensures that each zone always occurs in the solution together with its dummy zone. The original distances are used between the zones and the dummy zones, where each zone is responsible for the distance going to the zone and the dummy zone is responsible for the distance coming from the zone. The distances between all zones and the distances between all dummy zones are set to infeasible, it means that a very large value is selected for these distances in order to make them unelectable from the solver.

2.3   Motion Planning

The aim of the offline motion planning architecture is find the correct robot arm joint values in order to avoid collisions between from one task and the following one. The planning and the optimization are performed over a configuration space of the robot kinematic (joint positions) and dynamic variables (joints velocity and acceleration) in order to plan a motion. A valid robot joints configuration is called key-point and it corresponds to a collision free placement of the robot in its physical workspace. The temporal sequence of these key-points is called the trajectory. The planners will add other configurations among each couple of key-points with the aim of avoiding collisions. The collision checking between two configurations is performed using a linear interpolation of the robot motions. Each algorithm performs a backward configuration search: from the last key-point to the first one. The software architecture core can be split in three steps as shown in the Figure 3.

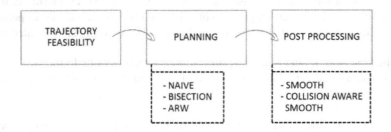

Fig. 3. Motion planning architecture overview

Fig. 4. Representation of smooth perturbation action. The middle points are moved towards the straight line.

In the first step, the trajectory feasibility is checked. The algorithm checks if each trajectory keypoint corresponds to a configuration reachable by the robot and it is not colliding. If the first step ends in a good way, the motion planners are executed in a hierarchical order, from the most simple and fast to the most effective but slower. A planner is executed only if the previous one fails to find a solution following this order:

1. *Naive*. Given the configuration sequence, the algorithm will check if each couple of points is connectible[2] otherwise it will try to add a point between them. Typically the middle point of three points, may include a collision or the three points are not connectible, then the algorithm will attempt to reposition this point editing each single point dimension with various correction factors.
2. *Bisection*. This algorithm uses a logic that is similar to the previous one with the following two main different features:
   (a) A middle point dimension is moved using perturbation of random points over a normal distribution.
   (b) When a collision free middle point is found, the connectible test is performed. But in this case each segment (first-middle and middle-second key-points) is treated recursively using a divide and conquer technique.
3. *ARW*. The Adaptive Random Walks algorithm is part of the Probabilistic Roadmap Methods. The proposed algorithm turns out to be simple to implement, and the solution it produces can be easily and efficiently optimized. Furthermore, the algorithm can incorporate adaptive components in order to be adapted to particular problems. Proofs of the theoretical soundness of the algorithm are provided in [4].

After the kinematic evaluation, the optimization algorithms will edit the key-points in order to make a smoother robot trajectory. All the algorithms that optimize the trajectory will be computed:

1. *Smooth*. When the feasible motion path has been computed, it is not rare that the final path has been filled with redundant points that makes the robot motions jerky. In order to avoid motion that stress robot mechanics and increase the motion time, several actions are performed:
   – If two points are connectible and the are some middle points, the lasts will be deleted.
   – Given each consecutive 3-tuple points, the middle one is moved using a perturbation method. The perturbation pushes the middle point straight to the line connecting the first and the third point (Figure 4).
2. *Collision Aware Smooth*. At this point, the motion plan is smooth, collision free but discrete. The resulted trajectory is smooth and time saving, but it does not consider the distance from the objects. This smooth planner keeps key-points to a minimum distance without loosing the trajectory smooth property built from the previous plan step.

---

[2] Two key-points are connectible if the robot motions needed to reach the second point starting from the first one are collision free.

3   Results and Case Study

The system has been evaluated on the Thermobot [1] test product shown in Figure 5. The first test focuses on the reliability of the system, where the zones over the product are labeled with consecutive numbers (see Figure 5). After the system computation, the output sequence is a reasonable one, 4-3-2-1, where the robot should spend 4.599 seconds to transitional movements. The worst case is the sequence 3-1-2-4, with a transitional trajectories time of 5.654 seconds. On average, this will save half second for each inspected product. This appears to be a good result considering the large number of pieces made in a factory.

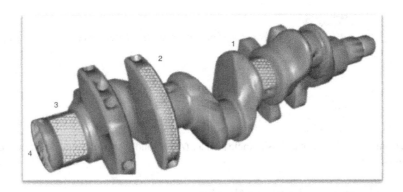

Fig. 5. Zones over a mechanical engine part: the crankshaft

The second set of tests focus on the performance of the motion planning architecture provided by the WorkCellSimulator. A good performance of the motion planning module is a must in order to compute the cost matrix for the ATSP solver (see Figure 2). The architecture is compared with a successful single shot algorithm, the ARW. Several trials with different trajectory sizes (Figures 6, 7) have been performed. Further, Figure 8 shows that the WorkCellSimulator motion planning architecture (hierarchical set of algorithms and heuristics) has higher performance than a single algorithm. That is because the mixed policy built inside the simulator is more flexible than a general purpose algorithm like ARW. Looking deeply, the standard deviation of the computational times is straightforward that the architecture is more stable in terms of response times. Which is a strong requirement for applications used in industrial processes.

Trajectory Size (Points)	Trial 1	Trial 2	Trial 3	Trial 4	Average	StdDev
20	4,71620	5,06383	4,99058	4,94046	4,92777	0,12979
50	11,24590	11,71840	11,73470	12,11530	11,70358	0,30829
80	16,06670	16,65910	16,56760	16,52070	16,45353	0,22881

Fig. 6. WorkCellSimulator planning architecture performance in different size trajectories

Trajectory Size (Points)	Trial 1	Trial 2	Trial 3	Trial 4	Average	StdDev
20	20,84690	16,30030	17,85460	22,17530	19,29428	2,33171
50	44,21270	34,50470	40,99020	36,79550	39,12578	3,74624
80	58,57220	45,83820	59,26940	53,26120	54,23525	5,37613

Fig. 7. ARW performance in different size trajectories

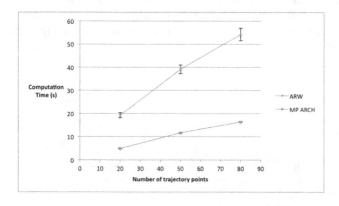

Fig. 8. Comparison between a classic single planner (ARW) and WorkCellSimulator motion planning architecture

4   Conclusions and Future Works

The paper presented the development and validation of a motion optimization system for the manufacturing quality inspection process. A robot equipped with a vision system has to cover a complex solid part. To correctly simulate the task execution, WorkCellSimulator was integrated with a module able to plan the minimum coverage of the path according to predefined temporal constraints. As a result, given a set of inspection points and a time within which they must be inspected, the system checks the points validity (i.e. every point must be reachable by the robot, and not cause collisions) and deletes those which do not satisfy such requirements. The ATSP algorithm orders the remaining points and forms the minimum coverage path observing the time constraints. The computed path is the trajectory the robot has to follow to inspect the product.

The use case proves that the system is able to select the most suitable inspection strategy according to the process cycle time.

As future work, we envision to be able to implement dynamic planning. It will include a dynamic path planning, collision avoidance and on-line simulation. In detail, an on-line work-cell simulation will be implemented in order to simulate the path of the robot in real time and to make continuously available information about potential collisions so that a dynamic adaptation of the planned motion will be possible. When the work cell is equipped with a system able to forward dynamic feedback to the simulator, the dynamic planning will adapt the motion of the robot according to this feedback; in the detection of cracks, for example, if the vision system provides feedback to the simulator, the latter will dynamically and locally adapt the collision-free path of the robot in order to optimize the image quality.

References

1. Thermobot project, http://thermobot.eu/
2. Govindaraju, M., Mital, A., Subramani, B.: A comparison between manual and hybrid methods in parts inspection. Integrated Manufacturing Systems 9, 344–349 (1998)
3. Applegate, D., Cook, W., Rohe, A.: Chained lin-kernighan for large traveling salesman problems. INFORMS Journal on Computing 15(1), 82–92 (2003)
4. Carpin, S., Pillonetto, G.: Motion planning using adaptive random walks. IEEE Transactions on Robotics 21(1), 129–136 (2005)
5. Chin, R.T., Harlow, C.A.: Automated visual inspection: A survey. IEEE Transaction on Pattern Analysis and Machine Intelligence PAMI-4(6), 557–573 (1982)
6. Coren, S., Girgus, J.S.: Visual spatial illusions: Many explanations. Science 179, 503–504 (1973)
7. Liangsiri, J., Corstack, H.-A., Höfling, M.: Simulation in quality management an approach to improve inspection planning, Schottland, September 5-8 (2004)
8. Radford, G.S.: The Control of Quality in Manufacturing. Ronald Press Co., New York (retrieved November 16, 2013), OCLC 1701274
9. Reinelt, G.: TSPLIB—A traveling salesman problem library. ORSA Journal on Computing 3(4), 376–384 (1991)
10. Schoonard, J.W., Gould, J.D.: Field of view and target uncertainty in visual search and inspection. In: Human Factors (February 1973)
11. Tonello, S., Zanetti, G.P., Finotto, M., Bortoletto, R., Tosello, E., Menegatti, E.: WorkCell-Simulator: A 3D simulator for intelligent manufacturing. In: Noda, I., Ando, N., Brugali, D., Kuffner, J.J. (eds.) SIMPAR 2012. LNCS, vol. 7628, pp. 311–322. Springer, Heidelberg (2012)
12. Wang, J.S.C.: Human reliability in visual inspection. Quality (September 1974)

Dealing with Conflicting Requirements in Robot System Engineering: A Laboratory-Based Course

Luca Gherardi[1], Davide Brugali[2], and Andrea Luzzana[2]

[1] ETH Zürich, Switzerland
lucagh@ethz.ch
[2] University of Bergamo, Bergamo, Italy
{andrea.luzzana,brugali}@unibg.it

Abstract. This paper presents a project-based laboratory for senior-level students in computer engineering that is based on the LEGO Mindstorms kits extended with a set of off-the-shelf microcontrollers and custom electronics. It is organized in an integrated set of projects, which individually cover a subset of typical issues and challenges involved in the development of a complete robotic system. The pedagogical goal is to equip students with an understanding of how engineering of complex projects is a multi-dimensional decision making process and with teamwork and self-learning skills.

1 Introduction

Robustness, versatility, low-cost, performance, and reusability are examples of conflicting requirements that make the process of engineering robotic systems a difficult and challenging endeavour [3]. Robotic system engineers should master highly heterogeneous technologies in order to exploit and integrate them in a consistent and effective way. Thus, from an educational point of view, robot system engineering is both a challenge and an opportunity [10].

Teaching robotic system engineering is challenging because Robotics is an experimental science that plays the role of integrator of the most advanced results in a large variety of research fields and thus is highly dependant on the evolution of the underlying technologies. Teaching robotic system engineering should therefore focus on providing students with the skills (1) to identify stable and varying aspects in the domain of robotic systems, (2) to analyze conflicting requirements arising from the need to exploit and integrate heterogeneous technologies, and (3) to perform careful multidimensional modelling and design of complex systems where properties are emerging from the interaction of constituent parts.

Learning robotic system engineering is an opportunity to discover how theoretical concepts in a variety of scientific disciplines typically learned in different classes can be applied in practice, and how synergies among disparate technological fields can be exploited to build complex systems [2].

Aim of this paper is to present a project-based laboratory that senior-level students in computer engineering take before graduation at the Computer science Department at the University of Bergamo. It is an optional laboratory that follows a compulsory half-year course in Robotics.

D. Brugali et al. (Eds.): SIMPAR 2014, LNAI 8810, pp. 554–565, 2014.
© Springer International Publishing Switzerland 2014

The pedagogical goal of this laboratory is to equip students with an understanding of how engineering of complex systems is a multi-dimensional decision making process, which consists in analyzing and eliciting conflicting requirements, identifying alternative designs, selecting, implementing, and verifying tradeoff solutions, and how complexity incorporates not only technological issues, but also the human organization.

For this purpose, the laboratory has been structured as a Problem-Based Learning (PBL) course, where students are assigned an open-ended engineering problem [9], which: a) requires more information than is initially available, b) admits multiple solution paths, c) changes as new information is obtained, d) requires collaboration among students. The laboratory described in this paper has several elements of novelty compared with the state of the art.

First, it covers a larger set of topics than other project-based courses (e.g. [7]), as it allows students to face an integrated set of challenges related to mechanical design, wireless communication protocol design, motor control, sensor data processing, microcontroller programming, and PC programming. This is highly appreciated by students since the curriculum in computer engineering at the University of Bergamo can be customized by including courses in mechatronics, and mechanical engineering.

Second, it addresses the various phases of the robot engineering process, from requirements elicitation and analysis, to system design and subsystem development, up to system integration and validation. A similar approach has been documented in [4], where a course in design and implementation of a small robot is described. The small robot is much simpler than the kind of robotic system developed during the project-based laboratory described in this paper.

Third, it uses the LEGO kit not for its simplicity as in [12], [5], [11], and [6] but for its versatility [13]. Indeed, the LEGO RCX has been replaced by a more powerful low cost microprocessor in order to control a larger number of motors and sensors than it is allowed by the RCX or the NXT devices.

Fourth, it is organized in an integrated set of projects, which individually cover the issues and challenges involved in the development of a specific subsystem of the complete robotic system. Each project is assigned to a small group of students, who have to complete their assignment taking into account the requirements of their subsystem and the constraints imposed by the other subsystems. This organization allows students to learn the importance of proper documentation of project results both as users and providers. In contrast, the courses described in the literature (e.g. [14], [6]) are typically organized as a set of simple and independent projects.

The paper is organized as follows. Section 2 summarizes the curriculum in computer science offered at the University of Bergamo. Section 3 presents the laboratory assignment and describes the LEGO robotic system that has been developed during the laboratory. Section 4 presents the organization of the laboratory in terms of student groups and activities. Section 5 illustrates the system engineering challenges faced by the students. Finally Section 6 reports on the lesson learned and on the project evaluation, and draws the relevant conclusions.

2   Course Description

The University of Bergamo offers a computer engineering degree organized in two levels (3 years and 2 years long). The project-based laboratory, presented in the paper is complementary to the course of Robotics, which is offered during the first semester of the last year of the second level degree, is mandatory in the Mechatronics and Industrial Informatics curricula and optional in the Networked Information Systems curriculum.

The objective of the Robotics course (9 CFUs)[1] is to provide an introduction to the fundamental concepts, models, and algorithms to develop software control systems for autonomous mobile manipulation robots. The key topics include: (a) robot kinematics, (b) motor control, (c) robot perception (laser, sonar, 2D-3D camera), (d) motion planning and navigation, (e) control and software architectures with a specific focus on reusing open source libraries. The course spans over 12 weeks in the first semester; it is made of lectures of 3 hours each, that are given twice a week for a total of 24 lectures.

Before the Robotics course, students follow several courses in computer science, control, electronics, and mechatronics, which provide the required background for the project-based laboratory described in this paper, such as: (a) high level programming languages (36 CFU), (b) embedded, real-time, and distributed system programming (15 CFU), (c) digital control and system identification (21 CFU), (d) multi-body systems modeling and design (6 CFU).

3   The LEGO Mobile Manipulator

The overall goal of the project-based laboratory, declared to the students during the first day, was the following. "*The final objective is the design and the realization of a mobile manipulator. The rover must be able to move towards a desired position (expressed in terms of x, y, θ with respect to the initial pose reference frame) while the arm to reach any pose in its 3D workspace (expressed in terms of joint positions). The human operator specifies the rover and arm target positions through a graphical user interface running on a standard PC. The effectiveness of the design should be evaluated in terms of* robustness *by defining a stress test for the hardware,* versatility *by analyzing the shape of the workspace, and* performance *by analyzing position accuracy and repeatability.*"

The assignment didn't specify any specific kinematic model, neither for the rover nor for the arm. The students were also free to decide the more appropriate localization mechanism to be used for computing the rover position (e.g. odometry, visual based), the number of computational nodes, and the distribution of functionality among the computational nodes.

The result of the laboratory-based course is the mobile manipulator robot depicted in Figure 1 (left). The robot is composed of an omnidirectional wheeled

---

[1] University Formative Credit (CFU):1 CFU correspond to 25 hours of study including homeworks.

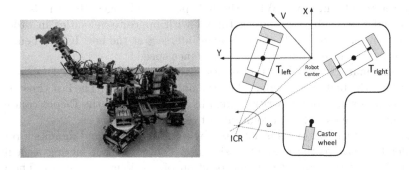

Fig. 1. The mobile manipulator (left) and the rover kinematic model (right)

rover and a 6 degrees of freedom (DOF) arm. The rover and the arm are controlled by two onboard microcontrollers that communicate with a remote PC workstation. The workstation executes a GUI that allows the user to specify a target position of the arm joints and a target position of the rover with respect to a global reference frame. A simple navigation algorithm localizes the robot using images captured by a ceiling camera, computes the trajectory (turn on place and move forward) from the current position to the target position and sends velocity commands to the rover MCU.

The robot has been built using six LEGO Mindstorms kits. In total, ten DC motors (9V, 300 mA), twelve rotary encoders with a resolution of 16 steps per revolution, and eight contact sensors were used. The motors allow a no-load maximum rotation speed of 360 rpm and a stall torque of 5.5 Ncm.

The LEGO RCX computational unit has been replaced by a more powerful STR32 microcontroller (MCU). The MCU interfaces the LEGO motors and sensors through custom electronic boards developed by the students during another course project. All the devices are power supplied by 3 cells LiPo batteries with a nominal voltage of 11.1 V and 2 A/h capacity. The MCU communicates with a remote PC over an 802.15.4 wireless network provided by Maxstream ZigBee modules [8] which establish a broadcast wireless connections offering a bitrate of 115200 bit/s.

3.1   The Robot Kinematics

The kinematic structure of the omnidirectional nonholonomic rover (see right part of Figure 1) is based on two separate differential drive subsystems (T_{left} and T_{right}), linked to a rigid platform by two passive steering axis, and a castor wheel. Each subsystem has a couple of actuated wheels coupled with a rotary encoder providing speed feedback and a third rotary encoder measuring the angular position of the steering axis.

The desired motion of the robot is specified by the linear velocity vector V and the rotational speed ω expressed in the robot reference frame (X, Y). These two parameters identify an unique instantaneous center of rotation (ICR) around which the robot will move. When the ICR position changes, the wheels of each differential drive subsystem are actuated with opposite velocities in order to rotate it on place so that the wheels axes intersect at the new ICR. Then, each wheel is actuated in order to reach a reference speed.

The kinematic structure of the robotic arm is that of a typical 7-DOF robotic arm, where the first axis is replaced by the underlying rover. The last three joints intersect in a single point (wrist center) in order to satisfy the Pieper condition and simplify the closed form solution of the inverse kinematics.

Each one of the six joints is actuated by a LEGO motor and mounts a rotary encoder to measure the angular position. A contact sensor, acting as a limit switch, is used to obtain the home position of the joint at startup. The arm MCU executes six separated closed loop position controllers.

4   Laboratory Organization

The objective of the project-based laboratory was to allow students to face the challenge of developing a complex system. Here, according to the etymology, complex does not mean complicated but interlaced. Indeed, the development of the LEGO robot described in Section 3 provides food for thought along two interlaced dimensions: spatial and temporal.

The spatial dimension is concerned with the modular structure of the robotic system (the rover, the arm, the onboard and the offboard computation). Considered the number of students, the development of the entire robot was broken down by the instructors into four projects (depicted in Figure 2), which were defined according to following principle: the projects (a) had to lead to the development of composable building blocks, so that they could be carried out concurrently, and (b) had to be interdependent, so that they could stimulate the discussion and the interaction between the groups.

The first two projects were assigned to groups of three students with a specific interest in mechatronics, while the other two projects to groups of four students with an interest in industrial informatics or information systems. Each project spanned a total of twelve weeks. Students carried on their projects during the sessions attended by the tutors (four hours per week) and met in the laboratory at least two additional times per week.

The temporal dimension is concerned with the development process, which requires the students to analyze, disentangle, and negotiate conflicting requirements, to revise design decisions according to ongoing work by other students, and to integrate heterogeneous technologies. The projects were structured in four phases, according on the typical design stages of mechatronic projects [14].

During the first phase (*Requirement elicitation and Technology assessment*), the four groups were invited to internally discuss the project assignment, to devise the requirements for the subsystem to be developed, to discuss these requirements with the other groups, to survey the available literature, and to get the necessary software tools.

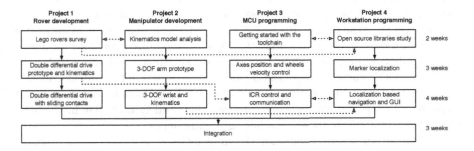

Fig. 2. The projects steps and dependencies (dashed arrows)

During the second and third phase (*Subsystem design and prototyping*), respectively, each group designed and developed a first prototype and the final version of its subsystem.

The fourth phase (*System integration and evaluation*) was for the integration of the system. It required the groups to coordinate their efforts in order to solve any inconsistencies in the software and in the hardware.

While the organization of the spatial dimension was fixed, the students had the possibility to discuss with the instructors the organization of activities carried out during the four development phases defined along the temporal dimension.

5 System Engineering Challenges

The students of the four projects faced several development challenges that allowed them to realize the complexity of system engineering and to learn the importance of negotiating conflicting requirements. The challenges can be grouped according to the development phases: requirement analysis, design and implementation, and integration. They are described in the next three subsections.

5.1 Challenge 1: Developing Feasible Requirements

During the first phase, the students faced the issue of analyzing the project assignment and eliciting the required functionality. The project assignment reflects a typical problem in system engineering: the customer needs are normally described as a wish list. In particular, the project assignment generically indicates that the robot has to be a mobile manipulator and that it has to be able to reach a pose in the 3D environment specified by the user.

The students of Project 1 analyzed different kinds of LEGO rovers documented in literature (such as [5]). The ambition of creating a kind of LEGO rover never developed before motivated the students to design an omnidirectional robot. Furthermore, the ominidirectional kinematics model would greatly satisfy the *versatility* requirement specified in the project assignment.

After a survey of the literature, the students quickly realized that omnidirectional rovers typically use Swedish wheels, which are not included in the LEGO

Mindstorms kit and cannot be easily built using LEGO bricks. They understood that in this case *Versatility* and *Reusability* are conflicting requirements.

Similarly, the students of Project 2 surveyed the literature on manipulator kinematic models. In order to satisfy the *Versatility* requirement, they evaluated the possibility to build a 7-DOF arm such as the Kuka LWR (3 DOF for the shoulder, 1 DOF for the elbow, and 3 DOF for the wrist). The students realized that such a robot would be difficult to build with LEGO bricks and moreover it would be an excessive weight for the rover. They understood that in this case *Versatility* and *Robustness* are conflicting requirements.

The two groups understood that the kinematics of the mobile manipulator had to be specified jointly. A viable alternative for building an omnidirectional rover has been identified by taking inspiration from [1]: the students of Project 1 decided to design a double differential drive rover, which is feasible reusing LEGO bricks and provides both stability and traction power (four motors for traction and steering). In order to take into account the payload limitations of the rover, the students of Project 2 decided to develop an arm with only 2 DOF for the shoulder since the missing DOF is provided by the rover.

The two groups discussed this choice with the students of Project 3, who emphasized the complexity of developing the control software for the double differential drive due to the need to synchronize and coordinate the motion of the two traction systems. They also pointed out that this issue would have affected the performance (position accuracy and repeatability) of both the rover and the arm. Here students understood that in this case *Robustness* and *Performance* are conflicting requirements.

The students of Project 1 raised a concern about the possibility to estimate the rover motion using only odometry due to the limited resolution of the encoders and the difficulty in controlling the double-differential rover. Two solutions were considered: using an onboard webcam to track visual markers placed on the floor in known positions or mounting the webcam on the ceiling in order to track a visual marker on the rover. Both solutions would satisfy the *Performance* requirement. The former solution would better satisfy the *Versatility* requirement, since the workspace would not be limited by the field of view of the camera mounted on the ceiling, but was immediately discarded because the students of Project 3 pointed out the limitations of the onboard MCU, which does not have enough power to process camera images. Here students understood the importance of *Resource constraints* in the design of embedded systems.

Students of Project 3 discussed with their colleagues of Project 4 about how to distribute the functionality of the robot between the MCUs and the workstation taking into account the low bitrate of the wireless communication and the different characteristics of the computational units. The MCU can perform real-time tasks by reacting to hardware interrupts in a very short time but has a limited computational power. On the contrary, the workstation PC has a high-frequency CPU but no efficient I/O mechanisms. Thus, the students agreed to implement the wheels closed-loop speed controller and ICR controller on the rover MCU, the joints closed-loop position controller on the arm MCU, and the image processing and GUI on the workstation.

5.2   Challenge 2: Integrating Heterogeneous Technologies

During the second and third phase, the students faced the issue of designing and implementing the four subsystems. In particular, they realized that the LEGO Mobile Manipulator is a good example of heterogeneous structures where properties (*Robustness, Versatility, Performance*) are emerging from the interaction of constituent parts and cannot be confined into individual subsystems.

The students of Project 2 faced several design issues due to the limited resolution of the encoders and the gears backlash. In particular they had to consider two conflicting requirements: position accuracy and repeatability. The former can be achieved by mounting the encoder between the motor shaft and the reduction gearbox of the joint. The latter, which is more important in industrial applications, can be achieved by mounting the encoder between the reduction gearbox and the joint shaft. The students understood that the performance of the robotic arm results from the specific integration of the mechanical subsystem and the sensor subsystem. Indeed, they realized that the position uncertainty due to the limited resolution of the encoder is higher than the gear backlash, thus repeatability could not be improved by mounting the encoder on the joint axis, while it was much easier to mount it on the motor axis.

Students of Project 2 realized that it was crucial to place the three motors of the wrist as much as possible close to the base of the arm in order to have a lower weight on the joints. This requirement could be met by building a complex differential transmission gearbox. As a result the joints of the wrist couldn't be moved independently requiring the definition of the transformation from joints velocity to speed of the motors. The students of Project 2 and Project 3 understood that systems engineering typically involves design decisions, whose effects are not local to individual subsystems but span over interconnected systems. Indeed, the design of the differential transmission implied a significant higher effort to implement the axis controllers on the MCU of the arm.

The students of Project 3 and Project 4 discussed the specification of a shared serial communication protocol between the MCUs and the remote workstation. They agreed on the packet length and structure, the commands identifiers and parameters, and the units of measurement of the exchanged data. The students understood the importance of separating the common interface between two interdependent functionalities from their specific implementations. Indeed, the students of the two groups could focus on the implementation of the functionality for motion control on the MCU and for navigation on the workstation independently. In particular, the students of Project 3 implemented the functions to read the encoders, to generate the PWM output for the motors, and to read the serial communication peripheral. The students of Project 4 implemented a simple GUI for sending commands to the rover and to the arm, using software libraries learned in previous courses. They also implemented a simple navigation algorithm that periodically localizes the rover using the ARTK+ library, computes the straight line between the rover current position and the target position, and generates the velocity commands to turn the rover on place and to drive it toward the target.

5.3   Challenge 3: Revising Requirements and Design Decisions

The development of the LEGO Mobile Manipulator has been a highly iterative process as is typical in complex systems engineering. The students had to solve some design problems that emerged only when they started testing and integrating the various subsystems.

The first prototype of the double differential drive had a notable limitation: the traction subsystems weren't able to steer more than 180 degrees because of the cables used for transmitting signals and power between the MCU, the motors and the encoders. Thus the students considered the possibility to improve the prototype in order to remove the steering limitation. They understood that the interface between the mechanical subsystem and the electronic subsystem was not well defined. They realized that a sliding contact along the turning axis of each traction system was needed. They faced here two conflicting requirements: *Performance* and *Reusability*, i.e they had to increase the steering capability of the rover using material available in the laboratory. The chosen approach was to build two sliding contacts using only LEGO bricks and copper wires. The rotor is made up of eight coaxial pulleys mounted on the revolving axis. Eight copper cables are rounded on each pulley and come out from the bottom of the rotor in order to be connected to two motors and two encoders. The stator is made up of sixteen coaxial vertical supports, which tense eight copper cables around the pulleys. These cables come out from the top of the stator in order to be connected to the MCU.

Once assembled, the LEGO mobile manipulator robot has been tested in order to validate the overall system and identify design errors. The following problems have been identified and solved during this phase:

- The load of the rover was higher than expected and not well balanced. As a consequence, the castor wheel was not able to turn adequately when the rover had to change direction. This problem has been mitigated by better distributing the load of the batteries.
- Oscillations in the motors movements led to a flickering motion of the rover. This problem has been addressed by better tuning the PI parameters of the wheel speed controllers.
- Several data packets were transmitted incorrectly during the communication between the workstation and the two MCUs on the robot. Students realized that the wireless communication in broadcast mode was unreliable and decided to implement a protocol that checks for corrupted packets in order to retransmit them.
- The marker localization algorithm was highly sensitive to the scene illumination due to the limited capability of the low-cost webcam. They suggested to use an additional light source to improve the scene illumination.

By integrating their subsystems and evaluating the resulting system, students had an additional opportunity to learn about the constraints that characterize systems engineering.

6 Evaluation and Concluding Remarks

Students were required to submit a technical documentation of their achievements at the end of each phase using the Trello (http://trello.com) collaboration tool, which provided each group of students with an individual project board and each student with an individual account. This system allowed the instructor to track the contribution of each student to the project development and assess the student learning (50% of the score). The documentation has been evaluated for completeness and adequacy of the bibliographic references and for the accuracy of the technical description of the proposed solution (e.g. the use of standard modeling languages, such as UML for documenting the software). The rest of the grade was based on oral questions designed to check to what extent students contributed to the project, their role in the group, and their understanding of the system requirements, the motivations underlying the design choices, and the correlation between design choices and system behaviour during the experimental evaluation of the robotic system functionality.

The analysis of the documentation and the oral exam clearly indicates that the students learned three fundamental lessons emerging from the challenges they faced during the development of the LEGO mobile manipulator.

The first lesson learned is that a careful analysis of the informal user's requirements (i.e. project assignment) and of the technical specifications (i.e. LEGO kit) must be performed in order to develop a good set of feasible requirements taking into account the resources available to the project (material, time, knowledge).

The second lesson learned is that robotic systems engineering is inherently complex due to the interdisciplinary skills required, the heterogeneous technologies involved, and the difficulty in characterizing the interactions among systems and subsystems.

The third lesson learned is that developing robotic systems is a highly iterative process that may require to revise initial requirements and design decisions. Even if the initial problem has been carefully decomposed in subproblems (the four projects), their individual solutions (the four subsystems) may not fit together particularly well at first.

The project-based laboratory has been introduced for the first time in the 2008-2009 session as complementary to the Robotic course. Beside the specific skills acquired through the project development, the positive effects of the laboratory on the student learning achievement can be measured indirectly by observing their grades attained for the Robotics course in each session.

As indicated in Table 1, in contrast to previous editions of the Robotics course, more students have passed the exam right after the end of the course and the average grades were higher. These results indicates that the project-based laboratory allowed the students to gain a better understanding of the theoretical

Table 1. Student attainment of the Robotics course before and after the introduction
of the project-based laboratory

Metric	2001-2008	2009-2013
Mean success rate (%)	73	87
Mean score (min 18, max 30)	25	27

concepts presented in the Robotics course. In addition the instructors observed
a more regular and involved students' partecipation during the classes.

With regard to the pedagogical objectives illustrated in Section 1, the development of LEGO robot has presented both strengths and weaknesses.

The proposed project-based laboratory offered the students the opportunity
to appreciate the multidisciplinary nature of robotics, and to investigate the close
relationship between software and hardware design. It is easily scalable and can
be offered to larger classes. For example, a fifth group of students could develop
a perception system, which uses the LEGO light sensor to drive the rover along
a visual path on the floor. A sixth group of students could use the same sensor
to recognize colored spots on a wall. In this case, the sensor could be mounted
on the arm. In both cases, additional conflicting requirements would emerge.

At the same time, the limitations of the LEGO kit generated a sense of frustra-
tion in the students, who got excited about creating an entire robot from scratch
but got disappointed about the high technological gap between the project-based
laboratory and other theoretical courses in their curriculum. More specifically,
the groups who developed the rover and the arm used a trial-and-error method
of direct implementation of the chosen kinematics model since the mechanical
properties of LEGO bricks (gears, wheels, pulley, joints) were not available for
performing a model-based design and evaluation of transmission efficiency, backlash, and wear as they learned in previous courses. In contrast, the students who
programmed the MCU followed the Ziegler-Nichols empirical method to tune
the PI parameters of the position and speed controllers

The validity of the approach has been evaluated by requesting the students
to fill an anonymous questionnaire, which is common to all the courses of the
Faculty of Engineering at the University of Bergamo. Table 2 summarizes the
results, which reports the mean and the spread of the scores for the project-
based laboratory presented in this paper and the mean of the scores for all the
courses of the Faculty of Engineering (the maximum score was ten). Overall the
project-based laboratory has been successful, as demonstrated by the high scores
of the first three questions. Students found it appropriate to have this course in
their curriculum, they were highly motivated to contribute to the success of the
team work, and considered the topic very interesting. The workload has been
perceived to be in line with other courses. Most students found unusual the lack
of a textbook and the need to search for adequate material by themselves.

Table 2. Scores of the evaluation questionnaires

Question	Mean	Spread	Mean (Faculty)
Curriculum Organization	7.9	1.5	7.4
Motivation	8.4	0.7	7.3
Interest in the topic	8.1	1.4	7.2
Workload adequacy	7.1	1.2	7.0
Teaching material adequacy	7.0	2.7	8.0
Assessment Method	7.2	1.7	7.9

References

1. Borenstein, J.: Experimental results from internal odometry error correction with the omnimate mobile robot. IEEE Transactions on Robotics and Automation 14(6), 963–969 (1998)
2. Brugali, D.: Exploiting the synergies between robotics and software engineering: A project-based laboratory. In: Global Engineering Education Conference (EDUCON). IEEE (2014)
3. Brugali, D., Gherardi, L., Biziak, A., Luzzana, A., Zakharov, A.: A reuse-oriented development process for component-based robotic systems. In: Noda, I., Ando, N., Brugali, D., Kuffner, J.J. (eds.) SIMPAR 2012. LNCS (LNAI), vol. 7628, pp. 361–374. Springer, Heidelberg (2012)
4. Crisman, J.: System design via small mobile robots. IEEE Trans. Educ. (1996)
5. Kim, S., Jeon, J.: Introduction for freshmen to embedded systems using lego mindstorms. IEEE Trans. Educ. 52(1), 99–108 (2009)
6. Kim, Y.: Control systems lab using a lego mindstorms nxt motor system. IEEE Trans. Educ. 54(3), 452–461 (2011)
7. Lee, C., Su, J., Lin, K., Chang, J., Lin, G.: A project-based laboratory for learning embedded system design with industry support. IEEE Trans. Educ. (2010)
8. Maxstream XBee ZigBee, http://www.digi.com/
9. O'Grady, M.J.: Practical problem-based learning in computing education. Trans. Comput. Educ. 12(3), 10:1–10:16 (2012)
10. Padir, T., Chernova, S.: Guest editorial special issue on robotics education. IEEE Transactions on Education 56(1), 1–2 (2013)
11. Papadimitriou, V., Papadopoulos, E.: Putting Low-Cost Commercial Robotics Component to the Test. IEEE Robotics & Automation Magazine 14, 99–110 (2007)
12. Ruiz del Solar, J.: Robotics-centered outreach activities: An integrated approach. IEEE Trans. Educ. 53(1), 38–45 (2010)
13. Ruzzenente, M., Koo, M., Nielsen, K., Grespan, L., Fiorini, P.: A review of robotics kits for tertiary education. In: Proc. Int. Workshop Teaching Robot. Teaching Robot., Integr. Robot. School Curric., Riva del Garda, Italy (2012)
14. Tutunji, T., Saleem, A., Rabbo, S.A.: An undergraduate mechatronics project class at philadelphia university, Jordan: Methodology and experience. IEEE Trans. Educ. 52(3), 365–374 (2009)

Using Augmented Measurements to Improve the Convergence of ICP

Jacopo Serafin and Giorgio Grisetti

Dept. of Computer, Control and Management Engineering,
Sapienza University of Rome, Via Ariosto 25, 00185, Rome, Italy
{serafin,grisetti}@dis.uniroma1.it

Abstract. Point cloud registration is an essential part for many robotics applications and this problem is usually addressed using some of the existing variants of the Iterative Closest Point (ICP) algorithm. In this paper we propose a novel variant of the ICP objective function which is minimized while searching for the registration. We show how this new function, which relies not only on the point distance, but also on the difference between surface normals or surface tangents, improves the registration process. Experiments are performed on synthetic data and real standard benchmark datasets, showing that our approach outperforms other state of the art techniques in terms of convergence speed and robustness.

Keywords: Point Cloud Registration, ICP, Surface Normals.

1 Introduction

Registering two point clouds is a building block of many robot applications such as simultaneous localization and mapping (SLAM), object recognition and detection, augmented reality and many others. This problem is commonly solved by variants of the Iterative Closest Point (ICP) algorithm proposed by Besl and McKay [1]. ICP tries to find a transformation that minimizes the distance of a set of corresponding points in the two clouds. At each iteration ICP refines the estimate of the transformation by alternating a search and an optimization routine. Given the current transform, the search looks for corresponding points in the two clouds. The optimization computes the transformation that results in the minimum distance between the corresponding points found by the search step. ICP is a very successful scheme and several variants of increasing performances have been proposed. If the correspondences are free from outliers and the measurements are affected by low noise, the transformation can be found directly by applying the Horn formula [3].

The whole concept at the base of ICP is that, at each iteration, an improved transformation with respect to the previous one is found. Such a transformation represents the new initial guess for the heuristic used to find the correspondences and allows to determine better associations at the next iteration. Accordingly, researchers focused on seeking for heuristics that provide "good" correspondences.

D. Brugali et al. (Eds.): SIMPAR 2014, LNAI 8810, pp. 566–577, 2014.
© Springer International Publishing Switzerland 2014

The original idea of picking up the closest points [1] has been progressively refined to consider features, curvature and other characteristics of the points. Pomerlau *et al.* [5] provided an excellent overview on these different variants.

ICP and its variants require multiple iterations because it does not exist an heuristic that provides the exact correspondences. Since the optimization requires linear time in the number of correspondences, the bottleneck of the computation is represented by the heuristic that has to compute them.

The main drawback of ICP in its original formulation is the assumption that the points in the two surfaces are exactly the same. This is clearly not true as the point clouds are obtained by sampling a set of points from the surface observed by the sensor. If the observer position changes, the chances that two points in the clouds are the same is very low. This is particularly evident at low sampling resolutions. Aware of this aspect, Magnusson *et al.* [4] proposed to approximate the surface with a set of Gaussians capturing the local statistics of the surface in the neighborhood of a point. In that representation, called the Normal Distrubution Transform (NDT), the correspondence search uses the Mahalanobis distance instead of the Euclidean one and the optimization tries to minimize it.

Similarly, Segal *et al* [6] proposed a refined version of ICP called *Generalized ICP* (GICP). The core idea behind this algorithm is to account for the shape of the surface which surrounds a point by approximating it with a planar patch. In the optimization, two corresponding patches are aligned onto each other, neglecting the error along their tangent direction. This can be straightforwardly implemented by minimizing the Mahalanobis distance of corresponding points, where the covariance matrix of a measurement is forced to have the shape of a disk aligned with the sampled surface. Thanks to the better rejection of false correspondences based on the surface normal cue and the more realistic objective function, NDT and GICP exhibit a substantially more stable convergence behavior.

In fact, within ICP and its variants, the optimization and the correspondence search are not independent. If the optimization is robust to outliers and exhibits a smooth behavior, the chances that it finds a better solution at the subsequent step increases. In this way an improvement is obtained at each iteration until a good solution is found. Despite NDT and GICP, the authors are unaware of other methods that improve the objective function.

Since point clouds are the effects of sampling a surface, the local characteristics of this surface play a role in the optimization. From this point of view, the objective function has to express some distance between *surface samples*, and the optimization algorithm has to determine the optimal alignment between these two set of samples. A surface sample, however, is not fully described just by 3D points, but it requires additional cues like the surface normal, the curvature and, potentially, the direction of the edge. Both NDT and GICP minimize a distance between corresponding points, while they neglect additional cues that can indeed play a role in determining the transformation and in rejecting outliers.

In this paper we propose a novel variant of the objective function which is optimized while searching for the transformation. This function depends not only on the relative point distance, but also on the difference between surface normals or tangents in case the point lies on an edge. We provide an iterative form for the optimization routine and we show through experiments performed on synthetic data and standard benchmark datasets that our approach outperforms other state of the art techniques, both in terms of convergence speed and robustness.

2 ICP

The problem of registering two point clouds consists in finding the rotation and the translation that maximizes the overlap between the two clouds. More formally, let $\mathcal{P}^{\mathrm{r}} = \{\mathbf{p}^{\mathrm{r}}_{1:N^{\mathrm{r}}}\}$ and $\mathcal{P}^{\mathrm{c}} = \{\mathbf{p}^{\mathrm{c}}_{1:N^{\mathrm{c}}}\}$ be the two set of points, we want to find the transformation $\mathbf{T}^*$ that minimizes the distance between corresponding points in the two scenes:

$$
\mathbf{T}^* = \operatorname*{argmin}_{\mathbf{T}} \sum_{\mathcal{C}} \overbrace{\left(\mathbf{p}^{\mathrm{c}}_i - \mathbf{T} \oplus \mathbf{p}^{\mathrm{r}}_j\right)^T \boldsymbol{\Omega}_{ij} \underbrace{\left(\mathbf{p}^{\mathrm{c}}_i - \mathbf{T} \oplus \mathbf{p}^{\mathrm{r}}_j\right)}_{\mathbf{e}_{ij}(\mathbf{t})}}^{\chi^2_{ij}} . \tag{1}
$$

In Eq. 1 the symbols have the following meaning:

- $\mathbf{T}$ is the transform that is updated at each step i of the iterative algorithm with the one found at iteration $i-1$;
- $\boldsymbol{\Omega}_{ij}$ is an information matrix that takes into account the noise properties of the sensor or of the surface;
- $\mathcal{C} = \{\langle i, j \rangle_{1:M}\}$ is a set of correspondences between points in the two clouds. $\langle i, j \rangle \in \mathcal{C}$ means that the point $\mathbf{p}^{\mathrm{r}}_j$ in the cloud $\mathcal{P}^{\mathrm{r}}$ corresponds to the point $\mathbf{p}^{\mathrm{c}}_i$ in the cloud $\mathcal{P}^{\mathrm{c}}$;
- $\mathbf{e}_{ij}(\mathbf{t})$ is the error function that computes the distance between the point $\mathbf{p}^{\mathrm{c}}_i$ and the corresponding point $\mathbf{p}^{\mathrm{r}}_j$ in the other cloud after applying the transformation $\mathbf{T}$;
- χ^2_{ij} is the $\boldsymbol{\Omega}_{ij}$-norm of the error $\mathbf{e}_{ij}(\mathbf{t})$;
- $\oplus$ is an operator that applies the transformation $\mathbf{T}$ to a point $\mathbf{p}$. If we use the homogeneous notation for transformations and points, $\oplus$ reduces to the matrix-vector product.

In general, the correspondences between two point clouds are not known. However, in presence of a good approximation for the initial transform, they can be "guessed" through some heuristic like nearest neighbour. In its most general formulation, ICP iteratively refines an initial transform $\mathbf{T}$ by searching for correspondences and finding the solution of Eq. 1. Such a new transformation is then used in order to compute the new correspondences. Eq. 1 describes the objective function used in the optimization of ICP, NDT and GICP. In the case of ICP, $\boldsymbol{\Omega}_{ij}$ is a diagonal matrix potentially scaled with a weight representing the confidence about the correctness of a correspondence. NDT computes the covariances Σ_i directly from the point cloud and it measures the distances by using the mean of the Gaussians rather than the points as shown in Eq. 2.

$$\mathbf{T}^* = \underset{\mathbf{T}}{\operatorname{argmin}} \sum_{\mathcal{C}} \left(\mu_i^{\mathrm{c}} - \mathbf{T} \oplus \mathbf{p}_j^{\mathrm{r}} \right)^T \Sigma_i^{-1} \left(\mu_i^{\mathrm{c}} - \mathbf{T} \oplus \mathbf{p}_j^{\mathrm{r}} \right) \ . \tag{2}$$

In GICP, $\Omega_{ij} = \Sigma_i^{-1}$ depends only on the ith point $\mathbf{p}_i^{\mathrm{c}}$ and its neighborhood. The covariance Σ_i is enforced to have a disk shape and to lie on the surface from where $\mathbf{p}_i^{\mathrm{c}}$ was sampled. In all cases, the difference $\mathbf{p}_i^{\mathrm{c}} - \mathbf{T} \oplus \mathbf{p}_j^{\mathrm{r}}$ is a 3D vector that measures the offset between two 3D points and the domain of the error function is $\Re^3$.

Since an increase in the dimensionality of the points makes the whole system more observable, less correspondences are required for the optimization process. By characterizing each point with other quantities to which a transform can be applied, we can achieve such an increase in the dimensionality. We propose, for this reason, the use of normals for quasi-planar regions and/or tangents for regions of high curvature.

3 Extended ICP

In this section we describe the extension of the model of ICP in order to consider also normals and tangents of the surface. We first illustrate the general concept and, subsequently, we focus on the case in which a local surface has either a normal, a tangent or none of the two. We conclude the section by sketching an algorithm to carry on the optimization.

3.1 Extending the Measurements

Let $\mathbf{n}_i$ be the normal of a point $\mathbf{p}_i$ belonging to a certain surface, and $\boldsymbol{\tau}_i$ its tangent if the point is part of an edge, we can then extend Eq. 1 as follows:

$$\begin{aligned}
\mathbf{T}^* = \underset{\mathbf{T}}{\operatorname{argmin}} \quad & \sum_{\mathcal{C}} \left(\mathbf{p}_i^{\mathrm{c}} - \mathbf{T} \oplus \mathbf{p}_j^{\mathrm{r}} \right)^T \Omega_{ij}^{\mathrm{p}} \left(\mathbf{p}_i^{\mathrm{c}} - \mathbf{T} \oplus \mathbf{p}_j^{\mathrm{r}} \right) \\
+ \quad & \sum_{\mathcal{C}} \left(\mathbf{n}_i^{\mathrm{c}} - \mathbf{T} \oplus \mathbf{n}_j^{\mathrm{r}} \right)^T \Omega_{ij}^{\mathrm{n}} \left(\mathbf{n}_i^{\mathrm{c}} - \mathbf{T} \oplus \mathbf{n}_j^{\mathrm{r}} \right) \\
+ \quad & \sum_{\mathcal{C}} \left(\boldsymbol{\tau}_i^{\mathrm{c}} - \mathbf{T} \oplus \boldsymbol{\tau}_j^{\mathrm{r}} \right)^T \Omega_{ij}^{\tau} \left(\boldsymbol{\tau}_i^{\mathrm{c}} - \mathbf{T} \oplus \boldsymbol{\tau}_j^{\mathrm{r}} \right) \ .
\end{aligned} \tag{3}$$

Here $\mathbf{n}_i^{\mathrm{c}}$, $\mathbf{n}_j^{\mathrm{r}}$ and Ω_{ij}^{n} represent respectively the normal of the point $\mathbf{p}_i^{\mathrm{c}}$ and $\mathbf{p}_i^{\mathrm{r}}$, and the information matrix of the correspondence among the two normals. Similarly, $\boldsymbol{\tau}_i^{\mathrm{c}}$, $\boldsymbol{\tau}_j^{\mathrm{r}}$ and Ω_{ij}^{τ} are the tangents and the information matrix of the correspondence among the two tangents. We recall that, if $\mathbf{T}$ is a transformation described by a rotation matrix $\mathbf{R}$ and a translation vector $\mathbf{t}$, the $\oplus$ operator has different definitions depending on its arguments:

$$\mathbf{T} \oplus \mathbf{x} = \begin{cases} \mathbf{R} \cdot \mathbf{x} + \mathbf{t} & \text{if } \mathbf{x} \text{ is a point} \\ \mathbf{R} \cdot \mathbf{x} & \text{if } \mathbf{x} \text{ is a tangent or a normal} \end{cases} \tag{4}$$

A Mahalanobis distance between two point clouds can be measured by considering also the *distances of corresponding normals* and *corresponding tangents* after applying the transformation $\mathbf{T}$, as shown in Eq. 3.

By defining an extended point $\bar{\mathbf{p}}$ as a vector consisting of a point $\mathbf{p}$, its normal $\mathbf{n}$ and its tangent $\boldsymbol{\tau}$, we have a straightforward modification of the $\oplus$ operator as

$$\bar{\mathbf{p}} = \big(\mathbf{p}, \mathbf{n}, \boldsymbol{\tau} \big)^T \qquad \mathbf{T} \oplus \bar{\mathbf{p}} = \big(\mathbf{R}\mathbf{p} + \mathbf{t}, \mathbf{R}\mathbf{n}, \mathbf{R}\boldsymbol{\tau} \big)^T \ . \tag{5}$$

Eq. 3 can be, then, compactly rewritten in terms of extended points as

$$\mathbf{T}^* = \operatorname*{argmin}_{\mathbf{T}} \sum_{C} \big(\bar{\mathbf{p}}_i^c - \mathbf{T} \oplus \bar{\mathbf{p}}_j^r \big)^T \bar{\boldsymbol{\Omega}}_{ij} \big(\bar{\mathbf{p}}_i^c - \mathbf{T} \oplus \bar{\mathbf{p}}_j^r \big) \ , \tag{6}$$

where $\bar{\boldsymbol{\Omega}}_{ij} = \operatorname{diag}(\boldsymbol{\Omega}_{ij}^{\mathrm{p}}, \boldsymbol{\Omega}_{ij}^{\mathrm{n}}, \boldsymbol{\Omega}_{ij}^{\tau})$ summarizes the contribution of $\boldsymbol{\Omega}_{ij}^{\mathrm{p}}$, $\boldsymbol{\Omega}_{ij}^{\mathrm{n}}$ and $\boldsymbol{\Omega}_{ij}^{\tau}$. The function $\operatorname{diag}(\mathbf{a}_1, \dots, \mathbf{a}_k)$ stands for a diagonal matrix whose entries, starting from the upper left corner, are $\mathbf{a}_1, \dots, \mathbf{a}_k$. If the point is not sampled from a locally planar surface nor from an edge, a reasonable distance metric is the Euclidean distance. For these points, we fall back to the ICP case, which is enclosed in Eq. 6 by setting the information matrices of the tangent and the normal to the null matrix: $\boldsymbol{\Omega}_{ij}^{\mathrm{n}} = \boldsymbol{\Omega}_{ij}^{\tau} = 0$.

When measuring the distance between two planar patches, it is reasonable to neglect displacements along the tangent direction of the plane, while errors along the normal direction should be more severely penalized. Additionally, the normals of the two planes should be as close as possible. However, *this constraint cannot be enforced when using only 3D points*. To obtain this behavior from the error function, we can impose $\boldsymbol{\Omega}_{ij}^{\mathrm{p}}{}^{-1}$ to be a disc lying on the surface around $\mathbf{p}_i^c$, as done in [6]. Since the tangent is not defined in a planar patch, we set $\boldsymbol{\Omega}_{ij}^{\tau} = 0$. Additionally, we set the covariance matrix $\boldsymbol{\Omega}_{ij}^{\mathrm{n}}{}^{-1}$ of the normal to have a shape which is elongated in the normal direction. In this way the error between the normals introduces a strong momentum that "forces" them to have the same direction.

Conversely, when measuring the distance between two edges, it is reasonable to slide them onto each other along the tangent direction. This behavior can be obtained by enforcing $\boldsymbol{\Omega}_{ij}^{\mathrm{p}}{}^{-1}$ to have a prolonged shape and to lie along the tangent direction. The tangents $\boldsymbol{\tau}$, instead, can be used to penalize two edges not lying on the same direction by setting $\boldsymbol{\Omega}_{ij}^{\tau}$ to have a shape which is elongated in the direction of $\boldsymbol{\tau}$. Since an edge has no normal, $\boldsymbol{\Omega}_{ij}^{\mathrm{n}}$ has to be set to 0.

The reader might notice that tangents and normals are mutually exclusive. Since the contributions of the tangent and the normal components to the χ_{ij}^2 have the same matrix dimensions, we can further simplify the extended point $\bar{\mathbf{p}}$ by partitioning it into an affine part $\mathbf{p}$, and in a linear part $\mathbf{l}$. The former is subject to translations and rotations, the latter only to the rotation. In this way it is possible to reduce the dimension of the error function and to speed up the calculation without loss of generality. We therefore define a compact form for an extended point $\tilde{\mathbf{p}}$ as

$$\tilde{\mathbf{p}} = \big(\mathbf{p}, \mathbf{l} \big)^T \qquad \mathbf{T} \oplus \tilde{\mathbf{p}} = \big(\mathbf{R}\mathbf{p} + \mathbf{t}, \mathbf{R}\mathbf{l} \big)^T \ . \tag{7}$$

Table 1. This table summarizes the components of the information matrix used in our algorithm, depending on the type of the structure around a point. $\mathbf{R}_{n_i}$ and $\mathbf{R}_{\tau_i}$ are two rotation matrices that bring the y axis respectively along the direction of the normal $\mathbf{n}_i$, or the tangent τ_i. ϵ is a small value (10^{-3} in our experiments).

Case	Ω_{ij}^{p}	Ω_{ij}^{n}	Ω_{ij}^{r}
planar	$\mathbf{R}_{n_i}\mathrm{diag}(\frac{1}{\epsilon},1,1)\mathbf{R}_{n_i}^T$	$\mathbf{R}_{n_i}\mathrm{diag}(\frac{1}{\epsilon},\frac{1}{\epsilon},1)\mathbf{R}_{n_i}^T$	0
edge	$\mathbf{R}_{\tau_i}\mathrm{diag}(\frac{1}{\epsilon},\frac{1}{\epsilon},1)\mathbf{R}_{\tau_i}^T$	0	$\mathbf{R}_{\tau_i}\mathrm{diag}(\frac{1}{\epsilon},\frac{1}{\epsilon},1)\mathbf{R}_{\tau_i}^T$
none	$\mathbf{I}$	0	0

According to the new formalism, the objective function in Eq. 6 becomes

$$\mathbf{T}^* = \operatorname*{argmin}_{\mathbf{T}} \sum_{\mathcal{C}} \left(\tilde{\mathbf{p}}_i^{\mathrm{c}} - \mathbf{T}\oplus\tilde{\mathbf{p}}_j^{\mathrm{r}}\right)^T \tilde{\Omega}_{ij} \underbrace{\left(\tilde{\mathbf{p}}_i^{\mathrm{c}} - \mathbf{T}\oplus\tilde{\mathbf{p}}_j^{\mathrm{r}}\right)}_{\tilde{\mathbf{e}}_{ij}(\mathbf{T})}, \qquad (8)$$

where $\tilde{\Omega}_{ij} = \mathrm{diag}(\Omega_{ij}^{\mathrm{p}}, \Omega_{ij}^{\mathrm{l}})$, and the information matrices must be modified according to Table 2

Table 2. This table summarizes the components of the information matrix for our algorithm when using a reduced representation

Case	$\mathbf{l}_i$	Ω_{ij}^{p}	Ω_{ij}^{l}
planar	$\mathbf{n}_i$	$\mathbf{R}_{n_i}\mathrm{diag}(\frac{1}{\epsilon},1,1)\mathbf{R}_{n_i}^T$	$\mathbf{R}_{n_i}\mathrm{diag}(\frac{1}{\epsilon},\frac{1}{\epsilon},1)\mathbf{R}_{n_i}^T$
edge	τ_i	$\mathbf{R}_{\tau_i}\mathrm{diag}(\frac{1}{\epsilon},\frac{1}{\epsilon},1)\mathbf{R}_{\tau_i}^T$	$\mathbf{R}_{\tau_i}\mathrm{diag}(\frac{1}{\epsilon},\frac{1}{\epsilon},1)\mathbf{R}_{\tau_i}^T$
none	0	$\mathbf{I}$	0

3.2 Carrying on the Optimization

In this section we present the procedure for the minimization described in Eq. 8 by using a strengthened least squares procedure. The input of this algorithm are two sets of extended points $\tilde{\mathbf{p}}_{1:n}^{\mathrm{c}}$ and $\tilde{\mathbf{p}}_{1:m}^{\mathrm{c}}$, a (noisy) set of candidate correspondences $\mathcal{C} = \langle i,j\rangle_{1:M}$ and the information matrix $\tilde{\Omega}_{ij}$, computed according to Table 2. The aim of this procedure is to find the transform $\mathbf{T}^*$ that minimizes the following objective or cost function

$$\mathbf{T}^* = \operatorname*{argmin}_{\mathbf{T}} \sum_{\mathcal{C}} \underbrace{\tilde{\mathbf{e}}_{ij}(\mathbf{T})^T \tilde{\Omega}_{ij} \tilde{\mathbf{e}}_{ij}(\mathbf{T})}_{\tilde{\chi}_{ij}^2}. \qquad (9)$$

Each correspondence contributes to the overall cost function by the scalar term $\tilde{\chi}_{ij}^2$.

As is well know, the minimizing $\mathbf{T}^*$ of Eq. 9 can be found by iteratively solving the following linear system:

$$\mathbf{H} \cdot \Delta \mathbf{T} = -\mathbf{b} \, , \tag{10}$$

where $\mathbf{H} = \sum_{\mathcal{C}} \mathbf{J}_{ij}^T \tilde{\mathbf{\Omega}}_{ij} \mathbf{J}_{ij}$ is the Hessian matrix, $\mathbf{b} = \sum_{\mathcal{C}} \mathbf{J}_{ij}^T \tilde{\mathbf{\Omega}}_{ij} \tilde{\mathbf{e}}_{ij}$ is the coefficient vector and $\mathbf{J}_{ij}$ is the Jacobian of the error function. At each iteration we compute an improved transform $\mathbf{T}'$ from the previous transform $\mathbf{T}$ by using $\mathbf{H}$ and $\mathbf{b}$. By solving the linear system in Eq. 10 we determine a perturbation $\Delta \mathbf{T}$ which is applied to the previous transform $\mathbf{T}$ in order to reduce the error. The transform $\mathbf{T}'$ of the next iteration is thus computed as

$$\mathbf{T}' = \Delta \mathbf{T} \oplus \mathbf{T}' \, . \tag{11}$$

For readers interested in further details on the derivation of Eq. 10 we suggest the work by Kümmerle et al. [2].

In our approach, a perturbation $\Delta \mathbf{T}$ is defined as a vector composed of two parts $(\Delta \mathbf{t} \ \Delta \mathbf{q})^T$ where $\Delta \mathbf{t} = (\Delta t_x \ \Delta t_y \ \Delta t_z)$ is a translation vector and $\Delta \mathbf{q} = (\Delta q_x \ \Delta q_y \ \Delta q_z)$ is the imaginary part of the normalized quaternion used to represent an incremental rotation. If $\Delta \mathbf{t} = 0$, the perturbation is the 4-by-4 identity matrix. Under this parameterization, the Jacobian $\mathbf{J}_{ij}$ with respect to the local perturbation $\Delta \mathbf{T}$ is computed as

$$\mathbf{J}_{ij} = \left. \frac{\partial \mathbf{e}_{ij} \left(\Delta \mathbf{T} \oplus \mathbf{T}^{(n)} \right)}{\partial \Delta \mathbf{T}} \right|_{\Delta \mathbf{T}=0} = \begin{pmatrix} -\mathbf{I} & 2[\mathbf{T} \oplus \mathbf{p}_j^r]_\times \\ \mathbf{0} & 2[\mathbf{T} \oplus \mathbf{l}_j^r]_\times \end{pmatrix} \, , \tag{12}$$

where $[\mathbf{x}]_\times$ is the cross product matrix of the vector $\mathbf{x}$. In practice, by exploiting the block structure and the sparsity of the Jacobian, it is possible to compute efficiently the linear system in Eq. 10.

In order to be robust to the presence of outliers, which usually significantly contribute to the error, the proposed scheme has to be further modified. To reduce the contribution of these wrong terms, we scale the information matrix of each correspondence whose χ^2 is greater than an acceptance threshold by a factor γ_{ij}.

$$\gamma_{ij} = \begin{cases} 1 & \text{if } \chi_{ij}^2 < K \\ \frac{K}{\chi^2} & \text{otherwise} \end{cases} \tag{13}$$

Even if the correct correspondences are rejected at the beginning of the iterative process, these will be considered again as the system converges towards a better solution, since their χ^2 will decrease.

In order to smooth the convergence it can be also added a damping factor to the linear system in Eq. 10. In practice, $\Delta \mathbf{T}$ is found by solving the damped linear system $(\mathbf{H} + \lambda \mathbf{I})\Delta \mathbf{T} = -\mathbf{b}$, since it prevents the solution to take too large steps that might be caused by nonlinearities or wrong correspondences.

3.3   Optimization Summary

In this subsection we wrap-up the ideas discussed above and we provide the sketch of an iterative algorithm the optimization of Eq. 8. At each iteration our algorithm computes an improved estimate $\mathbf{T}'$ from the current estimate $\mathbf{T}$ by executing the following steps:

1. Compute the information matrices $\tilde{\mathbf{\Omega}}_{ij}$ according to Table 2;
2. Compute the error vector $\tilde{\mathbf{e}}_{ij}$ as shown in Eq. 8;
3. Compute the Jacobian $\mathbf{J}_{ij}$ according to Eq. 12;
4. Compute the $\tilde{\chi}^2_{ij}$ as in Eq. 9 and the scaling factor γ_{ij} from Eq. 13;
5. Compute a scaled version of the Hessian and of the coefficient vector as:

$$\mathbf{H} = \sum_{\mathcal{C}} \gamma_{ij} \mathbf{J}_{ij}^T \tilde{\mathbf{\Omega}}_{ij} \mathbf{J}_{ij} \qquad \mathbf{b} = \sum_{\mathcal{C}} \gamma_{ij} \mathbf{J}_{ij}^T \tilde{\mathbf{\Omega}}_{ij} \tilde{\mathbf{e}}_{ij} \; ; \tag{14}$$

6. Solve the linear system of Eq. 10 to find an improved perturbation $\mathbf{\Delta T}$;
7. Compute the improved transformation $\mathbf{T}'$ as in Eq. 11.

4 Experiments

We validated our approach both on real and synthetic data. The real world experiments were conducted on publicly available benchmarking datasets, and they show the performances of our optimization algorithm when included in a full ICP system. The experiments on synthetic data, instead, allow to characterize the behavior of our approach under different levels of sensor noise and outlier ratios. Comparisons with NDT are not showed since it performs similarly to GICP because they rely on analogous representations of the points.

4.1 Real World Experiments

For the real world experiments we used the benchmarking datasets by Stuerm *et al.* [7]. Each dataset consists in a sequence of depth and RGB images acquired with a calibrated RGBD camera in a reference scene. Note that even if our approach is not restricted to the use of depth images, we decided to use these datasets since they are labeled with the ground truth of the transformations. We do not make use of the RGB channels.

In order to provide the input data to the algorithm illustrated in the previous section, we processed the point cloud $\mathcal{P}$ generated from each depth image by extracting the local surface characteristics from the neighborhood of each point $\mathbf{p}_i$. This process is performed by computing the parameters of a Gaussian $\mathcal{N}(\mu_i, \mathbf{\Sigma}_i)$ and taking all points that lie within a fixed ball centered in $\mathbf{p}_i$, as

$$\mu_i = \frac{1}{|\mathcal{P}_i|} \sum_{\mathbf{p}_k \in \mathcal{P}_i} \mathbf{p}_k \qquad \mathbf{\Sigma}_i = \frac{1}{|\mathcal{P}_i|} \sum_{\mathbf{p}_k \in \mathcal{P}_i} (\mathbf{p}_k - \mu_i)^T (\mathbf{p}_k - \mu_i) \; , \tag{15}$$

where $\mathcal{P}_i$ is the set of all points in $\mathcal{P}$ that are closer than a fixed distance from $\mathbf{p}_i$.

For determining if a point lies on a corner, an edge or a flat surface, we analyze the eigenvalues of its covariance matrix $\mathbf{\Sigma}_i$. If all eigenvalues have more or less the same magnitude, we assume the point is on a corner. If one of the eigenvalues is smaller with respect to the other two, we assume the point lies on an edge. Finally, if one of the eigenvalues is smaller of some order of magnitude with respect to the others then we assume the point is on a planar patch. This discrimination is necessary to compute the correct information matrices, according to Table 2.

Given two clouds to be aligned, we search the correspondences using a line of sight criterion over the depth images, we reject the correspondences whose normals are too different and we execute one iteration of optimization. Notice that ICP and GICP are special cases that can be captured by our algorithm just by modifying the way in which the information matrices are computed. To focus our analysis on the objective function we left all parts of the system unchanged, including the correspondence selection. This represents an advantage for plain ICP, since normally it does not rely on the normals in order to reject wrong associations.

For each dataset, we incrementally aligned one frame to the previous one. For each iteration of the alignment, we compared the difference between the current solution and the ground truth. Each attempted alignment produced a plot which shows the evolution of the rotational and translational error. For compactness, we provide in this paper only the average error plots obtained by averaging all errors of a run[1]. The reader who is interested in the individual plots of each alignment, can find them at http://www.dis.uniroma1.it/~serafin/publications/icp-augmented-measurements.

In order to measure the robustness of the alignments to wrong initial guesses we performed several runs of the experiments by considering a frame each N. Table 3 shows the average evolution of the rotational and the translational error on three different datasets and at different frame skips.

The plotted results point out that our novel objective function in general performs better than the other approaches, in particular in terms of convergence speed. This is true especially for the rotational part of the error since it is influenced directly by the normals. Also in the case where no frame was skipped (first column of Table 3), GICP required twice the number of iterations to converge to the results of our approach. Moreover, ICP and GICP showed much less robustness to frame skipping (second and third column of Table 3).

4.2   Experiments on Synthetic Data

We conducted experiments on synthetic data in order to assess the effects of the inliers and of the sensor error on our optimization function. To this end we generated a scene consisting of about 300k 3D points with normals and tangents. Then, we computed the correct correspondences and ideal measurements and we corrupted them. This process has been performed by injecting a variable fraction of random outliers and perturbing the measurements by adding Gaussian noise

---

[1] With run we denote all the alignment over a single dataset with a certain frame skip rate.

Table 3. Average evolution of the translational and rotational error for three different datasets at varying frame skip rates. Our approach is labeled "nicp" in the captions of the images.

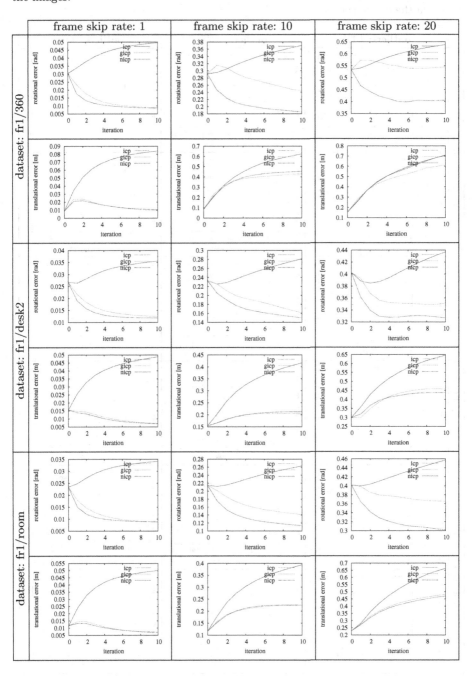

Table 4. Average evolution of the translational and rotational error at different outlier ratios and levels of noise affecting the measurements of the point (standard deviation, in meters) and the normals (standard deviation in degrees). Our approach is labeled "nicp" in the captions of the images.

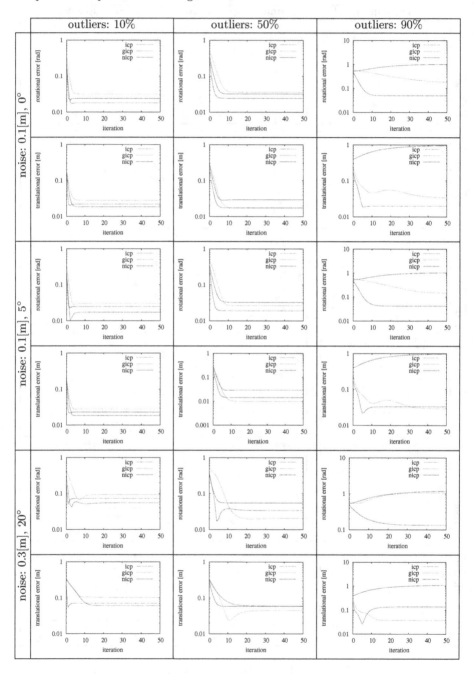

to the points and normal estimates. For each setting we ran our approach, ICP and GICP, and we plotted the evolution of the translational and rotational error. The results are shown in Table 4.

Overall the experiments on synthetic data reflect the behavior of the real world ones. Shortly, using additional information in the error function makes the approach more robust and accelerates the convergence. This is particularly true at high rates of outliers and sensor noise. Not surprisingly, instead, noise in the normals lowers the performances. In the unrealistic scenario in which every normal is affected by a 20° error at 90% of outliers the translational estimate becomes less accurate than GICP, but it still converges to a reasonable solution.

5   Conclusions

In this paper we proposed a novel optimization function to register point clouds using an ICP based algorithm that takes into account an augmented measurement vector. Statistical comparative experiments on real and synthetic data show that our approach performs better than other state of the art methods both in terms of convergence speed and robustness. As expected, the normals and the tangents of the surfaces showed an improvement in particular in the rotational part of the error, while keeping the translational one similar to the other approaches. A further enhancement could be obtained by finding an additional measurement, related to the translation, to be considered in the minimization of the cost function.

Acknowledgments. This work has partly been supported by the European Commission under FP7-600890-ROVINA.

References

1. Besl, P.J., McKay, N.D.: A method for registration of 3-D shapes. IEEE Transactions on Pattern Analysis and Machine Intelligence (1992)
2. Grisetti, G., Kummerle, R., Stachniss, C., Burgard, W.: A tutorial on graph-based slam. IEEE Intelligent Transportation Systems Magazine 2(4), 31–43 (2010)
3. Horn, B.K., Hilden, H.M., Negahdaripour, S.: Closed-form solution of absolute orientation using orthonormal matrices. Journal of the Optical Society of America (1988)
4. Magnusson, M., Duckett, T., Lilienthal, A.J.: Scan registration for autonomous mining vehicles using 3D-ndt. Journal on Field Robotics (2007)
5. Pomerleau, F., Colas, F., Siegwart, R., Magnenat, S.: Comparing icp variants on real-world data sets. Autonomous Robots (2013)
6. Segal, A.V., Haehnel, D., Thrun, S.: Generalized-ICP. In: Proc. of Robotics: Science and Systems, RSS (2009)
7. Sturm, J., Engelhard, N., Endres, F., Burgard, W., Cremers, D.: A benchmark for the evaluation of rgb-d slam systems. In: Proc. of the IEEE/RSJ Int. Conf. on Intelligent Robots and Systems, IROS (2012)

Design of a Kiosk Type Healthcare Robot System for Older People in Private and Public Places

Ho Seok Ahn[1], I-Han Kuo[2], Chandan Datta[1], Rebecca Stafford[3], Ngaire Kerse[4], Kathy Peri[5], Elizabeth Broadbent[3], and Bruce A. MacDonald[1]

[1] Department of Electrical and Computer Engineering, CARES,
University of Auckland, Auckland, New Zealand
{hs.ahn,chandan.datta,b.macdonald}@auckland.ac.nz
[2] Department of Computing, Unitec Institute of Technology, Auckland, New Zealand
ikuo@unitec.ac.nz
[3] Department of Psychological Medicine, CARES,
University of Auckland, Auckland, New Zealand
{r.stafford,e.broadbent}@auckland.ac.nz
[4] Department of General Practice and Primary Health Care, CARES,
University of Auckland, Auckland, New Zealand
n.kerse@auckland.ac.nz
[5] School of Nursing, CARES, University of Auckland, Auckland, New Zealand
k.peri@auckland.ac.nz

Abstract. In this paper, we introduce a healthcare robot system for older people and its experiments in private and public spaces. We designed a healthcare robot system and healthcare functionalities, and conducted a long-term study in a real environment. Our healthcare robot system consists of three parts: a kiosk type service robot platform, a healthcare software system with healthcare service modules, and a medical server system. 1) The kiosk type service robot platform is used for giving helpful information to older people through a touch screen. 2) The healthcare software system is designed to enable easy modification of healthcare service modules according to the purpose of the robot. 3) The medical server system stores health information of older people for managing their health conditions. For validating our software design and implementation in real environments, we deployed this healthcare robot system in private and public places of a retirement village. In these experiments, older people interacted with the robots and used healthcare functionalities for over 12 weeks. During the experiments, the robots sent records of the interactions to our medical server. The server provides this information to clinicians who are supervising the older peoples' health status. When the experiments were completed, the participants completed questionnaires. The results showed that older people in private places used the healthcare service for checking their health conditions, and older people in public places like to use the entertainment services. We confirmed that our kiosk type robot can help older people as well.

Keywords: Healthcare robot system, caring of older adults, health condition management, healthcare service, private homes, rest home lounges.

D. Brugali et al. (Eds.): SIMPAR 2014, LNAI 8810, pp. 578–589, 2014.
© Springer International Publishing Switzerland 2014

1 Introduction

Our society is rapidly moving toward an aged society with the older population rising sharply [1-2], which is a big concern for care service providers in the future [3-4]. Older people will be troubled with illness as a result of a degenerative loss of brain function [5]. Therefore, they will require long-term care, but it will be challenging to provide care due to the lack of care staff [6-9]. Animal therapy is one of the successful solutions to help older people in care facilities [10-11], but they may carry infectious diseases, and may bite or cause physical damage [12]. Instead of live animals, companion and assistant robots have been used, such as the therapeutic robot PARO, a baby harp seal robot intended to have a calming effect on patients in hospitals and nursing homes, similar to animal-assisted therapy [13-14]. The doglike robot AIBO developed by SONY achieved success in the robotics market [15]. People, who live alone as well as older people, feel happy when caring for and living with AIBO. Robots can also help older people by providing assistance with daily life and in managing people's conditions. Researchers have developed several types of companion and assistant robot systems and found that companion and assistant robots can have positive effects on both psychological and physical outcomes [16-19].

In our previous research, we have designed an assistant robot system to provide companionship and healthcare support to older people. We have studied how to improve quality of life and health conditions of older people through several long-term studies. Our first long-term study was an acceptability study with 53 participants from 2008 to 2009. This study found that robots are acceptable to older adults [20]. In our second long-term study, we deployed robots in a retirement village from 2010 to 2011. We asked residents and staff at a retirement village what they would like a robot to do and look like so we could design a dedicated healthcare robot appropriately [21, 30]. We developed a healthcare robot system HealthBots to do some of these tasks. We tested HealthBots in a cross-sectional study at a retirement village, and found that staff and residents could interact with the robot and that peoples' attitudes towards robots improved after meeting it [22]. After improving some aspects of HealthBots, we carried out a two-week observational study in the lobby of the retirement center to test aspects of feasibility and acceptance [24]. We carried out a range of experiments in private and public spaces in a retirement village and hospital from the fourth quarter of 2011 as our third long-term study [5, 12, 23, 31]. This study included six investigations, and five kinds of robot platforms such as PARO, Guide, Charlie, iRobi, and Friend robots: 1) A cross-over randomized trial in the independent units, 2) A non-randomized trial in the lounge areas of the rest homes and hospitals, 3) An observational study in the public areas, such as Reception, Café and Medical center, 4) An interview study with Paro and Guide robot in the dementia unit with residents, staff and relatives, 5) A randomized trial of Paro in the hospital and rest home, and 6) fall monitoring of the older people in daily life. We used Charlie and iRobi robots as healthcare robot platforms in the first study, and Charlie and Guide robots as healthcare robot platforms in the second study.

This paper focuses on the design of the healthcare robot system with the Charlie platform and Charlie experiments in the first and second investigation of our third long-term study. Fig. 1 shows the use of Charlie for measuring the vital signs of an older adult in a rest home. Charlie has healthcare functionalities including measuring vital signs, Skype calls, a brain fitness game, and some entertainment functions. Our healthcare robots manage the health status of older people by helping them to measure their vital signs and sending the results to the medical server for giving their medical information to doctors. In addition, older adults interact with the healthcare robots, play a brain fitness game, and watch music videos. The interaction histories are recorded in the medical server for analysis by clinicians. For validating the software design and implementation of HealthBors and its services in real environments, we conducted the studies at Selwyn Village in New Zealand, which has several levels of care including hospitals, rest homes, and private apartments. We have deployed three Charlie systems in private apartments in the first investigation, and two Charlie systems in public spaces (one at each at a rest home and a hospital) for over 12 weeks in the second investigation. Participants complete questionnaires rating the healthcare robot system.

Fig. 1. An older adult measures his blood pressure through our healthcare robot, Charlie, in a rest home. The robot helps older people to measure their vital signs without the aid of caregivers, nurses or family members, and records the data for healthcare providers to check.

2   Healthcare Robot System: HealthBots

2.1   Overview of Healthcare Robot System

We developed a healthcare robot system with a service robot platform, a software system with service modules, and a medical server system. We can use several kinds of service robot platforms as a healthcare robot system in HealthBots according to the users and purpose. Fig. 2 shows the Healthbots system overview with a kiosk type robot Charlie. Older adults can measure their vital signs, such as blood pressure. They also interact with healthcare robots for using healthcare service functions such as a brain fitness game and entertainment. The measured vital sign results and interaction records are sent to our medical server system, and then clinicians can review them for managing the health conditions of the older adults.

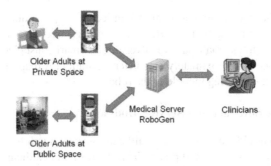

Fig. 2. Overview of the healthcare robot system, Healthbots. Robots help older adults in various spaces and send information such as vital signs and interaction records to the medical server, RoboGen. Doctors and psychologists access the medical server and check the health status of the older adults.

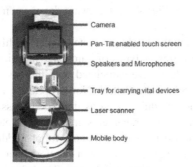

Fig. 3. The kiosk type robot platform, Charlie. It consists of a camera, a Pan-Tilt enabled touch screen, speakers, microphones, ultrasonic sensors, bumper sensors, a laser scanner, two single board computers and a 24V Li-Polymer battery.

2.2   Kiosk Type Service Robot Platform

The kiosk type robot platform Charlie is shown in Fig. 3. The robot platform is from Yujin robotics in South Korea and is originally designed as a serving robot in cafes and restaurants, and for assisting teachers in schools; it has a friendly appearance and tray for carrying items. Charlie is a differential drive mobile robot 1.2 meters high, powered by a 24V Li-Polymer battery, and consists of a camera, a rotatable touch screen, speakers, microphones, ultrasonic sensors, bumper sensors, a laser range finder and two single board computers. User responses were received via the touch screen and HealthBot responds to participants with synthesized speech, visual output on the screen, and movements. The touch screen helps the older people who have hearing or speaking difficulties by showing messages or pictures. Charlie's synthetic speech is generated through a diphone concatenation type synthesis implemented with Festival speech synthesis system [25] and used a New Zealand accented diphone voice developed at the University of Auckland [26]. Expression was added to the synthetic speech through an intonation modeling technique [27] called 'Say Emotional'. For map building and navigation, Charlie uses the StarGazer robot localization system [28]. The system requires small passive silver dot landmarks installed on the ceiling of the robot work-space at approximately one meter separation. A map of the area was built using the built-in map building module of the robot.

2.3   Healthcare Software and Service Modules

The HealthBots should have several healthcare service modules according to the purposes of deployment, users and places. This means that healthcare service modules should be modified easily without any changes of the HealthBots software architecture. In addition, various experts from health psychology, gerontology, health informatics as well as engineers should be able to modify the behavior scenario of HealthBots according to the requirements of experiments. For these reasons, we designed a behavior scenario based HealthBots software architecture comprising three logical layers as shown in Fig. 4: a hardware layer, a middleware layer, and a behavior layer [33].

The hardware layer is for the hardware systems of HealthBot, which consist of the operating system and two different types of hardware: proprietary and non-proprietary. Proprietary hardware is the hardware associated with the basic robot platform, such as two single board computers and controllers. Non-proprietary hardware is the hardware added for healthcare service modules, such as the blood pressure meter, blood oxygen saturation meter, blood glucose meter, cameras, microphones, etc.

The middleware layer consists of three parts: a robot middleware, service modules, and a behavior execution engine. The robot platform has a ROCOS framework developed by Yujin robotics as a robot middleware. The behavior execution engine starts and stops the service modules by commands from the behavior layer. The service modules communicate with several web-services for information retrieval and update, and are integrated with third-party applications for providing added functionality.

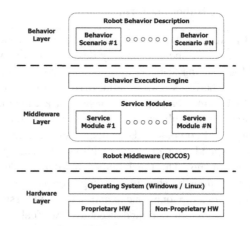

Fig. 4. Overview of the healthcare software system. It consists of three layers: a hardware layer, a middleware layer, and a behavior layer.

The behavior layer consists of a number of behavior scenario files, which are different according to the purpose of system and experiments. The behavior scenario files describe robot behavior as a finite state machine, which can easily be modified by various experts from health psychology, gerontology, and health informatics as well as by engineers. The front-end of the application with the selected behavior scenario is developed using Flash/ActionScript 3.0 and the back-end is developed using C++.

In this study, Charlie has three service modules: a blood pressure service module, an entertainment service module which contains music videos, and pictures, and a web surfing function. A brain fitness game service module plays brain games, developed by Dakim [29].

2.4   Medical Server System: RoboGen

We developed a medical server system, RoboGen [32], for storing health information including vital signs measurement records and records of interactions between HealthBots and their users. It hosts a website application portal for carers to log in and monitor on data from users of HealthBots. Users and family members as well as specialists such as doctors, nurses, and psychologists can access the user data through the RoboGen website. This central data server is built using the Microsoft ASP .NET and MVC framework and a Microsoft SQL server. The robot connects to RoboGen through web-services.

3   Experimental Method

3.1   Overview of Experiments

We had two different investigations with five Charlie robots by deploying in three different parts of Selwyn village in New Zealand: private apartments for the first investigation, a rest home and a hospital for the second investigation, and a total of 99 older adults used the robots (6 older adults in the private apartments, 60 older adults in the rest home, and 33 older adults in the hospital). Selwyn village is a non-profit retirement complex in Auckland, New Zealand. The 26 acre village has around 650 residents, and provides progressive care from independent living units through hospital and dementia care [22]. For the recruitment of participants, we presented our research, and residents who were interested in using robot were recruited voluntarily for these experiments.

The first investigation was done in private apartments with Charlie and iRobi robots, which were described on other publications [31]. In the experiments with Charlie in the first investigation, 6 older adults were recruited, and 3 older adults were given individual Charlie robots in their apartments for 6 weeks. The robots were then moved to 3 different apartments for another 3 residents.

The second investigation was done in a lounge of the rest home and the hospital with Charlie and Guide robots, which were described on other publications [5]. For the experiments with Charlie in the rest home, we deployed one Charlie robot in a lounge of the rest home, which accommodates 110 residents and employees 47 staff, and 60 older adults were recruited. For the experiments with Charlie in the hospital, we deployed another Charlie robot in a lounge to the hospital, which accommodates 67 residents and employees 51 staff, and 33 older adults were recruited. We continued our experiments in the rest home and the hospital for twelve weeks. After each interaction, users were able to rate the functionalities of the healthcare robot system.

Table 1.   Instructions and Wording of the Appropriate Healthcare Functionalities and the Suitability of using Kiosk type Healthcare Robot System Questionnaire. BP means the blood pressure measurement service module, EN means the entertainment service module, and BG means the brain fitness game service module.

Measure	Scale instructions	Items				
Usage of healthcare service module (same in BP, EN, BG)*	Please circle the number that best corresponds to how useful you find the healthcare service module. I think this service is …	0 Poor	1 Acceptable	2 Good	3 Excellent	
User satisfaction about the robot in private space (1 question)	Q1. Please circle the number that best corresponds to how much you enjoyed using the robot today.	0 Not at all	1 A little	2 Moder-ately	3 Quite a lot	4 Very much
User satisfaction about the robot in public space (4 Questions)	Q1. Please circle the number that best corresponds to how much you enjoyed using the robot.	0 Not at all	1 A little	2 Moder-ately	3 Quite a lot	4 Very much
	Q2. Please circle the number that best corresponds to how useful you found the robot.	0 Not at all	1 A little	2 Moder-ately	3 Quite a lot	4 Very much
	Q3. Please circle the number that best corresponds to how you would rate your interaction with the robot.	0 Not at all	1 A little	2 Moder-ately	3 Quite a lot	4 Very much
	Q4. Please circle the number that best corresponds to how much you would like to interact with the robot again.	0 Not at all	1 A little	2 Moder-ately	3 Quite a lot	4 Very much

3.2   Procedure

We demonstrated how to use the robots to interested staff and residents two weeks prior to starting the experiments. Staff managers were provided the duty phone number of the researchers to contact if there were any issues with the robots. Research assistants were available at the village to respond to any issues.

For the first investigation in the private apartments, participants were able to interact with the Charlie within their apartments as much or as little as they liked over the six week period. Six residents used Charlie robots. At first three participants used Charlie for six weeks, and then the other three participants used Charlie for six weeks. At the end of each interaction, participants had the opportunity to complete questionnaires on the robot about their satisfaction with each service module and their overall evaluation.

For the second investigation in the rest home and hospital, participants were able to interact with Charlie as much or as little as they liked over a twelve week period. When they interacted with Charlie, they entered their personal information so that their identity was known. At the end of each interaction, participants had the opportunity to complete questionnaires on the robot about their satisfaction with each service module and their overall evaluation. Some participants also completed written questionnaires about their quality of life, depression and perceptions of the robots, which are not the focus of this paper.

4   Experimental Results and Evaluations

As well as validating the HealthBots software design and implementation by a real, long term deployment in older care facilities, on multiple, heterogeneous robots, there are two aims of the analyses of the data gathered: 1) to determine the appropriate healthcare robot functions in the two different locations, 2) to evaluate the suitability of this healthcare robot system in the two different locations. Other papers on the results of the experiments conducted at this time at the village are published or in submission [5, 12, 20-24, 30-34].

4.1   Appropriate Healthcare Robot Functions According to Location

Firstly, six participants who were not familiar to robot used our HealthBots system including three main services, such as the blood pressure measurement, entertainment contents, and the brain fitness game, over a 12 week period, and we confirmed that the HealthBots software design and its services work well in real environments. Secondly, we found the appropriate healthcare functionalities according to the place the robot was deployed by measuring the usage of healthcare service modules. The instructions and wording of the rating questions on the robot are shown in Table 1. The items were the same in all service modules such as blood pressure measurement, entertainment, and brain fitness. Participants were asked how useful they found the healthcare service using a scale from 0 (Poor) to 3 (Excellent), after people used healthcare service modules. The questions were displayed on the robot itself and people answered by touching their selected answer on the screen. Then, Charlie sent the results to Robogen for storage.

Fig. 5 shows the average score of each healthcare service module according to its location. We found that participants liked to use three healthcare services overall, but there were differences according to the location. The participants in the private apartments were satisfied with the blood pressure measurement service and the brain fitness game service than entertainment service. Especially, the use of the entertainment service decreased as time went on. It may be that as older adults living independently are not in an environment that monitors their blood pressure every day, so they wanted to check their blood pressure in their homes. On the other hand, the participants in the public spaces were satisfied with the entertainment service. There were some differences between the participants in the rest home and the hospital. The participants in the rest home were satisfied with the brain fitness game service and entertainment service more than those in the hospital. On the other hand, the participants in the hospital were satisfied with the blood pressure measurement service more than those in the rest home.

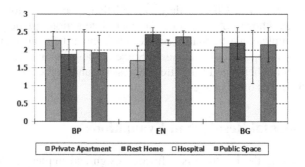

Fig. 5. The average score of each healthcare service module according to place. BP means the blood pressure measurement service module, EN means the entertainment service module, and BG means the brain fitness game service module. The data for the public space was obtained from the participants in the rest home and hospital, and used for comparing with the results of the private space.

4.2   Suitability of Using Our Healthcare Robot System According to Location

We evaluated the suitability of using the kiosk type healthcare robot system according to the place by measuring the user satisfaction with the robot. Questionnaires were different for different places; one question to the participants in the private apartments and four questions to the participants in the public spaces such as the rest home and the hospital. Instructions and wording of the questionnaire for each place are shown in Table 1. The questions were asked on the Charlie's touch-screen. Then, Charlie sent the results to the Robogen server for storage. Fig. 6 shows the average score on each question about the user satisfaction with the robot according to the location. The participants in the public spaces were satisfied with using the kiosk type robot, but the participants in the private apartments did not give high scores although they enjoyed using Charlie.

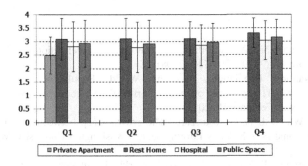

Fig. 6. The average score of each question about the user satisfaction about the robot according to place. Q1 is how much the user enjoys using the robot. Q2 is how useful the user found the robot. Q3 is how user would rate his interaction with the robot. Q4 is how much user would like to interact with the robot again. The data for the public space was obtained from the participants in the rest home and hospital, and used for comparing with the results of the private space.

5   Conclusions

We completed a 12-week study on appropriate services of a healthcare robot system for older people in private and public spaces. We designed the healthcare robot system, HealthBots, and deployed it to Selwyn village, which had several levels of care as well as various care facilities such as hospitals, rest homes, and private apartments. We used three Charlie robots in the private apartments, two Charlie robots in the public places, the rest home and the hospital, for the long-term studies. From the results, we found some important points, in addition to verifying that our software system was deployed and working on multiple, heterogeneous robots for a long period in different field environments. Older people in the private places (their own homes) used the healthcare service mostly for checking their health conditions. Older people in the public places used the entertainments functions most, especially in the rest home. We expect that the entertainment contents should be updated often when a robot is used for a long time to avoid the user becoming bored with the content. A kiosk type robot platform is quite good for the healthcare robot platform, but may be more acceptable in rest-home and hospital lounges than in private homes, which may be due to its size. In future work, we will study a cost benefit analysis when healthcare robot systems are employed in a family doctor's practice and in peoples' homes in the community.

Acknowledgment. This work was jointly supported by the Robot Pilot Project program of the Korea Ministry of Knowledge and Economy (MKE), Korea Institute for Robot Industry Advancement (KIRIA) and the New Zealand Ministry of Business, Innovation and Employment IIOF (13635). We thank Electronics and Telecommunications Research Institute (ETRI), Yujin Robot, ED, Isan, our colleagues from the University of Auckland HealthBots research team, and the residents and staff of Selwyn Village.

References

1. Lutz, W., Sanderson, W., Scherbov, S.: The coming acceleration of global population ageing. Nature 451(7179), 716–719 (2008)
2. United Nations Population Division, World Population Aging: 1950-2050, http://www.un.org/esa/population/publications/worldageing195 02050 (accessed February 19, 2012)
3. Super, N.: Who will be there to care? The growing gap between caregiver supply and demand. National Health Policy Forum, George Washington University, Washington, DC (2005)
4. United Nations Population Division, World Population Ageing 2009 (2012), http://www.un.org/esa/population/publications/WPA2009/WPA200 9_WorkingPaper.pdf
5. Robinson, H., MacDonald, B.A., Kerse, N., Broadbent, E.: Suitability of Healthcare Robots for a Dementia Unit and Suggested Improvements. Journal of the American Medical Directors Association 14(1), 34–40 (2012)
6. Jacobzone, S.: Coping with aging: International challenges. Health Aff. 2000 19, 213–225 (2000)
7. Slama, C.A., Bergman-Evans, B.: A troubling triangle. An exploration of loneliness, helplessness, and boredom of residents of a veterans home. Journal of Psychosocial Nursing and Mental Health Services 38(12), 36–43 (2000)
8. Jongenelis, K., Pot, A.M., Eisses, A.M., Beekman, A.T., Kluiter, H., Ribbe, M.W.: Prevalence and risk indicators of depression in elderly nursing home patients: The AGED study. Journal of Affective Disorders 83, 135–142 (2004)
9. Rossen, E.K., Knafl, K.A.: Older women's response to residential relocation: Description of transition styles. Qualitative Health Research 13(1), 20–36 (2003)
10. Raina, P., Waltner-Toews, D., Bonnett, B., Woodward, C., Abernathy, T.: Influence of companion animals on the physical and psychological health of older people: An analysis of a one-year longitudinal study. Journal of the American Geriatrics Society 7(3), 323–329 (1999)
11. Baun, M.M., Johnson, R.A., Fine Aubrey, H.: Human-animal interaction and successful aging. In: Handbook on Animal-assisted Therapy: Theoretical Foundations and Guidelines for Practice, pp. 283–299 (2010)
12. Robinson, H., MacDonald, B.A., Kerse, N., Broadbent, E.: The Psychosocial Effects of a Companion Robot: A Randomized Controlled Trial. Journal of the American Medical Directors Association 14(9), 661–667 (2013)
13. Shibata, T., Ohkawa, K., Tanie, K.: Spontaneous Behavior of Robots for Cooperation – Emotionally Intelligent Robot System. In: IEEE International Conference on Robotics & Automation (ICRA 1996), pp. 2426–2431 (1996)
14. Ahn, H.S., Choi, J.Y., Lee, D.-W.: A Behavior Combination Generating Method for Reflecting Emotional Probabilities using Simulated Annealing Algorithm. In: IEEE International Symposium on Robot and Human Interactive Communication (ROMAN 2011), pp. 192–197 (2011)
15. Fujita, M.: On activating human communications with pet-type robot AIBO. Proceedings of the IEEE 92(11), 1804–1813 (2004)
16. Reiser, U., Connette, C., Fischer, J., Kubacki, J., Bubeck, A., Weisshardt, F., Jacobs, T., Parlitz, C., Hagele, M., Verl, A.: Care-o-bot 3-creating a product vision for service robot applications by integrating design and technology. In: IEEE/RSJ International Conference on Intelligent Robots and Systems, pp. 1992–1998 (2009)

17. Ahn, H.S., Lee, D.-W., Choi, D., Lee, D.-Y., Lee, H., Baeg, M.-H.: Development of an Incarnate Announcing Robot System using Emotional Interaction with Humans. International Journal of Humanoid Robotics 10(2), 1–24 (2013)
18. Suga, K., Sato, M., Yonezawa, H., Naga, S., Shimizu, J., Morita, C.: Change in the concentration of salivary IgA by contact of elderly subjects with a pet robot. International Journal of Analytical Bio-Science 25, 251–254 (2002)
19. Wada, K., Shibata, T., Musha, T., Kimura, S.: Effects of robot therapy for demented patients evaluated by EEG. In: IEEE/RSJ International Conference on Intelligent Robots and Systems (IROS 2005), pp. 1552–1557 (2005)
20. Kuo, I.H., Rabindran, J.M., Broadbent, E., Lee, Y.I., Kerse, N., Stafford, R.M.Q., MacDonald, B.A.: Age and gender factors in user acceptance of healthcare robots. In: IEEE International Symposium on Robot and Human Interactive Communication (ROMAN 2009), pp. 214–219 (2009)
21. Broadbent, E., Tamagawa, R., Kerse, N., Knock, B., Patience, A., MacDonald, B.A.: Retirement home staff and residents' preferences for healthcare robots. In: IEEE International Symposium on Robot and Human Interactive Communication (ROMAN 2009), pp. 645–650 (2009)
22. Stafford, R.Q., Broadbent, E., Jayawardena, C., Unger, U., Kuo, I.H., Igic, A., Wong, R., Kerse, N., Watson, C., MacDonald, B.A.: Improved robot attitudes and emotions at a retirement home after meeting a robot. In: IEEE International Symposium on Robot and Human Interactive Communication, pp. 82–87 (2010)
23. Jayawardena, C., Kuo, I., Datta, C., Stafford, R.Q., Broadbent, E., MacDonald, B.A.: Design, implementation and field tests of a socially assistive robot for the elderly: HealthBot Version 2. In: RAS/EMBS International Conference on Biomedical Robotics and Biomechatronics, pp. 1837–1842 (2012)
24. Stafford, R.Q., MacDonald, B.A., Jayawardena, C., Wegner, D.M., Broadbent, E.: Does the Robot Have a Mind? Mind Perception and Attitudes Towards Robots Predict Use of an Eldercare Robot. International Journal of Social Robotics 6(1), 17–32 (2014)
25. Black, A.W., Taylor, P., Caley, R.: The festival speech synthesis system (2012), http://www.cstr.ed.ac.uk/projects/festival
26. Watson, C.I., Teutenberg, J., Thompson, L., Roehling, S., Igic, A.: How to build a New Zealand voice. In: Proceedings of the New Zealand Linguistic Society Conference (2009)
27. Igic, A., Watson, C.I., Teutenberg, J., Broadbent, E., Tamagawa, R., MacDonald, B.A.: Towards a flexible platform for voice accent and expression selection on a healthcare robot. In: Australasian Language Technology Association Workshop (2009)
28. Hagisonic, Localization System StarGazer for Intelligent Robots (2012), http://www.robotshop.com/media/files/pdf/stargazer_user_manu al_ver_04_080417(english).pdf
29. http://www.dakim.com/
30. Broadbent, E., Tamagawa, R., Patience, A., Knock, B., Kerse, N., Day, K., MacDonald, B.A.: Attitudes towards health care robots in a retirement village. Australasian Journal on Ageing 31(2), 115–120 (2012)
31. Datta, C., Yang, H.Y., Kuo, I.-H., Broadbent, E., MacDonald, B.A.: Software platform design for personal service robots in healthcare. In: IEEE International Conference on Robotics, Automation and Mechatronics, pp. 156–161 (2013)
32. Datta, C., Tiwari, P., Kuo, I., MacDonald, B.A.: End user programmingto enable closed-loop medication management using ahealthcare robot. In: Australasian Conference on Robotics & Automation (2011)
33. Jayawardena, C., Kuo, I.-H., Broadbent, E., MacDonald, B.A.: Socially Assistive Robot Health Bot: Design, Implementation, and Field Trials. IEEE Systems Journal (2014)

Author Index